THE WORLD'S CLASSICS

614

LATE VICTORIAN PLAYS

1890–1914

LATE VICTORIAN PLAYS

1890–1914

Edited
with an Introduction
by

GEORGE ROWELL

LONDON
OXFORD UNIVERSITY PRESS
NEW YORK TORONTO
1968

Oxford University Press, Ely House, London W.1
GLASGOW NEW YORK TORONTO MELBOURNE WELLINGTON
CAPE TOWN SALISBURY IBADAN NAIROBI LUSAKA ADDIS ABABA
BOMBAY CALCUTTA MADRAS KARACHI LAHORE DACCA
KUALA LUMPUR HONG KONG TOKYO

This volume of Late Victorian Plays 1890–1914
was first published in The World's Classics
in 1968

Set by Santype Ltd., Salisbury, and
printed in Great Britain at the
University Press, Oxford, by Vivian Ridler
Printer to the University

INTRODUCTION

In the twenty years covered by the plays in this volume English drama underwent both refinement and reform. The refinement was effected in the repertoire of the actor-managers which, previously derivative and trite, achieved in the Society drama independence and respectability. The call for reform was aimed against the dominance of the actor-managers' theatre and set up in competition 'repertory' theatres and 'social' or 'regional' drama. The two movements often overlapped: in the 1890s, when Pinero, Jones, and Wilde evolved Society drama, Shaw was already preaching the gospel of the theatre as a week-day pulpit; by 1914, when the first 'repertory' theatres were established and presenting Shaw's plays, together with Galsworthy's and Granville-Barker's, the Society drama had been taken over by Sutro and Maugham, who were filling West End theatres with their fashionable comedies. It is arbitrary and unprofitable to break off the history of the English theatre in 1901 or 1910, for the Victorian era continued, as far as the drama was concerned, until 1914, when it collapsed before the onslaught of the Great War. Consequently the title *Late Victorian Plays* is offered for this collection, rather than the more accurate but unwieldy 'Late Victorian, Edwardian, and Early Georgian Plays'.

The whole era represented in this volume saw the popularity of the Victorian theatre sustained, but playgoing taste transformed and English drama raised to the realm of literature for the first time since Sheridan and Goldsmith. The theatrical reforms of Robertson and the Bancrofts had found plenty of imitators, but their attempt to foster a native English comedy took twenty years to bear fruit. In the two decades which followed Robertson's death, the English theatre was dominated by Irving at the Lyceum, in a repertory of Shakespeare and melodrama, and by Gilbert and Sullivan at the Savoy. Leading actors of 'modern' drama, like the Bancrofts themselves, Hare, Wyndham, and the Kendals, revived Robertson or fell back on adaptations from the French. The accession in 1890 of George Alexander to the ranks of the actor-managers, however, not only made the St. James's a home of native English drama but spurred on his colleagues to stage original plays themselves. In the quarter-century which followed, London's actor-managers vied with each other to find and encourage new playwrights. Even when limited to one author for each actor-manager, the list is impressive, for it includes: Wilde at the St. James's (Alexander), Jones at the Criterion (Wyndham), Pinero at the Garrick (Hare), Haddon Chambers at the Haymarket (Tree), Barrie at the Duke of York's (Du Maurier), Maugham at the Vaudeville (Hawtrey), Sutro at the Garrick (Bourchier). All these authors wrote successfully for other theatres; their work and that of their sponsors set the tone of the late Victorian theatre—secure, profitable, socially acceptable.

At the same time this Society drama did not limit its appeal (as, for example, the Restoration drama had done) to 'High Society'. The late Victorian theatre remained fundamentally a popular theatre. True, its rowdier elements had been diverted to the rapidly expanding music hall, but the actor-managers did not play merely to the stalls, the obsolescent boxes, and the newly engineered circle. Each idol had his faithful following in the gallery, as well as more prosperous, though not fashionable, patrons in the upper circle. Their audiences were a cross-section of Victorian society, and if the fashionable dramas of the period seem to bear a strong family resemblance, it is because their creators evolved an entertainment with something in it for every part of the house: the authentic Mayfair and Belgravia settings and the titled *dramatis personae* appealed to the stalls and circle, but the highly dramatic—often melodramatic—situations kept the gallery enthralled. The English theatre between 1890 and 1914 was uniquely stable, and the price of that stability which its audiences paid was the predictability of its popular drama.

The Second Mrs. Tanqueray by Arthur Wing Pinero, though not the first Society drama, is singled out as the most significant, both for its serious tone and for its tragic denouement. It was in fact an extraordinarily courageous play for its author and his manager, Alexander, to offer in 1893. Pinero, apprenticed as an actor to Irving, had learnt his craft by adapting *pièces bien faites* for the Kendals and constructing the series of farces which still hold the stage. Nothing as uncompromising as *The Second Mrs. Tanqueray* had previously achieved performance—indeed Pinero's earlier essay, *The Profligate*, had been drastically modified by Hare to please the public. Paula Tanqueray and her interpreter, the unknown Mrs. Patrick Campbell, therefore caught the audience unawares; the impact was both immediate and profound, and though Pinero was to achieve many later successes, there can be no disputing William Archer's verdict: 'On May 27, 1893, Arthur Pinero planted a new milestone on the path of progress in the shape of *The Second Mrs. Tanqueray*.'[1]

The penalty he paid for pioneering Society drama was to be outstripped by his competitors, and in retrospect the play seems written to an overworked formula. 'The woman with a past' belongs to the past, and Pinero's much praised construction may appear to hinder rather than help the movement of the piece. But this is judgement from hindsight. *The Second Mrs. Tanqueray* was not merely the first 'problem play' to accept the inevitability of an unhappy ending. It depicted its heroine with greater insight and more feeling than any of Wilde's or Jones's characters, similarly *déclassées*; it offered two effectively contrasted portraits of social suicide by marriage, one comic (the Orreyeds), the other tragic (the Tanquerays); and it ventured to criticize the 'dual morality' which its audience held dear. When Ellean falls in love with one of Paula's former protectors, her step-mother comments bitterly:

She's a regular woman too. She could forgive *him* easily enough—but *me*! That's just a woman!

In the same way Aubrey Tanqueray blames himself as well as Hugh Ardale, the man in question, for Paula's death:

Curse him! Yes, I do curse him—him and his class! Perhaps I

[1] *The Old Drama and the New* (1923), p. 310.

curse myself too in doing it. He has only led 'a man's life'—just as I, how many of us, have done!

It is the 'man with a past' that Pinero judges and condemns.

Henry Arthur Jones, traditionally paired with Pinero as the major-domos of Society drama, achieved this status from a totally different origin. Flouting a Nonconformist background which had barred him from even entering a theatre, he learnt to construct effective melodramas, notably *The Silver King*, for Wilson Barrett, an actor-manager in the old tradition of spectacle and sensation. Popular success, however, spurred him on to proclaim the renaissance of English drama. When that renaissance came about, his own contribution was best seen in a series of comedies whose philosophy proved ultra-conservative but whose craftsmanship was impeccable.

Of these *The Liars* is outstanding in both respects. Its acceptance of the Victorian code is loyal to the point of servility: Sir Christopher Deering, after dissuading the ill-used Lady Jessica Nepean from leaving her husband for the faithful Edward Falkner, admits blandly:

> You know what we English are, Ned. We're not a bit better than our neighbours, but, thank God! we do pretend we are, and we do make it hot for anybody who disturbs that holy pretence.

In fact the 'holy pretences' of Victorian convention formed a recurring theme in Jones's work, whether they were treated seriously (in *Michael and His Lost Angel* and *Mrs. Dane's Defence*) or comically (in *The Case of Rebellious Susan* and *Whitewashing Julia*). The eloquence with which he preached the prejudices of his day has put him at a disadvantage beside Pinero, who laboured to denounce them, or Wilde, who could never be serious about anything for long. At Jones's best, however, as in *The Liars*, his story-telling is beyond reproach and his dialogue catches the rhythms and accent of fashionable Victorian Society as surely as Etherege reproduced the idiom of Restoration Society, even if it does not aspire to the satire of Wycherley or comprehend the poetry of Congreve.

Society drama held the stage firmly until 1914 and such

practitioners as R. C. Carton and Alfred Sutro were content to follow Jones's lead. The two later exponents represented here, however, varied the formula to their own taste. Hubert Henry Davies was not an ambitious writer and aimed no higher than pleasant entertainment. Several of his titles (*Lady Epping's Lawsuit*, *Mrs. Gorringe's Necklace*) suggest orthodox drawing-room comedy, but in *The Mollusc* he showed himself one of the few playwrights of the period to derive some part of his style directly from Robertson. The flower-arranging scene at the start of the second act displays all the dexterity for which Robertson's 'stage-management' was acclaimed, though the characterization it serves is understandably more subtle than that of *Caste* or *Ours*. In its control of sentiment, too, *The Mollusc* recalls the Robertsonian school of 'reserved force' which pervaded English acting after his death. Such a passage as the following seems to link the work of the Bancrofts at the Prince of Wales's with that of Charles Wyndham and Mary Moore at the Criterion:

Miss Roberts. Shall I tell you something? . . .

Tom. You must now you've begun. . . .

Miss Roberts. Well, don't look at me.

Tom. I'm ready. (*He looks at her, and then turns his back to her.*)

Miss Roberts. Suppose there was a girl, quite young, and not bad looking, and she knew that her chief value as a person was her looks and her youth, and a man—oh, I don't know how to say this——

Tom. I'm not looking.

Miss Roberts. He had great value as a person. He was kind and sensible, and brave, and he had done things. He wasn't young, but he couldn't have lived and still had a smooth face . . . and if he wanted to give her so much—such great things—don't you think she'd be proud to give him her one little possession, her looks and her youth?

But Davies's work looks forward as well as back. The very modesty of his means made him a bridge between the generations of playwrights separated by the Great War (in which he died). *The Mollusc*, with its small cast and unostentatious setting, points away from the Mayfair drawing-room of

Jones and Pinero towards the lounge-hall of the 1920s. Another portent is the easy, relaxed rhythm of the dialogue—suggesting in some measure the advent of Lonsdale and Coward and even more clearly of Van Druten. But the effect, though small-scale, is not insipid; Davies uses his miniature canvas to paint a shrewdly detailed portrait of a selfish but lovable woman.

St. John Hankin was not a Society dramatist in the sense of writing for the fashionable playgoer. None of his plays in fact achieved a West End production and his audience was to be found amongst the intellectual outposts of the theatre, both in London and the provinces. But his themes and settings (after experimenting with a 'middle-class comedy', *The Two Mr. Wetherbys*) challenged the fashionable playwrights on their own ground, treading it with a lightly ironic step. The background of *The Cassilis Engagement* (Deynham Abbey, Lady Marchmont, the Countess of Remenham, 'the Leicestershire Cassilises') suggests Society drama; indeed the play might, in Jones's or Pinero's hands, have made a suitably serious treatise on misalliance. Hankin is more concerned to expose his characters, revealing here the ruthless streak in Mrs. Cassilis and there the shallow streak in Ethel Borridge. This refusal to mix satire and sentiment, as Wilde and later Maugham mixed them so profitably, may account for the failure of his plays to reach the audience they reflect. His craftsmanship is confident, his attitude aloof, declining to identify himself with the beliefs, old or new, of his age. Perhaps this detachment held the seeds of the melancholy which led to his early death.

Those outposts which gave Hankin a hearing included the Stage Society and the Court Theatre under its celebrated Vedrenne-Barker management. Both enterprises can be traced back to the foundation of the Independent Theatre in 1891, a development which, though modest in scope, inaugurated the call for reform already noted. The avowed object of the Independent Theatre was 'to give special performances of plays which have a literary and artistic, rather than a commercial value', a description intended for the controversial Ibsen. Before long, controversy raged even more fiercely round a native dramatist, George Bernard Shaw, in whose plays, fleetingly and sometimes furtively staged, the young Granville-Barker began to be prominent. Shaw and Granville-Barker were the progenitors of English social drama, Shaw by inspiration rather than example, Granville-Barker by his achievements both as producer and playwright. When he staged *The Voysey Inheritance*[1] at the Court in 1905, it was the first of his own plays to be given public performance. In its elaborately middle-class setting and deliberately muted tone *The Voysey Inheritance* accurately reflects the spirit of English social drama and its revolt against the Mayfair melodrama of the fashionable theatre. But Granville-Barker, as playwright, producer, and actor, always strove to heighten realism with a touch of poetry, and the Voysey family transcend the Lincoln's Inn office and Chislehurst dining-room so carefully recreated here. In earlier—and later—plays this apparent contradiction between Granville-Barker's method and purpose produced a sense of strain; in *The Voysey Inheritance*, however, the diversity enriches rather than enfeebles.

One of Shaw's and Granville-Barker's aims at the Court was to widen the scope of contemporary drama by persuading established literary figures to write for the theatre. John Galsworthy, with Laurence Housman, John Masefield, and Gilbert Murray, was one of those who accepted the invitation, though Chesterton, Conrad, Kipling, and Wells were not to be drawn. In Galsworthy's case this introduction led him to write a series of plays in which English social drama reached its most uncompromising expression. *Justice*, produced by Granville-Barker some years later, is arguably Galsworthy's best play. What is beyond dispute is its conformity to Shaw's definition of 'blue-book drama'—drama which not only exposed social abuse but shamed authority into its reform. The picture of solitary confinement drawn in this play was, on his own admission, instrumental in persuading Winston Churchill, then Home Secretary, drastically to reduce its enforcement.

[1] Reprinted here in the revised (1934) version.

But *Justice* is more than a social document. It tells a story with the compassion characteristic of Galsworthy but also with force and feeling—two qualities less evident in his drama as a whole. The blows which fall on the wretched Falder in the last act derive from failings of character—his own and others'—with an inevitability that amply justifies Galsworthy's description of the play as 'a tragedy'. A comparison between *Justice* and *The Ticket-of-Leave Man*, the highly successful melodrama of 1863, illustrates the advance in the audience's taste which had taken place. Taylor, writing for the undiscriminating mid-Victorian public, presents his villains as stock stage types; Galsworthy, in a period of unprecedented Liberal revival, indicts no single individual but instead condemns the prejudices shared by his characters and his audience.

Amongst the provincial centres of social drama Lancashire, as given voice by the Manchester Gaiety Theatre, was pre-eminent, and Stanley Houghton, with Harold Brighouse, its most forceful spokesman. *Hindle Wakes*, the climax of Houghton's brief career, achieved immediate fame, even notoriety, but its qualities are more solid than those of a *succès de scandale*. The story is told with a lively logic, strongly—though unexpectedly in this North Country setting—influenced by Shaw, and this logic is even brought to bear on that favourite theme of Society dramatists, the dual morality. Beatrice Farrar, asked to forgive her fiancé for his illicit week-end with Fanny Hawthorn, replies:

Could you have forgiven me if I had done the same as you?
Alan (*surprised*). But—you—you couldn't do it!
Beatrice. Fanny Hawthorn did.
Alan. She's not your class.
Beatrice. She's a woman.
Alan. That's just it. It's different with a woman.
Beatrice. Yet you expect me to forgive you. It doesn't seem fair.
Alan. It isn't fair. But it's usual.

Unlike Pinero, however, Houghton was not afraid to pursue to its ultimate conclusion the case for a single morality:

Alan. But you didn't ever really love me?
Fanny. Love you? Good heavens, of course not! Why on earth

should I love you? You were just someone to have a bit of fun with. You were an amusement—a lark.

Alan (*shocked*). Fanny! Is that all you cared for me?

Fanny. How much more did you care for me?

Alan. But it's not the same. I'm a man.

Fanny. You're a man, and I was your little fancy. Well, I'm a woman, and *you* were *my* little fancy. You wouldn't prevent a woman enjoying herself as well as a man, if she takes it into her head?

In founding the Gaiety and calling into existence the Lancashire school of playwrights, the redoubtable Miss Horniman issued a challenge:

If Lancashire playwrights will send their plays to me I shall pledge myself to read them through. Let them write not as one dramatist does, about countesses and duchesses and society existing in imagination, but about their friends and enemies—about real life.[1]

Houghton's play meets her specifications, but adds a dry, dour humour of its own—a quality often lacking in the regional drama of the time, wherever it was set—which has ensured the survival of *Hindle Wakes*, when the work of other practitioners (McEvoy, Elizabeth Baker, Githa Sowerby) is quoted but unperformed.

Society drama, social drama—the two movements reacted, counteracted, and interacted during the last chapter of the Victorian theatre. Though they do not tell the whole story of the drama of that age—which included, for example, a successful though short-lived revival of English verse drama and fantasy and a longer-lived flowering of Irish poetic drama —they establish its tone. At one extreme the theatre was fashionable, ostentatious, superficial, at the other serious, progressive, homespun. The limitations of the actor-managers' theatre do not need enumeration. Those of the 'repertory' movement included a preoccupation with 'real life' which tended to cut off the pioneers of the English theatre from the dazzling advances in Continental stagecraft made by such masters as Reinhardt, Diaghilev, and the self-exiled

[1] Rex Pogson, *Miss Horniman and the Gaiety Theatre, Manchester* (1952), pp. 36–37.

Gordon Craig. But whatever the era's limitations, it was one of great importance in English drama.

A word should be added to explain three notable absentees from this volume. Oscar Wilde has some claim, through *Lady Windermere's Fan*, to be the forerunner of the Society dramatists and a stronger claim, through *The Importance of Being Earnest*, to have written the best play of his century. Both claims have been fully acknowledged by the wide availability of his plays in modern editions. George Bernard Shaw, who led the forces of reform against Society drama and inspired the writers of social drama, though they could never hope to emulate him, is similarly well served, both on the bookshelf and the playbill. William Somerset Maugham, who shrewdly turned himself into a Society dramatist when social drama proved unrewarding, is at his most characteristic as a playwright of the 1920s. These three writers have been—and will be—represented elsewhere.

GEORGE ROWELL

Department of Drama
University of Bristol
1967

CONTENTS

INTRODUCTION v

THE SECOND MRS. TANQUERAY 1
by Arthur W. Pinero
By permission of Messrs Samuel French Ltd.

THE LIARS *by* Henry Arthur Jones 81
By permission of Mrs. John Maxse, literary trustee of the late Henry Arthur Jones

THE MOLLUSC *by* Hubert Henry Davies 155
By permission of the literary trustee of the late H. H. Davies

THE CASSILIS ENGAGEMENT 213
by St. John Hankin

THE VOYSEY INHERITANCE 285
by Harley Granville-Barker
By permission of the Trustees of the Granville Barker Estates

JUSTICE *by* John Galsworthy 377
By permission of Messrs Gerald Duckworth & Co. Ltd.

HINDLE WAKES *by* Stanley Houghton 443

THE SECOND MRS. TANQUERAY

SIR ARTHUR WING PINERO

(1854–1934)

Born Islington, London. His family was of Portuguese extraction, the name being originally Pinheiro. Began work with his father in a lawyer's office but in 1874 joined the company at the Theatre Royal, Edinburgh. Acted with Irving at the Lyceum from 1876 to 1881 and with the Bancrofts at the Haymarket from 1881 to 1882, before concentrating on writing for the theatre. Knighted 1909.

His plays included *£200 a Year* (1877); *Daisy's Escape* (1879); *The Money Spinner* (1881); *The Squire* (1881); *Lords and Commons* (1883); *The Iron Master* (1884); *The Magistrate* (1885); *The Schoolmistress* (1886); *The Hobby Horse* (1886); *Dandy Dick* (1887); *Sweet Lavender* (1888); *The Profligate* (1889); *Lady Bountiful* (1891); *The Second Mrs. Tanqueray* (1893); *The Notorious Mrs. Ebbsmith* (1895); *Trelawny of the 'Wells'* (1898); *The Gay Lord Quex* (1899); *Iris* (1901); *Letty* (1903); *His House in Order* (1906); *The Thunderbolt* (1908); *Mid-Channel* (1909); *The 'Mind-the-Paint' Girl* (1912); *The Big Drum* (1915); *The Enchanted Cottage* (1922); *A Cold June* (1932).

The dates given here and later are of a play's first production.

THE SECOND MRS. TANQUERAY

A PLAY IN FOUR ACTS

by

Arthur W. Pinero

THE SECOND MRS. TANQUERAY

First produced at the St. James's Theatre, London, 27 *May* 1893, *with the following cast:*

AUBREY TANQUERAY	Mr. George Alexander
FRANK MISQUITH, Q.C., M.P.	Mr. Nutcombe Gould
GORDON JAYNE, M.D.	Mr. Murray Hathorn
MORSE	Mr. Alfred Holles
CAYLEY DRUMMLE	Mr. Cyril Maude
PAULA	Mrs. Patrick Campbell
ELLEAN	Miss Maude Millett
MRS. ALICE CORTELYON	Miss Amy Roselle
LADY ORREYED	Miss Edith Chester
SIR GEORGE ORREYED	Mr. Adolphus Vane-Tempest
CAPTAIN HUGH ARDALE	Mr. Ben Webster

THE SECOND MRS. TANQUERAY

ACT I

SCENE. AUBREY TANQUERAY'*s Chambers in the Albany—a richly and tastefully-decorated room. The wall* R. *is almost entirely taken up by a pair of doors which open into another room. Up* L., *at back, a small door supposed to lead to a bedchamber. At back* C., *a fireplace, with fire burning brightly. A luxurious easy chair on each side of the fireplace. On the* R. *of fireplace, against the wall, a writing-table and chair. On the writing-table, writing materials, a small cigar-cabinet, and lighted spirit-lamp. On the* L. *wall, a heavy curtain drawn over a large window. Down* R.C., *set obliquely to face audience, a sofa. Down* L.C., *a circular table laid for a dinner which has reached the stage of dessert. On this table, wines in decanters, flowers, fruit, plate, silver, coffee-cups, etc., etc. Round the table, at equal distances, four chairs. Other articles of furniture, bric-à-brac, china, pictures, lamps, candles, etc., about the room. Everything to suggest wealth and refinement.*

AUBREY TANQUERAY, MISQUITH, *and* JAYNE *are seated at the dinner-table,* L.C. AUBREY *is forty-two, handsome, winning in manner, his speech and bearing retaining some of the qualities of young manhood.* MISQUITH *is about forty-seven, genial and portly.* JAYNE *is a year or two* MISQUITH'*s senior; soft-speaking and precise—in appearance a type of the prosperous town physician.* MORSE, AUBREY'*s servant, takes the little cabinet of cigars and the spirit-lamp from table up* R.C., *places them beside* AUBREY, *and goes out, door* R.

Misquith. Aubrey, it is a pleasant yet dreadful fact to contemplate, but it's nearly fifteen years since I first dined with you. You lodged in Piccadilly in those days, over a hat-shop. Jayne, I met you at that dinner, and Cayley Drummle.

Jayne. Yes, yes. What a pity it is that Cayley isn't here to-night.

Aubrey. Confound the old gossip! His empty chair has been staring us in the face all through dinner. I ought to have told Morse to take it away.

Misquith. Odd, his sending no excuse.

Aubrey. I'll walk round to his lodgings later on and ask after him.

Misquith. I'll go with you.

Jayne. So will I.

Aubrey [*opening the cigar-cabinet*]. Doctor, it's useless to tempt you, I know. Frank—[MISQUITH *and* AUBREY *smoke*.] I particularly wished Cayley Drummle to be one of us to-night. You two fellows and Cayley are my closest, my best friends——

Misquith. My dear Aubrey!

Jayne. I rejoice to hear you say so.

Aubrey. And I wanted to see the three of you round this table. You can't guess the reason.

Misquith. You desired to give us a most excellent dinner.

Jayne. Obviously.

Aubrey [*hesitatingly*]. Well—I—(*Glancing at the clock*.] —Cayley won't turn up now.

[*He moves the candle from* R. *to* L. *of the table*.

Jayne. H'm, hardly.

Aubrey. Then you two shall hear it. Doctor, Frank, this is the last time we are to meet in these rooms.

Jayne. The last time?

Misquith. You're going to leave the Albany?

Aubrey. Yes. You've heard me speak of a house I built in the country years ago, haven't you?

Misquith. In Surrey.

Aubrey. Well, when my wife died I cleared out of that house and let it. I think of trying the place again.

Misquith. But you'll go raving mad if ever you find yourself down there alone.

Aubrey. Ah, but I shan't be alone, and that's what I wanted to tell you. I'm going to be married.

Jayne. Going to be married?

Misquith. Married?

Aubrey. Yes—to-morrow.

Jayne. To-morrow?

Misquith. You take my breath away! My dear fellow, I—I— of course, I congratulate you.

Jayne. And—so do I—heartily.

Aubrey. Thanks—thanks.

[*There is a moment or two of embarrassment*.

Misquith. Er—ah—this is an excellent cigar.

Jayne. Ah—um—your coffee is remarkable.

Aubrey. Look here; I daresay you two old friends think this treatment very strange, very unkind. So I want you to understand me. You know a marriage often cools friendships. What's the usual course of things? A man's engagement is given out, he is congratulated, complimented upon his choice; the church is filled with troops of friends, and he goes away happily to a chorus of good wishes. He comes back, sets up house in town or country, and thinks to resume the old associations, the old companionships. My dear Frank, my dear good doctor, it's very seldom that it can be done. Generally, a worm has begun to eat its way into those hearty, unreserved, prenuptial friendships; a damnable constraint sets in and acts like a wasting disease; and so, believe me, in nine cases out of ten a man's marriage severs for him more close ties than it forms.

Misquith. Well, my dear Aubrey, I earnestly hope——

Aubrey. I know what you're going to say, Frank. I hope so, too. In the meantime let's face dangers. I've reminded you of the *usual* course of things, but my marriage isn't even the conventional sort of marriage likely to satisfy society. Now, Cayley's a bachelor, but you two men have wives. By the by, my love to Mrs. Misquith and to Mrs. Jayne when you get home—don't forget that. Well, your wives may not—like—the lady I'm going to marry.

Jayne. Aubrey, forgive me for suggesting that the lady you are going to marry may not like our wives—mine at least; I beg your pardon, Frank.

Aubrey. Quite so; then I must go the way my wife goes.

Misquith. Come, come, pray don't let us anticipate that either side will be called upon to make such a sacrifice.

Aubrey. Yes, yes, let us anticipate it. And let us make up our minds to have no slow bleeding-to-death of our friendship. We'll end a pleasant chapter here to-night, and after to-night start afresh. When my wife and I settle down at Willowmere it's possible that we shall all come together. But if this isn't to be, for Heaven's sake let us recognize that it is simply because it *can't* be, and not wear hypocritical faces and suffer and be wretched. Doctor, Frank —[*Holding out his hands, one to* MISQUITH, *the other to* JAYNE.]—good luck to all of us!

Misquith. But—but—do I understand we are to ask nothing? Not even the lady's name, Aubrey?

Aubrey. The lady, my dear Frank, belongs to the next chapter, and in that her name is Mrs. Aubrey Tanqueray.

Jayne [*raising his coffee-cup*]. Then, in an old-fashioned way, I propose a toast. Aubrey, Frank, I give you 'The Next Chapter!'

[*They drink the toast, saying*, 'The Next Chapter!'

Aubrey. Doctor, find a comfortable chair; Frank, you too. As we're going to turn out by and by, let me scribble a couple of notes now while I think of them.

Misquith
Jayne } [*together*]. Certainly—yes, yes.

Aubrey. It might slip my memory when I get back.

[AUBREY *sits at the writing-table at the other end of the room, and writes.*

Jayne [*to* MISQUITH, *in a whisper*]. Frank—[MISQUITH *quietly leaves his chair and sits nearer to* JAYNE, *above table.*] What is all this? Simply a morbid crank of Aubrey's with regard to ante-nuptial acquaintances?

Misquith. H'm! Did you notice *one* expression he used?

Jayne. Let me think——

Misquith. 'My marriage is not even the conventional sort of marriage likely to satisfy society.'

Jayne. Bless me, yes! What does that suggest?

Misquith. That he has a particular rather than a general reason for anticipating estrangement from his friends, I'm afraid.

Jayne. A horrible *mésalliance*! A dairymaid who has given him a glass of milk during a day's hunting, or a little anaemic shopgirl! Frank, I'm utterly wretched!

Misquith. My dear Jayne, speaking in absolute confidence, I have never been more profoundly depressed in my life.

[MORSE *enters door* R.

Morse [*announcing*]. Mr. Drummle.

[CAYLEY DRUMMLE *enters briskly.* MISQUITH *and* JAYNE *rise.* MORSE *retires.* DRUMMLE *is a neat little man of about five-and-forty, in manner bright, airy, debonair, but with an undercurrent of seriousness.*

Drummle. I'm in disgrace; nobody realizes that more thoroughly than I do. Where's my host?

Aubrey [*who has risen*]. Cayley. [*He comes down* R.

Drummle [*shaking hands with him*]. Don't speak to me till I have tendered my explanation. A harsh word from anybody would unman me.

[MISQUITH *and* JAYNE *shake hands with* DRUMMLE.

Aubrey. Have you dined?

Drummle. No—unless you call a bit of fish, a cutlet, and a pancake dining.

Aubrey. Cayley, this is disgraceful.

Jayne [*coming down* L.]. Fish, a cutlet, and a pancake will require a great deal of explanation. [*He sits below the table.*

Misquith. Especially the pancake. My dear friend, your case looks miserably weak.

Drummle. Hear me! hear me!

Jayne. Now then!

Misquith. Come!

Aubrey. Well!

Drummle. It so happens that to-night I was exceptionally *early* in dressing for dinner.

Misquith. For which dinner—the fish and cutlet?

Drummle. For *this* dinner, of course—really, Frank! At a quarter to eight, in fact, I found myself trimming my nails, with ten minutes to spare. Just then enter my man with a note—would I hasten, as fast as cab could carry me, to old Lady Orreyed in Bruton Street?—'sad trouble'. Now, recollect, please, I had ten minutes on my hands, old Lady Orreyed was a very dear friend of my mother's, and was in some distress.

Aubrey. Cayley, come to the fish and cutlet?

Misquith
Jayne } [*together*]. Yes, yes, and the pancake!

Drummle [*with mock indignation*]. Upon my word! Well, the scene in Bruton Street beggars description; the women servants looked scared, the men drunk; and there was poor old Lady Orreyed on the floor of her boudoir like Queen Bess among her pillows.

Aubrey. What's the matter?

Drummle [*to everybody*]. You know George Orreyed?

Misquith. Yes.

Jayne. I've met him.

Drummle. Well, he's a thing of the past.

Aubrey. Not dead!

Drummle. Certainly, in the worst sense. He's married Mabel Hervey.

Misquith. What!

Drummle. It's true—this morning. The poor mother showed me his letter—a dozen curt words, and some of those ill-spelt.

Misquith [*walking up to the fireplace*]. I'm very sorry.

Jayne. Pardon my ignorance—who *was* Mabel Hervey?

Drummle. You don't——? Oh, of course not. [*He sits* L.C.] Miss Hervey—Lady Orreyed, as she now is—was a lady who would have been, perhaps had been, described in the reports of the Police or the Divorce Court as an actress. Had she belonged to a lower stratum of our advanced civilization she would, in the event of judicial inquiry, have defined her calling with equal justification as that of a dressmaker. To do her justice, she is a type of a class which is immortal. Physically, by the strange caprice of creation, curiously beautiful; mentally, she lacks even the strength of deliberate viciousness. [*He rises and moves* C.] Paint her portrait, it would symbolize a creature perfectly patrician; lance a vein of her superbly-modelled arm, you would get the poorest *vin ordinaire*! Her affections, emotions, impulses, her very existence—a burlesque! Flaxen, five-and-twenty, and feebly frolicsome, anybody's, in less gentle society I should say everybody's, property! That, Doctor, was Miss Hervey who is the new Lady Orreyed. Dost thou like the picture?

Misquith [*behind the table*]. Very good, Cayley! Bravo!

Aubrey [*rising and laying his hand on* DRUMMLE'*s shoulder*]. You'd scarcely believe it, Jayne, but none of us really know anything about this lady, our gay young friend here, I suspect, least of all.

Drummle. Aubrey, I applaud your chivalry.

Aubrey. And perhaps you'll let me finish a couple of letters which Frank and Jayne have given me leave to write. [*Returning to the writing-table*.] Ring for what you want, like a good fellow! [AUBREY *resumes his writing*.

Misquith [*to* DRUMMLE]. Still, the fish and cutlet remain unexplained.

Drummle. Oh, the poor old woman was so weak that I insisted upon her taking some food, and felt there was nothing for it but to sit down opposite her. The fool! the blackguard!

Misquith [*going to settee and sitting*]. Poor Orreyed! Well, he's gone under for a time.

Drummle. For a time! My dear Frank, I tell you he has absolutely ceased to be. [AUBREY, *who has been writing busily, turns his head towards the speakers and listens. His lips are set, and there is a frown upon his face*.] For all practical purposes you may regard him as the late George Orreyed. To-morrow the very characteristics of his speech, as we remember them, will have become obsolete.

Jayne. But surely, in the course of years, he and his wife will outlive——

Drummle. No, no, Doctor, don't try to upset one of my settled beliefs. You may dive into many waters, but there is *one* social Dead Sea——!

Jayne. Perhaps you're right.

Drummle. Right! Good God! I wish you could prove me otherwise! Why, for years I've been sitting, and watching and waiting.

Misquith. You're in form to-night, Cayley. May we ask where you've been in the habit of squandering your useful leisure?

Drummle. Where? On the shore of that same sea.

Misquith. And, pray, what have you been waiting for?

Drummle. For some of my best friends *to come up*. [AUBREY *utters a half-stifled exclamation of impatience; then he hurriedly gathers up his papers from the writing-table. The three men turn to him.*] Eh?

Aubrey [*pushing the chair in*]. Oh, I—I'll finish my letters in the other room if you'll excuse me for five minutes. Tell Cayley the news. [*He goes out* R.

Drummle [*hurrying to the door and speaking off*]. My dear fellow, my jabbering has disturbed you! I'll never talk again as long as I live!

Misquith. Close the door, Cayley. [DRUMMLE *shuts the door.*

Jayne. Cayley——

Drummle [*advancing to the dinner table* C.]. A smoke, a smoke, or I perish!

[*He selects a cigar from the little cabinet.* JAYNE *moves away from the table.*

Jayne. Cayley, marriages are in the air.

Drummle. Are they? Discover the bacillus, Doctor, and destroy it.

Jayne. I mean, among our friends.

Drummle [*cutting his cigar*]. Oh, Nugent Warrinder's engagement to Lady Alice Tring. I've heard of that. They're not to be married till the spring.

Jayne. Another marriage that concerns us a little takes place to-morrow.

Drummle. Whose marriage?

Jayne. Aubrey's.

Drummle. Aub——! [*Looking towards* MISQUITH.] Is it a joke?

Misquith [*standing* R.C.]. No.

Drummle [*walking slowly to* C., *looking from* MISQUITH *to* JAYNE]. To whom?

Misquith. He doesn't tell us.

Jayne. We three were asked here to-night to receive the announcement. Aubrey has some theory that marriage is likely to alienate a man from his friends, and it seems to me he has taken the precaution to wish us good-bye.

Misquith. No, no.

Jayne. Practically, surely.

Drummle [*thoughtfully*]. Marriage in general, does he mean, or *this* marriage?

Jayne. That's the point. Frank says——

Misquith. No, no, no; I feared it suggested——

Jayne. Well, well. [*To* DRUMMLE.] What do you think of it?

Drummle [*after a slight pause*]. Is there a light there?

[JAYNE *points to the spirit-lamp and walks up* L.C.

Drummle [*lighting his cigar*]. He—wraps the lady—in mystery —you say?

Misquith. Most modestly.

Drummle. Aubrey's—not—a very—young man.

Jayne [C.]. Forty-three.

Drummle. Ah! *L'âge critique!*

Misquith. A dangerous age—yes, yes.

Drummle. When you two fellows go home, do you mind leaving me behind here?

Misquith. Not at all.

Jayne. By all means.

Drummle. All right. [*Anxiously.*] Deuce take it, the man's second marriage mustn't be another mistake!

[*With his head bent he walks up to the fireplace.*

Jayne. You knew him in his short married life, Cayley. Terribly unsatisfactory, wasn't it?

Drummle. Well—— [*Looking at the door* R.] I quite closed that door?

Misquith. Yes.

[*He settles himself on the top end of the sofa;* JAYNE *is seated in an armchair.*

Drummle [*smoking, with his back to the fire*]. He married a Miss Herriott; that was in the year eighteen—confound dates—twenty years ago. She was a lovely creature—by Jove, she was; by religion a Roman Catholic. She was one of your cold sort, you know—all marble arms and black velvet. I remember her with painful distinctness as the only woman who ever made me nervous.

Misquith [*softly*]. Ha, ha!

Drummle. He loved her—to distraction, as they say. [*Glancing towards the door.*] Jupiter, how fervently that poor devil courted her! But I don't believe she allowed him even to squeeze her fingers. She *was* an iceberg! As for kissing, the mere contact would have given him chapped lips. However, he married her and took her away, the latter greatly to my relief.

Jayne. Abroad, you mean?

Drummle. Eh? Yes. I imagine he gratified her by renting a villa in Lapland, but I don't know. After a while they returned, and then I saw how woefully Aubrey had miscalculated results?

Jayne. Miscalculated——?

Drummle. He had reckoned, poor wretch, that in the early days of marriage she would thaw. But she didn't. I used to picture him closing his doors and making up the fire in the hope of seeing her features relax. Bless her, the thaw never set in! I believe she kept a thermometer in her stays and always registered ten degrees below zero. However, in time a child came—a daughter.

Jayne. Didn't that——?

Drummle. Not a bit of it; it made matters worse. Frightened at her failure to stir up in him some sympathetic religious belief, she determined upon strong measures with regard to the child. He opposed her for a miserable year or so, but she wore him down, and the insensible little brat was placed in a convent, first in France, then in Ireland. Not long afterwards the mother died—[*he comes down*]—strangely enough, of fever, the only warmth, I believe, that ever came to that woman's body.

Misquith. Don't, Cayley! [*He rises and slowly moves up* R.C.

Jayne. The child is living, we know.

Drummle. Yes, if you choose to call it living. Miss Tanqueray—a young woman of nineteen now—is in the Loretto convent at Armagh. She professes to have found her true vocation in a religious life, and within a month or two will take final vows.

[*He goes down* R.C. *and sits on the sofa.*

Misquith. He ought to have removed his daughter from the convent when the mother died.

[*He moves to front of the fire* C.

Drummle. Yes, yes, but absolutely at the end there was reconciliation between husband and wife, and she won his promise that the child should complete her conventual education. He reaped his reward. When he attempted to gain his girl's confidence and affection he was too late; he found that he was dealing with the spirit of the mother. You remember his visit to Ireland last month?

Jayne. Yes.

Drummle. That was to wish his girl good-bye.

Misquith. Poor fellow!

Drummle. He sent for me when he came back. I think he must have had a lingering hope that the girl would relent—would come to life, as it were—at the last moment, for, for an hour or so, in this room, he was terribly shaken. I'm sure he'd clung to that hope from the persistent way in which he kept breaking off in his talk to repeat one dismal word, as if he couldn't realize his position without dinning this damned word into his head.

Jayne. What word was that?

Drummle. Alone—alone. [AUBREY *enters* R.

Aubrey [*advancing to the fire*]. A thousand apologies!

Drummle [*gaily*]. We are talking about you, my dear Aubrey.

[*During the telling of the story*, MISQUITH *has risen and gone to the fire, and* DRUMMLE *has thrown himself full length on the sofa*. AUBREY *now joins* MISQUITH *and* JAYNE.

Aubrey [*between* MISQUITH *and* JAYNE]. Well, Cayley, are you surprised?

Drummle. Surp——! I haven't been surprised for twenty years.

Aubrey. And you're not angry with me?

Drummle. Angry! [*Rising*.] Because you considerately withhold the name of a lady with whom it is now the object of my life to become acquainted? My dear fellow, you pique my curiosity, you give zest to my existence! And as for a wedding, who on earth wants to attend that familiar and probably draughty function? Ugh! [*Crossing to the table* L.C.] My cigar's out.

Aubrey [*walking down* R.C.]. Let's talk about something else.

Misquith [*coming down, looking at his watch*]. Not to-night, Aubrey.

Aubrey. My dear Frank!

Misquith. I go up to Scotland to-morrow, and there are some little matters——

Jayne. I am off too.

Aubrey. No, no.

Jayne. I must: I have to give a look to a case in Clifford Street on my way home.

Aubrey [*going to the door* R.]. Well!

[MISQUITH *and* JAYNE *exchange looks with* DRUMMLE.

Aubrey [*opening the door and calling*]. Morse, hats and coats! [*Returning.*] I shall write to you all next week from Genoa or Florence. Now, Doctor, Frank, remember, my love to Mrs. Misquith and to Mrs. Jayne!

[MORSE *enters* R. *with hats and coats. He gives* MISQUITH'*s first, then* DRUMMLE'*s, then* JAYNE'*s.*

Misquith
Jayne } [*together*]. Yes, yes—yes, yes.

Aubrey. And your young people!

[*As* MISQUITH *and* JAYNE *put on their coats there is the clatter of careless talk.*

Jayne. Cayley, I meet you at dinner on Sunday.

Drummle. At the Stratfields'. That's very pleasant.

Misquith [*putting on his coat with* AUBREY'*s aid*]. Ah-h!

Aubrey. What's wrong?

Misquith. A twinge. Why didn't I go to Aix in August?

Jayne [*shaking hands with* DRUMMLE]. Good night, Cayley.

Drummle. Good night, my dear Doctor!

Misquith [*shaking hands with* DRUMMLE]. Cayley, are you in town for long?

Drummle. Dear friend, I'm nowhere for long. Good night.

Misquith. Good night.

[AUBREY, JAYNE, *and* MISQUITH *go out, followed by* MORSE; *the hum of talk is continued outside.*

Aubrey. A cigar, Frank?

Misquith. No, thank you.

Aubrey. Going to walk, Doctor?

Jayne. If Frank will.

Misquith. By all means.

Aubrey. It's a cold night.

[*The door is closed by* MORSE. DRUMMLE *remains standing* L.C. *with his coat on his arm and his hat in hand. The slam of the street door is heard off* R.

Drummle [*to himself, thoughtfully*]. Now then! What the devil——! [*After a short silence,* AUBREY *returns.*

Aubrey [*eyeing* DRUMMLE *a little awkwardly*]. Well, Cayley?

Drummle. Well, Aubrey?

[AUBREY *walks up to the fire and stands looking into it.* DRUMMLE *crosses to* R.C.

Aubrey. You're not going, old chap?

[DRUMMLE *deliberately puts his hat and coat on the sofa and sits.*

Drummle. No.

Aubrey [*after a slight pause, with a forced laugh*]. Hah! Cayley, I never thought I should feel—shy—with you. [*Going to fireplace.*

Drummle [*shortly*]. Why do you?

Aubrey. Never mind. [*Turns to fire.*

Drummle. Now, I can quite understand a man wishing to be married in the dark, as it were.

Aubrey. You can?

Drummle [*argumentatively*]. In your place I should very likely adopt the same course.

Aubrey. You think so?

Drummle. And if I intended marrying a lady not prominently in Society, as I presume you do—as I presume you do——

Aubrey. Well?

Drummle. As I presume you do, I'm not sure that *I* should tender her for preliminary dissection at afternoon tea-tables.

Aubrey. No?

Drummle. In fact, there is probably only one person—were I in your position to-night—with whom I should care to chat the matter over.

Aubrey. Who's that?

Drummle. Yourself, of course. [*Going to* AUBREY *and standing beside him.*] Of course, yourself, old friend.

Aubrey [*after a pause*]. I must seem a brute to you, Cayley. But there are some acts which are hard to explain, hard to defend——

Drummle. To defend——?

Aubrey. Some acts which one must trust to time to put right.

[*He sits* L.C. DRUMMLE *watches him for a moment, then takes up his hat and coat.*

Drummle. Well, I'll be moving.

Aubrey. Cayley! Confound you and your old friendship! Do you think I forget it? Put your coat down! Why did you stay behind here? Cayley, the lady I am going to marry is the lady—who is known as—Mrs. Jarman.

[*There is a pause.*

Drummle [*in a low voice*]. Mrs. Jarman! are you serious?

[*He walks up to the fireplace, where he leans upon the mantelpiece, uttering something like a groan.*

Aubrey [*starting up*]. As you've got this out of me I give you

Drummle [*offering his hand*]. Do prove it!

Aubrey [*taking his hand*]. We have spoken too freely of—of Mrs. Jarman. I was excited—angry. Please forget it!

Drummle. My dear Aubrey, when we next meet I shall remember nothing but my respect for the lady who bears your name.

[MORSE *enters, closing the door* R. *behind him carefully.*

Aubrey. What is it?

Morse [*hesitatingly*]. May I speak to you, sir? [DRUMMLE *wanders away up* L., *looking at the pictures. In an undertone.*] Mrs. Jarman, sir.

Aubrey [*softly to* MORSE]. Mrs. Jarman! Do you mean she is at the lodge in her carriage?

Morse. No, sir—here. [AUBREY *looks towards* DRUMMLE, *perplexed.*] There's a nice fire in your—in that room, sir.

[*Glancing in the direction of the door leading to the bedroom.*

Aubrey [*between his teeth, angrily*]. Very well.

[MORSE *retires.* AUBREY *moves up back of the sofa. Hearing the door close,* DRUMMLE *comes down.*

Drummle [*looking at his watch*]. A quarter to eleven—horrible. [*Crossing to sofa and taking up his hat and coat.*] Must get to bed—up late every night this week. [AUBREY *assists* DRUMMLE *with his coat, standing on his* L.; *and as he does so he looks towards the door up* L., *listening.*] Thank you. Well, good night, Aubrey. I feel I've been dooced serious, quite out of keeping with myself; pray overlook it.

Aubrey [*kindly*]. Ah, Cayley!

Drummle. And remember that, after all, I'm merely a spectator in life; nothing more than a man at a play, in fact; only, like the old-fashioned playgoer, I love to see certain characters happy and comfortable at the finish. You understand?

[*He delivers this speech with much surface gaiety, to hide deeper emotion.*

Aubrey. I think I do.

Drummle. Then, for as long as you can, old friend, will you—keep a stall for me?

Aubrey. Yes, Cayley.

Drummle [*gaily*]. Ah, ha! Good night! [*Bustling to the door.*] Don't bother! I'll let myself out! Good night! God bless yer!

[*He goes out;* AUBREY *follows him. The stage is empty for a moment, then* MORSE *enters by the other door up* L., *carrying some unopened letters which after a little consideration he places on the mantelpiece against the clock.* AUBREY *returns, walking across to* L.C. MORSE *goes to the door* R., *and stands waiting.*

Aubrey. Yes?

Morse. You hadn't seen your letters that came by the nine o'clock post, sir; I've put 'em where they'll catch your eye by and by.

Aubrey. Thank you.

Morse [*hesitatingly*]. Gunter's cook and waiter have gone, sir. Would you prefer me to go to bed?

Aubrey [*frowning*]. Certainly not.

Morse. Very well, sir. [*He goes out.*

Aubrey [*opening the upper door* L.]. Paula! Paula!

[*He goes* C. PAULA *enters and throws her arms round his neck. She is a young woman of about twenty-seven; beautiful, fresh, innocent-looking. She is in superb evening dress.*

Paula. Dearest!

Aubrey. Why have you come here?

Paula [*drawing back*]. Angry?

Aubrey. Yes—no. But it's eleven o'clock.

[*He shuts the door.*

Paula [*laughing*]. I know. [*Watching him.*

Aubrey. What on earth will Morse think? [*He returns.*

Paula. Do you trouble yourself about what servants *think*?

Aubrey. Of course.

Paula. Goose! They're only machines made to wait upon people—and to give evidence in the Divorce Court. [*Looking round.*] Oh, indeed! A snug little dinner!

Aubrey [*lightly*]. Three men.

Paula. [*suspiciously*]. Men?

Aubrey [*decisively*]. Men.

Paula [*penitently*]. Ah! [*Sitting* R. *of the table.*] I'm so hungry.

Aubrey. Let me get you some game pie, or some——

[*He moves to back of the table, as if going to the sideboard* L.

Paula. No, no, hungry for this. What beautiful fruit! I love fruit when it's expensive. [*He clears a space on the table, places a plate before her, and helps her to fruit.*] I haven't dined, Aubrey dear.

Aubrey. My poor girl! Why?

Paula. In the first place, I forgot to order any dinner, and my cook, who has always loathed me, thought he'd pay me out before he departed.

Aubrey. The beast!

Paula. That's precisely what I——

Aubrey. No, Paula!

Paula. What I told my maid to call him. What next will you think of me?

Aubrey [*sitting above the table*]. Forgive me. You must be starved.

Paula [*eating fruit*]. *I* didn't care. As there was nothing to eat, I sat in my best frock, with my toes on the dining-room fender, and dreamt, oh, such a lovely dinner-party.

Aubrey. Dear lonely little woman!

Paula. It was perfect. I saw you at the end of a very long table, opposite me, and we exchanged sly glances now and again over the flowers. We were host and hostess, Aubrey, and had been married about five years.

Aubrey [*kissing her hand*]. Five years.

Paula. And on each side of us was the nicest set imaginable—you know, dearest, the sort of men and women that can't be imitated.

Aubrey. Yes, yes. Eat some more fruit.

Paula. But I haven't told you the best part of my dream.

Aubrey. Tell me.

Paula. Well, although we had been married only such a few years, I seemed to know by the look on their faces that none of our guests had ever heard anything—anything—anything peculiar about the fascinating hostess.

Aubrey [*bending over her*]. That's just how it will be, Paula. The world moves so quickly. That's just how it will be.

Paula [*with a little grimace*]. I wonder! [*Glancing at the fire.*] Ugh! do throw another log on.

Aubrey [*rising and mending the fire*]. There. But you mustn't be here long.

Paula. Hospitable wretch! I've something important to tell you. [*He makes towards her. She stops him.*] No, stay where you are. [*Turning from him, her face averted.*] Look here, that was my dream, Aubrey; but the fire went out while I was dozing, and I woke up with a regular fit of the shivers. And the result of it all was that I ran upstairs and scribbled you a letter.

Aubrey [*another movement*]. Dear baby!

Paula. Remain where you are. [*Taking a letter from her pocket.*] This is it. [*Rising.*] I've given you an account of myself, furnished you with a list of my adventures since I—you know. [*Weighing the letter in her hand.*] I wonder if it would go for a penny. Most of it you're acquainted with; *I've* told you a good deal, haven't I?

Aubrey. Oh, Paula!

Paula. What I haven't told you I daresay you've heard from others. But in case they've omitted anything—the dears—it's all here.

Aubrey. Why in Heaven's name must you talk like this to-night?

Paula. It may save discussion by and by, don't you think? [*Holding out the letter.*] There you are.

Aubrey. No, dear, no. [*He takes the letter.*

Paula [R.C.]. Take it. Read it through after I've gone, and then—read it again, and turn the matter over in your mind finally. And if, even at the very last moment, you feel you—oughtn't to go to church with me, send a messenger to Pont Street, any time before eleven to-morrow, telling me that you're afraid, and I—I'll take the blow.

Aubrey [*quietly*]. Why, what—what do you think I am?

Paula. That's it. It's because I know you're such a dear good fellow that I want to save you the chance of ever feeling sorry you married me. I really love you so much, Aubrey, that to save you that I'd rather you treated me as—as the others have done.

Aubrey [*turning from her with a cry*]. Oh!

Paula [*after a slight pause*]. I suppose I've shocked you. I can't help it if I have.

[*She sits* R.C., *with assumed languor and indifference. He turns to her.*

Aubrey. My dearest, you don't understand me. I—I can't bear to hear you always talking about—what's done with. I tell you I'll never remember it; Paula, can't you dismiss it? Try. [*He kneels, impulsively, beside her.*] Darling, if we promise each other to forget, to forget, we're bound to be happy. After all, it's a mechanical matter; the moment a wretched thought enters your head, you quickly think of something bright—it depends on one's will. [*Referring to the letter he holds in his hand.*] Shall I burn this, dear? Let me, let me! [*Rising.*

Paula [*with a shrug of the shoulders*]. I don't suppose there's much that's new to you in it—just as you like.

[*He goes to the fire and burns the letter.*

Aubrey. There's an end of it. [*Returning to her*.] What's the matter?

Paula [*rising, coldly*]. Oh, nothing! [*Going up* L.C.] I'll go and put my cloak on.

Aubrey [*detaining her*]. What *is* the matter?

Paula [*pouting*]. Well, I think you might have said, 'You're very generous, Paula,' or at least, 'Thank you, dear,' when I offered to set you free.

Aubrey [*catching her in his arms*]. Ah!

Paula. Ah! ah! Ha, ha! It's all very well, but you don't know what it cost me to make such an offer. I do so want to be married.

Aubrey [*releasing her*]. But you never imagined——?

Paula. Perhaps not. And yet I *did* think of what I'd do at the end of our acquaintance if you had preferred to behave like the rest. [*Taking a flower from her bodice.*

Aubrey. Hush!

Paula [*indifferently*]. Oh, I forgot!

Aubrey. What would you have done when we parted?

Paula [*matter of fact*]. Why, killed myself.

Aubrey. Paula, dear!

Paula. It's true. [*She goes to him, putting the flower in his buttonhole*.] Do you know, I feel certain I should make away with myself if anything serious happened to me.

Aubrey. Anything serious! [*Blankly*.] What, has nothing ever been serious to you, Paula?

Paula. Not lately; not since a long while ago. [*Impressively*.] I made up my mind then to have done with taking things seriously. If I hadn't, I—— However, we won't talk about that.

Aubrey. But now, now, life will be different to you, won't it —quite different? Eh, dear?

Paula. Oh yes, now. [*Entreatively*.] Only, Aubrey, mind you keep me always happy.

Aubrey. I will try to.

Paula. I know I couldn't swallow a second big dose of misery. I know that if ever I felt wretched again—truly wretched—I should take a leaf out of Connie Tirlemont's book. You remember? [*With a look of horror*.] They found her——

[*She suddenly stops and looks down, as if she saw the lady in her 'mind's eye*.'

Aubrey. For God's sake, don't let your thoughts run on such things!

Paula [*laughing*]. Ha, ha, how scared you look! [*She goes up* L.C.; *then stops and looks at the clock.*] There, think of the time! Dearest, what will my coachman say! My cloak!

[*She runs off, gaily, by the upper door.* AUBREY *looks after her for a moment, then he walks up to the fire and stands warming his feet at the bars. As he does so he raises his head and observes the letters upon the mantelpiece. He takes one down quickly.*

Aubrey. Ah! Ellean! [*Opening the letter with a knife which he finds upon the writing-table and reading in a low voice.*] 'My dear father,—A great change has come over me. I believe my mother in Heaven has spoken to me, and counselled me to turn to you in your loneliness. At any rate, your words have reached my heart, and I no longer feel fitted for this solemn life. I am ready to take my place by you. Dear father, will you receive me?—Ellean.'

[PAULA *re-enters, dressed in a handsome cloak. He stares at her as if he hardly realized her presence. She goes down stage and picks up gloves that she has previously placed on* L.C. *table. Surprised at his silence, she turns to him.* AUBREY *comes* R. *of her.*

Paula. What are you staring at? Don't you admire my cloak?

Aubrey. Yes.

Paula [*petulantly*]. Couldn't you wait till I'd gone before reading your letters?

Aubrey [*putting the letter away*]. I beg your pardon.

Paula. Take me downstairs to the carriage. [*Slipping her arm through his.*] How I tease you! To-morrow! I'm so happy! [*They go out.*

THE CURTAIN FALLS.

ACT II

SCENE.—*A morning-room in* AUBREY TANQUERAY'*s house, 'Highercoombe', near Willowmere, Surrey—a bright and prettily furnished apartment of irregular shape. Down* R., *fireplace with fire burning. Up* R.C., *double doors opening into a small hall. Up* L.C., *a large recessed window through which is seen a view of extensive grounds. Down* L., *a door. Up* R., *a piano, open, and music-stool. Up* C., *a small table and two chairs. In the window-recess, a writing-table and library chair. On the blotting-book, an addressed letter stamped for the post. Down* R.C., *a circular table tastefully laid for breakfast —silver, flowers, fruit, etc. On the* R. *of this table, a settee to seat two persons; on the* L., *an armchair.* L.C., *a table; on the* L.

of this table, another settee to match its fellow. On the table, a newspaper. On the mantelpiece, a clock. Other articles of furniture to fill spaces—everything charming and tasteful.

TIME.—*A morning in early spring. The sun streams in through the window.*

AUBREY *and* PAULA *are seated* R.C. *at breakfast, and* AUBREY *is silently reading his letters. Two servants, a man and a woman, hand dishes and then retire, door* R.C. *After a little while* AUBREY *puts his letters aside and looks across to the window.*

Aubrey. Sunshine! Spring!

Paula [*glancing at the clock*]. Exactly six minutes.

Aubrey. Six minutes?

Paula. Six minutes, Aubrey dear, since you made your last remark.

Aubrey. I beg your pardon; I was reading my letters. Have you seen Ellean this morning?

Paula [*coldly*]. Your last observation but one was about Ellean.

Aubrey. Dearest, what *shall* I talk about?

Paula. Ellean breakfasted two hours ago, Morgan tells me, and then went out walking with her dog.

Aubrey. She wraps up warmly, I hope; this sunshine is deceptive.

Paula. I ran about the lawn last night, after dinner, in satin shoes. Were you anxious about me?

Aubrey. Certainly.

Paula [*melting*]. Really?

Aubrey. You make me wretchedly anxious; you delight in doing incautious things. You are incurable.

[*She rises and goes round back of the table to him.*

Paula. Ah, what a beast I am! [*Kissing him, then glancing at the letters by his side.*] A letter from Cayley?

Aubrey. He is staying very near here, with Mrs. —— Very near here.

Paula [*turning her face in the direction of the windows*]. With the lady whose chimneys we have the honour of contemplating from our windows? [*She moves over up* L.C.

Aubrey. With Mrs. Cortelyon—yes.

Paula. Mrs. Cortelyon! The woman who might have set the example of calling on me when we first threw out roots in this deadly-lively soil! Deuce take Mrs. Cortelyon!

[*She comes down.*

Aubrey. Hush! my dear girl!

Paula [*returning to her seat*]. Oh, I know she's an old acquaintance of yours—and of the first Mrs. Tanqueray. And she joins the rest of 'em in slapping the second Mrs. Tanqueray in the face. However, I have my revenge—she's six-and-forty, and I wish nothing worse to happen to any woman.

Aubrey. Well, she's going to town, Cayley says here, and his visit's at an end. He's coming over this morning to call on you. Shall we ask him to transfer himself to us? Do say yes.

Paula. Yes.

Aubrey [*gladly*]. Ah, ha! old Cayley!

Paula [*coldly*]. He'll amuse *you*.

Aubrey. And you too.

Paula. Because *you* find a companion, shall I be boisterously hilarious?

Aubrey. Come, come! He talks London, and you know you like that.

Paula. London! [*Putting her chair back*.] London or Heaven! which is farther from me?

Aubrey. Paula!

Paula. Oh! Oh, I am so bored, Aubrey!

[*She leans back wearily*.

Aubrey [*rising, gathering up his letters, looking at her puzzled and going to her, leaning over her shoulder*]. Baby, what can I do for you?

Paula. I suppose, nothing. You have done all you can for me.

Aubrey. What do you mean?

Paula. You have married me.

[*He walks away from her thoughtfully, to the writing-table. As he places his letters on the table he sees an addressed letter, stamped for the post, lying on the blotting-book; he picks it up*.

Aubrey [*in an altered tone*]. You've been writing this morning before breakfast?

Paula [*looking at him quickly, then away again*]. Er—that letter.

Aubrey [*coming towards her with the letter in his hand*]. To Lady Orreyed. Why?

Paula. Why not? Mabel's an old friend of mine.

Aubrey [C.]. Are you—corresponding?

Paula. I heard from her yesterday. They've just returned from the Riviera. She seems happy.

Aubrey [*sarcastically*]. That's good news.

Paula. Why are you always so cutting about Mabel? She's a kind-hearted girl. Everything's altered; she even thinks of letting her hair go back to brown. She's Lady Orreyed. She's married to George. What's the matter with her?

Aubrey [*turning away*]. Oh! [*He crosses to his seat again.*

Paula [*excitedly*]. You drive me mad sometimes with the tone you take about things! [*Jumping up.*] Great goodness, if you come to that, George Orreyed's wife isn't a bit worse than yours! [*She crosses to* C. *He faces her suddenly. Soberly.*] I suppose I needn't have made that observation.

Aubrey. No, there was scarcely a necessity.

[*He throws the letter on to the table* L.C., *and takes up the newspaper and sits* L.C.

Paula. I am very sorry. [*Advancing a step or two.*

Aubrey. All right, dear. [*With a nod, quietly.*

Paula [R. *of* L.C. *table, trifling with the letter*]. I—I'd better tell you what I've written. I meant to do so, of course. I—I've asked the Orreyeds to come and stay with us. [*He looks at her and lets the paper fall to the ground in a helpless way.*] George was a great friend of Cayley's. [*With rising anger.*] I'm sure *he* would be delighted to meet them here.

Aubrey [*throwing his head back, laughing mirthlessly*]. Ha, ha, ha! They say Orreyed has taken to tippling at dinner. Heavens above!

Paula [*walking away, throws letter down*]. Oh! I've no patience with you! You'll kill me with this life! [*She crosses to back of* R. *chair, selects some flowers from a vase on the table* R.C., *cuts and arranges them, and fastens them in her bodice.*] What is my existence Sunday to Saturday? In the morning, a drive down to the village with the groom, to give my orders to the tradespeople. At lunch, you and Ellean. [*Playing with nosegay off table.*] In the afternoon, a novel, the newspapers; if fine, another drive—*if* fine! Tea—you and Ellean. Then two hours of dusk; then dinner—you and Ellean. Then a game of Bésique, you and I, while Ellean reads a religious book in a dull corner. Then a yawn from me, another from you, a sigh from Ellean; three figures suddenly rise—'Good night, good night, good night!' [*Imitating a kiss.*] 'God bless you!' [*With an exaggerated sigh of dejection and putting nosegay in belt.*] Ah!

Aubrey. Yes, yes, Paula—yes, dearest—that's what it is *now*. But, by and by, if people begin to come round us——

Paula. Hah! [*Advancing to him and standing* R. *of the table*.] That's where we've made the mistake, my friend Aubrey! [*Pointing to the window*.] Do you believe these people will *ever* come round us? Your former crony, Mrs. Cortelyon? Or the grim old vicar, or that wife of his whose huge nose is positively indecent? Or the Ullathornes, or the Gollans, or Lady William Petres? I know better! And when the young ones gradually take the place of the old, there will still remain the sacred tradition that the dreadful person who lives at the top of the hill is never, under any circumstances, to be called upon! [*She moves* C.] And so we shall go on here, year in and year out, until the sap is run out of our lives, and we're stale and dry and withered from sheer, solitary respectability. Upon my word, I wonder we didn't see that we should have been far happier if we'd gone in for the devil-may-care, *café*-living sort of life in town! After all, *I* have a set and you might have joined it. It's true I did want, dearly, dearly, to be a married woman, but where's the pride in being a married woman among married women who are—married! If—— [*Seeing that* AUBREY'*s head has sunk into his hands*.] Aubrey! My dear boy! [*She goes to him*.] You're not—crying?

[*He looks up, with a flushed face*. ELLEAN *enters, door up* R.C., *dressed very simply for walking. She is a low-voiced, grave girl of about nineteen, with a face somewhat resembling a Madonna. Towards* PAULA *her manner is cold and distant*.

Aubrey [*in an undertone*]. Ellean!

Ellean. Good morning, Papa. [*Coming down* C.] Good morning, Paula.

[PAULA *puts her arms round* ELLEAN *and kisses her on the left cheek*. ELLEAN *makes little response*.

Paula. Good morning. [*Going to the piano—brightly*.] We've been breakfasting this side of the house, to get the sun.

[*She sits at the piano and rattles at a gay melody. Seeing that* PAULA'*s back is turned to them*, ELLEAN *goes to* AUBREY *and kisses him; he returns the kiss almost furtively. As they separate, the servants re-enter door up* R.C. *The manservant places the chair on which* PAULA *has been sitting* R. *of* L.C. *table. Then both servants proceed to carry out the breakfast-table*.

Aubrey [*to* ELLEAN *while this is going on*]. I guess where you've been: there's some gorse clinging to your frock.

Ellean [*removing a sprig of gorse from her skirt*]. Rover and I walked nearly as far as Black Moor. The poor fellow has a thorn in his pad; I am going upstairs for my tweezers.

Aubrey. Ellean! [*She returns to him.*] Paula is a little depressed—out of sorts. She complains that she has no companion.

Ellean. I am with Paula nearly all the day, Papa.

Aubrey. Ah, but you're such a little mouse. Paula likes cheerful people about her.

Ellean. I'm afraid I am naturally rather silent; and it's so difficult to seem to be what one is not.

Aubrey. I don't wish that, Ellean.

Ellean. I will offer to go down to the village with Paula this morning—shall I?

Aubrey [*touching her hand gently*]. Thank you—do.

Ellean. When I've looked after Rover, I'll come back to her.

[*She goes out, door down* L.; PAULA *ceases playing, and turns on the music-stool looking at* AUBREY.

Paula. Well, have you and Ellean had your little confidence?

[*She comes down to settee* R.C. *and sits.*

Aubrey. Confidence?

Paula. Do you think I couldn't feel it, like a pain between my shoulders?

Aubrey [*going to her*]. Ellean is coming back in a few minutes to be with you. [*Bending over her.*] Paula, Paula dear, is this how you keep your promise!

Paula. Oh! [*Rising impatiently and crossing swiftly to the settee* L.C., *where she sits, moving restlessly.*] I *can't* keep my promise; I *am* jealous; it won't be smothered. [*Vehemently.*] I see you looking at her, watching her; your voice drops when you speak to her. I know how fond you are of of that girl, Aubrey.

Aubrey. What would you have? I've no other home for her. She is my daughter.

Paula. She is your saint. Saint Ellean!

Aubrey [R.C.]. You have often told me how good and sweet you think her.

Paula [C.]. Good!—yes. Do you imagine *that* makes me less jealous? [*Going to him and clinging to his arm.*] Aubrey, there are two sorts of affection—the love for a woman you respect, and the love for a woman you—love. She gets the first from you: I never can.

Aubrey. Hush, hush! you don't realize what you say.

Paula. If Ellean cared for me only a little, it would be different. I shouldn't be jealous then. Why doesn't she care for me?

Aubrey. She—she—she will, in time.

Paula. You can't say that without stuttering.

Aubrey. Her disposition seems a little unresponsive; she resembles her mother in many ways; I can see it every day.

Paula. She's marble. It's a shame. There's not the slightest excuse; for all she knows, I'm as much a saint as she—only married. Dearest, help me to win her over!

Aubrey. Help you?

Paula. You can. [*Persuasively*.] Teach her that it is her duty to love me; she hangs on to every word you speak. I'm sure, Aubrey, that the love of a nice woman who believed me to be like herself would do me a world of good. You'd get the benefit of it as well as I. It would soothe me; it would make me less horribly restless; it would take this—this—mischievous feeling from me. [*Coaxingly*.] Aubrey!

Aubrey. Have patience; everything will come right.

Paula. Yes, if you help me.

Aubrey. In the meantime you will tear up your letter to Lady Orreyed, won't you?

Paula [*kissing his hand*]. Of course I will—anything!

[*She moves away from him to* L.C. *table and standing at back of it picks up letter*.

Aubrey. Ah, thank you, dearest! [*Laughing*.] Just imagine 'Saint Ellean' and that woman side by side!

[*He crosses* R. *to fire*.

Paula [*going back with a cry*]. Ah!

Aubrey. What?

Paula [*passionately*]. It's Ellean you're considering, not me! It's all Ellean with you! Ellean! Ellean!

[ELLEAN *re-enters, door down* L.

Ellean. Did you call me, Paula? [*Clenching his hands*, AUBREY *turns away and goes out door up* R.C.] Is Papa angry?

Paula [*shrugging her shoulders*]. I drive him distracted sometimes. [*Walking away to settee* R. *and sitting, petulantly*.] There, I confess it!

Ellean [*advancing*]. Do you? Oh, why do you?

Paula. Because I—because I'm jealous.

Ellean [*jealous*]. Jealous?

Paula. Yes—of you. [ELLEAN *is silent. Facing her.*] Well, what do you think of that?

Ellean. I knew it; I've seen it. It hurts me dreadfully. What do you wish me to do? [*By chair* L.C.] Go away?

Paula. Leave us! [*Beckoning her with a motion of the head.*] Look here! [ELLEAN *goes to* PAULA *slowly and unresponsively.*] You could cure me of my jealousy very easily. Why don't you—like me?

Ellean [*tremblingly*]. What do you mean by—like you? I don't understand.

Paula. Love me.

Ellean. Love is not a feeling that is under one's control. I shall alter as time goes on, perhaps. [*She moves* C.] I didn't begin to love my father deeply till a few months ago, and then I obeyed my mother.

Paula [*dryly*]. Ah, yes, you dream things, don't you—see them in your sleep? You fancy your mother speaks to you?

Ellean. When you have lost your mother it is a comfort to believe that she is dead only to this life, that she still watches over her child. I do believe that of my mother.

Paula [*slowly*]. Well, and so you haven't been bidden to love *me*?

Ellean [*after a pause, almost inaudibly*]. No. [*Moves to chair.*

Paula. Dreams are only a hash-up of one's day-thoughts, I suppose you know. Think intently of anything, and it's bound to come back to you at night. I don't cultivate dreams myself.

Ellean. Ah, I knew you would only sneer! [*She sits* L.C.

Paula. I'm not sneering; I'm speaking the truth. [*Rising.*] I say that if you cared for me in the daytime I should soon make friends with those nightmares of yours. [*Eyeing her askance, hesitatingly.*] Ellean, why don't you try to look on me as your second mother? [ELLEAN *gives* PAULA *a quick look, then sits motionless.*] Of course there are not many years between us, but I'm ever so much older than you—in experience. I shall have no children of my own, I know that; it would be a real comfort to me if you would make me feel we belonged to each other. Won't you? [ELLEAN *rises and stands front of* L.C. *table.*] Perhaps you think I'm odd—not nice. Well, the fact is I've two sides to my nature, and I've let the one almost smother the other. A few years ago I went through some trouble, and since then I haven't shed a tear. I believe if you put your arms round me just once I should run upstairs and have a good cry. There, I've talked to you as I've never talked to a woman in my life. Ellean, you seem to fear me. Don't! Kiss me! [*With a cry, almost of despair,* ELLEAN *turns from* PAULA, *and sinks on to the settee* L., *covering her face with her hands. Indignantly.*] Oh! Why is it! How dare you treat me like this? What do you mean by it? What do you mean? [*A* SERVANT *enters.*

Servant. Mr. Drummle, ma'am.

[CAYLEY DRUMMLE, *in riding dress, enters briskly and comes down to* PAULA. *The* SERVANT *retires.*

Paula [*recovering herself*]. Well, Cayley!

[*She crosses to the fireplace.*

Drummle [*shaking hands with her cordially*]. How are you? [*Shaking hands with* ELLEAN, *who rises.*] I saw you in the distance an hour ago, in the gorse near Stapleton's.

Ellean. I didn't see you, Mr. Drummle.

Drummle. My dear Ellean, it is my experience that no charming young lady of nineteen ever does see a man of forty-five. [*Laughing.*] Ha, ha!

Ellean [*crossing in front of him and going to the door*]. Paula, Papa wishes me to drive down to the village with you this morning. Do you care to take me?

Paula [*coldly*]. Oh, by all means. Pray tell Watts to balance the cart for three. [ELLEAN *goes out.*

Drummle [*crossing* R.C.]. How's Aubrey?

Paula. Very well—when Ellean's about the house.

Drummle. And you? I needn't ask.

Paula [*walking away to the window*]. Oh, a dog's life, my dear Cayley, mine.

Drummle [*crossing* R.C., *turning, watching her*]. Eh?

Paula. Doesn't that define a happy marriage? I'm sleek, well-kept, well-fed, never without a bone to gnaw and fresh straw to lie upon. [*Gazing out of the window.*] Oh, dear me!

Drummle [*to himself*]. H'm. [*Crossing to the fireplace—aloud.*] Well, I heartily congratulate you on your kennel. The view from the terrace here is superb.

Paula. Yes, I can see London.

Drummle. London! Not quite so far, surely?

Paula. I can. [*Turning.*] Also the Mediterranean, on a fine day. I wonder what Algiers looks like this morning from the sea! [*Coming down impulsively.*] Oh, Cayley, do you remember those jolly times on board Peter Jarman's yacht when we lay off——? [*Stopping suddenly, seeing* DRUMMLE *staring at her—half to herself.*] Good gracious! What are we talking about!

[*She moves* L.C. AUBREY *enters, door up* R.C., *which he leaves open.*

Aubrey [*coming down to* DRUMMLE]. Dear old chap! Has Paula asked you?

Paula. Not yet.

Aubrey. We want you to come to us, now that you're leaving Mrs. Cortelyon—at once, to-day. Stay a month, as long as you please—eh, Paula?

Paula. As long as you can possibly endure it—do, Cayley.

Drummle [*looking at* AUBREY]. Delighted. [*Advancing to* PAULA.] Charming of you to have me.

Paula. My dear man, you're a blessing. Ha! Ha! I must telegraph to London for more fish! A strange appetite to cater for! [*Almost childishly delighted.*] Something to do, to do, to do! [*She goes out, door down* L.

Drummle [L.C., *eyeing* AUBREY]. Well?

Aubrey [*with a wearied, anxious look*). Well, Cayley?

Drummle. How are you getting on?

Aubrey. My position doesn't grow less difficult. [*He goes up stage and shuts door; then comes down* R.C. *and sits.*] I told you, when I met you last week, of this feverish, jealous attachment of Paula's for Ellean?

Drummle. Yes. I hardly know why, but I came to the conclusion that you don't consider it an altogether fortunate attachment.

Aubrey [*troubled*]. Ellean doesn't respond to it.

Drummle. These are early days. Ellean will warm towards your wife by and by. [*Soothingly.*

Aubrey [*striking the arm of the settee nervously*]. Ah, but there's the question, Cayley!

Drummle. What question?

Aubrey. The question which positively distracts me. Ellean is so different from—most women; I don't believe a purer creature exists out of heaven. [*With difficulty.*] And I—I ask myself, am I doing right in exposing her to the influence of poor Paula's light, careless nature?

Drummle [*in a low voice*]. My dear Aubrey! [*He moves* L.C.

Aubrey. That shocks you! So it does me. [*Rising.*] I assure you I long to urge my girl to break down the reserve which keeps her apart from Paula, but somehow I can't do it—well, I don't do it. [DRUMMLE *sits* L.C.] How can I make you understand? But when you come to us you'll understand quickly enough. Cayley, there's hardly a subject you can broach on which poor Paula hasn't some strange, out-of-the-way thought to give utterance to; some curious, warped notion. They are not mere worldly thoughts—unless, good God! they belong to the little hellish world which our blackguardism has created: no, her ideas have too little calculation in them to be called worldly. But it makes it the more dreadful that such thoughts should be ready, spontaneous; that expressing them has become a perfectly natural process; that her words, acts even, have almost lost their proper significance for her, and seem beyond her control. [*Going to him.*] Ah, and the pain of listening to it all from the woman one loves, the woman one hoped to make happy and contented, who is really and truly a good woman, as it were, maimed! Well, this is my burden, and I shouldn't speak to you of it but for my anxiety about Ellean. Ellean! What is to be her future? It is in my hands; what am I to do? Cayley, when I remember how Ellean comes to me, from another world I always think, when I realize the charge that's laid on me, I find myself wishing, in a sort of terror, that my child were safe under the ground.

[*He walks away up to the writing-table and sits apart.* DRUMMLE *crosses to the fire thoughtfully.*

Drummle [R.]. My dear Aubrey, aren't you making a mistake?

Aubrey [*not turning*]. Very likely. What is it?

Drummle. A mistake, not in regarding your Ellean as an angel, but in believing that, under any circumstances, it would be possible for her to go through life without getting her white robe—shall we say, a little dusty at the hem? [*He moves to top end of settee* R.C. *and sits.*] Don't take me for a cynic. I am sure there are many women upon earth who are almost divinely innocent; but being on earth, they must send their robes to the laundry occasionally. Ah, and it's right that they should have to do so, for what can they learn from the checking of their little washing-bills but lessons of charity? Now I see but two courses open to you for the disposal of your angel.

Aubrey. Yes?

Drummle [*looking round at room*]. You must either restrict her to a paradise which is, like every earthly paradise, necessarily somewhat imperfect, or treat her as an ordinary flesh-and-blood young woman, and give her the advantages of that society to which she properly belongs.

Aubrey [*turning to* DRUMMLE]. Advantages?

Drummle. My dear Aubrey, of all forms of innocence mere ignorance is the least admirable. Take my advice, let her walk and talk and suffer and be healed with the great crowd. Do it, and hope that she'll some day meet a good, honest fellow who'll make her life complete, happy, secure. Now you see what I'm driving at.

Aubrey. A sanguine programme, my dear Cayley! [*Rising and coming down*.] Oh, I'm not pooh-poohing it. Putting sentiment aside, of course I know that a fortunate marriage for Ellean would be the best—perhaps the only—solution of my difficulty. But you forget the danger of the course you suggest.

Drummle. Danger?

Aubrey. If Ellean goes among men and women, how can she escape from learning, sooner or later, the history of—poor Paula's—old life?

Drummle. H'm! [*He rises*.] You remember the episode of the Jeweller's Son in the Arabian Nights? Of course you don't. [*Earnestly*.] Well, if your daughter lives, she *can't* escape—what you're afraid of. [AUBREY *gives a half-stifled exclamation of pain, leaves* DRUMMLE *and sits. Going to him*.] And when she does hear the story, surely it would be better that she should have some knowledge of the world to help her to understand it.

Aubrey. To understand!

Drummle. To understand, to—to philosophize.

Aubrey. To philosophize?

Dummle. Philosophy is toleration, and it is only one step from toleration to forgiveness.

Aubrey. You're right, Cayley; I believe you always are. Yes, yes. But, even if I had the courage to attempt to solve the problem of Ellean's future in this way, I—I'm helpless.

Drummle. How?

Aubrey. What means have I now of placing my daughter in the world I've left?

Drummle. Oh, some friend—some woman friend.

Aubrey [*in a low voice*]. I have none; they're gone.

Drummle. You're wrong there; I know one——

Aubrey [*rising—listening*]. That's Paula's cart. [*Walking across to the fireplace*.] Let's discuss this again.

Drummle [*going up to the window and looking out*]. It isn't the dog-cart. [*Turning to* AUBREY.] I hope you'll forgive me, old chap.

Aubrey. What for?

Drummle. Whose wheels do you think have been cutting ruts in your immaculate drive?

[*A* SERVANT *enters, door up* R.C.

Servant [*to* AUBREY]. Mrs. Cortelyon, sir.

Aubrey. Mrs. Cortelyon! [*After a short pause*.] Very well. [*The* SERVANT *withdraws*.] What on earth is the meaning of this?

Drummle [*coming down* C.]. Ahem! While I've been our old friend's guest, Aubrey, we have very naturally talked a good deal about you and yours.

Aubrey [*dryly*]. Indeed, have you?

Drummle. Yes, and Alice Cortelyon has arrived at the conclusion that it would have been far kinder had she called on Mrs. Tanqueray long ago. [*Slyly*.] She's going abroad for Easter before settling down in London for the season, and I believe she has come over this morning to ask for Ellean's companionship.

Aubrey. Oh, I see! [*Frowning*.] Quite a friendly little conspiracy, my dear Cayley!

Drummle. Conspiracy! Not at all, I assure you. [*Laughing*.] Ha, ha!

[ELLEAN *enters from the hall, door up* R.C., *with* MRS. CORTELYON, *a handsome, good-humoured, spirited woman of about forty-five*.

Ellean [*up* C.]. Papa——

[DRUMMLE *joins* ELLEAN *and stands talking when in doorway*.

Mrs. Cortelyon [*coming down to* AUBREY, *and shaking hands with him heartily*]. Well, Aubrey, how are you? I've just been telling this great girl of yours that I knew her when she was a sad-faced, pale baby. How is Mrs. Tanqueray? I have been a bad neighbour, and I'm here to beg forgiveness. Is she indoors?

Aubrey. She's upstairs putting on a hat, I believe.

Mrs. Cortelyon [*sitting* C., *comfortably*]. Ah! [*She looks round*.] We used to be very frank with each other, Aubrey. I suppose the old footing is no longer possible, eh?

Aubrey. If so, I'm not entirely to blame, Mrs. Cortelyon.

Mrs. Cortelyon. Mrs. Cortelyon? H'm! No, I admit it. But you must make some little allowance for me, *Mr. Tanqueray*. Your first wife and I, as girls, were like two cherries on one stalk, and then I was the confidential friend of your married life. That post, perhaps, wasn't altogether a sinecure. And now—well, when a woman gets to my age I suppose she's a stupid, prejudiced, conventional creature. However, I've got over it and—[*Giving him her hand.*]—I hope you'll be enormously happy and let me be a friend once more.

Aubrey. Thank you, Alice.

Mrs. Cortelyon. That's right. I feel more cheerful than I've done for weeks. But I suppose it would serve me right if the second Mrs. Tanqueray showed me the door. Do you think she will?

Aubrey [*listening*]. Here is my wife. [MRS. CORTELYON *rises and moves* C. *and* PAULA *enters, door down* L., *dressed for driving; she stops abruptly on seeing* MRS. CORTELYON. ELLEAN *slowly moves to window and sits.* DRUMMLE *remains standing in doorway. He afterwards moves down* R. *to fireplace* R.C.] Paula dear, Mrs. Cortelyon has called to see you.

[PAULA *starts, looks at* MRS. CORTELYON *irresolutely, then after a slight pause barely touches* MRS. CORTELYON'*s extended hand.*

Paula [*whose manner now alternates between deliberate insolence and assumed sweetness*]. Mrs.——? What name, Aubrey?

Aubrey. Mrs. Cortelyon.

Paula. Cortelyon? Oh, yes. Cortelyon.

Mrs. Cortelyon [*carefully guarding herself throughout against any expression of resentment*]. Aubrey ought to have told you that Alice Cortelyon and he are very old friends.

Paula. Oh, very likely he has mentioned the circumstance. I have quite a wretched memory.

Mrs. Cortelyon. You know we are neighbours, Mrs. Tanqueray.

Paula. Neighbours? Are we really? Won't you sit down? [*They both sit.* MRS. CORTELYON *sits* R.C., PAULA C.] Neighbours! That's most interesting!

Mrs. Cortelyon. Very near neighbours. You can see my roof from your windows.

Paula. I fancy I *have* observed a roof. But you have been away from home; you have only just returned.

Mrs. Cortelyon. I? What makes you think that?

Paula. Why, because it is two months since we came to Highercoombe, and I don't remember your having called.

Mrs. Cortelyon. Your memory is now terribly accurate. No, I've not been away from home, and it is to explain my neglect that I am here, rather unceremoniously, this morning.

Paula. Oh, to explain—quite so. [*With mock solicitude. She rises and goes to her.*] Ah, you've been very ill; I ought to have seen that before.

Mrs. Cortelyon. Ill!

Paula. You look dreadfully pulled down. We poor women show illness so plainly in our faces, don't we?

Aubrey [*behind table* L.C.—*anxiously*]. Paula dear, Mrs. Cortelyon is the picture of health.

Mrs. Cortelyon [*with some asperity*]. I have never *felt* better in my life.

Paula [*looking round innocently*]. Have I said anything awkward? [*Turning to* AUBREY.] Aubrey, tell Mrs. Cortelyon how stupid and thoughtless I always am!

[*She sits* L.C. DRUMMLE, *who has been watching the two ladies, is now on* MRS. CORTELYON'*s* R.

Mrs. Cortelyon [*aside to* DRUMMLE, *who is now standing close to her*]. Really, Cayley—— [*He soothes her with a nod and smile and a motion of his finger to his lip, then wanders away again up* R.] Mrs. Tanqueray, I am afraid my explanation will not be quite so satisfactory as either of those you have just helped me to. You may have heard—but, if you have heard, you have doubtless forgotten—that twenty years ago, when your husband first lived here, I was a constant visitor at Highercoombe.

Paula. Twenty years ago—fancy! I was a naughty little child then.

Mrs. Cortelyon. Possibly. Well, at that time, and till the end of her life, my affections were centred upon the lady of this house.

Paula. Were they? That was very sweet of you.

[ELLEAN *creeps down quietly to* MRS. CORTELYON, *listening intently to her.*

Mrs. Cortelyon. I will say no more on that score, but I must add this: when, two months ago, you came here, I realized, perhaps for the first time, that I was a middle-aged woman, and that it had become impossible for me to accept without some effort a breaking-in upon many tender associations. There, Mrs. Tanqueray, that is my confession. Will you try to understand it and pardon me?

Paula [*watching* ELLEAN—*sneeringly*]. Ellean dear, you appear to be very interested in Mrs. Cortelyon's reminiscences; I don't think I can do better than make you my mouthpiece—there is such sympathy between us. [*Leaning back languidly.*] What do you say—can we bring ourselves to forgive Mrs. Cortelyon for neglecting us for two weary months?

Mrs. Cortelyon [*to* ELLEAN, *pleasantly*]. Well, Ellean? [*With a little cry of tenderness* ELLEAN *impulsively sits beside* MRS. CORTELYON *and takes her hand.*] My dear child!

[ELLEAN *sits with* MRS. CORTELYON *on settee* R.

Paula [*in an undertone to* AUBREY]. Ellean isn't so very slow in taking to Mrs. Cortelyon!

Mrs. Cortelyon [*to* PAULA *and* AUBREY]. Come, this encourages me to broach my scheme. Mrs. Tanqueray, it strikes me that you two good people are just now excellent company for each other, while Ellean would perhaps be glad of a little peep into the world you are anxious to avoid. Now, I'm going to Paris to-morrow for a week or two before settling down in Chester Square, so—don't gasp, both of you!—if this girl is willing, and you have made no other arrangements for her, will you let her come with me to Paris, and afterwards remain with me in town during the Season? [ELLEAN *utters an exclamation of surprise.* PAULA *is silent. After a pause.*] What do you say?

Aubrey [L.C., *gently*]. Paula—Paula dear. [*Hesitatingly, moves* C.] My dear Mrs. Cortelyon, this is wonderfully kind of you; I am really at a loss to—eh, Cayley?

Drummle (*up stage, watching* PAULA *apprehensively*]. Kind! Now I must say I don't think so! I begged Alice to take *me* to Paris, and she declined. I am thrown over for Ellean! Ha! Ha!

Mrs. Cortelyon [*laughing*]. What nonsense you talk, Cayley!

[*The laughter dies out.* PAULA *remains quite still.*

Aubrey. Paula dear.

[*He crosses to* PAULA'*s chair and stands behind table.*

Paula [*slowly collecting herself*]. One moment. I—I don't quite—— [*To* MRS. CORTELYON.] You propose that Ellean leaves Highercoombe almost at once and remains with you some months?

Mrs. Cortelyon. It would be a mercy to me. You can afford to be generous to a desolate old widow. Come, Mrs. Tanqueray, won't you spare her?

Paula. Won't *I* spare her. [*Suspiciously.*] Have you mentioned your plan to Aubrey—before I came in?

Mrs. Cortelyon. No, I had no opportunity.

Paula. Nor to Ellean?

Mrs. Cortelyon. Oh, no.

Paula [*looking about her, in suppressed excitement*]. This hasn't been discussed at all, behind my back?

Mrs. Cortelyon. My dear Mrs. Tanqueray!

Paula [*forcing her chair back a little*]. Ellean, let us hear your voice in the matter!

Ellean. I should like to go with Mrs. Cortelyon——

Paula. Ah!

Ellean. That is, if—if——

Paula. If—if what?

Ellean [*looking towards* AUBREY, *appealingly*]. Papa?

Paula [*in a hard voice*]. Oh, of course—I forgot. [*To* AUBREY.] My dear Aubrey, it rests with you, naturally, whether I am —to lose—Ellean.

Aubrey [*brightly*]. Lose Ellean! [*Advancing to* PAULA.] There is no question of losing Ellean. [*Going to* C.] You would see Ellean in town constantly when she returned from Paris; isn't that so, Mrs. Cortelyon? [*Crosses more* R.C.

Mrs. Cortelyon. Certainly.

Paula [*laughing softly*]. Oh, I didn't know I should be allowed that privilege.

Mrs. Cortelyon. Privilege, my dear Mrs. Tanqueray!

Paula. Ha, ha! that makes all the difference, doesn't it?

Aubrey [*with assumed gaiety*]. All the difference? I should think so! [*To* ELLEAN, *laying his hand upon her head, tenderly.*] And you are quite certain you wish to see what the world is like on the other side of Black Moor?

Ellean [*in a low voice*]. If you are willing, Papa, I am quite certain. [*She rises.*

Aubrey [*looking at* PAULA *irresolutely, then speaking with an effort*]. Then I—I am willing.

Paula [*rising and striking the table lightly with her clenched hand*]. That decides it! [*There is a general movement.* AUBREY *and* ELLEAN *go up stage;* MRS. CORTELYON *advances to* PAULA; DRUMMLE *remains in front of fire. Excitedly to* MRS. CORTELYON, *who advances towards her.*] When do you want her?

Mrs. Cortelyon. We go to town this afternoon at five o'clock, and sleep to-night at Bayliss's. There is barely time for her to make her preparations.

Paula. I will undertake that she is ready.

Mrs. Cortelyon. I've a great deal to scramble through at home too, as you may guess. Good-bye!

[*She offers her hand.*

Paula [*turning away*]. Mrs. Cortelyon is going.

[PAULA *stands up* L.C., *looking out of the window, with her back to those in the room.* DRUMMLE *comes down to* MRS. CORTELYON.

Mrs. Cortelyon [*aside to* DRUMMLE]. Cayley——

Drummle [*aside to her*]. Eh?

Mrs. Cortelyon. I've gone through it, for the sake of Aubrey and his child, but I—I feel a hundred. Is that a madwoman?

Drummle. Of course; all jealous women are mad.

[*He goes up and exits* R. *with* AUBREY. MRS. CORTELYON *moves up stage* C.

Mrs. Cortelyon [*hesitatingly, to* PAULA]. Good-bye, Mrs. Tanqueray.

[PAULA *inclines her head with the slightest possible movement, then resumes her former position.* ELLEAN *comes from the hall and takes* MRS. CORTELYON *out of the room off* R. *After a brief silence,* PAULA *turns with a fierce cry, and hurriedly takes off her coat and hat, almost tearing them from her, and tosses them upon the settee* L.C. *Upon removing her hat, she stabs it viciously with long fastener.*

Paula. Oh! Oh! Oh! [*She drops into the chair* C. *as* AUBREY *returns; he stands up* R.C., *looking at her.*] Who's that?

Aubrey [*coming down*]. I. You have altered your mind about going out?

Paula. Yes. Please to ring the bell.

Aubrey [*touching the bell on wall* R.]. You are angry about Mrs. Cortelyon and Ellean. Let me try to explain my reasons—— [*He returns* C.

Paula. Be careful what you say to me just now! I have never felt like this—except once—in my life. [*With great intensity.*] Be careful what you say to me! [*A* SERVANT *enters, door* R.C. *Rising.*] Is Watts at the door with the cart?

Servant [*coming down*]. Yes, ma'am.

Paula [*picking up the letter which has been lying upon the table,* L.C.]. Tell him to drive down to the post office directly, with this.

Aubrey [*advancing a step*]. With that?

Paula [*calmly*]. Yes. My letter to Lady Orreyed.

[*She gives the letter to the* SERVANT, *who goes out.*

Aubrey [*quickly*]. Surely you don't wish me to countermand any order of yours to a servant? Call the man back—take the letter from him!

Paula. I have not the slightest intention of doing so.

Aubrey [*going to the door* R.C.]. I must, then. [*She snatches up her hat and coat and follows him.*] What are you going to do?

Paula. If you stop that letter, walk out of the house.

[*He hesitates, then leaves the door, and comes down* R.C.

Aubrey. I am right in believing that to be the letter inviting George Orreyed and his wife to stay here, am I not?

Paula. Oh yes—quite right.

Aubrey. Let it go; I'll write to him by and by.

Paula [*coming down to him and facing him*]. You dare!

Aubrey [*pained at her violence*]. Hush, Paula!

Paula. Insult me again and, upon my word, I'll go straight out of the house!

Aubrey. Insult you?

Paula. Insult me! What else is it? My God! what else is it? [*Throwing her hat and coat on table* C.] What do you mean by taking Ellean from me? [*She goes* C.

Aubrey. Listen——!

Paula. Listen to *me*! [*Volubly.*] And how do you take her? You pack her off in the care of a woman who has deliberately held aloof from me, who's thrown mud at me! Yet this Cortelyon creature has only to put foot here once to be entrusted with the charge of the girl you know I dearly want to keep near me! [*She moves* L.C.

Aubrey [*entreatingly*]. Paula dear! hear me——!

Paula. Ah! of course, of course! [*She speaks with passionate volubility and self-conviction.*] I can't be so useful to your daughter as such people as this; and so I'm to be given the go-by for any town friend of yours who turns up and chooses to patronize us! Hah! Very well, at any rate, as you take Ellean from me you justify my looking for companions where I can most readily find 'em.

[*She goes to back of table.*

Aubrey. You wish me to fully appreciate your reason for sending that letter to Lady Orreyed?

Paula [*taking up her hat and coat*]. Precisely—I do.

Aubrey [*facing her*]. And could you, after all, go back to associates of that order? It's not possible!

Paula [*mockingly*]. What, not after the refining influence of these intensely respectable surroundings? [*Going to the door down* L.] We'll see!

Aubrey. Paula!

Paula [*violently*]. We'll see!

[*She goes out. He stands still looking after her.*

THE CURTAIN FALLS.

ACT III

SCENE.—*The drawing-room at 'Highercoombe'. The scene is set obliquely and runs up the stage from* R. *to* L. *In the wall at back are a door opening into a small hall and two large French windows, sheltered by a verandah, leading into the garden. The door is* R., *the windows* R.C. *and* L.C. *In the wall on the* L. *are double doors, recessed, and a fireplace, the former up stage, the latter down stage. The fireplace is decorated with flowers; over the fireplace a large mirror; before the fireplace, a settee.* L.C., *a table. Above table, a chair; below table, a footstool. On the* R. *of table, an armchair. On the table, knick-knacks in silver—small hand-mirror, etc., also a book or two. Up* C., *between the windows, a settee.* R.C., *by the window, an armchair.* R.C., *down stage, a circular ottoman.* R., *a grand pianoforte, open, and music-stool. Music on or by the piano. Other articles of furniture to fill spaces. Flowers, lamps, etc. Everything costly and tasteful. The windows are open at the beginning of the act. Moonlight in the garden.*

LADY ORREYED, *a pretty, affected doll of a woman with a mincing voice and flaxen hair, is sitting on the ottoman* R.C., *her head resting against the drum, and her eyes closed.* PAULA, *looking pale, worn, and thoroughly unhappy, is sitting at a table* L.C. *Both are in sumptuous dinner-gowns.*

Lady Orreyed [*opening her eyes*]. Well, I never! I dropped off! [*Feeling her hair.*] Just fancy! Where are the men?

Paula [*icily*]. Outside, smoking.

[*A* SERVANT *enters door* R. *with coffee, which he hands to* LADY ORREYED. SIR GEORGE ORREYED *comes in by the window* L.C. *He is a man of about thirty-five, with a low forehead, a receding chin, a vacuous expression, and an ominous redness about the nose.*

Lady Orreyed [*taking coffee*]. Here's Dodo.

Sir George. I say, the flies under the verandah make you swear. [*He moves down* R.C. *The* SERVANT *hands coffee to*

PAULA, *who declines it, then to* SIR GEORGE, *who takes a cup. The* SERVANT *goes up* L.] Hi! wait a bit! [*He looks at the tray searchingly, then puts back his cup.*] Never mind. [*The* SERVANT *moves away. Quietly to* LADY ORREYED.] I say, they're dooced sparin' with their liqueur, ain't they?

[*The* SERVANT *goes out at window* R.C. *and off up* L.

Paula [*to* SIR GEORGE]. Won't you take coffee, George?

[LADY ORREYED *puts her coffee-cup on the piano.*

Sir George [*pulling his moustache*]. No, thanks. It's gettin' near time for a whisky and potass. [*Approaching* PAULA, *regarding* LADY ORREYED *admiringly.*] I say, Birdie looks rippin' to-night, don't she?

Paula. Your wife?

Sir George. Yaas—Birdie.

Paula. Rippin'?

Sir George. Yaas.

Paula. Quite—quite rippin'.

[*She rises and goes up* R.C. *He moves round to the settee* L. PAULA *watches him with distaste.* SIR GEORGE *falls asleep on the settee by fireplace.* LADY ORREYED *returns to the front seat of the ottoman.*

Lady Orreyed. Paula love, I fancied you and Aubrey were a little more friendly at dinner. You haven't made it up, have you?

Paula. We? Oh, no. We speak before others, that's all.

Lady Orreyed. And how long do you intend to carry on this game, dear?

Paula [*turning away impatiently*]. I really can't tell you.

Lady Orreyed. Sit down, old girl; don't be so fidgety. [PAULA *sits on the upper seat of the ottoman with her back to* LADY ORREYED.] Of course, it's my duty, as an old friend, to give you a good talking to—[PAULA *glares at her suddenly and fiercely. Unconsciously*] but really I've found one gets so many smacks in the face through interfering in matrimonial squabbles that I've determined to drop it.

Paula [*emphatically*]. I think you're wise.

Lady Orreyed. However, I must say that I do wish you'd look at marriage in a more solemn light—just as I do, in fact. It is such a beautiful thing—marriage, and if people in our position don't respect it, and set a good example by living happily with their husbands, what can you expect from the middle classes? When did this sad state of affairs between you and Aubrey actually begin?

Paula. Actually, a fortnight and three days ago; I haven't calculated the minutes.

Lady Orreyed. A day or two before Dodo and I turned up—arrived.

Paula. Yes. One always remembers one thing by another; we left off speaking to each other the morning I wrote asking you to visit us.

Lady Orreyed. Lucky for you I was able to pop down, wasn't it, dear?

Paula [*glaring at her again*]. Most fortunate.

Lady Orreyed. A serious split with your husband without a pal on the premises—I should say, without a friend in the house—would be most unpleasant.

Paula [*rising and turning to her abruptly*]. This place must be horribly doleful for you and George just now. At least you ought to consider him before me. Why don't you leave me to my difficulties? [*She sits beside her.*

Lady Orreyed. Oh, we're quite comfortable, dear, thank you—both of us. George and me are so wrapped up in each other, it doesn't matter where we are. I don't want to crow over you, old girl, but I've got a perfect husband.

[SIR GEORGE *is now fast asleep, his head thrown back and his mouth open, looking hideous.*

Paula [*glancing at* SIR GEORGE]. So you've given me to understand.

Lady Orreyed. Not that we don't have our little differences. Why, we fell out only this very morning. You remember the diamond and ruby tiara Charley Prestwick gave poor dear Connie Tirlemont years ago, don't you?

Paula [*emphatically*]. No, I do not.

Lady Orreyed. No? Well, it's in the market. Benjamin of Piccadilly has got it in his shop-window, and I've set my heart on it.

Paula. You consider it quite necessary?

Lady Orreyed. Yes, because what I say to Dodo is this—a lady of my station must smother herself with hair ornaments. It's different with you, love—people don't look for so much blaze from you, but I've got rank to keep up; haven't I?

Paula. Yes.

Lady Orreyed. Well, that was the cause of the little set-to between I and Dodo this morning. He broke two chairs, he was in such a rage. I forgot, they're your chairs; do you mind?

Paula. No.

Lady Orreyed. You know, poor Dodo can't lose his temper without smashing something; if it isn't a chair, it's a mirror; if it isn't that, it's china—a bit of Dresden for choice. Dear old pet! he loves a bit of Dresden when he's furious. He doesn't really throw things *at* me, dear; he simply lifts them up and drops them, like a gentleman. I expect our room upstairs will look rather wrecky before I get that tiara.

Paula. Excuse the suggestion, perhaps your husband can't afford it.

Lady Orreyed. Oh, how dreadfully changed you are, Paula! Dodo can always mortgage something, or borrow off his ma. What *is* coming to you!

Paula [*rising*]. Ah! [*She sits at the piano and touches the keys.*

Lady Orreyed [*turning to* PAULA]. Oh, yes, do play! That's the one thing I envy you for.

[*She rises and sits* R. *of the ottoman.*

Paula. What shall I play?

Lady Orreyed. What was that heavenly piece you gave us last night, dear?

Paula. A bit of Schubert. Would you like to hear it again?

Lady Orreyed [*thoughtfully*]. You don't know any comic songs, do you?

Paula. I'm afraid not.

Lady Orreyed [*settling herself*]. I leave it to you, then.

[PAULA *plays.* AUBREY *and* CAYLEY DRUMMLE *appear outside the window* L.C.; *they look into the room.*

Aubrey [*to* DRUMMLE, *drawing back*]. You can see her face in that mirror. Poor girl, how ill and wretched she looks.

Drummle. When are the Orreyeds going?

Aubrey [*entering the room*]. Heaven knows!

Drummle [*following* AUBREY]. But *you're* entertaining them; what's it to do with Heaven?

Aubrey. Do you know, Cayley, that even the Orreyeds serve a useful purpose? My wife actually speaks to me before our guests—think of that! I've come to rejoice at the presence of the Orreyeds!

Drummle. I daresay; we're taught that beetles are sent for a benign end.

Aubrey. Cayley, talk to Paula again to-night.

Drummle. Certainly, if I get the chance.

Aubrey. Let's contrive it. George is asleep; perhaps I can get that doll out of the way. [*They go down stage. As they advance into the room,* PAULA *abruptly ceases playing and finds interest in a volume of music.* SIR GEORGE *is now nodding and snoring apoplectically.*] Lady Orreyed, whenever you feel inclined for a game of billiards I'm at your service.

Lady Orreyed [*jumping up*]. Charmed, I'm sure! I really thought you'd forgotten poor little me. Oh, look at Dodo!

[*She crosses to him, back of table.*

Aubrey. No, no, don't wake him; he's tired.

Lady Orreyed. I must, he looks so plain. [*Rousing* SIR GEORGE.] Dodo! Dodo!

[*She lightly flicks his face with her fan.*

Sir George [*stupidly*]. 'Ullo!

Lady Orreyed. Dodo, dear, you were snoring.

Sir George. Oh, I say, you could 'a told me that by and by.

Aubrey. You want a cigar, George; come into the billiard-room. [*Giving his arm to* LADY ORREYED.] Cayley, bring Paula. [AUBREY *and* LADY ORREYED *go out door* L.

Sir George [*rising and going* C.]. Hey, what! Billiard-room! [*Looking at his watch.*] How goes the——? Phew! 'Ullo, 'Ullo! Whisky and Potass!

[*He goes rapidly after* AUBREY *and* LADY ORREYED. PAULA *resumes playing.* CAYLEY *remains* R.C.

Paula [*after a pause*]. Don't moon about after me, Cayley; follow the others.

Drummle. Thanks, by and by. [*Sitting* R.C. *on ottoman, facing her.*] That's pretty.

Paula [*after another pause, still playing*]. I wish you wouldn't stare so.

Drummle. Was I staring? I'm sorry. [*He rises and moves to the front of the ottoman; then glances at* PAULA *and finding her looking at him turns his back. She plays a little longer, then stops suddenly, rises, and goes to the window, where she stands looking out.* DRUMMLE *moves from the ottoman to the settee. Quietly.*] A lovely night.

Paula [*startled*]. Oh! [*Without turning to him.*] Why do you hop about like a monkey?

Drummle. Hot rooms play the deuce with the nerves. Now, it would have done you good to have walked in the garden with us after dinner and made merry. Why didn't you?

Paula [*in a hard voice*]. You know why.

Drummle. Ah, you're thinking of the—difference between you and Aubrey?

Paula. Yes, I *am* thinking of it.

Drummle. Well, so am I. How long——?

Paula. Getting on for three weeks.

Drummle. Bless me, it must be! And this would have been such a night to have healed it! Moonlight, the stars, the scent of flowers; and yet enough darkness to enable a kind woman to rest her hand for an instant on the arm of a good fellow who loves her. Ah, ha! it's a wonderful power, dear Mrs. Aubrey, the power of an offended woman! Only realize it! Just that one touch—the mere tips of her fingers—and, for herself and another, she changes the colour of the whole world!

Paula [*turning to him, calmly*]. Cayley, my dear man, you talk exactly like a very romantic old lady.

[*She leaves the window and sits* L.C. *playing with the knick-knacks on the table.*

Drummle [*to himself, thoughtfully*]. H'm, that hasn't done it! [*Rising and coming down.*] Well—ha, ha!—I accept the suggestion. [*Standing beside her.*] An old woman, eh?

Paula. Oh, I didn't intend——

Drummle. But why not? I've every qualification—well, almost. And I confess it would have given this withered bosom a throb of grandmotherly satisfaction if I could have seen you and Aubrey at peace before I take my leave to-morrow.

Paula [*looking up quickly*]. To-morrow, Cayley!

Drummle. I must.

Paula. Oh, this house is becoming unendurable.

Drummle. You're very kind. [*Slyly.*] But you've got the Orreyeds.

Paula [*fiercely*]. The Orreyeds! I—I hate the Orreyeds! I lie awake at night, hating them!

Drummle. Pardon me, I've understood that their visit is, in some degree, owing to—hem!—your suggestion.

Paula. Heavens! that doesn't make me like them better. Somehow or another, I—I've outgrown these people. This woman—I used to think her 'jolly!'—sickens me. I can't breathe when she's near me: the whiff of her handkerchief turns me faint! And she patronizes me by the hour, until I—I feel my nails growing longer with every word she speaks!

Drummle. My dear lady, why on earth don't you say all this to Aubrey?

Paula. Oh, I've been such an utter fool, Cayley!

Drummle [*soothingly*]. Well, well, mention it to Aubrey!

Paula. No, no, you don't understand. What do you think I've done?

Drummle. Done! What, *since* you invited the Orreyeds?

Paula. Yes; I must tell you——

Drummle [*disturbed*]. Perhaps you'd better not.

[*He moves* R.C.

Paula. Look here. I've intercepted some letters from Mrs. Cortelyon and Ellean to—him. [*Producing three unopened letters from the bodice of her dress.*] There are the accursed things! From Paris—two from the Cortelyon woman, the other from Ellean!

Drummle. But why—why?

Paula. I don't know. [*Rising and speaking with great volubility.*] Yes, I do! I saw letters coming from Ellean to her father; not a line to me—not a line. And one morning it happened I was downstairs before he was, and I spied this one lying with his heap on the breakfast-table, and I slipped it into my pocket—out of malice, Cayley, pure devilry! And a day or two afterwards I met Elwes the postman at the Lodge, and took the letters from him, and found these others amongst 'em. I felt simply fiendish when I saw them—fiendish! [*Returning the letters to her bodice.*] And now I carry them about with me, and they're scorching me like a mustard plaster! [*She moves up* R.C.

Drummle. Oh, this accounts for Aubrey not hearing from Paris lately!

Paula. That's an ingenious conclusion to arrive at! [*Pacing to and fro excitedly.*] Of course it does! [*With an hysterical laugh.*] Ha, ha!

Drummle. Well, well! [*Laughing.*] Ha, ha, ha!

Paula [*turning upon him*]. I suppose it *is* amusing!

Drummle [*with sudden gravity*]. I beg pardon.

Paula. Heaven knows I've little enough to brag about! I'm a bad lot, but not in mean tricks of this sort. [*She moves down* R., *then across the front of the ottoman to* C.] In all my life this is the most caddish thing I've done. How am I to get rid of these letters—that's what I want to know? [*Vehemently.*] How am I to get rid of them?

Drummle. If I were you I should take Aubrey aside and put them into his hands as soon as possible.

Paula. What! and tell him to his face that I——! No, thank you. [*Hesitatingly.*] I suppose *you* wouldn't like to——

Drummle. No, no; I won't touch 'em!

[*He moves to the other side of the* L.C. *table.*

Paula. And you call yourself my friend?

Drummle [*good-humouredly*]. No, I don't!

Paula. Perhaps I'll tie them together and give them to his man in the morning.

Drummle. That won't avoid an explanation.

Paula [*recklessly*]. Oh, then he must miss them——

Drummle. And trace them.

Paula [*throwing herself upon the ottoman* R.C.]. I don't care!

Drummle [*smiling and moving back of table*]. I know you don't; but—[*coaxingly*]—let me send him to you now, may I? [*Advancing to her.*

Paula. Now! What do you think a woman's made of? I couldn't stand it, Cayley. I haven't slept for nights; and last night there was thunder, too! I believe I've got the horrors.

Drummle [*taking the little hand-mirror from the table* L.C.]. You'll sleep well enough when you deliver those letters. [*Going to her.*] Come, come, Mrs. Aubrey—a good night's rest! [*Holding the mirror before her face.*] It's quite time.

[*She looks at herself for a moment, then snatches the mirror from him.*

Paula. You brute, Cayley, to show me that!

[*She puts it on* R. *seat.*

Drummle. Then—may I? Be guided by a fr—a poor old woman! May I?

Paula [*setting her teeth*]. You'll kill me, amongst you!

Drummle [*entreatingly*]. What do you say?

Paula [*after a pause*]. Very well. [*He nods his head and goes out rapidly, door up* L. *She looks after him for a moment, and calls* 'Cayley! Cayley!' *Rises and moves* C., *facing audience. Then she again produces the letters, deliberately, one by one, fingering them with aversion. Suddenly she starts, turning her head towards the door.*] Ah!

[AUBREY *enters quickly, door up* L.

Aubrey [*coming down on her* L.]. Paula!

Paula [*handing him the letters, her face averted*]. There! [*He examines the letters, puzzled, and looks at her inquiringly.*] They are many days old. I stole them, I suppose to make you anxious and unhappy.

[*He looks at the letters again, then lays them aside on the table* L.C.

Aubrey [*gently*]. Paula, dear, it doesn't matter.

Paula [*after a short pause*]. Why—why do you take it like this?

Aubrey. What did you expect?

Paula. Oh, but I suppose silent reproaches are really the severest. And then, naturally, you are itching to open your letters. [*She crosses the room to* L.C. *as if to go*.

Aubrey. Paula! [*He crosses* R.C. *She pauses*.] Surely, surely it's all over now?

Paula. All over! [*Mockingly*.] Has my stepdaughter returned then? When did she arrive? [*Standing at the door*.] I haven't heard of it!

Aubrey [*quietly*]. You can be very cruel.

Paula. That word's always on a man's lips; he uses it if his soup's cold. [*With another movement as if to go*.] Need we——

Aubrey. I know I've wounded you, Paula. But isn't there any way out of this?

Paula. When does Ellean return? [*She moves down* L.] To-morrow? Next week?

Aubrey [*wearily*]. Oh! Why should we grudge Ellean the little pleasure she is likely to find in Paris and in London. [*He moves* C.

Paula. I grudge her nothing, if that's a hit at me. But with that woman——! [*She sits* L. *on the settee*.

Aubrey. It must be that woman or another. You know that at present we are unable to give Ellean the opportunity of—of——

Paula. Of mixing with respectable people.

Aubrey. The opportunity of gaining friends, experience, ordinary knowledge of the world. If you are interested in Ellean, can't you see how useful Mrs. Cortelyon's good offices are?

Paula [*rising and going to him*]. May I put one question? At the end of the London season, when Mrs. Cortelyon has done with Ellean, is it understood that the girl comes back to us? [AUBREY *is silent*.] Is it? Is it?

Aubrey [*hesitatingly*]. Let us wait till the end of the season——

Paula. Oh! [*She goes down* L.] I knew it. You're only fooling me; you put me off with any trash. I believe you've sent Ellean away, not for the reasons you give, but because you don't consider me a decent companion for her, because you're afraid she might get a little of her innocence rubbed off in my company. [*She returns to* L. *of him*.] Come, isn't that the truth? Be honest! Isn't that it?

Aubrey. Yes. [*There is a moment's silence on both sides.*

Paula [*with uplifted hands as if to strike him*]. Oh!

Aubrey [*taking her by the wrists*]. Sit down. Sit down. [*He puts her into a chair; she shakes herself free with a cry. From this point to the end of the scene the man dominates.*] Now listen to me. Fond as you are, Paula, of harking back to your past, there's one chapter of it you always let alone. I've never asked you to speak of it; you've never offered to speak of it. I mean the chapter that relates to the time when you were—like Ellean. [*She attempts to rise; he restrains her.*] No, no.

Paula. I don't choose to talk about that time. I won't satisfy your curiosity.

Aubrey. My dear Paula, I have no curiosity—I know what you were at Ellean's age. [*She looks up.*] I'll tell you. You hadn't a thought that wasn't a wholesome one, you hadn't an impulse that didn't tend towards good, you never harboured a notion you couldn't have gossiped about to a parcel of children. [*She makes another effort to rise: he lays his hand lightly on her shoulder.*] And this was a very few years back—there are days now when you look like a schoolgirl—but think of the difference between the two Paulas. You'll have to think hard, because after a cruel life one's perceptions grow a thick skin. But, for God's sake, do think till you get these two images clearly in your mind, and then ask yourself what sort of a friend such a woman as you are to-day would have been for the girl of seven or eight years ago.

Paula [*rising*]. How dare you? I could be almost as good a friend to Ellean as her own mother would have been had she lived. I know what you mean. How dare you?

[*She nearly breaks down.*

Aubrey. You say that; very likely you believe it. But you're blind, Paula; you're blind. You! Every belief that a young pure-minded girl holds sacred—that you once held sacred—you now make a target for a jest, a sneer, a paltry cynicism. I tell you, you're not mistress any longer of your thoughts or your tongue. Why, how often, sitting between you and Ellean, have I seen her cheeks turn scarlet as you've rattled off some tale that belongs by right to the club or the smoking-room! ['Oh!' *from* PAULA.] Have you noticed the blush? If you have, has the cause of it ever struck you? And this is the girl you say you love, I admit that you *do* love, whose love you expect in return! Oh,

Paula, I make the best, the only, excuse for you when I tell you you're blind!

Paula [*with a restless movement of the hands*]. Ellean—Ellean blushes easily.

Aubrey. You blushed as easily a few years ago.

Paula [*after a short pause*]. Well! Have you finished your sermon?

Aubrey [*with a gesture of despair*]. Oh, Paula!

[*He leaves her, going up to the window* R.C. *and standing with his back to the room.*

Paula [*to herself*]. A few—years ago! [*She walks slowly towards the door* R., *then suddenly drops upon the ottoman in a paroxysm of weeping.*] Oh God! A few years ago!

Aubrey [*going to her*]. Paula!

Paula [*sobbing*]. Oh, don't touch me!

Aubrey. Paula!

Paula. Oh, go away from me! [*He goes back a few steps to* L.C., *and after a little while she becomes calmer and rises unsteadily; then in an altered tone.*] Look here——! [*He advances a step, front of table; she checks him with a quick gesture.*] Look here! Get rid of these people—Mabel and her husband—as soon as possible! I—I've done with them!

[*She gets up to the door.*

Aubrey [*in a whisper*]. Paula!

Paula. And then—then—when the time comes for Ellean to leave Mrs. Cortelyon, give me—give me another chance! [*He advances again, but she shrinks away.*] No, no!

[*She goes out by the door on the* R. *He sinks on to the settee, covering his eyes with his hands. There is a brief silence, then a* SERVANT *enters, door up* L. AUBREY *looks up quickly.*

Servant. Mrs. Cortelyon, sir, with Miss Ellean.

[AUBREY *rises to meet* MRS. CORTELYON, *who enters, followed by* ELLEAN, *both being in travelling dresses. The* SERVANT *withdraws.*

Mrs. Cortelyon [*shaking hands with* AUBREY C.]. Oh, my dear Aubrey! [*Moves over to* R.C.

Aubrey. Mrs. Cortelyon! [*Advancing to and kissing* ELLEAN L.C.] Ellean dear!

Ellean. Papa, is all well at home?

Mrs. Cortelyon [R.C.]. We're shockingly anxious.

Aubrey. Yes, yes, all's well. This is quite unexpected. [*To* MRS. CORTELYON.] You've found Paris insufferably hot?

Mrs. Cortelyon. Insufferably hot! Paris is pleasant enough. We've had no letter from you!

Aubrey. I wrote to Ellean a week ago.

Mrs. Cortelyon. Without alluding to the subject I had written to you upon. [ELLEAN *goes down* L.

Aubrey [*thinking*]. Ah, of course——

Mrs. Cortelyon. And since then we've both written and you've been absolutely silent. Oh, it's too bad!

Aubrey [*picking up the letters from the table,* L.C.]. It isn't altogether my fault. Here are the letters——

Ellean. Papa! [*She moves up* L. *and over to* MRS. CORTELYON.

Mrs. Cortelyon. They're unopened.

Aubrey. An accident delayed their reaching me till this evening. I'm afraid this has upset you very much.

[*He puts letters into his pocket.*

Mrs. Cortelyon [*fretfully*]. Upset me!

Ellean [*in an undertone to* MRS. CORTELYON, *behind her on* R.]. Never mind. Not now, dear—not to-night.

Aubrey. Eh?

Mrs. Cortelyon [*to* ELLEAN *aloud*]. Child, run away and take your things off. [*Sitting on ottoman.*] She doesn't look as if she'd journeyed from Paris to-day.

[ELLEAN *moves towards the door* L. AUBREY *meets her up* L.C. *and takes her hands.*

Aubrey. I've never seen her with such a colour.

Ellean [*to* AUBREY, *in a faint voice*]. Papa, Mrs. Cortelyon has been so very, very kind to me, but I—I have come home. [*She goes out, door up* L.

Aubrey [*follows her to the door*]. Come home! [*To* MRS. CORTELYON, *puzzled.*] Ellean returns to us, then?

[*He goes* C.

Mrs. Cortelyon. That's the very point I put to you in my letters, and you oblige me to travel from Paris to Willowmere on a warm day to settle it. I think perhaps it's right that Ellean should be with you just now, although I—— [*In an outburst.*] My dear friend, circumstances are a little altered.

Aubrey. Alice, you're in some trouble. [*He sits* L.C.

Mrs. Cortelyon. Well—yes, I *am* in trouble. You remember pretty little Mrs. Brereton who was once Caroline Ardale?

Aubrey. Quite well.

Mrs. Cortelyon. She's a widow now, poor thing. She has the *entresol* of the house where we've been lodging in the Avenue de Friedland. Caroline's a dear chum of mine; she formed a great liking for Ellean. [*Taking off her gloves.*

Aubrey. I'm very glad.

Mrs. Cortelyon. Yes, it's nice for her to meet her mother's friends. Er—that young Hugh Ardale the papers were full of some time ago—he's Caroline Brereton's brother, you know.

Aubrey. No, I didn't know. What did he do? I forget.

Mrs. Cortelyon. Checked one of those horrid mutinies at some far-away station in India, marched down with a handful of his men and a few faithful natives, and held the place until he was relieved. They gave him his company and a V.C. for it.

Aubrey. And he's Mrs. Brereton's brother?

Mrs. Cortelyon. Yes. He's with his sister—*was* rather—in Paris. He's home—invalided. [*Impatiently.*] Good gracious, Aubrey, why don't you help me out? Can't you guess what has occurred?

Aubrey [*quickly*]. Alice!

Mrs. Cortelyon. Young Ardale—Ellean!

Aubrey [*slowly*]. An attachment?

Mrs. Cortelyon. Yes, Aubrey. [*After a little pause.*] Well, I suppose I've got myself into sad disgrace. But really I didn't foresee anything of this kind. A serious, reserved child like Ellean, and a boyish, high-spirited soldier—it never struck me as being likely. [AUBREY *rises, turns away and paces to and fro thoughtfully, from* R. *to down* L.] I did all I could directly Captain Ardale spoke—wrote to you at once. Why on earth don't you receive your letters promptly, and when you do get them why can't you open them? I endured the anxiety till last night, and then made up my mind—home! Of course, it has worried me terribly. My head's bursting. Are there any salts about? [AUBREY *fetches a bottle from a cabinet and hands it to her.*] We've had one of those hateful smooth crossings that won't let you be properly indisposed.

Aubrey [*going* C.]. My dear Alice, I assure you I've no thought of blaming you.

Mrs. Cortelyon. That statement always precedes a quarrel.

Aubrey. I don't know whether this is the worst or the best luck. How will my wife regard it? Is Captain Ardale a good fellow?

Mrs. Cortelyon [*turning to him*]. My dear Aubrey, you'd better read up the accounts of his wonderful heroism. Face to face with death for a whole week; always with a smile and a cheering word for the poor helpless souls depending on him! Of course, it's that that has stirred the depths of your child's nature. I've watched her while we've been dragging the story out of him, and if angels look different from Ellean at that moment, I don't desire to meet any, that's all!

Aubrey. If you were in my position——? But you can't judge.

Mrs. Cortelyon. Why, if I had a marriageable daughter of my own and Captain Ardale proposed for her, naturally I should cry my eyes out all night—but I should thank Heaven in the morning.

Aubrey. You believe so thoroughly in him?

Mrs. Cortelyon [*laying her hand on* AUBREY'*s arm*]. Do you think I should have only a headache at this minute if I didn't! Look here, you've got to see me down the lane; that's the least you can do, my friend. [*She moves up* C.] Come into my house for a moment and shake hands with Hugh.

Aubrey. What, is he here?

Mrs. Cortelyon. He came through with us, to present himself formally to-morrow. Where are my gloves? [AUBREY *fetches them from the ottoman, and hands them to her*.] Make my apologies to Mrs. Tanqueray, please. She's well, I hope? [*Going towards the door up* L.] I can't feel sorry she hasn't seen me in this condition.

[ELLEAN *enters, door up* L.

Ellean [*to* MRS. CORTELYON]. I've been waiting to wish you good night. I was afraid I'd missed you.

Mrs. Cortelyon. Good night, Ellean.

Ellean [*in a low voice, embracing* MRS. CORTELYON]. I can't thank you. Dear Mrs. Cortelyon!

Mrs. Cortelyon [*her arms round* ELLEAN, *in a whisper to* AUBREY]. Speak a word to her.

[MRS. CORTELYON *goes out, door up* L.

Aubrey [*to* ELLEAN]. Ellean, I'm going to see Mrs. Cortelyon home. [*Going to the door*.] Tell Paula where I am; explain, dear.

Ellean [*her head drooping*]. Yes. [*She moves* R.C.—*quickly*.] Father! [*He turns to her*.] You are angry with me—disappointed?

Aubrey. Angry?—no.

Ellean. Disappointed?

Aubrey [*gently smiling, going to her and taking her hand*]. If so, it's only because you've shaken my belief in my discernment. I thought you took after your poor mother a little, Ellean; [*Looking into her face earnestly.*] but there's a look on your face to-night, dear, that I never saw on hers—never, never.

Ellean [*leaning her head on his shoulder—tearfully*]. Perhaps I ought not to have gone away?

Aubrey. Hush! You're quite happy?

Ellean. Yes.

Aubrey. That's right. Then, as you are quite happy there is something I particularly want you to do for me, Ellean.

Ellean. What is that?

Aubrey. Be very gentle with Paula. Will you?

[*She releases herself.*

Ellean [*slowly*]. You think I have been unkind.

Aubrey [*kissing her upon the forehead*]. Be very gentle with Paula.

[*He goes out, door up* L., *and she stands* C. *looking after him. A rose is thrown though the window and falls at her feet. She picks up the flower wonderingly and goes to the window.*

Ellean [*starting back*]. Hugh!

[HUGH ARDALE, *a handsome young man of about seven-and-twenty, with a boyish face and manner, appears outside the window.*

Hugh. Nell! Nelly dear!

Ellean [*alarmed*]. What's the matter?

Hugh. Hush! Nothing. It's only fun. [*Laughing.*] Ha, ha, ha! I've found out that Mrs. Cortelyon's meadow runs up to your father's plantation; I've come through a gap in the hedge. [*He remains at the window* R.C.

Ellean. Why, Hugh?

Hugh. I'm miserable at The Warren; it's so different from the Avenue de Friedland. [ELLEAN *moves down to* C.] Don't look like that! Upon my word I meant just to peep at your home and go back, but I saw figures moving about here, and came nearer, hoping to get a glimpse of you. [*Coming down* C.] Was that your father?

Ellean [*moving up to* L. *window*]. Yes.

Hugh. Isn't this fun! A rabbit ran across my foot while I was hiding behind that old yew.

Ellean [*going down* L.C.]. You must go away; it's not *right* for you to be here like this.

Hugh. But it's only fun, I tell you. You take everything so seriously. Do wish me good night.

Ellean. We have said good night.

Hugh. In the hall at The Warren, before Mrs. Cortelyon and a man-servant. Oh, it's so different from the Avenue de Friedland!

Ellean [*moving to him, giving him her hand hastily*]. Good night, Hugh.

Hugh. Is that all? We might be the merest acquaintances.

[*He momentarily embraces her, but she releases herself.*

Ellean. It's when you're like this that you make me feel utterly miserable. [*Throwing the rose from her angrily.*] Oh!

[*She moves* L.

Hugh [*drawing back*]. I've offended you now, I suppose?

Ellean. Yes.

Hugh. Forgive me, Nelly. Come into the garden for five minutes; we'll stroll down to the plantation.

Ellean. No, no.

Hugh. For two minutes—to tell me you forgive me.

Ellean. I forgive you.

Hugh. Evidently. [*He moves up to* R.C. *window.*] I shan't sleep a wink to-night after this. [ELLEAN *moves up to* R. *door.*] What a fool I am! [*Entreatively.*] Come down to the plantation. Make it up with me.

Ellean. There is somebody coming into this room. [*Holding door-handle.*] Do you wish to be seen here?

Hugh [*hurriedly*]. I shall wait for you behind that yew-tree. You *must* speak to me. Nelly!

[*He disappears off* L. ELLEAN *goes to* L.C. *window as* PAULA *enters door* R.

Paula [*with joyful surprise*]. Ellean!

Ellean. You—you are very surprised to see me, Paula, of course.

Paula. Why are you here? Why aren't you with—your friend? [*Contemptuously.*

Ellean. I've come home—if you'll have me. We left Paris this morning; Mrs. Cortelyon brought me back. She was here a minute or two ago; Papa has just gone with her to The Warren. He asked me to tell you.

Paula [*moving down* R.C.]. There are some people staying with us that I'd rather you didn't meet. It was hardly worth your while to return for a few hours.

Ellean. A few hours? [*She goes down* C.

Paula. Well, when do you go to London?

Ellean. I don't think I go to London, after all.

Paula [*eagerly*]. You—you've quarrelled with her?

[*She moves to her.*

Ellean [*moving to back of the chair*]. No, no, no, not that; but—Paula! [*In an altered tone.*] Paula!

Paula [*startled*]. Eh? [ELLEAN *goes deliberately to* PAULA *an. kisses her. Breathlessly,* R.C.] Ellean!

Ellean. Kiss *me.*

Paula. What—what's come to you?

Ellean. I want to behave differently to you in the future. Is it too late?

Paula. Too—late! [*Impulsively kissing* ELLEAN *and crying.*] No—no—no! No—no!

Ellean. Paula, don't cry.

Paula [*wiping her eyes*]. I'm a little shaky; I haven't been sleeping. It's all right—talk to me.

Ellean [*hesitatingly*]. There is something I want to tell you——

Paula. Is there—is there?

[*They sit together on the ottoman,* R.C., PAULA *taking* ELLEAN'*s hand.*

Ellean. Paula, in our house in the Avenue de Friedland, on the floor below us, there was a Mrs. Brereton. She used to be a friend of my mother's. Mrs. Cortelyon and I spent a great deal of time with her.

Paula [*suspiciously*]. Oh! [*Letting* ELLEAN'*s hand fall.*] Is this lady going to take you up in place of Mrs. Cortelyon?

Ellean. No, no. [*Falteringly.*] Her brother is staying with her—*was* staying with her. Her brother——

[*She breaks off in confusion.*

Paula [*looking into her face*]. Well?

Ellean [*almost inaudibly*]. Paula——

[*She rises and walks away to* L.C., PAULA *following her.*

Paula. Ellean! [*Taking hold of her.*] You're not in love! [ELLEAN *looks at* PAULA *appealingly.*] Oh! *You* in love! You! [*Suspiciously.*] Oh, this is why you've come home! Of course, you can make friends with me now! You'll leave us for good soon, I suppose; so it doesn't much matter being civil to me for a little while!

[*She goes round the front of the ottoman to the piano, where she stands facing* ELLEAN.

Ellean. Oh, Paula!

Paula. Why, how you have deceived us—all of us! We've

taken you for a cold-blooded little saint. The fools you've made of us! [*Bitterly.*] Saint Ellean! Saint Ellean!

Ellean [*passionately*]. Ah, I might have known you'd only mock me! [*She goes up* C. *to the settee.*

Paula [*her tone changing*]. Eh?

Ellean [R.C., *turning away*]. I—I can't talk to you. [*Sitting on the settee.*] You do nothing else but mock and sneer, nothing else. [*She cries.*

Paula [*to* C.*—following her penitently*]. Ellean dear! Ellean! I didn't mean it. I'm so horribly jealous, it's a sort of curse on me. [*Kneeling beside* ELLEAN *and embracing her.*] My tongue runs away with me. I'm going to alter, I swear I am. I've made some good resolutions, and, as God's above me, I'll keep them! If you *are* in love, if you *do* ever marry, that's no reason why we shouldn't be fond of each other. Come, you've kissed me of your own accord—you can't take it back. Now we're friends again, aren't we? Ellean dear! I want to know everything, everything. Ellean dear, Ellean!

Ellean. Paula, Hugh has done something that makes me very angry. He came with us from Paris to-day, to see Papa. He is staying with Mrs. Cortelyon and—[*She rises and goes down* R.C.] I ought to tell you——

Paula. Yes, yes. What? [*She rises and remains up* L.C.

Ellean. He has found his way by The Warren meadow through the plantation up to this house. He is waiting to bid me good night. [*Glancing towards the garden.*] He is—out there.

Paula [*pleased*]. Oh!

Ellean. What shall I do?

Paula [*moving to her*]. Bring him in to see me! Will you?

Ellean. No, no.

Paula. But I'm dying to know him. Oh, yes, you must. I shall meet him before Aubrey does. [*Coming down excitedly to table* L.C., *running her hands over her hair.*] I'm so glad. [ELLEAN *goes out by the window* L.C.] The mirror—mirror. What a fright I must look! [*Not finding the hand-glass on the table, she jumps on to the settee* L., *and surveys herself in the mirror over the mantelpiece, then returns to the* L.C. *chair and sits quietly down and waits.*] Ellean! Just fancy! Ellean!

[*After a pause* ELLEAN *enters by the window* L.C. *with* HUGH.

Ellean [C.]. Paula, this is Captain Ardale—Mrs. Tanqueray.

[PAULA *rises and turns, and she and* HUGH *stand staring blankly at each other for a moment or two; then* PAULA *advances and gives him her hand.*

Paula [*in a strange voice, but calmly*]. How do you do?

Hugh. How do you do?

Paula [*to* ELLEAN]. Mr. Ardale and I have met in London, Ellean. Er—Captain Ardale, now?

Hugh. Yes.

Ellean [L.C., *simply*]. In London?

Paula. They say the world's very small, don't they?

Hugh. Yes.

Paula. Ellean, dear, I want to have a little talk about you to Mr. Ardale—Captain Ardale—alone. [*Putting her arms round* ELLEAN, *and leading her to the door* L.] Come back in a little while. [ELLEAN *nods to* PAULA *with a smile and goes out, while* PAULA *stands watching her at the open door.*] In a little while—in a little—— [*Closing the door and coming down to* L.C. *and then taking a seat facing* HUGH, *who has not moved.*] Be quick! Mr. Tanqueray has only gone down to The Warren with Mrs. Cortelyon. What is to be done?

Hugh [*blankly*]. Done? [*He puts his hat on the ottoman.*

Paula [*sitting in chair* L.]. Done—done. [*Holding her brow.*] Something must be done. [*With great force.*

Hugh. I understood that Mr. Tanqueray had married a Mrs.—Mrs.——

Paula. Jarman?

Hugh. Yes.

Paula. I'd been going by that name. You didn't follow my doings after we separated.

Hugh. No.

Paula [*sneeringly*]. No.

Hugh. I went out to India.

Paula. What's to be done?

Hugh. Damn this chance!

[*He goes down* R., *and up round the ottoman.*

Paula [*bowing her head*]. Oh, my God!

Hugh [*back to* C.]. Your husband doesn't know, does he?

Paula. That you and I——?

Hugh. Yes.

Paula. No. He knows about others.

Hugh. Not about me. How long were we——?

Paula. I don't remember, exactly.

Hugh. Do you—do you think it matters?

Paula. His—his daughter. [*With a muttered exclamation he turns away and sits up* C., *with his head in his hands.*] What's to be done?

Hugh. I wish I could think.

Paula [*ramblingly*]. Oh! Oh! What happened to that flat of ours in Ethelbert Street?

[*She mechanically pushes her hair back from her left temple.*

Hugh. I let it.

Paula. All that pretty furniture?

Hugh. Sold it.

Paula. I came across the key of the escritoire the other day in an old purse! [*The three lines preceding she has sat quite quietly and retrospectively. Suddenly realizing the horror and hopelessness of her position, and starting to her feet with an hysterical cry of rage.*] What am I maundering about?

[*She strides across in front of the ottoman to the piano.*

Hugh. For God's sake, be quiet! Do let me think.

Paula [*pacing up to* R.]. This will send me mad! [*Suddenly turning and standing over him.*] You—you beast, to crop up in my life again like this!

Hugh [*rising, facing her*]. I always treated you fairly.

Paula [*weakly*]. O! I beg your pardon—I know you did—I—— [*She sinks on to the chair up* C., *crying hysterically.*

Hugh. Hush! [*He goes to her.*

Paula. She kissed me to-night! I'd won her over! I've had such a fight to make her love me! And now—just as she's beginning to love me, to bring this on her!

Hugh. Hush, hush! Don't break down!

[*He is apprehensive of someone coming into the room.*

Paula [*sobbing*]. You don't know! I—I haven't been getting on well in my marriage. It's been my fault. The life I used to lead spoilt me completely. But I'd made up my mind to turn over a new life from to-night. From to-night!

Hugh. Paula——

Paula. Don't you call me that!

[*She staggers down to* L.C. *chair.*

Hugh. Mrs. Tanqueray, there is no cause for you to despair in this way. It's all right, I tell you—it *shall* be all right.

Paula [*shivering*]. What are we to do? [*She sits* L.C.

Hugh. Hold our tongues. [*He moves down* C.

Paula [*staring vacantly*]. Eh?

Hugh. The chances are a hundred to one against any one ever turning up who knew us when we were together. Besides, no one would be such a brute as to split on us. If anybody did do such a thing we should have to lie! What are we upsetting ourselves like this for, when we've simply got to hold our tongues?

Paula. You're as mad as I am!

Hugh. Can you think of a better plan?

Paula. There's only one plan possible—[*Rising.*]—let's come to our senses!—Mr. Tanqueray must be told.

[*She crosses* R.

Hugh. Your husband! What, and I lose Ellean! I lose Ellean!

Paula [R.]. You've *got* to lose her.

Hugh [C.]. I *won't* lose her! I *can't* lose her!

[*He moves up* L.C.

Paula [R.]. Didn't I read of your doing any number of brave things in India? Why, you seem to be an awful coward!

Hugh. That's another sort of pluck altogether—[*Coming* C.]—I haven't this sort of pluck.

Paula. Oh, I don't ask *you* to tell Mr. Tanqueray. [*Determinedly.*] That's my job.

[*She sits on the front seat of the ottoman.*

Hugh [*crossing to her*]. You—you—you'd better! You——!

Paula [*rising*]. Don't bully me! I intend to.

Hugh [*taking hold of her; she wrenches herself free*]. Look here, Paula! I never treated you badly—you've owned it. Why should you want to pay me out like this? You don't know how I love Ellean!

Paula. Yes, that's just what I *do* know.

[*She crosses* L.C. *and sits.*

Hugh. I say you don't! [*Turning to her.*] She's as good as my own mother. I've been downright honest with her too. I told her, in Paris, that I'd been a bit wild at one time, and, after a damned wretched day, she promised to forgive me because of what I'd done since in India. She's behaved like an angel to me! Surely I oughtn't to lose her, after all, just because I've been like other fellows! No; I haven't been half as rackety as a hundred men we could think of. [*He tries to take her hands.*] Paula, don't pay me out for nothing; be fair to me, there's a good girl—be fair to me!

Paula [*crossing to* L.C.]. Oh, I'm not considering you at all! I advise you not to stay here any longer; Mr. Tanqueray is sure to be back soon.

Hugh [*taking up his hat and staggering up* R.C.]. What's the understanding between us then? What have we arranged to do?

Paula. I don't know what you're going to do. [*She moves down* L.C.] I've got to tell Mr. Tanqueray.

Hugh [*approaching her fiercely*]. By God, you shall do nothing of the sort!

Paula. You shocking coward!

Hugh. If you dare! [*Going up to the window* R.C.] Mind! If you dare!

Paula [*following him*]. Why, what would you do?

Hugh [*after a short pause, sullenly*]. Nothing. I'd shoot myself—that's nothing. Good night.

Paula. Good night.

[*He disappears. She walks unsteadily to the ottoman, and sits; and as she does so her hand falls upon the little silver mirror, which she takes up, staring at her own reflection.*]

THE CURTAIN FALLS.

ACT IV

The drawing-room at 'Highercoombe', the same evening.

PAULA *is still seated on the ottoman, looking vacantly before her, with the little mirror in her hand.* LADY ORREYED *enters, door* L.

Lady Orreyed. There you are! You never came into the billiard-room. Isn't it maddening—Cayley Drummle gives me sixty out of a hundred and beats me. I must be out of form, because I know I play remarkably well for a lady. [*Going to her.*] Only last month—— [PAULA *rises.*] Whatever is the matter with you, old girl?

Paula. Why?

Lady Orreyed [*staring*]. It's the light, I suppose. [PAULA *crosses to* L.C. *and replaces the mirror on the table.*] By Aubrey's bolting from the billiard-table in that fashion I thought perhaps——

Paula. Yes; it's all right.

Lady Orreyed. You've patched it up? [PAULA *nods. Going to her.*] Oh, I am jolly glad——! [*Kisses her.*] I mean——

Paula. Yes, I know what you mean. Thanks, Mabel.

Lady Orreyed. Now take my advice; for the future——

Paula [*abruptly*]. Mabel, if I've been disagreeable to you while you've been staying here, I—I beg your pardon.

[*She walks away and sits up* R.C.

Lady Orreyed. You disagreeable, my dear? I haven't noticed it. Dodo and me both consider you make a first-class hostess, but then you've had such practice, haven't you? [*Dropping on to the ottoman and gaping*.] Oh, talk about being sleepy——!

Paula. Why don't you——?

Lady Orreyed. Why, dear, I must hang about for Dodo. You may as well know it; he's in one of his moods.

[*She rises and joins* PAULA, *sitting on her* R.

Paula [*under her breath*]. Oh——!

Lady Orreyed. Now, it's not his fault; it was deadly dull for him while we were playing billiards. Cayley Drummle did ask him to mark, but I stopped that; it's so easy to make a gentleman look like a billiard-marker. This is just how it always is; if poor old Dodo has nothing to do, he loses count, as you may say.

Paula. Hark!

[SIR GEORGE ORREYED *enters, door* L., *walking slowly and deliberately; he looks pale and watery-eyed*.

Sir George [*with mournful indistinctness*]. I'm 'fraid we've lef' you a grea' deal to yourself to-night, Mrs. Tanqueray. Attra'tions of billiards. I apol'gize. [*He staggers in a gentlemanly way down* L.C. *to chair*.] I say, where's ol' Aubrey?

Paula [*without turning*]. My husband has been obliged to go out to a neighbour's house.

[*She rises and goes to the window*.

Sir George. I want his advice on a rather pressing matter connected with my family—my family. [*Sitting*.] To-morrow will do just as well.

Lady Orreyed [*aside to* PAULA]. This is the mood I hate so—drivelling about his precious family.

Sir George. The fact is, Mrs. Tanqueray, I am not easy in my min' 'bout the way I am treatin' my poor ol' mother.

Lady Orreyed [*to* PAULA]. Do you hear that? That's *his* mother, but *my* mother he won't so much as look at!

Sir George. I shall write to Bruton Street firs' thing in the morning.

Lady Orreyed [*to* PAULA]. Mamma has stuck to me through everything—well you know! [*Coming down* R.C.

Sir George. I'll get ol' Aubrey to figure out a letter. I'll drop a line to Uncle Fitz too—dooced shame of the ol' feller to chuck me over in this manner. [*Wiping his eyes.*] All my family have chucked me over.

Lady Orreyed [*rising*]. Dodo! [*She moves down* C.

Sir George. Jus' because I've married beneath me to be chucked over! [*Counting them on his fingers.*] Aunt Lydia, the General, Hooky Whitgrave, Lady Sugnall—my own dear sister!—all turn their backs on me. It's more than I can stan'!

Lady Orreyed [*approaching nearer to him with dignity*]. Sir George, wish Mrs. Tanqueray good night at once and come upstairs. Do you hear me?

Sir George [*rising angrily*]. Wha'——?

Lady Orreyed. Be quiet!

Sir George. You presoom to order me about!

Lady Orreyed. You're making an exhibition of yourself! [PAULA *rises.*

Sir George. Look 'ere——!

Lady Orreyed. Come along, I tell you!

[*He hesitates, utters a few inarticulate sounds, then snatches up a fragile ornament from the table, and is about to dash it on to the ground.* LADY ORREYED *retreats.* PAULA *comes down, and taking the ornament from him places it upon mantelshelf.*

Paula [C.]. George! [*He shakes* PAULA*'s hand.*

Sir George. Good ni', Mrs. Tanqueray.

Lady Orreyed [*to* PAULA]. Good night, darling. Wish Aubrey good night for me. Now, Dodo?

[*The first two sentences she says with affected sweetness, the last with great severity. She goes out, door* R.

Sir George [*to* PAULA]. I say, are you goin' to sit up for ol' Aubrey?

Paula. Yes.

Sir George. Shall I keep you comp'ny?

Paula. No, thank you, George.

Sir George. Sure?

Paula. Yes, sure.

Sir George [*shaking hands*]. Good night again.

Paula. Good night.

[*She turns away. He goes out, steadying himself carefully, door* R. DRUMMLE *appears outside the window* L.C.*, with a cap on his head and smoking.*

Drummle [*looking into the room, and seeing* PAULA]. My last cigar. Where's Aubrey?

Paula. Gone down to The Warren, to see Mrs. Cortelyon home.

Drummle [*entering the room*]. Eh? Did you say Mrs. Cortelyon?

Paula. Yes. She has brought Ellean back.

Drummle. Bless my soul! Why?

Paula [R.C.]. I—I'm too tired to tell you, Cayley. If you stroll along the lane you'll meet Aubrey. [*Sitting* R.C.] Get the news from him.

Drummle [*going up to the window*]. Yes, yes. [*Returning to* PAULA.] I don't want to bother you, only—the anxious old woman, you know. Are you and Aubrey——?

Paula. Good friends again?

Drummle [*nodding*]. Um.

Paula [*giving him her hand*]. Quite, Cayley, quite.

Drummle [*retaining her hand*]. That's capital. As I'm off so early to-morrow morning, let me say now—thank you for your hospitality.

[*He bends over her hand gallantly, then goes out by the window, up* L.C.

Paula [*to herself*]. 'Are you and Aubrey——?' 'Good friends again?' 'Yes.' 'Quite, Cayley, quite.'

[*There is a brief pause, then* AUBREY *enters hurriedly, door* L., *wearing a light overcoat and carrying a cap.*

Aubrey. Paula dear! Have you seen Ellean? [*Standing* C.

Paula. I found her here when I came down.

Aubrey. She—she's told you?

Paula. Yes, Aubrey.

Aubrey. It's extraordinary, isn't it! Not that somebody should fall in love with Ellean or that Ellean herself should fall in love. All that's natural enough, and was bound to happen, I suppose, sooner or later. But this young fellow! You know his history?

Paula [*startled*]. His history?

Aubrey. You remember the papers were full of his name a few months ago?

Paula. Oh, yes.

Aubrey. The man's as brave as a lion, there's no doubt about that; and at the same time, he's like a big good-natured schoolboy, Mrs. Cortelyon says. Have you ever pictured the kind of man Ellean would marry some day?

Paula. I can't say that I have.

Aubrey. A grave, sedate fellow I've thought about—hah! She has fallen in love with the way in which Ardale practically

laid down his life to save those poor people shut up in the Residency. [*Taking off his coat.*] Well, I suppose if a man can do that sort of thing, one ought to be content. And yet—— [*Throwing his coat on the settee.*] I should have met him to-night, but he'd gone out. [*Coming down to her.*] Paula dear, tell me how you look upon this business.
[*To chair* L.C. *and sitting.*

Paula. Yes, I will—I must. To begin with, I—I've seen Mr. Ardale. [*He rises and goes to her.*

Aubrey. Captain Ardale?

Paula. Captain Ardale.

Aubrey. Seen him?

Paula. While you were away he came up here, through our grounds, to try to get a word with Ellean. I made her fetch him in and present him to me.

Aubrey [*frowning*]. Doesn't Captain Ardale know there's a lodge and a front door to this place? Never mind! What is your impression of him?

Paula. Aubrey, do you recollect my bringing you a letter—a letter giving you an account of myself—to the Albany late one night—the night before we got married?

Aubrey. A letter?

Paula. You burnt it; don't you know?

Aubrey. Yes; I know.

Paula. His name was in that letter.

Aubrey [*going back from her slowly, and staring at her*]. I don't understand.

Paula [*with forced calmness*]. Well—Ardale and I once kept house together. [*He remains silent, not moving. After a pause.*] Why don't you strike me? Hit me in the face —I'd rather you did! Hurt me! hurt me!
[*She screams and nearly swoons.*

Aubrey [*after a pause*]. What did you—and this man—say to each other—just now?

Paula. I—hardly—know.

Aubrey. Think!

Paula. The end of it all was that I—I told him I must inform you of—what had happened . . . he didn't want me to do that . . . I declared I would . . . he dared me to. [AUBREY *advances a step and bends over her. Breaking down.*] Let me alone!—oh!

Aubrey. Where was my daughter while this went on?

Paula. I—I had sent her out of the room . . . that is all right.

Aubrey. Yes, yes—yes, yes.

[*Click of lock heard. He turns his head towards the door* L.

Paula [*nervously*]. Who's that?

[*He goes to the door, meeting a* SERVANT *who enters with a letter*.

Servant. The coachman has just run up with this from The Warren, sir. [AUBREY *takes the letter*.] It's for Mrs. Tanqueray, sir; there's no answer.

[*The* SERVANT *withdraws*. AUBREY *goes to* PAULA *and drops the letter into her lap; she opens it with uncertain hands*. AUBREY *moves* C.

Paula [*reading it to herself*]. It's from—him. [*Long pause*.] He's going away—or gone—I think. [*Rising in a weak way*.] What does it say? I never could make out his writing.

[*She gives the letter to* AUBREY *and stands near him looking at the letter over his shoulder as he reads. Letter to be written on two sides*.

Aubrey [*reading*]. 'I shall be in Paris by to-morrow evening. Shall wait there, at Meurice's, for a week, ready to receive any communication you or your husband may address to me. Please invent some explanation to Ellean. Mrs. Tanqueray, for God's sake, do what you can for me.'

[PAULA *and* AUBREY *speak in low voices, both still looking at the letter*.

Paula. Has he left The Warren, I wonder, already?

Aubrey. That doesn't matter.

Paula. No, but I can picture him going quietly off. Very likely he's walking on to Bridgeford or Cottering to-night, to get the first train in the morning. A pleasant stroll for him.

Aubrey. We'll reckon he's gone, that's enough.

Paula. That isn't to be answered in any way?

Aubrey. Silence will answer that.

Paula. He'll soon recover his spirits, I know.

Aubrey. You know. [*Offering her the letter*.] You don't want this, I suppose?

Paula. No.

Aubrey. It's done with—done with.

[*He tears the letter into small pieces. She has dropped the envelope; she searches for it, finds it, and gives it to him*.

Paula. Here!

Aubrey [*looking at the remnants of the letter*]. This is no good; I must burn it.

Paula. Burn it in your room.

Aubrey. Yes. [*Passively*.]

Paula. Put it in your pocket for now.

Aubrey [L. *in front of table*]. Yes.

[*He does so.* ELLEAN *enters, door* R., *comes down* R. *of settee, and they both turn, guiltily, and stare at her.*

Ellean [*after a short silence, wonderingly*]. Papa——

Aubrey. What do you want, Ellean?

Ellean [*moves down* R.]. I heard from Willis that you had come in; I only want to wish you good night. [PAULA *steals away, door* R. *without looking back. Puzzled.*] What's the matter? [*She crosses* C., *front of the ottoman, to* AUBREY.] Ah! [*Her head drooping.*] Of course, Paula has told you about Captain Ardale?

Aubrey. Well?

Ellean [*falteringly*]. Have you and he met?

Aubrey. No.

Ellean. You are angry with him; [*Laying her hand on his arm.*] so was I. But to-morrow when he calls and expresses his regret—to-morrow——

Aubrey. Ellean—Ellean!

Ellean. Yes, Papa?

Aubrey. I—I can't let you see this man again. [*He walks away from her up stage* R.C., *in a paroxysm of distress, then, after a moment or two, he returns to her and takes her to his arms.*] Ellean! my child!

Ellean [*releasing herself*]. What has happened, Papa? What is it?

Aubrey [*thinking out his words deliberately*]. Something has occurred, something has come to my knowledge, in relation to Captain Ardale, which puts any further acquaintanceship between you two out of the question.

Ellean. Any further acquaintanceship . . . out of the question?

Aubrey. Yes.

[*She sits* L.C. *He advances to her quickly, but she shrinks from him.*

Ellean. No, no—I am quite well. [*After a short pause.*] It's not an hour ago since Mrs. Cortelyon left you and me together here; you had nothing to urge against Captain Ardale then.

Aubrey. No.

Ellean. You don't know each other; you haven't even seen him this evening. Father!

Aubrey [*firmly*]. I have told you he and I have not met.

Ellean [*in chair*]. Mrs. Cortelyon couldn't have spoken against him to you just now. No, no, no; she's too good a friend to both of us. [*Turning to him.*] Aren't you going to give me some explanation? You can't take this position towards me—towards Captain Ardale—without affording me the fullest explanation.

Aubrey [*with difficulty, next to her*]. Ellean, there are circumstances connected with Captain Ardale's career which you had better remain ignorant of. It must be sufficient for you that I consider these circumstances render him unfit to be your husband.

Ellean. Father!

Aubrey. You must trust me, Ellean; you must try to understand the depth of my love for you and the—the agony it gives me to hurt you. You must trust me. [*He moves* R.C.

Ellean [*she rises and goes to him composedly*]. I will, Father; but you must trust me a little too. Circumstances connected with Captain Ardale's career?

Aubrey. Yes.

Ellean. When he presents himself here to-morrow of course you will see him and let him defend himself?

Aubrey. Captain Ardale will not be here to-morrow.

Ellean [*after a pause*]. Not! You have stopped his coming here?

Aubrey. Indirectly—yes.

Ellean. But just now he was talking to me at that window! Nothing had taken place then! And since then nothing can have——! [*Suddenly.*] Oh! Why—you have heard something against him from Paula.

Aubrey. From—Paula!

Ellean. She knows him.

Aubrey. Who has told you so?

Ellean. When I introduced Captain Ardale to her she said she had met him in London. Of course! It is Paula who has done this!

Aubrey [*crossing to her* C.—*in a hard voice*]. I—I hope you—you'll refrain from rushing at conclusions. There's nothing to be gained by trying to avoid the main point, which is that you must drive Captain Ardale out of your thoughts. Understand that! You're able to obtain comfort from your religion, aren't you? I'm glad to think that's so. I talk to you in a harsh way, Ellean, but I feel your pain almost as acutely as you do. [*Going to the door up* L.] I—I can't say anything more to you to-night.

Ellean [*turning* R.C.]. Father! [*He pauses at the door.*] Father, I'm obliged to ask you this; there's no help for it—I've no mother to go to. Does what you have heard about Captain Ardale concern the time when he led a wild, a dissolute life in London?

Aubrey [*returning to her slowly and staring at her*]. Explain yourself! [*To* C. *behind table.*

Ellean. He has been quite honest with me. One day—in Paris—he confessed to me—what a man's life is—what his life had been.

Aubrey [*under his breath*]. Oh!

Ellean [*tearfully*]. He offered to go away, not to approach me again.

Aubrey. And you—you accepted his view of what a man's life is!

Ellean. As far as *I* could forgive him, I forgave him.

Aubrey [*with a groan*]. Why, when was it you left us? It hasn't taken you long to get your robe 'just a little dusty at the hem!'

Ellean. What do you mean?

Aubrey. Hah! A few weeks ago my one great desire was to keep you ignorant of evil.

Ellean. Father, it is impossible to be ignorant of evil. Instinct, common instinct, teaches us what is good and bad. Surely I am none the worse for knowing what is wicked and detesting it!

Aubrey. Detesting it! Why, you *love* this fellow! [*He sits* L.C.

Ellean. Ah, you don't understand! [*She delivers this speech standing* R. *of* L.C. *chair, whereon* AUBREY *is seated.*] I have simply judged Captain Ardale as we all pray to be judged. I have lived in imagination through that one week in India when he deliberately offered his life back to God to save those wretched, desperate people. In his whole career I see nothing but that one week; those few hours bring him nearer the Saints, I believe, than fifty uneventful years of mere blamelessness would have done! [*Down* R.] And so, Father, if Paula has reported anything to Captain Ardale's discredit—— [*She moves* R.C.

Aubrey [*rising and going to her*]. Paula——!

Ellean. It *must* be Paula; it can't be anybody else.

Aubrey. You—you'll please keep Paula out of the question. Finally, Ellean, understand me—I have made up my mind.

[*Again going to the door up* L. *She follows him.*

Ellean. But wait—listen! [*She goes up* R.C.] I have made up my mind also.

Aubrey [*facing her*]. Ah! I recognize your mother in you now!

Ellean [*quickly*]. You need not speak against my mother because you are angry with me!

Aubrey [*unsteadily*]. I—I hardly know what I'm saying to you. In the morning—in the morning——

[*Moves to the door. He goes out. Suddenly she turns her head to listen. Then, after a moment's hesitation, she goes softly to the window* R.C., *and looks out under the verandah.*

Ellean [*in a whisper*]. Paula! Paula!

[PAULA *appears outside the window and steps into the room; her face is white and drawn, her hair is a little disordered.*

Paula [*huskily*]. Well?

Ellean. Have you been under the verandah all the while—listening?

Paula. N—no.

Ellean. You *have* overheard us—I see you have. And it *is* you who have been speaking to my father against Captain Ardale. Isn't it? [*Down* L.] Paula, why don't you own it or deny it?

Paula [*faintly*]. Oh, I—I don't mind owning it; why should I?

Ellean. Ah! You seem to have been very, very eager to tell your tale.

Paula. No, I wasn't eager, Ellean. I'd have given something not to have had to do it. I wasn't eager.

Ellean. Not! Oh, I think you might safely have spared us all for a little while.

[*She crosses back of table to the* L. *settee.*

Paula. But, Ellean, you forget I—I am your stepmother. It was my—my duty—to tell your father what I—what I knew——

Ellean. What you knew! Why, after all, what can you know! You can only speak from gossip, report, hearsay! How is it possible that you——! [*She stops abruptly and moves over to* PAULA. *The two women stand staring at each other for a moment; then* ELLEAN *backs away from* PAULA *slowly*.] Paula!

Paula [*advancing*]. What—what's the matter?

Ellean. You—you knew Captain Ardale in London!

Paula. Why—what do you mean?

Ellean. Oh!

[*She makes for the door* R., *but* PAULA *turns and catches her by the wrist.* ELLEAN *is now* R.C., PAULA C.

Paula. You shall tell me what you mean!

Ellean [*helplessly*]. Ah! [*Suddenly looking fixedly in* PAULA's *face*.] You *know* what I mean.

Paula [*still clutching her*]. You accuse me!

Ellean. It's in your face!

Paula [*hoarsely*]. You—you think I'm—that sort of creature, do you?

Ellean. Let me go!

Paula. Answer me! You've always hated me! [*Shaking her*.] Out with it!

Ellean. You hurt me!

Paula. You've always hated me! You shall answer me!

Ellean. Well, then, I have always—always——

Paula. What?

Ellean. I have always known what you were!

Paula. Ah! [*She releases her and feebly grasps back of* L.C. *chair*.] Who—who told you?

Ellean. Nobody but yourself. From the first moment I saw you I knew you were altogether unlike the good women I'd left; directly I saw you I knew what my father had done. You've wondered why I've turned from you! There—that's the reason! Oh, but this is a horrible way for the truth to come home to every one! Oh!

[*She moves down* R.C.

Paula [*madly*]. It's a lie! It's all a lie! [*Forcing* ELLEAN *down upon her knees*.] You shall beg my pardon for it. [ELLEAN *utters a loud shriek of terror*.] Ellean, I'm a good woman! I swear I am! I've always been a good woman! You dare to say I've ever been anything else! [*Throwing her off violently*.] It's a lie! [AUBREY *re-enters*.

Aubrey. Paula! [PAULA *staggers back up* C. *to* R.C. *window*. AUBREY *advances. Raising* ELLEAN.] What's this? What's this?

Ellean [*faintly*]. Nothing. [*She goes round the ottoman and leans upon it.*] It—it's my fault. Father, I—I don't wish to see Captain Ardale again.

[*She goes out, door* R., AUBREY *slowly following her to the door.*

Paula. Aubrey, she—she guesses.

Aubrey. Guesses?

Paula. About me—and Ardale.

Aubrey. About you—and Ardale?

Paula. She says she suspected my character from the beginning . . . that's why she's always kept me at a distance . . . and now she sees through——

[*She falters; he helps her to the ottoman* R.C., *where she sits.*

Aubrey [*bending over her*]. Paula, you must have said something—admitted something——

Paula. I don't think so. It—it's in my face.

Aubrey. What?

Paula. She tells me so. She's right! I'm tainted through and through; anybody can see it, anybody can find it out. You said much the same to me to-night.

Aubrey [*partly to himself, as if dazed*]. If she has got this idea into her head we must drive it out, that's all. We must take steps to—— What shall we do? We had better—better—— [*Sitting* L.C. *and staring before him.*] What—what?

Paula [*lifting her head, after a pause*]. Ellean! So meek, so demure! You've often said she reminded you of her mother. Yes, I know now what your first marriage was like.

Aubrey [*as before*]. We must drive this idea out of her head. We'll do something. What shall we do?

Paula. She's a regular woman too. She could forgive *him* easily enough—but *me*! That's just a woman!

Aubrey. What *can* we do?

Paula. Why, nothing! She'd have no difficulty in following up her suspicions. Suspicions! You should have seen how she looked at me! [*He buries his head in his hands. There is silence for a time, then she rises slowly, crosses to* L.C., *takes chair from behind table and sits beside him*]. Aubrey!

Aubrey. Yes. [*She looks at him pityingly.*

Paula [*moving slightly*]. I'm very sorry.

[*Without meeting her eyes, he lays his hand on her arm for a moment.*

Aubrey [*rousing himself*]. Well, we must look things straight in the face. [*Glancing round.*] At any rate, we've done with this.

Paula [*following his glance*]. I suppose so. [*After a brief pause.*] Of course, she and I can't live under the same roof any more. [*Abruptly.*] You know she kissed me to-night, of her own accord.

Aubrey. I asked her to alter towards you.

Paula [*disappointed*]. That was it, then.

Aubrey. I—I'm sorry I sent her away.

Paula. It was my fault; I made it necessary.

Aubrey. Perhaps now she'll propose to return to the convent —well, she must.

Paula. Would you like to keep her with you and—and leave me?

Aubrey. Paula——!

Paula. You needn't be afraid I'd go back to—what I was. I couldn't.

Aubrey. Sssh, for God's sake! We—you and I—we'll get out of this place . . . what a fool I was to come here again!

Paula. You lived here with your first wife!

Aubrey. We'll get out of this place and go abroad again, and begin afresh.

Paula. Begin afresh?

Aubrey. There's no reason why the future shouldn't be happy for us—no reason that I can see——

[*Almost discussing his own helplessness*

Paula [*abruptly*]. Aubrey!

Aubrey. Yes?

Paula [*matter of fact*]. You'll never forget this, you know.

Aubrey. This?

Paula. To-night, and everything that's led up to it. Our coming here, Ellean, our quarrels—cat and dog!—Mrs. Cortelyon, the Orreyeds, this man! What an everlasting nightmare for you!

Aubrey. Oh, we can forget it, if we choose.

Paula. That was always your cry. How *can* one do it?

Aubrey. We'll make our calculations solely for the future, talk about the future, think about the future.

Paula. I believe the future is only the past again, entered through another gate.

Aubrey. That's an awful belief.

Paula. To-night proves it. You must see now that, do what we will, go where we will, you'll be continually reminded of—what I was. I see it.

Aubrey. You're frightened to-night; meeting this man has

frightened you. But that sort of thing isn't likely to recur. The world isn't quite so small as all that.

Paula. Isn't it! The only great distances it contains are those we carry within ourselves—the distances that separate husbands and wives, for instance. And so it'll be with us. You'll do your best—oh, I know that—you're a good fellow. But circumstances will be too strong for you in the end, mark my words.

Aubrey. Paula——!

Paula. Of course I'm pretty now—I'm pretty still—and a pretty woman, whatever else she may be, is always—well, endurable. But even now I notice that the lines of my face are getting deeper; so are the hollows about my eyes. Yes, my face is covered with little shadows that usen't to be there. Oh, I know I'm 'going off'. I hate paint and dye and those messes, but, by and by, I shall drift the way of the others; I shan't be able to help myself. And then, some day—perhaps very suddenly, under a queer, fantastic light at night or in the glare of the morning—that horrid, irresistible truth that physical repulsion forces on men and women will come to you, and you'll sicken at me.

Aubrey. I——!

Paula [*she delivers this speech staring forward, as if she were looking at what she describes*]. You'll see me then, at last, with other people's eyes; you'll see me just as your daughter does now, as all wholesome folks see women like me. And I shall have no weapon to fight with—not one serviceable little bit of prettiness left me to defend myself with! A worn-out creature—broken up, very likely, some time before I ought to be—my hair bright, my eyes dull, my body too thin or too stout, my cheeks raddled and ruddled—a ghost, a wreck, a caricature, a candle that gutters, call such an end what you like! Oh, Aubrey, what shall I be able to say to you then? And this is the future you talk about! I know it—I know it! [*He is still sitting staring forward; she rocks herself to and fro as if in pain.*] Oh, Aubrey! Oh! Oh!

[*With a long, low wail she bends forward till her head almost touches her knees. He tries to comfort her. She straightens herself and lays her head upon his shoulder.*

Aubrey. Paula——!

Paula [*with a moan*]. Oh, and I wanted so much to sleep to-night! [*From the distance, in the garden* L., *there comes the sound of* DRUMMLE'*s voice; he is singing as he approaches the house. Listening.*] That's Cayley, coming back from The Warren. [*Starting up.*] He doesn't know, evidently. I—I won't see him!

[*She goes out quickly, door* R. DRUMMLE'*s voice comes nearer. By a strong effort* AUBREY *rouses himself and rises. For a moment he stands* C., *irresolute; then an idea comes to him. He puts the chair that* PAULA *has used back behind the table, snatches up a book, and sitting on settee* L. *makes a pretence of reading. After a moment or two,* DRUMMLE *appears at the window* L.C. *and looks in.*

Drummle. Aha! my dear chap!

Aubrey. Cayley?

Drummle [*coming into the room*]. I went down to The Warren after you.

Aubrey. Yes?

Drummle. Missed you. Well? I've been gossiping with Mrs. Cortelyon. [*Removing a handkerchief which he has tied round his throat.*] Confound you, I've heard the news!

Aubrey [*lowering his book*]. What have you heard?

Drummle. What have I heard! Why—Ellean and young Ardale! [*Checking himself—looking at* AUBREY *keenly.*] My dear Aubrey! Alice is under the impression that you are inclined to look on the affair favourably.

Aubrey [*rising and advancing to* DRUMMLE]. You've not—met Captain Ardale? [*Puts the book on the table.*

Drummle. No. Why do you ask? [*Hesitatingly.*] By the by, I don't know that I need tell you—but it's rather strange. He's not at The Warren to-night.

Aubrey. No?

Drummle [*quickly and lightly*]. He left the house half an hour ago, to stroll about the lanes; just now a note came from him, a scribble in pencil, simply telling Alice that she would receive a letter from him to-morrow. What's the matter? There's nothing very wrong, is there? My dear chap, pray forgive me if I'm asking too much.

Aubrey. Cayley, you—you urged me to send her away!

Drummle. Ellean! Yes, yes. But—but—by all accounts this is quite an eligible young fellow. Alice has been giving me the history——

Aubrey [*madly*]. Curse him! [*Hurling his book to the floor.*] Curse him! Yes, I do curse him—him and his class! Perhaps I curse myself too in doing it. He has only led 'a man's life'—just as I, how many of us, have done! The misery he has brought on me and mine it's likely enough we, in our time, have helped to bring on others by this leading 'a man's life'! But I do curse him for all that. My God, *I've* nothing more to fear—I've paid *my* fine! And so I can curse him in safety. Curse him! Curse him!

Drummle. In Heaven's name, tell me what's happened?

Aubrey [*gripping* DRUMMLE'*s arm*]. Paula! Paula!

Drummle. What?

Aubrey. They met to-night here. They—they—they're not strangers to each other.

Drummle. Aubrey! [*He moves slowly up* C.

Aubrey. Curse him! My poor, wretched wife! My poor, wretched wife!

[*He sinks into* L.C. *chair. The door* R. *opens and* ELLEAN *appears. The two men turn to her. There is a moment's silence.*

Ellean [*very quietly*]. Father . . . father . . . !

Aubrey. Ellean?

Ellean. I—I want you. [*He goes to her.*] Father . . . go to Paula! [*He looks into her face, startled.*] Quickly—quickly [*He passes her to go out, she seizes his arm, with a cry.* No, no; don't go!

[*He shakes her off and goes.* ELLEAN *staggers back towards* DRUMMLE.

Drummle [*to* ELLEAN]. What do you mean? What do you mean?

Ellean. I—I went to her room—to tell her I was sorry for something I had said to her. And I *was* sorry—I *was* sorry. I heard the fall. I—I've seen her. It's horrible.

Drummle. She—she has——!

Ellean. Killed—herself? [*Nodding.*] Yes—yes. So everybody will say. But I know—I helped to kill her. If I had only been merciful!

[*She beats her breast. She faints upon the ottoman. He pauses for a moment irresolutely—then he goes to the door* R., *opens it, and stands looking off.*

CURTAIN

THE LIARS

HENRY ARTHUR JONES

(1851–1929)

Born Grandborough, Buckinghamshire. Worked as draper's assistant and later commercial traveller until his play, *The Silver King*, was successfully produced in 1882. Spoke and wrote widely on the theatre's claim to artistic and social recognition, his publications on this theme including *The Renascence of the English Drama* (1895) and *The Foundations of a National Drama* (1913). In later life involved in political and ideological controversies with G. B. Shaw and H. G. Wells (in *My Dear Wells, A Manual for the Haters of England*, 1921, and elsewhere). Also published *Patriotism and Popular Education* (1919) and *What is Capital*? (1925).

His plays included *It's Only Round the Corner* (1879); *A Clerical Error* (1879); *The Silver King* (with H. A. Herman, 1882); *Saints and Sinners* (1884); *The Middleman* (1889); *Judah* (1890); *The Dancing Girl* (1891); *The Masqueraders* (1894); *The Case of Rebellious Susan* (1894); *Michael and His Lost Angel* (1896); *The Liars* (1897); *Mrs. Dane's Defence* (1900); *Whitewashing Julia* (1903); *Dolly Reforming Herself* (1908): *Mary Goes First* (1913); *The Lie* (1914).

THE LIARS

AN ORIGINAL COMEDY IN FOUR ACTS

by

Henry Arthur Jones

THE LIARS

First produced at the Criterion Theatre, London, 6 *October* 1897 *with the following cast:*

COLONEL SIR CHRISTOPHER DEERING	Mr. Charles Wyndham
EDWARD FALKNER	Mr. T. B. Thalberg
GILBERT NEPEAN	Mr. Herbert Standing
GEORGE NEPEAN	Mr. Leslie Kenyon
FREDDIE TATTON	Mr. Adolphus Vane-Tempest
ARCHIBALD COKE	Mr. Alfred Bishop
WAITER AT 'THE STAR AND GARTER'	Mr. Paul Berton
TAPLIN	Mr. R. Lambart
GADSBY	Mr. C. Terric
FOOTMAN	Mr. A. Eliot
MRS. CRESPIN	Miss Janette Steer
BEATRICE EBERNOE	Miss Cynthia Brooke
DOLLY COKE	Miss Sarah Brooke
FERRIS	Miss M. Barton
LADY ROSAMUND TATTON	Miss Irene Vanbrugh
LADY JESSICA NEPEAN	Miss Mary Moore

THE LIARS

ACT I

SCENE: *Interior of a large tent on the lawn of* FREDDIE TATTON'S *house in the Thames valley. The roof of the tent slopes up from the back of the stage. An opening at back discovers the lawn, a night scene of a secluded part of the Thames, and the opposite bank beyond. Small opening L. The tent is of Eastern material, splendidly embroidered in rich Eastern colours. The floor is planked and some rugs are laid down. The place is comfortably furnished for summer tea and smoking room. Several little tables, chairs and lounges, most of them of basket-work. On the table spirit-decanters, soda-water bottles, cigars, cigarettes, empty coffee cups, match-box, etc. Some plants in the corners. Lamps and candles lighted.*

TIME: *After dinner on a summer evening.*

Discover ARCHIBALD COKE *and* FREDDIE TATTON.

COKE, *a tall, pompous, precise man, about fifty, is seated at side table smoking.* FREDDIE, *a nervous, weedy little creature about thirty, with no whiskers, and nearly bald, with a squeaky voice, is walking about.*

Freddie [*very excited, very voluble, very squeaky*]. It's all very well for folks to say, 'Give a woman her head; don't ride her on the curb.' But I tell you this, Coke, when a fellow has got a wife like mine, or Jess, it's confoundedly difficult to get her to go at all, without a spill, eh?

Coke. It is perplexing to know precisely how to handle a wife—[*Drinks, sighs.*]—very perplexing!

Freddie. Perplexing? It's a d—ee—d silly riddle without any answer! You know I didn't want to have this house-party for the Regatta—[COKE *looks at him.*]—I beg your pardon. Of course I wanted to have you and Dolly, and I didn't mind Gilbert and Jess. But I didn't want to have Falkner here. He's paying a great deal too much attention to Jess, and Jess doesn't choke him off as she should. Well, I thoroughly made up my mind if Jess came, Falkner shouldn't.

Coke. Yes?

Freddie. Well, Rosamund said he should. So I stuck out, and she stuck out, in fact we both stuck out for a week. I was determined he shouldn't come.

Coke. Then why did you give in?

Freddie. I didn't.

Coke. But he's here!

Freddie. Yes; but only for a few days. Rosamund invited him, unknown to me, and then—well—you see, I was obliged to be civil to the fellow. [*Very confidential*.] I say, Coke—we're tiled in, aren't we? Candidly, what would you do if you had a wife like Rosamund?

Coke [*sententiously*]. Ah! Just so! [*Drinks*.

Freddie. You're the lucky man of us three, Coke.

Coke. I must own my wife has some good points——

Freddie. Dolly got good points! I should think she has!

Coke. But she's terribly thoughtless and frivolous.

Freddie. So much the better. Give me a woman that lets a man call his soul his own. That's all I want, Coke, to call my soul my own. And—[*resolutely*] some of these days—[*very resolutely*] I will, that's all!

[*Enter* MRS. CRESPIN, *a sharp, good-looking woman between thirty and thirty-five*.

Mrs. Crespin. Is Mr. Gilbert Nepean leaving for Devonshire to-night?

Freddie. Yes. He takes the eleven thirty-four slow and waits for the down fast at Reading.

Mrs. Crespin. To-night?

Freddie. Yes. His steward, Crampton, has been robbing him for years, and now the fellow has bolted with a heap of money and a farmer's wife.

Mrs. Crespin. Mr. Nepean must go to-night?

Freddie. Yes. Why?

Mrs. Crespin. Lady Jessica and Mr. Falkner have gone for a little moonlight row. I thought Mr. Nepean might like to stay and steer.

Freddie. Oh, Lady Jessica knows the river well.

Mrs. Crespin. Ah, then Mr. Nepean can look after the steward. After all, no husband need emphasize the natural absurdity of his position by playing cox to another man's stroke, need he?

[*Enter* COLONEL SIR CHRISTOPHER DEERING, *a genial handsome Englishman about thirty-eight, and* GEORGE NEPEAN, *a dark, rather heavy-looking man about the same age*.

Sir Christopher. Oh, nonsense, Nepean; you're mistaken!

George. You'd better say a word to Falkner——

Sir Christopher [*with a warning look*]. Shush!

George. If you don't, I shall drop a very strong hint to my brother.

Sir Christopher [*more peremptorily*]. Shush, shush!

Freddie. What's the matter?

Sir Christopher. Nothing, Freddie, nothing! Our friend here —[*Trying to link his arm in* GEORGE'*s*—GEORGE *stands off*.] is a little old-fashioned. He doesn't understand that in all really innocent flirtations ladies allow themselves a very large latitude indeed. In fact, from my very modest experience with the sex—take it for what it's worth—I should say the more innocent the flirtation, the larger the latitude the lady allows herself, eh, Mrs. Crespin?

Mrs. Crespin. Oh, we are all latitudinarians at heart.

Sir Christopher. Yes; but a lady who practises extensively as a latitudinarian rarely becomes a—a—a longitudinarian, eh?

Mrs. Crespin. Oh, I wouldn't answer for her! It's a horrid, wicked world; and if once a woman allows one of you wretches to teach her the moral geography of it, it's ten to one she gets her latitude and longitude mixed before she has had time to look at the map.

[*Goes up to opening, and looks off*.

Freddie [*to* SIR CHRISTOPHER]. I say, I'm awfully sorry about this. You know I told Rosamund how it would be if we had Falkner here——

Sir Christopher [*draws* FREDDIE *aside*]. Shush! Tell Lady Rosamund to caution Lady Jessica——

Freddie. I will. But Rosamund generally does just the opposite of what I tell her. Don't be surprised, old fellow, if you hear some of these days that I've—well, don't be surprised.

Sir Christopher. At what?

Freddie. Well, I shall—now, candidly, old fellow—we're tiled in, quite between ourselves—if you found yourself landed as I am, what would you do?

Sir Christopher. You mean if I found myself married?

Freddie. Yes.

Sir Christopher. I should make the best of it.

[GEORGE *comes up to them*. MRS. CRESPIN *comes from back of tent*.

George [*to* SIR CHRISTOPHER]. Then it's understood that you'll give Falkner a hint?

Sir Christopher. My dear fellow, surely your brother is the best judge———

George. Of what he doesn't see?

Sir Christopher. He's here.

George. He's leaving for Devonshire to-night—unless I stop him. Will that be necessary?

Sir Christopher. No. Falkner is my friend. I introduced him to Lady Jessica. If you insist, I'll speak to him. But I'm sure you're wrong. He's the very soul of honour. I didn't live with him out there those three awful years without knowing him.

George. I don't see what your living three years in Africa with him has got to do with it.

Mrs. Crespin. Let's see how it works out. Falkner behaves most gallantly in Africa. Falkner rescues Mrs. Ebernoe. Falkner splendidly avenges Colonel Ebernoe's death, and strikes terror into every slave-dealer's heart. Falkner returns to England covered with glory. A grateful nation goes into a panic of admiration, and makes itself slightly ridiculous over Falkner. Falkner is the lion of the season. Therefore we may be quite sure that Falkner won't make love to any pretty woman who comes in his way. It doesn't seem to work out right.

Sir Christopher. But Falkner is not an ordinary man, not even an ordinary hero.

Mrs. Crespin. My dear Sir Christopher, the one cruel fact about heroes is that they are made of flesh and blood! Oh, if only they were made of waxwork, or Crown Derby ware, or Britannia metal; but, alas and alas! they're always made of flesh and blood.

Coke. Where did Falkner come from? What were his people?

Sir Christopher. His grandfather was what Nonconformists call an eminent divine, his father was a rich city merchant; his mother was a farmer's daughter. Falkner himself is a—well, he's a Puritan Don Quixote, mounted on Pegasus.

Mrs. Crespin. Put a Puritan Don Quixote on horseback, and he'll ride to the—Lady Jessica, eh?

Sir Christopher. Hush! He'll love and he'll ride away.

Mrs. Crespin [*significantly*]. I sincerely hope so.

Coke. I must say that Falkner is less objectionable than Dissenters generally are. I have an unconquerable aversion to Dissenters.

Sir Christopher. Oh, I hate 'em! But they saved England, hang 'em! And I'm not sure whether they're not the soundest part of the nation to-day.

Mrs. Crespin. Oh, pray don't tell them so, just as they're getting harmless and sensible—and a little artistic.

[*A piano is played very softly and beautifully at a distance of some twenty yards. They all listen.*

Mrs. Crespin. Is that Mrs. Ebernoe?

Sir Christopher. Yes.

Mrs. Crespin. What a beautiful touch she has!

Sir Christopher. She has a beautiful nature.

Mrs. Crespin. Indeed! I thought she was a little stiff and unsociable. But perhaps we are too frivolous.

Sir Christopher. Perhaps. And she hasn't quite recovered from poor Ebernoe's death.

[*Enter* LADY ROSAMUND *and* DOLLY COKE *in evening dress.* DOLLY *is without any wrap on her shoulders.*

Mrs. Crespin. But that's nearly two years ago. Is it possible we still have women amongst us who can mourn two years for a man? It gives me hopes again for my sex.

Freddie [*his back to* LADY ROSAMUND]. I know jolly well Rosamund won't mourn two years for me.

Lady Rosamund [*a clear-cut, bright, pretty woman*]. You're quite right, Freddie, I shan't. But if you behave very prettily meantime, I promise you a decent six weeks. So be satisfied, and don't make a disturbance down there—[*With a little gesture pointing down.*] and create the impression that I wasn't a model wife.

[FREDDIE *makes an appealing gesture for sympathy to* SIR CHRISTOPHER.

Coke [*in a very querulous, pedantic tone to* DOLLY]. No wrap again! Really, my dear, I do wish you would take more precautions against the night air. If you should take influenza again——

Dolly [*a pretty, empty-headed little woman*]. Oh, my dear Archie, if I do, it is I who will have to cough and sneeze!

Coke. Yes; but it is I who will be compelled to listen to you. I do wish you would remember how very inconvenient it is for me when you have influenza.

Dolly. My dear, you can't expect me to remember *all* the things that are inconvenient to you. Besides, other people don't wrap up. Jessica is out on the river with absolutely nothing on her shoulders.

Mrs. Crespin. Is it not a physiological fact that when our hearts reach a certain temperature our shoulders may be, and often are, safely left bare?

[GEORGE NEPEAN *has been listening. He suddenly rises, comes some steps towards them as if about to speak, stops, then turns and exit with great determination.*

Sir Christopher. Mrs. Crespin, you saw that?

Mrs. Crespin. Yes. Where has he gone?

Sir Christopher. I suppose to tell his brother his suspicions. I'm sure you meant nothing just now, but—[*Glancing round.*]—we are all friends of Lady Jessica's, aren't we?

Mrs. Crespin. Oh, certainly. But don't you think you ought to get Mr. Falkner away?

Sir Christopher. He'll be leaving England soon. These fresh outbreaks amongst the slave-traders will give us no end of trouble, and the Government will have to send Falkner out. Meantime——

Mrs. Crespin. Meantime, doesn't Mrs. Ebernoe play divinely? [*Going off.*

Sir Christopher [*politely intercepting her*]. Meantime it's understood that nothing more is to be said of this?

Mrs. Crespin. Oh, my dear Sir Christopher, what more can be said? [*Exit.*

Sir Christopher [*holds the tent curtains aside for her to pass out; looks after her, shakes his head, perplexed, then turns to* COKE]. Coke, what do you say, a hundred up?

Coke [*rising*]. I'm agreeable! Dolly! Dolly!

[LADY ROSAMUND, DOLLY *and* FREDDIE *are chattering very vigorously together.*

Dolly [*doesn't turn round to him*]. Well?

[*Goes on chattering to* LADY ROSAMUND *and* FREDDIE.

Coke. You had a tiresome hacking cough, dear, during the greater portion of last night.

Dolly. Did I? [*Same business.*

Coke. It would be wise to keep away from the river.

Dolly. Oh, very well, dear. I'll try and remember.

[*Same business.*

Coke [*turns, annoyed, to* SIR CHRISTOPHER]. I'm a painfully light sleeper. The least thing disturbs me, and—[*Looks anxiously at* DOLLY *who is still chattering, then turns to* SIR CHRISTOPHER.] Do you sleep well?

Sir Christopher [*links his arm in* COKE'*s*]. Like a top. Never missed a night's rest in my life.

[*Takes* COKE *off at opening.*

Freddie [*has been talking angrily to* LADY ROSAMUND]. Very well then, what am I to do?

Dolly. Oh, do go and get a whisky and soda, there's a dear Freddie!

Freddie. That's all very well, but if Jessica goes and makes a fool of herself in my house, people will say it was my fault.

Lady Rosamund. What—example, or influence, or sheer desperate imitation?

Freddie [*pulls himself up, looks very satirical, evidently tries to think of some crushing reply without success*]. I must say, Rosamund, that your continued chaff of me and everything that I do is in execrable taste. For a woman to chaff her husband on all occasions is—well it's very bad taste, that's all I can say about it! [*Exit at back*.

Dolly. Freddie's getting a dreadful fidget. He's nearly as bad as Archie.

Lady Rosamund. Oh, my dear, he's ten times worse. One can't help feeling some small respect for Archie.

Dolly. Oh, do you think so? Well, yes, I suppose Archie is honourable and all that.

Lady Rosamund. Oh, all men are honourable. They get kicked out if they aren't. My Freddie's honourable in his poor little way.

Dolly. Oh, don't run Freddie down. I rather like Freddie.

Lady Rosamund. Oh, if you had to live with him——

Dolly. Well, he always lets you have your own way.

Lady Rosamund. I wish he wouldn't. I really believe I should love and respect him a little if he were to take me and give me a good shaking, or do something to make me feel that he's my master. But—[*Sighs*.] he never will! He'll only go on asking everybody's advice how to manage me—and never find out. As if it weren't the easiest thing in the world to manage a woman—if men only knew.

Dolly. Oh, do you think so? I wonder if poor old Archie knows how to manage me!

Lady Rosamund. Archie's rather trying at times.

Dolly. Oh, he is! He's so frumpish and particular, and he's getting worse.

Lady Rosamund. Oh, my dear, they do as they grow older.

Dolly. Still, after all, Freddie and Archie aren't quite so awful as Gilbert.

Lady Rosamund. Oh, Gilbert's a terror. I hope Jessica won't do anything foolish——

[*A very merry peal of laughter heard off, followed by* LADY JESSICA'*s voice.*

Lady Jessica [*heard off*]. Oh, no, no, no, no, no! Please keep away from my dress! Oh, I'm so sorry! [*Laughing a little.*] But you are—so—so— [*Another peal of laughter.*

Falkner [*heard off, a deep, rich, sincere, manly tone*]. So ridiculous? I don't mind that!

Lady Jessica [*heard off*]. But you'll take cold. Do go and change!

Falkner [*heard off*]. Change? That's not possible!

[LADY JESSICA *appears at opening at back, looking off, smothering her laughter. She is a very bright, pretty woman about twenty-seven, very dainty and charming. Piano ceases.*

Lady Jessica. Oh, the poor dear, foolish fellow! Look!

Lady Rosamund. What is it?

Lady Jessica. My ten-and-sixpenny brooch! He kept on begging for some little souvenir, so I took this off. That quite unhinged him. I saw he was going to be demonstrative, so I dropped the brooch in the river and made a terrible fuss. He jumped in, poor dear, and fished it up. It was so muddy at the bottom! He came up looking like a *fin-de-siècle* Neptune—or a forsaken merman—or the draggled figure-head of a penny Thames steamboat.

Lady Rosamund [*very seriously*] Jess, the men are talking about you.

Lady Jessica [*very carelessly*]. Ah, are they? Who is?

Lady Rosamund. My Freddie says that you——

Lady Jessica [*interrupting on 'says'*]. My dear Rosy, I don't mind what your Freddie says any more than you do.

Lady Rosamund. But George has been fizzing up all the evening.

Lady Jessica. Oh, let him fizz down again.

Lady Rosamund. But I believe he has gone to give Gilbert a hint——

Lady Jessica [*showing annoyance*]. Ah, that's mean of George! How vexing! Perhaps Gilbert will stay now.

Lady Rosamund. Perhaps it's as well that Gilbert should stay.

Lady Jessica. What? My dear Rosy, you know I'm the very best of wives, but it does get a little monotonous to spend all one's time in the company of a man who doesn't understand a joke—not even when it's explained to him!

Lady Rosamund. Jess, you really must pull up.

Dolly. Yes, Jess. Mrs. Crespin was making some very cattish remarks about you and Mr. Falkner.

Lady Jessica. Was she? Rosy, why do you have that woman here?

Lady Rosamund. I don't know. One must have somebody. I thought you and she were very good friends.

Lady Jessica. Oh, we're the best of friends, only we hate each other like poison.

Lady Rosamund. I don't like her. But she says such stinging things about my Freddie, and makes him so wild.

Lady Jessica. Does she? I'll ask her down for the shooting. Oh! I've got a splendid idea!

Lady Rosamund. What is it?

Lady Jessica. A new career for poor gentlewomen. You found a school and carefully train them in all the best traditions of the gentle art of husband-baiting. Then you invite one of them to your house, pay her, of course, a handsome salary, and she assists you in 'the daily round, the common task' of making your husband's life a perfect misery to him. After a month or so she is played out and retires to another sphere, and you call in a new—lady-help!

Lady Rosamund. Oh, I don't think I should care to have my Freddie systematically henpecked by another woman.

Lady Jessica. No; especially as you do it so well yourself. Besides, your Freddie is such a poor little pocket-edition of a man—I hope you don't mind my saying so——

Lady Rosamund. Oh, not at all. He's your own brother-in-law.

Lady Jessica. Yes; and you may say what you like about Gilbert

Dolly. Oh, we do, don't we, Rosy?

Lady Jessica. Do you? Well, what do you say?

Dolly. Oh, it wouldn't be fair to tell, would it, Rosy? But Mrs. Crespin said yesterday——

[LADY ROSAMUND *glances at* DOLLY *and stops her.*

Lady Jessica. About Gilbert?

Dolly. Yes.

Lady Jessica. Well, what did she say?

[DOLLY *glances at* LADY ROSAMUND *inquiringly.*

Lady Rosamund. No, Dolly, no!

Lady Jessica. Yes, Dolly! Do tell me.

Lady Rosamund. No, no!

Lady Jessica. I don't care what she said, so long as she didn't say that he could understand a joke. That would be shamefully untrue. I've lived with him for five years, and I'm sure he can't. But what did Mrs. Crespin say, Rosy?

Lady Rosamund. No, it really was a little too bad.

Dolly. Yes. I don't much mind what anybody says about Archie, but if Mrs. Crespin had said about him what she said about Gilbert——

Lady Jessica. But what did she say? Rosy, if you don't tell me, I won't tell you all the dreadful things I hear about your Freddie. Oh, do tell me! There's a dear!

Lady Rosamund. Well she said——

[*Begins laughing.* DOLLY *begins laughing.*

Lady Jessica. Oh, go on! go on! go on!

Lady Rosamund. She said—no, I'll whisper!

[LADY JESSICA *inclines her ear,* LADY ROSAMUND *whispers;* DOLLY *laughs.*

Lady Jessica. About Gilbert? [*Beginning to laugh.*

Lady Rosamund. Yes. [*Laughing.*

[*They all join in a burst of laughter which grows louder and louder. At its height enter* GILBERT NEPEAN. *He is a man rather over forty, much the same build as his brother* GEORGE; *rather stout, heavy figure, dark complexion; strong, immobile, uninteresting features; large, coarse hands; a habit of biting his nails. He is dressed in tweeds, long light ulster and travelling cap, which he does not remove. As he enters, the laughter, which has been very boisterous, suddenly ceases. He goes up to table without taking any notice of the ladies; very deliberately takes out cigar from case, strikes a match which does not ignite, throws it down with an angry gesture and exclamation; strikes another which also does not ignite; throws it down with a still angrier gesture and exclamation. The third match ignites, and he deliberately lights his cigar. Meantime, as soon as he has reached table,* LADY JESSICA, *who stands behind him, exchanges glances with* DOLLY *and* LADY ROSAMUND, *and makes a little face behind his back.* DOLLY *winks at* LADY JESSICA, *who responds by pulling a mock long face.* DOLLY *steals off.* LADY ROSAMUND *shrugs her shoulders at* LADY JESSICA, *who pulls her face still longer.* LADY ROSAMUND *steals quietly off after* DOLLY. GILBERT *is still busy with his cigar.* LADY JESSICA *does a little expressive pantomime behind his back.*

Gilbert. What's all this tomfoolery with Falkner?

Lady Jessica. Tomfoolery?

Gilbert. George says you are carrying on some tomfoolery with Falkner.

Lady Jessica. Ah! that's very sweet and elegant of George. But I never carry on any tomfoolery with anyone—because I'm not a tomfool, therefore I can't.

Gilbert. I wish for once in your life you'd give me a plain answer to a plain question.

Lady Jessica. Oh, I did once. You shouldn't remind me of that. But I never bear malice. Ask me another, such as—if a herring and a half cost three ha'pence, how long will it take one's husband to learn politeness enough to remove his cap in his wife's presence?

Gilbert [*instinctively takes off his cap, then glancing at her attitude, which is one of amused defiance, he puts the cap on again*]. There's a draught here.

Lady Jessica. The lamp doesn't show it. But perhaps you are right to guard a sensitive spot.

Gilbert. I say there's a confounded draught.

Lady Jessica. Oh, don't tell fibs, dear. Because if you do, you'll go—where you *may* meet me, and then we should have to spend such a very long time together.

Gilbert [*nonplussed, bites his nails a moment or two; takes out his watch*]. I've no time to waste. I must be down in Devonshire to-morrow to go into this business of Crampton's. But before I go, I mean to know the truth of this nonsense between you and Falkner.

Lady Jessica. Ah!

Gilbert. Shall I get it from you—or from him?

Lady Jessica. Wouldn't it be better to get it from me? Because he mightn't tell you *all*?

Gilbert. *All*? Then there is something to know?

Lady Jessica. Heaps. And if you'll have the ordinary politeness to take off that very ugly cap I'll be very sweet and obedient and tell you *all*.

Gilbert. Go on!

Lady Jessica. Not while the cap sits there!

[*Pointing to his head.*

Gilbert. I tell you I feel the draught.

[LADY JESSICA *rises, goes to the tent openings, carefully draws the curtains. He watches her, sulkily biting his nails.*

Lady Jessica. There! now you may safely venture to uncover the sensitive spot.

Gilbert [*firmly*]. No.

Lady Jessica. Very well, my dear. Then I shan't open my lips.

Gilbert. You won't?

Lady Jessica. No; and I'm sure it's far more important for you to know what is going on between Mr. Falkner and me than to have that horrid thing sticking on your head.

Gilbert [*takes a turn or two, bites his nails, at length sulkily flings the cap on the table*]. Now!

Lady Jessica. Mr. Falkner is very deeply attached to me, I believe.

Gilbert. He has told you so?

Lady Jessica. No.

Gilbert. No?

Lady Jessica. No; but that's only because I keep on stopping him.

Gilbert. You keep on stoppping him?

Lady Jessica. Yes; it's so much pleasanter to have him dangling for a little while, and *then*——

Gilbert. Then what?

Lady Jessica. Well, it is pleasant to be admired.

Gilbert. And you accept his admiration?

Lady Jessica. Of course I do. Why shouldn't I? If Mr. Falkner admires me, isn't that the greatest compliment he can pay to your taste? And if he spares you the drudgery of being polite to me, flattering me, complimenting me, and paying me the hundred delicate little attentions that win a woman's heart, I'm sure you ought to be very much obliged to him for taking all that trouble off your hands.

Gilbert [*furious*]. Now understand me. This nonsense has gone far enough. I forbid you to have anything further to say to the man.

Lady Jessica. Ah, you forbid me!

Gilbert. I forbid you. And, understand, if you do——

Lady Jessica. Ah, take care! Don't threaten me!

Gilbert. Do you mean to respect my wishes?

Lady Jessica. Of course I shall respect your wishes. I may not obey them, but I will respect them.

Gilbert [*enraged, comes up to her very angrily.*] Now, Jessica, once for all—

[*Enter* GEORGE; GILBERT *stops suddenly.*

George. The dog-cart's ready, Gilbert. What's the matter?

Gilbert. Nothing. [*To* LADY JESSICA.] You'll please to come on to me at Teignwick to-morrow.

Lady Jessica. Can't. I've promised to go to Barbara, and I must keep my promise, even though it parts me from you.

[*Enter* SERVANT *at back*.

Servant. You've only just time to catch the train, sir.

Gilbert. I'm not going.

Servant. Not going, sir?

Gilbert. No. [*Exit* SERVANT.

Lady Jessica [*appeals to* GEORGE]. Isn't it dear of him to stay here on my account when he knows he ought to be in Devon? Isn't it sweet to think that after five long years one has still that magnetic attraction for one's husband?

Gilbert. No. I'm hanged if I stay on your account. [*Goes up to opening, calls out*.] Hi! Gadsby! I'm coming! [*Comes back to* LADY JESSICA.] Understand, I expect you at Teignwick to-morrow.

Lady Jessica. Dearest, I shan't come.

Gilbert. I say you shall!

Lady Jessica. 'Shall' is not a pretty word for a husband to use.

[*Takes up the cap he has thrown down and stands twiddling the tassel*.

Gilbert. George, I expect this business of Crampton's will keep me for a week, but I can't tell. Look after everything while I'm away. [*Glancing at* LADY JESSICA. *To* LADY JESSICA.] You won't come to Teignwick?

Lady Jessica. I've promised Barbara. Here's your cap.

Gilbert. Good-bye, George!

[*Shakes hands with* GEORGE, *looks at* LADY JESSICA, *and is then going off at back*.

Lady Jessica. Ta ta, dearest! [*Going up to him*.

Gilbert [*turns, comes a step or two to* LADY JESSICA, *livid with anger; speaks in her ear*]. You'll go just one step too far some day, madam, and if you do, look out for yourself, for, by jove! I won't spare you!

[*Exit*. LADY JESSICA *stands a little frightened, goes up to opening at back, as if to call him back, comes down, takes up an illustrated paper*. GEORGE *stands watching her, smoking*.

Lady Jessica [*after a little pause*]. George, that was very silly of you to tell Gilbert about Mr. Falkner and me.

George. I thought you had gone far enough.

Lady Jessica. Oh no, my dear friend. You must allow me to be the best judge of how far——

George. How far you can skate over thin ice?

Lady Jessica. The thinner the ice the more delicious the fun, don't you think? Ah, you're like Gilbert. You don't skate —or joke.

George. You heard what Gilbert said?

Lady Jessica. Yes; that was a hint to you. Won't it be rather a tiresome task for you?

George. What?

Lady Jessica. To keep an eye on me, watch that I don't go that one step too far. And not quite a nice thing to do, eh?

George. Oh, I've no intention of watching you—— [*Enter* FALKNER *at back. Looking at the two.*] Not the least intention, I assure you. [*Exit.*

Lady Jessica. So to-morrow will break up our pleasant party.

Falkner [*about forty, strong, fine, clearly-cut features, earnest expression, hair turning gray, complexion pale, and almost gray with continued work, anxiety, and abstinence*]. And after to-morrow?

Lady Jessica. Ah, after to-morrow!

Falkner. When shall we meet again?

Lady Jessica. Shall we meet again? Yes, I suppose. Extremes do meet, don't they?

Falkner. Are we extremes?

Lady Jessica. Aren't we? I suppose I'm the vainest, emptiest, most irresponsible creature in the world——

Falkner. You're not! you're not! You slander yourself! You can be sincere, you can be earnest, you can be serious——

Lady Jessica. Can I? Oh, do tell me what fun there is in being serious! I can't see the use of it. There you are, for instance, mounted on that high horse of seriousness, spending the best years of your life in fighting African slave-traders and other windmills of that sort. Oh do leave the windmills alone! They'll all tumble by themselves by-and-by.

Falkner. I'm not going to spend the best years of my life in fighting slave-traders. I'm going to spend them—in loving you. [*Approaching her very closely.*

Lady Jessica. Oh, that will be worse than the windmills—and quite as useless. [*He is very near to her.*] If you please—you remember we promised to discuss all love-matters at a distance of three feet, so as to allow for the personal equation. Your three feet, please.

Falkner. When shall we meet again?

Lady Jessica. Ah, when? Where do you go to-morrow night, when you leave here?

Falkner. I don't know. Where do you?

Lady Jessica. To my cousin Barbara's.

Falkner. Where is that?

Lady Jessica. Oh, a little way along the river, towards town; not far from Staines.

Falkner. In what direction?

Lady Jessica. About two miles to the nor'-nor'-sou'-west. I never was good at geography.

Falkner. Is there a good inn near?

Lady Jessica. There's a delightful little riverside hotel, the Star and Garter, at Shepperford. They make a speciality of French cooking.

Falkner. I shall go there when I leave here to-morrow. May I call at your cousin's?

Lady Jessica. It wouldn't be wise. And I'm only staying till Monday.

Falkner. And then?

Lady Jessica. On Monday evening I go back to town.

Falkner. Alone?

Lady Jessica. No; with Ferris, my maid. Unless I send her on first.

Falkner. And you will?

Lady Jessica. No; I don't think so. But a curious thing happened to me the last time I stayed at Barbara's. I sent Ferris on with the luggage in the early afternoon, and I walked to the station for the sake of the walk. Well, there are two turnings, and I must have taken the wrong one.

Falkner. What happened?

Lady Jessica. I wandered about for miles, and at half-past seven I found myself, very hot, very tired, very hungry, and in a very bad temper, at the Star and Garter at Shepperford. That was on a Monday too.

Falkner. That was on a Monday?

Lady Jessica. Yes—hark! [*Goes suddenly to back, looks off.*] Oh, it's you, Ferris! What are you doing here?

[FERRIS, *a perfectly trained lady's maid, about thirty, dark, quiet, reserved, a little sinister-looking, appears at opening at back with wrap in hand.*

Ferris. I beg pardon, my lady. But I thought you might be getting chilly, so I've brought you this.

Lady Jessica. Put it on the chair.

Ferris. Yes, my lady. [*Puts wrap on chair and exit.*

Lady Jessica [*yawns*]. Heigho! Shall we go into the billiard room? [*Going.*

Falkner. No. [*Stopping her.*] How long do you mean to play with me?

Lady Jessica. Am I playing with you?

Falkner. What else have you done the last three months? My heart is yours to its last beat. My life is yours to its last moment. What are you going to do with me?

Lady Jessica. Ah, that's it! I'm sure I don't know. [*Smiling at him.*] What shall I do with you?

Falkner. Love me! love me! love me!

Lady Jessica. You are very foolish!

Falkner. Foolish to love you?

Lady Jessica. No; not foolish to love me. I like you for that. But foolish to love me so foolishly. Foolish to be always wanting to play Romeo, when I only want to play Juliet sometimes.

Falkner. Sometimes? When?

Lady Jessica. When I am foolish too—on a Monday evening.

[*She is going off; he intercepts her, clasps her.*

Falkner. Ah! will you drive me mad? Shall I tear you to pieces to find out if there is a heart somewhere within you?

Lady Jessica [*struggling*]. Hush! someone coming.

[FALKNER *releases her*. SIR CHRISTOPHER *saunters in at back*, *smoking*. *Exit* LADY JESSICA.

Sir Christopher. Drop it, Ned! Drop it, my dear old boy! You're going too far.

Falkner [*going off after* LADY JESSICA]. We won't discuss the matter, Kit.

Sir Christopher [*putting his arm in* FALKNER'*s*, *and holding him back*]. Yes we will, Ned. George Nepean has been making a row, and I—well, I stroked him down. I said you were the soul of honour——

Falkner [*disengaging himself*]. You were right. I am the soul of honour.

Sir Christopher. And that you didn't mean anything by your attentions to Lady Jessica.

Falkner. You were wrong. I do mean something.

Sir Christopher. Well, what?

Falkner [*going*]. That's my business—and Lady Jessica's.

Sir Christopher. You forget—I introduced you here.

Falkner. Thank you. You were very kind. [*Going off.*

Sir Christopher [*stopping him*]. No, Ned; we'll have this out, here and now, please.

Falkner [*angrily*]. Very well, let's have it out, here and now.

Sir Christopher [*with great friendship*]. Come, old boy,

there's no need for us to take this tone. Let's talk it over calmly, as old friends and men of the world.

Falkner. Men of the world! If there is one beast in all the loathsome fauna of civilization that I hate and despise, it is a man of the world! Good heaven, what men! what a world!

Sir Christopher. Quite so, old fellow. It is a beastly bad world—a lying, selfish, treacherous world! A rascally bad world every way. But bad as it is, this old world hasn't lived all these thousands of years without getting a little common sense into its wicked old noddle—especially with regard to its love affairs. And, speaking as an average bad citizen of this blackguardly old world, I want to ask you, Ned Falkner, what the devil you mean by making love to a married woman, and what good or happiness you expect to get for yourself or her? Where does it lead? What's to be the end of it?

Falkner. I don't know—I don't care! I love her!

Sir Christopher. But, my good Ned, she's another man's wife.

Falkner. She's married to a man who doesn't value her, doesn't understand her, is utterly unworthy of her.

Sir Christopher. All women are married to men who are utterly unworthy of them—bless 'em! All women are undervalued by their husbands—bless 'em! All women are misunderstood—bless 'em again!

Falkner. Oh, don't laugh it off like that. Look at that thick clown of a husband. They haven't a single idea, or thought, or taste in common.

Sir Christopher. That's her lookout before she married him.

Falkner. But suppose she didn't know, didn't understand. Suppose experience comes too late?

Sir Christopher. It generally does—in other things besides marriage!

Falkner. But doesn't it make your blood boil to see a woman sacrificed for life?

Sir Christopher. It does—my blood boils a hundred times a day. But marriages are made in heaven, and if once we set to work to repair celestial mistakes and indiscretions, we shall have our hands full. Come down to brass tacks. What's going to be the end of this?

Falkner. I don't know—I don't care! I love her!

Sir Christopher. You don't know? I'll tell you. Let's go over all the possibilities of the case. [*Ticking them off on his fingers.*] Possibility number one—you leave off loving her——

Falkner. That's impossible.

Sir Chrisopher. Possibility number two——you can, one or the other, or both of you, die by natural means; but you're both confoundedly healthy, so I'm afraid there's no chance of that. Possibility number three—you can die together by poison, or steel, or cold Thames water. I wouldn't trust *you* not to do a fool's trick of that sort; but, thank God, she's got too much sense. By the way, Ned, I don't think she cares very much for you——

Falkner. She will.

Sir Christopher. Well, well, we shall see. Possibility number four—you can keep on dangling at her heels, and being made a fool of, without getting any—'forrarder'.

Falkner. Mine is not a physical passion.

Sir Christopher [*looks at him for two moments*]. Oh, that be hanged!

Falkner. I tell you it is not.

Sir Christopher. Well then, it ought to be.

Falkner [*very angrily*]. Well then, it is! And say no more about it. What business is it of yours?

Sir Christopher. Possibility number five—a *liaison* with her husband's connivance. Gilbert Nepean won't make a *mari complaisant*. Dismiss that possibility.

Falkner. Dismiss them all.

Sir Christopher. Don't you wish you could? But you'll have to face one of them, Ned. Possibility number six—a secret *liaison*. That's nearly impossible in society. And do you know what it means? It means in the end every inconvenience and disadvantage of marriage without any of its conveniences and advantages. It means endless discomfort, worry, and alarm. It means constant sneaking and subterfuges of the paltriest, pettiest kind. What do you say to that, my soul of honour?

Falkner. I love her. I shall not try to hide my love.

Sir Christopher. Oh, then you want a scandal? You'll get it! Have you thought what sort of a scandal it will be? Remember you've stuck yourself on a pedestal, and put a moral toga on. That's awkward. It wants such a lot of living up to. Gilbert Nepean is a nasty cuss and he'll make a nasty fuss. Possibility number seven, *tableau* one—Edward Falkner on his moral pedestal in a toga-esque attitude, honoured and idolized by the British public. *Tableau* two—a horrible scandal, a field day for Mrs. Grundy; Edward Falkner is dragged from his pedestal, his toga is torn to pieces, his splendid reputation is blown to the winds, and he is rolled in the mud under the feet of the British public, who, six months ago, crowned him with garlands and shouted themselves hoarse in his praise. Are you prepared for that, my soul of honour?

Falkner. If it comes.

Sir Christopher [*shakes his head, makes a wry face, then proceeds*]. Possibility number eight. Last remaining possibility, only possible possibility—pull yourself together, pack up your traps, start to-morrow morning for Africa or Kamtschatka, Jericho or Hong-Kong. I'll go with you. What do you say?

Falkner. No.

Sir Christopher. No?

Falkner. I wonder at you, Deering—I wonder at you coming to lecture me on love and morality.

Sir Christopher. Ah, why?

Falkner [*with growing indignation*]. I love a woman with the deepest love of my heart, with the purest worship of my soul. If that isn't moral, if that isn't sacred, if that isn't righteous, tell me, in heaven's name, what is? And you come to lecture me with your cut and dried worldly-wise philosophy, your mean little maxims, you come to lecture me on love and morality—you!

Sir Christopher. Yes, I do! I may have had my attachments, I may have done this, that, and the other. I'm not a hero, I'm not on a pedestal, I never put on a moral toga. But I owe no woman a sigh or a sixpence. I've never wronged any friend's sister, or daughter, or wife. And I tell you this, Ned Falkner, you're a fool if you think that anything can come of this passion of yours for Lady Jessica, except misery and ruin for her, embarrassment and disgrace for you, and kicking out of decent society for both of you.

Falkner [*very firmly*]. Very well. And will you please be the first to cut me? Or shall I cut you?

Sir Christopher. You mean that, Ned?

Falkner. Yes; if I'm a fool, leave me to my folly. [*Very strongly*.] Don't meddle with me.

Sir Christopher. You do mean that, Ned? Our friendship is to end?

Falkner. Yes. [*Sits, takes up paper.*

Sir Christopher. Very well. You'll understand some day, Ned, that I couldn't see an old comrade, a man who stood shoulder to shoulder with me all these years—you'll understand I couldn't see him fling away honour, happiness, reputation, future, everything, without saying one word and trying to pull him up. Good-bye, old chap.

[*Going off.*

[FALKNER *springs up generously, goes to him warmly, holding out both hands.*

Falkner [*cries out*]. Kit!

Sir Christopher. Ned!

[*The two men stand with hands clasped for some time, then* FALKNER *speaks in a soft, low, broken voice.*

Falkner. I love her, Kit—you don't know how much. When I see her, that turn of her head, that little toss of her curls, the little roguish face she makes—God couldn't make her like that and then blame a man for loving her! If He did—well, right or wrong, I'd rather miss heaven than one smile, one nod, one touch of her finger-tips!

Sir Christopher. Oh, my poor dear old fellow, if you're as far gone as that, what the deuce am I to do with you?

[*Enter at back* BEATRICE EBERNOE, *a tall, dark woman, about thirty, very beautiful and spiritual.*

Beatrice. Ned, here's a messenger from the Colonial Office with a very urgent letter for you.

Falkner. For me?

[*Enter* SERVANT *at back, bringing letter to* FALKNER.

Servant. Important, sir. The messenger is waiting in the hall for your answer.

Falkner [*taking letter*]. Very well, I'll come to him.

[*Exit* SERVANT.

Falkner [*reading letter*]. More trouble out there. They want me to go out at once and negotiate. They think I could win over the chiefs and save a lot of bloodshed.

Sir Christopher. You'll go, Ned?

Falkner. I don't know.

Sir Christopher [*to* BEATRICE]. Help me to persuade him.

Beatrice. Can I? Have I any influence? Ned, for the sake of old days——

Falkner. Ah, no—let me be—I must think this over.

[*Exit with distracted manner.*

Beatrice. Have you spoken to him?

Sir Christopher. Yes; I gave him a thorough good slanging. Not a bit of use. When one of you holds us by a single hair, not all the king's horses and all the king's men can drag us back to that beggarly dusty old tow-path of duty.

Beatrice. I won't believe men are so weak.

Sir Christopher. Aren't we? There never was so sensible a man as I am in the management of other men's love affairs. You should have heard me lecture Ned. But once put me near you and I'm every bit as bad as that poor fool I've been basting!

[*Indicating* FALKNER *by inclination of the head towards the direction he has gone.*

Beatrice. Oh, no, Kit. I won't have you say that.

Sir Christopher. But I am. How beautifully you played just now!

Beatrice. Did I?

Sir Christopher. Don't do it again.

Beatrice. Why not?

Sir Christopher. It's taking an unfair advantage of me. You oughtn't to arouse those divine feelings in a man's heart. You oughtn't to make me feel like a martyr, or a king, or a saint in a cathedral window, with all heaven's sunlight streaming through me! You oughtn't to do it! Because devil a ha'porth of a king, or a martyr, or a saint is there in me—and after you've been playing to me and lifted me into that seventh heaven of yours, I feel so mean and shabby when I drop down to earth again, and find myself a hard, selfish man of the world.

Beatrice. Oh, I think there's a great deal of the martyr and saint and king in you.

Sir Christopher. Do you? I believe there is! I know there would be if you'd only screw me up to it—and keep me screwed up. Beatrice, there's nothing I couldn't do if you would only——

Beatrice [*going away from him*]. Kit, you mustn't speak of this again. I can't quite forget.

Sir Christopher. There's no need. While he was alive I never had one disloyal thought towards him. Now he's dead, who could be so fitted to take care of his dearest treasure as his oldest friend?

Beatrice [*going away*]. I can't quite forget.

Sir Christopher. But you're young. What do you mean to do with your life?

Beatrice. I'd some thoughts of entering a sisterhood.

Sir Christopher. Ah, no! Surely there are plenty of dear good ugly women in the world who can do that.

Beatrice. But I must enjoy the luxury of self-sacrifice. Tell me how I can drink the deepest of that cup.

Sir Christopher. Marry me. I'll give you the most splendid opportunities. Now if you and I were to join our forces, and take our poor Ned in hand, and——

Beatrice. Hush!

[FALKNER *re-enters, evidently very much distracted.*

Sir Christopher [*after a little pause, goes up to him*]. Well, Ned, what are you going to do?

Falkner [*in an agony of indecision*]. I don't know! I don't know!

Sir Christopher. You'll go, Ned? I'll go with you!

[*Enter* LADY JESSICA *at back.*

Beatrice. You'll go, Ned?

Lady Jessica. Go? Where?

Falkner. Nowhere. I shan't go, Kit. The man's waiting. I must give him my answer.

[*Exit* L. LADY JESSICA *looks after him.* SIR CHRISTOPHER *shrugs his shoulders at* BEATRICE.

Sir Christopher. Not all the king's horses, nor all the king's men.

CURTAIN.

(*Five days pass between Acts I and II.*)

ACT II

SCENE: *Private sitting-room in the Star and Garter, Shepperford-on-Thames, a room in a small high-class riverside hotel, furnished in the usual incongruous hotel fashion. Large French windows both right and left take up a good part of the back of the stage, and open upon a veranda which runs along outside. The pillars and roof of the veranda are smothered with trails of flowers and creeping plants. Beyond the veranda and very near to it is the Thames with opposite bank. Door down stage right. A sofa down stage right. A sideboard left. On the sideboard, plates, knives, forks, etc., dishes of fine peaches, grapes and strawberries, and a bottle each of hock, claret, and champagne, as described in the text. A small table with writing materials at back between windows. A small table with white cloth laid, down stage, a little to the left of centre. A fireplace down stage left.*

Discover FALKNER *in evening dress and French* WAITER.

Falkner [*menu in hand*]. *Crème à la Reine.* We might have some trifle before the soup.

Waiter. Anchovy salad? Caviare?

Falkner. Caviare.

Waiter. *Bien, m'sieu*. At what hour will m'sieu dine?

Falkner. I don't know; I'm not sure that my friend will come at all. But tell the cook to have everything prepared, so that we can have dinner very soon after my friend arrives.

Waiter. *Bien, m'sieu*.

Falkner [*reading menu*]. Caviare. *Crème à la Reine. Rouget à l'Italienne*. Whitebait. *Petites Timbales à la Lucullus. Mousse de Foies Gras en Belle Vue*. Is your cook equal to those *entrées*?

Waiter. Oh, sir, he is equal to anything. Trust to me, sir The cook shall be *magnifique*. The dinner shall be *magnifique*.

Falkner [*continuing*]. *Poulardes poêlées, sauce Arcadienne. Selle de Mouton. Ortolans. Salade. Asperges en Branches. Pouding Mousseline, sauce Églantine. Soufflé Glacé à l'Ananas*. Dessert? [WAITER *points to the dessert on the sideboard*.] And the wines?

Waiter [*pointing to the wines on the sideboard*]. Ayala, seventy-four. Johannisberg, sixty-eight. Château Haut-Brion, seventy-five. I have brought them from London myself. We have not these vintages here.

Falkner. Good.

Waiter. It is but one friend that m'sieu expect?

Falkner. Only one friend.

Waiter. *Bien, m'sieu*.

[*Exit*. FALKNER *alone walks restlessly about the room for a few seconds, comes down; is arrested by something he hears outside the door, shows great delight*.

[*Re-enter* WAITER.

Waiter. A lady; she say will Mr. Falkner please to see her? She have lost her way.

Falkner. Show her in. [*Exit* WAITER.

[FALKNER *alone walks eagerly about room for a few seconds; his manner very eager and impatient and quite different from what it had been before. Re-enter* WAITER, *showing in* LADY JESSICA *most charmingly and coquettishly dressed in summer outdoor clothes. She comes in rather tempestuously, speaking as she enters, and going up to* FALKNER.

Lady Jessica [*all in a breath*]. Oh, my dear Mr. Falkner, I've been staying with my cousin, and I was walking to the station, and by some unlucky chance I must have taken the wrong turning, for instead of finding myself at the station, I found myself here; and as I'm very hungry, would you think it very dreadful if I asked you to give me just a mere mouthful of dinner?

Falkner [*intensely calm low voice*]. I'm delighted. [*To* WAITER.] Will you let us have dinner as soon as it is ready?

Waiter. In half an hour, sir. And the friend, sir?

Fqlkner. The friend?

Waiter. The friend that m'sieu expect—the friend of the dinner?

Falkner. Oh, yes—if he comes, show him in.

Lady Jessica [*alarmed*]. You don't expect——

Falkner [*glancing at* WAITER]. Hush!

Waiter [*absolutely impassive face*]. *Bien, m'sieu!* [*Exit.*

Falkner. I'm so glad you've come. Look. [*Holding out his hand.*] I'm trembling with delight. I knew you would be here.

Lady Jessica. I'm sure you didn't, for I didn't know myself two hours ago. It was only by chance that I happened to take the wrong turning.

Falkner. No; the right turning. And not by chance. It was not chance that brought you to me.

Lady Jessica. Oh, please, not that strain. I can't play up to it. Sit down and let us discuss something mundane—say dinner.

Falkner [*giving her the menu*]. I hope you'll like what I've ordered. I sent the waiter up to London for some of the dishes and the wines.

Lady Jessica [*takes menu, looks at it, shows mock terror*]. What? You surely don't expect my poor little appetite to stand up to this dinner. Oh, let me be a warning to all, never take the wrong turning when it may lead to a menu like this.

Falkner. That's for your choice. You don't suppose I'd offer you anything but the very best.

Lady Jessica. Yes, but a little of the very best is all I want; not all of it.

Falkner. Take all of it that I can set before you.

Lady Jessica. Oh, but think—there may be other deserving ladies in the world.

Falkner. There is but you.

Lady Jessica [*looks at him very much amused*]. And I came here to cure you of this folly. Ah, me! [*Reading the menu.*] *Mousse de Foies Gras. Poulardes poêlées, sauce Arcadienne*—what is *sauce Arcadienne*?

Falkner. I don't know. Love is the sauce of life. Perhaps it's that.

Lady Jessica. Yes, but don't dish it up too often or too strong. It's sure to be wasted.

Falkner. My love for you is not wasted.

Lady Jessica. No?

Falkner. You'll return it. You'll love me at last.

Lady Jessica. Shall I? *Crème à la Reine. Rouget à l'Italienne*. And if I did, what then?

Falkner. Join your life to mine. Come to Africa with me.

Lady Jessica [*shakes her head*]. Impossible! We should only shock the British public. They wouldn't understand us. *Ortolans. Salade. Asperges en Branches*. Besides, what would everybody say?

Falkner. We shouldn't hear them.

Lady Jessica. No; but they'd be talking all the same. Ha, ha! They'd call us the eloping philanthropists.

Falkner. Would that matter?

Lady Jessica. Oh, yes. A philanthropist may not elope. A tenor may. Doesn't it show the terrible irony there is in the heart of things, that the best meaning philanthropist in the world may not elope with his neighbour's wife? *Pouding Mousseline, sauce Églantine*. What makes you so eager to go hunting slave-traders in Africa?

Falkner. My father spent half his fortune putting slavery down. My grandfather spent half his life and died a pauper for the same cause.

Lady Jessica. Well then, you should send a subscription to the Aborigines' Protection Society. That is how I keep up our family traditions.

Falkner. How?

Lady Jessica. My father had a shocking reputation, and my grandfather, Beau Lillywhite—Oh! [*Shrug*.] So I follow in their footsteps—at a respectful distance. I flirt with you. *Soufflé Glacé à l'Ananas*. There's no flirting in Central Africa, I suppose?

Falkner. No flirting. Only heat and hunger and thirst, and helpless misery prolonged to a horrible death.

Lady Jessica [*genuinely moved*]. Oh, I'm so sorry! Don't think me heartless about *that*. Perhaps if I had lived amongst it as you have——

Falkner. Ah, if you had! you'd do as I ask you. You'd give all your heart to me, you'd give all your woman's care and tenderness to them, and you'd never hear one whisper of what people said of you.

Lady Jessica [*looking at him with real admiration*]. How earnest you are! How devoted!

[*Enter* WAITER *with knives and forks; he goes to table and begins laying it. They move away from each other.*

Lady Jessica [*to* WAITER]. What is *sauce Arcadienne*?

WAITER. *Pardon!* The cook is splendid. He is *magnifique*—but he has—[*gesture*] *renversé* the *sauce Arcadienne* all over the shop.

Falkner. It doesn't matter.

Lady Jessica. Oh, I had set my heart on *sauce Arcadienne*.

Falkner. The cook must make some more *sauce Arcadienne*.

Waiter. Ah, that is impossible till the middle of the night.

Ldy Jessaica. Ah, what a pity! It is the one thing I long for, *sauce Arcadienne*.

Falkner. Why?

Lady Jessica. Because I don't know what it is.

Waiter. He will give you some *sauce Marguerite*.

Lady Jessica. What is *sauce Marguerite?*

Waiter [*all the while laying table*]. Ah, it is *délicieuse*. It is the very best sauce that is in all the world.

Lady Jessica. *Va pour la sauce Marguerite!* Oh, this dinner!

[*A barrel organ strikes up outside.*

Waiter. Ah, there is the beast of the organ man.

Lady Jessica. No, let him be. I like music—and monkeys. [*To* FALKNER.] Tell them to make haste.

Falkner. Hurry the dinner.

Waiter. *Bien, m'sieu!* [*Exit*.

Lady Jessica [*taking out watch*]. Half-past seven, I've not an hour to stay.

Falkner. Yes, your life if you will.

Lady Jessica. Ah, no! You must be sensible. Think! what could come of it if I did love you? I should only break your heart or—what would be far worse—break my own.

Falkner. Break it then—or let me break it. It's better to feel, it's better to suffer, than to be meanly happy. I love you, but I'd rather smother you in tears and blood than you should go on living this poor little heartless, withered life, choked up with all this dry society dust. Oh, can't I make you feel? Can't I make you live? Can't I make you love me?

Lady Jessica [*after a moment's pause, looking at him with great admiration*]. Perhaps I do in my heart of hearts!

Falkner. Ah! [*Springs to seize her; she struggles with him.*

Lady Jessica. Mr. Falkner! Mr. Falkner! If you please. Do you hear? Mr. Falkner! [*Tears herself free.*] Will you please go and stop that horrid organ? Will you please?

[FALKNER *bows, exit at door.* LADY JESSICA *panting, flurried, out of breath, goes up to the window fanning herself with handkerchief, passes on to veranda, stays there for a few moments fanning herself, suddenly starts back alarmed, comes into room, stands frightened, listening.* GEORGE NEPEAN *appears on veranda, comes up to window, looks in.*

Lady Jessica [*trying to appear indifferent*]. Ah, George!

George. I thought I caught sight of you. May I come in?

Lady Jessica. Certainly.

George [*entering*]. I'm not intruding?

Lady Jessica. Intruding? Oh, no. Have you heard from Gilbert?

George. Yes, I had a letter this morning. He may be back in two or three days.

Lady Jessica [*embarrassed*]. Yes?

[*A pause. The organ outside stops in the middle of a bar.*

George [*glancing at table*]. You're dining here?

Lady Jessica. Yes; just a small party. What brings you here?

George. I was going on to some friends at Hersham. I was waiting for the ferry when I caught sight of you. [*Glancing at table and sideboard.*] You're giving your friends rather a good dinner.

Lady Jessica. H'm, rather. I've heard the cooking's very good here. [*A little pause.*] There's a nest of cygnets outside. Have you seen them?

George. No.

Lady Jessica. Do come and look at them; they are so pretty.

[*Going off at window followed by* GEORGE *when* FALKNER *enters at door. The two men look at each other.* LADY JESSICA *shows very great confusion and embarrassment. A long awkward pause.* GEORGE *looks very significantly at the sideboard and table.*

George [*to* LADY JESSICA]. Gilbert must know of this. You understand? [*Bows. Exit by window and veranda.*

Lady Jessica [*who has stood frightened and confused*]. Did you hear? What can I do? What can I do?

Falkner [*calm, triumphant*]. You must join your life to mine now.

Lady Jessica. No, no! If you wish me ever to have one kind thought of you, get me out of this! Do something, find somebody to dine with us. Understand me, I know myself, if this leads to a scandal, I shall hate you in a week. Oh, do something! do something!

Falkner. Be calm. Be sure I'll do all I can to save you from a scandal. If that is impossible, be sure I'll do all I can to protect you from it.

Lady Jessica. Ah, no! Save me from it. I can't face it. I can't give up my world, my friends. Oh, what can I do? I'll go back to town——

Falkner. What good will that do? You had far better stay now. Sit down, be calm. Trust to me.

Lady Jessica. Oh, you are good, and I'm such a coward.

Falkner. Let us think what is the best thing to do.

Lady Jessica. Can't we get somebody to dine with us?

Lady Rosamund [*heard outside*]. Oh, can't you wait, Freddie?

Lady Jessica [*looking off*]. Hark! Rosy!

[*Goes up to window.*

Freddie [*heard off*]. What! Row two more miles without a drink?

Lady Jessica. She's there in a boat with Freddie and another man. The men are landing. If we could only get them to stay and dine with us! We must! Go and find George Nepean and bring him back here. Make haste. When you come back, I'll have Rosy here.

Falkner. In any case rely on me. I'm as firm as the earth beneath you. [*Exit at door.*

Lady Jessica [*goes up to window. Calls off*]. Rosy! Rosy! Come here! Yes, through there. Shush!

[LADY ROSAMUND *appears in the veranda.*

Lady Rosamund. Jess! What's the matter? [*Entering room.*

Lady Jessica. Everything. You and Freddie must stay and dine here.

Lady Rosamund. We can't, we're going on to dine with Mrs. Crespin at her new place, and we've got Jack Symons with us.

Lady Jessica. *Va pour* Jack Symons, whoever he may be! He must stay and dine too!

Lady Rosamund. Impossible. Mrs. Crespin has asked some people to meet us. As her place is on the river Jack proposed we should row down and dress there. What are you doing here? I thought you were at Barbara's.

Lady Jessica. I was going back to town to-night. I thought I'd walk to the station—it's so delightful across the fields. Well, you know the path, I went on all right till I came to those two turnings, and then—I must have taken the wrong one, for, instead of finding myself at the station, I found myself here.

Lady Rosamund. Well?

Lady Jessica. I'd been wandering about for over an hour, I was very hungry; I remembered Mr. Falkner was staying here; so I came in and asked him to give me some dinner.

Lady Rosamund. It was very foolish of you!

Lady Jessica. Yes, especially as George Nepean was waiting for the ferry and caught sight of me on the veranda.

Lady Rosamund. George Nepean!

Lady Jessica. He came in, saw Mr. Falkner, put a totally wrong construction on it all, and threatened to let Gilbert know.

Lady Rosamund. How could you be so imprudent, Jess? You must have known that——

Lady Jessica. Oh, don't stand there rowing me. Help me out of this and I promise you I won't get into another.

Lady Rosamund. Why didn't you explain to George how it happened?

Lady Jessica. So I would. Only when he came in I was alone. I felt sure he would put a wrong construction on it, so I told him I was dining here with a little party—then Mr. Falkner came in, and I was too confused to say anything. Besides I couldn't very well tell him the truth, because——

Lady Rosamund. Because what?

Lady Jessica. Well, it's very curious, but the last time I was staying with Barbara the very same thing happened.

Lady Rosamund. What?

Lady Jessica. I was walking to the station, and I must have taken the wrong turning, for, instead of finding myself at the station, I found myself here.

Lady Rosamund. What, twice?

Lady Jessica. Yes.

Lady Rosamund. Oh, impossible!

Lady Jessica. No, it isn't; for it actually happened.

Lady Rosamund. Do you mean to tell me that you——

Lady Jessica [*taking her up on the* '*tell*']. Yes, I do. The sign-post is most deceptive.

Lady Rosamund. It must be.

Lady Jessica. But the other time it was really a mistake, and I dined here all alone.

Lady Rosamund. Honour?

Lady Jessica. Really, really honour!

Lady Rosamund. I cannot imagine how you, a woman of the world——

Lady Jessica. Oh, do not nag me. Mr. Falkner has gone for George. You must stay here and tell George you are dining with me.

Lady Rosamund. What about Freddie and Jack? See if they've come back to the boat.

Lady Jessica. [*looking off at window*]. Not yet. Here's Mr. Falkner—alone. [*Re-enter* FALKNER *at window.*]—Well, where is he?

Falkner [*to* LADY ROSAMUND]. How d'ye do? [*To* LADY JESSICA.] He took a fly that was waiting outside and drove to the post-office. I went there and made inquiries. He stopped, sent off a telegram——

Lady Jessica. That must have been to Gilbert.

Falkner. Then he drove off towards Staines. Shall I follow him?

Lady Jessica. Yes. No. What's the use? He may be anywhere by now.

Lady Rosamund. Besides we can't stay to dinner.

Lady Jessica. You must—you must! I must be able to tell Gilbert that somebody dined with me.

Lady Rosamund. Jess, I'll write to George when I get back to-night, and tell him that I dined with you here.

Lady Jessica. Oh, you good creature! No! Write now, on the hotel paper. Then he'll see you were actually here.

Lady Rosamund. Pens, ink, and paper.

Falkner [*at table up stage*]. Here!

[LADY ROSAMUND *seats herself at table.*

Lady Jessica. Rosy, I've got a better plan than that.

Lady Rosamund. What?

Lady Jessica. Could you be in town to-morrow morning?

Lady Rosamund. Yes—why?

Lady Jessica. Write to George to call on you there. I'll drop in a little before he comes. Then we can see what frame of mind he is in, and explain things accordingly. We can manage him so much better between us.

Lady Rosamund. Very well, make haste. [*Looks off at window.*] Mr. Falkner, will you go into the bar, run up against my husband and his friend, and keep them busy there till I get back into the boat.

Falkner. Very well. [*Exit at door.*

Lady Rosamund. Now, what shall I say?

Lady Jessica [*dictating*]. 'My dear George'——

Lady Rosamund [*writing*]. 'My dear George'—Oh, this pen!

[*Throws away the pen, takes up another, tries it.*

Lady Jessica. We must make it very short and casual, as if you didn't attach must importance to it.

Lady Rosamund [*throws away second pen*]. That's as bad!

Lady Jessica [*taking out a gold stylograph, giving it to* LADY ROSAMUND]. Here's my stylograph. Take care of it. It was a birthday present.

Lady Rosamund. 'Monday evening. My dear George'——

Lady Jessica [*dictating*]. 'Jess has told me that you have just been here and that you were surprised at her presence. She fears you may have put a wrong construction on what you saw. She was too flurried at the moment to explain. But if you will kindly call on me to-morrow, Tuesday morning, at Cadogan Gardens at'—what time will suit you?

Lady Rosamund. Twelve?

Lady Jessica. Yes, and I'll be there a few minutes before.

Lady Rosamund [*writing*]. 'Twelve'.

Lady Jessica [*dictating*]. 'I will give you a full explanation. You will then see how very simple the whole affair was, and how little cause you had for your suspicions of her.' That will do, won't it?

Lady Rosamund. Yes, I think. 'Yours sincerely'— no, 'Yours affectionately, Rosy.'

Lady Jessica. 'P.S. You had perhaps better say nothing about this to Gilbert until after we have met. When you see how trifling the matter is, you can tell Gilbert or not, as you please.'

Lady Rosamund [*writing*]. 'As you please. George Nepean, Esquire.' What's his number?

Lady Jessica. Two-twenty.

Lady Rosamund [*writing*]. 'Two-twenty, Sloane Street.'

Lady Jessica. What about Freddie? Shall we tell him?

Lady Rosamund. Oh, no! I wouldn't trust my Freddie in a matter of this kind. He'd put a wrong construction on it—men always do. [*Puts letter in envelope, seals it.*

Lady Jessica. But if George asks him?

Lady Rosamund. Freddie won't come up to town to-morrow.

We'll see how George takes it, and we'll keep Freddie out of it, if we can. [*She has risen, leaving stylograph on writing-table, where it remains. She seals letter.*] Stamp?

Lady Jessica. I've got one in my purse. [*Takes letter.*

Lady Rosamund [*has caught sight of the menu, has taken it up*]. Jess, you'll go straight to the station now?

Lady Jessica. Yes, I'm awfully hungry——

Lady Rosamund. Yes, but I don't think this dinner would agree with you. [*Puts the menu down significantly.*

Lady Jessica. Very well. But I am hungry.

Lady Rosamund. And Jess, if I get you out of this—you won't take the wrong turning again?

Lady Jessica. No! No!

Lady Rosamund. Honour?

Lady Jessica. Honour! Really, really honour! Rosy, you know this is only a silly freak—nothing more.

Lady Rosamund. I may be sure of that, Jess? Honour?

Lady Jessica. Honour! Really, really honour!

Lady Rosamund [*kisses her*]. I must be going. To-morrow!

Lady Jessica. To-morrow at Cadogan Gardens, ten minutes to twelve. [*Rings bell.*

Lady Rosamund [*at window*]. Those men are in the boat. My Freddie is looking for me. What shall I tell him?

[*Exit at window.* LADY JESSICA *goes up to window, keeping well behind curtains. Looks off for a few seconds, then comes down. Enter* WAITER.

Lady Jessica [*giving letter*]. Please get that posted at once.

Waiter [*taking letter*]. *Bien, madame.*

[*Exit with letter. Re-enter* FALKNER *at window.*

Lady Jessica. They've gone?

Falkner. Yes. What have you done?

Lady Jessica. Rosy has written to George to come and see her to-morrow morning at Cadogan Gardens. You had better come too.

Falkner. At what time?

Lady Jessica. Say a quarter to one. George will have gone by then and we can tell you if he accepts our explanation.

Falkner. What is the explanation to be?

Lady Jessica. That Rosy and I were dining together here, that she hadn't arrived, that you happened to come into the room, and that George saw you and put a wrong construction on it. That will be all right, won't it?

Falkner. Yes—I daresay. I wish it had been possible to tell the truth.

Lady Jessica. The truth? What truth? Rosy was actually here, and she *might* have stayed and dined with me—only she didn't—and—well, if it isn't the truth, it's only a little one.

Falkner. I think those things are all the same size.

Lady Jessica. Oh, please don't be disagreeable, just at our last moment too.

Falkner. Our last moment? Ah, no, no, no! [*Approaching her.*

Lady Jessica. Ah, yes, yes, yes! I promised Rosy I'd go straight to the station——

Falkner. There's no train till eight fifty. What harm can there be in your staying to dinner now?

Lady Jessica. I promised Rosy I wouldn't. I'm fearfully hungry—— [*Enter* WAITER *with letter on salver.*

Waiter [*advancing with letter on salver to* LADY JESSICA]. Pardon, is this letter for madame?

Lady Jessica [*takes letter, shows fright*]. Yes. Excuse me. Who brought it? [*Opens letter, takes out telegram.*

Waiter. She is here in the passage.

Lady Jessica [*opens telegram; shows great alarm. Goes to door*]. Ferris.

Ferris [*coming to door*]. Yes, my lady.

Lady Jessica. Come in.

Waiter. *Bien, madame.* [*Exit.*

Lady Jessica. When did this telegram come?

Ferris. This afternoon, my lady. The moment I got in, Mr. Rawlins said to me, 'Mr. Nepean is coming back to-night; I've just had a telegram from him to get his room ready. And this telegram is for her ladyship,' he said, and he gave me that telegram. 'What time will her ladyship be back to-night?' he said. 'I don't know,' I said. 'Where is her ladyship now?' he said. 'I don't know,' I said.

Lady Jessica. You didn't know?

Ferris. No, my lady.

Lady Jessica. Then why did you come here?

Ferris. The other night when I was bringing your ladyship's shawl to the tent, I happened to hear you mention this hotel. I didn't think anything of it, your ladyship, and I didn't in the least expect to find you here, I assure your ladyship. But I thought your ladyship would like to be apprised that Mr. Nepean is coming home to-night, and so I came, as I may say by pure chance, my lady; just as you might have come yourself, my lady.

Lady Jessica. Quite right, Ferris. [*To* FALKNER.] Mr. Nepean is coming home to-night. He reaches Paddington at ten.

Ferris. I've got a cab outside, my lady, and I've looked out the trains. If we make haste, we can drive over to Walton and just catch a train there. But we haven't a moment to spare.

Lady Jessica. Come then.

Ferris. I hope I've done right, my lady?

Lady Jessica. Quite right, Ferris. No. please don't trouble to come out, I'd rather you didn't. Rosy and I will dine with you some other night. Goodnight. [*Exit* FERRIS.

Falkner [*seizing* LADY JESSICA'*s hands*]. And to-morrow?

Lady Jessica. To-morrow? [*Grimace.*] *Petits rows conjugals—sauce tartare.*

[*Exit at door.* FALKNER *enraged, sulky, disappointed, takes several turns about the room, kicks a hassock savagely. Enter* WAITER *with two little morsels of caviare.*

Falkner. What's that?

Waiter. Caviare on toast.

Falkner. Hang the caviare. Bring in the soup.

Waiter. Ah, it is not yet ready, two, three minutes. I am very sorry, but the cook say the *sauce Marguerite*——

Falkner. What about it?

Waiter. It will not be made.

Falkner. Very well.

Waiter. And the *salade*?

Falkner. What about the salad?

Waiter. Will m'sieu mix it?

Falkner. No, mix it yourself.

Waiter. *Bien, m'sieu.* [*Going off.*

Falkner. Waiter!

Waiter. Sir!

Falkner [*pointing to the cover laid for* LADY JESSICA]. Take those confounded things away.

Waiter. Sir!

Falkner. Take those confounded things away; I'm going to dine alone.

Waiter. *Bien, m'sieu.*

[*Takes up the second cover, and the one plate of caviare, leaving the other on the table in* FALKNER'*s place. Is going off with them.*

Falkner. Bring in the soup.

Waiter. *Bien, m'sieu.*

[*Exit with things, leaving door open.* SIR CHRISTOPHER'*s voice heard outside.*

Sir Christopher. Mr. Falkner.

Waiter. Yes, sir. In number ten, sir.

Sir Christopher. Has he dined?

Waiter. Not yet, sir. What name, sir?

Sir Christopher. Oh never mind my name. Show me in.

Waiter [*at door, announcing*]. The friend of the dinner.

[*Enter* SIR CHRISTOPHER *in morning dress. Exit* WAITER.

Sir Christopher [*very cordially*]. Ah, dear old boy, here you are. [*Shaking hands cordially.*] All alone?

Falkner. [*very sulkily*]. Yes.

Sir Christopher [*looking at table*]. You haven't dined?

Falkner. No.

Sir Christopher. That's all right. I'll join you. What's the matter?

Falkner. Nothing.

Sir Christopher. Nothing?

Falkner [*very sulky throughout*]. No. What should be?

Sir Christopher. You look upset.

Falkner. Not at all.

Sir Christopher. That's all right. [*Going up to table very ravenously.*] I say, old chap, dinner won't be long, eh?

Falkner. No, why?

Sir Christopher. I'm famished. I was over at Hounslow, I had no end of work to get through, so I stuck to it. I've had nothing but a biscuit and a glass of sherry since breakfast. I was going up to town for dinner, then I remembered you wrote to me from here; so I thought I'd run over on the chance of finding you. And here you are. [*Cordially.*] Well, how are you?

Falkner. I'm very well.

Sir Christopher. That's all right. And, and—about the lady?

Falkner. What about her?

Sir Christopher. You're going to behave like a good true fellow and give her up, eh?

Falkner. Yes, I suppose.

Sir Christopher. That's all right. Love 'em, worship 'em, make the most of 'em! Go down on your knees every day and thank God for having sent them into this dreary world for our good and comfort. But, don't break your heart over 'em. Don't ruin your career for 'em! Don't lose a night's rest for 'em! They aren't worth it—except one! [*Very softly*.

Falkner [*same sulky mood*]. You're full of good advice.

Sir Christopher. It's the only thing I am full of. I say, old fellow, could you hurry them up with the dinner?

[FALKNER *goes and rings bell*.

Sir Christopher [*casually taking up the menu*]. No, Ned; they're not worth it, bless their hearts. And the man who— [*Suddenly stops, his face illuminated with delighted surprise*.] Ned!

Falkner. What?

Sir Christopher [*pointing to the menu*]. This isn't the menu for to-night?

Falkner. Yes.

Sir Christopher [*incredulously*]. No! Dear old fellow! [*Looking at him with great admiration*.] Dear old fellow! I say, Ned, you do yourself very well when you're all alone.

Falkner. Why shouldn't I?

Sir Christopher. Why shouldn't you? Why shouldn't you?

[*Reading menu*.

Falkner. Why shouldn't I? Excuse me a moment.

[*Exit at door*. SIR CHRISTOPHER, *left alone, reads over the menu, showing great satisfaction, then goes up to sideboard, takes up the bottles of wine, looks at them, shows great satisfaction, rubs his hands, comes up to writing table, happens to catch sight of the stylograph pen, picks it up, is arrested by something inscribed on it, shows astonishment, comes down stage looking at it intently, puzzled and surprised. As* WAITER *re-enters with soup*, SIR CHRISTOPHER *puts stylograph in pocket*.

Waiter [*putting soup on table*]. Mr. Falkner say will you please excuse him? He has gone to London just now, this minute.

Sir Christopher. Gone to London!

Waiter. On very important business. He say will you please make yourself at home with the dinner?

Sir Christopher [*puzzled*]. Gone to London! What on earth— [*Resolutely and instantly takes seat at head of table*.] Serve up the dinner! Sharp!

Waiter. Caviare on toast?

Sir Christopher. Oh, damn the caviare! Open the champagne!

[*Takes the morsel of caviare and throws it down his throat; helps himself to soup, peppers it vigorously, meantime* WAITER *opens champagne and pours out a glass.*

Sir Christopher. The fish! Quick! and the *entrées*, bring them both up at the same time—bring up the whole bag of tricks!!

[SIR CHRISTOPHER *throws spoonful after spoonful of soup down his throat. The organ outside strikes up in the middle of the bar at which it left off, a very rowdy street tune.*

CURTAIN.

(*One night passes between Acts II and III.*)

ACT III

SCENE: LADY ROSAMUND'*s drawing-room, Cadogan Gardens, a very elegant modern apartment, furnished in good taste. Door at back. Door right. Large bow window forming an alcove up stage right. Fireplace left.* LADY ROSAMUND *discovered in out-door morning dress.* FOOTMAN *showing in* LADY JESSICA *at back.*

Footman [*announces*]. Lady Jessica Nepean.

[*Exit* FOOTMAN.

Lady Rosamund. Well, dear?

Lady Jessica [*kisses* LADY ROSAMUND *very affectionately*]. Oh, Rosy——

Lady Rosamund. What's the matter?

Lady Jessica. Directly you had gone Ferris came in with a telegram from Gilbert, saying he was coming home last night. Of course I flew back to town. When I got there I found a later telegram saying he hadn't been able to finish his business, and that he would come back to-day.

Lady Rosamund [*taking letter from pocket*]. He reaches Paddington at twelve.

Lady Jessica. How do you know?

Lady Rosamund [*giving letter*]. Read that.

Lady Jessica [*looking at handwriting*]. From George Nepean.

Lady Rosamund. Yes. He came here an hour ago to see me, and left that note. I'm afraid George means to be very horrid.

Lady Jessica [*reading*]. 'Dear Lady Rosamund, I shall, of course, be quite ready to listen to any explanation you may have to offer. I will come back to Cadogan Gardens on my return from Paddington. I am now on my way there to meet Gilbert, who arrives from Devon at twelve. It is only fair to tell you that on leaving Lady Jessica last evening I telegraphed him I had a most serious communication to make to him, and that on his arrival I shall tell him exactly what I saw.' George does mean to be horrid.

[*Retaining letter.*

Lady Rosamund. I cannot imagine how you——

Lady Jessica. Oh, do not preach. I tell you it was the sign-post. It is most deceptive.

Lady Rosamund. It must be. The next time you come to that sign-post——

Lady Jessica. I shall know which turning to take! You needn't fear.

Lady Rosamund. My Freddie's in a small fever.

Lady Jessica. What about?

Lady Rosamund. My coming up to town this morning.

Lady Jessica. You're sure he'll stay down there? He won't come up and—interfere?

Lady Rosamund. Oh no, poor old dear! I snubbed him thoroughly and left him grizzling in his tent, like Achilles. He'll stay there all day, fuming and trying to screw up his courage to have a tremendous row with me when I get back to dinner this evening. I know my Freddie so well!

[FREDDIE *saunters in at back, half timid, half defiant.*

Lady Rosamund [*looking at him with amused surprise*]. Hillo, my friend! Hillo!

Freddie [*very severe and dignified, takes no notice of her*]. How do, Jess?

[LADY JESSICA *alternately reads* GEORGE'*s letter and looks at* FREDDIE.

Lady Rosamund. What has brought you to town?

Freddie. I came up with a purpose.

Lady Rosamund. Oh, don't say that. People are always so horrid who do things with a purpose.

Freddie. I came up with Mrs. Crespin. She has lost the address of the cook that you gave her last evening. I told her you were in town. She will call here for it.

Lady Rosamund [*sweetly*]. Very well.

Freddie. Do you intend to stay in, or go out this morning?

Lady Rosamund. That depends. I may stay in—or I may go out. What are you going to do?

Freddie. That depends. I may stay in—or—I may go out.

Lady Rosamund. Very well, dear, do as you please. I'll take the alternative. [*To* LADY JESSICA.] Come and take your things off in my room.

Lady Jessica [*glancing at* FREDDIE]. But don't you think——

Freddie [*rising with great dignity, placing himself in front of them*]. I have come up to town this morning, because for the future I intend to place everything in this house on a new basis, an entirely opposite basis from that on which it now stands.

Lady Rosamund. You're going to turn all the furniture upside down! Oh, I wouldn't!

Freddie. Hitherto I have been content to be a cipher in this establishment. I will be a cipher no longer.

Lady Rosamund. No, I wouldn't. Come along, Jess!

Lady Jessica. But—— [*Showing* GEORGE'*s letter.*

Lady Rosamund. We'll talk it over upstairs. Run away to your club, Freddie, and think over what figure you would like to be. I daresay we can arrange it.

[*Exit* LADY ROSAMUND, R., *taking off* LADY JESSICA, *and closing the door rather sharply behind her.*

Freddie [*left alone, marches up to the door, calls out in a forcible-feeble scream*]. I will not be a cipher! I will not be a cipher! [*Comes to centre of stage, gesticulates, his lips moving, sits down very resolutely, and then says in a tone of solemn conviction.*] I will *not* be a cipher!

[*Enter* FOOTMAN *at back, announcing.*

Footman. Sir Christopher Deering!

[*Enter* SIR CHRISTOPHER. *Exit* FOOTMAN.

Sir Christopher [*shaking hands*]. I've just come on from Lady Jessica's. They told me I should find her here.

Freddie. She's upstairs with my wife.

Sir Christopher. Can I see her for a few minutes?

Freddie. I don't know. Deering, old fellow, we're tiled in, aren't we? If I ask your advice——

Sir Christopher. Certainly, Freddie. What is it?

Freddie. I've been married for seven years——

Sir Christopher. Seven years is it? It doesn't seem so long.

Freddie. Oh, doesn't it? Yes, it does. Rosy and I have never quite hit it off from the first.

Sir Christopher. No? How's that?

Freddie. I don't know. When I want to do anything, she

doesn't. When I want to go anywhere she won't. When I like anybody, she hates them. And when I hate anybody, she likes them. And—well—there it is in a nutshell.

Sir Christopher. Hum! I should humour her a little, Freddie—let her have her own way. Try kindness.

Freddie. Kindness? I tell you this, Deering, kindness is a grand mistake. And I made that grand mistake at starting. I began with riding her on the snaffle. I ought to have started on the curb, eh?

Sir Christopher. Well, there's something to be said for that method in some cases. Kindness won't do, you say? Why not try firmness?

Freddie. I have.

Sir Christopher. Well?

Freddie. Well, firmness is all very well, but there's one great objection to firmness.

Sir Christopher. What's that?

Freddie. It leads to such awful rows, and chronic rowing does upset me so. After about two days of it, I feel so seedy and shaky and nervous, I don't know what to do. [*Has a sudden wrathful outburst.*] And she comes up as smiling as ever!

Sir Christopher. Poor old fellow!

Freddie. I say, Deering, what would you advise me to do?

Sir Christopher. Well, it requires some consideration——

Freddie [*with deep conviction*]. You know, Deering, there must be some way of managing them.

Sir Christopher. One would think so. There must be some way of managing them!

Freddie [*has another wrathful outburst*]. And I used to go and wait outside her window, night after night, for hours! What do you think of that?

Sir Christopher. I should say it was time very badly laid out.

Freddie [*pursuing his reminiscences*]. Yes, and caught a chill on my liver and was laid up for six weeks.

Sir Christopher. Poor old fellow!

Freddie. I say, Deering, what would you do?

Sir Christopher. Well—well—it requires some consideration.

Freddie [*walking about*]. You know, Deering, I may be an ass——

Sir Christopher. Oh!

Freddie [*firmly*]. Yes. I may be an ass, but I'm not a *silly* ass! I may be a fool, but I'm not a *d—ee—d* fool! Now there's something going on this morning between Rosamund and

Jess. They're hobnobbing and whispering, and when two of 'em get together——

Sir Christopher. Oh, my dear fellow, when two women get together, do you think it can ever be worth a man's while to ask what nonsense or mischief they're chattering? By the way, did you say that I could see Lady Jessica?

Freddie. She's upstairs with Rosy. I'll send her to you. Deering, if you were married, would you be a cipher in your own house?

Sir Christopher. Not if I could help it.

Freddie [*very determinedly*]. Neither will I.

[*Exit* R. SIR CHRISTOPHER, *left alone, takes out the stylograph and looks at it carefully. In a few seconds enter* LADY JESSICA, R. *As she enters he drops left hand which holds the stylograph.*

Sir Christopher. How d'ye do?

Lady Jessica. How d'ye do? You wish to see me?

[SIR CHRISTOPHER *presents the stylograph,* LADY JESSICA *shows alarm.*

Sir Christopher. I see from the inscription that this belongs to you.

Lady Jessica [*taking stylograph*]. Where did you find it?

Sir Christopher. In a private sitting-room at the Star and Garter at Shepperford.

Lady Jessica. I must have left it there some time ago. I could not imagine where I had lost it. Thank you so much.

Sir Christopher. Pray don't mention it. Good morning.

[*Is going.*

Lady Jessica. Good morning. [SIR CHRISTOPHER *has got to door at back.*] Sir Christopher—[SIR CHRISTOPHER *stops.*] You were at Shepperford——?

Sir Christopher. Last evening.

Lady Jessica. Pretty little spot.

Sir Christopher. Charming.

Lady Jessica. And a very good hotel?

Sir Christopher. First class. Such splendid cooking!

Lady Jessica. The cooking's good, is it?—oh, yes, I dined there once, some time ago.

Sir Christopher. I dined there last night.

Lady Jessica. Did you? At the *table d'hôte*?

Sir Christopher. No, in a private sitting room. Number ten.

Lady Jessica. With a friend, I suppose?

Sir Christopher. No. All alone.

Lady Jessica. All alone? In number ten?

Sir Christopher. All alone. In number ten.

Lady Jessica. I suppose you—I suppose——

Sir Christopher. Suppose nothing except that I had a remarkably good dinner, that I picked up that stylograph and brought it up to town with me last night. And there is an end of the whole matter, I assure you. Good morning. [*Going.*

Lady Jessica. Good morning. Sir Christopher—you—[SIR CHRISTOPHER *is again arrested at the door*] you—a—— [SIR CHRISTOPHER *comes down to her.*] I may trust you?

Sir Christopher. If I can help you—yes.

Lady Jessica. Nothing—nothing is known about my being there?

Sir Christopher. Your being there?

Lady Jessica [*after a pause—embarrassed*]. I was to have dined in number ten.

Sir Christopher. All alone?

Lady Jessica [*same embarrassed manner*]. No—with Mr. Falkner. I was coming up to town from my cousin's. I started to walk to the station. I must have taken the wrong turning, for instead of finding myself at the station, I found myself at the Star and Garter. I was very hungry and I asked Mr. Falkner to give me a mere mouthful of dinner.

Sir Christopher. A mere mouthful.

Lady Jessica. And then George Nepean caught sight of me, came in, saw Mr. Falkner, and telegraphed my husband that I—of course Gilbert will believe the worst, and I—oh, I don't know what to do?

Sir Christopher. Can I be of any service?

Lqdy Jessica. How would you advise me to—to get out of it?

Sir Christopher. Let us go over the various possibilities of the case. There are only two.

Lady Jessica. What are they?

Sir Christopher. Possibility number one—get out of it by telling fibs. Possibility number two—get out of it by telling the truth. Why not possibility number two?

Lady Jessica. Oh, I couldn't!

Sir Christopher. Couldn't what?

Lady Jessica. Tell my husband that I was going to dine with Mr. Falkner.

Sir Christopher. But it was quite by accident?

Lady Jessica. Oh, quite! Quite!

Sir Christopher. Well——?

Lady Jessica. But if Gilbert made inquiries——

Sir Christopher. Well?

Lady Jessica. It was such a very good dinner that Mr. Falkner ordered.

Sir Christopher. It was! It was! If he didn't expect you, why did he order that very excellent dinner?

Lady Jessica. I'm sure you ought to be the last person to ask that, for it seems you ate it.

Sir Christopher. I did.

Lady Jessica. It's an ill wind that blows nobody good!

Sir Christopher. I'm not grumbling at the wind, or at the dinner, but if I'm to help you out of this, you had better tell me all the truth. Especially as I'm not your husband. Now frankly, is this a mere indiscretion, or——

[*Looking at her.*

Lady Jessica. A mere indiscretion, nothing more. Honour—really, really honour.

Sir Christopher. A mere indiscretion that will never be repeated.

Lady Jessica. A mere indiscretion that will never be repeated. You believe me?

Sir Christopher [*looking at her*]. Yes, I believe you, and I'll help you.

Lady Jessica. Thank you! Thank you!

Sir Christopher. Now did Falkner expect you?

Lady Jessica. He ought not.

Sir Christopher. He ought not. But he did.

Lady Jessica. I told him I shouldn't come.

Sir Christopher. Which was exactly the same as telling him you would.

Lady Jessica. Have you seen Mr. Falkner?

Sir Christopher. Only for a minute just before dinner. He came up to town.

Lady Jessica. Without any dinner?

Sir Christopher. Without any dinner. To come back to these two possibilities.

Lady Jessica. Yes, Rosy and I have decided on—on——

Sir Christopher. On possibility number one, tell a fib. I put that possibility first out of natural deference and chivalry towards ladies. The only objection I have to telling fibs is that you get found out.

Lady Jessica. Oh, not always! I mean, if you arrange things not perhaps exactly as they were, but as they ought to have been.

Sir Christopher. I see. In that way a lie becomes a sort of idealized and essential truth——

Lady Jessica. Yes. Yes——

Sir Christopher. I'm not a good hand at—idealizing.

Lady Jessica. Ah, but then you're a man! No, I can't tell the truth. Gilbert would never believe me. Would you—after that dinner?

Sir Christopher. The dinner would be some tax on my digestion.

[LADY ROSAMUND *enters* R., *followed by* FREDDIE, *with a self-important and self-assertive air.*

Lady Rosamund. Good morning, Sir Christopher.

Sir Christopher [*shaking hands*]. Good morning, Lady Rosamund.

Lady Rosamund. Jess, I've had to tell Freddie.

Lady Jessica. And I've had to tell Sir Christopher. He was at Shepperford last evening, and he has promised to help us.

Freddie. I must say, Jess, that I think you have behaved—well—in a—confounded silly way.

Lady Jessica. That is perfectly understood.

Freddie [*solemnly*]. When a woman once forgets what is due——

Lady Jessica. Oh, don't moralize! Rosy, Sir Christopher, do ask him not to improve the occasion.

Sir Christopher. The question is, Freddie, whether you will help us in getting Lady Jessica out of this little difficulty.

Freddie. Well, I suppose I must join in.

Lady Jessica. Now, Rosy, do you fully understand——

Sir Christopher. I don't think I do. What is the exact shape which possibility number one has taken—or is going to take?

Lady Rosamund. Jess and I had arranged to have a little *tête-à-tête* dinner at Shepperford. Jess got there first. I hadn't arrived. George saw Jess at the window, and came in. At that moment Mr. Falkner happened to come into the room, and Jess knowing that appearances were against her, was confused, and couldn't on the spur of the moment give the right explanation.

Sir Christopher. I suppose the waiter will confirm that right explanation?

Lady Jessica. The waiter? I hadn't thought of that. Waiters will confirm anything, won't they? Couldn't you settle with the waiter?

Sir Christopher. Well, I——

Lady Jessica. You did have the dinner, you know!

Sir Christopher. Very well. I'll settle with the waiter.

[*Enter* FOOTMAN.

Footman [*at back, announcing*]. Mrs. Crespin.

[*Enter* MRS. CRESPIN. *Exit* FOOTMAN.

Mrs. Crespin [*shows a little surprise at seeing them all, then goes very affectionately to* LADY ROSAMUND]. Good morning, dear. Good morning, Sir Christopher. [SIR CHRISTOPHER *bows. To* FREDDIE.] I've seen you [*Goes to* LADY JESSICA.] Good morning, dearest. [*Kisses her.*

Lady Jessica. Good morning, dearest. [*Kisses her.*

Mrs. Crespin [*to* LADY JESSICA. *Looking anxiously at her*]. You're looking pale and worried.

Lady Jessica. Me? Oh no, I'm sure I don't, do I?

Sir Christopher. Not to masculine eyes.

Mrs. Crespin [*to* LADY ROSAMUND]. Dear, I've lost the address of that cook. Would you mind writing it out again?

Lady Rosamund. Certainly.

[*Goes to writing table and writes.*

Mrs. Crespin [*to* LADY JESSICA]. What's the matter with our dear friend George Nepean?

Lady Jessica. Matter?

Mrs. Crespin. I ran against him in a post office on my way from Paddington just now.

Lady Jessica. Yes?

Mrs. Crespin. Your husband is quite well, I hope?

Lady Jessica. My husband? Oh, quite! He always is quite well. Why?

Mrs. Crespin. George Nepean seemed so strange.

Lady Jessica. How?

Mrs. Crespin. He said he was going to Paddington to meet your husband—and he made so much of it.

Lady Jessica. Ah! You see, my husband is a big man, so naturally George would make much of it.

Mrs. Crespin. I always used to go to the station to meet my husband—when I had one.

Lady Jessica [*a little triumphantly*]. Ah! Rosy and I know better than to kill our husbands with too much kindness.

Mrs. Crespin. Still, I think husbands need a little pampering——

Sir Christopher. Not at all. The brutes are so easily spoilt. A little overdose of sweetness, a little extra attention from a wife to her husband, and life is never the same again!

Freddie [*who has been waiting eagerly to get a word in*]. I suppose you didn't mention anything to George Nepean about our dining with you last evening?

Mrs. Crespin [*alert*]. Did I? Let me see! Yes! Yes! I did mention that you were over. Why?

[*They all look at each other.*

Freddie. Oh, nothing, nothing!

Mrs. Crespin. I'm so sorry. Does it matter much?

Lady Jessica. Not in the least.

Lady Rosamund. Oh, not in the least.

Freddie. Not in the least.

Sir Christopher. Not at all.

Mrs. Crespin. I'm afraid I made a mistake.

Lady Rosamund. How?

Mrs. Crespin. Your husband——

Lady Rosamund. Oh, my dear, what does it matter what my Freddie says or does or thinks, eh, Freddie? [*Frowning angrily aside at* FREDDIE.] There's the address of the cook.

[*Giving the paper on which she had been writing.*

Mrs. Crespin Thank you so much. Good morning, dearest.

[*Kiss.*

Lady Rosamund. Good morning, dearest. [*Kiss.*

Mrs. Crespin [*going to* LADY JESSICA]. Good-bye, dearest.

[*Kiss.*

Lady Jessica. Good-bye, dearest. [*Kiss.*

Mrs. Crespin [*very sweetly shaking hands*]. Good-bye, Sir Christopher.

Sir Christopher. Good-bye. [LADY ROSAMUND *rings bell.*

Mrs. Crespin. You are quite sure that I didn't make a mistake in telling George Nepean that Lady Rosy and Mr. Tatton dined with me last evening?

Sir Christopher. It was the truth, wasn't it?

Mrs. Crespin. Of course it was.

Sir Christopher. One never makes a mistake in speaking the truth.

Mrs. Crespin. Really? That's a very sweeping assertion to make.

Sir Christopher. I base it on my constant experience—and practice. [FOOTMAN *appears at door at back.*

Mrs. Crespin. You find it always answers to tell the truth?

Sir Christopher. Invariably.

Mrs. Crespin. I hope it will in this case. Good-bye! Good-bye! Good-bye!

[*Exit* MRS. CRESPIN. *Exit* FOOTMAN. *They all stand looking at each other, nonplussed.* SIR CHRISTOPHER *slightly touching his head with perplexed gesture.*

Sir Christopher. Our fib won't do.

Lady Rosamund. Freddie, you incomparable nincompoop!

Freddie. I like that! If I hadn't asked her, what would have happened? George Nepean would have come in, you'd have plumped down on him with your lie, and what then? Don't you think it's jolly lucky I said what I did?

Sir Christopher. It's lucky in this instance. But if I am to embark any further in these imaginative enterprises, I must ask you, Freddie, to keep a silent tongue.

Freddie. What for?

Sir Christopher. Well, old fellow, it may be an unpalatable truth to you, but you'll never make a good liar.

Freddie. Very likely not. But if this sort of thing is going on in my house, I think I ought to.

Lady Rosamund. Oh, do subside, Freddie, do subside!

Lady Jessica. Yes, George—and perhaps Gilbert—will be here directly. Oh, will somebody tell me what to do?

Sir Christopher. We have tried possibility number one. It has signally failed. Why not possibility number two?

Lady Jessica. Tell the truth? My husband would never believe it! Besides, he threatened that he wouldn't spare me. And he won't. No! No! No! Somebody dined with me last night, or was going to dine with me, and that somebody was a woman. [*Enter* FOOTMAN *at back.*

Footman [*announcing*]. Mrs. Coke!

[*Enter* DOLLY. *Exit* FOOTMAN.

Lady Jessica [*goes affectionately and a little hysterically to her*]. Dolly! How good of you! [*Kissing her.*

Dolly. What's the matter?

Lady Jessica. Dolly, you dined with me, or were going to dine with me at the Star and Garter at Shepperford last evening. Don't say you can't, and didn't, for you must and did!

Dolly. Of course I'll say anything that's—necessary.

Lady Jessica. Oh, you treasure!

Dolly. But I don't understand——

[LADY JESSICA *takes her aside and whispers eagerly.*

Sir Christopher [*glancing at* LADY JESSICA *and* DOLLY]. Possibility number one—with variations. I'm not required any further. [*Takes up his hat and is about to bolt.*

Lady Rosamund. Oh, Sir Christopher, you won't desert us?

Sir Christopher. Certainly not, if I can be of any use. But if this is to be a going concern, don't you think the fewer partners the better?

Lady Rosamund. Oh, don't go. You can help us so much.

Sir Christopher. How?

Lady Rosamund. Your mere presence will be an immense moral support to us.

Sir Christopher [*uncomfortable*]. Thank you! Thank you!

Lady Rosamund. You can come to our assistance whenever we are in the lurch, corroborate us whenever we need corroboration—and——

Sir Christopher. Bolster up generally.

Lady Rosamund. Yes. Besides, everybody knows you are such an honourable man. I feel they won't suspect you.

Sir Christopher [*uncomfortable*]. Thank you! Thank you!

Dolly [*to* LADY JESSICA]. Very well, dear. I quite understand. After George went away, you were so upset at his suspicions that you came back to town without any dinner. Did I stay and have the dinner?

Sir Christopher. No, no. I wouldn't go so far as that.

Dolly. But what did I do? I must have dined somewhere, didn't I? Not that I mind if I didn't dine anywhere. But won't it seem funny if I didn't dine somewhere?

Lady Jessica. I suppose it will.

Dolly. Very well then, where did I dine? Do tell me. I know I shall get into an awful muddle if I don't know. Where did I dine? [*Enter* FOOTMAN *at back.*

Footman [*announcing*]. Mr. George Nepean.

[*Enter* GEORGE NEPEAN. *Exit* FOOTMAN.

George [*enters very frigidly, bows very coldly. Very stiffly*]. Good morning, Lady Rosamund! [*To the others—bowing.*] Good morning.

Lady Rosamund [*very cordially*]. My dear George, don't take that tragic tone. [*Insists on shaking hands.*] Anyone would suppose that something dreadful was the matter. I've just explained to Sir Christopher your mistake of last night.

George. My mistake?

Lady Jessica. You shouldn't have left so hurriedly, George. I sent Mr. Falkner after you to explain. Dolly, tell him.

Dolly. Jess and I had arranged to have a little dinner all by our two selves——

George. Indeed!

Dolly. There's nothing strange in that, Sir Christopher?

Sir Christopher. Not at all. I am sure any person of either sex would only be too delighted to dine *tête-à-tête* with you.

Dolly. And when I got there, I found poor Jess in an awful state. She said you had come into the room and had made the most horrid accusations against her, poor thing!

George. I made no accusation.

Lady Jessica. What did you mean by saying that Gilbert must know?

George. Merely that I should tell him what I saw.

Lady Jessica. And have you told him?

George. Yes, on his arrival an hour ago.

Lady Jessica. Where is he?

George. Round at Sloane Street waiting till I have heard Lady Rosamund's explanation.

Lady Rosamund. Well, you have heard it. Or, rather, it's Dolly's explanation. The whole thing is so ridiculously simple. I think you ought to beg Jess's pardon.

George. I will when I am sure that I have wronged her.

Freddie. Oh, come, I say, George! you don't refuse to take a lady's word——

Lady Rosamund. Freddie, subside!

Dolly [*to* GEORGE]. Poor Jess was so much upset by what you said that she couldn't eat any dinner, she nearly had hysterics, and when she got a little better, she came straight up to town, poor thing!

George. What was Mr Falkner doing there?

Lady Jessica. He was staying in the hotel and happened to come into the room at that moment. [*A little pause.*

Lady Rosamund. Is there anything else you would like to ask?

George. No.

Lady Rosamund. And you're quite satisfied?

George. The question is not whether I'm satisfied, but whether Gilbert will be. I'll go and fetch him. Will you excuse me? [*Going.*

Sir Christopher [*stops him*]. Nepean, I'm sure you don't wish to embitter your brother and Lady Jessica's whole future life by sowing jealousy and suspicion between them. Come now, like a good fellow, you'll smooth things over as much as you can.

George. I shall not influence my brother one way or the other. He must judge for himself.

[*Exit at back.* SIR CHRISTOPHER *shrugs his shoulders.*

Dolly. I got through very well, didn't I? [*To* LADY JESSICA.

Lady Jessica. Yes, dear. Thank you so much. But George didn't seem to believe it, eh?

Freddie. It's so jolly thin. A couple of women dining together! Why should a couple of women want to dine together? Oh, it's too thin, you know!

Lady Jessica. And you don't think Gilbert will believe it? He must! he must! Oh, I begin to wish that we had tried——

Sir Christopher. Possibility number two. I'm afraid it's too late now.

Lady Jessica. Oh, what shall I do? Do you think Gilbert will believe Dolly?

Lady Rosamund. He must if Dolly only sticks to it.

Dolly. Oh, I'll stick to it. Only I should like to know where I dined. Where did I dine?

[*Enter* FOOTMAN *at back, comes up to* DOLLY.

Footman. If you please, ma'am, Mr. Coke is waiting for you below.

Dolly [*with a scream*]. Oh, dear! Oh, dear! I'd quite forgotten!

Lady Rosamund. What?

Dolly. I arranged to meet Archie here and take him on to the dentist's. [*To* FOOTMAN.] Tell Mr. Coke I'll come in a moment. [*Exit* FOOTMAN.

Dolly [*to* LADY JESSICA]. Dear, I must go——

Lady Jessica. You can't! You must stay now and tell Gilbert—mustn't she, Sir Christopher?

Sir Christopher. I'm afraid you must, Mrs. Coke. You are our sheet-anchor.

Dolly. But what can I tell Archie?

Lady Rosamund. Can't you put him off, send him away?

Dolly. What excuse can I make? He is so fidgety and inquisitive. He'll insist on knowing everything. No, I must go.

Lady Jessica [*desperate*]. You can't! You can't! You must stay! Couldn't we tell Archie and ask him to help us?

Dolly. Oh, I wouldn't tell Archie for the world. He wouldn't understand.

[*Enter, door at back,* ARCHIBALD COKE, *in very correct frock coat, very prim and starchy.*

Coke. Good morning, Rosy! Freddie! Sir Christopher! [*Nodding all round.*] Now, Dolly, are you ready?

Dolly. I—I——

Lady Jessica. She can't go, Archie.

Coke. Can't go?

Lady Jessica. She—she isn't well.

Coke. Not well? [*Alarmed.*] Not influenza again?

Dolly. No, not influenza. But I'd rather not go.

Coke. Oh, nonsense, nonsense! I cannot take the gas alone. [*To* SIR CHRISTOPHER.] I've a terrible dread of the gas. I'm sure they'll give me too much some day. Now, Dolly.

Lady Rosamund [*to* SIR CHRISTOPHER]. Gilbert will be here directly. Can't you get him away?

Sir Christopher. Coke, your wife isn't just the thing, as you can see. I'll go to the dentist's with you. Come along! [*Linking his arm with* COKE'*s*.] I'll see they give you the right dose.

Coke [*resisting*]. No. My wife is the proper person to go to the dentist with me, and see that the gas is rightly administered. Come, Dolly!

Lady Jessica [*comes desperately to* COKE]. Dolly can't go.

Coke. Why not?

Lady Jessica. She must stay here and tell Gilbert that she dined with me last evening.

Coke. Tell Gilbert that she dined with you last evening! What for?

Sir Christopher [*aside to* LADY ROSAMUND]. We're taking too many partners into this concern.

Coke. She dined with me. Why should she tell Gilbert she dined with you?

Lady Jessica. If you must know, I was coming to the station from Barbara's and I must have taken the wrong turning——

Coke [*very suspicious*]. The wrong turning?

Lady Jessica. Yes, for instead of finding myself at the station I found myself at the Star and Garter.

Coke. The Star and Garter?

Lady Jessica. And as I was frightfully hungry I asked Mr. Falkner to give me a little dinner.

Coke. A little dinner?

Lady Jessica. George Nepean happened to come in, and seeing the dinner things laid, actually suspected me of dining with Mr. Falkner! And he has told Gilbert, and don't you see—if Dolly will only say that it was she who was dining with me—don't you see?

Coke. No, I don't. I cannot lend myself to anything of the sort. And I expressly forbid Dolly to say that she dined with you.

Lady Jessica. But she has said so. She has just told George Nepean.

Coke. Told George Nepean!

Dolly. I couldn't leave poor Jess in a scrape. And now I have said so, I must stick to it, mustn't I? You wouldn't have me tell another one now.

Coke. Well, I'm surprised! Really, I consider it quite disgraceful.

Freddie. Look here, Coke, we can't let Gilbert think that Jess was dining with Falkner, can we? He'd only make a howling scandal, and drag us all into it. We've got to say something. I know it's jolly thin, but can you think of a better one?

Coke. No, and I decline to have anything to do with this! I should have thought my character was too well known for me to be asked to a—a— It is too disgraceful! I will not lend my countenance to anything of the kind!

Lady Rosamund. Very well then, will you please take yourself off and leave us to manage the affair ourselves?

Coke. No, I will not forfeit my self-respect, I will not permit my wife to forfeit her self-respect by taking part in these proceedings. Really, it is—it is—it is too disgraceful!

[LADY JESSICA *suddenly bursts into tears, sobs violently*.

Sir Christopher [*comes up to him very calm, touches him on the shoulder*]. Coke, I assure you that theoretically I have as great an objection to lying as you or any man living. But Lady Jessica has acted a little foolishly. No more. Of that I am sure. If you consent to hold your tongue, I think Gilbert Nepean will accept your wife's explanation and the affair will blow over. If, however, you insist on the truth coming out, what will happen? You will very likely bring about a rupture between them, you may possibly place Lady Jessica in a position where she will have no alternative but to take a fatal plunge, and you will drag yourself and your wife into a very unpleasant family scandal. That's the situation.

Coke. But it places me in a very awkward position. No, really, I cannot consent—I'm an honourable man.

Sir Christopher. So are we all, all honourable men. The curious thing is that ever since the days of the Garden of Eden, women have had a knack of impaling us honourable men on dilemmas of this kind, where the only alternative is to be false to the truth or false to them. In this instance I think we may very well keep our mouths shut without suffering any violent pangs of conscience about the matter. Come now!

Coke [*sits down overwhelmed*]. Well, understand me, if I consent to keep my mouth shut, I must not be supposed to countenance what is going on. That is quite understood?

Sir Christopher. Oh, quite! Quite! We'll consider you as strictly neutral. Then you will?

Coke [*rising up, violently*]. No! On second thoughts, I really cannot! I cannot!

Lady Rosamund. Very well! Then will you go away and leave us to manage it as we can?

Coke. And I had arranged to take the gas so comfortably this morning. It's most unfair to place me in a position of this kind. I must protest—I really——

[*Enter* FOOTMAN.

Footman [*at back, announcing*]. Mr. Gilbert Nepean. Mr. George Nepean.

[*Enter* GILBERT *and* GEORGE NEPEAN. *Exit* FOOTMAN.

Lady Rosamund [*advances very cordially to* GILBERT, *who does not respond*]. Good morning, Gilbert.

Gilbert. Good morning. Good morning, Coke.

Coke [*very uncomfortable*]. Good morning.

Gilbert [*nodding*]. Freddie! Deering! [*Looks at* LADY JESSICA, *who looks at him. They do not speak. Pause, looking round.*] I thought I was coming here for a private explanation.

[SIR CHRISTOPHER *takes up his hat quickly. Is going to bolt.*

Lady Rosamund. No, Sir Christopher. If Gilbert is determined to carry this any further we shall need the unbiased testimony of an impartial friend, so that people may know exactly what did occur. Please stay.

Sir Christopher [*puts down hat*]. Whew! [*To himself.*]

Lady Rosamund. Gilbert, don't be foolish. Everybody here knows all about the stupid affair of last evening.

Gilbert. Everybody here knows? Well, I don't. I shall be glad to be informed.

[*Looks around.* COKE *shows symptoms of great discomfort.*

Sir Christopher. Nepean, I'm sure you don't wish to make any more than is necessary of Lady Jessica's trifling indiscretion——

Gilbert. I wish to make no more of it than the truth, and I'll take care that nobody makes less of it. Now—[*To* LADY JESSICA, *very furiously*.]—you were dining with this fellow, Falkner, last evening?

Lady Jessica. No.

Gilbert. No? Then whom did you dine with?

Lady Jessica. If you speak like that I shan't answer you.

Gilbert. Will you tell me what I ask?

Lady Jessica. No!

Gilbert. I can't get the truth from you. Perhaps, as you all know, somebody else will oblige me. Coke——

Coke [*most uncomfortable*]. Really, I—I don't know all the particulars, and I would prefer not to be mixed up in your private affairs.

Gilbert. Deering—you?

Sir Christopher. My dear fellow, I only know what I've heard, and hearsay evidence is proverbially untrustworthy. Now, if I may offer you a little advice, if I were you I should gently take Lady Jessica by the hand, I should gently lead her home, I should gently use all those endearing little arts of persuasion and entreaty which a husband may legitimately use to his wife, and I should gently beguile her into telling me the whole truth. I should believe everything she told me, I shouldn't listen to what anybody else said, and I should never mention the matter again. Now, do as I tell you, and you'll be a happy man to-morrow, and for the rest of your life. [*Pause.*

Gilbert [*looks at* LADY JESSICA]. No. [SIR CHRISTOPHER *shrugs his shoulders, and retires.*] I came here for an explanation, and I won't go till I've got it.

Lady Rosamund. My dear Gilbert, we're patiently waiting to give you an explanation, if you'll only listen to it. Dolly, do tell him how it all happened, and let him see what a donkey he is making of himself.

Dolly. Yes, Gilbert, I wish you wouldn't get in these awful tempers. You frighten us so that in a very little while we shan't know whether we're speaking the truth, or whether we're not.

Gilbert. Go on! Go on!

Dolly. Jess and I had arranged to have a little *tête-à-tête* dinner at Shepperford and talk over old times, all by our two selves [COKE *gets very uncomfortable*]—hadn't we, Jess? Rosy, you heard us arranging it all?

Lady Rosamund. Yes, on the last night you were at our place.

Dolly. Yes, Well, Jess got there first and then Mr. Falkner happened to come into the room, and then George happened to come into the room, and wouldn't wait to listen to Jess's explanation, would he, Jess? Well, when I got there, I found Jess in strong hysterics, poor old dear! I couldn't get her round for ever so long. And as soon as she was better she came straight up to town. And that's all. [*Pause.*

Gilbert. And what did you do?

Dolly. I came up to town, too.

Gilbert. Without any dinner?

Dolly. Eh?

Gilbert. Where did you dine?

Dolly. I didn't really dine anywhere—not to say dine. I had some cold chicken and a little tongue when I got home. [*Pause.*] And a tomato salad.

Coke [*very much shocked at* DOLLY]. Oh, of all the—— [SIR CHRISTOPHER *nudges him to be quiet.*

Gilbert. Coke, what do you know of this?

Coke. Well—I know what Dolly has just told you.

Gilbert. You allow your wife to dine out alone?

Coke. Yes—yes—on certain occasions.

Gilbert. And you knew of this arrangement?

Coke. Yes—at least, no—not before she told me of it. But after she told me, I did know.

George. But Jessica said that she expected a small party.

Dolly. I was the small party.

Gilbert [*to* COKE]. What time did Dolly get home last evening?

Coke. Eh? Well, about——

Dolly. A little before nine.

George. Impossible! I was at Shepperford after half past seven. If Lady Jessica had hysterics, and you stayed with her, you could scarcely have reached Kensington before nine.

Dolly. Well, perhaps it was ten. Yes, it was ten.

Gilbert. Coke, were you at home last evening when your wife got back?

Coke. I? No—yes, yes—no—not precisely.

Gilbert [*growing more indignant*]. Surely you must know whether you were at home or not when your wife returned?

Coke. No, I don't. And I very much object to be cross-questioned in this manner. I've told you all I know and—I—I withdraw from the whole business. Now, Dolly, are you ready?

Gilbert. No, stop! I want to get to the bottom of this and I will. [*Coming furiously to* LADY JESSICA.] Once more, will you give me your version of this cock-and-bull story?

[*Enter* FOOTMAN *at back*.

Footman [*announcing*]. Mr. Falkner!

Gilbert. Ah!

Sir Christopher. Nepean! Nepean! Control yourself!

[*Enter* FALKNER. *Exit* FOOTMAN.

Gilbert. Let me be, Deering. [*Going to* FALKNER.] You were at Shepperford last evening. My wife was there with you?

Falkner. I was at Shepperford last evening. Lady Jessica was there. She was dining with Lady Rosamund——

Lady Rosamund. No! No!

Gilbert. Lady Jessica was dining with Lady Rosamund?

Falkner. I understood her to say so, did I not, Lady Rosamund?

Lady Rosamund. No! No! It was Mrs. Coke who was dining with Lady Jessica.

Falkner. Then I misunderstood you. Does it matter?

Gilbert. Yes. [*Going to him*.] I want to know what the devil you were doing there?

Sir Christopher. Nepean! Nepean!

Gilbert. Do you hear? What the devil were you doing there? Will you tell me, or——

[*Trying to get at* FALKNER. SIR CHRISTOPHER *holds him back*.

Lady Jessica [*rises very quietly*]. Mr. Falkner, tell my husband the truth.

Falkner. But, Lady Jessica——

Lady Jessica. Yes, if you please—the truth, the whole truth, and nothing but the truth. Tell him all. I wish it.

Gilbert. You hear what she says. Now then, the truth—and be damned to you!

Falkner [*looks round, then after a pause, with great triumph*]. I love Lady Jessica with all my heart and soul! I asked her to come to me at Shepperford last evening. She came. Your brother saw us and left us. The next moment Lady Rosamund came, and she had scarcely gone when the maid came with your telegram and took Lady Jessica back to town. If you think there was anything more on your wife's side than a passing folly and amusement at my expense, you will wrong her. If you think there is anything less on my side than the deepest, deepest, deepest love and worship, you will wrong me. Understand this. She is guiltless. Be sure of that. And now you've got the truth, and be damned to *you*. [*Goes to door at back—turns.*] If you want me, you know where to find me. [*To* LADY JESSICA.] Lady Jessica, I am at your service—always!

[*Exit at back. They all look at each other.*

Sir Christopher [*very softly to himself*]. Possibility number two—with a vengeance!

CURTAIN.

(*A few hours from morning till evening pass between Acts III and IV.*)

ACT IV

SCENE: *Drawing-room in* SIR CHRISTOPHER'*s flat in Victoria Street. At back left a large recess, taking up half the stage. The right half is taken up by an inner room furnished as library and smoking-room. Curtains dividing library from drawing-room. Door up stage,* L. *A table down stage,* R. *The room is in great confusion, with portmanteau open, clothes, etc., scattered over the floor; articles which an officer going to Central Africa might want are lying around.*

Time: night, about half-past nine o'clock. SIR CHRISTOPHER *and* TAPLIN *are busy packing. Ring at door.*

Sir Christopher. See who it is, Taplin; and come back and finish packing the moment I am disengaged.

[*Exit* TAPLIN. *He re-enters in a few moments showing in* BEATRICE *in evening dress.* SIR CHRISTOPHER *goes to her, and shakes hands cordially. Exit* TAPLIN.

Beatrice. I was out dining when you called. But I got your message and I came on at once.

Sir Christopher. I couldn't wait. I had to come back and pack. [*Going on with his packing.*] I haven't one half-moment to spare.

Beatrice. When do you start?

Sir Christopher. To-morrow morning. It's very urgent. I've been at the War Office all the afternoon. You'll excuse my going on with this. I've three most important duties to fulfil to-night.

Beatrice. What are they?

Sir Christopher [*packing*]. I've got to pack. I've got to persuade Ned to come out there with me—if I can. And I've got [*Looking straight at her.*] to make you promise to be my wife when I come home again.

Beatrice. Oh, Kit, you know what I've told you so often!

Sir Christopher [*packing always*]. Yes, and you're telling it me again, and wasting my time when every moment is gold. Ah, dear, forgive me, you know I think you're worth the wooing. And you know I'm the man to woo you. And you know I'm ready to spend three, five, seven, fourteen or twenty-one years in winning you. But if you'd only say 'Yes' this minute, and let me pack and see Ned, you'd save me such a lot of trouble. And I'll do all the love-making when I come back.

Beatrice. Where is Ned?

Sir Christopher. Playing the fool for Lady Jessica. Poor fellow! There never was but one woman in this world that was worth playing the fool for, and I'm playing the fool for her. I've sent for Ned to come here. That's a digression. Come back to brass-tacks. You'll be my wife when I come home?

Beatrice. Let me think it over, Kit.

Sir Christopher. No. You've had plenty of time for that. I can't allow you to think it over any longer.

Beatrice. But it means so much to me. Let me write to you out there.

Sir Christopher [*very determinedly*]. No. [*Leaves his packing, takes out his watch.*] It's a little too bad of you when I'm so pressed. [*Comes to her.*] Now, I can only give you five minutes, and it must absolutely be fixed up in that time. [*Coming to her with great tenderness and passion.*] Come, my dear, dear chum, what makes you hesitate to give yourself to me? You want me to come well out of this, don't you?

Beatrice. You know I do!

Sir Christopher. Then you don't love your country if you won't have me. Once give me your promise, and it will give me the pluck of fifty men! Don't you know if I'm sure of you I shall carry everything before me?

Beatrice. Will you? Will you? But if you were to die——

Sir Christopher. I won't die if you're waiting to be my wife when I come home. And you will? You will? I won't hear anything but 'Yes'. You shan't move one inch till you've said 'Yes'. Now! say it! Say 'Yes!' Say 'Yes'—do you hear?

Beatrice [*throwing herself into his arms*]. Yes! Yes! Yes! Take me! Take me!

Sir Christopher [*kissing her very reverently*]. My wife when I come home again. [*A pause.*

Beatrice. You know, Kit, I can love very deeply.

Sir Christopher. And so you shall, when I come home again. And so will I when I come home again. [*Looking at his watch.*] A minute and a quarter! I must get on with my packing. Play something to me while I pack.

Beatrice [*going to piano. Stops*]. Kit, there will be some nursing and other woman's work out there?

Sir Christopher. Yes, I suppose——

Beatrice. I'll come with you.

Sir Christopher. Very well. How long will it take you to pack?

Beatrice. Half an hour.

Sir Christopher. All right! I must wait here for Ned. Come back and have some supper by-and-by?

Beatrice. Yes—in half an hour.

Sir Christopher. We might be married at Cairo—on our way out?

Beatrice. Just as you please.

Sir Christopher. Or before we start to-morrow morning?

Beatrice. Will there be time?

Sir Christopher. Oh, I'll find time for that! What do you say?

Beatrice. Just as you please.

Sir Christopher. Very well, I'll fix that up. [*Enter* TAPLIN.

Taplin. Mr. Gilbert Nepean is below, Sir Christopher.

Sir Christopher [*glancing at his packing*]. Show him up, Taplin. [*Exit* TAPLIN.

Sir Christopher [*holding* BEATRICE'*s hand*]. To-morrow morning, then?

Beatrice. Yes, I've given you some trouble to win me, Kit?

Sir Christopher. No more than you're worth.

Beatrice. I'll give you none now you have won me.

[*Enter* TAPLIN.

Taplin [*announcing*]. Mr. Gilbert Nepean.

[*Enter* GILBERT NEPEAN. *Exit* TAPLIN.

Beatrice. How d'ye do?

Gilbert. How d'ye do? [*Shaking hands*.

Beatrice. And good-bye. [*To* SIR CHRISTOPHER.] No, I won't have you come down all those stairs, indeed I won't. *Au revoir*. [*Exit*.

Gilbert. Excuse my coming at this hour.

Sir Christopher. I'm rather pressed. What can I do for you?

Gilbert. I've been down to Shepperford this afternoon. It seems you dined there last evening.

Sir Christopher. I did.

Gilbert. I want to get all the evidence.

Sir Christopher. What for?

Gilbert. To guide me in my future action. Deering, I trust you. Can I take that fellow's word that my wife is guiltless?

Sir Christopher. I'm sure you can.

Gilbert. How do you know?

Sir Christopher. Because he'd give his head to tell you that she is not.

Gilbert. Why?

Sir Christopher. It would give him the chance he is waiting for—to take her off your hands.

Gilbert. Take her off my hands—he's waiting for that?

Sir Christopher. Don't you see he is? And don't you see that you're doing your best to make him successful?

Gilbert. How?

Sir Christopher. Don't think when you've married a woman that you can sit down and neglect her. You can't. You've married one of the most charming women in London, and when a man has married a charming woman, if he doesn't continue to make love to her, some other man will, such are the sad ways of humankind. How have you treated Lady Jessica?

Gilbert. But do you suppose I will allow my wife to go out dining with other men?

Sir Christopher. The best way to avoid that is to take her out to dinner yourself—and to give her a good one. Have you dined to-night?

Gilbert. Dined? No! I can't dine till I know what to believe.

Sir Christopher. The question is, what do you want to believe? If you want to believe her innocent, take the facts as they stand. If you want to believe her guilty, continue to treat her as you are doing, and you'll very soon have plenty of proof. And let me tell you, nobody will pity you. Do you want to believe her innocent?

Gilbert. Of course I do.

Sir Christopher. Where is she?

Gilbert. I don't know—at home, I suppose.

Sir Christopher. Go home to her—don't say one word about what has happened, and invite her out to the very best dinner that London can provide.

Gilbert. But after she has acted as she has done?

Sir Christopher. My dear fellow, she's only a woman. I never met but one woman that was worth taking seriously. What are they? A kind of children, you know. Humour them, play with them, buy them the toys they cry for, but don't get angry with them. They're not worth it, except one! Now I must get on with my packing.

[SIR CHRISTOPHER *sets to work packing*. GILBERT *walks up and down the room, biting his nails, deliberating*. GILBERT, *after a moment or two, speaks*.

Gilbert. Perhaps you're right, Deering.

Sir Christopher. Oh, I know I am!

Gilbert. I'll go to her.

Sir Christopher [*busy packing*]. Make haste, or you may be too late.

[GILBERT *goes to door*. *At that moment enter* TAPLIN.

Taplin [*announcing*]. Mr. Falkner!

[*Enter* FALKNER. *Exit* TAPLIN. GILBERT *and* FALKNER *stand for a moment looking at each other*. *Exit* GILBERT; FALKNER *looks after him*.

Sir Christopher. Well?

Falkner [*very elated*]. You want to see me?

Sir Christopher. Yes. You seem excited.

Falkner. I've had some good news.

Sir Christopher. What?

Falkner. The best. She loves me.

Sir Christopher. You've seen her?

Falkner. No.

Sir Christopher. Written to her?

Falkner. Yes. I've just had this answer. [*Taking out letter*.

Sir Christopher. Where is she?

Falkner. Still at her sister's. [*Reading*.] 'I shall never forget the words you spoke this morning. You were right in saying that your love would not be wasted. I have learned at last what it is worth. You said you would be at my service always. Do not write again. Wait till you hear from me, and the moment I send for you, come to me.' I knew I should win her at last, and I shall!

Sir Christopher. *Après?*

Falkner. What does it matter? If I can persuade her I shall take her out to Africa with me.

Sir Christopher. Africa? Nonsense! There's only one woman in the world that's any use in that part of the globe, and I'm taking her out myself.

Falkner. Beatrice?

Sir Christopher. We are to be married to-morrow morning.

Falkner. I congratulate you—with all my heart.

[*Shaking hands warmly*.

Sir Christopher. Thank you. [*Pause*.] You'll come with us, Ned?

Falkner. If she will come too.

Sir Christopher. Oh, we can't have her.

Falkner. Why not?

Sir Christopher. In the first place, she'd be very much in the way. In the second place—it's best to be frank—Lady Deering will not recognize Lady Jessica.

Falkner. Very well. [*Turns on heel*.] Good-night, Kit!

[*Very curtly*.

Sir Christopher. No. [*Takes out watch. Glances at packing*.] Now, my dear old Ned, you're still up that everlasting *cul-de-sac*—playing the lover to a married woman, and I've got to drag you out of it.

Falkner. It's no use, Kit. My mind is made up. Let me go.

Sir Christopher. To the devil with Lady Jessica? No, I'm going to stop you.

Falkner. Ah, you'll stop me! How?

Sir Christopher. There was a time when one whisper would have done it. [*Whispers*.] Duty. [FALKNER *moves uneasily away. Follows him up*.] You know that you're the only man who can treat peaceably with the chiefs. You know that your going out may save hundreds, perhaps thousands, of lives.

Falkner. I'm not sure of that.

Sir Christopher. You're not sure? Well then, for Heaven's sake, try it—put it to the test. But you know there's every chance. You know the whole country is waiting for you to declare yourself. You know that you have a splendid chance of putting the crown on your life's work, and you know that if you don't seize it, it will be because you stay here skulking after her!

Falkner. Skulking!

Sir Christopher. What do you call it? What will everybody call it? Ned, you've faced the most horrible death day after day for months. You've done some of the bravest things out there that have been done by any Englishman in this generation; but if you turn tail now there's only one word will fit you to the end of your days, and that word is 'Coward'!

Falkner. Coward!

Sir Christopher. Coward! And there's only one epitaph to be written on you by-and-by—'Sold his honor, his fame, his country, his duty, his conscience, his all, for a petticoat!'

Falkner. Very well, then, when I die write that over me. I tell you this, Kit, if I can only win her—and I shall, I shall, I feel it—she'll leave that man and come to me; and then!—I don't care one snap of the fingers if Africa is swept bare of humanity from Cairo to Cape Town, and from Teneriffe to Zanzibar! Now argue with me after that!

Sir Christopher. Argue with you? Not I! But I wish to God there was some way of kidnapping fools into sense and reason, and locking them up there for the rest of their lives.

[*Enter* TAPLIN.

Taplin [*announcing*]. Lady Jessica Nepean, Lady Rosamund Tatton.

[*Enter* LADY JESSICA *and* LADY ROSAMUND. *Exit* TAPLIN. LADY JESSICA *shows delighted surprise at seeing* FALKNER, *goes to him cordially*. LADY ROSAMUND *tries to stop* LADY JESSICA *from going to* FALKNER.

Lady Jessica [*to* FALKNER]. I didn't expect to find you here.

Falkner. I am waiting for you.

Lady Rosamund [*interposing*]. No, Jess, no. Sir Christopher! [*Aside to him.*] Help me to get her away from him.

[LADY JESSICA *and* FALKNER *are talking vigorously together*.

Sir Christopher. One moment. Perhaps we may as well get this little matter fixed up here and now. [*Takes out watch, looking ruefully at his packing.*] Lady Jessica, may I ask what has happened since I left you this morning?

Lady Jessica. Nothing. My husband went away in a rage. I've stayed with Rosy all day.

Lady Rosamund. We've been talking it all over.

Lady Jessica. Oh, we've been talking it all over—[*Gesture.*] —and over and over, till I'm thoroughly—*seasick* of it!

Lady Rosamund. And so I persuaded her to come and talk it over with you.

Sir Christopher [*glancing at his packing*, to LADY JESSICA]. You can't arrive at a decision?

Lady Jessica. Oh, yes, I can; only Rosy won't let me act on it.

Lady Rosamund. I should think not.

Sir Christopher. What is your decision?

Lady Jessica. I don't mind for myself. I feel that everything is in a glorious muddle and I don't care how I get out of it, or whether I get out of it at all.

Sir Christopher. But on the whole the best way of getting out of it is to run away with Mr. Falkner?

Lady Jessica. Mr. Falkner has behaved splendidly to me.

Sir Christopher. He has! Dear old fellow! He's a brick! [*Giving* FALKNER *an affectionate little hug around the shoulders.*] And I'm quite sure that in proposing to ruin your reputation, and make you miserable for life, he is actuated by the very best intentions.

Lady Jessica. I don't care whether I'm happy or miserable for the rest of my life.

Sir Christopher. You don't care now, but you will to-morrow morning, and next week, and next year, and all the years after.

Lady Jessica. No, I shan't! I won't!

Falkner. I'll take care, Lady Jessica, that you never regret this step. Your mind is quite made up?

Lady Jessica. Yes, quite.

Falkner. Then no more need be said.

[*Offering arm. Gesture of despair from* LADY ROSAMUND. SIR CHRISTOPHER *soothes her.*

Sir Christopher. One moment, Ned! [*Takes out his watch, looks ruefully at his packing, half aside.*] Good lord! when shall I get on with my packing? [*Puts watch in pocket, faces* FALKNER *and* LADY JESSICA *very resolutely.*] Now! I've nothing to say in the abstract against running away with another man's wife! There may be planets where it is not only the highest ideal morality, but where it has the further advantage of being a practical way of carrying on society. But it has this one fatal defect in our country to-day—it won't work! You know what we English are, Ned. We're not a bit better than our neighbours, but, thank God! we do pretend we are, and we do make it hot for anybody who disturbs that holy pretence. And take my word for it, my dear Lady Jessica, my dear Ned, it won't work. You know it's not an original experiment you're making. It has been tried before. Have you ever known it to be successful? Lady Jessica, think of the brave pioneers who have gone before you in this enterprise. They've all perished, and their bones whiten the anti-matrimonial shore. Think of them! Charley Gray and Lady Rideout—flitting shabbily about the Continent at cheap *table d'hôtes* and gambling clubs, rubbing shoulders with all the blackguards and *demi-mondaines* of Europe. Poor old Fitz and his beauty—moping down at Farnhurst, cut by the county, with no single occupation except to nag and rag each other to pieces from morning to night. Billy Dover and Polly Atchison——

Lady Jessica [*indignant*]. Well!

Sir Christopher. ——cut in for fresh partners in three weeks. That old idiot, Sir Bonham Dancer—paid five thousand pounds damages for being saddled with the professional strong man's wife. George Nuneham and Mrs. Sandys—George is conducting a tramcar in New York, and Mrs. Sandys—Lady Jessica, you knew Mrs. Sandys, a delicate, sweet little creature, I've met her at your receptions—she drank herself to death, and died in a hospital. [LADY JESSICA *moves a little away from* FALKNER, *who pursues her*.] Not encouraging, is it? Marriage may be disagreeable, it may be unprofitable, it may be ridiculous; but it isn't as bad as that! And do you think the experiment is going to be successful in *your* case? Not a bit of it! [FALKNER *is going to speak*.] No, Ned, hear me out. [*Turns to* LADY JESSICA.] First of all there will be the shabby scandal and dirty business of the divorce court. You won't like that. It isn't nice! You won't like it. After the divorce court, what is Ned to do with you. Take you to Africa? I do implore you, if you hope for any happiness in that state to which it is pleasing Falkner and Providence to call you, I do implore you, don't go out to Africa with him. You'd never stand the climate and the hardships, and you'd bore each other to death in a week. But if you don't go out to Africa, what are you to do? Stay in England, in society? Everybody will cut you. Take a place in the country? Think of poor old Fitz down at Farnhurst! Go abroad? Think of Charley Gray and Lady Rideout. Take any of the other dozen alternatives and find yourself stranded in some shady hole or corner, with the one solitary hope and ambition of somehow wriggling back into respectability. That's your side of it, Lady Jessica. As for Ned here, what is to become of him? [*Angry gesture from* FALKNER.] Yes, Ned, I know you don't want to hear, but I'm going to finish. Turn away your head. This is for Lady Jessica. He's at the height of his career, with a great and honourable task in front of him. If you turn him aside you'll not only wreck and ruin your own life and reputation, but you'll wreck and ruin his. You won't! You won't! His interests, his duty, his honour all lie out there. If you care for him, don't keep him shuffling and malingering here. Send him out with me to finish his work like the good, splendid fellow he is. Set him free, Lady Jessica, and go back to your home. Your husband has been here. He's sorry for what is past, and he has promised to treat you more kindly in the future. He's waiting at home to take you out. You missed a very good dinner last night. Don't miss another to-night. I never saw a man in a better temper than your husband. Go to him, and do, once for all, have done with this other folly. Do believe me, my dear Ned, my dear Lady Jessica, before it is too late, do believe me, it won't work, it won't work, it won't work! [*A little pause.*

Lady Jessica. I think you're the most horrid man I ever met!

Sir Christopher. Because I've told you the truth.

Lady Jessica. Yes, that's the worst of it! It is the truth.

Lady Rosamund. It's exactly what I've been telling her all the afternoon.

Falkner. Lady Jessica, I want to speak to you alone.

Lady Jessica. What's the use? We've got to part.

Falkner. No! No!

Lady Jessica. Yes, my friend. I won't ruin your career. We've got to part: and the fewer words the better.

Falkner. I can't give you up.

Lady Jessica. You must! Perhaps it's best. You can always cherish your fancy portrait of me, and you'll never find out how very unlike me it is. And I shall read about you in the newspapers and be very proud—and—come along, Rosy!

[*Going off.* FALKNER *is going after her.*

Sir Christopher [*stopping him*]. It can answer no purpose, Ned.

Falkner. What the devil has it got to do with you? You've taken her from me. Leave her to me for a few minutes. Lady Jessica, I claim to speak to you alone.

Lady Jessica. It can only be to say 'Good-bye'.

Falkner. I'll never say it.

Lady Jessica. Then I must. Good-bye!

Falkner. No—say it to me alone.

Lady Jessica. It can only be that—no more——

Falkner. Say it to me alone. [*Pointing to curtains.*

Lady Jessica. Rosy, wait for me. I won't be a minute.

[*Going to* FALKNER. LADY ROSAMUND *makes a little movement to stop her*. SIR CHRISTOPHER *by a gesture silences* LADY ROSAMUND *and allows* LADY JESSICA *to pass through the curtains where* FALKNER *has preceded her*.

Sir Christopher [*to* LADY JESSICA]. Remember his future is at stake as well as yours. Only the one word.

Lady Jessica [*as she passes through curtains*]. Only the one word.

Sir Christopher [*to* LADY ROSAMUND]. You'll excuse my packing. I've not a moment to waste. [*Enter* TAPLIN.

Taplin. Mr. Gilbert Nepean, Sir Christopher; he says he must see you.

Sir Christopher. You didn't say Lady Jessica was here?

Taplin. No, Sir Christopher.

Sir Christopher. I'll come to him.

[*Exit* TAPLIN. LADY ROSAMUND *passes between the curtains*. SIR CHRISTOPHER *is going to door, meets* GILBERT NEPEAN *who enters very excitedly*.

Gilbert. Deering, she's not at home! She's not at her sister's. You don't think she has gone to that fellow?

Sir Christopher. Make yourself easy. She is coming back to you.

Gilbert. Where is she?

Sir Christopher. Will you let me take a message to her? May I tell her that for the future you will treat her with every kindness and consideration?

Gilbert. Yes—yes. Say—oh—tell her what you please. Say I know I've behaved like a bear. Tell her I'm sorry, and if she'll come home I'll do my best to make her happy in future.

Sir Christopher. And [*Taking out watch*.] it's rather too late for dinner, may I suggest an invitation to supper?

Gilbert. Yes—yes.

Sir Christopher. Lady Rosamund——

[*Peeping through curtains*. LADY ROSAMUND *enters*.

Gilbert. You——

[*Going towards curtains*. SIR CHRISTOPHER *intercepts him*.

Lady Rosamund. We stepped over to ask Sir Christopher's advice.

Sir Christopher. And, strange to say, they've taken it.

Gilbert [*trying to get to curtains*]. Where is Jessica?

Sir Christopher [*stopping him*]. No. I'm to take the message. Lady Jessica, your husband is waiting to take you to supper. [*To* GILBERT.] At the Savoy?

Gilbert. Anywhere—I don't mind.

Sir Christopher. At the Savoy. You've only just time to go home and dress.

[LADY JESSICA *draws curtains aside, turns and throws a last agonized adieu to* FALKNER *who stands speechless and helpless*. LADY JESSICA *then controls her features and comes out to* GILBERT. *The curtains close.*

Gilbert. Will you come home and dress and go to the Savoy to supper? [*Offering arm.*

Lady Jessica. Delighted. [*Taking his arm.*

Gilbert. And you, Rosy?

Lady Rosamund. I can't. [*Looking at watch.*] It's nearly ten o'clock! Good-night, Sir Christopher. Good-night, dearest. [*Kissing* LADY JESSICA.] Good-night, Gilbert. Take care of her, or you'll lose her. Excuse my running away, I must get back to my poor old Freddie.

[*Exit* LADY ROSAMUND. FALKNER'*s face appears through the curtains*. LADY JESSICA *sees it*.

Sir Christopher. Good-night, Lady Jessica, and good-bye!

Lady Jessica. Good-night, Sir Christopher, and—[*At* FALKNER.] one last 'Good-bye.'

[*She looks towards curtains as if about to break away from* GILBERT *and go to* FALKNER.

Sir Christopher. Good-night, Nepean!

Gilbert. Good-night, Deering.

Sir Christopher. Try and keep her. She's worth the keeping.

Gilbert. I'll try. What would you like for supper, Jess?

Lady Jessica. Could they give me some *sauce Arcadienne*?

[*Looking at* FALKNER. *Exeunt* LADY JESSICA *and* GILBERT. SIR CHRISTOPHER *goes towards door with them;* FALKNER *comes forward in great despair from curtains, throws himself into chair against table, buries his face in his hands*.

Sir Christopher [*goes to him very affectionately*]. Come! Come! My dear old Ned! This will never do! And all for a woman! They're not worth it. [*Softly*.] Except one! They're not worth it. Come, buckle on your courage! There's work in front of you, and fame, and honour! And I must take you out and bring you back with flying colours! Come! Come! My dear old fellow!

Falkner. Let me be for a minute, Kit. Let me be!

[*Enter* BEATRICE. SIR CHRISTOPHER *goes to her*.

Beatrice. What's the matter?

Sir Christopher. Hush! Poor old chap! He's hard hit! Everybody else seems to be making a great mess of their love affairs. We won't make a mess of ours?

Beatrice. No. [*Goes to* FALKNER.] You'll get over this, Ned? We'll help you. You'll get over it?

Falkner [*rising with great determination*]. Yes, I shall pull round. I'll try! I'll try! To-morrow, Kit? We start to-morrow?

Sir Christopher [*putting one arm around each affectionately*]. To-morrow! My wife! My friend! My two comrades!

CURTAIN.

THE MOLLUSC

HUBERT HENRY DAVIES

(1869–1917)

Born Woodley, Cheshire, and educated Manchester Grammar School. Worked in textile industry until 1893 when he went to the U.S.A. and was employed in a shipping office in San Francisco and elsewhere. His early play, *The Weldons*, was produced at the Empire Theatre, New York, in 1899. Returned to England in 1901. On the outbreak of war volunteered for hospital service in France and continued with these duties until his health broke down in 1916.

His plays included *Mrs. Gorringe's Necklace* (1903); *Cousin Kate* (1903); *Captain Drew on Leave* (1905); *The Mollusc* (1907); *Lady Epping's Lawsuit* (1908); *A Single Man* (1910); *Doormats* (1912); *Outcast* (1914).

THE MOLLUSC

A COMEDY IN THREE ACTS

by

Hubert Henry Davies

THE MOLLUSC

First produced at the Criterion Theatre, London, 15 *October* 1907, *with the following cast:*

Tom Kemp	Sir Charles Wyndham
Mr. Baxter	Mr. Sam Sothern
Mrs. Baxter	Miss Mary Moore
Miss Roberts	Miss Elaine Innescourt

THE MOLLUSC

ACT I

SCENE. MRS. BAXTER'*s sitting room. A pleasant, well-furnished room. French windows open to the garden, showing flower-beds in full bloom, it being summer time. As the audience looks at the stage there is a door on the left hand side at the back, and from the door a few stairs lead down to the room. Nearer and also on this side is a fireplace. Against this same wall is a flower pot on a table containing a plant in bloom. There is plenty of comfortable furniture about the room.*

It is evening after dinner. Lamps are lighted and the windows closed. MR. BAXTER, *a man about forty, is seated near a lamp reading* Scribner's Magazine. *The door opens and* MISS ROBERTS *comes in. She is a pretty, honest-looking English girl about twenty-four. She comes towards* MR. BAXTER.

Miss Roberts. Mr. Baxter—are you very busy?

Mr. Baxter. No, Miss Roberts.

Miss Roberts. I want to speak to you.

Mr. Baxter. Yes. Won't you sit down?

Miss Roberts. Thank you. [*She does so.*] We shall soon be beginning the summer holidays, and I think after this term you had better have another governess for the girls.

Mr. Baxter. You want to leave us?

Miss Roberts. I don't *want* to. I shall be very sorry indeed to go. You and Mrs. Baxter have always been so kind to me. You never treated me like a governess.

Mr. Baxter. You have been with us so long. We have come to look on you as one of the family.

Miss Roberts. I can't tell you how often I have felt grateful. I don't want to leave you at all, and it will almost break my heart to say good-bye to the children, but I *must* go.

Mr. Baxter [*anxiously*]. You are not going to be married?

Miss Roberts [*smiling*]. Oh, no—nothing so interesting—I'm sorry to say.

Mr. Baxter. Have you told my wife you think of leaving?

Miss Roberts [*slightly troubled*]. I began to tell Mrs. Baxter several times; at the beginning of the term and three or four times since—but she was always too busy or too tired to attend to me; each time she asked me to tell her some other time—until I don't quite know what to do. That's why I've come to *you.*

Mr. Baxter [*slightly disconcerted*]. But it's not *my* place to accept your notice.

Miss Roberts. I know—but if I might explain to *you*——

Mr. Baxter. Certainly.

Miss Roberts. It's this. I can't teach the girls anything more. Gladys is nearly twelve and Margery, though she is only nine, is very bright; she often asks me the most puzzling questions—and the truth is—I have not had a good enough education myself to take them any further.

Mr. Baxter. Aren't they rather young to go to school?

Miss Roberts. I think you need a governess with a college education, or, at any rate, someone who doesn't get all at sea in algebra and Latin.

Mr. Baxter. I should have thought you might read and study.

Miss Roberts. I used to think so—but I find I haven't the time.

Mr. Baxter [*thoughtfully*]. Too much is expected of you besides your duties as the children's governess. I've noticed that—but I don't quite see how I can interfere.

Miss Roberts. Please don't trouble, and don't think I'm complaining. I am always glad to be of use to Mrs. Baxter. It's not for my own sake I want a change; it's for the girls'. This is their most receptive age. What they are taught, and *how* they are taught *now*, will mean so much to them later on. I can't bear to think they may suffer all their lives through *my* ignorance.

Mr. Baxter [*politely*]. Oh—I'm sure——

Miss Roberts. It's very kind of you to say so—but I know what it is. I have suffered myself for want of a thorough education. Of course I had the ordinary kind, but I was never brought up to know or do anything special. I found myself at a great disadvantage when I had to turn to, and earn my own living.

Mr. Baxter. Gladys and Margery won't have to earn their own livings.

Miss Roberts. No one used to think that I should have to earn mine—till one day—I found myself alone and poor—after the shipwreck—when my father and mother—and my sister——

[*She turns her head away to hide her emotion from* MR. BAXTER.

Mr. Baxter [*kindly*]. We shall all miss you very much when you go. [*Leaning towards her.*] I shall miss you very much. [*She nods.*] We've had such good walks and talks and games of chess.

Miss Roberts [*brightly*]. Yes! I've enjoyed them all.

Mr. Baxter. I hope you have a nice place to go to.

Miss Roberts [*simply*]. I haven't any place to go to. I hoped Mrs. Baxter would help me find a new situation. I can't get one very well without her help, as this is the only place where I have ever been a governess, and after being here four years—[*Smiles.*] I must ask Mrs. Baxter to give me a good character.

Mr. Baxter [*meditatively*]. Four years—it doesn't seem like four years. I don't know though—in some ways it seems as if you had always been here. [*Looking at* MISS ROBERTS.] It is very honest of you to give up a good situation for a conscientious reason like this.

Miss Roberts. I don't know.

Mr. Baxter [*as an afterthought*]. I suppose it really is your reason for leaving?

Miss Roberts [*laughing*]. It's not very nice of you to compliment me on my honesty one minute and doubt it the next.

Mr. Baxter [*seriously*]. No, Miss Roberts, no. I don't doubt it. I was only wondering. I thought perhaps there might be some other reason why you find it difficult to live here—why you think it would be wiser not to stay——

Miss Roberts [*innocently*]. No——

Mr. Baxter. I see. Well—as I leave everything to do with the girls' education to Mrs. Baxter—perhaps you will tell *her.* Tell her what you have told *me.*

Miss Roberts. And—will you sit in the room?

Mr. Baxter. Why? What is going to be the difficulty?

Miss Roberts [*embarrassed*]. I can't explain very well to you —but if you wouldn't mind sitting in the room. [*She rises.*] I think I hear Mrs. Baxter coming.

[MRS. BAXTER *enters. She is a pretty woman about thirty-five, vague in her movements and manner of speaking. She comes down the room as she speaks.*

Mrs. Baxter. I've been wondering where *Scribner's Magazine* is.

Mr. Baxter. I have it. Have you been looking for it?

Mrs. Baxter. No—not looking—only wondering.

Mr. Baxter. Do you want it?

Mrs. Baxter [*pleasantly*]. Not if you are reading it—though I was just half-way through a story.

Mr. Baxter. Do take it.

Mrs. Baxter [*taking magazine*]. Don't you really want it?

[*She looks about, selecting the most comfortable chair.*

Mr. Baxter. It doesn't matter.

Mrs. Baxter [*smiling*]. Thank you. [*She sits.*] Oh, Miss Roberts, I wonder if you could get me the cushion out of that chair? [*Pointing to a chair near a window.*

Miss Roberts. Certainly.

[*She brings the cushion to* MRS. BAXTER *and places it behind her back.*

Mrs. Baxter [*settling herself*]. Thank you. Now I'm quite comfortable—unless I had a footstool.

Miss Roberts. A footstool?

[*She gets a footstool, brings it to* MRS. BAXTER *and places it under her feet.*

Mrs. Roberts [*without an attempt to move while* MISS ROBERTS *is doing this*]. Don't trouble, Miss Roberts, I didn't mean *you* to do that. *I* could have done it. [*When* MISS ROBERTS *has placed the footstool.*] Oh, how kind of you, but you ought not to wait on me like this. [*Smiles sweetly.*] The paper-knife please. Who knows where it is? [MISS ROBERTS *takes the paper-knife from* MR. BAXTER *and gives it to* MRS. BAXTER. *To* MR. BAXTER.] I didn't see you were using it, dear, or I wouldn't have asked for it. [*To* MISS ROBERTS.] As you're doing nothing, would you mind cutting some of these pages? I find there are still a few uncut. [*She gives the magazine and paper-knife to* MISS ROBERTS, *then says, smiling sweetly*] Your fingers are so much cleverer than mine. [MISS ROBERTS *begins cutting the magazine.* MRS. BAXTER *leans back comfortably in her chair and says to* MR. BAXTER.] Why don't you get something to do?

Mr. Baxter [*rising*]. I'm going to my room to have a smoke.

[MISS ROBERTS *puts the magazine on the table and goes to* MR. BAXTER *with the paper-knife in her hand.*

Miss Roberts. No, Mr. Baxter, please, I want you to help me out. I want you to stay while I tell Mrs. Baxter.

Mrs. Baxter. What's all this mystery? [*Seriously.*] Take care you don't snap that paper-knife in two, Miss Roberts.

[MR. BAXTER *sits down again.*

Miss Roberts [*to* MRS. BAXTER]. I was telling Mr. Baxter before you came into the room——

Mrs. Baxter [*holding out her hand*]. Give me the paper-knife.

[MISS ROBERTS *gives her the paper-knife, which she examines carefully.*

Miss Roberts. I told you at the beginning of term, and several times since——

Mrs. Baxter. It would have been a pity if that paper-knife had been snapped in two. [*She looks up pleasantly at* MISS ROBERTS.] Yes, Miss Roberts?

Miss Roberts. I was saying that I thought——

[MRS. BAXTER *drops the paper-knife accidentally on the floor.*

Mrs. Baxter. Oh, don't trouble to pick it up. [MISS ROBERTS *picks up the paper-knife and holds it in her hand.*] Oh, thank you, I didn't mean you to do that.

Miss Roberts. I was saying——

Mrs. Baxter. It isn't chipped, is it?

Miss Roberts [*nearly losing her temper*]. No.

[*She marches to the table and lays the paper-knife down.*

Mrs. Baxter. It would have been a pity if that paper-knife had been chipped.

Miss Roberts [*facing* MRS. BAXTER *with determination, and speaking fast and loud*]. I said I must leave at the end of the term.

Mrs. Baxter [*blandly*]. Aren't you happy with us, Miss Roberts?

Miss Roberts. Oh, yes, thank you. Very.

Mrs. Baxter. Really happy, I mean.

Mr. Baxter. Miss Roberts feels that Gladys and Margery are getting too old for her to teach.

Miss Roberts [*glancing her gratitude to* MR. BAXTER *for helping her*]. Yes. [*To* MRS. BAXTER.] I've taught them all I know; they need someone cleverer; there ought to be a change.

Mrs. Baxter. I think you do very nicely.

Miss Roberts. You don't know how ignorant I am.

Mrs. Baxter [*sweetly*]. You do yourself an injustice, dear Miss Roberts.

[MISS ROBERTS *turns appealingly to* MR. BAXTER.

Mr. Baxter. It was the algebra, I think you said, Miss Roberts, that you found so especially difficult.

Miss Roberts. Yes. I've no head for algebra.

Mrs. Baxter [*cheerfully*]. Neither have I, but I don't consider myself a less useful woman for that.

Miss Roberts. You're not a governess.

Mrs. Baxter. Who said I was? Don't let us wander from the point, Miss Roberts.

[MISS ROBERTS *looks appealingly at* MR. BAXTER *again*.

Mr. Baxter. The Latin——

Miss Roberts. Yes, I give myself a lesson at night to pass on to them in the morning—that's no way to do, just keeping a length ahead.

Mrs. Baxter. Perhaps Mr. Baxter will help you with the Latin. Ask him.

Miss Roberts. I'm afraid even that——

Mrs. Baxter. Mr. Baxter's a very good Latin scholar. [*Smiling at* MR. BAXTER.] Aren't you, dear?

Mr. Baxter [*reluctantly*]. I read Virgil at school. I haven't looked at him since. After a time one's Latin gets rusty.

Mrs. Baxter [*cheerfully*]. Rub it up. We might begin now, while you're doing nothing. Ask Miss Roberts to bring you the books.

Mr. Baxter. Oh, no, dear.

Mrs. Baxter. Why shouldn't we improve our minds?

[*She leans her head back on the cushions.*

Mr. Baxter. Not after dinner. [*To* MISS ROBERTS.] I don't see why you want to teach the girls Latin.

Miss Roberts. Mrs. Baxter said she wished them to have a smattering of the dead languages.

Mrs. Baxter [*complacently*]. I learnt Latin. I remember so well standing up in class and reciting 'Hic—haec—hoc'—accusative 'hinc—honc—huc.'

Mr. Baxter [*correcting her*]. Hoc.

Mrs. Baxter. Huc, my dear, in *my* book. And the ablative was hibus.

Mr. Baxter. Hibus!

[MR. BAXTER *and* MISS ROBERTS *both laugh*.

Mrs. Baxter [*making wild serious guesses*]. Hobibus—no, wait a minute—that's wrong—don't tell me. [*She closes her eyes and murmurs*.] Ablative—ho—hi—hu—no; it's gone. [*She opens her eyes and says cheerfully*.] Never mind. [*To* MISS ROBERTS.] What were we talking about?

Miss Roberts. *My ignorance* of Latin.

Mrs. Baxter. I can't say that *my knowledge* of it has ever been of much service to me. I think Mr. Baxter is quite right. Why teach the girls Latin? Suppose we drop it from the curriculum and take up something else on Latin mornings——

Miss Roberts [*earnestly to* MRS. BAXTER]. I wonder if you realize how much all this means to the girls? Their future is *so* important.

Mrs. Baxter [*with the idea of putting* MISS ROBERTS *in her place*]. Of course it is important, Miss Roberts. It is not necessary to tell a mother how important her girl's future is—but I don't suppose we need settle it this evening. [*Wishing to put an end to the discussion, she rises, walks towards the table on which stands the flower pot and says amiably*] How pretty these flowers look growing in this pot.

Miss Roberts. Would you rather we discussed it to-morrow, Mrs. Baxter?

Mrs. Baxter. To-morrow will be my brother's first day here, and he will have so much to tell me after his long absence. I don't think to-morrow would be a good day.

Miss Roberts. The day after?

Mrs. Baxter. Oh, really, Miss Roberts, I can't be pinned down like that. [*She moves towards* MR. BAXTER.] Aren't you and Miss Roberts going to play chess?

Mr. Baxter [*rising*]. Miss Roberts seems so anxious to have this thing decided. I told her that anything to do with the girls' education was left to *you.*

Mrs. Baxter. Need it be settled this minute?

Miss Roberts [*going towards* MRS. BAXTER]. I've tried so often to speak to you about it and something must be done.

Mrs. Baxter [*resigning herself*]. Or course—if you insist upon it—I'll do it now. I'll do anything any of you wish. [*She sits down.*] I've had a slight headache all day—it's rather worse since dinner; I really ought to be in in bed, but I wanted to be up when Tom comes. If I begin to discuss this now I shall be in no state to receive him—but, of course—if you insist——

Miss Roberts. I don't want to tire you.

Mrs. Baxter. It *would* tire me very much.

Miss Roberts. Then I suppose we must put it off again.

Mrs. Baxter [*smiling*]. I think that would be best. We must thrash it our properly—some day.

[*She leans back in her chair.*

Mr. Baxter [*to* MISS ROBERTS, *sighing*]. I suppose we may as well play chess?

Miss Roberts [*with resignation*]. I suppose so.

[MR. BAXTER *and* MISS ROBERTS *sit at a table and arrange the chess men.*

Mrs. Baxter [*finding her place in her magazine, begins to read. After a slight pause, she says*]. What an abominable light! I can't possibly see to read. I suppose, Miss Roberts, you couldn't possibly carry that lamp over to this table, could you? [MISS ROBERTS *makes a slight movement as though she would fetch the lamp.*] It's too heavy, isn't it?

Mr. Baxter. Much too heavy!

Mrs. Baxter. I thought so. I'm afraid I must strain my eyes. I can't bear to sit idle.

Mr. Baxter [*rising*]. I'll carry the lamp over.

Mrs. Baxter [*quickly*]. No, no! You'd spill it. Call one of the servants; wouldn't that be the simplest plan?

Mr. Baxter. The simplest plan would be for you to walk over to the lamp.

Mrs. Baxter. Certainly, dear, if it's too much trouble to call one of the servants. [*She rises and carries her magazine to a chair by the lamp.*] I wouldn't have said anything about the lamp if I'd thought it was going to be such a business to move it. [*She sits and turns over a page or two while* MR. BAXTER, *who has returned to his seat, and* MISS ROBERTS *continue arranging the chess board.* MRS. BAXTER *calls gaily over her shoulder*] Have you checkmated Mr. Baxter yet, Miss Roberts?

Miss Roberts. I haven't finished setting the board.

Mrs. Baxter. How slow you are. [*She turns a page or two idly, then says seriously to* MR. BAXTER] Dear, you'll be interested to know that I don't think the housemaid opposite is engaged to young Locker. I believe it's the cook.

Mr. Baxter. Very interesting, dear. [*To* MISS ROBERTS.] It's you to play.

[*After three moves of chess,* MRS. BAXTER *says.*

Mrs. Baxter. Oh, here's such a clever article on wasps. It seems that wasps—I'll read you what it says. [*She clears her throat.*] Wasps——

Mr. Baxter [*plaintively*]. Dulcie, dear, it's impossible for us to give our minds to the game if you read aloud.

Mrs. Baxter [*amiably*]. I'm so sorry, dear. I didn't mean to disturb you. I think you'd have found the article instructive. If you want to read it afterwards, it's page 32, if you can remember that. 'Wasps and all about them.' I'll dog-ear the page. Oh, I never looked out Tom's train. Miss Roberts, you'll find the time-table on the hall table. [MISS ROBERTS *rises and* MRS. BAXTER *goes on*] Or if it isn't there, it may be——

Miss Roberts [*quickly*]. I know where it is. [*She goes out.*

Mrs. Baxter. What has Miss Roberts been saying to you about leaving?

Mr. Baxter. Only what she said to you.

Mrs. Baxter. I hope she won't leave me before I get suited. I shall never find any one else to suit me. I don't know what I should do without Miss Roberts.

[MISS ROBERTS *re-enters with small time-table.*

Miss Roberts. Here it is!

Mrs. Baxter [*cheerfully*]. Thank you, Miss Roberts, but I've just remembered he isn't coming by train at all; he's coming in a motor car.

Mr. Baxter. All the way from London?

Mrs. Baxter. Yes, at least I think so. It's all in his letter—who knows what I did with Tom's letter?

Miss Roberts [*making a slight movement as if to go*]. Shall I go and look?

Mrs. Baxter. Hush. I'm trying to think where I put it. [*Staring in front of her.*] I had it in my hand before tea; I remember dropping it—I had it again after tea; I remember thinking it was another letter, but it wasn't. That's how I know. [*Then to the others.*] I'm surprised neither of you remembers where I put it.

Miss Roberts. I'd better go and look. [*She moves to go.*

Mr. Baxter. I think I hear a motor coming.

[*He goes and looks through the window.*

Mrs. Baxter [*in an injured tone*]. It's too late now, Miss Roberts. Mr. Baxter thinks he hears a motor coming.

Mr. Baxter. Yes, it is a car; I see the lamps. It must be Tom.

Mrs. Baxter [*smiling affectionately*]. Dear Tom, how nice it will be to see him again. [*To* MR. BAXTER.] Aren't you going to the hall to meet Tom?

Mr. Baxter. Yes, of course. [*He goes out.*

Mrs. Baxter. You've never seen my brother Tom.

Miss Roberts. No, I don't think he's been home since I came to you.

Mrs. Baxter. No, I was trying to count up this afternoon how many years it would be since Tom was home. I've forgotten again now, but I know I did it; you'd have been surprised.

Tom [*outside*]. Where is she?

[*Confused greetings between* TOM *and* MR. BAXTER *are heard.* MRS. BAXTER *rises smiling, and goes towards the stairs.*

Mrs. Baxter. That's Tom's voice.

[TOM KEMP *enters, followed by* MR. BAXTER. TOM *is a cheerful, genial, high-spirited man about forty-five; he comes downstairs, where* MRS. BAXTER *meets him. He takes her in both arms and kisses her on each cheek.*

Tom. Well, child, how are you—bless you.

Mrs. Baxter. Oh, Tom, it *is* nice to see you again.

Tom [*holding her off and looking at her*]. You look just the same.

Mrs. Baxter. So do you, Tom. I'm so glad you haven't grown fat.

Tom [*laughing*]. No chance to grow fat out there. Life is too strenuous. [*He turns to* MR. BAXTER *and gives him a slap on the back*.] Well, Dick, you old duffer.

Mrs. Baxter. Tom.

Tom [*turning to her*]. Yes.

Mrs. Baxter. I want to introduce you to Miss Roberts.

[TOM *gives* MISS ROBERTS *a friendly hand-shake.*

Tom. How d'you do, Miss Roberts?

Mrs. Baxter. Are you very tired, Tom?

Tom. Tired—no—never tired. [*Smiling at* MRS. BAXTER.] You look splendid. [*He holds her by her shoulders.*

Mrs. Baxter [*languidly*]. I'm pretty well.

Tom [*spinning* MRS. BAXTER *round*]. Never better.

Mrs. Baxter [*disliking such treatment*]. I'm pretty well.

[*She wriggles her shoulders and edges away.*

Mr. Baxter [*to* TOM]. Have you dined?

Tom. Magnificently. Soup—fish—chops—roast beef]—*To* MISS ROBERTS.] You must live in Colorado, Miss Roberts, if you want to relish roast beef.

Mr. Baxter. But you've driven from London since dinner. [*To* MRS. BAXTER.] I suppose we can raise him a supper?

Mrs. Baxter. If the things aren't all put away.

Tom [*turning from* MISS ROBERTS]. No—see here—hold on—I dined at the Inn.

Mrs. Baxter [*smiling graciously*]. Oh, I was just going to offer to go into the kitchen and cook you something myself. [*She sits.*

Tom. I was late getting in and I wasn't sure what time you dined. [*To* MR. BAXTER.] Now, Dick, tell me the family history.

Mr. Baxter [*scratching his head, says slowly*]. The family history?

Mrs. Baxter [*calling out suddenly*]. His! Ablative—his.

Tom. Eh?

Mrs. Baxter [*gravely to* TOM]. Hic—haec—hoc. His—his—his.

Tom [*looking blankly at* MISS ROBERTS *and* MR. BAXTER]. *What's* the matter?

Mrs. Baxter [*smiling as she explains*]. I was giving them a Latin lesson before you came.

Tom [*amused*]. You?

Mrs. Baxter [*conceitedly*]. I never think we were meant to spend all our time in frivolous conversation.

Tom [*amused, turning to* MR. BAXTER]. Dulcie, giving you a Latin lesson?

Mr. Baxter [*sadly*]. I suppose she really thinks she was by now.

Tom [*walking about*]. It's bully to be home again. I felt like a kid coming here—slipping along in the dark—with English trees and English hedges and English farms flitting by. No one awake but a few English cows, standing in the fields—up to their knees in mist. It looked like dreams—like that dream I sometimes have out there in Colorado. I dream I've just arrived in England—with no baggage and nothing on but my pyjamas.

Mrs. Baxter. What *is* he talking about?

Miss Roberts. I know what you mean!

Tom. I guess you've had that dream yourself. No, I mean you know how I must have felt.

Miss Roberts. Like a ghost revisiting its old haunts.

Tom [*sitting near* MISS ROBERTS]. Like the ghost of the boy I used to be. I thought you'd understand. You look as if you would.

Mrs. Baxter. I'm so glad you haven't married some nasty common person in America.

Tom [*chaffingly to her*]. I thought you would be. That's why I didn't do it. [*He talks to* MISS ROBERTS.

Mrs. Baxter [*laughing as she turns to say to* MR. BAXTER]. He's always so full of fun.

Miss Roberts. I once dreamed I was in Colorado—but it was only from one of those picture post-cards you sent. I have never travelled.

Tom. And how did Colorado look in your dreams?

Miss Roberts [*recalling her vision of Colorado*]. Forests——

Tom. That's right. Pine forests stretching away, away—down below there in the valley—a sea of tree-tops waving—waving—waving for miles.

Miss Roberts. And mountains.

Tom. Chains of mountains—great blue mountains streaked with snow—range beyond range. Oh! it's grand! it's great!

Miss Roberts. I should love to see it.

Mrs. Baxter. I think you are much better off where you are, Miss Roberts.

Tom. It's great, but it's not gentle like this. It doesn't make you want to cry. It only makes you want to say your prayers.

Mrs. Baxter [*laughing as she turns to* MR. BAXTER]. Isn't he droll?

Miss Roberts. I know what you mean.

Tom. *You* know. I thought *you'd* know. Here it comes so close to you; it's so cosy and personal. They've nothing like our orchards and lawns out there. [*Rising suddenly*.] I want to smell the garden. [*He goes to the window*.

Mr. Baxter. No! Tom, Tom!

Mrs. Baxter. Don't open the window; we shall all catch cold.

Tom [*laughing, as he comes towards* MRS. BAXTER]. Dear old Dulcie, same as ever.

Mrs. Baxter [*smiling*]. All of us are not accustomed to living in tents and huts and such places.

Tom. What are you going to do with me in the morning?

Mrs. Baxter. We might all take a little walk, if it's a nice day.

Tom. A little walk!

Mrs. Baxter. If we're not too tired after the excitement of your arrival.

Tom. What time's breakfast?

Mr. Baxter. Quarter to nine.

Mrs. Baxter. We drift down about half-past.

Tom. What! You've got an English garden, and it's summer time and you aren't all running about outside at six o'clock in the morning?

Miss Roberts. I am.

Tom. *You* are? Yes, I thought *you* would be. You and I must have a walk before breakfast to-morrow morning.

Miss Roberts [*smiling*]. Very well.

Mrs. Baxter. Don't overdo yourself, Miss Roberts, before

you begin the duties of the day. [*To* TOM.] Miss Roberts is the children's governess.

Tom. Oh? [*To* MISS ROBERTS.] Do you rap them over the knuckles? And stick them in the corner?

Miss Roberts [*answering him in the same spirit of raillery*]. Oh, yes—pinch them and slap them and box their ears.

Mrs. Baxter [*leaning forward in her chair, thinking this may be true*]. I hope you don't do anything of the sort, Miss Roberts.

Miss Roberts. Oh, no! not really, Mrs. Baxter. [*She rises.*] I think I'll say good-night.

Tom. Don't go to bed yet, Miss Roberts.

Mrs. Baxter [*yawning*]. It's about time we all went.

Tom [*to* MRS. BAXTER]. You, too?

Mrs. Baxter. What time is it?

Tom [*looking at his watch*]. Twenty minutes past ten.

Mrs. Baxter. How late.

Tom. Call that late?

Mrs. Baxter. Ten is our bedtime. [*She rises.*] Come along, Miss Roberts; we shan't be fit for anything in the morning if we don't bustle off to bed. [*She suppresses a yawn.*

Miss Roberts. Good-night, Mr. Baxter.

[*She shakes hands with him.*

Mr. Baxter. Good-night.

Miss Roberts [*shaking hands with* TOM]. Good-night.

Tom. Good-night, Miss Roberts; sleep well.

Miss Roberts. I always do.

Mrs. Baxter. Will you give me the magazine off the table, Miss Roberts, to take upstairs? [TOM *goes to the table and hands the magazine to* MISS ROBERTS, *who brings it to* MRS. BAXTER. *To* MISS ROBERTS.] You and I needn't say good-night. We shall meet on the landing.

[*Turns over the pages of the magazine.*

Miss Roberts. Good-night, everybody.

Tom [*following* MISS ROBERTS *to the foot of the stairs*]. Good-night, Miss Roberts. [MISS ROBERTS *goes out.*] Nice girl, Miss Roberts.

Mrs. Baxter. She suits me very well.

Mr. Baxter. She says she is going to leave.

Tom. Leave—Miss Roberts mustn't leave!

Mrs. Baxter. I don't think she meant it. Don't sit up too late, Tom, and don't hurry down in the morning. Would you like your breakfast in bed?

Tom [*laughing*]. In bed?

Mrs. Baxter. I thought you'd be so worn out after your journey.

Tom. Heavens, no, that's nothing. Good-night, little sister. [*He kisses her.*

Mrs. Baxter. Good-night, Tom. It's so nice to see you again. [*Then to* MR. BAXTER.] Try not to disturb me when you come up-stairs. [*Speaking through a yawn as she goes towards the door.*] Oh, dear, I'm so sleepy. [*She goes out.*

Mr. Baxter [*smiling at* TOM]. Well, Tom!

Tom [*smiling at* MR. BAXTER]. Well, Dick, how's everything? Business pretty good?

Mr. Baxter. So, so.

Tom. That's nice.

Mr. Baxter. I don't go into the city every day now, two or three times a week. I leave my partners to attend to things the rest of the time—they seem to get on just as well without me.

Tom. I dare say they would. [*Taking out his cigarette case.*] I suppose I may smoke?

Mr. Baxter [*doubtfully*]. Here?

Tom. Well, don't you smoke here?

Mr. Baxter. You may. She won't smell it in the morning. [TOM *laughs and takes out a cigarette.*] Tom, if ever you get married don't give in to your wife's weaknesses in the first few days of the honeymoon—you'll want to then, but don't. It becomes a habit. What's the use of saying that to you? I suppose you'll never marry now. [*He sits down.*

Tom [*quite annoyed*]. Why not? Why shouldn't I marry? I don't see why you think I shan't marry. How long has she been here? [*He lights a cigarette.*

Mr. Baxter. Who?

Tom. Miss Roberts.

Mr. Baxter. Oh!

Tom. Weren't we talking of Miss Roberts?

Mr. Baxter. No.

Tom. Oh, well, we are now.

Mr. Baxter. She's been here about four years. I'm so sorry she wants to leave. I don't want her to go at all.

Tom. Nor do I. Rather nice for you, Dick. A pretty wife and a pretty governess. [*He nudges him.*

Mr. Baxter. Tom, don't do that.

[*He defends himself by putting up his hands.*

Tom. Very well, I won't.

Mr. Baxter [*embarrassed and slightly annoyed*]. Why do you say that?

Tom. Only chaffing. [*He sees the chess-board.*] Who's been playing chess?

Mr. Baxter. Miss Roberts and I.

Tom. Does Miss Roberts play chess? I must get her to teach me—let me see if I can remember any of the moves. [*He sits by the table and moves the chess men about idly as he talks.*] She is far too good to be your governess.

Mr. Baxter [*enthusing*]. You've noticed what an unusual woman she is?

Tom. Charming!

Mr. Baxter. Isn't she?

Tom. And so pretty!

Mr. Baxter. Very pretty.

Tom. She'll make a good wife for some man.

Mr. Baxter [*reluctantly*]. I suppose so—some time.

Tom. I should make love to her if I lived in the same house.

Mr. Baxter. But if you were married?

Tom. I'm not!

Mr. Baxter [*slowly and thoughtfully*]. No.

[*There is a moment's pause.*

Tom. Let's change the subject, and talk about Miss Roberts. Tell me things about her.

Mr. Baxter. She's an orphan.

Tom. Poor girl.

Mr. Baxter. She's no near relations.

Tom. Lucky fellow.

Mr. Baxter. She's wonderful with the children.

Tom. Make a good mother.

Mr. Baxter. And so nice, so interesting, so good, such a companion. I can't find a single fault in her. She's a woman in a thousand, in a million.

Tom. I say, you'd better not let Dulcie hear you talk like that.

Mr. Baxter [*seriously*]. I don't. [TOM *laughs.*] I was only saying that to show you how well she suits us.

Tom. Of course.

Mr. Baxter. How well she suits Dulcie.

Tom. Oh, Dulcie, of course.

Mr. Baxter. I can't think what Dulcie will do without her; she's got so used to her. Miss Roberts waits on Dulcie hand and foot.

Tom [*indignantly*]. What a shame!

Mr. Baxter. Isn't it?

Tom. Why should Dulcie be waited on hand and foot?

Mr. Baxter. I don't know. She's so—well, not exactly ill.

Tom. Ill? She's as strong as a horse, always was.

Mr. Baxter. Yes, I can't remember when she had anything really the matter with her, but she always seems so tired—keeps wanting to lie down—she's not an invalid, she's a——

Tom. She's a mollusc.

Mr. Baxter. What's that?

Tom. Mollusca, subdivision of the animal kingdom.

Mr. Baxter. I know that.

Tom. I don't know if the Germans have remarked that mammalia display characteristics commonly assigned to mollusca. I suppose the scientific explanation is that a mollusc once married a mammal and their descendants are the human mollusc.

Mr. Baxter [*much puzzled*]. What *are* you talking about?

Tom. People who are like a mollusc of the sea, which clings to a rock and lets the tide flow over its head. People who spend all their energy and ingenuity in sticking instead of moving, in whom the instinct for what I call molluscry is as dominating as an inborn vice. And it is so catching. Why, one mollusc will infect a whole household. We all had it at home. Mother was quite a famous mollusc in her time. She was bedridden for fifteen years, and then, don't you remember, got up to Dulcie's wedding, to the amazement of everybody, and tripped down the aisle as lively as a kitten, and then went to bed again till she heard of something else she wanted to go to—a garden party or something. Father, he was a mollusc, too; he called it being a conservative; he might just as well have stayed in bed, too. Ada, Charlie, Emmeline, all of them were more or less mollusky, but Dulcibella was the queen. You won't often see such a fine healthy specimen of a mollusc as Dulcie. I'm a born mollusc.

Mr. Baxter [*surprised*]. You?

Tom. Yes, I'm energetic now, but only artificially energetic. I have to be on to myself all the time; make myself do things. That's why I chose the vigorous West, and wandered from camp to camp. I made a pile in Leadville. I gambled it all away. I made another in Cripple Creek. I gave it away to the poor. If I made another, I should chuck it away. Don't you see why? Give me a competence, nothing to work for, nothing to worry about from day to day—why, I should become as famous a mollusc as dear old mother was.

Mr. Baxter. Is molluscry the same as laziness?

Tom. No, not altogether. The lazy flow with the tide. The mollusc uses forces to resist pressure. It's amazing the amount of force a mollusc will use, to do nothing, when it would be so much easier to do something. It's no fool, you know, it's often the most artful creature, it wriggles and squirms, and even fights from the instinct not to advance. There are wonderful things about molluscry, things to make you shout with laughter, but it's sad enough, too—it can ruin a life so, not only the life of the mollusc, but all the lives in the house where it dwells.

Mr. Baxter. Is there no cure for molluscry?

Tom. Well, I should say once a mollusc always a mollusc. But it's like drink, or any other vice. If grappled with it can be kept under. If left to itself, it becomes incurable.

Mr. Baxter. Is Dulcie a very advanced case?

Tom. Oh, very!!!

Mr. Baxter. Oh!

Tom. But let us hope not incurable. You know better than I how far she has gone. Tell me.

Mr. Baxter [*seriously*]. She's certainly getting worse. For instance, I can remember the time when she would go to church twice a Sunday, walk there and back; now she drives once, and she keeps an extra cushion in the pew, sits down for the hymns and makes the girls find her places.

Tom. Do you ever tell her not to mollusc so much?

Mr. Baxter. I used to, but I've given up now.

Tom. Oh, you must never give up.

Mr. Baxter. The trouble is she thinks she's so very active.

Tom. Molluscs always think that.

Mr. Baxter. Dulcie thinks of something to be done and tells me to do it, and then, by some mental process, which I don't pretend to grasp, she thinks she's done it herself. D'you think she does that to humbug me?

Tom. I believe there's no dividing line between the conscious and subconscious thoughts of molluscs. She probably humbugs herself just as much as she humbugs you.

Mr. Baxter. Oh!

Tom. You must be firm with her. The next time she tells you to do a thing, tell her to do it herself.

Mr. Baxter. I tried that. The other day, for instance, she wanted me to set a mouse-trap in her dressing-room; well, I was very busy at the time, and I knew there were no mice there, so I refused. It meant getting the cheese and everything.

Tom [*trying not to appear amused*]. Of course. And what did she say when you refused to set the mouse-trap?

Mr. Baxter. She began to make me sorry for her; she has no end of ways of making me sorry for her, and I've a very tender heart; but that day I just didn't care. I had the devil in me, so I said—set it yourself.

Tom. Bravo.

Mr. Baxter. We got quite unpleasant over it.

Tom. And which of you set the mouse-trap in the end?

Mr. Baxter. Miss Roberts. [TOM *rises and moves away to hide his amusement from* MR. BAXTER.] It's always like that. She makes Miss Roberts do everything. For instance, Dulcie used to play chess with me of an evening, now she tells Miss Roberts to. She used to go walks with me, now she sends Miss Roberts. Dulcie was never energetic, but we used to have some good times together; now I can't get her to go anywhere or do anything.

Tom. Not very amusing for *you*.

Mr. Baxter. It does rather take the fun out of everything.

Tom. How did you come to let her get so bad?

Mr. Baxter [*simply*]. I fell in love with her. That put me at her mercy.

[*There is a moment's silence, then* TOM *says with decision.*

Tom. I must take her in hand.

Mr. Baxter. I wish you would.

Tom. I'll make her dance.

Mr. Baxter. Don't be hard on her.

Tom. No, but firm. I'll show her what firmness is. A brother is the best person in the world to undertake the education of a mollusc. His firmness will be tempered with affection, and his affection won't be undermined with sentimentality. I shall start in on Dulcie the first thing to-morrow morning.

Mr. Baxter. And now what do you say to getting our candles?

Tom [*following* MR. BAXTER *towards the stairs*]. Come along. I'm ready—must have a good night's rest if I'm to tackle Dulcie in the morning. I don't anticipate any trouble. A woman isn't difficult to deal with if you take her the right way. Leave her to me, old man. You just leave her to me! [*They go up the stairs as the curtain falls.*

ACT II

SCENE. *The same scene on the following morning. The French windows are wide open, displaying a view of the garden bathed in sunshine.*

MRS. BAXTER *is lounging in an armchair reading a novel.* TOM *enters with an enormous bunch of wild flowers, foxgloves, meadowsweet, etc.*

Tom. Look!

Mrs. Baxter. Oh, how pretty! We must put them in water. Where's Miss Roberts?

Tom. In the schoolroom. They are at their lessons.

Mrs. Baxter. Then we must wait. What a pity. I hope they won't die.

Tom. Is Miss Roberts the only person in this house who can put these flowers in water?

Mrs. Baxter. The servants are always busy in the morning.

Tom. Why can't *you* do it?

Mrs. Baxter. I have other things to do.

Tom. What?

Mrs. Baxter. Numerous things. Do you think a woman never has anything to do?

Tom [*coming to her and tapping her on the shoulder*]. Get up and do them yourself.

Mrs. Baxter [*amiably*]. While you sit still in this chair. All very fine!

Tom. I'll help you.

Mrs. Baxter [*rising lazily*]. Very well. Bring me the vases and some water. [*She smells the flowers.*

Tom. Vases. [*Pointing to two vases on the mantelpiece.*] Will these do?

Mrs. Baxter. Yes. Get those.

Tom [*pointing to another vase on the table*]. And *that*. *You* must get that one. We will divide the labour. [*He gets the two vases.* MRS. BAXTER *has not stirred.*] Where's yours?

Mrs. Baxter [*smiling pleasantly*]. I thought *you* were going to get the vases.

Tom. We were going to do this work between us. Get your vase.

Mrs. Baxter [*laughing*]. Oh, Tom—what a boy you are still.

Tom. Why should I get all the vases? [*Talking seriously to her.*] You know, Dulcie, you'd feel better if you ran about a little more.

Mrs. Baxter [*pleasantly*]. You'd save time, dear, if you'd run and get that vase yourself instead of standing there telling *me* to.

[TOM *puts the vases on the table. Then he goes and takes up the other vase.*

Tom. Oh, very well. It's not worth quarreling about.

Mrs. Baxter. No, don't let us quarrel the first morning you are home.

Tom [*bringing the vase and putting it before her*]. There!

Mrs. Baxter. Thank you, Tom. You'll find a tap in the wall outside the window and a little watering-can beside it.

Tom. I got the vases.

Mrs. Baxter. Please bring me the water, Tom. These poppies are beginning to droop already.

Tom. I *won't* get the water. You must get it yourself.

Mrs. Baxter [*smiling*]. Very well. Wait till I go upstairs and put on my hat.

Tom. To go just outside the window?

Mrs. Baxter. I can't go into the hot sun without a hat.

Tom. Rats!

Mrs. Baxter [*seriously*]. It's *not* rats. Dr. Ross said I must *never* go out in the sun without a hat.

Tom. That much won't hurt you.

Mrs. Baxter. I don't mind, of course. But *you* must take the consequences if I have a sunstroke. Dick will be furious when he hears I've been out in the sun without a hat. You wouldn't like me to make Dick furious, would you, Tom? [TOM *touches her and points to the window, then folds his arms. There is a slight pause while she waits for* TOM *to offer to go.*] If you think it's too much trouble to step outside the window I'll go all the way upstairs for my hat. I suppose all these pretty flowers will be quite dead by the time I come back.

Tom [*exasperated*]. Oh, very well, I'll get the water.

[*He goes out into the garden.*

Mrs. Baxter [*calling*]. Try not to scratch the can, and be sure you don't leave the tap to dribble.

Tom [*outside*]. Oh, the tap's all right.

[*She occupies herself by smelling the flowers.* TOM *re-enters almost immediately with a little watering-can.*

Tom. Here's the water.

Mrs. Baxter. Thank you, Tom. Work seems like play when we do it between us. Fill the vases.

Tom. I won't. [*He puts the can on the table.*

Mrs. Baxter. Well, wait while I go and get an apron.

Tom. You don't want an apron for that.

Mrs. Baxter. I'm not going to risk spilling the water all down this dress; I only put it on so as to look nice for you. I won't be a minute.

Tom. Stay where you are. [*Muttering to himself as he fills the vases.*] An apron to fill three vases. You might as well put on your boots or get an umbrella or a waterproof.

[*He is about to set the can on the floor.*

Mrs. Baxter [*quickly*]. Don't put it on the carpet. Put it on the gravel outside.

Tom. Put it on the gravel yourself.

[TOM *holds the can for her to take. She elaborately begins to wind a handkerchief round her right hand.*

Mrs. Baxter. It's no use both of us wetting our hands.

[TOM *grumbling goes to the window and pitches the can outside.*

Tom. Now I hope I've scratched the can, and I'm sorry I didn't leave the tap to dribble.

Mrs. Baxter. Naughty, naughty. Do you remember, Tom, when we were all at home together, you always did the flowers?

Tom. I'm not going to do them now.

Mrs. Baxter. You did them so tastefully. No one could do flowers like you. I remember Aunt Lizzie calling one day and saying if we hired a florist to arrange our flowers we couldn't have got prettier effects than you got.

Tom. Get on with those flowers.

Mrs. Baxter. When I did the flowers, Mamma used to say the drawing-room used to look like a rubbish heap.

Tom [*loudly*]. Get on with those flowers.

Mrs. Baxter. I should so like Miss Roberts to see the way you can arrange flowers.

Tom. Get on——

Mrs. Baxter [*wheedling him*]. Do arrange one vase—only one, just to show Miss Roberts.

Tom [*weakening*]. Well, only one. You must do the other two.

[*He begins to put the flowers in water.* MRS. BAXTER *watches him a moment, then she sinks into the handiest armchair.*

Mrs. Baxter [*after a slight pause*]. How well you do it.

Tom [*suddenly realizing the situation*]. No, no, I won't. [*He flings the flowers on the table.*] Oh, you are artful. You've done nothing; I've done everything; I got the flowers, the vases, the water—everything, and now not another stalk will I touch. I don't care if they die; their blood will be on your head, not mine.

[*He sits down and folds his arms. A pause.*

Mrs. Baxter [*serenely*]. If you won't talk, I may as well go on reading my novel. It's on the table beside you. Would you mind passing it?

Tom. Yes, I would.

Mrs. Baxter. Throw it.

Tom. I shan't.

Mrs. Baxter. I thought you'd cheer us up when you came home, but you just sit in my chair doing nothing.

Tom [*turning on her and saying gravely*]. Dulcie, it grieves me very much to see you such a mollusc.

Mrs. Baxter. What's a mollusc?

Tom. You are.

Mrs. Baxter [*puzzled*]. A mollusc? [*Gaily.*] Oh, I know, one of those pretty little creatures that live in the sea—or am I thinking of a sea anemone?

Tom. It's dreadful to see a strong healthy woman so idle.

Mrs. Baxter [*genuinely amazed*]. I idle? Oh, you're joking.

Tom. What are you doing but idling now? [*Approaching her and saying roughly.*] Get up, and do those flowers. Get out of that chair this minute.

Mrs. Baxter [*rising and smiling*]. I was only waiting for *you.* I thought we were going to do the flowers together.

Tom. No, we won't do them together; if we do them together I shall be doing them by myself before I know where I am. [*He sits again.*

Mrs. Baxter. I don't call that fair, to promise to help me with the flowers, and then just to sit and watch. I don't think Colorado is improving you. You've become so lazy and underhand.

Tom [*indignantly*]. What do you mean?

Mrs. Baxter. What I mean to say is, you undertook to help me with the flowers, and now you try to back out of it. Perhaps you call that sharp in America, but in England we should call it unsportsmanlike.

Tom [*picking up the flowers and throwing them down*

disgustedly]. Oh, why did I ever go and gather all this rubbish?

[MR. BAXTER *enters and comes down the stairs.*

Mr. Baxter. Half-past eleven, dear.

Mrs. Baxter. Thank you, dear.

Tom. Half-past eleven, dear—thank you, dear—what does that mean?

Mr. Baxter. Lunch.

Tom. Already?

Mr. Baxter. Not real lunch.

Mrs. Baxter. We always have cake and milk in the dining-room at half-past eleven. We think it breaks up the morning more. Aren't you coming?

Tom. Cake and milk at half-past eleven; what an idea! No, thank you.

Mrs. Baxter. I shall be glad of the chance to sit down. I've had a most exhausting morning. [*She goes out.*

Mr. Baxter. Have you been taking her in hand?

Tom [*pretending not to comprehend*]. I beg your pardon?

Mr. Baxter. You said you were going to take her in hand, first thing this morning.

Tom. Oh, yes, so I did. So I have done—in a way—not seriously, of course—not the first morning.

Mr. Baxter. You said you were going to show her what firmness was.

Tom. Well, so I did, but never having had any firmness from you, she doesn't know it when she sees it. [MR. BAXTER *is about to put some of the flowers in a vase.*] What are you doing?

Mr. Baxter. They're dying for want of water.

Tom. But I said she must put them in water herself.

Mr. Baxter. Oh, I see, discipline.

Tom. Exactly.

Mr. Baxter. What happened?

Tom [*pointing to the flowers*]. Can't you see what's happened? There they are still. [*Angrily.*] We've spent hours wrangling over those damned flowers. It may seem paltry to make such a fuss over anything so trivial, but it's the principle of the thing; if I give in at the start, I shall have to give in to the finish.

Mr. Baxter. Like me.

Tom. Yes, like you. When she comes back from the dining-room, I'll make her do those flowers herself, if I have to stand over her all the morning.

Mr. Baxter [*looking at* TOM *with admiration*]. That's the spirit. If only I had begun like that the very first morning of our honeymoon.

Tom [*with great determination*]. I'll stand no nonsense. She *shall* do the flowers herself. [MISS ROBERTS *enters.*

Miss Roberts. Mrs. Baxter sent me to do the flowers.

[*She comes immediately to the table and begins putting the flowers in water.* TOM *and* MR. BAXTER *look at each other.*

Tom [*to him*]. Shall I tell her not to?

Mr. Baxter. Then Dulcie will tell her she is to.

Tom. Then we shall have to humiliate Dulcie before Miss Roberts.

Mr. Baxter. Yes.

Tom. I don't want to do that.

Mr. Baxter. No.

Tom. I'm not giving in.

Mr. Baxter. No.

Tom. Don't gloat.

Mr. Baxter. I'm not gloating.

Tom. You are. You're gloating because I've had to give in the way *you* always do.

Miss Roberts [*to* MR. BAXTER]. The girls have been asking if I thought they could have a half-holiday in honour of their uncle's arrival.

Mr. Baxter. I don't see why not.

Miss Roberts. If you think they'd be in the way, I might take them off to the woods for the day.

Mr. Baxter. Yes.

Miss Roberts. I thought as it's so fine we might take our lunch with us, and have a picnic.

Tom. Why don't we all go a picnic?

Mr. Baxter. All who?

Tom. You and I and the girls and Miss Roberts and Dulcie.

Mr. Baxter. You'll never get Dulcie on a picnic, will he, Miss Roberts?

Tom. Why not?

Mr. Baxter. Too much exertion.

Miss Roberts [*still busy filling the vases*]. I think Mrs. Baxter would go if Mr. Kemp asked her.

[TOM *looks at* MR. BAXTER *as soon as* MISS ROBERTS *has spoken and* MR. BAXTER *looks dubious.*

Tom [*in a lower voice, to* MR. BAXTER]. I don't want Miss Roberts to think that I can't master Dulcie; besides, a picnic, the very thing to make her run about, but we must approach her tactfully and keep our tempers. I lost mine over the flowers, otherwise I've not the least doubt I could have made her do them; we must humour Dulcie and cajole her. Whisk her off to the woods in a whirl of gaiety; you go dancing into the dining-room like this. [*Assuming great jollity.*] We're all going off on a picnic.

Mr. Baxter. Oh, no.

Tom. Why not?

Mr. Baxter. It wouldn't be me.

Tom. Well, er—[*Glancing at* MISS ROBERTS.] go and—er—[*Glancing again at* MISS ROBERTS.] Oh, go and say whatever you like. But be jolly about it; full of the devil.

[*He takes* MR. BAXTER *by the arm and pushes him towards the stairs.*

Mr. Baxter [*imitating* TOM *as he goes*]. We're all going off on a picnic. [*He stops at the top of the stairs and says seriously.*] It wouldn't be me. [*He exits.*

Tom. So you're not one of the cake and milk brigade?

Miss Roberts. No.

Tom. I thought you wouldn't be.

Miss Roberts. Aren't you going to join them?

Tom. No, I don't want to eat cake in the middle of the morning. I'm like you. We seem to have a lot of habits in common.

Miss Roberts. Do you think so?

Tom. Don't you?

Miss Roberts. I haven't thought.

[*She takes a vase to the mantelpiece.* TOM *watches her and follows with the other vase.* MISS ROBERTS *takes the vase from* TOM *and puts it on the mantelpiece.*

Tom. Didn't we have a nice walk together?

Miss Roberts. Yes; don't you love being out in the early morning?

Tom. I'm up with the sun at home out West. I live out-of-doors out there.

Miss Roberts. How splendid!

Tom. You're the kind of girl for Colorado.

Miss Roberts [*pleased*]. Am I?

Tom. Can you ride?

Miss Roberts. Yes, but I don't get any opportunities now.

Tom. Got a good nerve?

Miss Roberts. I broke a colt once; he'd thrown three men, but he never threw me!

Tom [*smiling at her*]. Well done!

Miss Roberts. I didn't mean to boast, but I'd love to do it again.

Tom. I should love to see you mounted on a mustang, flying through our country.

Miss Roberts. With the tree-tops waving down in the valley, and the great blue mountains you told us about, stretching away—away——

Tom [*watching her with admiration*]. You certainly ought to come to Colorado.

Miss Roberts. Nothing so thrilling could happen to me.

[*She returns to the table and picks up the remaining flowers.*

Tom [*following her*]. Why? You've nothing to do but get on the boat and take the train from New York, and I'd meet you in Denver.

Miss Roberts [*laughing*]. It's so nice to have someone here to make us laugh.

Tom [*a little hurt*]. Oh, I was being serious.

Miss Roberts [*seriously*]. Do you really think Colorado would be a good place for a girl like me to go to? A governess!

Tom. Yes, yes, a girl who has to earn her own living has a better time of it out there than here, more independence, more chance, more life.

Miss Roberts [*thoughtfully*]. I do know an English lady in Colorado Springs, at least a great friend of mine does, and I'm sure I could get a letter to her.

Tom [*cheerfully*]. You don't want any letters of introduction; you've got me.

Miss Roberts [*smiling*]. Yes, but that is not quite the same thing.

Tom. No, I suppose not; no, I see: well, can't you write to your friend and tell her to send that letter on at once?

Miss Roberts [*amused*]. You talk as if it were all settled.

Tom. I wish it were.

Miss Roberts [*not noticing that he is flirting with her, she says thoughtfully*]. I wish I knew what to do about leaving here.

Tom. You told me you had already given my sister notice.

Miss Roberts. She won't take it.

Tom. She can't make you stay if you want to go.

Miss Roberts [*smiling, but serious*]. It's not as simple as that. After Mrs. Baxter has treated me so well, I should be making a poor return, if I left her before she found someone to take my place. On the other hand, my duty to the children is to leave them.

Tom. A real old-fashioned conscience.

Miss Roberts. One must think of the others.

Tom. It seems to me you're always doing that.

Miss Roberts. If you knew how I sometimes long to be free to do whatever I like just for one day. When I see other girls—girls who don't work for a living—enjoying themselves—it comes over me so dreadfully what I am missing. From the schoolroom window I can see the tennis club, and while I am giving Gladys and Margery their geography lesson, I hear them calling 'Play! Fifteen love!' and see the ball flying and the girls in their white dresses, talking to such nice-looking young men.

Tom. Um, yes. Don't *you* ever talk to any of those nice-looking young men?

Miss Roberts. Of course not.

Tom. How's that?

Miss Roberts. Governesses never do. We only pass them by as we walk out with the children, or see the backs of their heads in church. Or if we are introduced, as I was to one at the Rectory one day—the occasion is so unusual we feel quite strained and nervous—and can't appear at our best. So that they don't want to pursue the acquaintance even if they could.

Tom. You don't seem strained and nervous as you talk to me.

Miss Roberts [*innocently*]. You don't seem like the others. [*She meets his eyes—smiles at him and says.*] I must go back to the schoolroom. [*She rises.*

Tom [*rising and coming to* MISS ROBERTS]. Not yet. Don't go yet. I want you to stay here—talking to me. You are sure to hear my little nieces shrieking about in the garden when they have done their cake.

[MRS. BAXTER *enters, followed by* MR. BAXTER.

Mrs. Baxter. Oh, I hurried back to finish the flowers, but I see you have done them. Thank you.

Miss Roberts. You asked me to do them, Mrs. Baxter.

Mrs. Baxter [*smiling*]. Oh, no, Miss Roberts—I think you are mistaken. I only said they were there waiting to be done.

[*She sits in an armchair and begins to read a novel.*

Tom [*in an undertone to* MR. BAXTER]. Have you told her about the picnic?

Mr. Baxter. There was no suitable opportunity—so——

Tom. You're a coward! [*He pushes past him.* TOM *then motions to* MR. BAXTER *to speak to* MRS. BAXTER. *He refuses.* TOM, *assuming great cheerfulness, addresses* MRS. BAXTER.] We are all going off on a picnic.

Mrs. Baxter [*pleasantly*]. Oh.

Tom. Yes. We four and the girls. [*Whispering to* MR. BAXTER.] Back me up.

Mr. Baxter [*rubbing his hands together, and trying to assume jollity*]. Won't that be fun?

Mrs. Baxter [*brightly*]. I think it would be great fun——

Tom. Ah.

Mrs. Baxter. ——Some day.

Tom. Why not to-day?

Mrs. Baxter. Why to-day?

Tom [*at a loss for an answer, appeals to* MR. BAXTER *and* MISS ROBERTS]. Why to-day?

Miss Roberts. In honour of Mr. Kemp's arrival, and it's such a fine day—and——

Mrs. Baxter. You will find the girls in the schoolroom—dear.

Tom [*very jolly*]. Shall she go and get them ready?

Mrs. Baxter [*innocently*]. What for?

Tom. The picnic.

Mrs. Baxter. I thought it had been decided not to go to-day.

Mr. Baxter [*losing his temper*]. Oh, Dulcie—you know quite well——

Tom [*signing to* MR. BAXTER *to keep quiet*]. Sh! [*Turning to* MRS. BAXTER *and pretending to make a meek, heartfelt appeal.*] Please let us go to-day. It's in honour of my arrival. I shall be *so* hurt if I don't have a picnic in honour of my arrival.

Mrs. Baxter. Suppose it rains.

Tom [*at a loss for an answer, appealing to the others*]. Suppose it rains?

Miss Roberts [*at the window*]. I can't see a single cloud.

Mr. Baxter. The glass has gone up.

Tom. It won't rain if we take plenty of umbrellas and mackintoshes and our goloshes.

Mrs. Baxter. I think we are all too tired.

Tom [*scouting the idea*]. Too tired!

[MR. BAXTER *and* TOM *get together.*

Mrs. Baxter. I suppose it is the excitement of Tom's arrival which is making us feel so next-dayish.

Tom. Next-dayish!

Mrs. Baxter. You especially. You were very irritable over the flowers. You ought to go and lie down.

[*She takes up her novel and opens it as if she considered the argument over.* MISS ROBERTS *watches them anxiously.* MR. BAXTER *makes an emphatic gesture, expressing his strong feelings on the subject.*

Tom [*clutching his arm*]. We *must* keep our tempers. We *must* keep our tempers.

Mr. Baxter. Shall we poke fun at her?

Tom. No, no, we'll try a little coaxing first. [*He takes a chair, places it close beside* MRS. BAXTER *and sits. Smiling affectionately at* MRS. BAXTER.] Dear Dulcie.

Mrs. Baxter [*smiling affectionately at* TOM *and patting his knees*]. Dear Tom.

Tom. We shall have such a merry picnic.

Mrs. Baxter. It *would* have been nice, wouldn't it?

Tom. Under a canopy of green boughs with the sunbeams dropping patterns on the carpet of moss at our feet.

Mrs. Baxter. Spiders dropping on our hats.

Tom. Dear, interesting little creatures, and so industrious.

Mrs. Baxter. Ants up our arms.

Tom [*laughing*]. Lizards up our legs. Frogs in our food. Oh, we shall get back to Nature. [TOM *and* MRS. BAXTER *both laugh heartily, both in the greatest good-humour.* MR. BAXTER *and* MISS ROBERTS *also laugh.*] Then it's settled.

Mrs. Baxter. Yes, dear—it's settled.

Tom [*thinking he has won*]. Ah!

Mrs. Baxter. We'll all stay quietly at home.

[*She resumes the reading of her book.* TOM *is in dismay.*

Mr. Baxter. The girls will be greatly disappointed.

Tom [*with emotion*]. Poor girls! A day in the woods. [*With mock pathos.*] Think what that means to those poor girls.

Mrs. Baxter [*rising and saying seriously to* MISS ROBERTS]. Miss Roberts, you might go to the schoolroom and tell Gladys and Margery that Mamma says they may have a half-holiday and go for a picnic in the woods.

[TOM *winks at* MR. BAXTER. *The three look at each other agreeably surprised.*

Miss Roberts [*moving towards the stairs*]. Thank you. Thank you very much, Mrs. Baxter. I'll go and get them ready at once. [*She goes out.*

Tom. I knew we only had to appeal to her heart.

Mr. Baxter. We shall want twelve hard-boiled eggs.

Tom. And some ginger-beer.

Mr. Baxter. A ham.

Tom. A few prawns.

Mrs. Baxter [*looking out of the window to which she has strolled*]. I am glad Miss Roberts and the girls have got such a fine day for their picnic.

[TOM *and* MR. BAXTER *look at each other in dismay.*

Mr. Baxter [*after a pause*]. After leading us on to believe——

Tom [*in great good humour*]. Can't you see she's teasing us? [*Going to* MRS. BAXTER, *he playfully pinches her ear.*] Mischievous little puss!

Mrs. Baxter [*gravely to* MR. BAXTER]. Dear, I should like to speak to you.

Mr. Baxter. Shall we go to my room?

Mrs. Baxter. I don't see why we need trouble to walk across the hall. [*Glancing at* TOM.] We may get this room to ourselves by and by. [*She sits down.*

Tom [*cheerfully taking the hint*]. All right—all right. I'll go and make preparations for the picnic. Don't keep us waiting, Dulcie. Prawns—hams—ginger-beer——

[*He runs off.*

Mr. Baxter [*slightly peevish*]. I wish you would enter more into the spirit of the picnic. It would do you good to go to a picnic.

Mrs. Baxter. I don't like the way Tom is carrying on with Miss Roberts. Last evening they monopolized the conversation. This morning—a walk before breakfast. Just now—as soon as my back is turned—at it again. I don't like it—and it wouldn't do me any good at all to go to a picnic.

Mr. Baxter. Tom seems so set on our going.

Mrs. Baxter. Tom is set on making *me* go. Tom has taken upon himself to reform my character. He thinks I need stirring up.

Mr. Baxter [*embarrassed*]. What put such an idea as that into your head?

Mrs. Baxter [*looking him straight in the eye*]. The clumsy way you both go about it. [MR. BAXTER *looks exceedingly uncomfortable.*] . . . It wouldn't deceive any woman. It wouldn't suit me at all if Tom became interested in Miss Roberts. I could never find another Miss Roberts. She understands my ways so well, I couldn't possibly do without her; not that I'm thinking of myself; I'm thinking only of her good. It's not right for Tom to come here turning her head, and I don't suppose the climate of Colorado would suit her.

Mr. Baxter. I don't think we need worry yet. They only met yesterday.

Mrs. Baxter. That is so like you, dear—to sit and let everything slip past you like the—what was that funny animal Tom mentioned—the mollusc. I prefer to take action. We must speak to Tom.

Mr. Baxter. You'll only offend him if you say anything to him.

Mrs. Baxter. I've no intention of saying anything. I think it would come much better from you.

Mr. Baxter [*with determination*]. *I* shan't interfere.

Mrs. Baxter [*trying to work on his feelings*]. It's not often I ask you to do anything for me, and I'm not strong.

Mr. Baxter [*feeling uncomfortable*]. I shouldn't know what to say to Tom, or how to say it.

Mrs. Baxter [*approaching* MR. BAXTER]. You know the way men talk to each other. Go up to him and say, 'I say, old fellow, that little governess of ours. Hands off, damn it all.' [MRS. BAXTER *nudges* MR. BAXTER *in a masculine way.* MR. BAXTER *laughs and retreats a little.* MRS. BAXTER *is mightily offended.*] I don't consider that trifling with a young girl's affections is food for laughter.

Mr. Baxter [*trying to conceal his amusement*]. I think I'll go and join Tom.

Mrs. Baxter. Will you tell him we wish him to pay less [MISS ROBERTS *enters*] attention to——

[*She sees* MISS ROBERTS.

Mr. Baxter. We'll see. [*He goes out.*

Mrs. Baxter. I know what *that* means.

Miss Roberts [*coming to* MRS. BAXTER]. If you please, Mrs. Baxter, I'm having such trouble with Gladys and Margery. They want to go to the picnic in their Sunday hats, and I say they must go in their everyday ones.

Mrs. Baxter. If there's going to be any trouble about the matter, let them have their own way.

Miss Roberts. Thank you. [*She is going out.*

Mrs. Baxter. Oh, Miss Roberts. [MISS ROBERTS *stops.*] I want a word with you before you start off on your picnic. Sit down, dear. [MISS ROBERTS *sits down.*] You know how devoted I am to my brother Tom.

Miss Roberts [*with smiling enthusiasm*]. I don't wonder. He's delightful. So amusing, so easy to get on with.

Mrs. Baxter. Yes, but of course we all have our faults, and a man who gets on easily with one will get on easily with another. Always mistrust people who are easy to get on with.

Miss Roberts [*solemnly*]. Oh—do you mean he isn't quite honest?

Mrs. Baxter [*indignantly*]. Nothing of the sort. You mustn't twist my meanings in that manner. You might get me into great trouble.

Miss Roberts. I'm so sorry, but I thought you were warning me against him,

Mrs. Baxter [*confused*]. Yes—no—yes—and no. [*Recovering herself.*] I am sure you will take what I'm going to say as I mean it, because—[*Smiles at her.*] I am so fond of you. Ever since you came to us I have wished to make you one of the family. When I say one of the family, I mean in the sense of taking your meals with us. Mr. Baxter and the girls and I are so much attached to you. We should like to keep you with us always.

Miss Roberts. I *must* leave at the end of the term.

Mrs. Baxter. We won't go into all that now.

Miss Roberts. But——

Mrs. Baxter [*smiling and raising her hand in protestation, says politely*]. Try not to interrupt. [*Seriously.*] I should say that a man of Tom's age who has never married would be a confirmed bachelor. He might amuse himself here and there with a pretty girl, but he would never think of any woman seriously.

Miss Roberts [*embarrassed*]. I can't think why you are saying this to me.

Mrs. Baxter [*plunging at last into her subject*]. To speak quite frankly—as a sister—I find your attitude towards my brother Tom a trifle too encouraging. Last evening, for instance, you monopolized a good deal of the conversation—and this morning you took a walk with him before breakfast—and altogether—[*very sweetly*] it looks just a little bit as if you were trying to flirt—doesn't it?

Miss Roberts [*with suppressed rage*]. I'm not a flirt!

Mrs. Baxter. I didn't say you were—I said——

Miss Roberts. I'm *not* a flirt—I'm *not*.

Mrs. Baxter. We'll say no more about it. It was very hard for me to have to speak to you. You have no idea how difficult I found it.

Miss Roberts. Mrs. Baxter, you have often been very kind to me, and I don't want to forget it—but I'd rather not be treated as one of the family any more. I want my meals in the schoolroom, and I mustn't be expected to sit in the drawing-room.

Mrs. Baxter. Upsetting the whole machinery of the house.

Miss Roberts. I can't go on meeting him at table and everywhere.

Mrs. Baxter. I don't see why not.

Miss Roberts. I shouldn't know where to look or what to say.

Mrs. Baxter. Look out of the window and converse on inanimate objects.

Miss Roberts [*mumbles angrily*]. I will not look out of the window and converse on inanimate objects.

Mrs. Baxter [*putting up a warning hand*]. Hush, hush, hush!

Miss Roberts. Please understand I won't be one of the family, and I won't go to the picnic.

[*She goes hurriedly into the garden.*

Mrs. Baxter. Oh, oh, naughty girl!

[TOM *and* MR. BAXTER *enter.*

Tom. Cook thinks the large basket and the small hamper will suffice. She *said* suffice.

Mrs. Baxter. I'm very sorry, Tom, but it is out of the question for us to go to a picnic to-day.

Mr. Baxter. Oh, Dulcie.

Tom. Too late to back out.

Mrs. Baxter. *I* haven't backed out. It's Miss Roberts.

Tom. We can't have a picnic without Miss Roberts.

Mr. Baxter. What's the matter with her?

Mrs. Baxter [*solemnly*]. Miss Roberts and I have had *words.* [TOM *whistles quietly.*

Mr. Baxter. What about?

Mrs. Baxter. Never you mind.

Tom. Oh, it can't be such a very dreadful quarrel between two such nice sensible women. I guess you were both in the right. [*To* MR. BAXTER.] I guess they were both in the wrong. [*Taking* MRS. BAXTER *by the arm and cajoling her.*] Come along. Tell us all about it.

Mrs. Baxter [*withdrawing her arm*]. No, Tom, I can't.

Tom. Then suppose I go to Miss Roberts and get her version.

Mrs. Baxter [*in dismay*]. Oh, no, that wouldn't do at all.

Tom. I only want to make peace. [*To* MR. BAXTER.] Wouldn't it be better if they told me and let me make it up for them?

Mr. Baxter. Why you?

Tom. A disinterested person.

Mrs. Baxter. But you are not.

[*Putting her hand over her mouth.*

Tom [*turns quickly to* MRS. BAXTER]. What?

Mrs. Baxter. I'm not going to say any more.

[*She sits down.*

Tom [*seriously*]. You *must*. If your quarrel concerns *me*, I have a right to know all about it.

Mr. Baxter [*motioning to* MRS. BAXTER]. You are only putting ideas into their heads.

Tom [*turning sharply on* MR. BAXTER]. Putting what ideas into their heads? [*It dawns upon him what the subject of the quarrel has been.*] Oh! [*To* MRS. BAXTER.] You don't mean to say you spoke to her about— [*He stops embarrassed.*] What have you said to her?

Mrs. Baxter. I decline to tell you.

Tom. Then I shall ask *her*. [*Going.*

Mrs. Baxter [*quickly*]. No, no, Tom. I—prefer to tell you myself. I spoke very nicely to her. I forget how the conversation arose, but I think I did say something to the effect that young girls ought to be careful not to have their heads turned by men years older than themselves. [*She looks significantly at* TOM, *who turns away angrily.*] Instead of thanking me, she stamped and stormed and was very rude to me—very rude. I simply said [*in a very gentle tone*] Oh, Miss Roberts! [*Rousing herself as she describes* MISS ROBERTS' *share in the scene.*] But she went on shouting, 'I won't go a picnic, I won't go a picnic!' and bounced out of the room. It just shows you how you can be deceived in people, and I have been so good to that girl.

Tom [*coming towards* MRS. BAXTER]. I'm very angry—with you—very angry.

Mrs. Baxter. I simply gave her a word of counsel which she chose to take in the wrong spirit.

Tom. You interfered. You meddled. It's too bad of you, Dulcie. It's unbearable.

Mr. Baxter [*watching* TOM]. The way you take it anyone would think you had fallen in love with our Miss Roberts since yesterday.

Mrs. Baxter. Yes—wouldn't any one?

Tom [*addressing them both*]. Would there be anything so strange in that? Perhaps I have, I don't know—perhaps as you imply I'm old enough to know better. I don't know. All I know is, I think her the most charming girl I ever met.

I've not had time to realize what this is; one must wait and see; give the seed a chance to produce a flower—not stamp on it. [*To* MRS. BAXTER.] You might have left things alone, when all was going so pleasantly. I was just beginning to think—beginning to feel—wondering if perhaps—later on—— Now you've spoilt everything.

Mrs. Baxter [*tearful and angry*]. I won't stay here to be abused. [*Going to the window.*] You've done nothing else all morning. I'm tired of being taken in hand and improved. No one likes to be improved.

[MRS. BAXTER *goes out through the window.*

Tom. I don't want to be unkind to her—but you know how a man feels. He doesn't like any one meddling when he's just beginning to——

Mr. Baxter [*showing embarrassment all through the early part of this scene.*] I agree with Dulcie. It would not be suitable for you to marry Miss Roberts.

Tom. She's as good as any of us.

Mr. Baxter [*hesitatingly*]. It's not that. Miss Roberts from her position here—alone in the world but for us—and having lived here so long—is—in a sense—under my protection.

Tom. I don't see that, but go on.

Mr. Baxter. I feel—in a certain degree—responsible for her. I think it is my duty—and Dulcie's duty—to try and stop her making what we both feel would be an unsuitable marriage.

Tom. It's a little early to speak of our marriage, but why should it be unsuitable?

Mr. Baxter. We don't wish her to marry you.

Tom. Why? Give me a reason.

Mr. Baxter. Why do you press me for a reason?

Tom. Because this is very important to me. You have constituted yourself her guardian. I have no objection to *that*, but I want to get at your objection to me as a husband to her. I'm in a position to marry. I'd treat her well if she'd have me. We'd be as happy as the day is long in our little home in the mountains——

Mr. Baxter [*unable to restrain himself*]. You married to her? Oh, no—oh, no, I couldn't bear that.

[*He sinks into a chair and leans his head on his hands.*

Tom [*completely taken aback*]. Dick, think what you're saying.

Mr. Baxter. I couldn't help it. You made me say it—talking of taking her away—right away where I shall never see her again. I couldn't stand my life here without her.

Tom. Dick, Dick!

Mr. Baxter. She knows nothing of how I feel; it's only this moment I realized myself what she is to me.

Tom. Then from this moment you ought never to see her again.

Mr. Baxter. That's impossible.

Tom. Think of Dulcie, and the girl herself; she can't live in the house with you both now.

Mr. Baxter. She's lived with us for four years, and no one has ever seen any harm in it; nothing is changed.

Tom. From the moment you realized what she is to you, everything is changed.

Mr. Baxter. There has never been anything to criticize in my conduct to Miss Roberts, and there won't be anything.

Tom. She is the object of an affection, which you, as a married man, have no right to feel for her. I don't blame you entirely. I blame Dulcie for throwing you so much together. I remember all you said last evening. Dulcie used to play chess with you, now she tells Miss Roberts to; Dulcie used to go for long walks with you, now she sends Miss Roberts. Out of your forced companionship has sprung this, which she ought to have foreseen.

Mr. Baxter. Nothing is confessed or understood; I don't see that Miss Roberts is in any danger.

Tom. She is alone. She has no confidant, no friend, no outlet for the natural desires of youth, for love, for someone to love. She finds you sympathetic—you know the rest.

Mr. Baxter. It is jealousy that is at the bottom of your morality.

Tom. It won't do, Dick. It's a most awful state of things.

Mr. Baxter. If you think that, I wonder you stay here.

Tom. Very well, if you mean I ought to clear out.

[*He goes towards the door.*

Mr. Baxter [*following after* TOM]. No, Tom. Look here, I didn't mean that; but you see, you and I can't discuss this without losing our tempers, so if your visit to us is to continue mutually pleasant, as I hope it will, we'd better avoid the topic in future.

Tom. Then you mean to keep Miss Roberts here indefinitely—compromised?

Mr. Baxter. It's no use going over the ground; we don't see things from the same point of view, so don't let us go on discussing. [*He goes up the stairs and then turns to* TOM.] Tom, you might trust me.

[MR. BAXTER *goes out.* TOM *remains in deep thought, then suddenly makes a determined movement, then stops and sighs.* MISS ROBERTS *enters from the garden. She hesitates timidly when she sees him.*

Miss Roberts. Mrs. Baxter sent me to get her magazine.

Tom. Where is my sister?

Miss Roberts. Sitting in the garden.

[*She takes up the magazine and is going out again.*

Tom. I—[MISS ROBERTS *stops.*] I—want to tell you something.

Miss Roberts. I can't stay.

Tom. I ask you as a great favour to me to hear me.

Miss Roberts. I ought not to stay.

Tom. I didn't think you'd refuse me when I asked you like that.

Miss Roberts [*hesitating*]. I can't stay long.

Tom. Won't you sit down while I tell you? [*He indicates a chair.* MISS ROBERTS *comes to the chair and sits.*] I want to tell you about myself, and my life in Colorado.

Miss Roberts [*nervously*]. I don't think I can stay if it's just to talk and hear stories of Colorado.

Tom [*smiling*]. Did you have enough of my stories this morning?

Miss Roberts. Oh, no, I was quite interested in what you said, but I——

Tom. You *were* interested. I knew it by your eyes. Why, you even thought you'd like to go there yourself some time.

Miss Roberts. I've changed my mind. I've quite given up that idea now.

Tom. You'd like it out there. I'm sure you would; it's a friendly country; no one cares who you are, but only what you are, so you soon make friends. That's right. That gives every one a chance, and it's good in this way, it makes a man depend on himself, it teaches him to think clearly and decide quickly; in fact he has to keep wide awake if he wants to succeed. That's the kind of training I've had. I've been from mining camp to mining camp—I've tried my luck in half the camps in California and Colorado. Sometimes it was good, sometimes bad, but take it altogether, I've done well. [*Making the next point clearly and delicately.*] I've got something saved up, and I can always make good money, anywhere west of Chicago.

[*Laughing*.] Now I'm talking like a true American; they always begin by telling you how much they've got. You'll forgive me, won't you? It's force of habit. Now what was I saying? [*Seriously*.] We learn to decide quickly in everything; you find me somewhat abrupt; it's only that. I make up my mind all at once, and once it's made up, that's finished—I don't change. [*Hesitating slightly*.] The first time I saw you I made up my mind—I said that's the girl for me, that's the girl I want for my wife. [*Leans towards her*.] Will you be my wife?

Miss Roberts [*rising and very much moved and distressed*]. Oh, no, I can't. I didn't know what was coming, or I wouldn't have listened, I wouldn't indeed.

Tom [*following her*]. I've been too abrupt. I warned you I was like that; I make up my mind I want something, and the next thing is, I go straight away and ask for it. That's too quick for you. You want time to think—well, take time to think it over. [MISS ROBERTS *turns to him quickly*.] Don't tell me yet; there's no hurry. I'm not going back for a month or two.

Miss Roberts. I'm very much obliged to you for asking me to marry you, but I can't.

Tom. Never?

Miss Roberts. No, never! I don't think so.

Tom. Eh? That sounds like hope.

Miss Roberts [*quickly*]. I didn't mean it to sound like hope.

Tom. It didn't seem that way last evening when we were talking about the forests and the mountains, and I was telling you how it felt to be back—or this morning when we were getting flowers, or afterwards when we sat here, while they were eating their cake and milk; it seemed to me we were getting on famously.

Miss Roberts [*appealingly*]. Oh, please don't go on. I can't bear it. You only distress me. [*She sobs.*

Tom. Oh! [*Pausing and looking at her, he sees that she means it and is really distressed.*] I'm sorry.

[*He goes out abruptly.* MISS ROBERTS *is weeping bitterly.* MR. BAXTER *enters. He comes downstairs towards her and looks down at her with affectionate concern.* MISS ROBERTS *does not notice his presence till he speaks.*

Mr. Baxter. What is it?

Miss Roberts [*trying to control her sobs*]. Nothing.

Mr. Baxter. You are in trouble. You are in great trouble—can't you tell me—can't I do anything?

Miss Roberts. No.

Mr. Baxter. Wouldn't it do you good to tell somebody? Don't you want someone to tell it all to?

Miss Roberts. I want—— [*She falters.*

Mr. Baxter. What is it you want?

Miss Roberts. I think I want a mother.

[*The effort of saying this brings on her tears afresh; she stands weeping bitterly.* MR. BAXTER *puts his arm about her and draws her gently to him. She yields herself naturally and sobs on his shoulder.* MR. BAXTER *murmurs and soothes her.*

Mr. Baxter. Poor child! Poor child! [*While they are in this sentimental position* TOM *and* MRS. BAXTER *appear at the window. They see* MR. BAXTER *and* MISS ROBERTS *but are unseen by them.* MISS ROBERTS *disengages herself from* MR. BAXTER *and goes out sobbing without perceiving* TOM *and* MRS. BAXTER. MR. BAXTER *watches* MISS ROBERTS *off, then turns and sees* MRS. BAXTER *for the first time; he becomes very embarrassed under her steady disapproving eyes. To* MRS. BAXTER.] Do you want me to explain?

Mrs. Baxter [*coldly*]. Not at present, thank you, Richard.

Mr. Baxter. I was only——

Mrs. Baxter. Not now. I prefer to consider my position carefully before expressing my astonishment and indignation.

Mr. Baxter. Well, if you won't let me explain——

[*He turns to the window and sees* TOM. *He looks appealingly at him.* TOM *ignores him and walks past him.* MR. BAXTER *shrugs his shoulders and goes out through the window.*

Mrs. Baxter. I don't know which of them I feel angriest with.

Tom. Dick, of course.

Mrs. Baxter [*tearfully*]. For thirteen years no man has ever kissed me—except you—Dick—and Uncle Joe—and Dick's brother—and old Mr. Redmayne—and the Dean when he came back from the Holy Land. [*Working herself into a rage.*] I'll never speak to Dick again. I'll bundle Miss Roberts out of the house at once.

Tom. Do it discreetly. Send her away certainly but don't do anything hastily.

Mrs. Baxter. I'm not the woman to put up with that sort of thing.

Tom [*persuasively*]. Don't be hard on her; don't be turning her into the street; make it look as if she were going on a holiday. Pack her off somewhere with the children for a change of air, this afternoon.

Mrs. Baxter. It's most inconvenient; everything will be upside down. [*Calming herself, she sits in an armchair.*] You're right. I mustn't be too hasty; better wait a few days, till the end of the term, or even till after we come home from the seaside, then pack her off. [*Pause.*] Unless it blows over.

Tom [*astonished and going to her quickly*]. Blows over! It won't blow over while *she's* in the house. [*Very seriously.*] You're up against a serious crisis. Take warning from what you saw and save your home from ruin. [MRS. BAXTER, *awed and impressed by this, listens attentively.*] You've grown so dependent on Miss Roberts, you've almost let her slip into your place; if you want to keep Dick, you must begin an altogether different life, not to-morrow—— [MRS. BAXTER *shakes her head.*] Not next week——[MRS. BAXTER *shakes her head again.*] Now! [MRS. BAXTER'*s face betrays her discontent at the unattractive prospect he offers her.*] *You* be his companion, *you* play chess with him, *you* go walks with him, sit up with him in the evenings, get up early in the morning. Be gay and cheerful at the breakfast table. When he goes away, see him off; when he comes home, run to meet him. Learn to do without Miss Roberts, and make him forget her.

Mrs. Baxter. Very well. [*Rising.*] She shall leave this house directly—directly I recover.

Tom. Recover from what?

Mrs. Baxter. From the shock. Think of the shock I've had; there's sure to be a reaction. I shouldn't wonder if I had a complete collapse. It's beginning already. [*She totters and goes towards staircase.*] Oh, dear, I feel so ill. Please call Miss Roberts.

Tom. You were going to learn to do without Miss Roberts.

Mrs. Baxter. That was before I was ill. I can't be ill without Miss Roberts.

[*Puts her hand to her side, turns up her eyes and groans as she totters out.*

Tom. Oh! Oh! You mollusc!

THE CURTAIN FALLS

ACT III

SCENE. *The same scene one week later. The only difference to the appearance of the room is that there is the addition of an invalid couch with a little table beside it.*

TOM *is in an armchair reading a newspaper.* MISS ROBERTS *comes in carrying two pillows, a scent bottle, and two fans. The pillows she lays on the couch.*

Miss Roberts. She is coming down to-day.

Tom [*betraying no interest at all*]. Oh!

Miss Roberts. Aren't you pleased?

Tom. I think it's about time.

Miss Roberts. How unsympathetic you are—when she has been so ill. For a whole week she has never left her room.

Tom. And refuses to see a doctor.

Miss Roberts. She says she doesn't think a doctor could do anything for her.

Tom. Except make her get up. Oh, no! I forgot—it's their business to keep people in bed.

Miss Roberts. You wouldn't talk like that if you'd seen her as I have, lying there day after day, so weak she can only read the lightest literature, and eat the most delicate food.

Tom. She won't let me in her room.

Miss Roberts. She won't have any one but Mr. Baxter and me.

Tom. It's too monstrous. What actually happened that day?

Miss Roberts. Which day?

Tom. The day you turned me down. [MISS ROBERTS *looks at him troubled. He looks away sadly.*] What happened after that?

Miss Roberts. I was still upset when Mr. Baxter came in and tried to comfort me.

Tom [*grimly*]. I remember.

Miss Roberts. You know he's a kind fatherly little man.

Tom. Oh—fatherly!

Miss Roberts. Yes, I wept on his shoulder just as if he'd been an old woman.

Tom. Ah! An old woman! I don't mind that.

Miss Roberts. Then I went to the schoolroom. Presently in walked Mrs. Baxter. She seemed upset too, for all of a sudden she flopped right over in the rocking-chair.

Tom. The only comfortable chair in that room.

Miss Roberts. Oh, don't say that. Then I called Mr. Baxter;

when he came, she gripped his hand and besought him never to leave her. I was going to leave them alone together, when she gripped my hand and besought me never to leave her either.

Tom. Did you promise?

Miss Roberts. Of course. I thought she was dying.

Tom [*scouting the idea*]. Dying? What made you think she was dying?

Miss Roberts. She said she was dying.

Tom. Well, what happened after she gripped you both in her death struggles?

Miss Roberts. We got her to bed, where she has remained ever since.

Tom. And here we are a week later, all four of us just where we were, only worse. What's to be done?

Miss Roberts. We must go on as we are for the present.

Tom. Impossible!

Miss Roberts. Till you go. Then Mr. Baxter and I——

Tom. More impossible!

Miss Roberts [*innocently*]. Poor Mr. Baxter; he will miss you when you go; I shall do my best to comfort him.

Tom. That's most impossible.

Miss Roberts. He must have someone to take care of him while his wife is ill.

Tom. You don't really think she has anything the matter with her?

Miss Roberts. I can't imagine anyone who is not ill stopping in bed a week; it must be so boring.

Tom. To a mollusc there is no pleasure like lying in bed feeling strong enough to get up.

Miss Roberts. But it paralyses everything so. Mr. Baxter can't go to business; I never have an hour to give to the girls; they're running wild and forgetting the little I ever taught them. I can't believe she would cause so much trouble deliberately.

Tom. Not deliberately, no. It suited Dulcie to be ill, so she kept on telling herself that she was ill till she thought she was, and if we don't look out, she will be. It's all your fault.

Miss Roberts. Oh—how?

Tom. You make her so comfortable, she'll never recover till you leave her.

Miss Roberts. I've promised never to leave her till she recovers.

Tom. A death-bed promise isn't binding if the corpse doesn't die.

Miss Roberts. I don't think you quite understand how strongly I feel my obligation to Mrs. Baxter. Four years ago I had almost nothing, and no home; she gave me a home; I can't desert her while she is helpless, and tells me twenty times a day how much she needs me.

Tom. She takes advantage of your old-fashioned conscience.

Miss Roberts. I wish she would have a doctor.

Tom [*with determination*]. She shall have me.

Miss Roberts. But suppose you treat her for molluscry, and you find out she has a real illness—think how dreadful you would feel.

Tom. That's what I've been thinking. That's why I've been sitting still doing nothing for a week. I do believe I'm turning into a mollusc again. It's in the air. The house is permeated with molluscular microbes. I'll find out what is the matter with Dulcie to-day; if it's molluscry I'll treat her for it myself, and if she's ill she shall go to a hospital.

Miss Roberts [*going to the bottom of the stairs*]. I think I hear her coming downstairs. Yes, here she is. Don't be unkind to her.

Tom. How is one to treat such a woman? I've tried kindness—I've tried roughness—I've tried keeping my temper—I've tried losing it—I've tried the serious tack—and the frivolous tack—there isn't anything else. [*As* MR. *and* MRS. BAXTER *appear.*] Oh! for heaven's sake look at this!

[*He takes his paper and sits down, ignoring them both.* MR. BAXTER *is carrying* MRS. BAXTER *in his arms.* MRS. BAXTER *is charmingly dressed as an invalid, in a peignoir and cap with a bow. She appears to be in the best of health, but behaves languidly.*

Mrs. Baxter [*as* MR. BAXTER *carries her down the stairs*]. Take care of the stairs, Dick. Thank you, darling! How kind you are to me. [*Nods and smiles to* MISS ROBERTS.] Dear Miss Roberts! [*To* MR. BAXTER.] I think you'd better put me down, dear—I feel you're giving way. [*He lays her on the sofa.* MISS ROBERTS *arranges the cushions behind her head.*] Thank you—just a little higher with the pillows; and mind you tuck up my toes. [MISS ROBERTS *puts some wraps over her—she nods and smiles at* TOM.] And what have you been doing all this week, Tom?

Tom [*without looking up*]. Mollusking.

Mrs. Baxter [*laughs and shakes her hand playfully at* TOM].

How amusing Tom is. I don't understand half his jokes. [*She sinks back on her cushions with a little gasp.*] Oh, dear, how it tires me to come downstairs. I wonder if I ought to have made the effort. [TOM *laughs harshly.*

Mr. Baxter [*reprovingly*]. Tom!

[MISS ROBERTS *also looks reprovingly at* TOM.

Mrs. Baxter. Have you no reverence for the sick?

Tom. You make me sick.

Mrs. Baxter. Miss Roberts, will you give me my salts, please.

Miss Roberts. They're on the table beside you, Mrs. Baxter.

Mrs. Baxter. Hand them to me, please. [MISS ROBERTS *picks up the salts where they stand within easy reach of* MRS. BAXTER *if she would only stretch out her hand.* MR. BAXTER *makes an attempt to get the salts.*] Not you, Dick; you stay this side, and hold them to my nose. The bottle is so heavy. [MISS ROBERTS *gives the salts to* MRS. BAXTER, *who gives them to* MR. BAXTER, *who holds them to* MRS. BAXTER'*s nose.*] Delicious!

Tom [*rising quickly and going towards* MRS. BAXTER]. Let me hold it to your nose. I'll make it delicious.

Mrs. Baxter [*briskly*]. No, thank you; take it away, Miss Roberts. I've had all I want.

[*She gives the bottle to* MISS ROBERTS.

Tom. I thought as much.

Mrs. Baxter [*feebly*]. My fan.

Mr. Baxter [*anxiously*]. A fan, Miss Roberts—a fan!

[MISS ROBERTS *takes a fan and gives it to* MR. BAXTER.

Mrs. Baxter. Is there another fan?

Mr. Baxter [*anxiously*]. Another fan, Miss Roberts—another fan! [MISS ROBERTS *gets another fan.*

Mrs. Baxter. If you could make the slightest little ruffle of wind on my right temple.

[MISS ROBERTS *stands gently fanning* MRS. BAXTER'*s right temple.* MR. BAXTER *also fans her.* TOM *twists his newspaper into a fan.*

Tom. Would you like a ruffle of wind on your left temple?

Mrs. Baxter [*briskly*]. No, no—no more fans—take them all away—I'm catching cold. [MISS ROBERTS *takes the fan from* MR. BAXTER *and lays both fans on the table.* MRS. BAXTER *smiles feebly at* MR. BAXTER *and* MISS ROBERTS. TOM *goes back to his chair and sits.*] My dear kind nurses!

Miss Roberts. Is there anything else I can do for you?

Mrs. Baxter. No, thank you. [*They turn away.*] Yes, hold my hand. [MISS ROBERTS *holds her hand. Then to* MR. BAXTER.] And you hold this one.

[MR. BAXTER *holds* MRS. BAXTER'*s other hand. She closes her eyes.*

Tom. Would you like your feet held?

Mr. Baxter [*holding up his hands to silence* TOM]. Hush, she's trying to sleep.

Tom [*going to her, says in a hoarse whisper*]. Shall I sing you to sleep? [MR. BAXTER *pushes* TOM *away.* TOM *resists.*

Mr. Baxter. Come away—she'll be better soon. [*They leave her.*] Oh, Tom, if you knew how I blame myself for this; it's all through me she's been brought so low; ever since the day she caught me comforting Miss Roberts. How she must have suffered, and she's been so sweet about it.

Mrs. Baxter [*opens her eyes*]. I don't feel any better since I came downstairs. [MISS ROBERTS *comes back to the sofa.*

Mr. Baxter. I wish you'd see a doctor.

Mrs. Baxter. As if a country doctor could diagnose me.

Tom. Have a baronet from London.

Mrs. Baxter. Later on, perhaps, unless I get well without.

Tom. Then you do intend to recover?

Mrs. Baxter. We hope, with care, that I may be able to get up and go about as usual in a few weeks' time.

Tom. When I've gone back to Colorado? [*He pushes* MR. BAXTER *out of the way and approaches* MRS. BAXTER.] I guess you'd be very much obliged to me if I cured you.

Mrs. Baxter [*speaking rapidly and with surprising energy*]. Yes, Tom, of course I should. But I've no confidence in you, and Dr. Ross once said a doctor could do nothing for a patient who had no confidence in him. [*Smiling at* TOM.] I'm so sorry, Tom; I wish I had confidence in you.

Tom. I have confidence in myself enough for two.

Mrs. Baxter. Dr. Ross said that wasn't at all the same thing. I wish you'd stand farther off; you make it so airless when you come so close. [*She waves him off with her hand.*

Tom. I'm not going to touch you.

Mrs. Baxter [*relieved*]. Oh, well, that's another matter. I thought you were going to force me up. Try to, rather. Do what you like, as long as you don't touch me or make me drink anything I don't like. I mean that I ought not to have.

Mr. Baxter. I wish we could think of some way to make our darling better.

Tom. I've heard of people who couldn't get up having their beds set on fire.

[*He picks up a box of matches and goes towards* MRS. BAXTER. MR. BAXTER *runs excitedly towards her to shield her.*

Mr. Baxter. No, Tom—Miss Roberts!

[MISS ROBERTS *also attempts to shield* MRS. BAXTER.

Mrs. Baxter [*taking a hand of* MR. BAXTER *and a hand of* MISS ROBERTS—*serenely*]. My dear ones, he doesn't understand—he wouldn't really do it.

Tom. Wouldn't he? [*He puts the matches back.*

Mrs. Baxter. To show him I'm not afraid, leave me alone with him.

Tom. Going to try and get round me, too? That's no good.

Mrs. Baxter [*affectionately to* MR. BAXTER *and* MISS ROBERTS]. You need a rest, I'm sure—both of you. Miss Roberts, will you go to the library for me, and change my book?

Miss Roberts. With pleasure.

Mrs. Baxter. Bring me something that won't tax my brain.

Miss Roberts [*soothingly*]. Yes, yes, something trashy—very well. [*She goes out.*

Mr. Baxter [*impulsively*]. I need a walk too. I'll go with Miss Roberts. [*About to follow her.*

Mrs. Baxter [*quickly pulling him back*]. No, you won't, Dick. I want you to go upstairs and move my furniture. The wash-stand gets all the sun, so I want the bed where the wash-stand is, and the wash-stand where the bed is. I wouldn't trouble you, dear, but I don't like to ask the servants to push such heavy weights.

Mr. Baxter. I'll do anything, dear, to make you more comfortable.

Mrs. Baxter. Do it quietly, so that I shan't be disturbed by the noise as I lie here. [*Closes her eyes.*

Mr. Baxter. Darling.

[*He kisses her tenderly on the brow, then tiptoes to the stairs motioning* TOM *to keep quiet.* TOM *stamps heavily on the ground with both feet.* MR. BAXTER, *startled, signs to* TOM *to keep quiet; then goes out.*

Mrs. Baxter [*smiling and murmuring*]. Dear Dick!

Tom. Poor Dick!

Mrs. Baxter [*plaintively*]. Poor Dulcie!

Tom. Look here, Dulciebella, it's no use trying to get round me. I know you. I've seen you grow up. Why, even in your cradle you'd lie by the hour, gaping at the flies, as if the world contained nothing more important. I used to tickle you, to try and give you a new interest in life, but you never disturbed yourself till bottle time. And afterwards; don't I know every ruse by which you'd make other people run about, when you thought you were playing tennis, standing on the front line, tipping at any ball that came near enough for you to spoil—[*He thumps the cushions.*] and then taking all the credit if your partner won the set? [*Again he thumps the cushions. Each time* MRS. BAXTER *looks startled and attempts to draw them from him.*] And if a ball was lost, would you help to look for it? [TOM *gesticulates*—MRS. BAXTER *watches him in alarm.*] Not you. You'd pretend you didn't see where it went. Those were the germs of mulluscry in infancy—and this is the logical conclusion—you lying there with a bow in your cap—[*He flicks her cap with his hand.*] having your hands held.

Mrs. Baxter [*in an injured tone*]. You have no natural affection.

Tom. I've a solid, healthy, brotherly affection for you, without a spark of romance.

Mrs. Baxter. Other people are much kinder to me than you are.

Tom. Other people only notice that you look pretty and interesting lying there—they wouldn't feel so sorry for you if you were ugly—[MRS. BAXTER *smiles.*] You know that; that's why you stuck that bow in your bonnet. [*He flicks her cap again.*] You can't fool me. [*Moves away.*

Mrs. Baxter [*sweetly yet maliciously*]. No, dear, I saw that the morning you made me do the flowers.

Tom [*exasperated at the remembrance of his failure*]. Get up! [*Thumps the table.*

Mrs. Baxter. I can't get up.

Tom. Lots of people think every morning that they can't get up, but they do.

Mrs. Baxter. Lots of people do lots of things I don't.

Tom. How you can go on like this after what you saw—Dick and Miss Roberts a week ago—after the warning I gave you then. I thought the fundamental instinct in any woman was self-preservation, and that she would make every effort to keep her husband by her. You don't seem to care—to indulge your molluscry you throw those two more and more together.

Mrs. Baxter. I don't see how you make that out.

Tom. There they are, both spending the whole of their time waiting on you.

Mrs. Baxter. In turns—never together—and I always have one or the other with me.

Tom [*taking it all in, he laughs and says with admiration and astonishment*]. Oh! Oh! I see. Lie still, hold them both to you and hold them apart. That's clever.

Mrs. Baxter. Your way was to pack Miss Roberts off; the result would have been that Dick would be sorry for her and blame me. *My* way, Dick is sorry for me, and blames himself, as long as Miss Roberts is here to remind him.

Tom. You can't keep this game up forever.

Mrs. Baxter [*complacently*]. When I feel comfortable in my mind that the danger has quite blown over—[*She suddenly remembers she is giving herself away too much.*] Oh, but Tom, I hope you don't think I planned all this like a plot, and got ill on purpose?

Tom. Who knows? It may have been a plot, or suggestions may have arisen like bubbles in the subconscious caverns of your mollusc nature.

Mrs. Baxter [*offended*]. It was bubbles.

Tom. You don't know which it was any more than anybody else. Think what this means for the others—there's your husband growing ill with anxiety, neglecting his business—your children running wild when they ought to be at school—Miss Roberts wasting her life in drudgery. All of them sacrificed so that you may lie back and keep things as they are. But you can't keep things as they are; they'll get worse, unless you get on to yourself and buck up. It's that, or the break up of your home. Now Miss Roberts' presence in the house has ceased to be a danger—[MRS. BAXTER *smiles*] for the moment. But you wait! Wait till this invalid game is no longer a novelty, and Dick grows tired of being on his best behaviour—or wait till he finds himself in some trouble of his own, then see what happens. He won't turn to you, he'll spare you—he'll turn to his friend, his companion, the woman he has come to rely on—because you shirked your duties on to her, and pushed her into your place. And there you'll be left, lying, out of it, a cypher in your own home.

Mrs. Baxter [*pleasantly*]. Do you know, Tom, I sometimes

think you would have made a magnificent public speaker.

[TOM *is angry. He conveys to the audience by his manner in the next part of the scene that he is trying to change his tactics. He sits.*

Tom. I wonder where those two are now?

Mrs. Baxter. Miss Roberts has gone to the library, and Dick is upstairs moving my furniture.

Tom [*gazing up at the ceiling*]. I haven't heard any noise of furniture being moved about.

Mrs. Baxter [*smiling*]. I asked him to do it quietly.

Tom. Miss Roberts has had more than time to go to the library and back.

Mrs. Baxter [*growing uneasy and sitting up*]. You don't think he's gone too?

Tom [*in an offhand way*]. That's what I should do. Pretend to you I was going upstairs to move furniture, and I should move out after her.

Mrs. Baxter. It's the first time I've let them out of my sight together since—[*She sits bolt upright.*] Go and see if they're coming. [*She points to the window.*

Tom. They'd be careful not to be seen from this window.

Mrs. Baxter [*excitedly*]. They may be in the arbour.

Tom. It's a very good place.

Mrs. Baxter. Go and look.

Tom. I won't.

Mrs. Baxter. Then I will!

[*She springs off the couch and runs towards the window.*

Tom. I thought I should make you get up.

Mrs. Baxter [*brought suddenly to realize what she has done*]. Oh!

Tom. Now that you are up, better go and look in the arbour.

Mrs. Baxter. If I do catch them again, of course there will be only one thing for me to do.

Tom. What's that?

Mrs. Baxter. The girls and I must come out and rough it with you in Colorado. [*She goes out through the window.*

Tom [*protesting vehemently*]. No, you don't! I won't have that! Not at any price. There's no room for you in Colorado. Oh, dear! What a dreadful thought! [MISS ROBERTS *comes in wearing her hat and carrying the library book in her hand.*] Thank goodness, they were not in the arbour.

Miss Roberts. What?

Tom. Oh, never mind, never mind.

Miss Roberts [*surprised at not seeing* MRS. BAXTER *on the couch*]. Why, where is she?

Tom. Gone for a chase round the garden.

Miss Roberts. A chase?

Tom. A wild goose chase. Leave her alone—she needs exercise. You see I was right; she was mollusking.

Miss Roberts. And she wasn't really ill?

Tom [*quickly*]. Now seize this opportunity to give her notice. Have a plan. Know where you're going to or we shall have —'Dear Miss Roberts—stay with us till you find a place'— and the whole thing over again.

Miss Roberts [*taking off her hat, says thoughtfully*]. I don't know where I can go at a moment's notice. I suppose you don't actually know of anyone in Colorado who wants a governess?

Tom. No, I can't say I do.

Miss Roberts. Then I suppose it must be the Governesses' Home.

Tom [*kindly*]. We shall hear from you from time to time, I hope?

Miss Roberts [*pleased*]. Oh, yes, if you wish to.

Tom. You'll write sometimes—[MISS ROBERTS *looks up hopefully. But when he says 'to my sister,' she is disappointed.*] to my sister?

Miss Roberts [*disappointed*]. Oh, yes.

Tom. And in that way I shall hear of you.

Miss Roberts [*sadly*]. If you remember to ask. But people so soon forget, don't they?

Tom. I shan't forget. I don't want you to forget me.

Miss Roberts. It won't make much difference to you in Colorado whether you're remembered or forgotten by me.

Tom. I like to know there are people here and there in the world who care what happens to me.

Miss Roberts [*faltering*]. That's something, isn't it?

Tom. It's a real thing to a man who lives out of his own country; we spend a lot of time just thinking of the folks at home.

Miss Roberts. Do you?

Tom [*looks at her face*]. How young you are—there isn't a line in your face. [*She smiles at him.*] You will let me hear how you get on? [*Moves away.*

Miss Roberts [*disappointed*]. If there's anything to tell. Some people have no history.

Tom. Yours hasn't begun yet—your life is all before you.

Miss Roberts. A governess's life isn't much.

Tom. You won't always be a governess. You'll marry a young man, I suppose. I hope he'll be worthy of you.

Miss Roberts [*wistfully*]. Would he have to be young for that?

Tom. It's natural; I suppose it's right—anyway it can't be helped. A man doesn't realize that he's growing old with the rest of the world; he notices that his friends are. He can't see himself—so he doesn't notice that he, too—he gets a shock now and then—but . . . well, then he gets busy about something else and forgets.

Miss Roberts. Forgets?

Tom. Or tries to. I almost wish I'd never come to England. It was easier out there to get busy and forget.

Miss Roberts. You'll find that easy enough when you go back.

Tom [*shaking his head*]. Too much has happened; more than I can forget. But I must buck up because I have to be jolly as a duty to my neighbours, and then your letters—they'll cheer me. And when that inevitable letter arrives to tell me you've found happiness, I shall send you my kindest thoughts and best wishes, and try not to curse the young devil whoever he is. So you see we can always be friends, can't we? In spite of the blunder I made a week ago. Don't quite forget me—[*Taking her hands and shaking them.*] when he comes along.

[*He goes and sits on the couch disconsolately.*

Miss Roberts. Shall I tell you something?

Tom. What?

Miss Roberts. Oh, no—I can't!

Tom. You must now you've begun.

Miss Roberts. I daren't.

Tom. I want you to.

Miss Roberts. Well, don't look at me.

Tom. I'm ready.

[*He looks at her, and then turns his back to her.*

Miss Roberts. Suppose there was a girl, quite young, and not bad looking, and she knew that her chief value as a person was her looks and her youth, and a man—oh, I don't know how to say this——

Tom. I'm not looking.

Miss Roberts. He had great value as a person. He was kind and sensible, and brave, and he had done things. He wasn't young, but he couldn't have lived and still had a smooth face, so she liked him all the better for not having a smooth face—his face meant things to a girl, and if he wanted to give her so much—such great things—don't you think she'd be proud to give him her one little possession, her looks and her youth?

Tom. You don't mean us? [*He turns to her.*

Miss Roberts [*overcome with confusion*]. Don't look at me. I'm ashamed. [*Covers her face with her hands.* TOM *goes to her, gently draws her hands from her face and holds them both in his.*] I wouldn't have dared to tell you, only I couldn't let you go on thinking what you were thinking. When you asked me to marry you a week ago and I said 'No'—it was only because I was so hurt—my pride was hurt and I thought—oh, never mind now—I wanted to say 'Yes' all the time.

Tom [*looking at her and saying to himself, as if he scarcely believed it*]. I am really going to take her with me to Colorado.

[*Kisses her. After a slight pause* MR. BAXTER *enters limping painfully.*

Mr. Baxter. I've sprained my ankle—moving that washstand.

Tom. Oh, my poor old chap—what can we do for you?

Miss Roberts. You ought to have some lint and a bandage. [*To* TOM.] You'll find it in a cupboard in the spare room—your room.

Tom. All right—hold on while I go and get it.

[*He puts* MR. BAXTER*'s hand on the post of the stairs; then he goes out.*

Miss Roberts. Hold on to me, Mr. Baxter.

[*She supports him.* MRS. BAXTER *enters from the garden without seeing* MR. BAXTER *and* MISS ROBERTS.

Mrs. Baxter. They're not in the arbour. [*Catching sight of them.*] What again?

Miss Roberts. He's sprained his ankle.

Mrs. Baxter [*rushing to him*]. Sprained his ankle—oh, my poor Dick!

Mr. Baxter [*looking surprised at* MRS. BAXTER]. What, you up—running about?

Mrs. Baxter. I've taken a sudden turn for the better.

Mr. Baxter [*mournfully*]. I wish you'd taken it a bit sooner; making me move that damned old washstand. [*Then suddenly.*] Oh, my foot!

Mrs. Baxter. Let me help you to my couch.

[TOM *comes in with bandages.*

Mr. Baxter. You wouldn't know how. [*Pushes her away.* MRS. BAXTER *gives an exclamation of horror. Turning to* MISS ROBERTS.] Miss Roberts!

Mrs. Baxter. Let me!

Mr. Baxter. No, no—not now. [*As* MISS ROBERTS *assists him to the sofa.*] You see, she's used to helping people, and you're not.

[MISS ROBERTS *kneels and begins to untie his shoe-lace.*

Mrs. Baxter [*to* TOM]. He refuses my help.

Tom. He turns to the woman he has come to rely on. Now is your chance. Seize it; you may never get another.

Mr. Baxter. I want a pillow for my foot.

Miss Roberts [*rising*]. A pillow for your foot?

Tom [*to* MRS. BAXTER]. Go on—go on—get it.

Mrs. Baxter [*running for the pillow*]. A pillow for his foot. [*She anticipates* MISS ROBERTS, *snatches the pillow and brings it to* MR. BAXTER, *then, looking indignantly at* MISS ROBERTS *she raises* MR. BAXTER'*s sprained foot with one hand as she places the pillow under it with the other.* MR. BAXTER *utters a yell of pain.*] Oh, my poor Dick, I'm so sorry. Did I hurt you?

Mr. Baxter [*looking at her in wonder*]. Why, Dulcie, but it seems all wrong for me to by lying here, while you wait on me.

Mrs. Baxter. I want you to rely on me, dear, so that when you're in trouble, you'll turn to me. What can I do for your poor foot? We must get some—some——

Tom. Bandages. [*Throwing bandages to* MRS. BAXTER.

Mrs. Baxter. Yes, and some—some arnica. Miss Roberts never thought of arnica.

Miss Roberts. I'll go and look for it.

[*She makes a slight movement.*

Mrs. Baxter [*pleasantly*]. Don't trouble, Miss Roberts, I will go myself directly. [*Then to* MR. BAXTER.] You know, dear, we must learn to do without Miss Roberts.

Tom. You'll have to. She's coming back to Colorado with me.

Mrs. Baxter [*going to* MISS ROBERTS]. Tom, this is news. Dear Miss Roberts, I'm so glad.

Mr. Baxter [*holding out his hand to* TOM]. So am I.

[TOM *shakes hands with* MR. BAXTER.

Mrs. Baxter. But oh, how we shall miss you.

Miss Roberts. I hope I'm not being selfish!

Mrs. Baxter. Oh, no, no, dear. I'm glad you're going to make

Tom happy. We shall do very well here; it's high time the children went to school. I've been thinking about it for a long time. [*She kneels by* MR. BAXTER.] And now that I'm so much better, I shall be able to do more for my husband, play chess with him—go walks with him——Tom shall never have another chance to call me a mollusc.

Tom. Bravo! Bravo!

Mr. Baxter. Dulcie!

Mrs. Baxter. Dearest!

Miss Roberts [*to* TOM]. You've worked a miracle!

Tom [*quietly to* MISS ROBERTS]. Were those miracles permanent cures? [*Shakes his head.*] We're never told! We're never told!

THE END

THE CASSILIS ENGAGEMENT

ST. JOHN EMILE CLAVERING HANKIN

(1869–1909)

Born Southampton. Educated Malvern and Merton College, Oxford. Worked as journalist in India and London, contributing to *The Saturday Review* and *The Times*, amongst other publications. Two of his series of articles from *Punch* were collected and published as *Mr. Punch's Dramatic Sequels* (1901) and *Lost Masterpieces* (1904). Gave up journalism in 1905. His health deteriorated and he was drowned in the River Ithon while undergoing treatment at Llandrindod Wells.

His plays included *The Two Mr. Wetherbys* (1903); *The Return of the Prodigal* (1905); *The Charity that Began at Home* (1906); *The Cassilis Engagement* (1907); *The Last of the De Mullins* (1908). He also translated *Les Trois Filles de M. Dupont* from Brieux (1905) and wrote two short plays, *The Burglar who Failed* (1908) and *The Constant Lover* (produced posthumously in 1912). *Thompson,* left unfinished on his death, was completed by George Calderon and produced in 1913.

THE CASSILIS ENGAGEMENT

A COMEDY FOR MOTHERS

by

St. John Hankin

THE CASSILIS ENGAGEMENT

First produced before the Stage Society at the Imperial Theatre, London, 10 *February* 1907 *with the following cast:*

MRS. CASSILIS	Miss Evelyn Weeden
LADY MARCHMONT	Miss Gertrude Burnett
THE COUNTESS OF REMENHAM	Miss Florence Haydon
MRS. HERRIES	Miss K. M. Romsey
MRS. BORRIDGE	Miss Clare Greet
LADY MABEL VENNING	Miss Isabel Roland
ETHEL BORRIDGE	Miss Maudi Darrell
THE RECTOR	Mr. F. Morland
MAJOR WARRINGTON	Mr. Sam Sothern
GEOFFREY CASSILIS	Mr. Langhorne Burton
WATSON	Mr. Ralf Hutton
DORSET	Miss Margaret Mackenzie

The Play produced by Miss Madge McIntosh.

NOTE: *The Leicestershire Cassilises pronounce their name as it is spelt.*

THE CASSILIS ENGAGEMENT

ACT I

SCENE. *The white drawing-room at Deynham Abbey, a very handsome room furnished in the Louis Seize style. There are big double doors at the back, and a large tea-table with tea-cups, etc., on cloth, stands rather to the left of it. There is a large French window open on the left of the stage, with a sofa in front of it facing the view. On the opposite side of the room is the fireplace, but there is no fire as the month is August. Two or three armchairs stand near it. When the curtain rises the* RECTOR *is standing judicially on hearthrug. He seems about to hum a tune, but thinks better of it.* MRS. HERRIES *is standing by window. Presently she crosses to her husband, and sits in one of the armchairs. The* RECTOR *is a rubicund, humorous-looking man of fifty; his wife a prosperous-looking lady a few years younger.*

Mrs. Herries. I wonder what can be keeping Mrs. Cassilis?

Rector [*back to fire*]. My dear, I told you we oughtn't to have called. On so sad an occasion——

Mrs. Herries. My dear Hildebrand, it's just on these sad occasions that a visit is so consoling. One should always call after a birth, a funeral——

Butler [*showing in* LADY REMENHAM *and her daughter*]. I will tell Mrs. Cassilis you are here, my lady. She will be down in a moment.

Lady Remenham. Thank you. How do you do, Mrs. Herries? How do you do, Rector?

[LADY REMENHAM *goes towards fireplace and shakes hands. She is a dignified old lady of about sixty. Her normal expression is one of placid self-assurance, but to-day she has the air of disapproving of something or somebody.* MABEL *is a very pretty girl of two and twenty.* LADY REMENHAM *seats herself comfortably by* MRS. HERRIES. MABEL *goes over to window, where the* RECTOR *joins her.*

Mrs. Herries. How do you do, Lady Remenham?

Rector. How do you do, Mabel?

Lady Remenham. You've heard this dreadful news, haven't you? [RECTOR *makes sympathetic gesture.*

Mrs. Herries. Yes. Poor Mrs. Cassilis.

Lady Remenham. Poor Adelaide, indeed! That unhappy boy!

But there! How any mother can allow such a thing to happen passes my comprehension. To get engaged!

Rector [*nods sympathetically*]. Just so.

Lady Remenham. Engagements are such troublesome things. They sometimes even lead to marriage. But we'll hope it won't be as bad as that in this case. You've not heard who she is, I suppose?

Mrs. Herries [*shaking her head mournfully*]. No.

Lady Remenham. Ah. Someone quite impossible, of course. Otherwise Adelaide would have told me in her letter.

Mrs. Herries. I'm afraid so.

Lady Remenham [*irritably*]. It's really extremely wicked of Geoffrey. And so silly, too!—which is worse. A temporary infatuation I could understand, terminated by some small monetary payment. It would have been regrettable, of course, but young men are like that. And Adelaide could have stopped it out of his allowance. But an engagement! I am quite shocked at her.

Mabel [*at window, turning to her mother*]. Don't you think, mamma, we might leave Mrs. Cassilis to manage her son's affairs her own way?

Lady Remenham. She has *not* managed them. That's exactly what I complain of. I can't altogether acquit the Rector of some blame in the matter. He was Geoffrey's tutor for years. They used to say in *my* young days, 'Train up a child in the way he should go——'

Rector [*attempting a mild jest*]. And when he's grown up he'll give you a great deal of anxiety. So they did! So they did!

Lady Remenham [*severely*]. That is not the ending *I* remember.

Rector. That is the Revised Version.

[MRS. HERRIES *frowns. She feels this is not a moment for levity.*

Lady Remenham. I dare say. They seem to alter everything nowadays. But, if so, I hardly see the use of education.

Rector [*obstinately cheerful*]. I have long been of that opinion, Lady Remenham.

[MRS. CASSILIS, *in a charming flutter of apologies, enters at this moment. She is a very pretty woman of forty, tall and graceful, and exquisitely dressed.*

Mrs. Cassilis. You *must* forgive me all of you. I had some letters to finish. [*General handshake. Kiss to* MABEL.] Dear Mabel. How do you do, Mrs. Herries?

Rector. How do you do, Mrs. Cassilis?

Lady Remenham. My dear Adelaide, *what* a charming gown!

But you always do have the most delightful clothes. Where *do* you get them?

Mrs. Cassilis. Clarice made this.

[*Two* FOOTMEN *bring the tea-table down into the middle of the room. The* BUTLER, *who has brought in a teapot on a salver, places it on the table, and brings up a chair for* MRS. CASSILIS. *The* FOOTMEN *go out.*

Lady Remenham. Clarice? The wretch! She always makes my things atrociously. If only I had your figure!

Mrs. Cassilis. Excuse me, dear. [*To* BUTLER.] The carriage has gone to the station to meet Lady Marchmont, Watson?

Butler. Yes, madam. It started five minutes ago.

[*Exit* BUTLER.

Mrs. Cassilis [*to* LADY REMENHAM]. I'm so glad you like it.

[*Goes to tea-table and seats herself.*

Lady Remenham. Is Margaret coming to stay with you?

Mrs. Cassilis. Yes, for ten days.

Lady Remenham [*drawing chair up to table*]. And now will you please pour out my tea? I have come here to scold you, and I shall require several cups.

Mrs. Cassilis [*quite cheerful*]. To scold *me*? Won't you all bring your chairs to the table? [*They all do so.*] Rector, where are you? [*To* LADY REMENHAM.] Cream?

Lady Remenham. Thank you. And a small lump.

Mrs. Cassilis. And why am I to be scolded?

Lady Remenham. You know quite well. [*Sternly.*] Adelaide, what is this I hear about Geoffrey's engagement?

Mrs. Cassilis [*not at all disturbed*]. Oh, that? Yes, Geoffrey has got engaged to a girl in London. Isn't it *romantic* of him! I know nothing whatever about her except that I believe she has no money, and Geoffrey is over head and ears in love with her.

Mrs. Herries [*blandly*]. My dear Mrs. Cassilis, I should have thought *that* was quite enough!

Mrs. Cassilis. Rector, will you cut that cake? It's just by your hand.

Lady Remenham [*refusing to be diverted from the task of cross-examination*]. Where did he meet her?

Mrs. Cassilis. In an omnibus, I understand.

Lady Remenham [*scandalized*]. An omnibus!

Mrs. Cassilis. Yes. That was so *romantic*, too! One of the horses fell down, and she was frightened. They thought she was going to faint. Geoffrey got her out, took charge of her, discovered her address, and took her home. Wasn't it *clever* of him? Of course, she asked him to come in. He was introduced to her mother. And now they're engaged. [*Gives cup to* RECTOR.

Lady Remenham [*with awful dignity*]. And what is the name of this young person?

Mrs. Cassilis. Borridge.

Lady Remenham. Borridge! Mabel, my love, pray remember if ever you come home and inform me that you are engaged to a person of the name of Borridge I shall whip you. [*Puts down cup.*

Mabel. Very well, mamma.

Mrs. Cassilis. Another cup?

Lady Remenham. Thank you. Rather less sugar this time. [*Gives cup.*] I never could understand why you let Geoffrey be in London at all. Alone too. Young men ought never to be allowed out alone at his age. They are so susceptible.

Mabel. Geoffrey has his profession, mamma.

Mrs. Cassilis. Geoffrey's at the Bar, you know.

Lady Remenham. The Bar! What business had Geoffrey to be at the Bar! Deynham has the best shooting in the Shires, and in the winter there's the hunting. What more does he want? It's disgraceful.

Rector [*another mild effort at humour*]. My dear Lady Remenham, you're sure you're not confusing the *Bar* with the *Dock*?

Mrs. Herries. Hildebrand!

Lady Remenham [*impatiently*]. The Bar is a good enough profession, of course. But only for *very* younger sons. Geoffrey will have Deynham some day, and twelve thousand a year. I don't think Adelaide need have made a little attorney of him.

Mrs. Cassilis. Young men must do *something*, don't you think?

Lady Remenham [*briskly*]. Certainly not! It's this vulgar Radical notion that people ought to *do* things that is ruining English Society. What did Mr. Borridge *do*, by the way?

Mrs. Cassilis [*hesitates*]. He was a bookmaker, I believe.

Lady Remenham [*triumphantly*]. There, you see! That's what comes of *doing* things!

Mrs. Cassilis [*slight shrug. Pouring herself out more tea, and still quite unruffled*]. Well, I'm afraid there's no use in discussing it. They're engaged, and Miss Borridge is coming down here.

Mrs. Herries. Coming here!

Lady Remenham. Coming here! ! !

Mrs. Cassilis. Yes. On a visit. With her mother.

Lady Remenham [*putting down her cup with a touch of solemnity*]. Adelaide, are you—excuse my asking the question—are you *quite* in your right mind?

Mrs. Cassilis [*laughing*]. I believe so.

Lady Remenham. You've noticed nothing? No dizziness about the head? No singing in the ears? (MRS. CASSILIS *shakes her head.*] And yet you ask this young woman to stay with you! *And* her mother! Neither of whom you know anything whatever about!

Mrs. Cassilis. Another cup?

[LADY REMENHAM *shakes her head irritably.*

Lady Remenham. Is *Mr.* Borridge—Ugh!—coming too?

Mrs. Cassilis. He is dead, I believe.

Lady Remenham. That, at least, is satisfactory.

Mabel. Mamma!

Lady Remenham. Mabel, I shall do my duty whatever happens. [*Turning to* MRS. CASSILIS *again.*] And does Mrs. Borridge carry on the business? I think you said he was a *boot*-maker?

Mabel. Book-maker.

Mrs. Cassilis [*refusing to take offence*]. No. I believe he left her some small annuity.

Lady Remenham. Annuity? Ah, dies with her, of course?

Mrs. Cassilis. No doubt.

Lady Remenham [*gasps*]. Well, Adelaide, I never should have believed it of you. To ask these people to the house!

Mrs. Cassilis. Why shouldn't I ask them? Geoffrey tells me Ethel is charming.

Lady Remenham. Ethel?

Mrs. Cassilis. Miss Borridge.

Lady Remenham. Bah!

[*Enter* BUTLER, *showing in another visitor. This is* LADY MARCHMONT, MRS. CASSILIS'*s sister. She is a woman of about five-and-forty. She wears a light travelling cloak. She is not unlike* MRS. CASSILIS *in appearance and manner, but is of a more delicate, fragile type.*

Butler. Lady Marchmont.

Mrs. Cassilis [*rising*]. Ah, Margaret. How glad I am to see you. Some more tea, Wilson.

Lady Marchmont [*kisses her*]. Not for me, please. No,

really. My doctor won't *hear* of it. Hot water with a little milk is the most he allows me. How do you do, dear? [*Shaking hands with the others.*] How do you do? How do you do? [BUTLER *goes out.*

Mrs. Cassilis. How's the General?

Lady Marchmont. Very gouty. His temper this morning was atrocious, poor man.

Lady Remenham [*shakes her head*]. You bear it like a saint, dear.

Lady Marchmont [*philosophically, sitting in armchair after laying aside her cloak*]. Yes—I go away a good deal. He finds my absence very soothing. That's why I was so glad to accept Adelaide's invitation when she asked me.

Mrs. Cassilis. My dear, you'll be invaluable. I look to you to help me with my visitors.

Lady Remenham. Poor Margaret. But you always were so unselfish.

Lady Marchmont. Are they *very*——?

Lady Remenham. Very.

Mrs. Cassilis [*laughing*]. My dear, Lady Remenham knows nothing whatever about them.

Lady Remenham [*firmly*]. I know everything about them. The girl has no money. She has no position. She became engaged to Geoffrey without your knowledge. She has a perfectly dreadful mother. And her name is Borridge.

Lady Marchmont [*raising her brows*]. When are they coming?

Mrs. Cassilis. I expect them in half an hour. The carriage was to go straight back to the station to meet them.

Lady Remenham [*ruffling her feathers angrily*]. I hope Geoffrey is conscious of the folly and wickedness of his conduct.

Lady Marchmont. Where is he, dear?

Mrs. Cassilis. He's down here with me—and as happy as possible, I'm glad to say.

Lady Remenham. Extraordinary! But the young men of the present day *are* extraordinary. Young men nowadays seem always to be either irreclaimably vicious or deplorably silly. I prefer them vicious. They give less trouble. My poor brother Algernon—you remember Algernon, don't you, Rector? He was another of your pupils.

Rector [*sighs*]. Yes, I remember.

Mrs. Herries. Major Warrington hasn't been down for quite a long time, has he?

Lady Remenham. No. We don't ask him to Milverton now.

He comes to us in London, but in the country one has to be more particular. He really is dreadfully dissipated. Always running after some petticoat or other. Often more than one. But there is safety in numbers, don't you think?

Rector. Unquestionably.

Lady Remenham. Algernon always says he is by temperament a polygamist. I don't know what he means. However, I've no anxiety about *him. He never* gets engaged. He's far too *clever* for that. I wonder if he could help you out of this dreadful entanglement? In a case of this kind one should have the very best advice.

Mrs. Cassilis [*laughing*]. I shall be delighted to see Major Warrington—though not for the reason you suggest.

Lady Remenham. Well, I'll ask him down. Remenham won't like it. He disapproves of him so much. He gets quite virtuous about it. But that sort of moral indignation should never be allowed to get out of hand, should it? [RECTOR *nods.*] Besides, he's away just now. I'll write to Algernon directly I get back, and I'll bring him over to dinner one day next week. Say Thursday?

Lady Marchmont. Do, dear. I adore Major Warrington.

Lady Remenham. I dare say. [*Preparing to go.*] He's not *your* brother. Meantime, I can ask him whether he knows anything against Mrs. Borridge. But he's sure to. He knows nearly all the detrimental people in London, especially if their daughters are in the least attractive.

Mrs. Cassilis [*smiling*]. You'll come *with* him on Thursday, won't you? And Mabel? [MABEL *rises.*

Lady Remenham. Perhaps that will be best. Then I can keep my brother within bounds. Poor Algernon is apt to take too much champagne unless I am there to prevent him. And now dear, I really must go. [*She and* MABEL *go up towards door.*] Good-bye.

Mrs. Cassilis. You won't stay to meet Mrs. Borridge?

Lady Remenham [*shudders*]. I think not. Thursday will be *quite* soon enough. Good-bye, Mrs. Herries. [*As they reach door* GEOFFREY *opens it, and almost runs into her arms.*] Ah, *here* is the young man who is causing us all this distress.

Geoffrey. I, Lady Remenham? [*Shakes hands.*] How do you do, Aunt Margaret? [*Shakes hands with others.*

Lady Remenham [*shakes hands*]. You. What do you *mean* by getting engaged to someone we none of us know anything about?

Mabel. Mamma!

Lady Remenham. I consider your conduct perfectly heartless. Its foolishness needs no comment from me.

Geoffrey. Really, Lady Remenham——

Lady Remenham. Tut, tut, sir. Don't 'really' me. I'm ashamed of you. And now I'll be off before I quarrel with you.

[*Sweeps out, followed by* MABEL. GEOFFREY *opens door for them, and then takes them down to their carriage.*

Mrs. Herries. I think we ought to be going, too. Come, Hildebrand. [*Shakes hands.* MRS. CASSILIS *rings.*

Rector. Good-bye, Mrs. Cassilis. Let's hope everything will turn out for the best.

Mrs. Herries. It never does. Good-bye.

Mrs. Cassilis [*going towards door with* RECTOR]. Good-bye. [*Shakes hands warmly.*] And you'll both come and dine on Thursday, won't you? To-morrow week that is. Major Warrington will want to see his old tutor.

Rector. You're very good. [*He and* MRS. HERRIES *go out.*

Mrs. Cassilis [*returning to her sister*]. Dear Lady Remenham! What nonsense she talks.

Lady Marchmont. People who talk as much as that must talk a good deal of nonsense, mustn't they? Otherwise they'd have nothing to say. [*Re-enter* GEOFFREY.

Geoffrey. Lady Remenham seems ruffled.

Lady Marchmont. About your engagement? I'm not surprised.

Geoffrey. I don't see what it's got to do with her.

Lady Marchmont. You must make allowance for a mother's feelings, my dear Geoffrey.

Geoffrey [*pats* MRS. CASSILIS'*s hand, then goes to tea-table and helps himself to tea*]. Lady Remenham isn't my mother. She's my god-mother.

Lady Marchmont. She's Mabel's mother.

Mrs. Cassilis. Sh! Margaret.

Lady Marchmont. My dear, there's no use making mysteries about things. Geoffrey was always supposed to be going to marry Mabel ever since they were children. He knows that.

Geoffrey. That was only boy and girl talk.

Lady Marchmont. For you, perhaps.

Geoffrey. And for her. Mabel never expected——

[*Pause. He thinks.*

Lady Marchmont. Did you ever ask her?

Geoffrey. But I never supposed——

Lady Marchmont. I think you *should* have supposed. A boy

should be very careful how he encourages a girl to think of him in that way.

Geoffrey. But I'd no idea. Of course, I *like* Mabel. I like her awfully. We're like brother and sister. But beyond that—— [*Pause*.] Mother, do *you* think I've behaved badly to Mabel?

Mrs. Cassilis [*gently*]. I think perhaps you've a little disappointed her.

Geoffrey [*peevishly*]. Why didn't somebody *tell* me? How was I to know?

Lady Marchmont. My dear boy, we couldn't be expected to know you were absolutely blind.

Mrs. Cassilis. Margaret, you're not to scold Geoffrey. I won't allow it.

Geoffrey. Mother, dear—you won't allow this to make any difference? With Ethel, I mean?

Mrs. Cassilis. Of course not, Geoffrey. [*Lays hand on his.*

Geoffrey [*earnestly*]. She's so fond of me. And I'm so fond of her. We were made for each other. I couldn't bear it if you were unkind to her.

Mrs. Cassilis. My dear Geoffrey. I'm sure Ethel is everything that is sweet and good, or my boy wouldn't love her. And I intend to fall in love with her myself directly I set eyes on her.

Geoffrey. Dear mother! [*Pats her hand affectionately. Pause; then, thoughtfully*.] I'm afraid you'll find *her* mother rather trying—at first. She's not quite a lady, you know. . . . But she's very good-natured.

Mrs. Cassilis [*cheerfully*]. Well, well, we shall see. And now run away, dear, and leave me to talk to Margaret, and I'll undertake that all symptoms of crossness shall have disappeared before our visitors arrive.

Geoffrey. All right, mother. [*Kisses her and goes out.*

Lady Marchmont [*looking after him reflectively*]. How you spoil that boy!

Mrs. Cassilis [*lightly*]. What else should I do with him? He's my only one. Mothers always spoil their sons, don't they? And quarrel with their daughters. More marriages are due to girls being unhappy at home than most people imagine.

Lady Marchmont. And yet Geoffrey wants to leave you, apparently.

Mrs. Cassilis [*smiling bravely; but her eyes have a suspicion of moisture in them*]. Evidently I didn't spoil him enough.

Lady Marchmont [*washing her hands of the whole affair*]. Well, I'm glad you're pleased with this engagement.

Mrs. Cassilis [*sudden change of manner. Her face loses its brightness, and she suddenly seems to look older*]. *Pleased* with it! Do you really believe that?

Lady Marchmont. Didn't you say so?

Mrs. Cassilis [*shrugs*]. To Lady Remenham and Mrs. Herries. Yes.

Lady Marchmont. And to Geoffrey.

Mrs. Cassilis. And Geoffrey, too. [*Half to herself.*] Mothers can't always be straightforward with their sons, can they?

Lady Marchmont. Why not?

[*There is a pause while* MRS. CASSILIS *makes up her mind whether to answer this or not. Then she seems to decide to speak out. She moves nearer to her sister, and when she begins her voice is very firm and matter-of-fact.*

Mrs. Cassilis. My dear Margaret, what would *you* do if your son suddenly wrote to you that he had become engaged to a girl you knew nothing whatever about, a girl far beneath him in social rank?

Lady Marchmont [*firmly*]. I should have forbidden the engagement. Forbidden it absolutely.

Mrs. Cassilis. Without seeing the girl?

Lady Marchmont. Certainly. The mere fact of her accepting my son before I had ever set eyes on her would have been quite enough.

Mrs. Cassilis. But supposing your son were of age and independent?

Lady Marchmont [*impatiently*]. Geoffrey isn't independent.

Mrs. Cassilis. He has five hundred a year.

Lady Marchmont [*contemptuously*]. What's *that*?

Mrs. Cassilis. Besides, Geoffrey knows I should always be willing to help him.

Lady Marchmont. That's just it. He ought *not* to have known. You ought to have made it clear to him from the first that if he married without your consent he would never have a penny from you, either now or at your death. Deynham isn't entailed, fortunately.

Mrs. Cassilis. But, my dear, I couldn't *disinherit* Geoffrey! How could I?

Lady Marchmont [*shrugs*]. You could have threatened to. And then the girl wouldn't have accepted him.

Mrs. Cassilis. I don't know. [*Thoughtfully.*] Five hundred a year may seem a considerable sum to her.

Lady Marchmont [*horrified*]. Is it as bad as that?

Mrs. Cassilis [*trying to smile*]. Besides, she may be really in love with him.

Lady Marchmont [*snappish*]. What *has* that to do with it?

Mrs. Cassilis. Young people. In love. They are seldom prudent, are they?

Lady Marchmont. Still, I should have forbidden the engagement.

Mrs. Cassilis. And then?

Lady Marchmont. What do you mean?

Mrs. Cassilis. If Geoffrey had defied me? Boys can be very obstinate.

Lady Marchmont. I should have refused ever to see him again.

Mrs. Cassilis. Ah, Margaret, I couldn't do that. Geoffrey is everything I have. He is my only son, my joy and my my pride. I couldn't quarrel with him whatever happened. [LADY MARCHMONT *leans back with gesture of impatience.*] No, Margaret, my plan was the best.

Lady Marchmont. What *is* your plan?

Mrs. Cassilis [*quite practical*]. My plan is to give the thing a fair trial. Ask her down here. Ask her mother down here. And see what happens.

Lady Marchmont [*looking at her narrowly*]. Nothing else?

Mrs. Cassilis. Nothing else—at present.

Lady Marchmont. You could have done that without sanctioning the engagement.

Mrs. Cassilis. Yes. But love thrives on opposition. There's a fascination about a runaway match. It has romance. Whereas there's no romance at all about an ordinary wedding. It's only dull and rather vulgar. [*Wearily.*] And, after all, the girl *may* be presentable.

Lady Marchmont. Borridge! [*Crisply.*] I'm not very sanguine about *that*.

Mrs. Cassilis. Anyhow, she's pretty, and Geoffrey loves her. That's all we know about her at present.

Lady Marchmont. Wretched boy. To think he should have allowed himself to be caught in this way! . . . Don't you think you might have asked the daughter *without* the mother?

Mrs. Cassilis. So Geoffrey suggested. He seemed rather nervous about having her here. She's rather a terrible person, I gather. But I said as we were marrying into the family, we mustn't be unkind to her. [*With a slow smile.*] Poor boy, he rather blenched at that. I think he hadn't associated *Mrs.* Borridge with his matrimonial schemes. It's just as well he should do so at once, don't you think?

Butler. Mrs. and Miss Borridge.

[*Enter* MRS. BORRIDGE *and* ETHEL. *Both rise.* LADY MARCHMONT *turns sharp round to look at the newcomers.* MRS. CASSILIS *goes up to meet them with her sweet smile. Nothing could be more hospitable than her manner or more gracious than her welcome. The change from the* MRS. CASSILIS *of a moment before, with the resolute set of the lips and the glitter in the eyes, to this gentle, caressing creature, does the greatest credit to her powers of self-control.* LADY MARCHMONT *notices it, and is a little shocked.*

Mrs. Cassilis. How do you do? *How* do you do, my dear? [*Kisses* ETHEL.] Tell Mr. Geoffrey, Watson. I hope you've not had a tiring journey, Mrs. Borridge? [*Exit* BUTLER.

Mrs. Borridge. Not at all, Mrs. Cassilis. We 'ad—had—the compartment to ourselves, bein' first class. As I says to my girlie, 'They'll very likely send the carridge to meet us, and it looks better for the servants.'

[MRS. BORRIDGE *comes down stage. She is a large, gross woman, rather over-dressed in inexpensive materials. Too much colour in her hat and far too much in her cheeks. But a beaming, good-natured harridan for all that. As a landlady you would rather like her. She smiles nervously in* LADY MARCHMONT'*s direction, not sure whether she ought to say anything or wait to be introduced. Her daughter keeps by her side, watching to see she doesn't commit herself, and quite sure that she will.* ETHEL *is pretty but second-rate; she has had the sense to dress simply and therefore is less appallingly out of the picture than her far more amiable mother.*

Mrs. Cassilis. Let me introduce you. Mrs. Borridge—Lady Marchmont, Miss Borridge. [LADY MARCHMONT *bows.*

Mrs. Borridge [*extends gloved hand*]. How do you do, Lady Marchmont? Proud, I'm sure.

[LADY MARCHMONT *finds nothing to say, and for the moment there is a constrained pause. Then enter* GEOFFREY *hurriedly.*

Geoffrey [*with as much heartiness as he can muster, but it rings a little hollow*]. How do you do, Mrs. Borridge?

Ethel, dear, how long have you been here? I didn't hear you come. [*Kisses her.*

Ethel. We've only just got here.

Mrs. Borridge [*subsiding into an armchair*]. Don't apologise, Geoffy. Your ma's been entertaining us most kind.

Geoffrey [*with a look of gratitude to* MRS. CASSILIS]. Dear mother.

Mrs. Borridge. Well, how *are* you, Geoffy? You *look* first-rate.

Geoffrey. Oh, I'm all right.

Mrs. Borridge. And what a fine 'ouse—house—you've got! Quite a palace, I declare!

Geoffrey. I'm glad you like it.

Mrs. Borridge. And it'll all be yours some day. Won't it?

Ethel [*pulls her sleeve*]. Mother!

Geoffrey. That's as my mother decides.

Mrs. Borridge. Then you're sure to 'ave it. I know what mothers are! And what a 'andsome room, too. Quite like the Metropole at Brighton.

[*Enter* MRS. CASSILIS'*s maid. She is in a perfectly plain black dress, and looks enormously more like a lady than* ETHEL.

Maid. Can I have your keys, madam?

Mrs. Borridge [*surprised*]. My keys?

Maid. The keys of your trunks, madam.

Mrs. Borridge. Certainly not. Who ever 'eard of such a thing?

Maid. I thought you might wish me to unpack for you, madam.

Mrs. Borridge [*bristling*]. Oh. *Did* you! I don't want no strange girls ferriting in *my* boxes. [ETHEL *nudges her arm.*] What *is* it, Eth? Oh, very well. But I'm not going to let her all the same. No, thank you.

Mrs. Cassilis [*quite self-possessed.* LADY MARCHMONT *nervously avoids her eye*]. Mrs. Borridge will unpack for herself, Dorset. [MAID *bows, and turns to go out.*] Wait a moment. [MAID *pauses at door.*] Would you like to take off your things at once, Mrs. Borridge? If so, Dorset shall show you your room. And I'll have some tea sent up to you there. You'll want it after your journey. [*Feels teapot.*] This is quite cold. What do you say, Ethel?

Ethel. Thank you, Mrs. Cassilis. A cup of tea would be very nice.

Mrs. Cassilis. Show Mrs. Borridge her room, Dorset

[MRS. BORRIDGE *rises.*] And take her up some tea. Dinner will be at eight. You'll ring if there's anything you want, won't you?

Mrs. Borridge. Thank you, Mrs. Cassilis.

[MRS. BORRIDGE *waddles out, beaming. She feels that her first introduction to the houses of the great has gone off successfully.* GEOFFREY *holds the door open for them, and gives* ETHEL *a sly kiss in passing.* MRS. CASSILIS *makes no sign, but one can feel her shudder at the sound.* GEOFFREY *comes down to her a moment later, brimming with enthusiasm.*

Geoffrey. Well, mother, *what* do you think of her? Isn't she *sweet?*

Mrs. Cassilis [*gently*]. She's very pretty, Geoff.

[*Lays hand on his.*

Geoffrey. And *good*! You don't know how *good* she is!

Mrs. Cassilis. So long as she's good to my boy that's all I ask.

Geoffrey. Dearest mother. [*Kisses her demonstratively.*] Now I'll go and dress.

[*Goes out quickly, with a boyish feeling that he has been rather too demonstrative for a true-born Englishman. There is a long pause, during which* LADY MARCHMONT *looks at her sister,* MRS. CASSILIS *at nothing. The latter is evidently in deep thought, and seems to have almost forgotten her sister's presence. At last* LADY MARCHONT *speaks with the stern accent of 'I told you so.'*

Lady Marchmont. And *that's* the girl your son is to marry.

Mrs. Cassilis. Marry her! Nonsense, my dear Margaret.

THE CURTAIN FALLS

ACT II

SCENE. *The lawn at Deynham. Time, after breakfast the following morning. Under a tree stand two or three long wicker chairs, with bright red cushions. On the right stands the house, with windows open on to the terrace. A path on the left leads to the flower garden, and another on the same side to the strawberry beds.*

When the curtain rises, MRS. CASSILIS *comes on to the terrace, followed by* ETHEL, *and a little later by* MRS. BORRIDGE. *The last-named is flushed with food, and gorgeously arrayed in a green silk blouse. She is obviously in the best of spirits, and is generally terribly at ease in Zion.*

Mrs. Cassilis. Shall we come out on the lawn? It's such a perfect morning.

Ethel. That *will* be jolly, Mrs. Cassilis. [*They come down.*] When I'm in the country I shall always eat too much breakfast and then spend the morning on a long chair digesting it. So will mother.

Mrs. Borridge. How you go on, dearie!

Mrs. Cassilis. Try this chair, then. [*Slightly moving the chair forward.*] Mrs. Borridge, what kind of chair do *you* like?

Mrs. Borridge. This'll do. I'm not particular. [*Subsides into another long chair.*] Am I showing my ankles, Eth?

Ethel. Sh! mother! [*Giggles.*

Mrs. Borridge. Well, I only asked, dearie.

Mrs. Cassilis. I wonder if you'd like a cushion for your head? Try this.

[*Puts vivid red cushion behind* MRS. BORRIDGE'*s vivid green blouse. The effect is electrifying.*

Mrs. Borridge. That's better.

[MRS. CASSILIS *sinks negligently in wicker chair and puts up white lace parasol.*

Ethel [*sigh of content*]. I call this Heaven, Mrs. Cassilis.

Mrs. Cassilis. That's right, my dear. Are you fond of the country?

Ethel. I don't know. I've never been there so far. Not to the real country, I mean. Mums and I have a week at Brighton now and then. And once we went for a month to Broadstairs after I had the measles. But that's not exactly country, is it?

Mrs. Cassilis. You're sure to like it. Geoffrey loves it. He's never so happy as when he's pottering about Deynham with his gun.

Ethel. Doesn't he get tired of that?

Mrs. Cassilis. Oh, no. Beside, he doesn't do that all the year round. He rides a great deal. We've very good hunting at Deynham. Are you fond of horses?

Ethel. I can't bear them, Mrs. Cassilis.

Mrs. Borridge. When she was a little tot her father put 'er—her—on a pony and she fell off. It didn't hurt 'er, but the doctor said 'er nerve was shook. And now she can't bear 'orses.

Mrs. Cassilis. What a pity! I do hope you won't be dull while you're with us. Perhaps you're fond of walking?

Ethel. Yes. I don't mind walking—for a little. If there's anything to walk *to*.

Mrs. Cassilis. We often walk up Milverton Hill on fine afternoons to see the view. It's the highest point about here.

Ethel [*stifling a yawn*]. Is it, Mrs. Cassilis?

Mrs. Cassilis. And no doubt we shall find other things to amuse you. What *do* you like?

Ethel. Oh, shops and theatres, and lunching at restaurants and dancing, and, oh, lots of things.

Mrs. Cassilis. I'm afraid we've no shops nearer than Leicester, and that's twelve miles away. And we've no restaurants at all. But I daresay we could get up a dance for you.

Ethel [*clapping her hands*]. That'll be *sweet*. I simply *love* dancing. And all the rest of the time I shall sit on the lawn and grow fat, like mummy. [*Protest from* MRS. BORRIDGE.] Oh, yes, I shall.

Mrs. Borridge. Ethel, don't be saucy.

Ethel [*laughing*]. Mummy, if you scold me you'll have to go in. It's far too hot to be scolded.

Mrs. Borridge. Isn't she a spoilt girl, Mrs. Cassilis? What they taught you at that boarding school, miss, *I* don't know. Not manners, *I* can see.

Ethel [*ruffling her mother's wig*]. There! there! mums. Was 'em's cross?

Mrs. Borridge [*pettishly*]. Stop it, Ethel, stop it, I say. Whatever will Mrs. Cassilis think of you!

Mrs. Cassilis [*smiling sweetly*]. Don't scold her, Mrs. Borridge. It's so pleasant to see a little high spirits, isn't it?

Mrs. Borridge [*beaming*]. Well, if *you* don't mind, Mrs. Cassilis, *I* don't. But it's not the way girls were taught to behave in *my* young days.

Ethel [*slight yawn*]. That was so long ago, mums!

Mrs. Cassilis [*rising*]. Well, I must go and see after my housekeeping. Can you entertain each other while I'm away for a little? My sister will be down soon, I hope. She had breakfast in her room. And Geoffrey will be back in half an hour. I asked him to ride over to Milverton for me with a note.

Ethel. We shall be all right, Mrs. Cassilis. Mother'll go to sleep. She always does if you make her too comfortable. And then she'll snore, won't you, mums?

[MRS. CASSILIS *goes into the house, smiling bravely to the last.*

Mrs. Borridge [*alarmed*]. Ethel, you shouldn't talk like that before Mrs. Cassilis. She won't like it.

Ethel. Oh, yes she will. And I'm going to make her like *me* awfully. What lovely clothes she has! I wish *you* had lovely clothes, mums.

Mrs. Borridge. What's the matter with my clothes, dearie? I 'ad on my best silk last night. And I bought this blouse special in the Grove only a week ago so as to do you credit.

Ethel. I know. Still . . . . Couldn't you have chosen something *quieter*?

Mrs. Borridge. Oh, no, dearie. I 'ate quiet things.

Ethel. *H*ate, mother.

Mrs. Borridge. *H*ate, then. Give me something *cheerful.*

Ethel [*hopelessly*]. Very well, mummy.

Mrs. Borridge [*imploring*]. But *do* be careful what you say before Mrs. Cassilis. She's not used to girls being so free.

Ethel. Oh, yes she is, mums. All girls are like that nowadays. All girls that are ladies, I mean. They bet, and talk slang, and smoke cigarettes, and play bridge. I know all about that. I've read about it in the *Ladies' Mail.* One of them put ice down her young man's back at dinner, and when he broke off his engagement she only laughed.

Mrs. Borridge [*lamentably*]. Oh, dear, I hope there won't be ice for dinner to-night.

Ethel [*laughing*]. Poor mums, don't be anxious. I'll be *very* careful, I promise you.

Mrs. Borridge [*complaining*]. You're so 'eadstrong. And I *do* want to see you married and respectable. I wasn't always respectable myself, and I know what it means for a girl. Your sister Nan, she's gay, she is. She 'adn't no ambition. An' look what she is now!

Ethel [*looking round nervously*]. If Geoff were to hear of it!

Mrs. Borridge. 'E won't. Not 'e! I've seen to that.

Ethel. These things always get known somehow.

Mrs. Borridge. Nan's changed 'er name. Calls 'erself Mrs. Seymour. An' she never comes to see us now. If she did, I'd show 'er the door fast enough. Disgracin' us like that!

Ethel. Poor Nan!

Mrs. Borridge [*warmly*]. Don't you pity 'er. She don't deserve it. She treated us like dirt. She's a bad 'un all through. I've done things myself as I didn't ought to 'ave done. But I've always *wanted* to be respectable. But it's not so easy when you've your living to make and no one to look to. [ETHEL *nods.*] Yes, I've 'ad my bad times, dearie. But I've pulled through them. And I *made* your father marry me. No one can deny that. It wasn't easy. An' I had to give him all my savings before e'd say 'Yes'. And even then I wasn't 'appy till we'd been to church. But 'e did marry me in the end. An' then *you* was born, an' I says my girl shall be brought up respectable. She shall be a lady. And some day, when she's married an' ridin' in her carriage, she'll say, 'It's all mother's doing.' [*Wipes her eyes in pensive melancholy.*

Ethel. How long *were* you married to father, mums?

Mrs. Borridge. Only eight years, dearie. Before that I was 'is 'ousekeeper.

Ethel. His, mummy.

Mrs. Borridge. Very well, dearie. [*With quiet satisfaction.*] Father drank 'isself to death the year Bend Or won the Derby. [*Shaking her head.*] He lost a pot o' money over that, and it preyed on 'is mind. So he took to drink. If he 'adn't insured 'is life an' kep' the premiums paid we shouldn't 'ave been in the 'ouse, that's where we should 'ave been, dearie.

Ethel. Poor dad!

Mrs. Borridge. Yes. 'E 'ad 'is faults. But 'e was a kind-'earted man, was Joe Borridge. 'E died much respected. [*Cheering up.*] An' now you're engaged to a *real* gentleman! *That's* the sort for my Eth!

Ethel. Oh! sh! mums. [*Looking round nervously.*

Mrs. Borridge. No one'll hear. And if they do, what's the harm? You've got 'is promise.

*Ethel. H*is, mother.

Mrs. Borridge. You can hold 'im—him—to it.

Ethel [*nodding*]. Yes. Besides, Geoff's awfully in love with me. And I really rather like *him*, you know—in a way.

Mrs. Borridge. I know, dearie. Still, I'd get something from 'im on paper if I was you, something that'll 'old 'im. The men takes a bit of 'olding nowadays. They're that slippy! You get something that'll 'old 'em. That's what I always say to girls. Letters is best. Oh, the chances I've seen missed through not gettin' something on paper!

Ethel [*confidently*]. You needn't worry, mummy. Geoff's all right.

Mrs. Borridge. I dare say. Still, I'd like something the lawyers can take hold of. Geoff may get tired of *you*, dearie. Men are that changeable. *I* know them!

Ethel [*viciously*]. He'd better not! I'd make him *pay* for it!

Mrs. Borridge. So you could, dearie, if you 'ad somethin' on paper. [ETHEL *shrugs impatiently.*] Well, if you won't, you won't. But if anything happens don't say I didn't warn you, that's all. I wish Geoffy was a lord, like Lord Buckfastleigh.

Ethel. I don't.

Mrs. Borridge. Well, not *just* like Buckfastleigh, per'aps But still a lord. You never did like Buckfastleigh.

Ethel. That old beast!

Mrs. Borridge [*remonstrating*]. He's been a good friend to us dearie. And he is an earl, whatever you may say.

Ethel. Pah!

Mrs. Borridge. And he's rich. Richer than Geoffy. And he's awfully sweet on you, dearie. I believe he'd 'ave married you if 'is old woman 'ad turned up 'er toes last autumn. And he's seventy-three. He wouldn't 'ave lasted long.

Ethel [*fiercely*]. I wouldn't marry him if he were twice as rich—and twice as old.

Mrs. Borridge [*placidly*]. I dare say you're right, dearie. He's a queer 'un is Buckfastleigh. But he offered to settle five thousand down if you'd go to Paris with 'im. Five thousand down on the nail. He wasn't what you'd call sober when he said it, but he meant it. I dare say he'd 'ave made it seven if you hadn't boxed 'is ears. [ETHEL *laughs.*] Wasn't I savage when you did that, dearie! But you was right as it turned out. For Geoffy proposed next day. And now you'll be a real married woman. There's nothing like being married. It's so respectable. When you're married you can look down on people. And that's what every woman wants. That's why I pinched and screwed and sent you to boarding school. I said my girlie shall be a real lady. And she is. [*Much moved at the reflection.*

Ethel. Is she, mums?

Mrs. Borridge. Of course, dearie. That's why she's 'ere. Deynham Abbey, *two* footmen in livery, fire in 'er bedroom, evenin' dress every night of 'er life. *Lady* Marchmont invited to meet her! Everythin' tip top! And it's not a bit too good for my girl. It's what she was made for.

E hel [*thoughtfully*]. I wish Johnny Travers had had some money. Then I could have married him.

Mrs. Borridge. Married 'im—him! Married a auctioneer's clerk without twopence to bless 'isself. I should think not indeed! Not likely!

Ethel. Still, I was awfully gone on Johnny.

Mrs. Borridge [*decidedly*]. Nonsense, Eth. I should 'ope we can look 'igher than *that*!

Ethel. Sh! mother. Here's Geoff.

[GEOFFREY, *in riding breeches, comes out of the house.*

Geoffrey. Good morning, dear. [*Kisses* ETHEL.] I thought I should be back earlier, but I rode over to Milverton for the mater. [*To* MRS. BORRIDGE.] Good morning.

Mrs. Borridge [*archly*]. You 'aven't no kisses to spare for *me*, 'ave you, Geoffy? Never mind. You keep 'em all for my girl. She's worth 'em.

Geoffrey [*caressing her hand*]. Dear Ethel.

Mrs. Borridge. How well you look in those riding togs, Geoffrey! Don't 'e, Eth?

[*Endeavouring to hoist herself out of her chair.*

Ethel [*smiling at him*]. Geoff always looks well in everything.

Mrs. Borridge. Well, I'll go indoors and leave you two to spoon. That's what you want, *I* know. I'll go and talk to your ma. [*Waddles off into the house, beaming.*

Geoffrey [*picking rose and bringing it to* ETHEL]. A rose for the prettiest girl in England.

Ethel. Oh, Geoff, do you think so?

Geoffrey. Of course. The prettiest and the best.

[*Takes her hand.*

Ethel. You do really love me, Geoff, don't you?

Geoffrey. Do you doubt it? [*Kisses her.*

Ethel. No; you're much too good to me, you know.

Geoffrey. Nonsense, darling.

Ethel. It's the truth. You're a gentleman and rich, and have fine friends. While mother and I are common as common.

Geoffrey [*firmly*]. You're *not.*

Ethel. Oh, yes we are. Of course, I've been to school, and been taught things. But what's education? It can't alter how we're made, can it? And she and I are the same underneath.

Geoffrey. Ethel, you're not to say such things, or to think them.

Ethel. But they're true, Geoff.

Geoffrey. They're not. [*Kisses her.*] Say they're not.

Ethel [*shakes her head*]. No.

Geoffrey. Say they're *not.* [*Kisses her.*] *Not*!

Ethel. Very well. They're not.

Geoffrey. That's right. [*Kiss.*] There's a reward.

Ethel [*pulling herself away*]. I wonder if I did right to say 'Yes' when you asked me, Geoff? Right for *you*, I mean.

Geoffrey. Of course you did, darling. You love me, don't you?

Ethel. But wouldn't it have been best for you if I'd said 'No'? Then you'd have married Lady Somebody or other, with lots and lots of money, and lived happy ever afterwards.

Geoffrey [*indignantly*]. I shouldn't.

Ethel. Oh, yes, you would.

Geoffrey. And what would *you* have done, pray?

Ethel. Oh, I should have taken up with someone else, or perhaps married old Buckfastleigh when his wife died.

Geoffrey. Ethel!

Ethel. I should. I'm not the sort to go on moping for long. I should have been awfully down for a bit, and missed you every day. But by and by I should have cheered up and married someone else. I could have done it. I could!

Geoffrey. And what about *me*?

Ethel. Wouldn't you have been happier in the end, dear? I'm not the sort of wife you ought to have married. Some day I expect you'll come to hate me. [*Sighs*.] Heigho.

Geoffrey [*softly*]. You know I shan't, dear.

Ethel. But I did so want to marry a gentleman. Mother wanted it, too. [*Quite simply*.] So I said 'Yes', you see.

Geoffrey [*drawing her to him*]. Darling!

[*Kisses her tenderly*.

Ethel. Geoff, what did *your* mother say when you told her we were engaged? Was she dreadfully down about it?

Geoffrey. No.

Ethel. On your honour?

Geoffrey. On my honour. Mother never said a single word to me against it. Lady Marchmont scolded me a bit. She's my aunt, you see.

Ethel. Old cat!

Geoffrey. And so did Lady Remenham. She's my godmother. But mother stood up for us all through.

Ethel [*sighs*]. I shall never get on with all your fine friends, Geoff.

Geoffrey. You will. Anyone who's as pretty as my Ethel can get on anywhere.

Ethel. Yes, I *am* pretty, aren't I? I'm glad of that. It makes a difference, doesn't it?

Geoffrey. Of course. In a week, you'll have them all running after you.

Ethel [*clapping her hands*]. Shall I, Geoff? Won't that be splendid! [*Kisses him.*] Oh, Geoff, I'm so happy. When shall we be married?

Geoffrey. I'm afraid not till next year, dear. Next June, mother says.

Ethel [*pouting*]. That's a *long* way off, Geoff.

Geoffrey. Yes, but mother says you're to be here a *great* deal between now and then, almost all the time, in fact. So it won't be so bad, will it?

Ethel. Why does your mother want it put off till then?

Geoffrey. Something about the London season, she said. We shall be married in London, of course, because your mother's house is there.

Ethel. Oh, yes, of course.

Geoffrey. And besides, mother says she never believes in very short engagements. She says girls sometimes don't quite know their own minds. I said I was sure *you* weren't like that. But she asked me to promise, so I did.

Ethel. Well, that's settled then. [*Jumping up.*] And won't it be nice to be *married*? Really *married*! . . . And now I want to *do* something. I'm tired of sitting still. What shall it be?

Geoffrey [*with brilliant originality*]. We might go for a walk up Milverton Hill. The view there's awfully fine. [*Looks at watch.*] But there's hardly time before lunch.

Ethel. Besides, I should spoil my shoes.

[*Puts out foot, the shoe of which is manifestly not intended for country walking.*

Geoffrey. Suppose we go to the strawberry beds and eat strawberries?

Ethel. Oh, yes, that'll be splendid. I can be so deliciously greedy over strawberries.

[*Puts her arm in his, and he leads her off to the strawberry beds. As they go off,* MRS. CASSILIS, LADY MARCHMONT, *and* MRS. BORRIDGE *come down from terrace.*

Mrs. Cassilis. Going for a stroll, dears?

Geoffrey. Only as far as the strawberry beds, mother dear.

Mrs. Cassilis. Oughtn't dear Ethel to have a hat? The sun is very hot here.

Ethel. I've got a parasol, Mrs. Cassilis.

[*They disappear down the path.*

Mrs. Borridge [*rallying her*]. You weren't down to breakfast, Lady Marchmont.

Lady Marchmont. No, I—had a headache.

Mrs. Cassilis. Poor Margaret.

Mrs. Borridge [*sympathetically*]. It's 'eadachy weather, isn't it?

[*Subsiding into a chair.* MRS. BORRIDGE *makes it a rule of life never to stand when she can sit.*

Lady Marchmont. I suppose it is.

Mrs. Borridge. Or perhaps it was the oyster patties last night? I've often noticed after an oyster I come over quite queer. Specially if it isn't *quite* fresh.

Lady Marchmont. Indeed!

Mrs. Borridge. Yes. But crabs is worse. Crabs is simply poison to me.

Lady Marchmont [*faintly*]. How extraordinary.

Mrs. Borridge. They are, I do assure you. If I touch a crab I'm that ill nobody would believe it.

Mrs. Cassilis. Well, Margaret, I expect you oughtn't to be talked to or it will make your head worse. You stay here quietly and rest while I take Mrs. Borridge for a stroll in the garden.

Lady Marchmont. Thank you. [*Closing her eyes.*] My head is a little bad still.

Mrs. Borridge [*confidentially*]. Try a drop of brandy, Lady Marchmont. My 'usband always said there's nothing like brandy if you're feeling poorly.

Lady Marchmont. Thank you. I think I'll just try what rest will do.

Mrs. Cassilis [*making* LADY MARCHMONT *comfortable*]. I expect that will be best. Put your head back, dear. Headaches are such trying things, aren't they, Mrs. Borridge? This way. And you're to keep quite quiet till luncheon, Margaret.

[LADY MARCHMONT *closes her eyes, with a sigh of relief. After a moment enter* BUTLER *from house, with* MRS. HERRIES.

Butler. Mrs. Herries.

Lady Marchmont [*rises, and goes up to meet her*]. How do you do? Mrs. Cassilis is in the garden, Watson. [*To* MRS. HERRIES.] She has just gone for a stroll with Mrs. Borridge.

Mrs. Herries. Oh, pray don't disturb her. Pray don't. I can only stay for a moment. Literally a moment.

Lady Marchmont. But she would be so sorry to miss you. Will you let her know, Watson? She went that way.

[*Pointing to a path along which* MRS. CASSILIS *went a moment before.*

Butler. Yes, my lady.

Lady Marchmont. And how's the dear Rector? [*She and* MRS. HERRIES *sit*.] You've not brought him with you?

Mrs. Herries. No. He was too busy. There is always so much to do in these *small* parishes, isn't there?

Lady Marchmont. Indeed?

Mrs. Herries. Oh, yes. There's the garden—and the pigs. The Rector is devoted to his pigs, you know. And his roses.

Lady Marchmont. The Rector's roses are quite famous, aren't they?

[*But* MRS. HERRIES *has not come to Deynham to talk horticulture, but to inquire about a far more interesting subject. She looks round cautiously, and then, lowering her voice to an undertone, puts the important question*.

Mrs. Herries. And now tell me, dear Lady Marchmont, before Mrs. Cassilis comes back, what is she like?

Lady Marchmont. Really, dear Mrs. Herries. I think I must leave you to decide that for yourself.

Mrs. Herries [*sighs*]. So bad as that! The Rector feared so. And the mother? [*No answer*.] Just so! What a pity. An *orphan* is so much easier to deal with.

Lady Marchmont [*laughing slightly*]. You may be glad to hear that Mr. Borridge *is* dead.

Mrs. Herries. So Mrs. Cassilis said. How fortunate! How very fortunate!

[MRS. CASSILIS, *followed by* MRS. BORRIDGE, *return from their walk*. WATSON *brings up the rear*.

Mrs. Herries. *Dear* Mrs. Cassilis, how do you do? [*Sympathetically*.] *How* are you?

Mrs. Cassilis [*rather amused at* MRS. HERRIES'*s elaborate bedside manner*]. Quite well, thanks. It's Margaret who is unwell.

Mrs. Herries. Indeed! She didn't mention it.

Lady Marchmont [*hurriedly*]. I have a headache.

Mrs. Herries. I'm so *sorry*.

Mrs. Cassilis [*sweetly*]. You have heard of my son's engagement, haven't you. Dear Ethel is with us now, I'm glad to say. Let me introduce you to her mother.

Mrs. Herries. How do you do? [*Bows*.] What charming weather we're having, aren't we?

Mrs. Cassilis. You'll stay to luncheon now you are here, won't you? [MRS. BORRIDGE *subsides into a chair*.

Mrs. Herries. I'm afraid I mustn't. I left the Rector at home. He will be expecting me.

Mrs. Cassilis. Why didn't you bring him with you?

Mrs. Herries. So kind of you, dear Mrs. Cassilis. [*Nervously.*] But he hardly liked—— How is *poor* Geoffrey?

Mrs. Cassilis [*cheerfully*]. He's very well. He's in the kitchen garden with Ethel. At the strawberry beds. You'll see them if you wait.

Mrs. Herries [*hastily*]. I'm afraid I can't. In fact, I must run away at once. I only looked in in passing. It's nearly one o'clock, and the Rector always likes his luncheon at one. [*Shakes hands with gush of sympathetic fervour.*] Good-bye, dear Mrs. Cassilis. Good-bye, Mrs. Borridge. [*Bows.*

Mrs. Borridge [*stretching out her hand*]. Good-bye, Mrs.—I didn't rightly catch your name.

Mrs. Herries. Herries. Mrs. Herries.

[*Shakes hands nervously.*

Mrs. Borridge [*heartily*]. Good-bye, Mrs. 'Erris.

Mrs. Cassilis. And you're coming over to dine on Thursday? That's to-day week, you know. *And* the Rector, of course. You won't forget?

Mrs. Herries. With pleasure. Good-bye, Lady Marchmont.

[*Looks at* MRS. BORRIDGE, *who has turned away, then at* LADY MARCHMONT, *then goes off, much depressed, into the house. Pause.*

Mrs. Borridge. I think I'll be going in, too, Mrs. Cassilis, just to put myself straight for dinner.

Mrs. Cassilis. Yes. Do. Luncheon will be ready in half an hour. [MRS. BORRIDGE *waddles off into the house complacently.* LADY MARCHMONT *sinks limply into a chair, with a smothered groan.* MRS. CASSILIS *resumes her natural voice.*] How's your headache, Margaret? Better?

Lady Marchmont. Quite well. In fact, I never had a headache. That was a little deception on my part, dear, to excuse my absence from the breakfast table. Will you forgive me? [MRS. CASSILIS *nods without a smile. She looks perfectly wretched.* LADY MARCHMONT *makes a resolute effort to cheer her up by adopting a light tone, but it is obviously an effort.*] Breakfasts *are* rather a mistake, aren't they? So trying to the temper. And that awful woman. I felt a brute for deserting you. On the very first morning, too. But I didn't feel strong enough to face her again so soon. How *could* Geoffrey do it!

Mrs. Cassilis [*grimly*]. Geoffrey's not going to marry *Mrs.* Borridge.

Lady Marchmont. He's going to marry the daughter. And

she'll grow like her mother ultimately. All girls do, poor things.

Mrs. Cassilis [*sighs*]. Poor Geoffrey. I suppose there's something wrong in the way we bring boys up. When they reach manhood they seem quite unable to distinguish between the right sort of woman and—the other sort. A pretty face, and they're caught at once. It's only after they've lived for a few years in the world and got spoiled and hardened—got what we call experience, in fact—that they even begin to understand the difference.

Lady Marchmont [*decidedly*]. You ought to have sent Geoffrey to a public school. His father ought to have insisted on it.

Mrs. Cassilis. Poor Charley died when Geoff was only twelve. And when I was left alone I couldn't make up my mind to part with him. Besides, I hate the way public school boys look on women.

Lady Marchmont. Still, it's a safeguard.

Mrs. Cassilis [*dismally*]. Perhaps it is.

[*Neither of the sisters speaks for a moment. Both are plunged in painful thought. Suddenly* LADY MARCHMONT *looks up and catches sight of* MRS. CASSILIS'*s face, which looks drawn and miserable. She goes over to her with something like a cry.*

Lady Marchmont. My dear Adelaide, don't look like that. You frighten me.

Mrs. Cassilis [*pulling herself together*]. What's the matter?

Lady Marchmont. Your face looked absolutely *grey*! Didn't you sleep last night?

Mrs. Cassilis. Not very much. [*Trying to smile.*] Has my hair gone grey, too?

Lady Marchmont. Of course not.

Mrs. Cassilis. I feared it might.

Lady Marchmont. You poor dear!

Mrs. Cassilis [*impulsively*]. I *am* pretty still, am I not, Margaret?

Lady Marchmont. My dear, you look perfectly sweet, as you always do. Only there *are* one or two little lines I hadn't noticed before. But your *hair*'s lovely.

Mrs. Cassilis [*eagerly*]. I'm glad of that. I shall need all my looks now—for Geoffrey's sake.

Lady Marchmont [*puzzled*]. Geoffrey's?

Mrs. Cassilis. Looks mean so much to a man, don't they?

And he has always admired me. Now I shall want him to admire me more than ever.

Lady Marchmont. Why, dear?

Mrs. Cassilis [*with cold intensity*]. Because I have a rival.

Lady Marchmont. This detestable girl?

Mrs. Cassilis [*nods*]. Yes.

Lady Marchmont. My dear Adelaide, isn't it too late now?

Mrs. Cassilis. Too late? Why, the time has scarcely begun. At present Geoffrey is over head and ears in love with her. While that goes on we can do nothing. [*With absolute conviction*.] But it won't last.

Lady Marchmont [*surprised at her confidence*]. Won't it?

Mrs. Cassilis. No. That kind of love never does. It dies because it is a thing of the senses only. It has no foundation in reason, in common tastes, common interests, common associations. So it dies. [*With a bitter smile*.] *My* place is by its death-bed.

Lady Marchmont [*with a slight shudder*]. That sounds rather ghoulish.

Mrs. Cassilis. It *is*.

Lady Marchmont [*more lightly*]. Are you going to do anything to hasten its demise?

Mrs. Cassilis [*quite practical*]. Oh, yes. In the first place, they're to stay here for a *long* visit. I want them to feel thoroughly at home. Vulgar people are so much more vulgar when they feel at home, aren't they?

Lady Marchmont. You can hardly expect any change in that direction from *Mrs*. Borridge.

Mrs. Cassilis [*a short, mirthless laugh*]. I suppose not. [*Practical again*.] Then I shall ask lots of people to meet them. Oh, *lots* of people. So that Geoffrey may have the benefit of the contrast. I've asked Mabel to stay, by the way—for a week—to help entertain *dear* Ethel. When those two are together it should open Geoffrey's eyes more than anything.

Lady Marchmont. Love is blind.

Mrs. Cassilis [*briskly*]. It sees a great deal better than it used to do, dear. Far better than it did when *we* were young people. [*Pause*.

Lady Marchmont. Anything else?

Mrs. Cassilis. Not at the moment. [*A ghost of a smile*.] Yes, by the way. There's Major Warrington.

Lady Marchmont [*shocked*]. You're not really going to consult that dissipated wretch?

Mrs. Cassilis [*recklessly*]. I would consult the Witch of Endor if I thought she could help me—and if I knew her address. Oh, I'm prepared to go any lengths. I wonder if he would elope with her for a consideration?

Lady Marchmont [*horrified*]. Adelaide, you wouldn't do that. It would be dreadful. Think of the scandal.

Mrs. Cassilis. My dear, if she would elope with Watson, I'd raise his wages. [*Rises.*

Lady Marchmont. Adelaide!

Mrs. Cassilis [*defiantly*]. I *would.* Ah, Margaret, you've no children. [*Her voice quivering, and her eyes shining with intensity of emotion.*] You don't know how it feels to see your son wrecking his life and not be able to prevent it. I love my son better than anything else in the whole world. There is nothing I wouldn't do to save him. That is how mothers are made. That's what we're for.

Lady Marchmont [*slight shrug*]. Poor girl!

Mrs. Cassilis [*fiercely*]. You're *not* to pity her, Margaret. I forbid you. She tried to steal away my son.

Lady Marchmont. Still——

Mrs. Cassilis [*impatiently*]. Margaret, don't be sentimental. The girl's not in *love* with Geoffrey. Anyone can see that. She's in love with his position and his money, the money he will have some day. She doesn't really care two straws for him. It was a trap, a trap from the beginning, and poor Geoff blundered into it.

Lady Marchmont. She couldn't *make* the omnibus horse fall down!

Mrs. Cassilis. No. That was chance. But after that she set herself to catch him, and her mother egged her on no doubt, and taught her how to play her fish. And you pity her!

Lady Marchmont [*soothingly*]. I don't really. At least, I did for a moment. But I suppose you're right.

Mrs. Cassilis [*vehemently*]. Of course I'm right. I'm Geoffrey's mother. Who should know if I don't? Mothers have eyes. If she really cared for him I should know. I might try to blind myself, but I should *know*. But she doesn't. And she shan't marry him. She shan't!

Lady Marchmont. My dear, don't glare at me like that. *I'm* not trying to make the match.

Mrs. Cassilis. Was I glaring?

Lady Marchmont. You looked rather tigerish. [MRS. CASSILIS *gives short laugh. Pause.*] By the way, as she's *not* to be your daughter-in-law, is it necessary to be quite so affectionate to her all the time? It rather gets on my nerves.

Mrs. Cassilis. It is absolutely necessary. If there were any coolness between us the girl would be on her guard, and Geoffrey would take her side. That would be fatal. Geoffrey must never know how I feel towards her. No! When this engagement is broken off I shall kiss her affectionately at parting, and when the carriage comes round I shall shed tears.

Lady Marchmont [*wondering*]. Why?

Mrs. Cassilis. Because otherwise it would make a division between Geoffrey and me. And I couldn't bear that. I must keep his love whatever happens. And if I have to deceive him a little to keep it, isn't that what we women always have to do? In fact, I shall have to deceive everybody except you. Lady Remenham, Mrs. Herries, the whole county. If they once knew they would be sure to talk. Lady Remenham never does anything else, does she? And later on, when the engagement was all over and done with, Geoffrey would get to hear of it, and he'd never forgive me.

Lady Marchmont. My dear, your unscrupulousness appals me. [MRS. CASSILIS *shrugs impatiently*.] Well, it's not very *nice*, you must admit.

Mrs. Cassilis [*exasperated*]. Nice! Of course it's not *nice*! Good heavens, Margaret, you don't suppose I *like* doing this sort of thing, do you? I do it because I must, because it's the only way to save Geoffrey. If Geoffrey married her, he'd be miserable, and I won't have that. Of course, it would be *pleasanter* to be perfectly straightforward, and tell the girl I detest her. But if I did she'd marry Geoff if only to spite me. So I must trap her as she has trapped him. It's not a *nice* game, but it's the only possible one. [*More calmly*.] Yes, I must be on the best of terms with Ethel. [*With a smile of real enjoyment at the thought*.] And *you* must make friends with that appalling mother.

Lady Marchmont [*firmly*]. *No*, Adelaide! I refuse!

Mrs. Cassilis [*crosses to her*]. You must. You *must*!

[*Takes her two hands and looks into her eyes.*

Lady Marchmont [*giving way, hypnotized*]. Very well. I'll do my best. [MRS. CASSILIS *drops her hands, and turns away with a sigh of relief*.] But I shan't come down to breakfast! There are limits to my endurance. [*Plaintive*.] And I do so hate breakfasting in my room. The crumbs always get into my bed.

Mrs. Cassilis [*consoling her*]. Never mind. When we've won you shall share the glory.

Lady Marchmont [*doubtfully*]. You're going to win?

Mrs. Cassilis [*nods*]. I'm going to win. I've no doubt whatever about that. I've brains and she hasn't. And brains always tell in the end. Besides, she did something this morning which made me sure that I should win.

Lady Marchmont [*trying to get back her old lightness of tone*]. She didn't eat with her knife?

Mrs. Cassilis [*resolutely serious*]. No. She *yawned.*

Lady Marchmont [*puzzled*]. Yawned?

Mrs. Cassilis. Yes. Three times. When I saw that I knew that I should win.

Lady Marchmont [*peevish*]. My dear Adelaide, what *do* you mean?

Mrs. Cassilis. Girls like that can't endure boredom. They're used to excitement, the vulgar excitement of Bohemian life in London. Theatres, supper parties, plenty of fast society. She owned as much this morning. Well, down here she shall be dull, oh, how *dull*! I will see to that. The curate shall come to dinner. And old Lady Bellairs, with her tracts and her trumpet. I've arranged that it shall be a *long* engagement. She shall yawn to some purpose before it's over. And when she's bored she'll get cross. You'll see. She'll begin to quarrel with her mother, and nag at Geoffrey —at everyone, in fact, except me. *I* shall be too sweet to her for that. [*With a long look into her sister's eyes.*] And that will be the beginning of the end.

Lady Marchmont [*turning away her eyes with something like a shiver*]. Well, dear, I think your plan diabolical. [*Rising.*] But your courage is perfectly splendid, and I love you for it. [*Lays hand on her shoulder for a moment caressingly.*] And now I'll go in and get ready for lunch.

[LADY MARCHMONT *turns to go into the house. As she does so the* BUTLER *comes out, followed by* MABEL *in riding habit.* MRS. CASSILIS'*s manner changes at once. The intense seriousness with which she has been talking to her sister disappears in an instant, and instead you have the charming hostess, without a care in the world, only thinking of welcoming her guest and making her comfortable. It is a triumph of pluck—and breeding.*

Butler. Lady Mabel Venning.

Mrs. Cassilis [*rising*]. Ah, Mabel, dear, how are you? [*Kisses her*.] You've ridden over? But you're going to *stay* here, you know. Haven't you brought your things?

Mabel. Mamma is sending them after me. It was such a perfect morning for a ride. How do you do, Lady Marchmont? [*Shaking hands*.

Mrs. Cassilis. That's right. Watson, tell them to take Lady Mabel's horse round to the stables. She will keep it here while she is with us. [*To* MABEL.] Then you'll be able to ride every day with Geoffrey. [*To* LADY MARCHMONT.] Poor Ethel doesn't ride. Isn't it unfortunate?

Lady Marchmont. Very!

Mrs. Cassilis. She and Geoffrey are down at the strawberry beds spoiling their appetites for luncheon. Would you like to join them?

Mabel. I think not, thanks. It's rather hot, isn't it? I think I'd rather stay here with you.

Mrs. Cassilis. As you please, dear. [*They sit*.

Mabel. Oh, before I forget, mamma asked me to tell you she telegraphed to Uncle Algernon yesterday, and he's coming down next Wednesday. She had a letter from him this morning by the second post. It came just before I started. Such a funny letter. Mamma asked me to bring it to you to read.

Mrs. Cassilis [*taking letter, and reading it aloud to her sister*]. 'My dear Julia—I am at a loss to understand to what I owe the honour of an invitation to Milverton. I thought I had forfeited all claim to it for ever. I can only suppose you have at last found an heiress to marry me. If this is so I may as well say at once that unless she is both extremely rich and extremely pretty I shall decline to entertain her proposal. My experience is that that is a somewhat unusual combination. I will be with you next Wednesday.—Your affectionate brother, A. L. Warrington.' [*Giving back letter*.] That's right, then. And now I think I'll just go down to the kitchen garden and tell Geoffrey you're here. [*Rises*.] No, don't come too. You stay and entertain Margaret.

[*She goes off by the path leading to the strawberry beds*.

Lady Marchmont. Dear Major Warrington. He always was the most delightfully witty, wicked creature. I'm so glad he's coming while I'm here. Adelaide must be sure and ask him over.

Mabel. Uncle Algernon is coming over to dine this day week—with mamma.

Lady Marchmont. To be sure; I remember.

[*Enter* GEOFFREY *quickly from garden*.

Geoffrey. Halloa, Mabel. How do you do? [*Shaking hands*.] I didn't know you were here.

Mabel. Mrs. Cassilis has just gone to tell you.

Geoffrey. I know. She met us as we were coming back from eating strawberries. We've been perfect pigs. She and Ethel will be here in a moment. I ran on ahead.

Lady Marchmont [*rising*]. Well, it's close on lunch time. I shall go in and get ready.

[LADY MARCHMONT *goes off into the house, leaving the young people together. They begin to chatter at once with the easy familiarity of long acquaintance*.

Geoffrey. You rode over? [*Sitting on the arm of her chair*.

Mabel. Yes, on Basil. He really is the sweetest thing. I like him much better than Hector.

Geoffrey. Poor old Hector. He's not so young as he was.

Mabel. No.

[GEOFFREY *suddenly remembers that there is something more important than horses which he has to say before* ETHEL *arrives. He hesitates for a moment, and then plunges into his subject*.

Geoffrey. Mabel. . . . There's something I want to ask you.

Mabel. Is there?

Geoffrey. Yes. But I don't know how to say it.

[*Hesitates again*.

Mabel [*smiling*]. Perhaps you'd better not try, then?

Geoffrey. I must. I feel I ought. It's about something Aunt Margaret said yesterday. . . . [*Blushing a little*.] Mabel, did you ever . . . did I ever. . . did I ever do anything to make you think I . . . I was going to ask you to marry me?

[*Looking her bravely in the face*.

Mabel [*turning her eyes away*]. No, Geoff.

Geoffrey. Sure?

Mabel. Quite sure.

Geoffrey. I'm glad.

Mabel [*looking up, surprised*]. Why, Geoff?

Geoffrey. Because from what Aunt Margaret said I was

afraid, without intending it, I'd . . . I—hadn't been quite honourable.

Mabel [*gently*]. You have always been everything that is honourable, Geoff. And everything that is kind.

Geoffrey [*relieved*]. Thank you, Mabel. You're a brick, you know. And we shall always be friends, shan't we?

Mabel. Always. [*Rises.*

Geoffrey. And you'll be friends with Ethel, too?

Mabel. If she'll let me.

Geoffrey. Of course she'll let you. She's the dearest girl. She's ready to be friends with everybody. And she'll *love* you, I know. [*Stands up.*] You promise? [*Holds out hand.*

Mabel [*takes it*]. I promise.

[MRS. CASSILIS *and* ETHEL *enter at this moment from garden.* MRS. CASSILIS *has her arm in* ETHEL'*s, and they make a picture of mutual trust and affection which would make* LADY MARCHMONT *scream. Luckily she is safely in her room washing her hands.* MRS. CASSILIS *smiles sweetly at* MABEL *as she speaks, but does not relax her hold on her future daughter-in-law.*

Mrs. Cassilis. Not gone in to get ready yet, Mabel?

Mabel. No. Lady Marchmont only went a minute ago.

Mrs. Cassilis [*to* ETHEL]. You've not met Mabel yet, have you? I must introduce you. Miss Borridge—Lady Mabel Venning. [*Sweetly.*] I want you two to be *great* friends! [*They shake hands.*] And now come in and get ready for luncheon.

[*They all move towards the house as the curtain falls.*

ACT III

SCENE. *The smoking room at Deynham. A week has elapsed since the last act, and the time is after dinner. The room has two doors, one leading to the hall and the rest of the house, the other communicating with the billiard-room. There is a fire-place on the left, in which a fire burns brightly. A writing table occupies the centre of the stage. Further up is a grand piano. By its side a stand with music on it. Obviously a man's room from the substantial writing table, with the cigar box on it, and the leather-covered armchairs. The* Field *and the* Sportsman *lie on a sofa hard by. The room is lighted by lamps. The stage is empty when the curtain rises.*

GEOFFREY *enters from hall. He crosses to the door of the billiard-room, opens it, and looks in. Then turns and speaks to* MAJOR WARRINGTON, *who has just entered from hall.* WARRINGTON *is a cheerful, rather dissipated-looking man of five and forty.*

Geoffrey. It's all right, Warrington. They've lighted the lamps.

Warrington. Good. [*Strolling across toward fireplace.*

Geoffrey [*at door of billiard-room*]. How many will you give me?

Warrington. Oh, hang billiards. I'm not up to a game to-night. That was only an excuse to get away from the women. I believe that's why games were invented. But if you *could* get me a whisky and soda I should be your eternal debtor. Julia kept such an infernally strict watch on me all the evening that I never got more than a glass and a half of champagne. A fellow can't get along on *that*, can he?

Geoffrey. I'll ring.

Warrington. Do. There's a good fellow. [GEOFFREY *rings.*] Every man requires a certain amount of liquid per day. I've seen the statistics in the *Lancet*. But Julia never reads the *Lancet*. Women never do read anything, I believe.

Geoffrey. Have another cigar?

Warrington. Thanks. Don't mind if I do. [*Takes one and lights it.*] Aren't you going to?

Geoffrey [*who looks seedy and out of spirits*]. No, thanks. [*Enter* FOOTMAN, *with whisky and soda.*] Whisky and soda, James.

Footman. Yes, sir. [*Puts it on small table and goes out.*

Warrington. Off your smoke?

Geoffrey. Yes. [*Pouring whisky.*] Say when.

Warrington. When. [*Takes soda.*] You're not going to have one?

Geoffrey. No.

Warrington. Off your drink?

Geoffrey. Yes.

Warrington. That's bad. What's the matter?

[*Selects comfortable easy chair and sits lazily.*

Geoffrey. Oh, nothing. I'm a bit out of sorts, I suppose.

Warrington. How well your mother looks to-night, by the way! Jove, what a pretty woman she is!

Geoffrey. Dear mother.

Warrington [*sips whisky meditatively*]. How does she like this marriage of yours?

Geoffrey [*off-hand*]. All right.

Warrington. Ah. [*Nods.*] Bites on the bullet. No offence, my dear fellow. I like her pluck.

Geoffrey [*exasperated*]. I assure you, you're mistaken. My mother's been kindness itself over my engagement. She's never said a word against if from the first. I believe she's the only person in this infernal county who hasn't.

Warrington. Except myself.

Geoffrey. Except yourself. And *you* think me a thundering young fool.

Warrington. Oh, no.

Geoffrey. Oh, yes. I could see you looking curiously at me all through dinner—when you weren't eating—as if I were some strange beast. You think I'm a fool, right enough.

Warrington [*stretching himself luxuriously*]. Not at all. Miss Borridge is a very pretty girl, very bright, very amusin'. I sat next her at dinner, you know. Not quite the sort one *marries*, perhaps—as a rule——

Geoffrey [*crossly*]. What do you mean?

Warrington [*shrugs*]. Anyhow, *you're* going to marry her. So much the better for *her*. What amuses me is your bringing her old reprobate of a mother down here. The cheek of it quite takes away my breath.

Geoffrey [*peevish*]. What's the matter with her mother? She's common, of course, and over-eats herself, but lots of people do that. And she's good-natured. That's more than some women are.

Warrington [*looking thoughtfully at the end of his cigar*]. Still, she's scarcely the sort one introduces to one's *mother*, eh? But I'm old-fashioned, no doubt. There's no saying what you young fellows will do. Your code is peculiarly your own.

[*Wanders across in quest of another whisky and soda.*

Geoffrey [*restively*]. Look here, Warrington, what do you mean?

Warrington [*easily*]. Want to hit me in the eye, don't you? *I* know. Very natural feeling. Lots of people have it.

Geoffrey [*sulkily*]. Why shouldn't I introduce her to my mother?

Warrington. Well, she's a disreputable old woman, you know. She lived with Borridge for years before he married her. The other daughter's——[*Shrugs shoulders.*] And then to bring her down here and introduce her to Julia! Gad, I like your humour.

Geoffrey [*much perturbed at his companion's news*]. Are you sure?

Warrington [*nonchalantly*]. Sure? Why, it's common knowledge. Everybody knows old Borridge, and most people loathe her. I don't. I rather like her in a way. She's so vulgar. Flings her aitches about with reckless indifference. And I like her affection for that girl. She's really fond of *her*. So much the worse for you, by the way. You'll never be able to keep them apart.

Geoffrey [*irritably*]. Why should I want to keep them apart?

Warrington. Why should you——?[*Drinks.*] Oh, well, my dear chap, if *you're* satisfied——

Geoffrey [*low voice*]. Her sister . . . ? Poor Ethel! Poor Ethel!

Warrington [*with a good-natured effort to make the best of things*]. My dear chap, don't be so down in the mouth. There's no use fretting. I'd no idea you were so completely in the dark about all this, or I wouldn't have told you. Cheer up.

Geoffrey [*huskily*]. I'm glad you told me.

Warrington. To think you've been engaged all this time and never found it out. What amazing innocence! [*Chuckling.*] Ha! Ha! . . . Ha! Ha! Ha!

Geoffrey. Don't. [*Sinks on to sofa with a groan.*

Warrington. Sorry, my dear boy. But it's so devilish amusing.

Geoffrey. How blind I've been! How utterly blind!

Warrington [*shrugs shoulders*]. Well, I rather like a chap who's a bit of an ass myself.

Geoffrey. Poor mother!

Warrington. Doesn't she know? Not about old Borridge? [GEOFFREY *shakes his head.*] She must! Women always do. They have an instinct about these things that is simply uncanny. It's often highly inconvenient, too, by the way. She probably says nothing on *your* account.

Geoffrey [*dismally*]. Perhaps so. Or Ethel's. She's been wonderfully kind to Ethel ever since she came down. Perhaps that's the reason. [*Rises.*] After all, it's not Ethel's fault.

Warrington. Of course not. [*Looks at him curiously, then with an instinct of kindliness, goes to him and lays hand on shoulder.*] Well, here's luck, my dear boy, and I won't say may you never repent it, but may you put off repenting it as long as possible. That's the best one can hope of most marriages.

Geoffrey [*drily*]. Thanks!

Warrington. Well, it's been an uncommon amusin' evening.

Mrs. Herries' face has been a study for a lifetime. And as for Julia's—oh, outraged respectability! What a joy it is!

[*Further conversation is interrupted by the entrance of the other guests from the hall. These are* LADY REMENHAM, LADY MARCHMONT, MRS. HERRIES, MRS. BORRIDGE, ETHEL, *and* MABEL. *Last of all comes the* RECTOR, *with* MRS. CASSILIS. *They enter with a hum of conversation.*

Rector [*to his hostess*]. Well, he's a disreputable poaching fellow. It's no more than he deserved.

Mrs. Cassilis [*nods dubiously*]. Still, I'm sorry for his wife.

Mrs. Herries. I'll send down to her in the morning and see if she wants anything.

Mrs. Borridge [*beaming with good humour*]. So this is where you gentlemen have got to!

Geoffrey. I brought Major Warrington to smoke a cigar.

Lady Remenham [*looking fixedly at whisky, then at* WARRINGTON]. Algernon!

Warrington [*protesting*]. My dear Julia, I believe there is nothing unusual in a man's requiring *one* whisky and soda at this time in the evening.

Lady Remenham. I trust it has been only one.

[*Sits on sofa, where she is jointed by* LADY MARCHMONT.

Warrington [*changing the subject*]. Whom have you been sending to jail for poaching now, Rector? No Justice's justice, I hope?

Rector. Old Murcatt. He's one of Mrs. Cassilis's tenants. A most unsatisfactory fellow. He was caught red-handed laying a snare in the Milverton woods. It was a clear case.

[ETHEL *stifles a yawn.*

Ethel. I should have thought there was no great harm in that.

Rector. My dear young lady!

Mrs. Cassilis. Take care, Ethel dear. An Englishman's hares are sacred.

Mrs. Borridge. How silly! I can't bear 'are myself.

[*Seats herself massively in armchair in front of piano. An awkward silence follows this insult to hares. As it threatens to grow oppressive, the* RECTOR *tries what can be done with partridges to bridge the gulf.*

Rector. You'll have plenty of partridges this year, Mrs. Cassilis. We started five coveys as we drove here.

Mrs. Cassilis [*acknowledging his help with a smile*]. We generally have a good many.

[ETHEL, *stifling another yawn, strolls to piano, opens it, and strikes a note or two idly.*

Mabel. You play, I know, Ethel. Won't you play something?

Ethel [*sulkily*]. No.

[*Turns away, closing piano sharply. Another constrained silence.*

Mrs. Herries. I saw you out riding to-day, Mabel. I looked in at Dobson's cottage. Poor fellow, I'm afraid he's very ill.

Mabel. Yes. I was with Geoffrey. We had a long ride, all through Lower Milverton and Carbury to Mirstoke. It was delightful.

Mrs. Borridge [*to* MRS. HERRIES]. Your husband has a lot of that sort of thing to do down here, I suppose, Mrs. 'Erris?

Mrs. Herries [*with frosty politeness*]. When people are ill they generally like a visit from a clergyman, don't they?

Mrs. Borridge [*bluntly*]. Well, there's no accounting for tastes. My 'usband, when he was ill, wouldn't 'ave a parson *near* 'im. Said it gave 'im the creeps.

[*Another silence that can be felt.* WARRINGTON'*s shoulders quiver with delight, and he chokes hurriedly into a newspaper.*

Lady Marchmont [*crossing to fire, with polite pretence that it is the physical, not the social, atmosphere that is freezing her to the bone*]. How sensible of you to have a fire, Adelaide.

Mrs. Cassilis [*throwing her a grateful look*]. It is pleasant, isn't it? These July evenings are often cold in the country.

[ETHEL *stifles a prodigious yawn.*

Geoffrey [*going to her*]. Tired, Ethel?

Ethel [*pettishly*]. No.

[*Glowers at him. He turns away with slight shrug. There is yet another awkward pause.*

Mrs. Cassilis [*rising nervously*]. Won't somebody play billiards? Are the lamps lighted, Geoffrey?

Geoffrey. Yes, mother.

Mrs. Cassilis. Or shall we play pyramids? Then we can all join in. [*Persuasively.*] *You'll* play, Mrs. Borridge, I'm sure?

Mrs. Borridge [*beaming*]. I'm on.

Mrs. Cassilis. You, Lady Remenham?

Lady Remenham. No, thanks. Mrs. Herries and I are going to stay by the fire and talk about the Rector's last sermon.

[*The* RECTOR *raises hands in horror.*

Mrs. Cassilis. You, Margaret?

Lady Marchmont. No, really. I've never played pyramids in my life.

Mrs. Borridge [*in good humour*]. Then it's 'igh time you began, Lady Marchmont. *I'll* teach you.

[MRS. CASSILIS *looks entreaty*. LADY MARCHMONT *assents, smiling*.

Lady Marchmont. Very well. To please you, dear Mrs. Borridge!

[LADY MARCHMONT *goes off to billiard-room, followed a moment later by* MABEL.

Mrs. Cassilis. You, Mabel? That's three. Ethel four.

Ethel. No, thank you, Mrs. Cassilis. I won't play.

Mrs. Borridge. Why not, Eth? You're a nailer at pyramids.

Ethel [*pettishly*]. Because I'd rather not, mother. [*Turns away.*

Mrs. Borridge. All right, dearie. You needn't snap my nose off.

[*Goes off to billiard-room with unruffled cheerfulness.*

Mrs. Cassilis. Geoffrey five. The Rector six.

Rector. Very well, if you won't play for money. I've no conscientious objections to playing for money, but whenever I do it I always lose. Which comes to the same thing.

[*Follows* MRS. BORRIDGE *off.*

Mrs. Cassilis. You, Major Warrington, of course?

Warrington [*laughing*]. No, thanks. I shall stay here and flirt with Mrs. Herries.

Mrs. Cassilis. Very well. How many did I say? Six, wasn't it? And myself seven. Coming, Geoff?

Geoffrey. All right mother.

[GEOFFREY *looks doubtfully at* ETHEL *for a moment, and even takes a step towards her, but she takes no notice of him. Baffled, he turns to his mother, who leads him off after the others.* LADY REMENHAM *settles herself comfortably in armchair above the fireplace.* MRS. HERRIES *takes another by her, and they begin to gossip contentedly.* ETHEL *looks sullenly in their direction.* WARRINGTON *makes a valiant effort to retrieve his glass from the mantelpiece, with a view to replenishing it with whisky.*

Lady Remenham. Now, Mrs. Herries, draw up that chair to the fire, and we'll talk scandal.

Warrington [*stretching out hand towards glass*]. The Rector's sermon, Julia!

Lady Remenham. Algernon! [*He stops dead.*]

[ETHEL *seats herself in the armchair behind the writing*

table, puts her elbows on the table, and glares into vacancy, looking rather like a handsome fury. Presently WARRINGTON *joins her. She yawns with unaffected weariness.* WARRINGTON *looks at her with an amused smile.*

Warrington. Bored, Miss Borridge?

Ethel. I wonder.

Warrington [*draws up chair by her*]. I don't. [*She laughs.*] Life isn't very lively down here till the shooting begins.

Ethel [*drumming with her fingers on table*]. I don't shoot. So I'm afraid that won't help me much.

Warrington. I remember. Nor ride, I think you told me?

Ethel [*yawns*]. Nor ride.

Warrington. Gad. I'm sorry for you.

Ethel [*looking curiously at him*]. I believe you really are.

Warrington. Of course I am.

Ethel. I don't know about 'of course'. Except for Mrs. Cassilis—and poor Geoff—who doesn't count—I don't find much sympathy in *this* part of the country. Heigho! How they hate me!

Warrington [*protesting*]. No. No.

Ethel. Oh, yes, they do. Every one of them. From Watson, who pours out my claret at dinner, and would dearly love to poison it, to your sister, who is glaring at us at this moment.

[*As, indeed,* LADY REMENHAM *is doing with some intensity. She highly disapproves of her brother's attentions to* ETHEL, *but as there is no very obvious method of stopping them, she says nothing. Presently she and* MRS. HERRIES *begin a game of bezique, and that for the time, at least, distracts her attention from her brother's depravity.*

Warrington [*looking up and laughing*]. Dear Julia. She never has any manners.

Ethel. She's no worse than the rest. Mrs. Herries would do just the same if she dared. And as for Mabel——!

Warrington. Don't hit it off with Mabel?

Ethel. Oh, we don't quarrel, if that's what you mean, or call one another names across the table. I wish we did. I could beat her at that. We're as civil as the Devil. [*He laughs.*] What *are* you laughing at?

Warrington. Only at the picturesqueness of your language.

Ethel [*shrugs*]. Yes, Mabel despises me, and I *hate* her.

Warrington. Why?

Ethel [*wearily*]. Because we're different, I suppose. She's everything I'm not. She's well-born and well-bred. Her father's an earl. Mine was a bookmaker.

Warrington. Is that all?

Ethel [*bitterly*]. No. She's running after Geoffrey. [WARRINGTON *looks incredulous.*] She is!

Warrington [*raising eyebrows*]. Jealous?

Ethel. Yes. I am jealous. Little beast! [*Picks up flimsy paper knife.*] I'd like to *kill* her.

[*Makes savage jab with knife. It promptly breaks.*

Warrington [*taking pieces out of her hand*]. Don't be violent.

[*Carries pieces blandly to fire.* ETHEL *stares straight in front of her. Meantime* LADY REMENHAM *has been conversing in an undertone with* MRS. HERRIES, *occasionally glancing over her shoulder at the other two. In the sudden hush which follows* WARRINGTON'*s movement towards the fireplace her voice suddenly becomes alarmingly audible.*

Lady Remenham. Such a common little thing, too! And *I* don't even call her pretty.

Mrs. Herries. It's curious how Mrs. Cassilis seems to have taken to her.

Lady Remenham. Yes. She even tolerates that awful mother. [*Irritably.*] What *is* it, Algernon?

Warrington [*blandly*]. Only a little accident with a paper knife.

[LADY REMENHAM *grunts.* WARRINGTON *returns to* ETHEL.

Mrs. Herries [*lowering her voice discreetly*]. For Geoffrey's sake, of course. She's so devoted to him.

Lady Remenham. It may be that. *I'm* inclined to think her mind has given way a little. I asked her about it last week.

[*The two ladies drop their voices again to a murmur, but* ETHEL *has heard the last remark or two, and looks like murder.*

Warrington [*sitting by* ETHEL *and resuming interrupted thread*]. You were going to tell me what makes you think Mabel is in love with Geoffrey.

Ethel. Was I?

Warrington. Weren't you?

Ethel. Well, perhaps I will.

Warrington. Go ahead.

Ethel. She's staying here, and they're always together.

They ride almost every morning. I can't ride, you know. And Geoffrey loves it.

Warrington. You should take to it.

Ethel. I did try one day. They were just starting when I suddenly said I'd like to go with them.

Warrington [*starting*]. What did they say to that?

Ethel. Oh, Mabel pretended to be as pleased as possible. She lent me an old habit, and Geoff said they'd let me have a horse that was as quiet as a lamb. Horrid kicking beast!

Warrington. What horse was it?

Ethel. It was called Jasmine, or some such name.

Warrington. Mrs. Cassilis's mare? Why, my dear girl, she hasn't a kick in her.

Ethel. Hasn't she! . . . Anyhow, we started. So long as we walked it was all right, and I began to think I might actually get to like it. But soon we began to trot—and that was *awful.* I simply screamed. The beast stopped at once. But I went on screaming till they got me off.

Warrington. What did Geoffrey say?

Ethel. Nothing. But he looked terrible. Oh, how he despised me!

Warrington. Poor girl.

Ethel. They brought me back, walking all the way. And Geoff offered to give up riding in the mornings if I liked. [WARRINGTON *whistles.*] But, of course, I had to say no. So now they go out together every day, and often don't come back till lunch.

Warrington. And what do *you* do?

Ethel [*wearily*]. I sit at home and yawn and yawn. [*Does so.*] Mrs. Cassilis takes me out driving sometimes. She does what she can to amuse me. But of course she's busy in the mornings.

Warrington. What does Mrs. Borridge do?

Ethel. Lady Marchmont looks after her. I believe she gets a kind of pleasure in leading her on and watching her make a fool of herself. Old cat! And mother sees nothing. She's as pleased with herself as possible. She's actually made Lady Marchmont promise to come and stay with us in London!

Warrington. Bravo, Mrs. Borridge!

Ethel. So I sit here in the drawing-room with a book or the newspaper and I'm bored! bored!

Warrington. And Geoffrey?

Ethel. He doesn't seem to notice. If I say anything to him about it he just says I'm not *well*! He's very kind and tries to find things to amuse me, but it's a strain. And so it goes on day after day. Heigho! [*A short silence.*

Warrington. Well, my dear, I admire your courage.

Ethel [*surprised*]. What do you mean?

Warrington. A lifetime of this! Year in year out. Till you can yawn yourself decently into your grave.

Ethel [*alarmed*]. But it won't always be like this. We shan't *live* here, Geoff and I.

Warrington. Oh, yes, you will. Mrs. Cassilis was talking only at dinner of the little house she was going to furnish for you both down here, just on the edge of the Park. So that you could always be near her.

Ethel. But Geoff has his profession.

Warrington. His profession is only a name. He makes nothing at it. And never will. Geoffrey's profession is to be a country gentleman and shoot pheasants.

Ethel. But we shall have a house in London as well.

Warrington [*shaking his head*]. Not you. As long as his mother lives Geoffrey will be dependent on her, you know. He has nothing worth calling an income of his own. And he's proud. He won't accept more from her than he's obliged even if her trustees would allow her to hand over anything substantial to him on his marriage—which they wouldn't.

Ethel [*defiantly*]. I shall refuse to live down here.

Warrington. My dear, you won't be asked. You'll have to live where Mrs. Cassilis provides a house for you. Besides, Geoff will prefer it. He likes the country, and he's devoted to his mother.

Ethel. Phew!

Warrington. Happily, it won't last for ever. I dare say you'll have killed poor Mrs. Cassilis off in a dozen years or so. Though you never know how long people will last nowadays, by the way. These modern doctors are the devil.

Ethel. Kill her off? What do you mean? I don't want to kill Mrs. Cassilis. I like her.

Warrington [*looking at her in genuine astonishment*]. My dear young lady, you don't suppose you'll be able to *stand* this sort of thing, do you? Oh, no. You'll kick over the traces, and there'll be no end of a scandal, and Geoff'll blow his brains out—if he's got any—and she'll break her heart, and that'll be the end of it.

Ethel [*fiercely*]. It won't.

Warrington. Oh, yes, it will. You don't know what Country Society is. The dullness of it! How it eats into your bones. *I* do.

Ethel. Does it bore *you*, too?

Warrington. Bore? It bores me to *tears*! I'm not a bad lot, really. At least, no worse than most middle-aged bachelors. But Julia thinks me an utterly abandoned character, and I take care not to undeceive her. Why? Because I find Milverton so intolerable. I used to come down every Christmas. One of those ghastly family reunions. A sort of wake without the corpse. At last I couldn't stand it, and did something perfectly outrageous. I forget what, but I know the servants all gave warning. So now I'm supposed to be thoroughly disreputable, and that ass Remenham won't have me asked to the house. Thank Heaven for that.

Ethel. But Geoff likes the country.

Warrington. I dare say. But Geoffrey and I are different. So are Geoffrey and you. You and I are town birds. He's a country bumpkin. *I* know the breed!

Ethel [*in horror*]. And I shall have to stand this all my life! All my life! [*Savagely.*] I won't! I won't!

Warrington [*calmly*]. You will!

Ethel. I won't, I tell you! [WARRINGTON *shrugs.*] It's too sickening. [*Pause. She seems to think for a moment, then grasps him by the arm and speaks eagerly, dropping her voice, and looking cautiously over towards the others.*] I say, let's go off to Paris, you and I, and leave all this. It'd be awful fun.

Warrington [*appalled, rising*]. Hush! Hush! For God's sake. Julia'll hear.

Ethel [*almost in a whisper*]. Never mind. What does it matter? Let's go. You'd enjoy it like anything. We'll have no end of a good time.

Warrington [*shaking himself free, desperately*]. My dear young lady, haven't I just told you that I'm not that sort at all? I'm a perfectly respectable person, of rather austere morality than otherwise.

Ethel. Rot! You'll come? [*Grasping his arm again.*]

Warrington. No, I won't. I decline. I can't go off with the girl my host is going to marry. It wouldn't be decent. Besides, I don't want to go off with anybody.

Ethel [*her spirits dropping to zero*]. You won't?

Warrington [*testily*]. No, I won't. And, for goodness' sake, speak lower. Julia's listening with all her ears.

Ethel [*with a bitter laugh*]. Poor Major Warrington! How I scared you!

Warrington. I should say you did. I'm not so young as I was. A few years ago, a little thing like that never made me turn a hair. Now I can't stand it.

[*Subsiding into chair, and wiping the perspiration from his brow.*

Ethel. You've gone through it before, then?

Warrington. More than once, my dear.

Ethel [*dismally*]. And now *you'll* look down on me, too.

Warrington [*trying to cheer up*]. On the contrary, I admire you immensely. In fact, I don't know which I admire more, your pluck or your truly marvellous self-control. To ask me to go off with you without letting Julia hear! [*Looking anxiously towards her.*] It was masterly.

Ethel [*sighs*]. Well, I suppose I shall have to marry Geoff after all.

Warrington. I suppose so. Unless you could go off with the Rector?

[*She laughs shrilly. The two ladies turn sharply and glare.*

Ethel. Now I've shocked your sister again.

Warrington. You have. She thinks I'm flirting with you. That means I shan't be asked down to Milverton for another five years. Thank heaven for that! Ah, here are the billiard players.

[*He rises, with a sigh of relief. The conversation has been amusing, but not without its perils, and he is not altogether sorry to have it safely over.* ETHEL *remains seated, and does not turn round. The billiard players troop in, headed by* MABEL, GEOFFREY *holding open the door for them.*

Geoffrey [*to* MABEL]. You fluked outrageously, you know.

Mabel [*entering*]. I didn't!

Geoffrey. Oh, yes, you did. Didn't she, mother?

Mrs. Cassilis [*smiling at her*]. Disgracefully.

Mrs. Borridge. You'll soon learn, Lady Marchmont, if you practise a bit.

Lady Marchmont. Do you think so?

Lady Remenham. Well, who won, Rector?

Mrs. Borridge. I did!

Lady Remenham. Indeed?

[*Turns frigidly away, losing all interest at once.*

Mrs. Borridge [*obstinately cheerful and friendly*]. Why didn't *you* play, Mrs. 'Erris?

Mrs. Herries [*frigid smile*]. I never play games.

Mrs. Borridge. You should learn. I'd teach you.

Mrs. Herries [*who longs to be as rude as* LADY REMENHAM *but has not quite the courage*]. Thank you. I fear I have no time.

[*Joins* LADY REMENHAM *again, ruffling her feathers nervously.*

Mrs. Cassilis. Ethel, dear, we missed *you* sadly. I hope you haven't been dull?

Ethel [*with hysterical laugh*]. Not at all. Major Warrington has been entertaining me.

Rector. I suspect Miss Borridge felt there would be no opponent worthy of her steel.

[ETHEL *shrugs her shoulders rudely. He turns away.*

Mrs. Cassilis [*as a last resort*]. I wonder if we could have some music now. Mabel, dear, won't you sing to us?

Mabel. I've got nothing with me.

Geoffrey. Do sing, Mabel. There'll be lots of things you know here. [*Opens the piano.*] Let me find something. Schumann?

Mabel [*shakes head*]. I think not.

[*Joins him in searching music stand.*

Mrs. Cassilis. Sing us that Schubert song you sang when we were dining with you last, dear.

Mabel. Very well. Where's Schubert, Geoffrey?

Ethel [*to* WARRINGTON]. Do you see that?

[*Watching* GEOFFREY'*s and* MABEL'*s heads in close proximity. Seems as if she were about to jump from her chair.* WARRINGTON *restrains her by a hand on her arm.*

Warrington. Sh! Be quiet, for heaven's sake.

Ethel [*hisses*]. The little *cat*!

Mabel. Here it is. Geoff, don't be silly. [*Turns to piano.*

Mrs. Cassilis. Can you see there?

Mabel. Yes, thank you.

[*She sings two verses of Schubert's 'Adieu', in German, very simply, in a small but sweet voice. While she sings the behaviour of the guests affords a striking illustration of the English attitude towards music after dinner.* GEOFFREY *stands by piano prepared to turn over when required.* LADY REMENHAM *sits on sofa in an attitude of seraphic appreciation of her daughter's efforts.* LADY MARCHMONT, *by her side, is equally enthralled—and thinks of something else.* MRS. HERRIES *gently beats time with her fan.* MRS. CASSILIS *is sweetly appreciative. The* BORRIDGES, *on the contrary, fall sadly below the standard of polite attention, required of them.* ETHEL, *who has begun by glaring defiantly at* MABEL *during the first few bars of the song, rapidly comes to the conclusion that she can't sing, and decides to ignore the whole performance.* MRS. BORRIDGE *begins by settling herself placidly to the task of listening. She is obviously puzzled and rather annoyed when the song turns out to be German, but decides to put up with it with a shrug, hoping it will soon be over. At the end of the first verse she turns to* MRS. CASSILIS *to begin to talk, but that lady, with a smile and a gesture, silences her, and the second verse begins. At this* MRS. BORRIDGE'*s jaw falls, and, after a few bars, she frankly addresses herself to slumber. Her purple, good-natured countenance droops upon her shoulder as the verse proceeds, and when she wakes up at the end it is with a visible start.* WARRINGTON, *meantime, has disgraced himself in the eyes of his sister by talking to* ETHEL *during the opening bars of the second verse, and has only been reduced to silence by the stony glare which she thenceforward keeps fixed upon him till the last bar. In self-defence, he leans back in his chair and contemplates the ceiling resolutely.*

Geoffrey [*clapping*]. Bravo! Bravo!

Rector. Charming, charming.

Lady Marchmont [*to* LADY REMENHAM]. What a sweet voice she has.

Mrs. Cassilis. Thank you, dear.

Rector [*to* MABEL, *heartily*]. Now we must have another.

Geoffrey. Do, Mabel.

Mabel. No. That's quite enough.

Rector [*with resolute friendliness*]. Miss Borridge, *you* sing I'm sure?

Mrs. Borridge. Do, dearie. [*To* LADY REMENHAM.] My girl has a wonderful voice, Lady Remling. Quite like a professional. Old Jenkins at the Tiv. used to say she'd make a fortune in the 'alls.

Lady Remenham [*frigidly*]. Indeed?

Ethel. I don't think I've any songs anyone here would care for.

Mrs. Borridge. Nonsense, dearie. You've lots of songs. Give them 'The Children's 'Ome'.

Ethel [*rising*]. Well, I'll sing if you like.

Geoffrey [*going to her*]. Shall I find you something, Ethel?

Ethel [*snaps*]. No!

[GEOFFREY *turns away snubbed, and joins* MABEL. ETHEL *goes to the piano, where she is followed a moment later by* WARRINGTON, *who stands behind it, facing audience, and looking much amused as her song proceeds.* ETHEL *takes her seat at piano. There is a moment's pause while she darts a glance at* GEOFFREY *standing with* MABEL. *Then she seems to make up her mind, and without prelude of any kind, plunges into the following refined ditty:—*

When Joey takes me for a walk, me an' my sister Lue,
'E puts 'is arms round both our waists, as lots o' men will do.
We don't allow no liberties, and so we tells 'im plain,
And Joey says 'e's sorry—but 'e does the same again!

[*Spoken.*] Well, we're not going to have that, you know. Not likely! We're not that sort. So we just says to 'im:—

Stop that, Joey! Stow it, Joe!
Stop that ticklin' when I tell yer toe.
You're too free to suit a girl like me,
Just you stop that ticklin' or I'll slap yer.

When Joe an' me is man an' wife—I thinks 'e loves me true,
I 'ope 'e'll go on ticklin' me—and leave off ticklin' Lue.
'E'll have to leave the girls alone, and mind what 'e's about,
Or 'im an' me an' Lucy 'ill precious soon fall out.

[*Spoken.*] Yes. I'm not going to put up with that sort of thing once we're married. Not I. If 'e tries it on I shall just sing out straight:—

Now then, all of you.

[*Looks across impudently towards* LADY REMENHAM, *who bristles with indignation.*

Stop that, Joey! Chuck it, Joe!
Stop that ticklin' when I tell yer toe!
You're too free to suit a girl like me,
Just you drop that ticklin' or I'll slap yer!

[*Sings chorus fortissimo, joined by her delighted mother and by* WARRINGTON, *who beats time sonorously on top of the piano. For this attention she slaps him cordially on the cheek at the last line, by way of giving an artistic finish to the situation, and then rises, flushed and excited, and stands by the piano, looking defiantly at her horrified audience.*

Warrington. Splendid, by Jove! Capital!

[*That, however, is clearly not the opinion of the rest of the listeners, for the song has what is called a 'mixed' reception. The ladies, for the most part, had originally settled themselves into their places prepared to listen to anything which was set before them with polite indifference. A few bars, however, suffice to convince them of the impossibility of that attitude.* LADY REMENHAM, *who is sitting on the sofa by* LADY MARCHMONT, *exchanges a horrified glance with that lady, and with* MRS. HERRIES *on the other side of the room.* MABEL *looks uncomfortable. The* RECTOR *feigns abstraction.* MRS. CASSILIS *remains calm and sweet, but avoids everyone's eye, and more particularly* GEOFFREY'*s, who looks intensely miserable. But* WARRINGTON *enjoys himself thoroughly, even down to the final slap, and as for* MRS. BORRIDGE, *her satisfaction is unmeasured. She beats time to the final chorus, wagging her old head and joining in in stentorian accents, finally jumping up from her chair, clapping her hands, and crying, 'That's right, Eth. Give 'em another.' In fact, she feels that the song has been a complete triumph for her daughter, and a startling vindication of old Jenkins's good opinion of her powers. Suddenly, however, she becomes conscious of the horrified silence which surrounds her. The cheers die away on her lips. She looks round the room, dazed and almost frightened, then hurriedly reseats herself in her chair, from which she has risen in her excitement, straightens her wig, and—there is an awful pause.*

Mrs. Cassilis [*feeling she must say something*]. Won't you come to the fire, Ethel? You must be cold out there.

Ethel. Thank you, Mrs. Cassilis. I'm not cold.

Warrington. Jove. Miss Borridge, I'd no idea you could sing like that.

Ethel [*with a sneer*]. Nor had Geoffrey.

Lady Remenham [*rising*]. Well, we must be getting home. Geoffrey, will you ask if the carriage is round.

Geoffrey. Certainly, Lady Remenham. [*Rings*.

Mrs. Herries. We must be going, too. Come, Hildebrand. [*Rising also*.

Lady Remenham. Are you coming with us, Mabel?

Mrs. Cassilis. Oh, no, I can't spare Mabel yet. She has promised to stay a few days more.

Lady Remenham. Very well. [*Enter* BUTLER.

Geoffrey. Lady Remenham's carriage.

Butler. It's at the door, sir.

Geoffrey. Very well. [*Exit* BUTLER.

Lady Remenham. Good-bye, then, dear. Such a pleasant evening. Good night, Mabel. We shall expect you when we see you. [*General leave-takings*.

Mrs. Herries. Good-bye, Mrs. Cassilis.

Mrs. Borridge. Good night, Lady Remling.

[*Holds out hand with nervous cordiality*.

Lady Remenham. Good night.

[*Sweeps past her with icy bow*, MRS. BORRIDGE *retires crushed to a chair by fire, and consoles herself with illustrated paper*.

Lady Remenham [*to* WARRINGTON, *who is devoting his last moments to* MISS BORRIDGE]. Algernon.

Warrington. Coming, Julia. [*To* ETHEL.] See you in London, then?

Geoffrey [*stiffly*]. You'll take another cigar, Warrington—to light you home?

Warrington. Thanks. Don't mind if I do.

[GEOFFREY *hands box*.

Lady Remenham [*sternly*]. Algernon. We're going to get on our wraps.

[MRS. CASSILIS *and* LADY REMENHAM, MRS. HERRIES *and the* RECTOR, *go out*.

Warrington. All right, Julia. I shall be ready as soon as you are.

Geoffrey [*motioning to whisky*]. Help yourself, Warrington.

[*Goes out after the others*.

Warrington [*to* ETHEL, *after helping himself to drink*]. Well, my dear, I'm afraid you've done it *this* time!

Ethel. Done what?

Warrington. Shocked them to some purpose! It was magnificent, but it was scarcely tactics, eh?

Ethel. I suppose not. [*Fiercely.*] But I *wanted* to shock them! Here have they been despising me all the evening for nothing, and when that detestable girl with a voice like a white mouse sang her German jargon, praising her sky-high. I said I'd show them what singing means! And I did!

Warrington. You certainly did! Ha! Ha! You should have seen Julia's face when you boxed my ears. If the earth had opened her mouth and swallowed you up like Korah, Dathan and the other fellow, it couldn't have opened wider than Julia's.

Ethel. Well, she can scowl if she likes. She can't hurt me now.

Warrington. I'm not so sure of that.

Ethel. She'll have to hurry up. We go to-morrow.

Warrington. Ah, I didn't know. Well, there's nothing like exploding a bomb before you leave, eh? Only it's not always safe—for the operator.

Geoffrey [*re-entering with* MRS. CASSILIS]. The carriage is round, Warrington. Lady Remenham's waiting.

Warrington. The deuce she is. [*Swallows whisky and soda.*] I must fly. Good-bye again. Good-bye, Mrs. Cassilis. A thousand thanks for a most interesting evening.

[WARRINGTON *goes out with* GEOFFREY. *Pause.* ETHEL *stands sullen by fireplace.*

Mrs. Borridge [*yawning cavernously*]. Well, I think I shall turn in. Good night, Mrs. Cassilis. [*General handshakes.*] Coming, Eth?

Ethel. In a moment, mother.

[MRS. BORRIDGE *waddles out, with a parting smile from* LADY MARCHMONT. GEOFFREY *returns from seeing* WARRINGTON *off the premises.* MRS. BORRIDGE *wrings his hand affectionately in passing.*

Lady Marchmont. I must be off, too. And so must you, Mabel. You look tired out.

[*Kisses* MRS. CASSILIS. GEOFFREY *opens door for them.*

Mabel. I am a little tired. Good night.

[*Exeunt* LADY MARCHMONT *and* MABEL.

Geoffrey. Are you going, mother?

Mrs. Cassilis. Not at once. I've a couple of notes to write.

[GEOFFREY *crosses to fire.* MRS. CASSILIS *goes to writing table centre, sits facing audience, and appears to begin to write notes.* GEOFFREY *goes up to* ETHEL *thoughtfully. A silence. Then he speaks in a low tone.*

Geoffrey. Ethel.

Ethel. Yes. [*Without looking up.*]

Geoffrey. Why did you sing that song to-night?

Ethel [*with a sneer*]. To please Lady Remenham!

Geoffrey. But, Ethel! That's not the sort of song Lady Remenham likes at all.

Ethel [*impatiently*]. To shock her, then.

Geoffrey. Ethel!

Ethel. I think I managed it, too!

Geoffrey. I don't understand. You're joking, aren't you?

Ethel. Joking!

Geoffrey. I mean, you didn't really do it on purpose to make Lady Remenham angry. I'm sure you didn't.

Ethel [*very distinctly*]. I tell you I did it on purpose, deliberately, to shock Lady Remenham. I suppose I ought to know.

Geoffrey [*astonished*]. But why? What made you do such a thing?

Ethel [*savagely*]. I did it because I chose. Is that plain enough?

Geoffrey. Still, you must have a *reason*. [*No answer, suspiciously*.] Did that fellow Warrington tell you to sing it?

Ethel [*snaps*]. No.

Geoffrey. I thought perhaps. . . . Anyhow, promise me not to sing such a song again here. [*Silence*.] You will promise?

Ethel. Pooh!

Geoffrey. Ethel, be reasonable. You must know you can't go on doing that sort of thing here. When we are married we shall live down here. You must conform to the ideas of the people round you. They may seem to you narrow and ridiculous, but you can't alter them.

Ethel. *You* don't think them narrow and ridiculous, I suppose?

Geoffrey. No. In this case I think they are right. In many cases.

Ethel. Sorry I can't agree with you.

Geoffrey [*gently*]. Ethel, dear, don't let's quarrel about a silly thing like this. If you are going to marry me you *must* take my judgement on a matter of this kind.

Ethel [*defiantly*]. *Must* I?

Geoffrey. Yes.

Ethel. Then I won't. So there. I shall do just exactly as I please. And if you don't like it you can do the other thing. I'm not going to be bullied by you.

Geoffrey [*reasoning with her*]. My dear Ethel, I'm sure I am never likely to bully you, or to do or say anything that is unkind. But on a point like this I can't give way.

Ethel. Very well, Geoff. If you think that you'd better break off our engagement, that's all.

Geoffrey. Ethel! [*With horror.*]

Ethel [*impatiently*]. Well, there's nothing to make faces about, is there?

Geoffrey. You don't *mean* that. You don't mean you *want* our engagement to come to an end.

Ethel. Never mind what *I* want. What do *you* want?

Geoffrey [*astonished*]. Of course I want it to go on. You know that.

Ethel [*gesture of despair*]. Very well, then. You'd better behave accordingly. And now, if you've finished your lecture, I'll go to bed. Good night.

[*Goes out, with a nod to* MRS. CASSILIS, *who kisses her good night gently.* GEOFFREY *holds door open for her to go out, then goes and stands by fire.* MRS. CASSILIS, *who has watched this scene while appearing to be absorbed in her notes, now rises to go to her room.*

Mrs. Cassilis [*cheerfully*]. Well, I must be off, too! Good night, Geoffrey. [*Kisses him.*

Geoffrey [*absently*]. Good night, mother. [MRS. CASSILIS *goes slowly towards door.*] Mother.

Mrs. Cassilis [*turning*]. Yes, Geoff.

Geoffrey. Mother, you don't think I was unreasonable in what I said to Ethel, do you?

Mrs. Cassilis [*seems to think it over*]. No, Geoff.

Geoffrey. Or unkind?

Mrs. Cassilis. No, Geoff.

Geoffrey. I was afraid. She took it so strangely.

Mrs. Cassilis. She's rather over-excited to-night, I think. And tired, no doubt. [*Encouragingly.*] She'll be all right in the morning.

Geoffrey. You think I did right to speak to her about that song?

Mrs. Cassilis. Quite right, dear. Dear Ethel still has a little to learn, and, of course it will take time. But we must be patient. Meantime, whenever she makes any little mistake, such as she made to-night, I think you should certainly speak to her about it. It will be such a help to her! I don't mean *scold* her, of course, but speak to her gently and kindly, just as you did to-night.

Geoffrey [*despondently*]. It didn't seem to do any good.

Mrs. Cassilis. One never knows, dear. Good night.

[*Kisses him and goes out. He stands thoughtfully looking into the fire, and the curtain falls.*

ACT IV

SCENE. *The morning-room at Deynham. Time, after breakfast next day. A pleasant room, with French windows at the back open on to terrace. The sun is shining brilliantly. There is a door to hall on the left. On the opposite side of the room is the fireplace.*

When the curtain rises MABEL *and* GEOFFREY *are on the stage.* GEOFFREY *stands by the fireplace.* MABEL *is standing by the open window. He looks rather out of sorts and dull.*

Mabel. What a lovely day!

Geoffrey [*absently*]. Not bad. [*Pulls out cigarette case.*

Mabel. I'm sure you smoke too much, Geoffrey.

Geoffrey [*smiles*]. I think not.

[*Enter* MRS. CASSILIS *from hall.*

Mrs. Cassilis. Not gone out yet, dears? Why, Mabel, you've not got your habit on.

Mabel. We're not going to ride this morning.

Mrs. Cassilis [*surprised*]. Not going to ride?

Mabel. No. We've decided to stay at home to-day for a change.

Mrs. Cassilis. But why, dear?

Mabel [*hesitating*]. I don't know. We just thought so. That's all.

Mrs. Cassilis. But you must have some reason. You and Geoffrey haven't been quarrelling, have you?

Mabel [*laughing*]. Of course not.

Mrs. Cassilis. Then why aren't you going to ride?

Mabel. Well, we thought Ethel might be dull if we left her all alone.

Mrs. Cassilis. Nonsense, dears. *I'll* look after Ethel. Go up and change, both of you, at once. Ethel would be dreadfully grieved if you gave up your ride for her. Ethel's not selfish. She would never allow you or Geoffrey to give up a pleasure on her account. [*Crosses to bell.*

Geoffrey. Well, Mabel, what do you say? [*Going to window.*] It is a ripping day.

Mabel. If Mrs. Cassilis thinks so.

Mrs. Cassilis. Of course I think so. Run away, dears, and

get your things on. I'll tell them to send round the horses. [*Rings.*

Geoffrey. All right. Just for an hour. Come on, Mabel. I'll race you to the end of the passage.

[*They run out together, nearly upsetting* FOOTMAN *who enters at the same moment.*

Mrs. Cassilis. Lady Mabel and Mr. Geoffrey are going out riding. Tell them to send the horses round. And tell Hallard I want to see him about those roses. I'm going into the garden now.

Footman. Very well, madam. [*Exit* FOOTMAN.

[MRS. CASSILIS *goes out into the garden. A moment later* MRS. BORRIDGE *and* ETHEL *come in from the hall.*

Mrs. Borridge [*looking round, then going to easy-chair*]. Mrs. Cassilis isn't here?

Ethel [*sulky*]. I dare say she's with the housekeeper.

Mrs. Borridge. Very likely. [*Picks up newspaper.*] Give me a cushion, there's a good girl. [ETHEL *does so.*] Lady Marchmont isn't down yet, I suppose.

Ethel. No. [*Turns away.*

Mrs. Borridge [*putting down paper*]. What's the matter, dearie? You look awfully down.

Ethel. Nothing.

[*Goes to window and stares out into the sunlight.*

Mrs. Borridge. I wish Lady Marchmont came down to breakfast of a morning.

Ethel [*shrugs*]. Do you?

Mrs. Borridge. Yes. It's dull without her. She and I are getting quite chummy.

Ethel [*irritably, swinging round*]. Chummy! My dear mother, Lady Marchmont's only laughing at you.

Mrs. Borridge. Nonsense, Ethel. Laughing at *me*, indeed! I should like to see her!

Ethel. That's just it, mother. You never will.

Mrs. Borridge. Pray, what do you mean by *that*, miss?

Ethel [*hopeless*]. Oh, it doesn't matter.

[*Goes to fireplace and leans arm on mantelpiece, depressed.*

Mrs. Borridge. Now you're sneering at me, and I won't 'ave it—have it. [*Silence.*] Do you 'ear?

Ethel. Yes, I *h*ear. [*Stares down at fender.*

Mrs. Borridge. Very well, then. Don't let me 'ave any more of it. [*Grumbling to herself.*] Laughing, indeed! [*Pause. Recovering her composure.*] Where's Geoffy?

Ethel. I don't know.

Mrs. Borridge. Out riding, I suppose?

Ethel. Very likely.

Mrs. Borridge. 'E only finished breakfast just before us.

Ethel. *H*e, mother.

Mrs. Borridge. Dear, dear, 'ow you do go on! You leave my aitches alone. *They're* all right.

Ethel [*sighs*]. I wish they were! [*Pause*.] You've not forgotten we're going away to-day, mother?

Mrs. Borridge. To-day? 'Oo says so?

Ethel. We were only invited for a week.

Mrs. Borridge. Were we, dearie? I don't remember.

Ethel. *I* do. There's a train at 12.15, if you'll ask Mrs. Cassilis about the carriage.

Mrs. Borridge [*flustered*]. But I've not let Jane know. She won't be expecting us.

Ethel. We can telegraph.

Mrs. Borridge. Can't we stay another day or two? I'm sure Mrs. Cassilis won't mind. And I'm very comfortable here.

Ethel [*firmly*]. *No*, mother.

Mrs. Borridge. Why not?

Ethel [*exasperated*]. In the first place because we haven't been asked. In the second, because I don't want to.

Mrs. Borridge. Don't want to?

Ethel [*snappishly*]. No. I'm sick and tired of this place.

Mrs. Borridge. Are you, dearie? I thought we were gettin' on first rate.

Ethel. *Did* you? Anyhow, we're going, thank goodness, and that's enough. Don't forget to speak to Mrs. Cassilis. I'll go upstairs and pack.

[*As she is crossing the room to go out* MRS. CASSILIS *enters from garden and meets her. She stops.* MRS. CASSILIS *kisses her affectionately*.

Mrs. Cassilis. Going out, Ethel dear? Good morning. [*Greets* MRS. BORRIDGE.

Ethel. Good morning.

Mrs. Cassilis [*putting her arm in* ETHEL'*s and leading her up to to window*]. Isn't it a lovely day? I woke at five. I believe it was the birds singing under my window.

Ethel. Did you, Mrs. Cassilis? [*Enter* LADY MARCHMONT.

Lady Marchmont. Good morning Adelaide. [*Kisses her*.] Late again, I'm afraid. [*Shakes hands with* ETHEL.

Mrs. Cassilis [*sweetly*]. Another of your headaches, dear? I'm so sorry.

Lady Marchmont [*ignoring the rebuke*]. Good morning, Mrs. Borridge. I hope *you* slept well.

Mrs. Borridge. Sound as a bell. But, then, I was always a one-er to sleep. My old man, when 'e was alive, used to say 'e never knew anyone sleep like me. And snore! Why 'e declared it kep' 'im awake 'alf the night. But *I* never noticed it.

Lady Marchmont [*sweetly*]. That must have been a great consolation for Mr. Borridge.

Mrs. Borridge. Your 'usband snore?

Lady Marchmont [*laughing*]. No.

Mrs. Borridge. Thinks it's low per'aps .... They used to say snorin' comes from sleepin with your mouth open, but *I* don't know. What do *you* think?

Lady Marchmont. I really don't know, dear Mrs. Borridge. I must think it over.

[LADY MARCHMONT *takes chair by* MRS. BORRIDGE. *They converse in dumb show.* ETHEL *and* MRS. CASSILIS *come down stage.*

Mrs. Cassilis. What a pretty blouse you've got on to-day, dear.

Ethel. Is it, Mrs. Cassilis?

Mrs. Cassilis. Sweetly pretty. It goes so well with your eyes. You've lovely eyes, you know.

Ethel. Do you think so?

Mrs. Cassilis. Of course. So does Geoff.

Ethel [*disengaging herself*]. Oh, Geoff——Well, I must go upstairs. [*To* MRS. BORRIDGE *in passing*.] Don't forget, mummy. [*Exit* ETHEL.

Mrs. Borridge. What, dearie? Oh, yes. Ethel says we must be packin' our traps, Mrs. Cassilis.

Mrs. Cassilis [*startled*]. Packing?

Mrs. Borridge. Yes. She says we mustn't outstay our welcome. She's proud, is my girlie.

Mrs. Cassilis [*with extreme cordiality*]. But you're not thinking of leaving us? Oh, you mustn't do that. Geoff would be so disappointed. And so should I.

Mrs. Borridge. I don't *want* to go, I'm sure. Only Ethel said——

Mrs. Cassilis. There must be some mistake. I counted on you for quite a long visit.

Mrs. Borridge. Ethel said we were only asked for a week.

Mrs. Cassilis. But that was before I really knew you, wasn't it? It's quite different now.

Mrs. Borridge [*purring delightedly*]. If you feel that, Mrs. Cassilis——

Mrs. Cassilis. Of course I feel it. I hope you'll stay quite a *long* time yet.

Mrs. Borridge [*complacent, appealing to* LADY MARCHMONT, *who nods sympathy*]. There! I told Ethel how it was.

Mrs. Cassilis [*anxious*]. Ethel doesn't *want* to go, does she?

Mrs. Borridge. Oh, *no.* She'd be delighted to stop on. Only she thought——

Mrs. Cassilis [*determined to leave* MRS. BORRIDGE *no opportunity to hedge*]. Very well, then. That's settled. You'll stay with us till Geoff and I go to Scotland. That won't be till the middle of August. You promise?

Mrs. Borridge. Thank you, Mrs. Cassilis. I call that *real* hospitable! [*Rising.*] And now I'll run upstairs and tell my girl, or she'll be packing my black satin before I've time to stop her. She's so 'asty. And I always say nothing spoils things like packing, especially satins. They do crush so.

[MRS. BORRIDGE *waddles out. As soon as the door closes* MRS. CASSILIS *heaves a deep sigh of relief, showing how alarmed she had been lest the* BORRIDGES *should really take their departure. For a moment there is silence. Then* LADY MARCHMONT, *who has watched this scene with full appreciation of its ironic humour, speaks.*

Lady Marchmont. How you fool that old woman!

Mrs. Cassilis. So do *you*, dear.

Lady Marchmont. Yes. You'll make me as great a hypocrite as yourself before you've done. When you first began I was shocked at you. But now I feel a dreadful spirit of emulation stealing over me.

Mrs. Cassilis [*grimly*]. There's always a satisfaction in doing a thing well, isn't there?

Lady Marchmont. You must feel it, then.

Mrs. Cassilis. Thanks.

Lady Marchmont [*puzzled*]. Do you really want these dreadful people to stay all that time?

Mrs. Cassilis. Certainly. And to come back, if necessary, in October.

Lady Marchmont. Good heavens! Why?

Mrs. Cassilis [*sitting*]. My dear Margaret, as long as that woman and her daughter are here we *may* get Geoffrey out of their clutches. I thought we should manage it last night. Last night was a terrible disillusionment for him, poor boy. But I was wrong. It was too soon.

Lady Marchmont. By the way, what did that amusing wretch Major Warrington advise?

Mrs. Cassilis. I didn't consult him. I'd no opportunity. Besides, I couldn't have trusted him. He might have gone over to the enemy.

Lady Marchmont. Yes. He was evidently attracted to the girl.

Mrs. Cassilis. I suppose so. Major Warrington isn't fastidious where women are concerned.

Lady Marchmont. Still, he knew, of course.

Mrs. Cassilis. Only what Lady Remenham would have told him. However, his visit wasn't altogether wasted, I think.

Lady Marchmont. That song, you mean.

Mrs. Cassilis. Yes. He gave poor Ethel a glimpse of the Paradise she is turning her back on for ever. London, music-hall songs, rackety bachelors. And that made her reckless. The contrast between Major Warrington, and, say, our dear Rector, can hardly fail to have gone home to her.

[*Further conversation is interrupted by the entrance of* ETHEL, *in the worst of tempers.* MRS. CASSILIS *is on her guard at once.*

Ethel [*bursting out*]. Mrs. Cassilis——

Mrs. Cassilis [*very sweetly, rising and going to her*]. Ethel, dear, what *is* this I hear? You're not going to run away from us?

Ethel [*doggedly*]. Indeed, we must, Mrs. Cassilis. You've had us for a week. We really musn't stay any longer.

Mrs. Cassilis. But, my dear, it's *delightful* to have you.

Mrs. Borridge [*who has followed hard after her daughter and now enters, flushed and rather breathless*]. There, you see, dearie! What did I tell you?

Mrs. Cassilis. Geoff would be *terribly* distressed if you went away. He'd think I hadn't made you comfortable. He'd scold me dreadfully.

Ethel. I don't think Geoff will care.

[MRS. BORRIDGE *appeals mutely for sympathy to* LADY MARCHMONT, *who hastens to give it in full measure.*

Mrs. Cassilis [*great solicitude*]. My dear, you've not had any little difference with Geoff? Any quarrel?

Ethel. No.

Mrs. Cassilis. I was so afraid——

Ethel. Still, we oughtn't to plant ourselves on you in this way.

Mrs. Borridge. Plant ourselves! Really, dearie, how can you say such things? Plant ourselves!

Ethel. Oh, do be quiet, mother. [*Stamps her foot*.

Mrs. Cassilis [*soothing her*]. Anyhow, you can't possibly go to-day. The carriage has gone to Branscombe, and the other horse has cast a shoe. And to-morrow there's a dinner party at Milverton. You'll stay for *that*?

Ethel. You're very kind, Mrs. Cassilis, but——

Mrs. Cassilis [*leaving her no time to withdraw*]. That's right, my dear. You'll stay. And next week we'll have some young people over to meet you, and you shall dance all the evening.

Mrs. Borridge. There, Ethel!

Ethel [*hopeless*]. Very well. If you really wish it.

Mrs. Cassilis. Of course I wish it. I'm *so* glad. I shan't be able to part with you for a *long* time yet.

[*Kisses her tenderly. But* ETHEL *seems too depressed to answer to these blandishments*.

Lady Marchmont [*under her breath*]. Really, Adelaide!

Mrs. Cassilis [*sweetly*]. Into the garden, did you say, Margaret? [*Taking her up towards window*.] Very well. The sun *is* tempting, isn't it?

[MRS. CASSILIS *and her sister sail out*. ETHEL *and her mother remain, the former in a condition of frantic exasperation*.

Ethel. Well, mother, you've done it!

Mrs. Borridge [*snapping. She feels she is being goaded unduly*]. Done what, dearie?

Ethel [*impatiently*]. Oh, you know.

Mrs. Borridge. Do you mean about staying on here? But what could I do? Mrs. Cassilis wouldn't *let* us go. You saw that yourself.

Ethel. You might have stood out.

Mrs. Borridge. I did, dearie. I stood out as long as ever I could. But she wouldn't hear of our goin'. You saw that yourself.

Ethel. Well, mother, don't say I didn't warn you, that's all.

Mrs. Borridge. Warn me, dearie?

Ethel [*breaking out*]. That I was tired of this place. Sick and tired of it! That it was time we were moving.

Mrs. Borridge [*placidly*]. Is that all? I'll remember. [*Pause*.] How far did you get with the packing?

Ethel [*impatiently*]. I don't know.

Mrs. Borridge. You hadn't packed my black satin?

Ethel. I don't know. Yes, I think so. I'm not sure. Don't *worry*, mother.

Mrs. Borridge [*lamentably*]. It'll be simply covered with creases. I know it will. Run up at once, there's a good girl, and shake it out.

Ethel [*snaps*]. Oh, bother!

Mrs. Borridge. Then I must. How tiresome girls are! Always in the tantrums!

[*Poor old* MRS. BORRIDGE *ambles out, grumbling.* ETHEL, *left alone, sits scowling furiously at the carpet and biting her nails. There is a considerable pause, during which her rage and weariness are silently expressed. Then* GEOFFREY *and* MABEL *enter, quite cheerful, in riding things. They make a curious contrast to the almost tragic figure of sulkiness which meets their eyes.*

Geoffrey [*cheerfully*]. Hullo, Ethel! There you are, are you?

Ethel [*sulky*]. You can see me, I suppose.

Mabel. We didn't get our ride after all.

Ethel. Didn't you? [*Turns away.*

Mabel. No. Basil has strained one of his sinews, poor darling. He'll have to lie up for a day or two.

Geoffrey. Isn't it hard luck? It would have been such a glorious day for a ride. We were going round by Long Winton and up to Tenterden's farm and——

Ethel [*snaps*]. You needn't trouble to tell me. I don't want to hear. [*There is an awkward pause after this explosion.*

Mabel. I think I'll go up and change my habit, Geoff.

[GEOFFREY *nods, and* MABEL *goes out.* GEOFFREY *after a moment goes up to* ETHEL, *and lays a hand gently on her shoulder.*

Geoffrey. What is it, Ethel? Is anything the matter?

Ethel [*shaking him off fiercely*]. Please don't touch me.

Geoffrey. Something has happened. What is it?

Ethel [*savagely*]. Nothing's happened. Nothing ever does happen here.

[GEOFFREY *tries to take her hand. She pulls it pettishly away. He slightly shrugs his shoulders. A long pause. He rises slowly and turns towards door.*

Ethel [*stopping him*]. Geoff!

Geoffrey. Yes. [*Does not turn his head.*

Ethel. I want to break off our engagement.

Geoffrey [*swinging round, astonished, and not for a moment taking her seriously*]. My dear girl!

Ethel. I think it would be better. Better for both of us.

Geoffrey [*still rallying her*]. Might one ask why?

Ethel. For many reasons. Oh, don't let us go into all that. Just say you release me and there's an end.

Geoffrey [*more serious*]. My dear Ethel. What *is* the matter? Aren't you well?

Ethel [*impatiently*]. I'm perfectly well.

Geoffrey. I don't think you are. You look quite flushed. I wish you'd take more exercise. You'd be ever so much better.

Ethel [*goaded to frenzy by this well-meant suggestion,* GEOFFREY'*s panacea for all human ills*]. Geoffrey, you're simply maddening. Do please understand that I know when I'm well and when I'm ill. There's nothing whatever the matter with me. I believe you think everything in life would go right if only everyone took a cold bath every morning and spent the rest of the day shooting partridges.

Geoffrey [*quite simply*]. Well, there's a lot in that, isn't there?

Ethel. Rubbish!

Geoffrey [*struck by a brilliant idea*]. It's not that silly business about the riding again, is it?

Ethel [*almost hysterical with exasperation*]. Oh, no! no! *Please* believe that I'm not a child, and that I know what I'm saying. *I want to break off our engagement.* I don't think we're suited to each other.

Geoffrey [*piqued*]. This is rather sudden, isn't it?

Ethel [*sharply*]. How do you know it's sudden?

Geoffrey. But isn't it?

Ethel. No. It's not.

Geoffrey [*struck by a thought*]. Ethel, has my mother——?

Ethel. Your mother has nothing whatever to do with it.

Geoffrey. She hasn't said anything?

Ethel. Your mother has been everything that's kind and good. In fact, if it hadn't been for her I think I should have broken it off before. But I didn't want to hurt her.

[GEOFFREY *rises, and paces the room up and down for a moment in thought. Then he turns to her again.*

Geoffrey. Ethel, you mustn't come to a decision like this hastily. You must take time to consider.

Ethel. Thank you. My mind is quite made up.

Geoffrey. Still, you might think it over for a day or two—a week, perhaps. It [*Hesitates.*] . . . it wouldn't be fair of me to take you at your word in this way.

Ethel. Why not?

Geoffrey [*hesitates*]. You might—regret it afterwards.

Ethel [*with a short laugh*]. You're very modest.

Geoffrey [*nettled*]. Oh, I'm not vain enough to imagine that you would find anything to regret in *me*. *I'm* a commonplace fellow enough. But there are other things which a girl has to consider in marriage, aren't there? Position. Money. If you broke off our engagement now, mightn't you regret these later on—[*Slight touch of bitterness.*] however little you regret *me*?

Ethel [*touched*]. Geoff, dear, I'm sorry I hurt you. I didn't mean to. You're a good fellow. Far too good for me. And I know you mean it kindly when you ask me to take time, and all that. But my mind's quite made up. Don't let's say any more about it.

Geoffrey [*slowly, and a little sadly*]. You don't love me any more, then?

Ethel. No. [*Decisively.*] I don't love you any more. Perhaps I never did love you really, Geoff. I don't know.

Geoffrey. I loved *you*, Ethel.

Ethel. I wonder.

Geoffrey. You know I did.

Ethel. You thought you did. But that's not always the same thing, is it? Many a girl takes a man's fancy for a moment. Yet people say one only loves once, don't they? [*Pause.*

Geoffrey [*hesitating again*]. Ethel . . . I don't know how to say it. . . . You'll laugh at me again. . . . But . . . you're sure you're not doing this on *my* account?

Ethel. On *your* account?

Geoffrey. Yes. To spare me. Because you think I ought to marry in my own class, as Lady Remenham would say?

Ethel. No.

Geoffrey. Quite sure?

Ethel [*nods*]. Quite. [*Turns away.*

Geoffrey [*frankly puzzled*]. Then I *can't* understand it!

Ethel [*turning on him impatiently*]. My dear Geoff, is it impossible for you to understand that I don't *want* to marry you? That if I married you I should be bored to death? That I *loathe* the life down here among your highly respectable friends? That if I had to *live* here with you I should yawn myself into my grave in six months?

Geoffrey [*astonished*]. Don't you *like* Deynham?

Ethel. No. I *detest* it. Oh, it's pretty enough, I suppose, and the fields are very green, and the view from Milverton Hill is much admired. And you live all alone in a great park, and you've horses and dogs, and a butler and two footmen. But that's not enough for *me*. I want life, people, *lots* of people. If I lived down here I should go blue-mouldy in three weeks. I'm town-bred, a true cockney. I want streets and shops and gas lamps. I don't want your carriage and pair. Give me a penny omnibus.

Geoffrey. Ethel!

Ethel. Now you're shocked. It *is* vulgar, isn't it? But *I'm* vulgar. And I'm not ashamed of it. Now you know.

[*Another pause.* GEOFFREY, *in pained surprise, ponders deeply. At last he speaks.*

Geoffrey. It's all over, then?

Ethel [*nodding flippantly*]. All over and done with. I surrender my claim to everything, the half of your wordly goods, of your mother's wordly goods, of your house, your park, your men-servants and maid-servants, your aristocratic relations. Don't let's forget your aristocratic relations. I surrender them all. There's my hand on it.

[*Stretches it out.*

Geoffrey [*pained*]. Don't, Ethel.

Ethel [*with genuine surprise*]. My dear Geoff, you don't mean to say you're *sorry*! You ought to be flinging your cap in the air at regaining your liberty. Why, I believe there are tears in your eyes! Actually tears! Let me look.

[*Turns his face to her.*

Geoffrey [*pulling it away sulkily*]. You don't suppose a fellow *likes* being thrown over like this, do you?

Ethel. Vanity, my dear Geoff! Mere vanity.

Geoffrey [*hotly*]. It's not!

Ethel [*suddenly serious*]. Geoff, do you *want* our engagement to go on? Do you *want* to marry me still? [*He turns to her impulsively.*] Do you *love* me still? [*Checks him.*] No, Geoff. Think before you speak. On your honour! [GEOFFREY *is silent.*] There, you see! Come, dear, cheer up. It's best as it is. Give me a kiss. The last one. [*She goes to* GEOFFREY *and holds up her face to be kissed. He kisses her on the forehead.*] And now I'll run upstairs and tell mother. [*Laughs.*] Poor mother! Won't she make a shine!

[ETHEL *goes out recklessly.* GEOFFREY, *left alone, looks round the room in a dazed way. Takes out cigarette case automatically, goes to writing table for match.*

Just as he is lighting cigarette MRS. CASSILIS *enters from garden, followed a moment later by* LADY MARCHMONT. *He throws cigarette away unlighted.*

Mrs. Cassilis. All alone, Geoffrey?

Geoffrey. Yes, mother.

Mrs. Cassilis. Where's Ethel?

Geoffrey. Mother—Ethel's . . . [*Sees* LADY MARCHMONT. *Pause.*] Good morning, Aunt Margaret.

Lady Marchmont. Good morning.

Mrs. Cassilis. Well, dear?

Geoffrey. Mother—[*Plunging into his subject.*] a terrible thing has happened. Ethel was here a moment ago, and she has broken off our engagement.

Lady Marchmont. Broken it off!

Mrs. Cassilis [*immensely sympathetic*]. Broken it off, dear? Surely not?

Geoffrey. Yes.

Mrs. Cassilis. Oh, *poor* Geoffrey. [*Going to him.*] Did she say why?

Geoffrey [*dully*]. Only that it had all been a mistake. She was tired of it all, and didn't like the country, and—that's all, I think.

Mrs. Cassilis [*anxious*]. My poor boy. And I thought her so happy with us. [*Laying hand caressingly on his shoulder as he sits with head bowed.*] You don't think we've been to blame—*I've* been to blame—in any way, do you? Perhaps we ought to have amused her more.

Geoffrey. Not you, mother. You've always been sweet and good to her. Always. She said so.

Mrs. Cassilis. I'm glad of that, dear.

[*Enter* MRS. BORRIDGE, *furiously angry, followed by* ETHEL, *vainly trying to detain or silence her.* GEOFFREY *retreats up stage, where* MRS. BORRIDGE *for a moment does not notice him.*

Mrs. Borridge [*raging*]. Where's Geoff? Leave me alone, Ethel. Where's Geoff?

Ethel. He's not here, mother. And Mrs. Cassilis is. Do be quiet.

Geoffrey [*coming between them*]. I'm here. What is it, Mrs. Borridge?

Mrs. Borridge. Oh, Geoffy, what *is* this Ethel's been telling me? You haven't reely broke off your engagement, have you?

Ethel. Nonsense, mother. *I* broke it off, as I told you.

Mrs. Borridge. But you didn't mean it, dearie. It's all a mistake. Just a little tiff.

Ethel [*firmly*]. No!

Mrs. Borridge [*obstinately*]. Yes, it is. It'll blow over. You wouldn't be so unkind to poor Geoffy.

Ethel. Mother, don't be a fool. It doesn't take anybody in. Come upstairs and let's get on with our packing.

Mrs. Borridge [*stamps foot*]. Be quiet, Ethel, when I tell you. Lady Marchmont, won't you speak to her? Undutiful girl. I should like to *whip* her!

[ETHEL *turns away in despair.*

Lady Marchmont [*soothingly*]. Ah, well, dear Mrs. Borridge, perhaps young people know best about these things.

Mrs. Borridge [*excited and angry*]. Know best! know best! How should they know best? They don't know *anything*. They're as ignorant as they are uppish. [*Growing tearful.*] And to think 'ow I've worked for that girl! 'Ow I've slaved for 'er, denied myself for 'er. [*Breaking down.*] I did so want 'er to be respectable. I 'aven't always been respectable myself, and I know the value of it.

[*Subsides into chair, almost hysterical, and no longer realising what she is saying.*

Ethel. Oh, hush, mother!

Mrs. Borridge [*angry again*]. I won't 'ush, so there! I'm your mother, and I won't be trod on. *I* find someone to marry you—a better match than ever you'll find for yourself, miss—and this is 'ow I'm treated! [*Begins to cry.*

Ethel [*taking her arm*]. Mother, mother, do come away.

Mrs. Borridge [*breaking down altogether*]. And now to 'ave to begin all over again. And young men ain't so green as they used to be. Not by a long way. They're cunning, most of them. They take a deal of catchin'. And I'm getting' an old woman. Oh, she might 'ave spared me this.

Mrs. Cassilis [*almost sorry for her*]. Mrs. Borridge—Mrs. Borridge.

Mrs. Borridge [*refusing to be comforted*]. But she's no natural affection. That's what it is. She doesn't love 'er mother. She's 'eadstrong and wilful, and never paid the least attention to what I told 'er. [*Burst of tears.*] But I do think she might 'ave let '*im* break it off. Then there'd 'ave been a breach of promise, and that's always something. That's what I always say to girls: 'Leave *them* to break it off, dearies. And then there'll be a breach of promise, *and* damages.' That's if you've got something on paper. But—

[*Fresh burst of tears.*] she never *would* get anything on paper. She never paid the least regard to her old mother. She's an undutiful girl, and that's 'ow it is.

[*Goes off into incoherent sobs.*

Butler. Lady Remenham.

Mrs. Cassilis [*rising hastily*]. The drawing-room, Watson.

[*She is, however, too late to stop* WATSON *from showing in* LADY REMENHAM.

Lady Remenham [*sailing in, with breezy cheerfulness*]. How do you do, Adelaide? How do you do, Margaret? I've just driven Algernon to the station, and I thought I'd leave this for you as I passed. [*Gives book.*

Mrs. Borridge. She's an undutiful daughter. That's what she is. [*Snorting and sobbing.*

Lady Remenham [*perceiving for the first time that something unusual is going on*]. Eh?

Mrs. Cassilis. Mrs. Borridge is not quite herself just now. Dear Ethel has decided that she does not wish to continue her engagement to my son, and Mrs. Borridge has only just heard the news.

Lady Remenham [*scarcely able to believe her ears*]. Not wish——!

Mrs. Cassilis [*hastily, checking her*]. No. This has naturally upset us all very much. It was so very sudden.

Lady Remenham. Well, I must say——

[*Luckily she does not do so, but takes refuge in silence.*

Mrs. Borridge [*burst of grief*]. Oh, why didn't she get something on paper? Letters is best. Men are that slippy! I always told her to get something on paper.

[*Breaks down completely.*

Ethel. Come away, mother. [*Takes her firmly by the arm.*] Will you please order the carriage, Mrs. Cassilis?

[*Leads* MRS. BORRIDGE *off, sobbing and gulping to the last.*

Lady Remenham [*sitting down, with a triumphant expression on her amiable countenance*]. Geoffrey, will you tell the coachman to drive round to the stables? *I* shall stay to luncheon!

[*It is impossible adequately to represent the tone in which* LADY REMENHAM *announces this intention. It is that of a victorious general occupying the field, from which he has beaten the enemy with bag and baggage. Luckily,* GEOFFREY *is too depressed to notice anything. He goes out without a word—and the curtain falls.*

THE VOYSEY INHERITANCE

HARLEY GRANVILLE-BARKER
1877—1946

Born Kensington, London. His mother was a professional reciter, he appeared on the stage as a child and subsequently acted in London and the provinces. Achieved some pre-eminence in productions for William Poel and the Stage Society. Began to direct productions for the latter and established himself as a leading English producer at the Court Theatre (1904–7) and elsewhere, especially for Charles Frohman's repertory season at the Duke of York's, 1910, and in his Shakespearean productions at the Savoy (1912–14). His first wife was the actress Lillah McCarthy. After his second marriage in 1918 to an American, Helen Huntington, he left the theatre but continued to write and translate plays and to comment on the drama. Director of the British Institute in Paris, 1937–9. During the 1939–45 war lectured at American Universities.

His plays included *The Weather-Hen* (with Berte Thomas, 1899); *The Marrying of Ann Leete* (1902); *Prunella* (with Laurence Housman, 1904); *The Voysey Inheritance* (1905); *Waste* (1907); *The Madras House* (1910); *The Secret Life* (published 1923); *His Majesty* (published 1928).

His adaptations included *Anatol* (from Arthur Schnitzler, published 1911); *Collected Plays by Gregorio Martinez Sierra* (with Helen Granville-Barker, published 1923); *Doctor Knock* (from Jules Romains, published 1925); *Four Plays by Serafin and Joaquín Alvarez Quintero* (with Helen Granville-Barker, published 1927).

His writings on the theatre included *Scheme and Estimates for a National Theatre* (with William Archer, 1904, revised 1930); *The Exemplary Theatre* (1922); *Prefaces to Shakespeare: 1st Series* (1927), *2nd Series* (1930), *3rd Series* (1937), *4th Series* (1945), *5th Series* (1947); *On Dramatic Method* (1931); *A Companion to Shakespeare Studies* (with G. B. Harrison, 1934); *The Use of the Drama* (1945).

THE VOYSEY INHERITANCE

A PLAY IN FIVE ACTS

by

Harley Granville-Barker

THE VOYSEY INHERITANCE

First produced at the Court Theatre, London, 7 November 1905, *with the following cast:*

MR. VOYSEY	Mr. A. E. George
MRS. VOYSEY	Miss Florence Haydon
TRENCHARD VOYSEY, K.C.	Mr. Eugene Mayeur
HONOR VOYSEY	Miss Geraldine Olliffe
MAJOR BOOTH VOYSEY	Mr. Charles Fulton
MRS. BOOTH VOYSEY	Miss Grace Edwin
CHRISTOPHER	Master Harry C. Duff
EDWARD VOYSEY	Mr. Thalberg Corbett
HUGH VOYSEY	Mr. Dennis Eadie
MRS. HUGH VOYSEY	Miss Henrietta Watson
ETHEL VOYSEY	Miss Alexandra Carlisle
DENIS TREGONING	Mr. Frederick Lloyd
ALICE MAITLAND	Miss Mabel Hackney
MR. BOOTH	Mr. O. B. Clarence
THE REV. EVAN COLPUS	Mr. Edmund Gwenn
PEACEY	Mr. Trevor Lowe
PHOEBE	Miss Gwynneth Galton
MARY	Mrs. Fordyce

THE VOYSEY INHERITANCE

ACT I

The Office of Voysey and Son is in the best part of Lincoln's Inn. Its panelled rooms give out a sense of grandmotherly comfort and security, very grateful at first to the hesitating investor, the dubious litigant. MR. VOYSEY*'s own room, into which he walks about twenty past ten of a morning, radiates enterprise besides. There is polish on everything; on the windows, on the mahogany of the tidily packed writing-table that stands between them, on the brasswork of the fireplace in the other wall, on the glass of the firescreen which preserves only the pleasantness of a sparkling fire, even on* MR. VOYSEY*'s hat as he takes it off to place it on the little red-curtained shelf behind the door.* MR. VOYSEY *is sixty or more and masterful; would obviously be master anywhere from his own home outwards, or wreck the situation in his attempt. Indeed there is sometimes a buccaneering air in the twist of his glance, not altogether suitable to a family solicitor. On this bright October morning,* PEACEY, *the head clerk, follows just too late to help him off with his coat, but in time to take it and hang it up with a quite unnecessary subservience. Relieved of his coat,* MR. VOYSEY *carries to his table the bunch of beautiful roses he is accustomed to bring to the office three times a week and places them for a moment only near the bowl of water there ready to receive them while he takes up his letters. These lie ready too, opened mostly, one or two private ones left closed and discreetly separate. By this time the usual salutations have passed,* PEACEY*'s 'Good morning, sir';* MR. VOYSEY*'s 'Morning, Peacey.' Then as he gets to his letters* MR. VOYSEY *starts his day's work.*

Mr. Voysey. Any news for me?

Peacey. I hear bad accounts of Alguazils Preferred, sir.

Mr. Voysey. Oh . . . who from?

Peacey. Merrit and James's head clerk in the train this morning.

Mr. Voysey. They looked all right on . . . Give me *The Times.* [PEACEY *goes to the fireplace for* The Times; *it is warming there.* MR. VOYSEY *waves a letter, then places it on the table.*] Here, that's for you . . . Gerrard's Cross business. Anything else?

Peacey [*as he turns* The Times *to its Finance page*]. I've made the usual notes.

Mr. Voysey. Thank'ee.

Peacey. Young Benham isn't back yet.

Mr. Voysey. Mr. Edward must do as he thinks fit about that. Alguazils, Alg—oh, yes.

[*He is running his eye down the columns.* PEACEY *leans over the letters.*

Peacey. This is from Mr. Leader about the codicil . . . You'll answer that?

Mr. Voysey. Mr. Leader. Yes. Alguazils. Mr. Edward's here, I suppose.

Peacey. No, sir.

Mr. Voysey [*his eye twisting with some sharpness*]. What!

Peacey [*almost alarmed*]. I beg pardon, sir.

Mr. Voysey. Mr. Edward.

Peacey. Oh, yes, sir, been in his room some time. I thought you said Headley; he's not due back till Thursday.

[MR. VOYSEY *discards* The Times *and sits to his desk and his letters.*

Mr. Voysey. Tell Mr. Edward I've come.

Peacey. Yes, sir. Anything else?

Mr. Voysey. Not for the moment. Cold morning, isn't it?

Peacey. Quite surprising, sir.

Mr. Voysey. We had a touch of frost down at Chislehurst.

Peacey. So early!

Mr. Voysey. I want it for the celery. All right, I'll call through about the rest of the letters.

[PEACEY *goes, having secured a letter or two, and* MR. VOYSEY *having sorted the rest* (*a proportion into the waste-paper basket*) *takes up the forgotten roses and starts setting them into a bowl with an artistic hand. Then his son* EDWARD *comes in.* MR. VOYSEY *gives him one glance and goes on arranging the roses, but says cheerily . . .*

Mr. Voysey. Good morning, my dear boy.

[EDWARD *has little of his father in him and that little is undermost. It is a refined face, but self-consciousness takes the place in it of imagination, and in suppressing traits of brutality in his character it looks as if the young man had suppressed his sense of humour too. But whether or no, that would not be much in evidence now, for* EDWARD *is obviously going through some experience which is scaring him* (*there is no better word). He looks not to have slept for a night or two, and his standing there, clutching and unclutching the bundle of papers he carries, his eyes on his father, half appealingly but half accusingly too, his whole being altogether so unstrung and desperate , makes* MR. VOYSEY'*s uninterrupted arranging of the flowers seem very calculated indeed. At last the little tension of silence is broken.*

Edward. Father . . .

Mr. Voysey. Well?

Edward. I'm glad to see you.

[*This is a statement of fact. He doesn't know that the commonplace phrase sounds ridiculous at such a moment.*

Mr. Voysey. I see you've the papers there.

Edward. Yes.

Mr. Voysey. You've been through them?

Edward. As you wished me . . .

Mr. Voysey. Well? [EDWARD *doesn't answer. Reference to the papers seem to overwhelm him with shame.* MR. VOYSEY *goes on with cheerful impatience.*] Now, now, my dear boy, don't take it like this. You're puzzled and worried, of course. But why didn't you come down to me on Saturday night? I expected you . . . I told you to come. Your mother was wondering why you weren't with us for dinner yesterday.

Edward. I went through everything twice. I wanted to make quite sure.

Mr. Voysey. I told you to come to me.

Edward [*he is very near crying*]. Oh, Father!

Mr. Voysey. Now look here, Edward, I'm going to ring and dispose of these letters. Please pull yourself together.

[*He pushes the little button on his table.*

Edward. I didn't leave my rooms all day yesterday.

Mr. Voysey. A pleasant Sunday! You must learn, whatever the business may be, to leave it behind you at the office. Life's not worth living else.

[PEACEY *comes in to find* MR. VOYSEY *before the fire ostentatiously warming and rubbing his hands.*

Oh, there isn't much else, Peacey. Tell Simmons that if he satisfies you about the details of this lease it'll be all right. Make a note for me of Mr. Granger's address at Mentone.

Peacey. Mr. Burnett . . . Burnett and Marks . . . has just come in, Mr. Edward.

Edward [*without turning*]. It's only fresh instructions. Will you take them?

Peacey. All right.

[PEACEY *goes, lifting his eyebrows at the queerness of* EDWARD*'s manner. This* MR. VOYSEY *sees, returning to his table with a little scowl.*

Mr. Voysey. Now sit down. I've given you a bad forty-eight hours, have I? Well, I've been anxious about you. Never mind, we'll thresh the thing out now. Go through the two accounts. Mrs. Murberry's first . . . how do you find it stands?

Edward [*his feelings choking him*]. I hoped you were playing some joke on me.

Mr. Voysey. Come now.

[EDWARD *separates the papers precisely and starts to detail them; his voice quite toneless. Now and then his father's sharp comments ring out in contrast.*

Edward. We've got the lease of her present house, several agreements . . . and here's her will. Here's an expired power of attorney . . . over her securities and her property generally . . . it was made out for six months.

Mr. Voysey. She was in South Africa.

Edward. Here's the Sheffield mortgage and the Henry Smith mortgage with Banker's receipts . . . her Banker's to us for the interest up to date . . . four and a half and five per cent. Then . . . Fretworthy Bonds. There's a note scribbled in your writing that they are at the Bank; but you don't say what bank.

Mr. Voysey. My own.

Edward [*just dwelling on the words*]. Your own. I queried that. There's eight thousand five hundred in three and a half India stock. And there are her Banker's receipts for cheques on account of those dividends. I presume for those dividends.

Mr. Voysey. Why not?

Edward [*gravely*]. Because then, Father, there are her Banker's half-yearly receipts for other sums amounting to an average of four hundred and twenty pounds a year. But I find no record of any capital to produce this.

Mr. Voysey. Go on. What do you find?

Edward. Till about three years back there seems to have been eleven thousand in Queenslands which would produce

. . . did produce exactly the same sum. But after January of that year I find no record of them.

Mr. Voysey. In fact the Queenslands are missing, vanished?

Edward [*hardly uttering the word*]. Yes.

Mr. Voysey. From which you conclude?

Edward. I supposed at first that you had not handed me all the papers . . .

Mr. Voysey. Since Mrs. Murberry evidently still gets that four twenty a year somehow; lucky woman.

Edward [*in agony*]. Oh!

Mr. Voysey. Well, we'll return to the good lady later. Now let's take the other.

Edward. The Hatherley Trust.

Mr. Voysey. Quite so.

Edward [*with one accusing glance*]. Trust.

Mr. Voysey. Go on.

Edward. Father . . .

[*His grief comes uppermost again and* MR. VOYSEY *meets it kindly.*

Mr. Voysey. I know, my dear boy. I shall have lots to say to you. But let's get quietly through with these details first.

Edward [*bitterly now*]. Oh, this is simple enough. We're young Hatherley's trustees till he comes of age. The property was thirty-eight thousand invested in Consols. Certain sums were to be allowed for his education; we seem to be paying them.

Mr. Voysey. Regularly?

Edward. Quite. But where's the capital?

Mr. Voysey. No record?

Edward. Yes . . . a note by you on a half sheet: Refer Bletchley Land Scheme.

Mr. Voysey. Oh . . . we've been out of that six years or more! He's credited with the interest on his capital?

Edward. With the Consol interest.

Mr. Voysey. Quite so.

Edward. The Bletchley scheme paid seven and a half.

Mr. Voysey. At one time. Have you taken the trouble to calculate what will be due from us to the lad?

Edward. Yes . . . capital and interest . . . about forty-six thousand pounds.

Mr. Voysey. A respectable sum. In five years' time?

Edward. When he comes of age.

Mr. Voysey. That gives us, say, four years and six months in which to think about it.

[EDWARD *waits, hopelessly, for his father to speak again; then says* . . .

Edward. Thank you for showing me these, sir. Shall I put them back in your safe now?

Mr. Voysey. Yes, you'd better. There's the key. [EDWARD *reaches for the bunch, his face hidden.*] Put them down. Your hand shakes . . . why, you might have been drinking. I'll put them away later. It's no use having hysterics, Edward. Look your trouble in the face.

[EDWARD'*s only answer is to go to the fire, as far from his father as the room allows. And there he leans on the mantelpiece, his shoulders heaving.*

I'm sorry, my dear boy. I wouldn't tell you if I could help it.

Edward. I can't believe it. And that you should be telling me . . . such a thing.

Mr. Voysey. Let yourself go . . . have your cry out, as the women say. It isn't pleasant, I know. It isn't pleasant to inflict it on you.

Edward [*able to turn to his father again; won round by the kind voice*]. How long has it been going on? Why didn't you tell me before? Oh, I know you thought you'd pull through. But I'm your partner . . . I'm responsible too. Oh, I don't want to shirk that . . . don't think I mean to shirk that, Father. Perhaps I ought to have discovered . . . but those affairs were always in your hands. I trusted . . . I beg your pardon. Oh, it's us . . . not you. Everyone has trusted us.

Mr. Voysey [*calmly and kindly still*]. You don't seem to notice that I'm not breaking my heart like this.

Edward. What's the extent of . . . ? Are there other accounts . . . ? When did it begin? Father, what made you begin it?

Mr. Voysey. I didn't begin it.

Edward. You didn't? Who then?

Mr. Voysey. My father before me. [EDWARD *stares.*] That calms you a little.

Edward. But how terrible! Oh, my dear father . . . I'm glad. But . . .

Mr. Voysey [*shaking his head*]. My inheritance, Edward.

Edward. My dear father!

Mr. Voysey. I had hoped it wasn't to be yours.

Edward. But you mean to tell me that this sort of thing has been going on here for years? For more than thirty years!

Mr. Voysey. Yes.

Edward. That's a little hard to understand . . . just at first, sir.

Mr. Voysey [*sententiously*]. We do what we must in this world, Edward. I have done what I had to do.

Edward [*his emotion well cooled by now*]. Perhaps I'd better just listen while you explain.

Mr. Voysey [*concentrating*]. You know that I'm heavily into Northern Electrics.

Edward. Yes.

Mr. Voysey. But you don't know how heavily. When I got the tip the Municipalities were organising the purchase, I saw of course the stock must be up to a hundred and forty-five—a hundred and fifty in no time. Now Leeds has quarrelled with the rural group . . . there'll be no general settlement for ten years. I bought at ninety-five. What are they to-day?

Edward. Seventy-two.

Mr. Voysey. Seventy-one and a half. And in ten years I may be . . . ! I'm not a young man, Edward. That's mainly why you've had to be told.

Edward. With whose money are you so heavily into Northern Electrics?

Mr. Voysey. The firm's money.

Edward. Clients' money?

Mr. Voysey. Yes.

Edward [*coldly*]. Well . . . I'm waiting for your explanation, sir.

Mr. Voysey [*with a shrug*]. Children always think the worst of their parents, I suppose. I did of mine. It's a pity.

Edward. Go on, sir, go on. Let me know the worst.

Mr. Voysey. There's no immediate danger. I should think anyone could see that from the figures there. There's no real risk at all.

Edward. Is that the worst?

Mr. Voysey [*his anger rising*]. Have you studied these two accounts or have you not?

Edward. Yes, sir.

Mr. Voysey. Well, where's the deficiency in Mrs. Murberry's income . . . has she ever gone without a shilling? What has young Hatherley lost?

Edward. He stands to lose . . .

Mr. Voysey. He stands to lose nothing if I'm spared for a little, and you will only bring a little common sense to bear and try to understand the difficulties of my position.

Edward. Father, I'm not thinking ill of you . . . that is, I'm trying not to. But won't you explain how you're justified . . . ?

Mr. Voysey. In putting our affairs in order?

Edward. Are you doing that?

Mr. Voysey. What else?

Edward [*starting patiently to examine the matter*]. How bad were things when you came into control?

Mr. Voysey. Oh, I forget.

Edward. You can't forget.

Mr. Voysey. Well . . . pretty bad.

Edward. How was it my grandfather . . . ?

Mr. Voysey. Muddlement . . . timidity! Had a perfect mania for petty speculation. He'd no capital . . . no real credit . . . and he went in terror of his life. My dear Edward, if I hadn't found out in time, he'd have confessed to the first man who came and asked for a balance sheet.

Edward. How much was he to the bad then?

Mr. Voysey. Oh . . . a tidy sum.

Edward. But it can't have taken all these years to pay off. . . .

Mr. Voysey. Oh, hasn't it!

Edward [*making his point*]. Then how does it happen, sir, that such a recent trust as young Hatherley's has been broken into?

Mr. Voysey. Well, what could be safer? There is no one to interfere, and we haven't to settle up for five years.

Edward [*utterly beaten*]. Father, are you mad?

Mr. Voysey. Mad? I wish everybody were as sane. As a trustee the law permits me to earn for a fund three and a half per cent . . . and that I do . . . punctually and safely. Now as to Mrs. Murberry . . . those Fretworthy Bonds at my bank . . . I've borrowed five thousand on them. But I can release them to-morrow if need be.

Edward. Where's the five thousand?

Mr. Voysey. I needed it . . . temporarily . . . to complete a purchase . . . there was that and four thousand more out of the Skipworth fund.

Edward. But, my dear father——

Mr. Voysey. Well?

Edward [*summing it all up very simply*]. It's not right.

[MR. VOYSEY *considers his son for a moment with a pitying shake of the head.*

Mr. Voysey. That is a word, Edward, which one should learn to use very carefully. You mean that from time to time I have had to go beyond the letter of the law. But consider the position I found myself in. Was I to see my father ruined and disgraced without lifting a finger to help him? I paid back to the man who was most involved in my father's mistakes every penny of his capital . . . and he never even knew the danger he'd been in . . . never had one uneasy moment. It was I that lay awake. I have now somewhere a letter from that man written as he lay dying . . . I'll tell you who it was, old Thomson the physiologist . . . saying that only his perfect confidence in our conduct of his affairs had enabled him to do his life's work in peace. Well, Edward, I went beyond the letter of the law to do that service . . . to my father . . . to old Thomson . . . to Science . . . to Humanity. Was I right or wrong?

Edward. In the result, sir, right.

Mr. Voysey. Judge me by the result. I took the risk of failure . . . I should have suffered. I could have kept clear of the danger if I'd liked.

Edward. But that's all past. The thing that concerns me is what you are doing now.

Mr. Voysey [*gently reproachful*]. My boy, can't you trust me a little? It's all very well for you to come in at the end of the day and criticise. But I who have done the day's work know how that work had to be done. And here's our firm, prosperous, respected and without a stain on its honour. That's the main point, isn't it?

Edward [*quite irresponsive to this pathetic appeal*]. Very well, sir. Let's dismiss from our minds any prejudice about behaving as honest firms of solicitors do behave . . .

Mr. Voysey. We need do nothing of the sort. If a man gives me definite instructions about his property, I follow them. And more often than not he suffers.

Edward. But if Mrs. Murberry knew . . .

Mr. Voysey. Well, if you can make her understand her affairs . . . financial or other . . . it's more than I ever could. Go and knock it into her head, then, if you can, that four hundred and twenty pounds of her income hasn't, for the last eight years, come from the place she thinks it's come from, and see how happy you'll make her.

Edward. But is that four hundred and twenty a year as safe as it was before you . . . ?

Mr. Voysey. Why not?

Edward. What's the security?

Mr. Voysey [*putting his coping stone on the argument*]. My financial ability.

Edward [*really not knowing whether to laugh or cry*]. Why, one'd think you were satisfied with this state of things.

Mr. Voysey. Edward, you really are most unsympathetic and unreasonable. I give all I have to the firm's work . . . my brain . . . my energies . . . my whole life. I can't, so to speak, cash in my abilities at par . . . I wish I could. If I could establish every one of these people with a separate and consistent bank balance to-morrow . . . naturally I should do it.

Edward [*thankfully able to meet anger with anger*]. Do you mean to tell me that you couldn't somehow have put things straight before now?

Mr. Voysey. So easy to talk, isn't it?

Edward. If thirty years of this sort of thing hasn't brought you hopelessly to grief . . . why, there must have been opportunities . . .

Mr. Voysey. Must there! Well, I hope that when I'm under the ground, you may find them.

Edward. I?

Mr. Voysey. And put everything right with a stroke of your pen, if it's so easy!

Edward. I!

Mr. Voysey. You're my partner and my son. You inherit the problem.

Edward [*realising at last that he has been led to the edge of this abyss*]. Oh no, Father.

Mr. Voysey. Why else have I had to tell you all this?

Edward [*very simply*]. Father, I can't. I can't possibly. I don't think you've any right to ask me.

Mr. Voysey. Why not, pray?

Edward. It's perpetuating the dishonesty.

[MR. VOYSEY *hardens at the unpleasant word.*

Mr. Voysey. You don't believe that I've told you the truth.

Edward. I want to believe it.

Mr. Voysey. It's no proof . . . my earning these twenty or thirty people their incomes for the last . . . how many years?

Edward. Whether what you've done has been wrong or right . . . I can't meddle in it.

[*For the moment* MR. VOYSEY *looks a little dangerous.*

Mr. Voysey. Very well. Forget all I've said. Go back to your room. Get back to your drudgery. A life's work—my life's work—ruined! What does that matter?

Edward. Whatever did you expect of me?

Mr. Voysey [*making a feint at his papers*]. Oh, nothing. [*Then he slams them down with great effect.*] Here's a great edifice built up by years of labour and devotion and self-sacrifice . . . a great arch you may call it . . . a bridge to carry our firm to safety with honour. My work! And it still lacks the key-stone. Just that! And it may be I am to die with my work incomplete. Then is there nothing that a son might do? Do you think I shouldn't be proud of you, Edward . . . that I shouldn't bless you from . . . wherever I may be, when you had completed my life's work . . . with perhaps just one kindly thought of your father?

[*In spite of this oratory, the situation is gradually impressing* EDWARD.

Edward. What will happen if I leave the firm now?

Mr. Voysey. I shall see that you are not held responsible.

Edward. I wasn't thinking of myself, sir.

Mr. Voysey. Well, I shan't mind the exposure. It won't make me blush in my coffin. And you're not so quixotic, I hope, as to be thinking of the feelings of your brothers and sisters. Considering how simple it would have been for me to go to my grave and let you discover the whole thing afterwards, the fact that I didn't, that I take thought for the future of you all . . . well, I did hope it might convince you that I . . . ! But there . . . consult your own safety.

[EDWARD *has begun to pace the room; indecision growing upon him.*

Edward. It's a queer dilemma to be facing.

Mr. Voysey. My dear boy . . . don't think I can't appreciate the shock it has been to you. After all, I had to go through it, you know. And worse!

Edward. Why worse?

Mr. Voysey. Well . . . I was a bit younger. And my poor dear Dad was on the edge of the precipice . . . all but over it. I'm not landing you in any such mess, Edward. On the contrary! On the contrary!

Edward. Yes. I came this morning thinking that next week would see us in the dock together.

Mr. Voysey. And I suppose if I'd broken down and begged your pardon for my folly, you'd have done anything for me, gone to prison smiling, eh?

Edwvrd. I suppose so.

Mr. Voysey. Oh, it's easy enough to forgive. I'm sorry I can't assume sack-cloth and ashes to oblige you. [*Now he begins to rally his son; easy in his strength.*] My dear

Edward, you've lived a quiet humdrum life up to now, with your poetry and your sociology and your agnosticism and your ethics of this and your ethics of that! . . . and you've never before been brought face to face with any really vital question. Now don't make a fool of yourself just through inexperience. I'm not angry at what you've said to me. I'm willing to forget it. And it's for your own sake and not for mine, Edward, that I do beg you to . . . to . . . be a man and take a man's view of the position you find yourself in. It's not a pleasant position, I know . . . but we must take this world as we find it, my dear boy.

Edward. You should have told me before you took me into partnership.

[*Oddly enough it is this last flicker of rebellion which breaks down* MR. VOYSEY'*s caution. Now he lets fly with a vengeance.*

Mr. Voysey. Should I be telling you at all if I could help it? Don't I know you're about as fit for the job as a babe unborn? I've been hoping and praying for these three years past that you'd show signs of shaping into something. But I'm in a corner . . . and am I to see things come to smash simply because of your scruples? If you're a son of mine you'll do as I tell you. Hadn't I the same choice to make? D'you suppose I didn't have scruples? If you run away from this, Edward, you're a coward. My father was a coward and he suffered for it to the end of his days. I was more of a sick-nurse to him here than a partner. Good lord! . . . of course it's pleasant and comfortable to keep within the law . . . then the law will look after you. Otherwise you have to look pretty sharp after yourself. You have to cultivate your own sense of right and wrong . . . deal your own justice. But that makes a bigger man of you, let me tell you. How easily . . . how easily could I have walked out of my father's office and left him to his fate! But I didn't. I thought it my better duty to stay and . . . yes, I say it with reverence . . . to take up my cross. Well, I've carried that cross pretty successfully. And what's more, it's made a happy . . . a self-respecting man of me. I don't want what I've been saying to influence you, Edward. You are a free agent. You must consult your conscience and decide upon your own course of action. Now don't let's discuss the matter any more for the moment. [EDWARD *looks at his father with clear eyes.*

Edward. Don't forget to put these papers away.

Mr. Voysey. Are you coming down to Chislehurst soon? We've got Hugh and his wife, and Booth and Emily, and Christopher for two or three days, till he goes back to school.

Edward. How is Chris?

Mr. Voysey. All right again now . . . grows more like his father. Booth's very proud of him. So am I.

Edward. I think I can't face them all just at present.

Mr. Voysey. Nonsense.

Edward [*a little wave of emotion going through him*]. I feel as if this thing were written on my face. How I shall get through business I don't know!

Mr. Voysey. You're weaker than I thought, Edward.

Edward [*a little ironically*]. I've always wondered why I was such a disappointment to you, Father. Though you've been very kind about it.

Mr. Voysey. No, no. I say things I don't mean sometimes.

Edward. You should have brought one of the others into the firm . . . Trenchard or Booth.

Mr. Voysey [*hardening*]. Trenchard! [*He dismisses that.*] Heavens, you're a better man than Booth. Edward, you mustn't imagine that the whole world is standing on its head merely because you've had an unpleasant piece of news. Come down to Chislehurst to-night . . . well, say to-morrow night. It'll be good for you . . . stop your brooding. That's your worst vice, Edward. You'll find the household as if nothing had happened. Then you'll remember that nothing really has happened. And presently you'll see that nothing need happen, if you keep your head. I remember times . . . when things have seemed at their worst . . . what a relief it's been to me . . . my romp with you all in the nursery just before your bed-time. And, my dear boy, if I knew that you were going to inform the next client you met of what I've just told you . . .

Edward [*with a shudder*]. Father!

Mr. Voysey. . . . and that I should find myself in prison to-morrow, I wouldn't wish a single thing I've ever done undone. I have never wilfully harmed man or woman. My life's been a happy one. Your dear mother has been spared to me. You're most of you good children and a credit to what I've done for you.

Edward [*the deadly humour of this too much for him*]. Father!

Mr. Voysey. Run along now, run along. I must finish my letters and get into the City.

[*He might be scolding a schoolboy for some trifling fault.* EDWARD *turns to have a look at the keen unembarrassed face.* MR. VOYSEY *smiles at him and proceeds to select from the bowl a rose for his buttonhole.*

Edward. I'll think it over, sir.

Mr. Voysey. That's right! And don't brood.

[*So* EDWARD *leaves him; and having fixed the rose in his buttonhole to his satisfaction he rings his table telephone and calls through to the listening clerk.*

Send Atkinson to me, please.

[*Then he gets up, keys in hand, to lock away Mrs. Murberry's and the Hatherley Trust papers.*

ACT II

The Voysey dining-room at Chislehurst, when children and grandchildren are visiting, is dining-table and very little else. And at the moment in the evening when five or six men are sprawling back in their chairs, and the air is clouded with smoke, it is a very typical specimen of the middle-class English domestic temple. It has the usual red-papered walls, the usual varnished woodwork which is known as grained oak; there is the usual hot, mahogany furniture; and, commanding point of the whole room, there is the usual black-marble sarcophagus of a fireplace. Above this hangs one of the two or three oil-paintings, which are all that break the red pattern of the walls, the portrait, painted in 1880, *of an undistinguished-looking gentleman aged sixty; he is shown sitting in a more graceful attitude than it could ever have been comfortable for him to assume.* MR. VOYSEY'*s father it is, and the brass plate at the bottom of the frame tells us that the portrait was a presentation one. On the mantelpiece stands, of course, a clock; at either end a china vase filled with paper spills. And in front of the fire—since that is the post of vantage—stands at this moment* MAJOR BOOTH VOYSEY. *He is the second son, of the age that it is necessary for a Major to be, and of the appearance of many ordinary Majors in ordinary regiments. He went into the army because he thought it would come up to a schoolboy's idea of it; and, being there, he does his little all to keep it to this. He stands astride, hands in pockets, coat-tails through his arms, half-smoked cigar in mouth, moustache bristling. On either side of him sits at the table an old gentleman; the one is* MR. EVAN COLPUS, *the vicar of their parish, the other* MR. GEORGE

BOOTH, a friend of long standing, and the MAJOR's godfather. MR. COLPUS is a harmless enough anachronism, except for the comparative waste of £400 a year in which his stipend involves the community. Leaving most of his parochial work to an energetic curate, he devotes his serious attention to the composition of two sermons a week. MR. GEORGE BOOTH, on the contrary, is as gay an old gentleman as can be found in Chislehurst. An only son, his father left him at the age of twenty-five a fortune of a hundred thousand pounds. At the same time he had the good sense to dispose of his father's business, into which he had been most unwillingly introduced five years earlier, for a like sum before he was able to depreciate its value. It was MR. VOYSEY's invaluable assistance in this transaction which first bound the two together in great friendship. Since that time MR. BOOTH has been bent on nothing but enjoying himself. He has even remained a bachelor with that object. Money has given him all he wants, therefore he loves and reverences money; while his imagination may be estimated by the fact that he has now reached the age of sixty-five, still possessing more of it than he knows what to do with. At the head of the table, meditatively cracking walnuts, sits MR. VOYSEY. He has his back to the conservatory door. On MR. VOYSEY's left is DENIS TREGONING, a nice enough young man. And at the other end of the table sits EDWARD, not smoking, not talking, hardly listening, very depressed. Behind him is the ordinary door of the room, which leads out into the dismal, draughty hall. The MAJOR's voice is like the sound of a cannon through the tobacco smoke.

Major Booth Voysey. Certainly . . . I am hot and strong for conscription . . . and the question will be to the fore again very shortly.

Mr. George Booth. My dear boy . . . the country won't hear of it . . .

Major Booth Voysey. I differ from you. If we . . . the army . . . if the men who have studied the subject . . . the brains of the army . . . say as one man to the country: Conscription is once more necessary for your safety . . . what answer has the country? What? There you are! None.

Tregoning. You try . . . and you'll see.

Major Booth Voysey. If the international situation grows more threatening I shall seriously consider going on half-pay for a bit and entering the House. And . . . I'm not a conceited man . . . but I believe that if I speak out upon a subject I understand, and only upon that subject, the House . . . and the country . . . will listen.

Mr. George Booth. The gentlemen of England have always risen to an emergency. Why . . . old as I am . . . I would shoulder a musket myself if need be. But . . .

Major Booth Voysey. Just one moment. Our national safety is not the only question. There's the stamina of the race . . . deplorably deteriorated! You should just see the fellars that try to enlist nowadays. Horrid little runts . . . with their stinkin' little fags . . . hangin' out of the corners of their slobberin' little mouths. What England wants is chest. Chest and discipline. And conscription . . .

Mr. Voysey [*with the crack of a nut*]. Your godson talks a deal, don't he? You know, when our Major gets into a club, he gets on the committee . . . gets on any committee to enquire into anything . . . and then goes on at 'em just like this. Don't you, Booth?

[BOOTH *knuckles under easily enough to his father's sarcasm.*

Major Booth Voysey. Well, sir, people tell me I'm a useful man on committees.

Mr. Voysey. I don't doubt it . . . your voice must drown all discussion.

Major Booth Voysey. You can't say I don't listen to you, sir.

Mr. Voysey. I don't . . . and I'm not blaming you. But I must say I often think what a devil of a time the family will have with you when I'm gone. Fortunately for your poor mother, she's deaf.

Major Booth Voysey. Well, sir . . . it might be my duty . . . as eldest son . . . Trenchard not counting . . .

Mr. Voysey [*with the crack of another nut*]. Trenchard not counting. Oh, certainly . . . bully them. Never mind whether you're right or wrong . . . bully them. I don't manage things that way myself, but I think it's your best chance.

Major Booth Voysey [*with some discomfort*]. Ha! If I were a conceited man, sir, I could trust you to take it out of me.

Mr. Voysey [*as he taps* MR. BOOTH *with the nutcrackers*]. Help yourself, George, and drink to your godson's health. Long may he keep his chest notes! Never heard him on parade, have you?

Tregoning. There's one thing you learn in the army . . . and that's how to display yourself. Booth makes a perfect firescreen. But I believe after mess that position is positively rushed.

Major Booth Voysey [*cheered to find an opponent he can tackle*]. If you want a bit of fire, say so, you sucking Lord Chancellor. Because I mean to allow you to be my brother-in-law, you think you can be impertinent.

[*So* TREGONING *moves to the fire and that changes the conversation.*

Mr. Voysey. Vicar, the port's with you. Help yourself and send it on.

Mr. Colpus. Thank you . . . I have had my quantum.

Mr. Voysey. Nonsense!

Mr. Colpus. Well . . . a teeny weeny drain!

Mr. Voysey. By the way . . . did you see Lady Mary yesterday? Is she going to help us clear off the debt on the chapel?

Mr. Colpus. Well, no . . . I'm afraid she isn't.

Mr. Voysey. Why not?

Mr. Colpus. Well . . . the fact is she's quite angry.

Mr. Voysey. What about?

Mr. Colpus. I regret to tell you . . . it's about Hugh's fresco.

Major Booth Voysey. Ah . . . I knew there'd be trouble!

Mr. Colpus. Someone has let it out to her that the Apostles are all portraits of people . . . and she strongly disapproves.

Major Booth Voysey. So do I.

Mr. Colpus. Indeed, I fear she's writing to you to say that as Hugh is your son she thinks you should have kept him under better control. I said I'd done all I could. And I did argue with him. First of all, you know, he wanted to make them local people . . . the butcher and the plumber and old Sandford. He said the fifteenth-century Florentines always did it. I said: My dear Hugh, we are not fifteenth-century Florentines . . . .

Major Booth Voysey. Hugh's no good at a likeness. I don't believe anyone would have known.

Mr. Colpus. But all he said was: Ha! Ha! Then I didn't see the thing for a week, and . . . oh, far worse! . . . he'd made them all quite well-known public characters! And as it was in tempera, he couldn't alter it without taking the wall down.

Mr. Voysey. What's the debt now?

Mr. Colpus. Three hundred pounds nearly.

Mr. Voysey. I shall have to stump up, I suppose.

Major Booth Voysey. Anonymously. What?

Mr. Voysey. George Booth . . . will you go halves?

Mr. George Booth. Certainly not. I can't see what we wanted the chapel for at all. Eight hundred pounds and more . . . !

Mr. Colpus. People do drop in and pray. Oh . . . I've seen them.

Mr. George Booth. Well, Vicar . . . it's your business, of course . . . but I call it a mistake to encourage all this extra religion. Work on week-days . . . church on Sundays. That was the rule when I was young.

Mr. Voysey. You can't stop people praying.

Mr. George Booth. But why make a show of it? What's the result? Hugh's a case in point. When he was a boy . . . mad about religion! Used to fast on Fridays! I remember your punishing him for it. Now look at him. What his beliefs are now . . . well, I'd rather not know. And with Edward here . . .

Edward. With me?

Mr. George Booth. Up at Cambridge . . . wanted to turn Papist, didn't you? And now . . . I suppose you call yourself a free thinker.

Edward. I don't call myself anything.

Mr. George Booth. Keep to the middle of the road . . . that's what I'd tell any young man.

Tregoning. Safety first.

Mr. George Booth. Certainly. For what should be a man's aim in life? I have always known mine, and . . . though far be it from me to boast . . . I look back to nothing I need regret . . . nothing the whole world might not know. I don't speak of quite personal affairs. Like most other men, I have been young. But all that sort of thing is nobody's business but one's own. I inherited a modest fortune. I have not needed to take the bread out of other men's mouths by working. My money has been wisely administered . . . well, ask your father about that . . . and has . . . . . . not diminished. I have paid my taxes without grumbling. I have never wronged any man. I have never lied about anything that mattered. I have left theories to take care of themselves and tried to live the life of an English gentleman. And I consider there is no higher . . . at any rate no more practical ideal.

Major Booth Voysey [*not to be outdone by this display of virtue*]. Well, I'm not a conceited man, but——

Tregoning. I hope you're sure of that, Booth.

Major Booth Voysey. Shut up. I was going to say when my

young cub of a brother-in-law-to-be interrupted me, that Training, for which we all have to be thankful to you, sir, has much to do with it. [*Suddenly he pulls his trousers against his legs.*] I say, I'm scorching. Try one of those new cigars, Denis?

Tregoning. No, thank you.

Major Booth Voysey. I will.

[*He glances round;* TREGONING *sees a box on the table and reaches it. The* VICAR *gets up.*

Mr. Colpus. Must be taking my departure.

Mr. Voysey. Already!

Major Booth Voysey [*frowning upon the cigar-box*]. No, not those. The Ramon Allones. Why on earth doesn't Honor see they're here?

Mr. Voysey. Spare time for a chat with my wife before you go. She has ideas about a children's tea-fight.

Mr. Colpus. Certainly I will.

Major Booth Voysey [*scowling helplessly around*]. My goodness! . . . one can never find anything in this house.

Mr. Voysey. My regards to Mrs. Colpus. Hope her lumbago will be better.

Mr. Colpus. These trials are sent us.

[*He is sliding through the half-opened door when* ETHEL *meets him, flinging it wide. She is the younger daughter, the baby of the family, but twenty-three now.*

Mr. Voysey. I say! It's cold again to-night! An ass of an architect who built this place . . . such a draught between these two doors.

[*He gets up to draw the curtain. When he turns* MR. COLPUS *has disappeared, while* ETHEL *has been followed into the room by* ALICE MAITLAND, *who shuts the door after her.* MISS ALICE MAITLAND *is a young lady of any age to thirty. Nor need her appearance alter for the next fifteen years; since her nature is healthy and well-balanced. It mayn't be a pretty face, but it has alertness and humour; and the resolute eyes and eyebrows are a more innocent edition of* MR. VOYSEY'*s, who is her uncle.* ETHEL *goes straight to her father (though her glance is on* DENIS *and his on her) and chirps, birdlike, in her spoiled-child way.*

Ethel. We think you've stayed in here quite long enough.

Mr. Voysey. That's to say, Ethel thinks Denis has been kept out of her pocket much too long.

Ethel. Ethel wants billiards. . . . Father . . . what a dessert you've eaten. Greedy pig!

[ALICE *is standing behind* EDWARD, *considering his hair-parting apparently.*

Alice. Crack me a filbert, please, Edward . . . I had none.

Edward [*jumping up, rather formally well-mannered*]. I beg your pardon, Alice. Won't you sit down?

Alice. No.

Mr. Voysey [*taking* ETHEL *on his knee*]. Come here, puss. Have you made up your mind yet what you want for a wedding present?

Ethel [*rectifying a stray hair on his forehead*]. After mature consideration, I decide on a cheque.

Mr. Voysey. Do you!

Ethel. Yes. I think that a cheque will give most scope to your generosity. If you desire to add any trimmings in the shape of a piano or a Persian carpet you may . . . and Denis and I will be grateful. But I think I'd let yourself go over a cheque.

Mr. Voysey. You're a minx.

Major Booth Voysey [*giving up the cigar search*]. Here, who's going to play?

Mr. George Booth [*pathetically, as he gets up*]. Well, if my wrist will hold out . . .

Major Booth Voysey [*to* TREGONING]. No, don't you bother to look for them. [*He strides from the room, his voice echoing through the hall.*] Honor, where are those Ramon Allones?

Alice [*calling after*]. She's in the drawing-room with Auntie and Mr. Colpus.

Mr. Voysey. Now I suggest that you and Denis go and take off the billiard table cover. You'll find folding it up a very excellent amusement.

[*He illustrates his meaning with his table napkin and by putting together the tips of his forefingers, roguishly.*

Mr. George Booth. Ah ha! I remember that being done in some play . . .

Ethel. Dear father . . . you must try not to be roguish. You won't get a blush or a giggle out of either of us. Denis . . . come her and kiss me . . . before everybody.

Tregoning. I shall do nothing of the sort.

Ethel. If you don't I swear I won't marry you. Come along. I detest self-conscious people. Come on. [DENIS *gives her a shamefaced peck on one cheek.*] That's a nice sort of kiss, too! If it wasn't for having to send back the presents I wouldn't marry you. [*She goes off.*

Denis. Women have no shame.

[*The* MAJOR *comes stalking back, followed in a fearful flurry by his elder sister,* HONOR. DENIS *follows* ETHEL. *Poor* HONOR (*her female friends are apt to refer to her as Poor* HONOR) *is a phenomenon common to most large families. From her earliest years she has been bottle-washer to her brothers. They were expensively educated, but she was grudged schooling. Her fate is a curious survival of the intolerance of parents towards daughters until the vanity of their hunger for sons has been gratified. In a less humane society she would have been exposed at birth. Yet* HONOR *is not unhappy in her survival, even if at this moment her life is a burden.*

Major Booth Voysey. Honor, they are not in the dining-room.

Honor. But they must be!—where else can they be?

[*She has a habit of accentuating one word in each sentence and often the wrong one.*

Major Booth Voysey. That's what you ought to know.

Mr. Voysey [*as he moves towards the door*]. Well . . . will you have a game?

Mr. George Booth. I'll play you fifty up, not more. I'm getting old.

Mr. Voysey [*stopping at a dessert dish*]. Yes, these are good apples of Bearman's. Six of my trees spoilt this year.

Honor. Here you are, Booth.

[*She triumphantly discovers the discarded box, at which the* MAJOR *becomes pathetic with indignation.*

Major Booth Voysey. Oh, Honor, don't be such a fool. I want the Ramon Allones.

Honor. I don't know the difference.

Major Booth Voysey. No, you don't, but you might learn.

Mr. Voysey [*in a voice like the crack of a very fine whip*]. Booth!

Major Booth Voysey [*subduedly*]. What is it, sir?

Mr. Voysey. Look for your cigars yourself. Honor, go back to your reading or your sewing or whatever you were fiddling at, and fiddle in peace.

[MR. VOYSEY *departs, leaving the room rather hushed.* MR. BOOTH *has not waited for this parental display. Then* ALICE *insinuates a remark very softly.*

Alice. Have you looked in the library?

Major Booth Voysey [*relapsing to an injured mutter*]. Where's Emily?

Honor. Upstairs with little Henry, he woke up and cried.

Major Booth Voysey. Letting her wear herself to rags over the child . . .

Honor. Well, she won't let me go.

Major Booth Voysey. Why don't you stop looking for those cigars?

Honor. If you don't mind, I want a lace doily, now I am here.

Major Booth Voysey. I daresay they're in the library. What a house! [*He departs*.

Honor. Booth is so trying.

Alice. Honor, why do you put up with it?

Honor. Someone has to.

Alice [*discreetly nibbling a nut, which* EDWARD *has cracked for her*]. I'm afraid I think Master Major Booth ought to have been taken in hand early . . . with a cane.

Honor [*as she vaguely burrows into corners*]. Papa did. But it's never prevented him booming at us . . . oh, ever since he was a baby. Now he's flustered me so I simply can't remember which set of them it was.

Alice. The Pettifers wished to be remembered to you, Edward.

Honor. I'd better take one of each. [*But she goes on looking*.] I sometimes think, Alice, that we're a very difficult family . . . except perhaps Edward.

Edward. Why except me?

Honor. And you were always difficult . . . to yourself. [*Then she starts to go, threading her way through the disarranged chairs*.] Mr. Colpus will shout so at Mother, and she doesn't like people to think she's so very deaf. . . . I thought Mary Pettifer looking old . . .

[*She talks herself out of the room*.

Alice [*after her*]. She's getting old. I was glad not to spend August abroad for once. We drove into Cheltenham for a dance. I golfed a lot.

Edward. How long were you with them?

Alice. A fortnight. It doesn't seem three months since I was here.

Edward. I'm down so seldom.

Alice. I might be one of the family . . . almost.

Edward. You know they're always pleased.

Alice. Well, being a homeless person! But what a cartload

to descend . . . yesterday and to-day. The Major and Emily. . . . Emily's not at all well. Hugh and Mrs. Hugh. And me. Are you staying?

Edward. No. I must get a word with my father.

Alice. Edward . . . you look more like half-baked pie-crust than usual. I wish you didn't sit over your desk quite so much.

Edward [*a little enviously*]. You're very well.

Alice. I'm always well and nearly always happy.

[MAJOR BOOTH *returns. He has the right sort of cigar in his mouth and is considerably mollified.*

Alice. You found them?

Major Booth Voysey. Of course they were there. Thank you very much, Alice. Now I want a knife.

Alice. I must give you a cigar-cutter for Christmas, Booth.

Major Booth Voysey. Beastly things, I hate 'em. [*He eyes the dessert disparagingly.*] Nothing but silver ones. [EDWARD *hands him a carefully opened pocket-knife.*] Thank you, Edward. And I must take one of the candles. Something's gone wrong with the library ventilator and you can never see a thing in that room.

Alice. Is Mrs. Hugh there?

Major Booth Voysey. Writing letters. Things are neglected here, Edward, unless one is constantly on the look out. The Pater only cares for his garden. I must speak seriously to Honor.

[*He has returned the knife, still open, and having now lit his cigar at the candle he carries this off.*

Edward [*giving her a nut, about the fifteenth*]. Here. 'Scuse fingers.

Alice. Thank you. [*Looking at him, with her head on one side and her face more humorous than ever.*] Edward, why have you given up proposing to me?

[*He starts, flushes; then won't be outdone in humour.*

Edward. One can't go on proposing for ever.

Alice. Have you seen anyone you like better?

Edward. No.

Alice. Well . . . I miss it.

Edward. What satisfaction did you find in refusing me?

Alice [*as she weighs the matter*]. I find satisfaction in feeling that I'm wanted.

Edward. Without any intention of giving . . . of throwing yourself away.

Alice [*teasing his sudden earnestness*]. Ah, now we come from mere vanity to serious questions.

Edward. Mine was a very serious question.

Alice. But, Edward, all questions are serious to you. You're a perfect little pocket-guide to life . . . every question answered; what to eat, drink and avoid, what to believe and what to say. Some things are worth bothering over... and some aren't.

Edward. One lays down principles.

Alice. I prefer my plan. I always do what I know I want to do. Crack me another nut.

Edward. Haven't you had enough?

Alice. I know I want one more.

[*He cracks another with a sigh which sounds ridiculous in that connection.*

I know it just as I knew I didn't want to marry you . . . each time. I didn't say No on principle . . . or because I thought it wouldn't be wise. That's why I want you to keep on asking me. Because at any moment I might say Yes. And then I suppose I should find that it was simply a habit you'd got into . . . and that you didn't want me after all. Still, take another chance. Take it now!

Edward. No . . . I think not . . . now.

Alice. Edward! There's nothing wrong, is there?

Edward. Nothing at all.

[*They are interrupted by the sudden appearance of* MRS. HUGH VOYSEY, *a brisk, bright little woman, in an evening gown which she has bullied a cheap dressmaker into making look exceedingly smart.* BEATRICE *is hard and clever. But if she keeps her feelings buried pretty deep it is because they are precious to her; and if she is impatient with fools it is because her own brains have had to win her everything in the world, so perhaps she does overvalue them a little. She speaks always with great decision and little effort.*

Beatrice. I believe I could write business letters upon an island in the middle of Fleet Street. But while Booth is poking at a ventilator with a billiard cue . . . no, I can't. The Vicar's in the drawing-room . . . and my bedroom's like an ice-house.

[*She goes to the fireplace, waving her half-finished letter.* BOOTH *appears at the door, billiard cue in hand, and says solemnly . . .*

Major Booth Voysey. Edward, I wish you'd come and have a look at this ventilator, like a good fellow.

[*Then he turns and goes again, obviously with the weight of an important matter on his shoulders. With the ghost of a smile* EDWARD *gets up and follows him.*

Alice. No one has a right to be as good and kind as Edward is. It encourages the rotters.

[*With which comment she joins* BEATRICE *at the fireplace.*

Beatrice. A satisfactory day's shopping?

Alice. 'M. The baby bride and I bought clothes all the morning. Then we had lunch with Denis and bought furniture

Beatrice. Nice furniture?

Alice. Very good and very new. They neither of them know what they want. [*Then suddenly throwing up her chin and exclaiming.*] Beatrice . . . why do women get married? Oh, of course . . . if you're caught young! With Ethel and Denis now . . . they're two little birds building their nest and it's all ideal. They'll soon forget they've ever been apart.

[*Now* HONOR *flutters into the room, patient but wild-eyed.*

Honor. Mother wants last week's *Notes and Queries.* Have you seen it?

Beatrice [*exasperated at the interruption*]. No.

Honor. It ought not to be here. [*So she proceeds to look for it.*] Hugh had it.

Beatrice. Lit his pipe with it.

Honor. Oh, d'you think so?

[*So she gives up the search and flutters out again.*

Alice. This is a most unrestful house.

Beatrice. I once thought of putting the Voyseys into a book of mine. Then I concluded they'd be as dull there as they are anywhere else.

Alice. They're not duller than most of the rest of us.

Beatrice. But how very dull that is!

Alice. They're a little noisier and perhaps not quite so well-mannered. But I love them . . . in a sort of way.

Beatrice. I don't. I should have thought love was just what they couldn't inspire.

Alice. Hugh's not like the others.

Beatrice. He has most of their bad points. But I don't love Hugh.

Alice [*her eyebrows up, though she smiles*]. Beatrice, you shouldn't say so.

Beatrice. Sounds affected, doesn't it?

Alice [*her face growing a little thoughtful*]. Beatrice . . . were you in love with Hugh when you married him? Don't answer if you don't want to.

Beatrice. I married him for his money.

Alice. He hadn't much.

Beatrice. I had none . . . and I wanted to chuck journalism and write books. Yes, I loved him enough to marry him. But with some of us . . . that's not much.

Alice. But you thought you'd be happy?

Beatrice [*considering carefully*]. No, I didn't. I hoped he'd be happy. Dear Alice, how ever should you understand these things? You've eight hundred a year.

Alice. What has that to do with it?

Beatrice [*putting her case very precisely*]. Fine feelings, my dear, are as much a luxury as clean gloves. From seventeen to twenty-eight I had to earn my own living . . . and I'm no genius. So there wasn't a single thing I ever did quite genuinely for its own sake. No . . . always with an eye to bread-and-butter . . . pandering to the people who were to give me that. I warned Hugh . . . he took the risk.

Alice. What risk?

Beatrice. That one day I'd find I could get on better without him.

Alice. And if he can't without you?

Beatrice. One should never let one's happiness depend on other people. It's degrading . . .

[*The conservatory door opens and through it come* MR. VOYSEY *and* MR. BOOTH *in the midst of a discussion.*

Mr. Voysey. My dear man, stick to the shares and risk it.

Mr. George Booth. No, of course if you seriously advise me. . . .

Mr. Voysey. I never advise greedy children; I let 'em overeat 'emselves and take the consequences.

Alice [*shaking a finger*]. Uncle Trench, you've been in the garden without a hat after playing billiards in that hot room.

Mr. George Booth. We had to give up . . . my wrist was bad. They've started pool.

Beatrice. Is Booth going to play?

Mr. Voysey. We left him instructing Ethel how to hold a cue.

Beatrice. I can finish my letter.

[*Off she goes.* ALICE *is idly following with a little paper her hand has fallen on behind the clock.*

Mr. Voysey. Don't run away, my dear.

Alice. I'm taking this to Auntie. . . *Notes and Queries* . . . she wants it.

Mr. Voysey. This room's cold. Why don't they keep the fire up? [*He proceeds to put coals on it.*

Mr. George Booth. It was too hot in the billiard room. You know, Voysey . . . about those Alguazils?

Mr. Voysey [*through the rattling of the coals*]. What?

Mr. George Booth [*trying to pierce the din*]. Those Alguazils.

[MR. VOYSEY *with surprising inconsequence points a finger at the silk handkerchief across* MR. BOOTH'*s shirt front.*

Mr. Voysey. What have you got your handkerchief there for?

Mr. George Booth. Measure of precau——[*At that moment he sneezes.*] Damn it . . . if you've given me a chill dragging me through your infernal garden . . .

Mr. Voysey [*slapping him on the back*]. You're an old crock.

Mr. George Booth. Well, I'll be glad of a winter in Egypt. [*He returns to his subject.*] And if you think seriously that I ought to sell out of the Alguazils before I go . . . ? Well . . . you'll have them. You can sell out if things look bad.

[*At this moment* PHOEBE, *the middle-aged parlourmaid, comes in, tray in hand. Like an expert fisherman* MR. VOYSEY *lets loose the thread of the conversation.*

Mr. Voysey. D'you want to clear?

Phoebe. It doesn't matter, sir.

Mr. Voysey. No, go on . . . go on.

[*So* MARY, *the young housemaid, comes in as well, and the two start to clear the table. All of which fidgets poor* MR. BOOTH *considerably. He sits shrivelled up in the armchair by the fire; and now* MR. VOYSEY *attends to him.*

Mr. Voysey. George . . . I've told you again and again that you ought not to run after high interest as you do.

Mr. George Booth. Yes . . . but one ought to see that one's money's put to good use.

Mr. Voysey. You're an old gambler.

Mr. George Booth [*propitiatingly*]. Ah, but then I've you to advise me. I do what you tell me in the end . . . you can't deny that.

Mr. Voysey. The man who don't know must trust in the man who do.

Mr. George Booth [*modestly insisting*]. There's ten thousand in Alguazils. What else could we put it into?

Mr. Voysey. I can get you something at four and a half.

Mr. George Booth. Oh, Lord!

Mr. Voysey [*with a sudden serious friendliness*]. I sometimes wish, George, that you'd look after your own affairs a little more than you do. You leave far too much in my hands. If I were a crook I could play Old Harry with them . . . and I doubt if you'd ever find out.

Mr. George Booth. But, of course, I shouldn't trust anybody. It's a question of knowing one's man . . . as I know you. Ah, my friend, what'll happen to your firm when you depart this life! . . . not before my time, I hope.

Mr. Voysey [*with a little frown*]. What d'ye mean?

Mr. George Booth. Edward's no use.

Mr. Voysey. I beg your pardon . . . very sound in business.

Mr. George Booth. May be . . . but I tell you he's no use. No personality.

Mr. Voysey. I fear you don't much like Edward.

Mr. George Booth [*with pleasant frankness*]. No, I don't.

Mr. Voysey. That's a pity. That's a great pity.

Mr. George Booth [*with a flattering smile*]. He's not his father and never will be. What's the time?

Mr. Voysey. Twenty past ten.

Mr. George Booth. I must be trotting.

[*As he goes to the door he meets* EDWARD, *who comes in apparently looking for his father; at any rate he catches his eye immediately, while* MR. BOOTH *obliviously continues.*

Mr. George Booth. I'll look into the drawing-room for a second. Stroll home with me?

Mr. Voysey. I can't.

Mr. George Booth [*mildly surprised at the short reply*]. Well, good-night. Good-night, Edward. [*He trots away.*

Mr. Voysey. Leave the table, Phoebe.

Phoebe. Yes, sir.

Mr. Voysey. You can come back in ten minutes.

[PHOEBE *and* MARY *depart and the door is closed. Alone with his son* MR. VOYSEY *does not move. His face grows a little keener, that's all.*

Mr. Voysey. Well, Edward?

[EDWARD *starts to move restlessly about, like a cowed animal in a cage; silently for a moment or two. Then when he speaks his voice is toneless, and he does not look at his father.*

Edward. Would you mind, sir, dropping with me for the future all these protestations about putting the firm's affairs straight . . . about all your anxieties and sacrifices. I see now, of course . . . a cleverer man than I could have seen it yesterday . . . that for some time, ever since, I suppose, you recovered from the first shock and got used to the double dealing, this hasn't been your object at all. You've used your clients' capital to produce your own income . . . to bring us up and endow us with. That ten thousand pounds to Booth for his boys; what you're giving Ethel on her marriage . . . ! It's odd it never struck me yesterday that my own pocket-money as a boy must have been drawn from some client's account. I suppose about half the sum you've spent on us first and last would have put things right?

Mr. Voysey. No, it would not.

Edward [*appealing for the truth*]. Come now . . . at some time or other!

Mr. Voysey. Well, if there have been good times there have been bad. At present the three hundred a year I'm to allow your sister is going to be rather a pull.

Edward. Three hundred a year . . . with things as they are! Since it isn't lunacy, sir, I can only conclude that you're enjoying yourself.

Mr. Voysey. Three trusts . . . two of them big ones . . . have been wound up within this last four years and the accounts have been above suspicion. What's the object of this rodomontade, Edward?

Edward. If I'm to remain in the firm, it had better be with a very clear understanding of things as they are.

Mr. Voysey [*firmly, not too anxiously*]. Then you do remain?

Edward [*in a very low voice*]. I must remain.

Mr. Voysey [*quite gravely*]. That's wise of you . . . I'm very glad.

Edward. But I make one condition. And I want some information.

Mr. Voysey. Well?

Edward. Of course no one has ever discovered . . . and no one suspects this state of things?

Mr. Voysey. Peacey knows.

Edward. Peacey!

Mr. Voysey. His father found out.

Edward. Oh. Does he draw hush-money?

Mr. Voysey [*curling a little at the word*]. I have made him a little present from time to time. But I might well have done that in any case. [*He becomes benevolent.*] Peacey's a devoted fellow. I couldn't do without him.

Edward [*with entire comprehension*]. No . . . it would hardly be wise to try. Well . . . the condition I make is a very simple one. It is that we should really try . . . as unobtrusively as you like . . . to put things straight.

Mr. Voysey [*with a little polite shrug*]. I've no doubt you'll prove an abler man of business than I have been.

Edward. To begin with we can halve what I draw from the firm.

Mr. Voysey. As you please.

Edward. And it seems to me that you can't give Ethel this thousand pounds dowry.

Mr. Voysey [*shortly, with one of the quick twists of his eye*]. I have given my word to Denis . . .

Edward. Since the money isn't yours to give.

Mr. Voysey [*in an indignant crescendo*]. I should not dream of depriving Ethel of what, as my daughter, she has every right to expect. I am surprised at your suggesting such a thing.

Edward [*pale and firm*]. I am set on this, Father.

Mr. Voysey. Don't be such a fool, Edward. What would it look like . . . suddenly refusing without rhyme or reason? What would old Tregoning think?

Edward. Oh, can't you see it's my duty to prevent this?

Mr. Voysey. Well . . . you can prevent it . . . by telling the nearest policeman. It is my duty to pay no more attention to such folly than a nurse pays to her child's tantrums. Understand, Edward, I don't want to force you to go on. Come with me gladly, or don't come at all.

Edward [*dully*]. It is my duty to be of what use I can to you, sir. Father, I want to save you if I can.

[*He flashes into this exclamation of almost broken-hearted affection.* MR. VOYSEY *looks at his son for a moment and his lip quivers. Then he steels himself.*

Mr. Voysey. Thank you! I have been saving myself quite satisfactorily for the last thirty years, and you must please believe that by this time I know my own business best.

Edward [*hopelessly*]. Can't we find the money some other way? How do you manage for your own income?

Mr. Voysey. I have a bank balance and a cheque book, haven't I? I spend what I think well to spend. What's the use of earmarking this or that as my own? You say none of it is my own. I might say it's all my own. I think I've earned it.

Edward [*anger coming on him*]. That's what I can't forgive. If you'd lived poor . . . if you'd really done all you could for your clients and not thought of your own pocket . . . then, even though things were no better than they are now . . . why, in a queer sort of way, I could have been proud of you. But, Father, do own the truth . . . I've a right to that from you at least. Didn't you simply seize this chance as a means of money-making?

Mr. Voysey [*with a sledge-hammer irony*]. Certainly. I sat that morning in my father's office, studying the helmet of the policeman in the street below, and thinking what a glorious path I had happened on to wealth and honour and renown. [*Then he begins to bully* EDWARD *in the kindliest way.*] My dear boy, you don't grasp the A.B.C. of my position. What has carried me to victory? The confidence of my clients. What has earned me that confidence? A decent life, my integrity, my brains? No, my reputation for wealth . . . that, and nothing else. Business nowadays is run on the lines of the confidence trick. What makes old George Booth so glad to trust me with every penny he possesses? Not affection . . . he's never cared for anything in his life but his collection of French prints.

Edward [*stupefied, helpless*]. Is he involved?

Mr. Voysey. Of course he's involved, and he's always after high interest, too . . . it's little one makes out of him. But there's a further question here, Edward. Should I have had confidence in myself, if I'd remained a poor man? No, I should not. In this world you must either be the master of money or its servant. And if one is not opulent in one's daily life one loses that wonderful . . . financier's touch. One must be confident oneself . . . and I saw from the first that I must at any cost inspire confidence. My whole public and private life has tended to that. All my surroundings . . . you and your brothers and sisters that I have brought into, and up, and put out in the world so worthily . . . you in your turn inspire confidence.

Edward. I sat down yesterday to try and make a list of the people who are good enough to trust their money to us. From George Booth with his money piling up while he sleeps . . . so he fancies . . . to Nursie with her savings, which she brought you so proudly to invest. But you've let those be, at least.

Mr. Voysey. Five hundred pounds. I don't know what I did with it.

Edward. But that's damnable.

Mr. Voysey. Indeed? I give her seventy-five pounds a year for it. Would you like to take charge of that account, Edward? I'll give you five hundred to invest to-morrow.

[EDWARD, *hopelessly beaten, falls into an almost comic state of despair.*

Edward. My dear father, putting every moral question aside . . . it's all very well your playing Robin Hood in this magnificent manner; but have you given a moment's thought to the sort of inheritance you'll be leaving me?

Mr. Voysey [*pleased for the first time*]. Ah! that's a question you have every right to ask.

Edward. If you died to-morrow could we pay eight shillings in the pound . . . or seventeen . . . or five? Do you know?

Mr. Voysey. And the answer is, that by your help I have every intention, when I die, of leaving a personal estate that will run into six figures. D'you think I've given my life and my talents for a less result than that? I'm fond of you all . . . and I want you to be proud of me . . . and I mean that the name of Voysey shall be carried high in the world by my children and grandchildren. Don't you be afraid, Edward. Ah, you lack experience, my boy . . . you're not full-grown yet . . . your impulses are a bit chaotic. You emotionalise over your work, and you reason about your emotions. You must sort yourself. You must realise that money-making is one thing, and religion another, and family life a third . . . and that if we apply our energies wholeheartedly to each of these in turn, and realise that different laws govern each, that there is a different end to be served, a different ideal to be striven for in each . . .

[*His coherence is saved by the sudden appearance of his wife, who comes round the door smiling benignly. Not in the least put out, in fact a little relieved, he greets her with an affectionate shout, for she is very deaf.*

Mr. Voysey. Hullo, Mother!

Mrs. Voysey. Oh, there you are, Trench. I've been deserted.

Mr. Voysey. George Booth gone?

Mrs. Voysey. Are you talking business? Perhaps you don't want me.

Mr. Voysey. No, no . . . no business.

Mrs. Voysey [*who has not looked for his answer*]. I suppose the others are in the billiard room.

Mr. Voysey [*vociferously*]. We're not talking business, old lady.

Edward. I'll be off, sir.

Mr. Voysey [*genial as usual*]. Why don't you stay? I'll come up with you in the morning.

Edward. No, thank you, sir.

Mr. Voysey. Then I'll be up about noon.

Edward. Good-night, Mother.

[MRS. VOYSEY *places a plump, kindly hand on his arm and looks up affectionately.*

Mrs. Voysey. You look tired.

Edward. No, I'm not.

Mrs. Voysey. What did you say?

Edward [*too weary to repeat himself*]. Nothing, Mother dear. [*He kisses her cheek, while she kisses the air.*

Mr. Voysey. Good-night, my boy.

[*Then he goes.* MRS. VOYSEY *is carrying her* Notes and Queries. *This is a dear old lady, looking older too than probably she is. Placid describes her. She has had a life of little joys and cares, has never measured herself against the world, never even questioned the shape and size of the little corner of it in which she lives. She has loved an indulgent husband and borne eight children, six of them surviving, healthy. That is her history.*

Mrs. Voysey. George Booth went some time ago. He said he thought you'd taken a chill walking round the garden.

Mr. Voysey. I'm all right.

Mrs. Voysey. D'you think you have?

Mr. Voysey [*in her ear*]. No.

Mrs. Voysey. You should be careful, Trench. What did you put on?

Mr. Voysey. Nothing.

Mrs. Voysey. How very foolish! Let me feel your hand. You are quite feverish.

Mr. Voysey [*affectionately*]. You're a fuss-box, old lady.

Mrs. Voysey [*coquetting with him*]. Don't be rude, Trench.

[HONOR *descends upon them. She is well into that nightly turmoil of putting everything and everybody to rights which always precedes her bed-time. She carries a shawl which she clasps round her mother's shoulders, her mind and gaze already on the next thing to be done.*

Honor. Mother, you left your shawl in the drawing-room. Oh . . . can't they finish clearing?

Mr. Voysey [*arranging the folds of the shawl with real tenderness*]. Now who's careless! [PHOEBE *comes into the room.*

Honor. Phoebe, finish here and then you must bring in the tray for Mr. Hugh.

Mrs. Voysey [*having looked at the shawl and* HONOR, *and connected the matter in her mind*]. Thank you, Honor. You'd better look after your father; he's been walking round the garden without his cape.

Honor. Papa!

Mr. Voysey. Phoebe, you get that little kettle and boil it, and brew me some whiskey and water. I shall be all right.

Honor [*fluttering more than ever*]. I'll get it. Where's the whiskey? And Hugh coming back at ten o'clock with no dinner. No wonder his work goes wrong. Here it is! Papa, you do deserve to be ill.

[*Clasping the whiskey decanter she is off again.* MRS. VOYSEY *sits at the dinner-table and adjusts her spectacles. She returns to* Notes and Queries, *one elbow firmly planted and her plump hand against her plump cheek. This is her favourite attitude; and she is apt, when reading, to soliloquize in her deaf woman's voice. At least, whether she considers it soliloquy or conversation is not easy to discover.* MR. VOYSEY *stands with his back to the fire, grumbling and pulling faces.*

Mrs. Voysey. This is a very perplexing correspondence about the Cromwell family. One can't deny the man had good blood in him . . . his grandfather Sir Henry, his uncle Sir Oliver . . .

Mr. Voysey. There's a pain in my back.

Mrs. Voysey. . . . and it's difficult to discover where the taint crept in.

Mr. Voysey. I believe I strained myself putting in those strawberry plants.

[MARY, *the house-parlourmaid, carries in a tray of warmed-up dinner for* HUGH *and plants it on the table.*

Mrs. Voysey. Yes, but then how was it he came to disgrace himself so? I believe the family disappeared. Regicide is a root and branch curse. You must read the letter signed C. W. A. . . . it's quite interesting. There's a misprint in mine about the first umbrella-maker . . . now where was it . . . [*And so the dear lady will ramble on indefinitely.*

ACT III

The dining-room looks very different in the white light of a July noon. Moreover, on this particular day, it isn't even its normal self. There is a peculiar luncheon spread on the table and on it are decanters of port and sherry; sandwiches, biscuits and an uncut cake; two little piles of plates and one little pile of napkins. There are no table decorations, and indeed the whole room has been made as bare and as tidy as possible. Such preparations denote one of the recognised English festivities, and the appearance of PHOEBE, *the maid, who has just completed them, the set solemnity of her face and the added touches of black to her dress and cap, suggest that this is probably a funeral. When* MARY *comes in, the fact that she has evidently been crying and that she decorously does not raise her voice above an unpleasant whisper makes it quite certain*

Mary. Phoebe, they're coming back . . . and I forgot one of the blinds in the drawing-room.

Phoebe. Well, pull it up quick and make yourself scarce. I'll open the door.

[MARY *got rid of,* PHOEBE *composes her face still more rigorously into the aspect of formal grief and, with a touch to her apron as well, goes to admit the funeral party. The first to enter are* MRS. VOYSEY *and* MR. BOOTH, *she on his arm; and the fact that she is in widow's weeds makes the occasion clear. The little old man leads his old friend very tenderly.*

Mr. George Booth. Will you come in here?

Mrs. Voysey. Thank you.

[*With great solicitude he puts her in a chair; then takes her hand.*

Mr. George Booth. Now I'll intrude no longer.

Mrs. Voysey. You'll take some lunch?

Mr. George Booth. No.

Mrs. Voysey. Not a glass of wine?

Mr. George Booth. If there's anything I can do just send round.

Mrs. Voysey. Thank you.

[*He reaches the door only to be met by the* MAJOR *and his wife. He shakes hands with them both.*

Mr. George Booth. My dear Emily! My dear Booth!

[EMILY *is a homely, patient, pale little woman of about thirty-five. She looks smaller than usual in her heavy black dress and is meeker than usual on an occasion of this kind. The* MAJOR, *on the other hand, though his grief is most sincere, has an irresistible air of being responsible for, and indeed rather proud of, the whole affair.*

Major Booth Voysey. I think it all went off as he would have wished.

Mr. George Booth [*feeling that he is called on for praise*]. Great credit . . . great credit.

[*He makes another attempt to escape and is stopped this time by* TRENCHARD VOYSEY, *to whom he is extending a hand and beginning his formula. But* TRENCHARD *speaks first.*

Trenchard. Have you the right time?

Mr. George Booth [*taken aback and fumbling for his watch*]. I think so . . . I make it fourteen minutes to one. [*He seizes the occasion.*] Trenchard, as a very old and dear friend of your father's, you won't mind me saying how glad I was that you were present to-day. Death closes all. Indeed . . . it must be a great regret to you that you did not see him before . . . before . . .

Trenchard [*his cold eye freezing this little gush*]. I don't think he asked for me.

Mr. George Booth [*stoppered*]. No? No! Well . . . well . . .

[*At this third attempt to depart he actually collides with someone in the doorway. It is* HUGH VOYSEY.

Mr. George Booth. My dear Hugh . . . I won't intrude.

[*Determined to escape, he grasps his hand, gasps out his formula and is off.* TRENCHARD *and* HUGH, *eldest and youngest son, are as unlike each other as it is possible for Voyseys to be, but that isn't very unlike.* TRENCHARD *has the cocksure manner of the successful barrister;* HUGH *the sweetly querulous air of diffidence and scepticism belonging to the unsuccessful man of letters or artist. The self-respect of* TRENCHARD'*s appearance is immense, and he cultivates that air of concentration upon any trivial matter, or even upon nothing at all, which will some day make him an impressive figure upon the Bench.* HUGH *is always vague, searching Heaven or the corners of the room for inspiration; and even on this occasion his tie is abominably crooked. The inspissated gloom of this assembly, to which each member of the family as he arrives adds his share, is unbelievable.* HUGH *is depressed partly at the inadequacy of his grief;* TRENCHARD *conscientiously preserves an air of the indifference which he feels;* BOOTH *stands statuesque at the mantelpiece; while* EMILY *is by* MRS. VOYSEY, *whose face in its quiet grief is nevertheless a mirror of many happy memories of her husband.*

Major Booth Voysey. I wouldn't hang over her, Emily.

Emily. No, of course not.

[*Apologetically she sits by the table.*

Trenchard. I hope your wife is well, Hugh?

Hugh. Thank you, Trench: I think so. Beatrice is in America . . . giving some lectures there.

Trenchard. Really!

[*Then comes in a small, well-groomed, bullet-headed schoolboy. This is the* MAJOR'*s eldest son. Looking scared and solemn, he goes straight to his mother.*

Emily. Now be very quiet, Christopher.

[*Then* DENIS TREGONING *appears.*

Trenchard. Oh, Tregoning, did you bring Honor back?

Denis. Yes.

Major Booth Voysey [*at the table*]. A glass of wine, Mother?

Mrs. Voysey. What?

[BOOTH *hardly knows how to turn his whisper decorously into enough of a shout for his mother to hear. But he manages it.*

Major Booth Voysey. Have a glass of wine?

Mrs. Voysey. Sherry, please.

[*While he pours it out with an air of its being medicine on this occasion and not wine at all,* EDWARD *comes quickly into the room, his face very set, his mind obviously on other matters than the funeral. No one speaks to him for the moment and he has time to observe them all.* TRENCHARD *is continuing his talk to* DENIS.

Trenchard. Give my love to Ethel. Is she ill that . . .

Tregoning. Not exactly, but she couldn't very well be with us. I thought perhaps you might have heard. We're expecting . . .

[*He hesitates with the bashfulness of a young husband.*

Trenchard. Indeed. I congratulate you. I hope all will be well. Please give my best love to Ethel.

Major Booth Voysey [*in an awful voice*]. Lunch, Emily?

Emily [*scared*]. I suppose so, Booth, thank you.

Major Booth Voysey. I think the boy had better run away and play . . . [*He checks himself on the word.*] Well, take a book and keep quiet; d'ye hear me, Christopher?

[CHRISTOPHER, *who looks incapable of a sound, gazes at his father with round eyes.* EMILY *whispers 'Library' to him and adds a kiss in acknowledgement of his good behaviour. After a moment he slips out, thankfully.*

Edward. How's Ethel, Denis?

Tregoning. A little smashed, of course, but no harm done . . . I hope. The doctor's a bit worried about her, though.

[ALICE MAITLAND *comes in, brisk and businesslike; a little impatient of this universal cloud of mourning.*

Alice. Edward, Honor has gone to her room; I must take her some food and make her eat it. She's very upset.

Edward. Make her drink a glass of wine, and say it is necessary she should come down here. And d'you mind not coming back yourself, Alice?

Alice [*her eyebrows up*]. Certainly, if you wish.

Major Booth Voysey [*overhearing*]. What's this? What's this?

[ALICE *gets her glass of wine and goes. The* MAJOR *is suddenly full of importance.*

Major Booth Voysey. What is this, Edward?

Edward. I have something to say to you all.

Major Booth Voysey. What?

Edward. Well, Booth, you'll hear when I say it.

Major Booth Voysey. Is it business? . . . because I think this is scarcely the time for business.

Edward. Why?

Major Booth Voysey. Do you find it easy to descend from your natural grief to the consideration of money? . . . I do not. [*He finds* TRENCHARD *at his elbow.*] I hope you are getting some lunch, Trenchard.

Edward. This is business and rather more than business, Booth. I choose now, because it is something I wish to say to the family, not write to each individually . . . and it will be difficult to get us all together again.

Major Booth Voysey [*determined at any rate to give his sanction*]. Well, Trenchard, as Edward is in the position of trustee . . . executor . . . I don't know your terms . . . I suppose . . .

Trenchard. I don't see what your objection is.

Major Booth Voysey [*with some superiority*]. Don't you? I should not call myself a sentimental man, but . . .

Edward. You had better stay, Denis; you represent Ethel.

Tregoning [*who has not heard the beginning of this*]. Why?

[HONOR *has obediently come down from her room. She is pale and thin, shaken with grief and worn out besides; for needless to say the brunt of her father's illness, the brunt of everything, has been on her. Six weeks' nursing, part of it hopeless, will exhaust anyone. Her handkerchief is to her eyes, and every minute or two they flood over with tears.* EDWARD *goes and affectionately puts his arm round her.*

Edward. My dear Honor, I am sorry to be so . . . so merciless. There! . . . there! [*He hands her into the room; then turns and once more surveys the family, who this time mostly return the compliment. Then he says shortly.*] I think you might all sit down. [*And then, since* BOOTH *happens to be conveniently near . . .*]
Shut the door, Booth.

Major Booth Voysey. Shut the door!

[*But he does so, with as much dignity as possible.* EDWARD *goes close to his mother and speaks very distinctly, very kindly.*

Edward. Mother, we're all going to have a little necessary talk over matters . . . now, because it's most convenient.

I hope it won't . . . I hope you won't mind. Will you come to the table?

[MRS. VOYSEY *looks up as if understanding more than he says.*

Mrs. Voysey. Edward . . .

Edward. Yes, Mother dear?

Major Booth Voysey [*commandingly*]. You'll sit here, Mother, of course.

[*He places her in her accustomed chair at the foot of the table. One by one the others sit down,* EDWARD *apparently last. But then he discovers that* HUGH *has lost himself in a corner of the room and is gazing into vacancy.*

Edward [*with a touch of kindly exasperation*]. Hugh, would you mind attending?

Hugh. What is it?

Edward. There's a chair.

[HUGH *takes it. Then for a moment—while* EDWARD *is trying to frame in coherent sentences what he must say to them—for a minute there is silence, broken only by* HONOR'*s sniffs, which culminate at last in a noisy little cascade of tears.*

Major Booth Voysey. Honor, control yourself.

[*And to emphasize his own perfect control he helps himself majestically to a glass of sherry. Then says . . .*

Major Booth Voysey. Well, Edward?

Edward. I'll come straight to the point which concerns you. Our father's will gives certain sums to you all . . . the gross amount would be something over a hundred thousand pounds. There will be no money.

[*He can get no further than the bare statement, which is received only with varying looks of bewilderment; until* MRS. VOYSEY, *discovering nothing from their faces, breaks this second silence.*

Mrs. Voysey. I didn't hear.

Hugh [*in his mother's ear*]. Edward says there's no money.

Trenchard [*precisely*]. I think you said . . . 'will be'.

Major Booth Voysey [*in a tone of mitigated thunder*]. Why will there be no money?

Edward [*letting himself go*]. Because every penny by right belongs to the clients father spent his life in defrauding. I mean that in its worst sense . . . swindling . . . thieving. And now I must collect every penny, any money that you can give me; put the firm into bankruptcy; pay back all we can. I'll stand my trial . . . it'll come to that with me . . . and the sooner the better. [*He pauses, partly for breath, and glares at them all.*] Are none of you going to speak? Quite right, what is there to be said? [*Then with a gentle afterthought.*] I'm sorry to hurt you, Mother.

[*The* VOYSEY *family seems buried deep beneath this avalanche of horror. All but* MRS. VOYSEY, *who has been watching* EDWARD *closely, and now says very calmly . . .*

Mrs. Voysey. I can't hear quite all you say, but I guess what it is. You don't hurt me, Edward . . . I have known of this for a long time.

Edward [*with a muted cry*]. Oh Mother, did he know you knew?

Mrs. Voysey. What do you say?

Trenchard [*collected and dry*]. I may as well tell you, Edward; I suspected everything wasn't right about the time of my last quarrel with my father. As there was nothing I could do I did not pursue my suspicions. Was father aware that you knew, Mother?

Mrs. Voysey. We never discussed it. There was once a great danger, I believe . . . when you were all younger . . . of his being found out. But we never discussed it.

Edward [*swallowing a fresh bitterness*]. I'm glad it isn't such a shock to all of you.

Hugh [*alive to the dramatic aspect of the matter*]. My God . . . before the earth has settled on his grave!

Edward. I thought it wrong to put off telling you.

[HONOR, *the word swindling having spelt itself out in her mind, at last gives way to a burst of piteous grief.*

Honor. Oh, poor papa! . . . poor papa!

Edward [*comforting her kindly*]. Honor, we shall want your help and advice.

[*The* MAJOR *has recovered from the shock, to swell with importance. It being necessary to make an impression, he instinctively turns first to his wife.*

Major Booth Voysey. I think, Emily, there was no need for you to be present at this exposure, and that now you had better retire.

Emily. Very well, Booth.

[*She gets up to go, conscious of her misdemeanour. But as she reaches the door, an awful thought strikes the* MAJOR.

Major Booth Voysey. Good Heavens . . . I hope the servants haven't been listening! See where they are, Emily . . . and keep them away . . . distract them. Open the door suddenly. [*She does so, more or less, and there is no one behind it.*] That's all right.

[*Having watched his wife's departure, he turns with gravity to his brother.*

Major Booth Voysey. I have said nothing as yet, Edward. I am thinking.

Trenchard [*a little impatient at this exhibition*]. That's the worst of these family practices . . . a lot of money knocking around and no audit ever required. The wonder to me is to find an honest solicitor of that sort anywhere.

Major Booth Voysey. Really, Trenchard!

Trenchard. Well, think of the temptation.

Edward. And most people are such innocents . . .

Trenchard. Of course the whole world is getting more and more into the hands of its experts . . .

Edward. Here were these funds . . . a kind of lucky bag into which he dipped.

Trenchard. But he must have kept accounts of some sort.

Edward. Scraps of paper. The separate funds . . . most of them I can't even trace. The capital doesn't exist.

Major Booth Voysey. Where's it gone?

Edward [*very directly*]. You've been living on it.

Major Booth Voysey. Good God!

Trenchard. What can you pay in the pound?

Edward. As we stand? . . . six or seven shillings, I daresay. But we must do better than that.

[*To which there is no response.*

Major Booth Voysey. All this is very dreadful. Does it mean beggary for the whole family?

Edward. Yes, it should.

Trenchard [*sharply*]. Nonsense.

Edward [*joining issue at once*]. What right have we to a thing we possess?

Trenchard. He didn't make you an allowance, Booth? Your capital's your own, isn't it?

Major Booth Voysey [*awkwardly placed between the two of them*]. Really . . . I . . . I suppose so.

Trenchard. How long have you had it?

Major Booth Voysey. Oh . . . when I married . . .

Trenchard. Then that's all right.

Edward [*vehemently*]. It was stolen money . . . it must have been.

Trenchard. Possibly . . . but possibly not. And Booth took it in good faith.

Major Booth Voysey. I should hope so!

Edward [*dwelling on the words*]. It's stolen money.

Major Booth Voysey [*bubbling with distress*]. I say, what ought I to do?

Trenchard. Do . . . my dear Booth? Nothing.

Edward [*with great indignation*]. Trenchard, we owe reparation.

Trenchard. No doubt. But to whom? From which client's account was Booth's money taken? You say yourself you don't know.

Edward [*grieved*]. Trenchard!

Trenchard. My dear Edward . . . the law will take anything it has a right to and all it can get; you needn't be afraid. But what about your position . . . can we get you clear?

Edward. Oh . . . I'll face the music.

[BOOTH'*s head has been turning incessantly from one to the other and by this he is just a bristle of alarm.*

Major Booth Voysey. But I say, you know, this is awful! Will the thing have to be made public?

Trenchard. No help for it.

[*The* MAJOR'*s jaw drops; he is speechless.* MRS. VOYSEY'*s dead voice steals in.*

Mrs. Voysey. What is all this?

Trenchard. I am explaining, Mother, that the family is not called upon to beggar itself in order to pay back to every client to whom Father owed a pound perhaps eight shillings instead of seven.

Mrs. Voysey. He will find that my estate has been kept separate.

Trenchard. I'm very glad to hear it, Mother.

[EDWARD *hides his face in his hands.*

Mrs. Voysey. When Mr. Barnes died, your father agreed to appointing another trustee.

Tregoning [*diffidently*]. I suppose, Edward, I'm involved?

Edward [*lifting his head quickly*]. Denis, I hope not. I didn't know that anything of yours. . . .

Tregoning. Yes . . . all I got under my aunt's will.

Edward. See how things are . . . I've not found a trace of that yet. We'll hope for the best.

Tregoning [*setting his teeth*]. It can't be helped.

[MAJOR BOOTH VOYSEY *leans over the table and speaks in the loudest of whispers.*

Major Booth Voysey. Let me advise you to say nothing of this to Ethel at such a critical time.

Tregoning. Thank you, Booth . . . naturally I shan't.

[HUGH, *by a series of contortions, has lately been giving evidence of a desire or intention to say something.*

Edward. Well, what is it, Hugh?

Hugh. I have been wondering . . . if he can hear this conversation.

[*Up to now it has all been meaningless to* HONOR, *in her nervous dilapidation; but this remark brings a fresh burst of tears.*

Honor. Oh, poor papa . . . poor papa!

Mrs. Voysey. I think I'll go to my room. I can't hear what any of you are saying. Edward can tell me afterwards.

Edward. Would you like to go too, Honor?

Honor [*through her sobs*]. Yes, please, I would.

Tregoning. I'll get out, Edward. Whatever you think fit to do . . . ! I'm on one side of the fence and Ethel's on the other, so to speak. I wish I'd more work on hand . . . for her sake . . . and the child's. That's all.

[*By this time* MRS. VOYSEY *and* HONOR *have been got out of the room.* TREGONING *follows them, and the four brothers are left together.* HUGH *is vacant,* EDWARD *does not speak,* BOOTH *looks at* TRENCHARD, *who settles himself to acquire information.*

Trenchard. How long have things been wrong?

Edward. He told me the trouble began in his father's time and that he'd been battling with it ever since.

Trenchard [*smiling*]. Oh, come now . . . that's hardly possible.

Edward. I believed him. Of course I've barely begun on the papers yet. But I doubt if I'll be able to trace anything more than twenty years back . . . unless it's to do with old George Booth's business.

Major Booth Voysey. But the Pater never touched his money . . . why, he was a personal friend.

Trenchard. How long now since he told you?

Edward. Last autumn.

Trenchard. What has been happening since?

Edward. He got ill in November . . . which didn't make him any easier to deal with. I began by trying to make him put some of the smaller people right. He said that was penny wise and pound foolish. So I've been doing what I could myself this last month or so. Oh . . . nothing to count.

Trenchard. He didn't think you'd actually take a hand?

Edward. First it was that he was in a corner and I was to help him out. Then we were to clean up the whole mess and have a quarter of a million to the good. That was in February . . . when the new Kaffir boom was on.

Trenchard. He was in that, was he?

Edward. Up to the neck. And I believe he'd have made a pile if he hadn't been ill. As it was, he got out fifteen thousand to the good.

Major Booth Voysey. Really!

Edward. I'm not sure he didn't only tell me because he wanted someone to boast to about his financial exploits.

Trenchard. Got more reckless as he got older, I suppose.

Edward. Oh . . . mere facts meant nothing to him. He drew up this will in May. He knew then he'd nothing to leave . . . on the balance. But there it all is . . . legacies to servants . . . and charities. And I'm the sole executor . . . with an extra thousand for my trouble!

Trenchard. Childish! Was I down for anything?

Edward. No.

Trenchard [*without resentment*]. How he did hate me!

Edward. You're spared the results of his affection anyway.

Trenchard. What on earth made you stay with him once you knew? [EDWARD *does not answer for a moment.*

Edward. I thought I might prevent things getting worse.

Trenchard. I'm afraid your position . . . at the best . . . is not a pleasant one.

Edward [*bowing his head*]. I know.

[TRENCHARD, *the only one of the three who comprehends, looks at his brother for a moment with something that might almost be admiration. Then he stirs himself.*

Trenchard. I must be off. Work waiting . . . end of term.

Major Booth Voysey. Shall I walk to the station with you?

Trenchard. I'll spend a few minutes with Mother. [*He says, at the door, very respectfully.*] You'll count on me for any professional help I can give, please, Edward.

Edward [*simply*]. Thank you, Trenchard.

[*So* TRENCHARD *goes. And the* MAJOR, *who has been endeavouring to fathom his final attitude, then comments—*

Major Booth Voysey. No heart, y'know! Great brain! If it hadn't been for that distressing quarrel, he might have saved our poor father. Don't you think so, Edward?

Edward. Perhaps.

Hugh [*giving vent to his thoughts at last with something of a relish*]. The more I think this out, the more devilishly humorous it gets. Old Booth breaking down by the grave . . . Colpus reading the service. . . .

Edward. Yes, the Vicar's badly hit.

Hugh. Oh, the Pater had managed his business for years.

Major Booth Voysey. Good God . . . how shall we ever look old Booth in the face again?

Edward. I don't worry about him; he can die quite comfortably enough on our six shillings in the pound. It's one or two of the smaller fry who will suffer.

Major Booth Voysey. Now, just explain to me . . . I didn't interrupt while Trenchard was speaking . . . of what exactly did this defrauding consist?

Edward. Speculating with a client's capital. You pocket the gains . . . and you keep paying the client his ordinary income.

Major Booth Voysey. So that he doesn't find it out?

Edward. Quite so.

Major Booth Voysey. In point of fact, he doesn't suffer?

Edward. He doesn't suffer till he finds it out.

Major Booth Voysey. And all that's wrong now is that some of their capital is missing.

Edward [*half amused, half amazed at this process of reasoning*]. Yes, that's all that's wrong.

Major Booth Voysey. What is the—ah—deficit?

[*The word rolls from his tongue.*

Edward. Anything between two and three hundred thousand pounds.

Major Booth Voysey [*impressed, and not unfavourably*]. Dear me . . . this is a big affair!

Hugh [*following his own line of thought*]. Quite apart from the rights and wrongs of this, only a very able man could have kept a straight face to the world all these years, as the Pater did.

Major Booth Voysey. But he often made money by these speculations?

Edward. Very often. His own expenditure was heavy . . . as you know.

Major Booth Voysey [*with gratitude for favours received*]. He was a very generous man.

Hugh. Did nobody ever suspect?

Edward. You see, Hugh, when there was any pressing danger . . . if a trust had to be wound up . . . he'd make a great effort and put the accounts straight.

Major Booth Voysey. Then he did put some accounts straight?

Edward. Yes, when he couldn't help himself.

[BOOTH *looks very inquiring, and then squares himself up to the subject.*

Major Booth Voysey. Now look here, Edward. You told us that he told you that it was the object of his life to put these accounts straight. Then you laughed at that. Now you tell me that he did put some accounts straight.

Edward [*wearily*]. My dear Booth, you don't understand.

Major Booth Voysey. Well, let me understand . . . I am anxious to understand.

Edward. We can't pay ten shillings in the pound.

Major Booth Voysey. That's very dreadful. But do you know that there wasn't a time when we couldn't have paid five?

Edward [*acquiescent*]. Perhaps.

Major Booth Voysey. Very well, then! If it was true about his father and all that . . . and why shouldn't we believe him if we can? . . . and he did effect an improvement, that's to his credit, isn't it? Let us at least be just, Edward.

Edward [*patiently polite*]. I am sorry if I seem unjust. But he has left me in a rather unfortunate position.

Major Booth Voysey. Yes, his death was a tragedy. It seems to me that if he had been spared he might have succeeded at length in this tremendous task and restored to us our family honour.

Edward. Yes, Booth, he sometimes spoke very feelingly of that.

Major Booth Voysey [*irony lost upon him*]. I can well believe it. And I can tell you that now . . . I may be right or I may be wrong . . . I am feeling far less concerned about the clients' money than I am at the terrible blow to the Family which this exposure will strike. Money, after all, can to a certain extent be done without . . . but honour. . . .

[*This is too much for* EDWARD.

Edward. Our honour! Does any one of you mean to give me a single penny towards undoing all the wrong that has been done?

Major Booth Voysey. I take Trenchard's word for it that that . . . is quite unnecessary.

Edward. Then don't talk to me about honour.

Major Booth Voysey [*somewhat nettled at this outburst*]. I am thinking of the public exposure. Edward, can't that be prevented?

Edward [*with quick suspicion*]. How?

Major Booth Voysey. Well, how was it being prevented before he died . . . before we knew anything about it?

Edward [*appealing to the spirits that watch over him*]. Oh, listen to this! First Trenchard . . . and now you! You've the poison in your blood, every one of you. Who am I to talk! I daresay so have I.

Major Booth Voysey [*reprovingly*]. I am beginning to think that you have worked yourself into rather an hysterical state over this unhappy business.

Edward [*rating him*]. Perhaps you'd have been glad . . . glad if I'd gone on lying and cheating . . . and married and begotten a son to go on lying and cheating after me . . . and to pay your interest in the lie and the cheat.

Major Booth Voysey [*with statesman-like calm*]. Look here, Edward, this rhetoric is exceedingly out of place. The simple question before us is . . . what is the best course to pursue?

Edward. There is no question before us. There's only one course to pursue.

Major Booth Voysey [*crushingly*]. You will let me speak, please. In so far as our poor father was dishonest to his clients, I pray that he may be forgiven. In so far as he spent his life honestly endeavouring to right a wrong which he had found already committed . . . I forgive him . . . I admire him, Edward . . . and I feel it my duty to—er—reprobate most strongly the—er—gusto with which you have been holding him up in memory to us . . . ten minutes after we'd been standing round his grave . . . as a monster of wickedness. I think I knew him as well as you . . . better. And . . . thank God! . . . there was not between him and me this . . . this unhappy business to warp my judgement of him. [*He warms to his subject.*] Did you ever know a more charitable man . . . a larger-hearted? He was a faithful husband . . . and what a father to all of us! . . . putting us out into the world and fully intending to leave us comfortably settled there. Further . . . as I see this matter, Edward . . . when as a young man he was told this terrible secret and entrusted with such a frightful task . . . did he turn his back on it like a coward? No. He went through it heroically to the end of his life. And, as he died, I imagine there was no more torturing thought than that he had left his work unfinished. [*He is pleased with this peroration.*] And now . . . if all these clients can be kept receiving their natural incomes . . . and if father's plan could be carried out, of gradually replacing the capital. . . .

[EDWARD *at this raises his head and stares with horror.*

Edward. You're asking me to carry on this . . . ? Oh, you don't know what you're talking about.

[*The* MAJOR, *having talked himself back to a proper eminence, remains good tempered.*

Major Booth Voysey. Well, I'm not a conceited man . . . but I do think that I can understand a simple financial problem when it has been explained to me.

Edward. You don't know the nerve . . . the unscrupulous daring it requires to. . . .

Major Booth Voysey. Of course, if you're going to argue round your own incompetence. . . .

Edward [*very straight*]. D'you want your legacy?

Major Booth Voysey [*with dignity*]. In one moment I shall get very angry. Here am I doing my best to help you and your clients . . . and there you sit imputing to me the most sordid motives. Do you suppose I should touch, or allow to be touched, the money which father has left us till every client's claim was satisfied?

Edward. My dear Booth, I know you mean well . . .

Major Booth Voysey. I'll come down to your office and work with you.

[*At this cheerful prospect even poor* EDWARD *can't help smiling.*

Edward. I'm sure you would.

Major Booth Voysey [*feeling that it is a chance lost*]. If the Pater had ever consulted me. . . .

[*At this point* TRENCHARD *looks round the door to say . . .*

Trenchard. Are you coming, Booth?

Major Booth Voysey. Yes, certainly. I'll talk this over with Trenchard. [*As he gets up and automatically stiffens, he is reminded of the occasion and his voice drops.*] I say . . . we've been speaking very loud. You must do nothing rash. I've no doubt he and I can devise something which will obviate . . . and then I'm sure I shall convince you. . . [*Glancing into the hall he apparently catches his eldes brother's impatient eye, for he departs abruptly, saying. . .* All right, Trenchard, you've eight minutes.

[BOOTH'*s departure leaves* HUGH, *at any rate, really at his ease.*

Hugh. This is an experience for you, Edward!

Edward [*bitterly*]. And I feared what the shock might be to you all! Booth has made a good recovery.

Hugh. You wouldn't have him miss such a chance of booming at us.

Edward. It's strange that people will believe you can do right by means which they know to be wrong.

Hugh [*taking great interest in this*]. Come, what do we know about right and wrong? Let's say legal and illegal. You're so down on the governor because he has trespassed against the etiquette of your own profession. But now he's dead . . . and if there weren't any scandal to think of . . . it's no use the rest of us pretending to feel him a criminal. Because we don't. Which just shows that money . . . and property . . . .

[*At this point he becomes conscious that* ALICE MAITLAND *is standing behind him, her eyes fixed on his brother. So he interrupts himself to ask . . .*

Hugh. D'you want to speak to Edward?

Alice. Please, Hugh.

Hugh. I'll go.

[*He goes, a little martyr-like, to conclude the evolution of his theory in soliloquy. His usual fate.* ALICE *still looks at* EDWARD, *and he at her rather appealingly.*

Alice. Auntie has told me.

Edward. He was fond of you. Don't think worse of him than you can help.

Alice. I'm thinking of you.

Edward. I may just escape.

Alice. So Trenchard says.

Edward. My hands are clean, Alice.

Alice. I know that.

Edward. Mother's not very upset.

Alice. She'd expected a smash in his lifetime.

Edward. I'm glad that didn't happen.

Alice. Yes. I've put Honor to bed. It was a mercy to tell her just at this moment. She can grieve for his death and his disgrace at the same time . . . and the one grief will soften the other perhaps.

Edward. Oh, they're all shocked enough at the disgrace . . . but will they open their purses to lessen the disgrace?

Alice. Will it seem less disgraceful to have stolen ten thousand pounds than twenty?

Edward. I should think so.

Alice. I should think so; but I wonder if that's the Law. If it isn't, Trenchard wouldn't consider the point. I'm sure Public Opinion doesn't say so . . . and that's what Booth is considering.

Edward [*with contempt*]. Yes.

Alice [*ever so gently ironical*]. Well, he's in the Army . . . he's almost in Society . . . and he has got to get on in both; one musn't blame him.

Edward [*very serious*]. But when one thinks how the money was obtained!

Alice. When one thinks how most money is obtained!

Edward. They've not earned it.

Alice [*her eyes humorous*]. If they had they might have given it to you and earned more. Did I ever tell you what my guardian said to me when I came of age?

Edward. I'm thankful you're out of the mess.

Alice. I shouldn't have been, but I was made to look after my affairs myself . . . much against my will. My guardian was a person of great character and no principles, the best and most lovable man I've ever met . . . I'm sorry you never knew him, Edward . . . and he said once to me: you've no moral right to your money . . . you've not earned it or deserved it in any way. So don't be either surprised or annoyed when any enterprising person tries to get it from you. He has at least as much moral right to it as you . . . if he can use it better perhaps he has more. Shocking sentiments, aren't they? But perhaps that's why I've less pity for some of these clients than you have, Edward.

[EDWARD *shakes his head, treating these paradoxes as they deserve.*

Edward. Alice . . . one or two of them will be beggared.

Alice [*sincerely*]. Yes, that is bad. What's to be done?

Edward. There's old nurse . . . with her poor little savings gone!

Alice. Something can be done for her . . . surely.

Edward. The Law's no respecter of persons . . . that's its boast. Old Booth with more than he wants will keep enough and to spare. My old nurse, with just enough, may starve. But it'll be a relief to clear out this nest of lies, even though one suffers one's self. I've been ashamed to walk into that office. I'll hold my head high in prison though.

[*He shakes himself stiffly erect, his chin high.* ALICE *quizzes him.*

Alcie. Edward, I'm afraid you're feeling heroic.

Edward. I!

Alice. You looked quite like Booth for the moment. [*This effectually removes the starch.*] Please don't glory in your martyrdom. It will be very stupid to send you to prison, and you must do your best to keep out. [*Her tone is most practical.*] We were talking about these people who'll be beggared.

Edward [*simply*]. I didn't mean to be heroic.

Alice. I know. But there's the danger in acting on principle . . . one begins to think more of one's attitude than of the use of what one is doing.

Edward. But I've no choice in the matter. There's only the one thing I can do.

Alice. Run the ship ashore? Well . . . if you say so!

Edward. Unless you expect me to take Booth's advice . . . turn honest cheat . . . juggle and speculate in the hope that . . . ! Oh, my dear Alice . . . no! If it were only a question of a few thousands . . . ! But I'm no good at that sort of thing anyway. It'd simply make matters worse. I've been sitting down . . . self-pityingly . . . under the shame of it all these months. I did . . . take a hand . . . and stop one affair going from bad to worse. I'd no right to. Sheer favouritism! I shall suffer for it now.

Alice. That's nobody's business but your own.

Edward. I could go on doing that . . . putting the worst cases straight . . . say for a year . . . or till I'm found out . . . as I almost certainly should be. For don't think I'd be any good at the game, Alice. [*Then his tone changes; he is glancing inward.*] But you know . . . there's something in me that'd rather like to try. [*He looks her full in the face.*] What do you say?

Alice [*catching her breath*]. Dear Edward . . . I can't advise.

Edward [*with grimly whimsical humour*]. You've undermined my principles. I must have some help in exchange.

Alice. I'm lawless at heart, I fear. Most women are. What would happen at the end of the year?

Edward. Then I should have to do what I ought to do now . . . send round a polite letter: Dear Sir or Madam . . . I am a thief . . . please call the police. For I can't succeed. Understand that. I can't make up a quarter of a million by careful management.

Alice. Will it be much worse for you . . . if at last they do call the police?

Edward. That . . . as you said . . . would be nobody's business but my own.

Alice. I'd do anything to help you . . . anything. That sounds like dear Booth . . . and it's just as silly.

Edward. Suppose I tackle the job?

Alice. Not because I want you to?

Edward. Do you? No . . . you shan't have to think that.

Alice. But my dear . . . I shall be so proud of you.

Edward. When I've failed?

Alice. I shan't think it failure.

Edward. Booth and Hugh and the rest must hold their tongues. I needn't have told them.

Alice. They'll do that much for you.

Edward. But I rather liked telling them too.

[*She is looking at him with suddenly shining eyes.*

Alice. Edward . . . I'm so happy. Suddenly . . . you're a different man.

Edward. Am I?

Alice. You've begun to be. It was in you to be . . . and I knew it. [*His face darkens.*

Edward. I wonder . . . I wonder if I'm not . . . already!

Alice. Why . . . ?

Edward. And if my father didn't begin . . . just like this? He told me he did. Doing the right thing in the wrong way . . . then doing the wrong thing . . . and coming to be what he was . . . and bringing me to this. Alice, suppose it's not failure I'm risking . . . but success. Yes, you're right . . . I feel a different man. [*She brings him help.*

Alice. I'll take that risk, my dear. I'll risk your turning crook. And it's a pretty big risk now for me.

[*He accepts it.*

Edward. Then there's no more to be said, is there?

Alice. Not for the moment. [*He does not ask what she means by this.*] I must go back to Honor. Horrid . . . if one knew it . . . to look comic when one is suffering. [*As she opens the door.*] And here's Booth back again.

Edward. Shall I tell him he has convinced me?

Alice [*mischievously*]. It would delight him. But I shouldn't.

ACT IV

MR. VOYSEY'*s room at the office is* EDWARD'*s room now. It has somehow lost that brilliancy which the old man's occupation seemed to give it. Perhaps it is only because this December morning is dull and depressing; but the fire isn't bright and the panels and windows don't shine as they did. There are no roses on the table either.* EDWARD, *walking in as his father did, hanging his hat and coat where his father's used to hang, is certainly the palest shadow of that other masterful presence. A depressed, drooping shadow, too. This may be what* PEACEY *feels; for he looks very surly as he obeys the old routine of following his chief to this room on his arrival. Nor has* EDWARD *so much as a glance for his confidential clerk. They exchange the most formal of greetings.* EDWARD *sits at his desk, on which lies the morning's pile of letters, unopened now.*

Peacey. Good morning, sir.

Edward. Good morning, Peacey. Any notes for me?

Peacey. Well, I've hardly been through the letters yet, sir.

Edward [*his eyebrows meeting*]. Oh . . . and I'm late myself.

Peacey. I'm very sorry, sir.

Edward. If Mr. Bullen calls, you had better show him those papers. Write to Metcalfe; say I've seen Mr. Vickery this morning and that we hope for a decision from Mr. Booth within a day or so. Better show me the letter.

Peacey. Very good, sir.

Edward. That's all, thank you.

[PEACEY *gets to the door, where he stops, looking not only surly but nervous now.*

Peacey. May I speak to you a moment, sir?

Edward. Certainly.

[PEACEY, *after a moment, makes an effort, purses his mouth and begins.*

Peacey. Bills are beginning to come in upon me as is usual at this season, sir. My son's allowance at Cambridge is now rather a heavy item of my expenditure. I hope that the custom of the firm isn't to be neglected now that you are the head of it, Mr. Edward. Two hundred your father always made it at Christmas . . . in notes if you please.

[*Towards the end of this* EDWARD *begins to pay attention. When he answers his voice is harsh.*

Edward. Oh to be sure . . . your hush money.

Peacey [*bridling*]. That's not a very pleasant word.

Edward. This is an unpleasant subject.

Peacey. Well, it's not one I wish to discuss. Mr. Voysey would always give me the notes in an envelope when he shook hands with me at Christmas.

Edward. Notes I understand. But why not a rise in salary?

Peacey. Mr. Voysey's custom, sir, from before my time. My father . . .

Edward. Yes. It's an hereditary pull you have over the firm, isn't it?

Peacey. When my father retired . . . he's been dead twenty-six years, Mr. Edward . . . he simply said: I have told the governor you know what I know. And Mr. Voysey said . . . I treat you as I did your father, Peacey. Never another word with him on the subject.

Edward. A very decent arrangement . . . and the thriftiest no doubt. Of the raising of salaries there might have been no end.

Peacey. Mr. Edward, that's uncalled for. We have served you and yours most faithfully. I know my father would sooner have cut off his hand than do anything to embarrass the firm.

Edward. But business is business, Peacey. Surely he could have had a partnership for the asking.

Peacey. That's another matter, sir.

Edward. Why?

Peacey. A matter of principle, if you'll excuse me. I must not be taken to approve of the firm's conduct. Nor did my dear father approve. And at anything like a partnership he would certainly have drawn the line.

Edward. My apologies.

Peacey. That's all right, sir. Always a bit of friction in coming to an understanding about anything, isn't there, sir? [*He is going when* EDWARD'*s question stops him.*

Edward. Why didn't you speak about this last Christmas?

Peacey. You were so upset about your father's death.

Edward. My father died the summer before that.

Peacey. Well . . . truthfully, Mr. Edward?

Edward. As truthfully as you think suitable.

[*The irony of this is wasted on* PEACEY, *who becomes pleasantly candid.*

Peacey. Well, I'd always thought there must be a smash when your father died . . . but it didn't come. I couldn't make you out. So I thought I'd better keep quiet for a bit and say nothing.

Edward. I see. Your son's at Cambridge?

Peacey. Yes.

Edward. I wonder you didn't bring him into the firm.

Peacey [*taking this very kind*]. Thank you. But James will go to the bar. He'll have to wait his chance, of course. But he's a clever lad. And it's a good use for one's savings.

Edward. I feel sure he'll do well. I'm glad to have had this little talk with you, Peacey. I'm sorry you can't have the money.

[*He returns to his letters, a little steely-eyed.* PEACEY *quite at his ease, makes for the door yet again, saying* . . .

Peacey. Oh, any time will do, sir.

Edward. You can't have it at all.

Peacey [*brought up short*]. Can't I?

Edward. No. This was one of the first things I made up my mind about. The firm's business is not carried on quite as it used to be. You may have noticed that you don't get the same little matters passing through your hands. In fact, we no longer make illicit profits out of our clients. So there are none for you to share. [PEACEY *bridles*.

Peacey. Mr. Edward . . . I'm sorry we began this discussion. You'll give me my two hundred, please . . . and we'll drop the subject.

Edward. Yes . . . I've no more to say.

Peacey. I want the money. And it's hardly gentlemanly in you, Mr. Edward, to try and get out of giving it me. Your father'd never have made such an excuse.

Edward. D'you think I'm lying to you?

Peacey. That is no business of mine, sir.

Edward. As long as the dividend is punctually paid.

Peacey. And there's no need to be sarcastic.

Edward. Would you rather I told you plainly what I think of you?

Peacey. That I'm a thief because I've taken money from a thief?

Edward. Worse! You're content to have others steal for you.

Peacey. And who isn't?

[EDWARD *is really pleased with the retort. He relaxes and changes his tone, which had indeed become a little bullying*.

Edward. Ah, my dear Peacey . . . I fear we musn't begin to talk economics. The present point is that I myself no longer receive these particular stolen goods. Therefore I can throw a stone at you. I have thrown it.

[PEACEY, *who would far sooner be bullied than talked to like this, turns very sulky indeed.*

Peacey. Then I resign my position here.

Edward. Very well.

Peacey. And I happen to think the secret's worth its price.

Edward. Perhaps someone will pay it you.

Peacey [*feebly threatening*]. Don't presume upon it's not being worth my while to make use of what I know.

Edward [*not unkindly*]. But, my good fellow, it happens to be the truth I'm telling you. I am doing a thankless . . . and an unpleasant . . . and a quite unprofitable job here. How can you hope to blackmail a man who has everything to gain by exposure and nothing to lose?

Peacey [*peeving*]. I don't want to ruin you, sir, and I have a great regard for the firm. But you must see that I can't have my income reduced in this way without a struggle.

Edward [*with great cheerfulness*]. Very well . . . struggle away.

Peacey [*his voice rising high and thin*]. But is it fair dealing on your part to dock the money suddenly like this? I have been counting on it most of the year, and I have been led into heavy expenses. Why couldn't you have warned me?

Edward. Yes, that's true, Peacey . . . it was stupid of me. I'm sorry.

[PEACEY *is a little comforted by this quite candid acknowledgement.*

Peacey. Things may get easier for you by and by.

Edward. Possibly.

Peacey. Will you reconsider the matter then?

[*At this insinuation* EDWARD *looks up, more than a little exasperated.*

Edward. Then you don't believe what I tell you?

Peacey. Yes, I do.

Edward. But you think that the fascination of swindling one's clients will finally prove irresistible?

Peacey. That's what your father found, I suppose you know.

[*This gives* EDWARD *such pause that he drops his masterful tone.*

Edward. I didn't.

Peacey. He got things as right as rain once.

Edward. Did he?

Peacey. So my father told me. But he started again.

Edward. Are you sure of this?

Peacey [*expanding pleasantly*]. Well, sir, I knew your father pretty well. And when I first came into the firm I simply hated him. He was that sour . . . so snappy with everyone . . . as if he had a grievance against the whole world.

Edward [*pensively*]. He had then . . . in those days!

Peacey. His dealings with his clients were no business of mine. I speak as I find. He came to be very kind to me . . . thoughtful and considerate. He was pleasant and generous to everyone . . .

Edward. So you have hopes of me yet?

Peacey [*who has a simple mind*]. No, Mr. Edward, no. You're different from your father . . . one must make up one's mind to that. And you may believe me or not, but I should be very glad to know that the firm was going straight again. I'm getting on in years myself now. I'm not much longer for the business, and there've been times when I have sincerely regretted my connection with it. If you'll let me say so, I think it's very noble of you to have undertaken the work you have. [*Then, as everything seems smooth again.*] And if you'll give me enough to cover this year's extra expense, I think I may promise you that I shan't expect money again.

Edward [*good-tempered, as he would speak to an importunate child*]. No, Peacey, no.

Peacey [*fretful again*]. Well, sir, you make things very difficult for me.

Edward. Here is a letter from Mr. Cartwright which you might attend to. If he wants an appointment with me, don't make one till the New Year. His case can't come on before February.

Peacey [*taking the letter*]. I show myself anxious to meet you in every way. . . . [*He is handed another.*]

Edward. 'Perceval Building Estate' . . . that's yours too.

Peacey [*putting them both down, resolutely*]. But I refuse to be ignored. I must consider my whole position. I hope I may not be tempted to make use of the power I possess. But if I am driven to proceed to extremities . . .

Edward [*breaking in upon this bunch of tags*]. My dear Peacey, don't talk nonsense . . . you couldn't proceed to an extremity to save your life. You've comfortably taken this money all these years. You'll find you're no longer capable of doing even such a slightly uncomfortable thing as tripping up your neighbour.

[*This does completely upset the gentle blackmailer. He loses one grievance in another.*

Peacey. Really, Mr. Edward, I am a considerably older man than you. These personalities . . . !

Edward. I'm sorry. Don't forget the letters.

Peacey. I will not, sir.

[*He takes them with great dignity and is leaving the room.*

Peacey. There's Mr. Hugh waiting.

Edward. To see me? Ask him in.

Peacey. Come in, Mr. Hugh, please.

[HUGH *comes in,* PEACEY *holding the door for him with a frigid politeness of which he is quite oblivious. At this final slight* PEACEY *goes out in dudgeon.*

Edward. How are you?

Hugh. I don't know.

[*And he throws himself into the chair by the fire.* EDWARD, *quite used to this sort of thing, goes quietly on with his work, adding encouragingly after a moment . . .*

Edward. How's Beatrice?

Hugh. Ink to the elbows. She's half-way through her new book.

[*He studies his boots with the gloomiest expression. And indeed, they are very dirty and his turned-up trousers are muddy at the edge. As he is quite capable of sitting silently by the fire for a whole morning* EDWARD *asks him at last . . .*

Edward. Do you want anything?

Hugh. Yes . . . I want five bob. I left home without a penny. I've walked.

Edward. From Highgate?

Hugh. Yes . . . by Hornsey and Highbury and Hackney and Hoxton. And I must have some lunch.

Edward. I can manage five bob . . .

[*He puts them on his table.*

Hugh. And Upper Holloway and Lower Holloway . . . and Pentonville . . . and Clerkenwell . . .

Edward. I don't know any of them.

Hugh. Nobody does . . . except the million people who live there. But that's London. And I also, my dear Edward, want it destroyed.

Edward. We are warned that . . . under certain circumstances . . . it may be.

Hugh. But why wait for mere foreigners to do the job? Why

not tackle it ourselves . . . and, in the inspiring words of Mr. Rockefeller, do it now?

Edward. And what about the people who live there?

Hugh. Why should they live there . . . or anywhere? Why should they live at all?

Edward. Well, they've their work to do . . . most of them. Incidentally . . . much as I love your society . . . so have I mine. And this morning I'm rather busy.

Hugh. Aha! There's the fatal word. We don't work, Edward, not one in a thousand of us. Work is creation. Is that what an outworn civilisation requires of us? Obviously not. It asks us to keep busy . . . and forget that to all these means there is no creative end at all. We've to keep our accounts straight . . . as you have to now . . . to keep the streets clean . . . and ourselves clean . . .

Edward. That at least may be called an end in itself.

Hugh. I'm not so sure. If it's merely a habit . .. all habits are bad habits. Why wash?

Edward. I seem to remember that, as a small boy, washing was not your strong point.

Hugh. I'm glad I had that much moral courage. On principle a man should not wash unless he feels an inward urge to wash. Did Michelangelo wash? Seldom!

Edward. Better his work than his company, then.

Hugh. I'm sick of this endless sham. But one can put some sort of an end to it . . . if not to all of it . . . to one's own small share in it. And I mean to. So that's that.

Edward. Suicide?

Hugh. Oh dear me no! Life's great fun if you could only live it. I mean to live it. Thanks for the five bob. [*He pockets it.*] And my first step is to hand you back for your wretched clients the money that the Pater settled on me . . . what there is left of it. And don't let me forget that I owe you this too.

Edward. But my dear Hugh, you can't afford . . .

Hugh. Aha! Another fatal word. Afford! Give a man an income . . . big or small . . . and he passes half his time thinking what he can or can't afford. The money has been a curse to me. It has never belonged to me . . .

Edward. No.

Hugh. Oh, never mind the legal . . . I mean in the real sense. How could it belong to me? I didn't create it . . . or even earn it. I've belonged to it. So there's the first step to being free. My spiritual history is a very interesting one, Edward. If it weren't for Beatrice I'd make a book of it.

Edward. Would it show her up badly?

Hugh. No . . . but writing's her job. One musn't poach.

Edward. She might make a book of it.

Hugh. Oh, it doesn't interest her. D'you remember the row there was at home when I said I meant to paint?

Edward. Very well.

Hugh. However . . . the Pater came down at last with two hundred a year. Studio rent, velvet coat, mutton chop cooked on the gas stove, and sardines for supper . . . that's what the art of painting meant to him. Then I got married to Beatrice . . . which was so unexpectedly moral of me that he sprang another two hundred. Well . . . I've kept busy. And I've learnt how to paint. And I do paint . . . other men's pictures.

Edward. Forgery?

Hugh. Yes . . . it is.

Edward. Are you joking?

Hugh. Not at all. Forty-nine out of fifty of us . . . if you put us to paint that table and chair . . . to begin with we don't see that table and chair! What we see is what we remember of some painting by Matisse or Picasso of some other table and chair. This world, my dear Edward, is growing fuller and fuller of paintings . . . and of paintings of paintings of paintings. And a couple of hundred of them must be mine. If I could afford it . . . aha, afford! . . . I'd buy them back and burn them. But the critics, dear Edward, much prefer paintings of paintings to paintings . . . for they know what to say about them. They rejoice when they see that bastard great-grandchild of Picasso's . . .

[EDWARD'*s table telephone rings.*

Edward. Yes? Yes . . . in two minutes. I must turn you out, Hugh. What does Beatrice say, by the by?

Hugh. About the money? Yes, there's that. I can't quite leave her with nothing.

Edward. Are you leaving her?

Hugh. We got married with the idea that we'd separate some time. And I can't be free unless I do.

Edward. I thought you were so fond of each other.

Hugh. I suppose in a sort of way we still are. We've always disagreed about everything. That used to be stimulating. But now when we argue we quarrel. And that's tiring.

Edward. Do they know down at home that you're not getting on?

Hugh. Emily may.

Edward. For heaven's sake keep a good face on things for Christmas.

Hugh. I don't believe I'll go down for Christmas.

Edward. Nonsense! You can't hurt Mother's feelings by . . .

Hugh. Do not expect me to pay homage to the Voysey family feelings. If we must have a hollow fraud to kow-tow before, there are many less brassy ones. Good lord . . . you're not still taken in by them, surely . . . after the way we've all treated you? Even I've shirked asking you how you've been getting on here . . . for fear you'd start telling me. How are things, though?

Edward. I've not done so badly. Better than I thought I should, really! I've righted what I thought the four most scandalous cases . . . somewhat to the prejudice of the rest.

Hugh. Then can't you cut free?

Edward. And go to gaol?

Hugh [*really startled by this*]. But they won't . . .

Edward. But they will.

Hugh. And at any moment . . . ?

Edward. Yes. I live on the brink. For the first month or so I thought every knock at the door meant a push over it. But nothing happens. There are days . . . you wouldn't believe it . . . when I quite forget that I'm a criminal. And . . . it's possible . . . nothing may happen. And . . . at this moment . . . I really don't know whether I want it to or not.

Hugh. I should take the plunge.

Edward. Why?

Hugh. The longer you wait the worse it'll be for you, won't it?

Edward. Yes.

Hugh. The thing's telling on you too.

Edward. I know. My barber tries to sell me hair restorer.

Hugh. On your faculties. The damn thing is swallowing you up. Don't let it. You've no right to let your life be brought to nothing.

Edward. Does my life matter?

Hugh. But of course.

Edward [*the iron in his soul*]. That's where we differ. Still, now I've scavenged up the worst of the mess . . . and can only sit here drudging . . . improving things by thirty shillings here . . . and by seven pounds two and sixpence there . . . I do begin to understand Father a little better.

Hugh [*cheerfully*]. Oh . . . I'm all for the Pater. He played a great game. And what this civilization needs . . . if we can't smash it up altogether . . . is a lot more men like him. . . .

[*The door is opened and* MR. GEORGE BOOTH *comes in. He looks older than he did and besides is evidently not in a happy frame of mind.*

Mr. George Booth. Hullo, Hugh. How are you, Edward?

Hugh. But what I'm going to do is to step out of my front door with five bob in my pocket. And I'll tramp . . . and I'll paint for my bread . . . the farmer . . . the farmer's wife . . . or his dog or his cow . . . an honest bit of work done with despatch for just what he thinks it's worth to him. And if I can earn my bread I'll know I'm some good . . . and if I can't I'll drown myself.

Edward. I should wait till the summer comes.

Hugh. I'll begin with your office boy. For two shillings I will do him a sketch of his spotty little countenance. Edward, may I propose it to him?

Edward. You may not. To begin with he can't afford two shillings. . . .

Hugh. Aha! Afford! And of course he's very busy too?

Edward. If he isn't, I'll sack him.

Hugh. Good God . . . what a world! Good-bye.

[HUGH *departs, not, we may be sure, to tramp the roads; but he has thoroughly enjoyed hearing himself talk.*

Edward. Will you come here . . . or will you sit by the fire?

Mr. George Booth. This'll do. I shan't keep you long.

Edward. Well . . . here's the Vickery correspondence. He will pay the extra rent, but . . .

Mr. George Booth [*nervously*]. Yes . . . it isn't really that I've come about.

Edward. No?

Mr. George Booth. Something less pleasant, I'm afraid.

Edward. Litigation? I trust not.

Mr. George Booth. No. . . . I'm getting too old to quarrel. No! I've made up my mind to withdraw my securities from the custody of your firm. I don't know what notice is usual.

[*He has got it out and feels better.* EDWARD *has awaited such a shock for so long that now it has come he finds he feels nothing.*

Edward. To a good solicitor . . . five minutes. Ten for a poor one. Have you any particular reason for doing this, Mr. Booth?

Mr. George Booth [*thankful to be able to talk and, so he thinks, stave off reproaches*]. Oh . . . naturally . . . naturally! You can't but know, Edward, that I have never been able to feel that implicit confidence in you . . . in your abilities, your personality, that's to say . . . which I reposed in your father. Well . . . hardly to be expected, was it?

Edward [*grimly acquiescent*]. Hardly.

Mr. George Booth. It's nothing against you. Men like your father are few and far between. I don't doubt that things go on here as they have always done. But since he died . . . I have not been happy about my affairs. It is a new experience for me . . . to feel worried . . . especially about money. The possession of money has always been something of a pleasure to me. And my doctor . . . I saw him again yesterday . . . he keeps me on a diet now . . . quite unnecessary . . . but he said that above all things I was not to worry. And, as I made up my mind upon the matter some time ago . . . in point of fact more than a year before your father died it was clear to me that I could not leave my interests in your hands as I had in his. . . .

Edward [*but this strikes* EDWARD *with the shock of a bullet*]. Did he know that?

Mr. George Booth. He must have guessed. I practically told him so. And I hoped he'd tell you . . . and so spare me the unpleasant necessity of hurting your feelings . . . as I fear I must be doing now.

Edward. Not at all. But we'll take it, if you please, that he never guessed. [*For with that thought of his father he really could not live.*] I can't induce you to change your mind?

Mr. George Booth. No. And I'd sooner you wouldn't try. I shall make a point of telling the family that you are in no way to blame. My idea is for the future to let my Bank . . .

Edward. For it's my duty to if I can. . . .

Mr. George Booth. Heavens above us, my dear Edward . . . the loss of one client . . . however important . . . !

Edward. I know. Well . . . here's the way out. And it isn't my fault.

Mr. George Booth. Forgive me for saying that your conduct seems to me a little lacking in dignity.

Edward [*patient; ironic*]. I'm sure it must. Will you walk off with your papers now? They'll make rather a cart-load.

Mr. George Booth. You'll have to explain matters a bit.

Edward [*grimly*]. Yes. I'd better. How much . . . Mr. Booth . . . do you think you're worth?

Mr. George Booth. God bless me . . . I know what I'm worth. I'm not a baby . . . or a woman. I have it all written down . . . more or less . . . in a little book.

Edward. I should like to see that little book. You'll get not quite half of that out of us.

Mr. George Booth. Don't be perverse, Edward. I said I had made up my mind to withdraw the whole. . . .

Edward. You should have made it up sooner.

Mr. George Booth. What's this all about?

Edward. The greater part of what is so neatly written down in that little book doesn't exist.

Mr. George Booth. Nonsense. It must exist. I don't want to realise. You hand me over the securities. I don't need to reinvest simply because . . .

Edward [*dealing his blow not unkindly, but squarely*]. I can't hand you over what I haven't got.

[*The old man hears the words. But their meaning . . .?*

Mr. George Booth. Is anything . . . wrong?

Edward. How many more times am I to tell you that we have robbed you of half your property?

Mr. George Booth [*his senses almost failing him*]. Say that again.

Edward. It's quite true.

Mr. George Booth. My money . . . gone?

Edward. Yes.

Mr. George Booth [*clutching at a straw of anger*]. You've been the thief . . . you . . . you . . . ?

Edward. I wouldn't tell you so if I could help it . . . my father.

[*This actually calls* MR. BOOTH *back to something like dignity and self-possession. He thumps* EDWARD'*s table furiously*.

Mr. George Booth. I'll make you prove that.

Edward. Oh, you've fired a mine.

Mr. George Booth [*scolding him well*]. Slandering your dead father, and lying to me . . . revenging yourself by frightening me . . . because I detest you!

Edward. Why . . . haven't I thanked you for pushing me over the edge? I do . . . I promise you I do.

Mr. George Booth [*shouting; and his courage fails him as he shouts*]. Prove it . . . prove it to me. You don't frighten me so easily. One can't lose half of all one has and then be told of it in two minutes . . . sitting at a table.

[*His voice tails off to a piteous whimper.*

Edward [*quietly now and kindly*]. If my father had told you this in plain words, you'd have believed him.

Mr. George Booth [*bowing his head*]. Yes.

[EDWARD *looks at the poor old thing with great pity.*

Edward. What on earth did you want to do this for? You need never have known . . . you could have died happy. Settling with all those charities in your will would have smashed us up. But proving your will is many years off yet, we'll hope.

Mr. George Booth [*pathetic and bewildered*]. I don't understand. No, I don't understand . . . because your father . . . ! But I must understand, Edward.

Edward. I shouldn't try to, if I were you. Pull yourself together, Mr. Booth. After all, this isn't a vital matter to you. It's not even as if you had a family to consider . . . like some of the others.

Mr. George Booth [*vaguely*]. What others?

Edward. Don't imagine your money has been specially selected for pilfering.

Mr. George Booth [*with solemn incredulity*]. One has read of this sort of thing. But I thought people always got found out.

Edward [*brutally humorous*]. Well . . . you've found us out.

Mr. George Booth [*rising to the full appreciation of his wrongs*]. Oh . . . I've been foully cheated!

Edward [*patiently*]. Yes . . . I've told you so.

Mr. George Booth [*his voice breaks, he appeals pitifully*]. But by you, Edward . . . say it's by you.

Edward [*unable to resist his quiet revenge*]. I've not the ability or the personality for such work, Mr. Booth . . . nothing but the remains of a few principles, which forbid me even to lie to you.

[*The old gentleman draws a long breath and then speaks with great awe, blending into grief.*

Mr. George Booth. I think your father is in Hell. I loved him, Edward . . . I loved him. How he could have had the heart! We were friends for fifty years. And all he cared for was to cheat me.

Edward [*venturing the comfort of an explanation*]. No . . . he didn't value money quite as you do.

Mr. George Booth [*with sudden shrill logic*]. But he took it. What d'you mean by that?

[EDWARD *leans back in his chair and changes the tenor of their talk.*

Edward. Well, you are master of the situation now. What are you going to do?

Mr. George Booth. To get the money back?

Edward. No, that's gone.

Mr. George Booth. Then give me what's left and——

Edward. Are you going to prosecute?

Mr. George Booth [*shifting uneasily in his chair*]. Oh, dear . . . is that necessary? Can't somebody else do that? I thought the law . . . ! What'll happen if I don't?

Edward. What do you suppose I'm doing here now?

Mr. George Booth [*as if he were being asked a riddle*]. I don't know.

Edward [*earnestly*]. When my father died, I began to try and put things straight. Then I made up my accounts . . . they can see who has lost and who hasn't and do as they please about it. And now I've set myself to a duller sort of work. I throw penny after penny hardly earned into the half-filled pit of our deficit. I've been doing that . . . for what it's worth . . . till this should happen. If you choose to let things alone . . . and hold your tongue . . . I can go on with the job till the next threat comes . . . and I'll beg that off too if I can. I've thought this my duty . . . and it's my duty to ask you to let me go on. [*He searches* MR. BOOTH'*s face and finds there only disbelief and fear. He bursts out.*] Oh you might at least believe me. It can't hurt you to believe me.

Mr. George Booth. You must admit, Edward, it isn't easy to believe anything in this office . . . just for the moment.

Edward [*bowing to the extreme reasonableness of this*]. I suppose not. I can prove it to you. I'll take you through the books . . . you won't understand them . . . but I could prove it.

Mr. George Booth. I think I'd rather not. Ought I to hold any further friendly communication with you now at all?

[*And at this he takes his hat.*

Edward [*with a little explosion of contemptuous anger*]. Certainly not. Prosecute . . . prosecute!

Mr. George Booth [*with dignity*]. Don't lose your temper. It's my place to be angry with you.

Edward. I shall be grateful if you'll prosecute.

Mr. George Booth. It's all very puzzling. I suppose I must prosecute. I believe you're just trying to practise on my goodness of heart. Certainly I ought to prosecute. Oughtn't I? I suppose I must consult another solicitor.

Edward [*his chin in the air*]. Why not write to *The Times* about it?

Mr. George Booth [*shocked and grieved at his attitude*]. Edward, how can you be so cool and heartless?

Edward [*changing his tone*]. D'you think I shan't be glad to sleep at night?

Mr. George Booth. You may be put in prison.

Edward. I am in prison . . . a less pleasant one than Wormwood Scrubs. But we're all prisoners, Mr. Booth.

Mr. George Booth [*wagging his head*]. Yes. This is what comes of your free-thinking and philosophy. Why aren't you on your knees?

Edward. To you?

[*This was not what* MR. BOOTH *meant, but he assumes a vicarious dignity of that sort.*

Mr. George Booth. And why should you expect me to shrink from vindicating the law?

Edward [*shortly*]. I don't. I've explained you'll be doing me a kindness. When I'm wanted you'll find me here at my desk. [*Then as an afterthought.*] If you take long to decide . . . don't alter your behaviour to my family in the meantime. They know the main points of the business, and . . .

Mr. George Booth [*knocked right off his balance*]. Do they? Good God! And I'm going there to dinner the day after to-morrow. It's Christmas Eve. The hypocrites!

Edward [*unmoved*]. I shall be there . . . that will have given you two days. Will you tell me then?

Mr. George Booth [*protesting violently*]. But I can't go . . . I can't have dinner with them. I must be ill.

Edward [*with a half-smile*]. I remember I went to dine at Chislehurst to tell my father of my decision.

Mr. George Booth [*testily*]. What decision?

Edward. To remain in the firm when I first learned what was happening.

Mr. George Booth [*interested*]. Was I there?

Edward. I daresay.

[MR. BOOTH *stands, hat, stick, gloves in hand, shaken by this experience, helpless, at his wits' end. He falls into a sort of fretful reverie, speaking half to himself, but yet as if he hoped that* EDWARD, *who is wrapt in his own thoughts, would have the decency to answer, or at least listen to what he is saying.*

Mr. George Booth. Yes, how often I dined with him! Oh, it was monstrous! [*His eyes fall on the clock.*] It's nearly lunch time now. D'you know I can still hardly believe it all. I wish I hadn't found it out. If he hadn't died, I should never have found it out. I hate to have to be vindictive . . . it's not my nature. I'm sure I'm more grieved than angry. But it isn't as if it were a small sum. And I don't see that one is called upon to forgive crimes . . . or why does the law exist? This will go near to killing me. I'm too old to have such troubles. It isn't right. And if I have to prosecute. . . .

Edward [*at last throwing in a word*]. Well . . . you need not.

Mr. George Booth [*thankful for the provocation*]. Don't you attempt to influence me, sir. [*He turns to go.*

Edward. And what's more . . . with the money you have left . . .

[EDWARD *follows him politely.* MR. BOOTH *flings the door open.*

Mr. George Booth. You'll make out a cheque for that at once, sir, and send it me.

Edward. You might . . .

Mr. George Booth [*clapping his hat on, stamping his stick*]. I shall do the right thing, sir . . . never fear.

[*So he marches off in fine style, he thinks, having had the last word and all. But* EDWARD*, closing the door after him, mutters . . .*

Edward. Save your soul . . . I'm afraid I was going to say.

ACT V

Naturally it is the dining-room which bears the brunt of what an English household knows as Christmas decorations. They consist chiefly of the branches of holly, stuck cock-eyed behind the top edges of the pictures. The one picture conspicuously not decorated is that which hangs over the fireplace, a portrait of MR. VOYSEY, *with its new gilt frame and its brass plate marking it also as a presentation. Otherwise the only difference between the dining-room's appearance at half-past nine on Christmas Eve and on any other evening in the year is that little piles of queer-shaped envelopes seem to be lying about, and quite a lot of tissue paper and string is to be seen peeping from odd corners. The electric light has been reduced to one bulb, but when the maid opens the door showing in* MR. GEORGE BOOTH *she switches on the rest.*

Mr. George Booth. No, no . . . in here will do. Just tell Mr. Edward.

Phoebe. Very well, sir.

[*She leaves him to fidget towards the fireplace and back, not removing his comforter or his coat, scarcely turning down the collar, screwing his cap in his hands. In a very short time* EDWARD *comes in, shutting the door and taking stock of the visitor before he speaks.*

Edward. Well?

Mr. George Booth [*feebly*]. I hope my excuse for not coming to dinner was acceptable. I did have . . . I have a very bad headache.

Edward. I daresay they believed it.

Mr. George Booth. I have come at once to tell you my decision.

Edward. What is it?

Mr. George Booth. I couldn't think the matter out alone. I went this afternoon to talk it over with the Vicar. After your father, he's my oldest friend now. [*At this* EDWARD'*s eyebrows contract and then rise.*] What a terrible shock to him!

Edward. Oh, three of his four thousand pounds are quite safe.

Mr. George Booth. That you and your father . . . you, whom he baptized . . . should have robbed him! I never saw a man so utterly prostrate with grief. That it should have been your father! And his poor wife . . . though she never got on with your father.

Edward [*with cheerful irony*]. Oh, Mrs. Colpus knows too, does she?

Mr. George Booth. Of course he told Mrs. Colpus. This is an unfortunate time for the storm to break on him. What with Christmas Day and Sunday following so close they're as busy as can be. He has resolved that during this season of peace and good-will he must put the matter from him if he can. But once Christmas is over . . . !

[*He envisages the old Vicar giving* EDWARD *a hell of a time then.*

Edward [*coolly*]. So you mean to prosecute. If you don't, you've inflicted on the Colpuses a lot of unnecessary pain and a certain amount of loss by telling them.

Mr. George Booth [*naïvely*]. I never thought of that. No, Edward, I have decided not to prosecute.

[EDWARD *hides his face for a moment.*

Edward. And I've been hoping to escape! Well, it can't be helped . . . [EDWARD *sets his teeth.*

Mr. George Booth [*with touching solemnity*]. I think I could not bear to see the family I have loved brought to such disgrace. And I want to ask your pardon, Edward, for some of the hard thoughts I have had of you. I consider this effort of yours a very striking one. You devote all the firm's earnings, I gather, to restoring the misappropriated capital. Very proper.

Edward. Mr. Booth . . . as I told you, you could help me . . . if you would. Your affairs, you see, are about the heaviest burden I carry.

Mr. George Booth. Why is that?

Edward. My father naturally made freest with the funds of the people who trusted him most.

Mr. George Booth. Naturally . . . you call it. Most unnatural, I think.

Edward [*finely*]. That also is true. And if you really want to help me, you could cut your losses . . . take interest only on the investments which do still exist. . . .

Mr. George Booth. No . . . forgive me . . . I have my own plan.

Edward. By prosecuting you'd be no better off . . .

Mr. George Booth. Quite so. The very first thing the Vicar said. He has an excellent head for business. Of course his interests are small beside mine. But we stand together . . .

[EDWARD *scents mischief and he looks straight at* MR. BOOTH . . . *very straight indeed.*

Edward. What is your plan?

Mr. George Booth. Its moral basis . . . I quote the Vicar . . . is this. You admit, I take it, that there were degrees of moral turpitude in your father's conduct . . . that his treachery was blacker by far in some cases than in others.

Edward. I think I won't make that admission for the moment.

Mr. Booth. What . . . to cheat and betray a life-long friend . . . and . . . and a man of God like the Vicar . . . is that no worse than a little ordinary trickiness? Now where are my notes? Our conditions are . . . one: we refrain from definitely undertaking not to prosecute . . . two: such securities as you have intact are to be returned to us at once . . .

Edward. Oh, certainly.

Mr. George Booth. Three: the interest upon those others that have been made away with is to be paid.

Edward. As it has been so far.

Mr. George Booth. We admit that. Four: the repayment of our lost capital is to be a first charge upon the . . . surplus earnings of the firm. There you are. And the Vicar and I both consider it very fair dealing.

Edward. Do you! [*He goes off into peals of laughter.*

Mr. George Booth. Edward . . . don't laugh!

Edward. But it's very, very funny!

Mr. George Booth. Stop laughing, Edward.

Edward. You refrain from undertaking not to prosecute . . . that's the neatest touch. That would keep me under your thumb, wouldn't it? [*Then with a sudden savage snarl.*] Oh, you Christian gentlemen!

Mr. George Booth. Don't be abusive, sir.

Edward. I'm giving my soul and body to restoring you and the rest of you to your precious money-bags. And you'll wring me dry . . . won't you? Won't you?

Mr. George Booth. Don't be rhetorical. The money was ours . . . we want it back. That's reasonable.

Edward [*at the height of irony*]. Oh . . . most!

Mr. George Booth. Any slight amendments to the plan . . . I'm willing to discuss them.

Edward [*as to a dog*]. Go to the devil.

Mr. George Booth. And don't be rude.

Edward. I'm sorry. [*There is a knock at the door.*] Come in.

[HONOR *intrudes an apologetic head.*

Honor. Am I interrupting business?

Edward [*mirthlessly joking*]. No. Business is over . . . quite over. Come in, Honor.

[HONOR *puts on the table a market basket bulging with little paper parcels, and, oblivious of* MR. BOOTH'*s distracted face, tries to fix his attention.*

Honor. I thought, dear Mr. Booth, perhaps you wouldn't mind carrying round this basket of things yourself. It's so very damp underfoot that I don't want to send one of the maids out to-night if I can possibly avoid it . . . and if one doesn't get Christmas presents the very first thing on Christmas morning quite half the pleasure in them is lost, don't you think?

Mr. George Booth. Yes . . . yes.

Honor [*fishing out the parcels one by one*]. This s a bell for Mrs. Williams . . . something she said she wanted so that you can ring for her, which saves the maids; cap and apron for Mary; cap and apron for Ellen; shawl for Davis when she goes out to the larder . . . all useful presents. And that's something for you . . . but you're not to look at it till the morning.

[*Having shaken each of them at the old gentleman, she proceeds to re-pack them. He is now trembling with anxiety to escape before any more of the family find him there.*

Mr. George Booth. Thank you . . . thank you. I hope my lot has arrived. I left instructions . . .

Honor. Quite safely . . . and I have hidden them. Presents are put on the breakfast-table to-morrow.

Edward [*with an inconsequence that still further alarms* MR. BOOTH]. When we were children our Christmas breakfast was mostly made off chocolates.

[*Before the basket is packed,* MRS. VOYSEY *sails slowly into the room, as smiling and as deaf as ever.* MR. BOOTH *does his best not to scowl at her.*

Mrs. Voysey. Are you feeling better, George Booth?

Mr. George Booth. No. [*Then he elevates his voice with a show of politeness.*] No, thank you; . . . I can't say I am.

Mrs. Voysey. You don't look better.

Mr. George Booth. I still have my headache. [*With a distracted shout.*] Headache!

Mrs. Voysey. Bilious, perhaps. I quite understand you didn't care to dine. But why not have taken your coat off? How foolish in this warm room!

Mr. George Booth. Thank you. I'm . . . just going.

[*He seizes the market basket. At that moment* MRS. HUGH *appears.*

Beatrice. Your shawl, Mother.

[*And she clasps it round* MRS. VOYSEY'*s shoulders.*

Mrs. Voysey. Thank you, Beatrice. I thought I had it on. [*Then to* MR. BOOTH, *who is now entangled in his comforter.*] A merry Christmas to you.

Beatrice. Good evening, Mr. Booth.

Mr. George Booth. I beg your pardon. Good evening, Mrs. Hugh.

Honor [*with sudden inspiration, to the company in general*]. Why shouldn't I write in here . . . now the table's cleared?

Mr. George Booth [*sternly, now he is safe by the door*]. Will you see me out, Edward?

Edward. Yes.

[*He follows the old man and his basket, leaving the others to distribute themselves about the room. It is a custom of the female members of the* VOYSEY *family, about Christmas time, to return to the dining-room, when the table has been cleared, and occupy themselves in various ways which involve space and untidiness.* BEATRICE *has a little work-basket containing a buttonless glove and such things, which she is rectifying.* HONOR'*s writing is done with the aid of an enormous blotting book, which bulges with apparently a year's correspondence. She sheds its contents upon the end of the dining-table and spreads them abroad.* MRS. VOYSEY *settles to the table near to the fire, opens the* Nineteenth Century *and is instantly absorbed in it.*

Beatrice. If there's anywhere else left in this house where one can write or sew or sit, I'd be glad to know of it. Christmas Tree in the back drawing-room and all the furniture in the front! Presents piled up under dusters in the library! My heap is very soft and bulgy. Honor . . . if you've given me an eiderdown quilt I'll never forgive you.

Honor. Oh, I haven't . . . I shouldn't think of it.

Beatrice. And to-morrow this room will look like a six P.M. bargain counter.

Honor. But . . . Beatrice . . . it's Christmas.

Beatrice. Noel . . . Noel! Where's Emily!

Honor. Well . . . I'm afraid she's talking to Booth.

Beatrice. If you mean that Booth is listening to her, I don't believe it. She has taken my fine scissors.

Honor. And I think she's telling him about you.

Beatrice. What . . . in particular . . . about me?

Honor. About you and Hugh.

Beatrice. Now whose fault is this? We agreed that nothing more was to be said till after Christmas.

Honor. But Edward knows . . . and Mother knows . . .

Beatrice. I warned Mother a year ago.

Honor. And Emily told me. And everyone seems to know except Booth. And it would be fearful if he found out. So I said: Tell him one night when he's in bed and very tired. But Emily didn't seem to think that would . . .

[*At this moment* EMILY *comes in, looking rather trodden upon.* HONOR *concludes in the most audible of whispers . . .*

Honor. Don't say anything . . . it's my fault.

Beatrice [*fixing her with a severe forefinger*]. Emily . . . have you taken my fine scissors?

Emily [*timidly*]. No, Beatrice.

Honor [*who is diving into the recesses of the blotting book*]. Oh, here they are! I must have taken them. I do apologise!

Emily [*more timidly still*]. I'm afraid Booth's rather cross. He's gone to look for Hugh.

Beatrice [*with a shake of her head*]. Honor . . . I've a good mind to make you do this sewing for me.

[*In comes the* MAJOR, *strepitant. He takes, so to speak, just enough time to train himself on* BEATRICE *and then fires.*

Major Booth Voysey. Beatrice, what on earth is this Emily has been telling me?

Beatrice [*with elaborate calm*]. Emily, what have you been telling Booth?

Major Booth Voysey. Please . . . please do not prevaricate. Where is Hugh?

Mrs. Voysey [*looking over her spectacles*]. What did you say, Booth?

Major Booth Voysey. I want Hugh, Mother.

Mrs. Voysey. I thought you were playing billiards together.

[EDWARD *strolls back from despatching* MR. BOOTH, *his face thoughtful.*

Major Booth Voysey [*insistently*]. Edward, where is Hugh?

Edward [*with complete indifference*]. I don't know.

Major Booth Voysey [*in trumpet tones*]. Honor, will you oblige me by finding Hugh and saying I wish to speak to him here immediately.

[HONOR, *who has leapt at the sound of her name, flies from the room without a word.*

Beatrice. I know quite well what you want to talk about, Booth. Discuss the matter by all means if it amuses you . . . but don't shout.

Major Booth Voysey. I use the voice Nature has gifted me with, Beatrice.

Beatrice [*as she searches for a glove button*]. Nature did let herself go over your lungs.

Major Booth Voysey [*glaring round with indignation*]. This is a family matter . . . otherwise I should not feel it my duty to interfere . . . as I do. Any member of the family has a right to express an opinion. I want Mother's. Mother, what do you think?

Mrs. Voysey [*amicably*]. What about?

Major Booth Voysey. Hugh and Beatrice separating.

Mrs. Voysey. They haven't separated.

Major Booth Voysey. But they mean to.

Mrs. Voysey. Fiddle-de-dee!

Major Booth Voysey. I quite agree with you.

Beatrice [*with a charming smile*]. Such reasoning would convert a stone.

Major Booth Voysey. Why have I not been told?

Beatrice. You have just been told.

Major Booth Voysey [*thunderously*]. Before.

Beatrice. The truth is, dear Booth, we're all so afraid of you.

Major Booth Voysey [*a little mollified*]. Ha . . . I should be glad to think that.

Beatrice [*sweetly*]. Don't you?

Major Booth Voysey [*intensely serious*]. Beatrice, your callousness shocks me. That you can dream of deserting Hugh . . . a man who, of all others, requires constant care and attention.

Beatrice. May I remark that the separation is as much Hugh's wish as mine?

Major Booth Voysey. I don't believe that.

Beatrice [*her eyebrows up*]. Really!

Major Booth Voysey. I don't imply that you're lying. But you must know that it's Hugh's nature to wish to do anything that he thinks anybody wishes him to do. All my life I've had to stand up for him . . . and, by Jove, I'll continue to do so.

Edward [*from the depths of his arm-chair*]. Booth . . . if you could manage to let this alone . . .

[*The door is flung almost off its hinges by* HUGH, *who then stands stamping and pale green with rage*.

Hugh. Look here, Booth . . . I will not have you interfering with my private affairs. Is one never to be free from your bullying?

Major Booth Voysey. You ought to be grateful.

Hugh. Well, I'm not.

Major Booth Voysey. This is a family affair.

Hugh. It is not!

Major Booth Voysey [*at the top of his voice*]. If all you can do is to contradict me . . . you'd better listen to what I've got to say . . . quietly.

[HUGH, *quite shouted down, flings himself petulantly into a chair. A hushed pause*.

Emily [*in a still small voice*]. Would you like me to go, Booth?

Major Booth Voysey [*severely*]. No, Emily. Unless anything has been going on which cannot be discussed before you. [*More severely still.*] And I trust that is not so.

Beatrice. Nothing at all appropriate to that tone of voice has been . . . going on. We swear it.

Major Booth Voysey. Why do you wish to separate?

Hugh. What's the use of telling you? You won't understand.

Beatrice [*who sews on undisturbed*]. We don't get on well together.

Major Booth Voysey [*amazedly*]. Is that all?

Hugh [*snapping at him*]. Yes, that's all. Can you find a better reason?

Major Booth Voysey [*with brotherly contempt*]. I've given up expecting common sense from you. But Beatrice . . . !

[*His tone implores her to be reasonable.*

Beatrice. Common sense is dry diet for the soul, you know.

Major Booth Voysey [*protesting*]. My dear girl . . . that sounds like a quotation from your latest book.

Beatrice. It isn't. I do think you might read that book . . . for the honour of the Family.

Major Booth Voysey [*successfully side-tracked*]. I bought it at once, Beatrice, and . . .

Beatrice. That's the principal thing, of course.

Major Booth Voysey [*. . . and discovering it*]. But do let us keep to the subject.

Beatrice [*with flattering sincerity*]. Certainly, Booth. And there is hardly any subject that I wouldn't ask your advice about. But upon this . . . please let me know better. Hugh and I will be happier apart.

Major Booth Voysey [*obstinately*]. Why?

Beatrice [*with resolute patience, having vented a little sigh*]. Hugh finds that my opinions distress him. And I have at last lost patience with Hugh.

Mrs. Voysey [*who has been trying to follow this through her spectacles*]. What does Beatrice say?

Major Booth Voysey [*translating into a loud sing-song*]. That she wishes to leave her husband because she has lost patience.

Mrs. Voysey [*with considerable acrimony*]. Then you must be a very ill-tempered woman. Hugh has a sweet nature.

Hugh [*shouting self-consciously*]. Nonsense, Mother.

Beatrice [*shouting good humouredly*]. I quite agree with you,

Mother. [*She continues to her husband in an even, just tone.*] You have a sweet nature, Hugh, and it is most difficult to get angry with you. I have been seven years working up to it. But now that I am angry I shall never get pleased again.

[*The* MAJOR *returns to his subject refreshed by a moment's response.*

Major Booth Voysey. How has he failed in his duty? Tell us. I'm not bigoted in his favour. I know your faults, Hugh.

[*He wags his head at* HUGH, *who writhes with irritation.*

Hugh. Why can't you leave them alone . . . leave us alone?

Beatrice. I'd state my case against Hugh if I thought he'd retaliate.

Hugh [*desperately rounding on his brother*]. If I tell you, you won't understand. You understand nothing! Beatrice thinks I ought to prostitute my art to make money.

Major Booth Voysey [*glancing at his wife*]. Please don't use metaphors of that sort.

Beatrice [*reasonably*]. Yes, I think Hugh ought to earn more money.

Major Booth Voysey [*quite pleased to be getting along at last*]. Well, why doesn't he?

Hugh. I don't want money.

Major Booth Voysey. How can you not want money? As well say you don't want bread.

Beatrice [*as she breaks off her cotton*]. It's when one has known what it is to be a little short of both . . .

[*Now the* MAJOR *spreads himself and begins to be very wise; while* HUGH, *to whom this is more intolerable than all, can only clutch his hair.*

Major Booth Voysey. You know I never considered art a very good profession for you, Hugh. And you won't even stick to one department of it. It's a profession that gets people into very bad habits, I consider. Couldn't you take up something else? You could still do those wood-cuts in your spare time to amuse yourself.

Hugh [*commenting on this with two deliberate shouts of stimulated mirth*]. Ha! Ha!

Major Booth Voysey. Well, it wouldn't much matter if you didn't do them at all.

Hugh. True!

[MRS. VOYSEY *leaves her arm-chair for her favourite station at the dining-table.*

Mrs. Voysey. Booth is the only one of you that I can hear at all distinctly. But if you two foolish young people think you want to separate . . . try it. You'll soon come back to each other and be glad to. People can't fight against nature for long. And marriage is a natural state . . . once you're married.

Major Booth Voysey [*with intense approval*]. Quite right, Mother.

Mrs. Voysey. I know.

[*She resumes the* Nineteenth Century. *And the* MAJOR, *to the despair of everybody, makes yet another start; trying oratory this time.*

Major Booth Voysey. My own opinion is, Beatrice and Hugh, that you don't realize the meaning of the word marriage. I don't call myself a religious man . . . but, dash it all, you were married in Church. And you then entered upon an awful compact . . . ! Surely, as a woman, Beatrice, the religious point of it ought to appeal to you. Good Lord . . . suppose everybody were to carry on like this! And have you considered that . . . whether you are right or whether you are wrong . . . if you desert Hugh you cut yourself off from the Family.

Beatrice [*with the sweetest of smiles*]. That will distress me terribly.

Major Booth Voysey [*not doubting her for a moment*]. Of course.

[HUGH *flings up his head, and finds relief at last in many words.*

Hugh. I wish to God I'd ever been able to cut myself off from the family! Look at Trenchard!

Major Booth Voysey [*gobbling a little at this unexpected attack*]. I do not forgive Trenchard for his quarrel with the Pater.

Hugh. He quarrelled because that was his best way of escape.

Major Booth Voysey. Escape from what?

Hugh. From tyranny . . . from hypocrisy . . . from boredom! . . . from his Happy English Home.

Beatrice [*kindly*]. Now, my dear . . . it's no use . . .

Major Booth Voysey [*attempting sarcasm*]. Speak so that Mother can hear you!

[*But* HUGH *isn't to be stopped now.*

Hugh. Why are we all dull, cubbish, uneducated . . . hopelessly middle-class!

Major Booth Voysey [*taking this as very personal*]. Cubbish!

Beatrice. Middle-class! Hugh . . . do think what you're saying.

Hugh. Upper middle-class, then. Yes . . . and snobbish too! What happens to you when you're born into that estate? What happened to us, anyhow? We were fed . . . we were clothed . . . we were taught and trained . . . and we were made comfortable. And that was the watchword given us: Comfort! You must work for a comfortable livelihood. You must practise a comfortable morality . . . and go to your parson for spiritual comfort . . . and he'll promise you everlasting comfort in heaven. Far better be born in a slum . . . with a drunkard for a father and a drab for a mother.

Major Booth Voysey. I never heard such lunacy.

Hugh. If you're nothing and nobody, you may find it in you to become something and somebody . . . and at least you learn what the world wants of you and what it doesn't. But do you think the world to-day couldn't do without us? Strip yourself of your comfortable income . . . as Edward here told you to . . . and step out into the street and see.

Major Booth Voysey [*ponderously*]. I venture to think . . .

Hugh. Oh no, you don't. You don't do either . . . and you'd better not try . . . for a little thinking might tell you that we and our like have ceased to exist at all. Yes, I mean it. Trenchard escaped in time. You went into the army . . . so how could you discover what a back number you are? But I found out soon enough . . . when I tried to express myself in art . . . that there was nothing to express . . . except a few habits, and tags of other people's thoughts and feelings. There is no Me . . . that's what's the matter. I'm an illusion. Not that it does matter to anyone but me. And look at Honor . . .

Major Booth Voysey. Honor leads a useful life . . . and a happy one. We all love her.

Hugh. Yes . . . and what have we always called her? Mother's right hand! I wonder they bothered to give her a name. By the time little Ethel came they were tired of training children. She was alive . . . in a silly, innocent sort of way. And then . . .

Beatrice. Poor little Ethel!

Major Booth Voysey. Poor Ethel!

[*They speak as one speaks of the dead.*

Hugh. And though your luck has been pretty poor, Edward, you've come up against realities at least . . . against something that could make a man of you. [*Then back to his humorous savagery.*] But if Booth thinks this world will stand still because he and his like want to be comfortable . . . that's where he's wrong.

Major Booth Voysey [*dignified and judicious*]. We will return, if you please, to the original subject of discussion. This question of a separation . . .

[HUGH *jumps up, past all patience.*

Hugh. Beatrice and I mean to separate. And nothing you may say will prevent it. The only trouble is money. She says we must have enough to live apart comfortably.

Beatrice [*in kindly irony*]. Yes . . . comfortably!

Hugh. And I daresay she's right . . . she generally is. So the question is: Can we raise it?

Major Booth Voysey. Well?

Hugh. Well . . . for the moment we can't.

Major Booth Voysey. Well, then?

Hugh. So we can't separate.

Major Booth Voysey. Then what in heaven's name have we been discussing it for?

Hugh. I haven't discussed it. I don't want to discuss it. Why can't you mind your own business? Now I'll go back to the billiard-room and my book.

[*He is gone before the* MAJOR *can recover his breath.*

Major Booth Voysey. I am not an impatient man . . . but really . . . !

Beatrice. Hugh's tragedy is that he is just clever enough to have found himself out . . . and no cleverer.

Major Booth Voysey [*magnanimous but stern*]. I will be frank. You have never made the best of Hugh.

Beatrice. No . . . at the worst it never came to that.

Major Booth Voysey. I am glad . . . for both your sakes . . . that you can't separate.

Beatrice. As soon as I am earning enough I shall walk off from him. [*The* MAJOR*'s manly spirit stirs.*

Major Booth Voysey. You will do nothing of the sort, Beatrice.

Beatrice [*unruffled*]. How will you stop me, Booth?

Major Booth Voysey. I shall tell Hugh he must command you to stay.

Beatrice [*with a little smile*]. I wonder would that make the difference. It was one of the illusions of my girlhood that I'd love a man who would master me.

Major Booth Voysey. Hugh must assert himself.

[*He begins to walk about, giving some indication of how it should be done.* BEATRICE*'s smile has vanished.*

Beatrice. Don't think I've enjoyed wearing the breeches . . . to use that horrid phrase . . . all through my married life. But someone had to plan and make decisions and do accounts. We weren't sparrows or lilies of the field . . . [*She becomes conscious of his strutting and smiles rather mischievously.*] Ah . . . if I'd married you, Booth!

[BOOTH'*s face grows beatific.*

Major Booth Voysey. Well, I own to thinking that I am a masterful man . . . that it's the duty of every man to be so. [*He adds forgivingly.*] Poor old Hugh!

Beatrice [*unable to resist temptation*]. If I'd tried to leave you, Booth, you'd have whipped me . . . wouldn't you?

Major Booth Voysey [*ecstatically complacent*]. Ha . . . well . . . !

Beatrice. Do say yes. Think how it will frighten Emily.

[*The* MAJOR *strokes his moustache and is most friendly.*

Major Booth Voysey. Hugh's been a worry to me all my life. And now . . . as head of the family . . . well, I suppose I'd better go and give the dear chap a quiet talking to. I see your point of view, Beatrice.

Beatrice. Why disturb him at his book?

[MAJOR BOOTH *leaves them, squaring his shoulders as becomes a lord of creation. The two sisters-in-law go on with their work silently for a moment; then* BEATRICE *adds . . .*

Beatrice. Do you find Booth difficult to manage, Emily

Emily [*putting down her knitting to consider the matter*]. No. It's best to let him talk himself out. When he has done that he'll often come to me for advice. But I like him to get his own way as much as possible . . . or think he's getting it. Otherwise he becomes so depressed.

Beatrice [*quietly amused*]. Edward shouldn't be listening to this. [*Then to him.*] Your presence profanes these Mysteries.

Edward. I won't tell . . . and I'm a bachelor.

Emily [*solemnly, as she takes up her knitting again*]. Do you really mean to leave Hugh?

Beatrice [*slightly impatient*]. Emily, I've said so.

[*They are joined by* ALICE MAITLAND, *who comes in gaily.*

Alice. What's Booth shouting about in the billiard-room?

Emily [*pained*]. Oh . . . on Christmas Eve, too!

Beatrice. Don't you take any interest in my matrimonial affairs?

[MRS. VOYSEY *shuts up the* Nineteenth Century *and removes her spectacles.*

Mrs. Voysey. That's a very interesting article. The Chinese Empire must be in a shocking state. Is it ten o'clock yet?

Edward. Past.

Mrs. Voysey [*as* EDWARD *is behind her*]. Can anyone see the clock?

Alice. It's past ten, Auntie.

Mrs. Voysey. Then I think I'll go to my room.

Emily. Shall I come and look after you, Mother?

Mrs. Voysey. If you'd find Honor for me, Emily.

[EMILY *goes in search of the harmless, necessary* HONOR, *and* MRS. VOYSEY *begins her nightly chant of departure.*

Mrs. Voysey. Good night, Alice. Good night, Edward.

Edward. Good night, Mother.

Mrs. Voysey [*with sudden severity*]. I'm not pleased with you, Beatrice.

Beatrice. I'm sorry, Mother.

[*But without waiting to be answered the old lady has sailed out of the room.* BEATRICE, EDWARD, *and* ALICE, *now left together, are attuned to each other enough to be able to talk with ease.*

Beatrice. But there's something in what Hugh says about this family. Had your great-grandfather a comfortable income, Edward?

Edward. I think so. It was his father made the money . . . in trade.

Beatrice. Which has been filtering away ever since. But fairly profitably, surely . . . to the rest of the world. You'd a great-aunt who was quite a botanist and an uncle who edited Catullus, hadn't you?

Edward. Yes. [*She is beginning to work out his theme.*

Beatrice. Well, that didn't pay them. Then there was the uncle killed in the Soudan. A captain's pension and no more wouldn't have been much for a widow and four children. . . .

Alice. Five.

Beatrice. Was it? Dear me . . . how prolific we were! And though I chaff Booth . . . I've seen him with his regiment giving weedy young slackers chest and biceps and making them 'decent chaps'. It takes a few generations, you know, to breed men who'll feel that it pays to do that for its own sake . . . and who'll be proud to do it. Oh, I can find a lot to say for the Upper Middle Class.

Edward. The family's petering out as its income does. D'you notice that? Six of us. But there are only Booth's two children.

Beatrice. It's more than the shrinking income that's doing it . . . more even than Hugh's 'worship of comfort'. Some fresh impulse to assert itself . . . I expect that is what a class needs to keep it socially alive. Well . . . your father developed one.

Edward. Not a very happy one!

Beatrice. It might have been . . . if he'd had the good sense to borrow the money for his financial operations just a little less casually.

Edward. D'you know what I think I've found out about him now?

Beatrice. Something interesting, I'm sure.

Edward. He did save my grandfather and the firm from a smash. That was true. A pretty capable piece of heroism! Then . . . six years after . . . he started on his own account . . . cheating again. I suppose he found himself in a corner . . .

Beatrice [*psychologically fascinated*]. Not a bit of it! He did it deliberately. One day when he was feeling extra fit he must have said to himself: Why not? . . . well, here goes! You never understood your father. I do . . . it's my business to.

Edward. He was an old scoundrel, Beatrice, and it's sophistry to pretend otherwise.

Beatrice. But he was a bit of a genius too. You can't be expected to appreciate that. It's tiresome work, I know . . . tidying up after these little Napoleons. He really did make money, didn't he, besides stealing it?

Edward. Lord, yes! And I daresay more than he stole. An honest two thousand a year from the firm. He had another thousand . . . and he spent about ten. He must have found the difference somewhere.

Beatrice. There you are, then. And we all loved him. You did, too, Alice.

Alice. I adored him.

Edward. He was a scoundrel and a thief.

Alice. I always knew he was a scoundrel of some sort. I thought he probably had another family somewhere.

Beatrice. Oh . . . what fun! Had he, Edward?

Edward. I fancy not.

Beatrice. No, he wasn't that sort . . . and it spoils the picture to overcrowd it.

Edward. Pleasant to be able to sit back and survey the business so coolly.

Beatrice. Somebody has to . . . some time or other . . . try to find a meaning in this and everything that happens . . . or we should run mad under what seems the wicked folly of it all. But it's only the flippant and callous little bit of me which writes my flippant and callous little books that sits back so coolly, Edward. And even that bit . . . when you're not looking . . . stands up to make you a pretty low bow. Aren't matters any better . . . aren't you nearly through?

Edward. Yes, they are better.

Beatrice. I'm glad. Have you ever been sorry that you didn't do the obviously wise thing . . . uncover the crime and let the law take its course?

Edward. Often.

Beatrice. Why did you take up the challenge single-handed . . . lawlessly . . . now that perhaps you can look back and tell?

[EDWARD *rather unwillingly, rather shyly, confesses . . .*

Edward. I think that I wanted . . . quite selfishly . . . a little vaingloriously, I daresay . . . to prove what my honesty was worth . . . what I was worth. And I was up against it. [*After which comes, perhaps, a more inward truth.*] And then, you know, I loved the Pater.

Beatrice [*touched*]. In spite of all?

Edward. Oh, yes. And I felt that if the worst of what he'd recklessly done was put right . . . it might be the better for him somehow.

[BEATRICE, *who has no such superstitious beliefs, lets this sink in on her nevertheless.*

Beatrice. Silence in the Court.

[*Another moment, and she collects her sewing, gets up and goes.* ALICE *has had all the while a keen eye on* EDWARD.

Alice. But something has happened since dinner.

Edward. Could you see that?

Alice. Tell me.

Edward [*as one throwing off a burden*]. The smash has come . . . and it's not my fault. Old George Booth . . .

Alice. I knew he'd been here.

Edward. He found out . . . I had to tell him. You can imagine him. I told him to take what was left of his money and prosecute. Well . . . he'll take what he can get and he won't prosecute. For he wants to bleed me, sovereign by sovereign as I earn sovereign by sovereign, till he has got the rest. And he has told the Vicar . . . who has told his wife . . . who has told the choir boys by this time I daresay. So it's a smash. And I thank God for it.

Alice [*quiet but intent*]. And what'll happen now?

Edward. One can't be sure. Gaol, possibly. I'll be struck off the Rolls anyhow. No more Lincoln's Inn for me.

Alice. And what then?

Edward. I don't know . . . and I don't care.

Alice [*still quieter*]. But I do.

Edward. Oh, I shan't shoot myself. I've never cared enough about my life to take the trouble to end it. But I'm damned tired, Alice. I think I could sleep for a week. I hope they won't undo what I've done, though. They won't find it very easy to . . . that's one thing. And I shan't help them Well, there it is. Nobody else knows yet. I like you to be the first to know. That's all. A Merry Christmas. Good night.

[*As he takes no more notice of her*, ALICE *gets up and goes to the door. There she pauses, and turns; and then she comes back to him.*

Alice. I'm supposed to be off to Egypt on the twenty-eighth for three months. No. I'm not ill. But, as I've never yet had anything to do except look after myself, the doctor thinks Egypt might be . . . most beneficial.

Edward. Well, you may find me still at large when you come back.

Alice. Oh, I'm not going . . . now.

Edward [*sharply*]. Why not? Good God . . . don't make it worse for me. To have you about while I'm being put through this . . . have you reading the reports the next morning . . . coming into Court perhaps to look pityingly at me! Go away . . . and stay away. That's all I ask.

Alice [*unperturbed*]. At the best, I suppose, you'll be left pretty hard up for the time being.

Edward. If His Majesty doesn't find me a new suit, they'll leave the clothes on my back.

Alice. What a good thing I've my eight hundred a year!

Edward [*with a gasp and a swallow*]. And what exactly do you mean by that?

Alice. Could they take my money as well . . . if we were married already? I've never been clear about married women's property. But you know. It's your business to. Could they?

Edward [*choking now*]. Are you . . . are you . . . ?

Alice. Because if they could it would be only sensible to wait a little. But if not . . . [EDWARD *hardens himself*.

Edward. Look here, now. Through these two damnable years there's only one thing I've been thanking God for . . . that you never did say Yes to me

Alice [*chaffing him tenderly*]. Four times and a half you proposed. The first time on a walk we took down in Devon . . . when you cut a stick of willow and showed me how to make a whistle from it. I have that still . . . and there are four and a half notches in it. The half was only a hint you dropped. But I could have caught you on it if I'd wanted to.

Edward. Well . . . you didn't.

Alice. No. But I kept the stick.

Edward. If you didn't care enough for me to marry me then . . .

Alice. Well . . . I didn't.

Edward. You don't suppose that now your eight hundred a year . . .

Alice. Are you still in love with me, Edward?

[EDWARD *sets his teeth against temptation*.

Edward. The answer must be No. [*She smiles*.

Alice. You're lying.

Edward. Can't we stop this? I've had about as much as I can stand.

Alice. Don't be so difficult. If I ask you to marry me, you'll refuse. And then what can I do? I can't coquet and be alluring. I don't know how.

Edward [*trying to joke his way out*]. Something to be thankful for!

Alice. But, my dear . . . I love you. I didn't before. I thought you were only a well-principled prig. I was wrong. You're a man . . . and I love you with all my heart and soul. Oh . . . please . . . please ask me to be your wife.

Edward [*for he resists happiness no more*]. If I've luck . . . if they let me go free . . .

Alice. No . . . now . . . now . . . while you're in trouble. I won't take you later . . . when the worst is over. I'm dashed if I do. I'll marry you to-morrow.

Edward [*objecting, but helplessly*]. That's Christmas Day.

Alice. And Boxing Day's next. Well, the old wretch of a Vicar can marry us on Saturday.

Edward [*giving his conscience one more hysterical chance*]. I haven't asked you yet.

Alice. I don't believe, you know, that they will put you in prison. It would be so extraordinarily senseless.

Edward. But now the scandal's out, we must go smash in any case.

Alice. You couldn't call them all together . . . get them round a table and explain? They won't all be like Mr. Booth and the Vicar. Couldn't we bargain with them to let us go on?

[*The 'we' and the 'us' come naturally.*

Edward. But . . . heavens above . . . I don't want to go on. You don't know what the life has been.

Alice. Yes, I do. I see when I look at you. But it was partly the fear, wasn't it? . . or the hope . . . that this would happen. Once it's all open and above-board . . . ! Besides . . . you've had no other life. Now there's to be ours. That'll make a difference.

Edward [*considering the matter*]. They just might agree . . . to syndicate themselves . . . and to keep me slaving at it.

Alice. You could make them.

Edward. I! I believe my father could have . . . if that way out had taken his fancy.

Alice [*her pride in him surging up*]. My dear . . . don't you know yourself yet . . . as I now know you, thank God? You're ten times the man he ever was. What was he after all but a fraud?

Edward [*soberly*]. Well . . . I'll try.

Alice [*gentle and grave*]. I'm sure you should. [*For a moment they sit quietly there, thinking of the future, uncertain of everything but one thing.*] The others must have gone up to bed. This is no way for an Upper Middle Class Lady to behave . . . sitting up hob-nobbing with you. Good night.

Edward. Good night. God bless you.

[*She is going again, but again she stops, and says half-humorously.*

Alice. But even now you haven't asked me.

Edward [*simply*]. Will you marry me?

Alice [*as simply in return*]. Yes. Yes, please. [*Then, moving nearer to him.*] Kiss me.

Edward [*half-humorously too*]. I was going to.

[*And he does, with a passion that has reverence in it too.*

Alice. Oh, my dear. My very dear. Till to-morrow then.

Edward. Till to-morrow.

[*She leaves him sitting there; a man conscious of new strength.*

JUSTICE

JOHN GALSWORTHY
(1867–1933)

Born Kingston Hill, Surrey. Educated Harrow and New College, Oxford. Called to the Bar, 1890, but never practised law. His first book, a collection of short stories entitled *From the Four Winds*, was published under the pseudonym John Sinjohn, 1897. His first novel to appear under his own name was *The Island Pharisees* (1904). Published *The Man of Property*, the first of his stories of the Forsyte family, 1906. The whole series was collected into three trilogies: *The Forsyte Saga* (1922), *A Modern Comedy* (1929), *End of the Chapter* (published posthumously, 1935). Awarded the Order of Merit, 1929, and the Nobel Prize for Literature, 1932.

His plays included *The Silver Box* (1906); *Strife* (1909); *Justice* (1910); *The Fugitive* (1913); *The Mob* (1914); *The Skin Game* (1920); *Loyalties* (1922); *Old English* (1924); *Escape* (1926).

JUSTICE

A TRAGEDY IN FOUR ACTS

by

John Galsworthy

JUSTICE

First produced at the Duke of York's Theatre, London, 21 *February* 1910, *with the following cast:*

James How	Mr. Sydney Valentine
Walter How	Mr. Charles Maude
Cokeson	Mr. Edmund Gwenn
Falder	Mr. Dennis Eadie
The Office-Boy	Mr. George Hersee
The Detective	Mr. Leslie Carter
The Judge	Mr. Dion Boucicault
The Old Advocate	Mr. Oscar Adye
The Young Advocate	Mr. Charles Bryant
The Prison Governor	Mr. Grendon Bentley
The Prison Chaplain	Mr. Hubert Harben
The Prison Doctor	Mr. Lewis Casson
Wooder	Mr. Frederick Lloyd
Moaney	Mr. Robert Pateman
Clipton	Mr. O. P. Heggie
O'Cleary	Mr. Whitford Kane
Ruth Honeywill	Miss Edyth Olive

Barristers, Solicitors, Spectators, Ushers, Reporters, Jurymen, Warders, Prisoners.

The play produced by Mr. Granville-Barker.

JUSTICE

ACT I

The scene is the managing clerk's room, at the offices of JAMES AND WALTER HOW, *on a July morning. The room is old-fashioned, furnished with well-worn mahogany and leather, and lined with tin boxes and estate plans. It has three doors. Two of them are close together in the centre of a wall. One of these two doors leads to the outer office, which is only divided from the managing clerk's room by a partition of wood and clear glass; and when the door into this outer office is opened there can be seen the wide outer door leading out on to the stone stairway of the building. The other of these two centre doors leads to the junior clerk's room. The third door is that leading to the partners' room.*

The managing clerk, COKESON, *is sitting at his table adding up figures in a pass-book, and murmuring their numbers to himself. He is a man of sixty, wearing spectacles; rather short, with a bald head, and an honest, pug-dog face. He is dressed in a well-worn black frock-coat and pepper-and-salt trousers.*

Cokeson. And five's twelve, and three—fifteen, nineteen, twenty-three, thirty-two, forty-one—and carry four. [*He ticks the page, and goes on murmuring.*] Five, seven, twelve, seventeen, twenty-four and nine, thirty-three, thirteen and carry one.

[*He again makes a tick. The outer office door is opened, and* SWEEDLE, *the office-boy, appears, closing the door behind him. He is a pale youth of sixteen, with spiky hair.*

Cokeson [*with grumpy expectation*]. And carry one.

Sweedle. There's a party wants to see Falder, Mr. Cokeson.

Cokeson. Five, nine, sixteen, twenty-one, twenty-nine—and carry two. Send him to Morris's. What name?

Sweedle. Honeywill.

Cokeson. What's his business?

Sweedle. It's a woman.

Cokeson. A lady?

Sweedle. No, a person.

Cokeson. Ask her in. Take this pass-book to Mr. James.

[*He closes the pass-book.*

Sweedle [*reopening the door*]. Will you come in, please?

[RUTH HONEYWILL *comes in. She is a tall woman, twenty-six years old, unpretentiously dressed, with black hair and eyes, and an ivory-white, clear-cut face. She stands very still, having a natural dignity of pose and gesture.*

[SWEEDLE *goes out into the partners' room with the pass-book.*

Cokeson [*looking round at* RUTH]. The young man's out. [*Suspiciously.*] State your business, please.

Ruth [*who speaks in a matter-of-fact voice, and with a slight West-country accent*]. It's a personal matter, sir.

Cokeson. We don't allow private callers here. Will you leave a message?

Ruth. I'd rather see him, please.

[*She narrows her dark eyes and gives him a honeyed look.*

Cokeson [*expanding*]. It's all against the rules. Suppose I had *my* friends here to see me! It'd never do!

Ruth. No, sir.

Cokeson [*a little taken aback*]. Exactly! And here you are wanting to see a *junior* clerk!

Ruth. Yes, sir; I must see him.

Cokeson [*turning full round to her with a sort of outraged interest*]. But this is a lawyer's office. Go to his private address.

Ruth. He's not there.

Cokeson [*uneasy*]. Are you related to the party?

Ruth. No, sir.

Cokeson [*in real embarrassment*]. I don't know what to say. It's no affair of the office.

Ruth. But what am I to do?

Cokeson. Dear me! I can't tell you that.

[SWEEDLE *comes back. He crosses to the outer office and passes through into it, with a quizzical look at* COKESON, *carefully leaving the door an inch or two open.*

Cokeson [*fortified by this look*]. This won't do, you know, this won't do at all. Suppose one of the partners came in!

[*An incoherent knocking and chuckling is heard from the outer door of the outer office.*

Sweedle [*putting his head in*]. There's some children outside here.

Ruth. They're mine, please.

Sweedle. Shall I hold them in check?

Ruth. They're quite small, sir.

[*She takes a step towards* COKESON.]

Cokeson. You mustn't take up his time in office hours; we're a clerk short as it is.

Ruth. It's a matter of life and death.

Cokeson [*again outraged*]. Life and death!

Sweedle. Here *is* Falder.

[FALDER *has entered through the outer office. He is a pale, good-looking young man, with quick, rather scared eyes. He moves towards the door of the clerks' office, and stands there irresolute.*

Cokeson. Well, I'll give you a minute. It's not regular.

[*Taking up a bundle of papers, he goes out into the partners' room.*

Ruth [*in a low, hurried voice*]. He's on the drink again. Will, He tried to cut my throat last night. I came out with the children before he was awake. I went round to you——

Falder. I've changed my digs.

Ruth. Is it all ready for to-night?

Falder. I've got the tickets. Meet me 11.45 at the booking office. For God's sake don't forget we're man and wife! [*Looking at her with tragic intensity*.] Ruth!

Ruth. You're not afraid of going, are you?

Falder. Have you got your things, and the children's?

Ruth. Had to leave them, for fear of waking Honeywill, all but one bag. I can't go near home again.

Falder [*wincing*]. All that money gone for nothing. How much *must* you have?

Ruth. Six pounds—I could do with that, I think.

Falder. Don't give away where we're going. [*As if to himself*.] When I get out there I mean to forget it all.

Ruth. If you're sorry, say so. I'd sooner he killed me than take you against your will.

Falder [*with a queer smile*]. We've *got* to go. I don't care; I'll have *you*.

Ruth. You've just to say; it's not too late.

Falder. It *is* too late. Here's seven pounds. Booking office —11.45 to-night. If you weren't what you are to me, Ruth——!

Ruth. Kiss me!

[*They cling together passionately, then fly apart just as* COKESON *re-enters the room.* RUTH *turns and goes out through the outer office.* COKESON *advances deliberately to his chair and seats himself.*

Cokeson. This isn't right, Falder.

Falder. It shan't occur again, sir.

Cokeson. It's an improper use of these premises.

Falder. Yes, sir.

Cokeson. You quite understand—the party was in some distress; and, having children with her, I allowed my feelings——[*He opens a drawer and produces from it a tract.*]. Just take this! 'Purity in the Home'. It's a well-written thing.

Falder [*taking it, with a peculiar expression*]. Thank you, sir.

Cokeson. And look here, Falder, before Mr. Walter comes, have you finished up that cataloguing Davis had in hand before he left?

Falder. I shall have done with it to-morrow, sir—for good.

Cokeson. It's over a week since Davis went. Now it won't do, Falder. You're neglecting your work for private life. I shan't mention about the party having called, but——

Falder [*passing into his room*]. Thank you, sir.

[COKESON *stares at the door through which* FALDER *has gone out; then shakes his head, and is just settling down to write, when* WALTER HOW *comes in through the outer office He is a rather refined-looking man of thirty-five, with a pleasant, almost apologetic voice.*

Walter. Good morning, Cokeson.

Cokeson. Morning, Mr. Walter.

Walter. My father here?

Cokeson [*always with a certain patronage as to a young man who might be doing better*]. Mr. James has been here since eleven o'clock.

Walter. I've been in to see the pictures, at the Guildhall.

Cokeson [*looking at him as though this were exactly what was to be expected*]. Have you now—ye-es. This lease of Boulter's—am I to send it to counsel?

Walter. What does my father say?

Cokeson. Aven't bothered him.

Walter. Well, we can't be too careful.

Cokeson. It's such a little thing—hardly worth the fees. I thought you'd do it yourself.

Walter. Send it, please. I don't want the responsibility.

Cokeson [*with an indescribable air of compassion*]. Just as you like. This 'right-of-way' case—we've got 'em on the deeds.

Walter. I know; but the intention was obviously to exclude that bit of common ground.

Cokeson. We needn't worry about that. We're the *right* side of the law.

Walter. I don't like it.

Cokeson [*with an indulgent smile*]. We shan't want to set ourselves up against the law. Your father wouldn't waste his time doing that.

[*As he speaks* JAMES HOW *comes in from the partners' room. He is a shortish man, with white side-whiskers, plentiful grey hair, shrewd eyes, and gold pince-nez.*

James. Morning, Walter.

Walter. How are you, father?

Cokeson [*looking down his nose at the papers in his hand as though deprecating their size*]. I'll just take Boulter's lease in to young Falder to draft the instructions.

[*He goes into* FALDER'S *room.*

Walter. About that right-of-way case?

James. Oh, well, we must go forward there. I thought you told me yesterday the firm's balance was over four hundred.

Walter. So it is.

James [*holding out the pass-book to his son*]. Three—five—one, no recent cheques. Just get me out the cheque-book.

[WALTER *goes to a cupboard, unlocks a drawer, and produces a cheque-book.*

James. Tick the pounds in the counterfoils. Five, fifty-four, seven, five, twenty-eight, twenty, ninety, eleven, fifty-two, seventy-one. Tally?

Walter [*nodding*]. Can't understand. Made sure it was over four hundred.

James. Give me the cheque-book. [*He takes the cheque-book and cons the counterfoils.*] What's this ninety?

Walter. Who drew it?

James. You.

Walter [*taking the cheque-book*]. July 7th? That's the day I went down to look over the Trenton Estate—last Friday week; I came back on the Tuesday, you remember. But look here, father, it was *nine* I drew a cheque for. Five guineas to Smithers and my expenses. It just covered all but half a crown.

James [*gravely*]. Let's look at that ninety cheque. [*He sorts the cheque out from the bundle in the pocket of the pass-book.*] Seems all right. There's no nine here. This is bad. Who cashed that nine-pound cheque?

Walter [*puzzled and pained*]. Let's see! I was finishing Mrs. Reddy's will—only just had time; yes—I gave it to Cokeson.

James. Look at that *ty*: that yours?

Walter [*after consideration*]. My *y*'s curl back a little; this doesn't.

James [*as* COKESON *re-enters from* FALDER'*s room*]. We must ask him. Just come here and carry your mind back a bit, Cokeson. D'you remember cashing a cheque for Mr. Walter last Friday week—the day he went to Trenton.

Cokeson. Ye-es. Nine pounds.

James. Look at this. [*Handing him the cheque.*

Cokeson. No! Nine pounds. My lunch was just coming in; and of course I *like* it hot; I gave the cheque to Davis to run round to the bank. He brought it back, all notes—you remember, Mr. Walter, you wanted some silver to pay your cab. [*With a certain contemptuous compassion.*] Here, let me see. You've got the wrong cheque.

[*He takes the cheque-book and pass-book from* WALTER.

Walter. Afraid not.

Cokeson [*having seen for himself*]. It's funny.

James. You gave it to Davis, and Davis sailed for Australia on Monday. Looks black, Cokeson.

Cokeson [*puzzled and upset*]. Why this'd be a felony! No, no! there's some mistake.

James. I hope so.

Cokeson. There's never been anything of that sort in the office the twenty-nine years I've been here.

James [*looking at cheque and counterfoil*]. This is a very clever bit of work; a warning to you not to leave space after your figures, Walter.

Walter [*vexed*]. Yes, I know—I was in such a tearing hurry that afternoon.

Cokeson [*suddenly*]. This has upset me.

James. The counterfoil altered too—very deliberate piece of swindling. What was Davis's ship?

Walter. *City of Rangoon*.

James. We ought to wire and have him arrested at Naples; he can't be there yet.

Cokeson. His poor young wife. I liked the young man. Dear, oh dear! In this office!

Walter. Shall I go to the bank and ask the cashier?

James [*grimly*]. Bring him round here. And ring up Scotland Yard.

Walter. Really?

[*He goes out through the outer office.* JAMES *paces the room. He stops and looks at* COKESON, *who is disconsolately rubbing the knees of his trousers.*

James. Well, Cokeson! There's something in character, isn't there?

Cokeson [*looking at him over his spectacles*]. I don't quite take you, sir.

James. Your story would sound d——d thin to anyone who didn't know you.

Cokeson. Ye-es! [*He laughs. Then with sudden gravity*.] I'm sorry for that young man. I feel it as if it was my own son, Mr. James.

James. A nasty business!

Cokeson. It unsettles you. All goes on regular, and then a thing like this happens. Shan't relish my lunch to-day.

James. As bad as that, Cokeson?

Cokeson. It makes you think. [*Confidentially*.] He must have had temptation.

James. Not so fast. We haven't convicted him yet.

Cokeson. I'd sooner have lost a month's salary than had this happen. [*He broods*.

James. I hope that fellow will hurry up.

Cokeson [*keeping things pleasant for the cashier*]. It isn't fifty yards, Mr. James. He won't be a minute.

James. The idea of dishonesty about this office—it hits me hard, Cokeson.

[*He goes towards the door of the partners' room*.

Sweedle [*entering quietly, to* COKESON *in a low voice*]. She's popped up again, sir—something she forgot to say to Falder.

Cokeson [*roused from his abstraction*]. Eh? Impossible. Send her away!

James. What's that?

Cokeson. Nothing, Mr. James. A private matter. Here, I'll come myself. [*He goes into the outer office as* JAMES *passes into the partners' room*.] Now, you really mustn't—we can't have anybody just now.

Ruth. Not for a minute, sir?

Cokeson. Reely! Reely! I can't have it. If you want him, wait about; he'll be going out for his lunch directly.

Ruth. Yes, sir.

[WALTER, *entering with the* CASHIER, *passes* RUTH *as she leaves the outer office*.

Cokeson [*to the* CASHIER, *who resembles a sedentary dragoon*]. Good-morning. [*To* WALTER.] Your father's in there.

[WALTER *crosses and goes into the partners' room*.

Cokeson. It's a nahsty, unpleasant little matter, Mr. Cowley. I'm quite ashamed to have to trouble you.

Cowley. I remember the cheque quite well. [*As if it were a liver*.] Seemed in perfect order.

Cokeson. Sit down, won't you? I'm not a sensitive man, but a thing like this about the place—it's not nice. I like people to be open and jolly together.

Cowley. Quite so.

Cokeson [*button-holing him, and glancing towards the partners' room*]. Of course he's a young man. I've told him about it before now—leaving space after his figures, but he *will* do it.

Cowley. I should remember the person's face—quite a youth.

Cokeson. I don't think we shall be able to show him to you, as a matter of fact.

[JAMES *and* WALTER *have come back from the partners' room*.

James. Good morning, Mr. Cowley. You've seen my son and myself, you've seen Mr. Cokeson, and you've seen Sweedle, my office boy. It was none of us, I take it.

[*The* CASHIER *shakes his head with a smile*.

James. Be so good as to sit here. Cokeson, engage Mr. Cowley in conversation, will you?

[*He goes towards* FALDER'*s room*.

Cokeson. Just a word, Mr. James.

James. Well?

Cokeson. You don't want to upset the young man in there, do you? He's a nervous young feller.

James. This must be thoroughly cleared up, Cokeson, for the sake of Falder's name, to say nothing of yours.

Cokeson [*with some dignity*]. That'll look after itself, sir. He's been upset once this morning; I don't want him startled again.

James. It's a matter of form; but I can't stand upon niceness over a thing like this—too serious. Just talk to Mr. Cowley.

[*He opens the door of* FALDER'*s room*.

James. Bring in the papers in Boulter's lease, will you, Falder?

Cokeson [*bursting into voice*]. Do you keep dogs?

[*The* CASHIER, *with his eyes fixed on the door, does not answer*.

Cokeson. You haven't such a thing as a bulldog pup you could spare me, I suppose?

[*At the look on the* CASHIER'*s face his jaw drops, and he turns to see* FALDER *standing in the doorway, with his eyes fixed on* COWLEY, *like the eyes of a rabbit fastened on a snake*.

Falder [*advancing with the papers*]. Here they are, sir.
James [*taking them*]. Thank you.
Falder. Do you want me, sir?
James. No, thanks!

[FALDER *turns and goes back into his own room. As he shuts the door* JAMES *gives the* CASHIER *an interrogative look, and the* CASHIER *nods.*

James. Sure? This isn't as we suspected.
Cowley. Quite. He knew me. I suppose he can't slip out of that room?
Cokeson [*gloomily*]. There's only the window—a whole floor and a basement.

[*The door of* FALDER'*s room is quietly opened, and* FALDER, *with his hat in his hand, moves towards the door of the outer office.*

James [*quietly*]. Where are you going, Falder?
Falder. To have my lunch, sir.
James. Wait a few minutes, would you? I want to speak to you about this lease.
Falder. Yes, sir. [*He goes back into his room.*
Cowley. If I'm wanted, I can swear that's the young man who cashed the cheque. It was the last cheque I handled that morning before my lunch. These are the numbers of the notes he had. [*He puts a slip of paper on the table; then, brushing his hat round.*] Good morning!
James. Good morning, Mr. Cowley!
Cowley [*to* COKESON]. Good morning.
Cokeson [*with stupefaction*]. Good morning.

[*The* CASHIER *goes out through the outer office.* COKESON *sits down in his chair, as though it were the only place left in the morass of his feelings.*

Walter. What are you going to do?
James. Have him in. Give me the cheque and the counterfoil.
Cokeson. I don't understand. I thought young Davis——
James. We shall see.
Walter. One moment, father: have you thought it out?
James. Call him in!
Cokeson [*rising with difficulty and opening* FALDER'*s door; hoarsely*]. Step in here a minute. [FALDER *comes in.*
Falder [*impassively*]. Yes, sir?
James [*turning to him suddenly with the cheque held out*]. You know this cheque, Falder?
Falder. No, sir.
James. Look at it. You cashed it last Friday week.

Falder. Oh! yes, sir; that one—Davis gave it me.

James. I know. And you gave Davis the cash?

Falder. Yes, sir.

James. When Davis gave you the cheque was it exactly like this?

Falder. Yes, I think so, sir.

James. You know that Mr. Walter drew that cheque for *nine* pounds?

Falder. No, sir—ninety.

James. Nine, Falder.

Falder [*faintly*]. I don't understand, sir.

James. The suggestion, of course, is that the cheque was altered; whether by you or Davis is the question.

Falder. I—I——

Cokeson. Take your time, take your time.

Falder [*regaining his impassivity*]. Not by me, sir.

James. The cheque was handed to Cokeson by Mr. Walter at one o'clock; we know that because Mr. Cokeson's lunch had just arrived.

Cokeson. I couldn't leave it.

James. Exactly; he therefore gave the cheque to Davis. It was cashed by you at 1.15. We know that because the cashier recollects it for the last cheque he handled before *his* lunch.

Falder. Yes, sir. Davis gave it to me because some friends were giving him a farewell luncheon.

James [*puzzled*]. You accuse Davis, then?

Falder. I don't know, sir—it's very funny.

[WALTER, *who has come close to his father, says something to him in a low voice*.

James. Davis was not here again after that Saturday, was he?

Cokeson [*anxious to be of assistance to the young man, and seeing faint signs of their all being jolly once more*]. No, he sailed on the Monday.

James. Was he, Falder?

Falder [*very faintly*]. No, sir.

James. Very well, then, how do you account for the fact that this nought was added to the nine in the counterfoil on or after *Tuesday*?

Cokeson [*surprised*]. How's that?

[FALDER *gives a sort of lurch; he tries to pull himself together, but he has gone all to pieces*.

James [*very grimly*]. Out, I'm afraid, Cokeson. The cheque-book remained in Mr. Walter's pocket till he came back from Trenton on Tuesday morning. In the face of this, Falder, do you still deny that you altered both cheque and counterfoil?

Falder. No, sir—no, Mr. How. I did it, sir; I did it.

Cokeson [*succumbing to his feelings*]. Dear, dear! what a thing to do!

Falder. I wanted the money so badly, sir. I didn't know what I was doing.

Cokeson. However such a thing could have come into your head!

Falder [*grasping at the words*]. I can't think, sir, really! It was just a minute of madness.

James. A long minute, Falder. [*Tapping the counterfoil.*] Four days at least.

Falder. Sir, I swear I didn't know what I'd done till afterwards, and then I hadn't the pluck. Oh, sir, look over it! I'll pay the money back—I will, I promise.

James. Go into your room.

[FALDER, *with a swift imploring look, goes back into his room. There is silence.*

James. About as bad a case as there could be.

Cokeson. To break the law like that—in here!

Walter. What's to be done?

James. Nothing for it. Prosecute.

Walter. It's his first offence.

James [*shaking his head*]. I've grave doubts of that. Too neat a piece of swindling altogether.

Cokeson. I shouldn't be surprised if he was tempted.

James. Life's one long temptation, Cokeson.

Cokeson. Ye-es, but I'm speaking of the flesh and the devil, Mr. James. There was a woman come to see him this morning.

Walter. The woman we passed as we came in just now. Is it his wife?

Cokeson. No, no relation. [*Restraining what in jollier circumstances would have been a wink.*] A married person, though.

Walter. How do you know?

Cokeson. Brought her children. [*Scandalized.*] There they were outside this office.

James. A real bad egg.

Walter. I should like to give him a chance.

James. I can't forgive him for the sneaky way he went to work—counting on our suspecting young Davis if the matter came to light. It was the merest accident the cheque-book stayed in your pocket.

Walter. It *must* have been the temptation of a moment. He hadn't time.

James. A man doesn't succumb like that in a moment, if he's a clean mind and habits. He's rotten; got the eyes of a man who can't keep his hands off when there's money about.

Walter [*dryly*]. We hadn't noticed that before.

James [*brushing the remark aside*]. I've seen lots of those fellows in my time. No doing anything with them except to keep 'em out of harm's way. They've got a blind spot.

Walter. It's penal servitude.

Cokeson. They're *nahsty* places—prisons.

James [*hesitating*]. I don't see how it's possible to spare him. Out of the question to keep him in this office—honesty's the *sine qua non*.

Cokeson [*hypnotized*]. Of course it *is*.

James. Equally out of the question to send him out amongst people who've no knowledge of his character. One must think of society.

Walter. But to brand him like this?

James. If it had been a straightforward case I'd give him another chance. It's far from that. He has dissolute habits.

Cokeson. I didn't say that—extenuating circumstances.

James. Same thing. He's gone to work in the most cold-blooded way to defraud his employers, and cast the blame on an innocent man. If that's not a case for the law to take its course, I don't know what is.

Walter. For the sake of his future, though.

James [*sarcastically*]. According to you, no one would ever prosecute.

Walter [*nettled*]. I hate the idea of it.

Cokeson. We must have protection.

James. This is degenerating into talk.

[*He moves towards the partners' room.*

Walter. Put yourself in his place, father.

James. You ask too much of me.

Walter. We can't possibly tell the pressure there was on him.

James. You may depend on it, my boy, if a man is going to do this sort of thing he'll do it, pressure or no pressure; if he isn't nothing'll make him.

Walter. He'll never do it again.

Cokeson [*fatuously*]. S'pose I were to have a talk with him. We don't want to be hard on the young man.

James. That'll do, Cokeson. I've made up my mind.

[*He passes into the partners' room.*

Cokeson [*after a doubtful moment*]. We must excuse your father. I don't want to go against your father; if he thinks it right.

Walter. Confound it, Cokeson! why don't you back me up? You know you feel——

Cokeson [*on his dignity*]. I really can't say what I feel.

Walter. We shall regret it.

Cokeson. He must have known what he was doing.

Walter [*bitterly*]. 'The quality of mercy is not strained.'

Cokeson [*looking at him askance*]. Come, come, Mr. Walter. We must try and see it sensible.

Sweedle [*entering with a tray*]. Your lunch, sir.

Cokeson. Put it down!

[*While* SWEEDLE *is putting it down on* COKESON'*s table, the detective*, WISTER, *enters the outer office, and, finding no one there, comes to the inner doorway. He is a square, medium-sized man, clean-shaved, in a serviceable blue serge suit and strong boots.*

Wister [*to* WALTER]. From Scotland Yard, sir. Detective-Sergeant Wister.

Walter [*askance*]. Very well! I'll speak to my father.

[*He goes in to the partners' room.* JAMES *enters.*

James. Morning! [*In answer to an appealing gesture from* COKESON.] I'm sorry; I'd stop short of this if I felt I could. Open that door. [SWEEDLE, *wondering and scared, opens it.*] Come here, Mr. Falder.

[*As* FALDER *comes shrinking out, the* DETECTIVE, *in obedience to a sign from* JAMES, *slips his hand out and grasps his arm.*

Falder [*recoiling*]. Oh! no—oh! no!

Wister. Come, come, there's a good lad.

James. I charge him with felony.

Falder. Oh, sir! There's someone—I did it for her. Let me be till to-morrow.

[JAMES *motions with his head. At that sign of hardness,* FALDER *becomes rigid. Then, turning, he goes out quietly in the* DETECTIVE'*s grip.* JAMES *follows, stiff and erect.* SWEEDLE, *rushing to the door with open mouth, pursues them through the outer office into the corridor. When they have all disappeared* COKESON *spins completely round and makes a rush for the outer office.*

Cokeson [*hoarsely*]. Here! Here! What are we doing?

[*There is silence. He takes out his handkerchief and mops the sweat from his face. Going back blindly to his table, he sits down, and stares blankly at his lunch.*

THE CURTAIN FALLS

ACT II

A Court of Justice, on a foggy October afternoon—crowded with barristers, solicitors, reporters, ushers, and jurymen. Sitting in the large, solid dock is FALDER, *with a warder on either side of him, placed there for his safe custody, but seemingly indifferent to and unconscious of his presence.* FALDER *is sitting exactly opposite to the* JUDGE, *who, raised above the clamour of the court, also seems unconscious of and indifferent to everything.* HAROLD CLEAVER, *the counsel for the Crown, is a dried, yellowish man, of more than middle age, in a wig worn almost to the colour of his face.* HECTOR FROME, *the counsel for the defence, is a young, tall man, clean-shaved, in a very white wig. Among the spectators, having already given their evidence, are* JAMES *and* WALTER HOW, *and* COWLEY, *the cashier.* WISTER, *the detective, is just leaving the witness-box.*

Cleaver. That is the case for the Crown, me lud!

[*Gathering his robes together, he sits down.*

Frome [*rising and bowing to the* JUDGE]. If it please your lordship and members of the jury. I am not going to dispute the fact that the prisoner altered this cheque, but I am going to put before you evidence as to the condition of his mind, and to submit that you would not be justified in finding that he was responsible for his actions at the time. I am going to show you, in fact, that he did this in a moment of aberration, amounting to temporary insanity, caused by the violent distress under which he was labouring. Gentlemen, the prisoner is only twenty-three years old. I shall call before you a woman from whom you will learn the events that led up to this act. You will hear from her own lips the tragic circumstances of her life, the still more tragic infatuation with which she has inspired the prisoner. This woman, gentlemen, has been leading a miserable existence with a husband who habitually ill-uses her, from whom she actually goes in terror of her life. I am not, of course, saying that it's either right or desirable for a young man to fall in love with a married woman, or that it's his business to rescue her from an ogre-like husband. I'm not saying anything of the sort. But we all know the power of the passion of love; and I would ask you to remember, gentlemen, in listening to her evidence, that, married to a drunken and violent husband, she has no power to get rid of him; for, as you know, another offence besides violence is necessary to enable a woman to obtain a divorce; and of this offence it does not appear that her husband is guilty.

Judge. Is this relevant, Mr. Frome?

Frome. My lord, I submit, extremely—I shall be able to show your lordship that directly.

Judge. Very well.

Frome. In these circumstances, what alternatives were left to her? She could either go on living with this drunkard, in terror of her life; or she could apply to the Court for a separation order. Well, gentlemen, my experience of such cases assures me that this would have given her very insufficient protection from the violence of such a man; and even if effectual would very likely have reduced her either to the workhouse or the streets—for it's not easy, as she is now finding, for an unskilled woman without means of livelihood to support herself and her children without resorting either to the Poor Law or—to speak quite plainly—to the sale of her body.

Judge. You are ranging far, Mr. Frome.

Frome. I shall fire point-blank in a minute, my lord.

Judge. Let us hope so.

Frome. Now, gentlemen, mark—and this is what I have been leading up to—this woman will tell you, and the prisoner will confirm her, that, confronted with such alternatives, she set her whole hopes on himself, knowing the feeling with which she had inspired him. She saw a way out of her misery by going with him to a new country, where they would both be unknown, and might pass as husband and wife. This was a desperate and, as my friend Mr. Cleaver will no doubt call it, an immoral resolution; but, as a fact, the minds of both of them were constantly turned towards it. One wrong is no excuse for another, and those who are never likely to be faced by such a situation possibly have the right to hold up their hands—as to that I prefer to say nothing. But whatever view you take, gentlemen, of this part of the prisoner's story—whatever opinion you form of the right of these two young people under such circumstances to take the law into their own hands—the fact remains that this young woman in her distress, and this young man, little more than a boy, who was so devotedly attached to her, *did* conceive this—if you like—reprehensible design of going away together. Now, for that, of course, they required money, and—they had none. As to the actual events of the morning of July 7th, on which this cheque was altered, the events on which I rely to prove the defendant's irresponsibility—I shall allow those events to speak for themselves, through the lips of my witnesses. Robert Cokeson.

[*He turns, looks round, takes up a sheet of paper, and waits.*

[COKESON *is summoned into the court, and goes into the witness-box, holding his hat before him. The oath is administered to him.*

Frome. What is your name?

Cokeson. Robert Cokeson.

Frome. Are you managing clerk to the firm of solicitors who employ the prisoner?

Cokeson. Ye-es.

Frome. How long had the prisoner been in their employ?

Cokeson. Two years. No, I'm wrong there—all but seventeen days.

Frome. Had you him under your eye all that time?

Cokeson. Except Sundays and holidays.

Frome. Quite so. Let us hear, please, what you have to say about his general character during those two years.

Cokeson [*confidentially to the jury, and as if a little surprised at being asked*]. He was a nice, pleasant-spoken young man. I'd no fault to find with him—quite the contrary. It was a *great* surprise to me when he did a thing like that.

Frome. Did he ever give you reason to suspect his honesty?

Cokeson. No! To have dishonesty in our office, that'd never do!

Frome. I'm sure the jury fully appreciate that, Mr. Cokeson.

Cokeson. Every man of business knows that honesty's the *sign qua nonne.*

Frome. Do you give him a good character all round, or do you not?

Cokeson [*turning to the* JUDGE]. Certainly. We were all very jolly and pleasant together, until this happened. Quite upset me.

Frome. Now, coming to the morning of the 7th of July, the morning on which the cheque was altered. What have you to say about his demeanour that morning?

Cokeson [*to the jury*]. If you ask me, I don't think he was quite *compos* when he did it.

Judge [*sharply*]. Are you suggesting that he was insane?

Cokeson. Not *compos*.

Judge. A little more precision, please.

Frome [*smoothly*]. Just tell us, Mr. Cokeson.

Cokeson [*somewhat outraged*]. Well, in my opinion—[*looking at the* JUDGE]—such as it is—he was jumpy at the time. The jury will understand my meaning.

Frome. Will you tell us how you came to that conclusion?

Cokeson. Ye-es, I will. I have my lunch in from the restaurant, a chop and a potato—saves time. That day it happened to come just as Mr. Walter How handed me the cheque. Well, I like it hot; so I went into the clerk's office and I handed the cheque to Davis, the other clerk, and told him to get change. I noticed young Falder walking up and down. I said to him: 'This is not the Zoological Gardens, Falder.'

Frome. Do you remember what he answered?

Cokeson. Ye-es: 'I wish to God it were!' Struck me as funny.

Frome. Did you notice anything else peculiar?

Cokeson. I did.

Frome. What was that?

Cokeson. His collar was unbuttoned. Now, I like a young man to be neat. I said to him: 'Your collar's unbuttoned.'

Frome. And what did he answer?

Cokeson. Stared at me. It wasn't nice.

Judge. Stared at you? Isn't that a very common practice?

Cokeson. Ye-es, but it was the look in his eyes. I can't explain my meaning—it was funny.

Frome. Had you ever seen such a look in his eyes before?

Cokeson. No. If I had I should have spoken to the partners. We can't have anything eccentric in our profession.

Judge. Did you speak to them on that occasion?

Cokeson [*confidentially*]. Well, I didn't like to trouble them without *prime facey* evidence.

Frome. But it made a very distinct impression on your mind?

Cokeson. Ye-es. The clerk Davis could have told you the same.

Frome. Quite so. It's very unfortunate that we've not got him here. Now can you tell me of the morning on which the discovery of the forgery was made? That would be the 18th. Did anything happen that morning?

Cokeson [*with his hand to his ear*]. I'm a little deaf.

Frome. Was there anything in the course of that morning—I mean before the discovery—that caught your attention?

Cokeson. Ye-es—a woman.

Judge. How is *this* relevant, Mr. Frome?

Frome. I am trying to establish the state of mind in which the prisoner committed this act, my lord.

Judge. I quite appreciate that. But this was long after the act.

Frome. Yes, my lord, but it contributes to my contention.

Judge. Well!

Frome. You say a woman. Do you mean that she came to the Office?

Cokeson. Ye-es.

Frome. What for?

Cokeson. Asked to see young Falder; he was out at the moment.

Frome. Did you see her.

Cokeson. I did.

Frome. Did she come alone?

Cokeson [*confidentially*]. Well, there you put me in a difficulty. I mustn't tell you what the office-boy told me.

Frome. Quite so, Mr. Cokeson, quite so——

Cokeson [*breaking in with an air of* '*You are young—leave it to me*']. But I think we can get round it. In answer to a question put to her by a third party the woman said to me: 'They're mine, sir.'

Judge. What are? What were?

Cokeson. Her children. They were outside.

Judge. How do you know?

Cokeson. Your lordship mustn't ask me that, or I shall have to tell you what I was told—and that'd never do.

Judge [*smiling*]. The office-boy made a statement.

Cokeson. Egg-zactly.

Frome. What I want to ask you, Mr. Cokeson, is this. In the course of her appeal to see Falder, did the woman say anything that you specially remember?

Cokeson [*looking at him as if to encourage him to complete the sentence*]. A leetle more, sir.

Frome. Or did she not?

Cokeson. She did. I shouldn't like you to have led me to the answer.

Frome [*with an irritated smile*]. Will you tell the jury what it was?

Cokeson. 'It's a matter of life and death.'

Foreman of the Jury. Do you mean the woman said that?

Cokeson [*nodding*]. It's not the sort of thing you like to have said to you.

Frome [*a little impatiently*]. Did Falder come in while she was there? [COKESON *nods*.] And she saw him, and went away?

Cokeson. Ah! there I can't follow you. I didn't see her go.

Frome. Well, is she there now?

Cokeson [*with an indulgent smile*]. No!

Frome. Thank you, Mr. Cokeson. [*He sits down.*

Cleaver [*rising*]. You say that on the morning of the forgery the prisoner was jumpy. Well, now, sir, what precisely do you mean by that word?

Cokeson [*indulgently*]. I *want* you to understand. Have you ever seen a dog that's lost its master? He was kind of everywhere at once with his eyes.

Cleaver. Thank you; I was coming to his eyes. You called them 'funny'. What are we to understand by that. Strange, or what?

Cokeson. Ye-es, funny.

Cleaver [*sharply*]. Yes, sir, but what may be funny to you may not be funny to me, or to the jury. Did they look frightened, or shy, or fierce, or what?

Cokeson. You make it very hard for me. I give you the word, and you want me to give you another.

Cleaver [*rapping his desk*]. Does 'funny' mean mad?

Cokeson. Not mad, fun——

Cleaver. Very well! Now you say he had his collar unbuttoned? Was it a hot day?

Cokeson. Ye-es; I think it was.

Cleaver. And did he button it when you called his attention to it?

Cokeson. Ye-es, I think he did.

Cleaver. Would you say that that denoted insanity?

[*He sits down.* COKESON, *who has opened his mouth to reply, is left gaping.*

Frome [*rising hastily*]. Have you ever caught him in that dishevelled state before?

Cokeson. No! He was *always* clean and quiet.

Frome. That will do, thank you.

[COKESON *turns blandly to the* JUDGE, *as though to rebuke counsel for not remembering that the* JUDGE *might wish to have a chance; arriving at the conclusion that he is to be asked nothing further, he turns and descends from the box, and sits down next to* JAMES *and* WALTER.

Frome. Ruth Honeywill.

[RUTH *comes into court, and takes her stand stoically in the witness-box. She is sworn.*

Frome. What is your name, please?

Ruth. Ruth Honeywill.

Frome. How old are you?

Ruth. Twenty-six.

Frome. You are a married woman, living with your husband? A little louder.

Ruth. No, sir; not since July.

Frome. Have you any children?

Ruth. Yes, sir, two.

Frome. Are they living with you?

Ruth. Yes, sir.

Frome. You know the prisoner?

Ruth [*looking at him*]. Yes.

Frome. What was the nature of your relations with him?

Ruth. We were friends.

Judge. Friends?

Ruth [*simply*]. Lovers, sir.

Judge [*sharply*]. In what sense do you use that word?

Ruth. We love each other.

Judge. Yes, but——

Ruth [*shaking her head*]. No, your lordship—not yet.

Judge. Not yet! H'm! [*He looks from* RUTH *to* FALDER.] Well!

Frome. What is your husband?

Ruth. Traveller.

Frome. And what was the nature of your married life?

Ruth [*shaking her head*]. It don't bear talking about.

Frome. Did he ill-treat you, or what?

Ruth. Ever since my first was born.

Frome. In what way?

Ruth. I'd rather not say. All sorts of ways.

Judge. I am afraid I must stop this, you know.

Ruth [*pointing to* FALDER]. *He* offered to take me out of it, sir. We were going to South America.

Frome [*hastily*]. Yes, quite—and what prevented you?

Ruth. I was outside his office when he was taken away. It nearly broke my heart.

Frome. You knew, then, that he had been arrested?

Ruth. Yes, sir. I called at his office afterwards, and [*pointing to* COKESON] that gentleman told me all about it.

Frome. Now, do you remember the morning of Friday, July 7th?

Ruth. Yes.

Frome. Why?

Ruth. My husband nearly strangled me that morning.

Judge. Nearly strangled you!

Ruth [*bowing her head*]. Yes, my lord.

Frome. With his hands, or——?

Ruth. Yes, I just managed to get away from him. I went straight to my friend. It was eight o'clock.

Judge. In the morning? Your husband was not under the influence of liquor then?

Ruth. It wasn't always that.

Frome. In what condition were you?

Ruth. In very bad condition, sir. My dress was torn, and I was half choking.

Frome. Did you tell your friend what had happened?

Ruth. Yes. I wish I never had.

Frome. It upset him?

Ruth. Dreadfully.

Frome. Did he ever speak to you about a cheque?

Ruth. Never.

Frome. Did he ever give you any money?

Ruth. Yes.

Frome. When was that?

Ruth. On Saturday.

Frome. The 8th?

Ruth. To buy an outfit for me and the children, and get all ready to start.

Frome. Did that surprise you, or not?

Ruth. What, sir?

Frome. That he had money to give you.

Ruth. Yes, because on the morning when my husband nearly killed me my friend cried because he hadn't the money to get me away. He told me afterwards he'd come into a windfall.

Frome. And when did you last see him?

Ruth. The day he was taken away, sir. It was the day we were to have started.

Frome. Oh, yes, the morning of the arrest. Well, did you see him at all between the Friday and that morning? [RUTH *nods.*] What was his manner then?

Ruth. Dumb-like—sometimes he didn't seem able to say a word.

Frome. As if something unusual had happened to him?

Ruth. Yes.

Frome. Painful, or pleasant, or what?

Ruth. Like a fate hanging over him.

Frome [*hesitating*]. Tell me, did you love the defendant very much?

Ruth [*bowing her head*]. Yes.

Frome. And had he a very great affection for you?

Ruth [*looking at* FALDER]. Yes, sir.

Frome. Now, ma'am, do you or do you not think that your danger and unhappiness would seriously affect his balance, his control over his actions?

Ruth. Yes.

Frome. His reason, even?

Ruth. For a moment like, I think it would.

Frome. Was he very much upset that Friday morning, or was he fairly calm?

Ruth. Dreadfully upset. I could hardly bear to let him go from me.

Frome. Do you still love him?

Ruth [*with her eyes on* FALDER]. He's ruined himself for me.

Frome. Thank you.

[*He sits down.* RUTH *remains stoically upright in the witness-box.*

Cleaver [*in a considerate voice*]. When you left him on the morning of Friday the 7th you would not say that he was out of his mind, I suppose?

Ruth. No, sir.

Cleaver. Thank you; I've no further question to ask you.

Ruth [*bending a little forward to the jury*]. I would have done the same for him; I would indeed.

Judge. Please, please! You say your married life is an unhappy one? Faults on both sides?

Ruth. Only that I never bowed down to him. I don't see why I should, sir, not to a man like that.

Judge. You refused to obey him?

Ruth [*avoiding the question*]. I've always studied him to keep things nice.

Judge. Until you met the prisoner—was that it?

Ruth. No; even after that.

Judge. I ask, you know, because you seem to me to glory in this affection of yours for the prisoner.

Ruth [*hesitating*]. I—I do. It's the only thing in my life now.

Judge [*staring at her hard*]. Well, step down, please.

[RUTH *looks at* FALDER, *then passes quietly down and takes her seat amongst the witnesses.*

Frome. I call the prisoner, my lord.

[FALDER *leaves the dock; goes into the witness-box, and is duly sworn.*

Frome. What is your name?

Falder. William Falder.

Frome. And age?

Falder. Twenty-three.

Frome. You are not married? [FALDER *shakes his head.*

Frome. How long have you known the last witness?

Falder. Six months.

Frome. Is her account of the relationship between you a correct one?

Falder. Yes.

Frome. You became devotedly attached to her, however?

Falder. Yes.

Judge. Though you knew she was a married woman?

Falder. I couldn't help it, your lordship.

Judge. Couldn't help it?

Falder. I didn't seem able to.

[*The* JUDGE *slightly shrugs his shoulders.*

Frome. How did you come to know her?

Falder. Through my married sister.

Frome. Did you know whether she was happy with her husband?

Falder. It was trouble all the time.

Frome. You knew her husband?

Falder. Only through her—he's a brute.

Judge. I can't allow indiscriminate abuse of a person not present.

Frome [*bowing*]. If your lordship pleases. [*To* FALDER.] You admit altering this cheque? [FALDER *bows his head.*

Frome. Carry your mind, please, to the morning of Friday, July the 7th, and tell the jury what happened.

Falder [*turning to the jury*]. I was having my breakfast when she came. Her dress was all torn, and she was gasping and couldn't seem to get her breath at all; there were the marks of his fingers round her throat; her arm was bruised, and the blood had got into her eyes dreadfully. It frightened me, and then when she told me, I felt—I felt—well—it was too much for me! [*Hardening suddenly.*] If you'd seen it, having the feelings for her that I had, you'd have felt the same, I know.

Frome. Yes?

Falder. When she left me—because I had to go to the office—

I was out of my senses for fear that he'd do it again, and thinking what I could do. I couldn't work—all the morning I was like that—simply couldn't fix my mind on anything. I couldn't think at all. I seemed to have to keep moving. When Davis—the other clerk—gave me the cheque—he said: 'It'll do you good, Will, to have a run with this. You seem half off your chump this morning.' Then when I had it in my hand—I don't know how it came, but it just flashed across me that if I put the *ty* and the nought there would be the money to get her away. It just came and went —I never thought of it again. Then Davis went out to his luncheon, and I don't really remember what I did till I'd pushed the cheque through to the cashier under the rail. I remember his saying 'Notes?' Then I suppose I knew what I'd done. Anyway, when I got outside I wanted to chuck myself under a bus; I wanted to throw the money away; but it seemed I was in for it, so I thought at any rate I'd save her. Of course the tickets I took for the passage and the little I gave her's been wasted, and all, except what I was obliged to spend on myself, I've restored. I keep thinking over and over however it was I came to do it, and how I can't have it all again to do differently!

[FALDER *is silent, twisting his hands before him.*

Frome. How far is it from your office to the bank?

Falder. Not more than fifty yards, sir.

Frome. From the time Davis went out to lunch to the time you cashed the cheque, how long do you say it must have been?

Falder. It couldn't have been four minutes, sir, because I ran all the way.

Frome. During those four minutes you say you remember nothing?

Falder. No, sir; only that I ran.

Frome. Not even adding the *ty* and the nought?

Falder. No, sir. I don't really.

[FROME *sits down, and* CLEAVER *rises.*

Cleaver. But you remember running, do you?

Falder. I was all out of breath when I got to the bank.

Cleaver. And you don't remember altering the cheque?

Falder [*faintly*]. No, sir.

Cleaver. Divested of the romantic glamour which my friend is casting over the case, is this anything but an ordinary forgery? Come.

Falder. I was half frantic all that morning, sir.

Cleaver. Now, now! You don't deny that the *ty* and the nought were so like the rest of the handwriting as to thoroughly deceive the cashier?

Falder. It was an accident.

Cleaver [*cheerfully*]. Queer sort of accident, wasn't it? On which day did you alter the counterfoil?

Falder [*hanging his head*]. On the Wednesday morning.

Cleaver. Was that an accident too?

Falder [*faintly*]. No.

Cleaver. To do that you had to watch your opportunity, I suppose?

Falder [*almost inaudibly*]. Yes.

Cleaver. You don't suggest that you were suffering under great excitement when you did that?

Falder. I was haunted.

Cleaver. With the fear of being found out?

Falder [*very low*]. Yes.

Judge. Didn't it occur to you that the only thing for you to do was to confess to your employers, and restore the money?

Falder. I was afraid. [*There is silence.*

Cleaver. You desired, too, no doubt, to complete your design of taking this woman away?

Falder. When I found I'd done a thing like that, to do it for nothing seemed so dreadful. I might just as well have chucked myself into the river.

Cleaver. You knew that the clerk Davis was about to leave England—didn't it occur to you when you altered this cheque that suspicion would fall on him?

Falder. It was all done in a moment. I thought of it afterwards.

Cleaver. And that didn't lead you to avow what you'd done?

Falder [*sullenly*]. I meant to write when I got out there—I would have repaid the money.

Judge. But in the meantime your innocent fellow-clerk might have been prosecuted.

Falder. I knew he was a long way off, your lordship. I thought there'd be time. I didn't think they'd find it out so soon.

Frome. I might remind your lordship that as Mr. Walter How had the cheque-book in his pocket till after Davis had sailed, if the discovery had been made only one day later Falder himself would have left, and suspicion would have attached to him, and not to Davis, from the beginning.

Judge. The question is whether the prisoner knew that suspicion would light on himself, and not on Davis. [*To* FALDER *sharply.*] Did you know that Mr. Walter How had the cheque-book till after Davis had sailed?

Falder. I—I—thought—he——

Judge. Now speak the truth—yes or no!

Falder [*very low*]. No, my lord. I had no means of knowing.

Judge. That disposes of your point, Mr. Frome.

[FROME *bows to the* JUDGE.

Cleaver. Has any aberration of this nature ever attacked you before?

Falder [*faintly*]. No, sir.

Cleaver. You had recovered sufficiently to go back to your work that afternoon?

Falder. Yes, I had to take the money back.

Cleaver. You mean the *nine* pounds. Your wits were sufficiently keen for you to remember that? And you still persist in saying you don't remember altering this cheque.

[*He sits down.*

Falder. If I hadn't been mad I should never have had the courage.

Frome [*rising*]. Did you have your lunch before going back?

Falder. I never ate a thing all day; and at night I couldn't sleep.

Frome. Now, as to the four minutes that elapsed between Davis's going out and your cashing the cheque: do you say that you recollect *nothing* during those four minutes?

Falder [*after a moment*]. I remember thinking of Mr. Cokeson's face.

Frome. Of Mr. Cokeson's face! Had that any connection with what you were doing?

Falder. No, sir.

Frome. Was that in the office, before you ran out?

Falder. Yes, and while I was running.

Frome. And that lasted till the cashier said: 'Will you have notes?'

Falder. Yes, and then I seemed to come to myself—and it was too late.

Frome. Thank you. That closes the evidence for the defence, my lord.

[*The* JUDGE *nods, and* FALDER *goes back to his seat in the dock.*

Frome [*gathering up notes*]. If it pleases your Lordship—Members of the Jury,—My friend in cross-examination has shown a disposition to sneer at the defence which has been set up in this case, and I am free to admit that nothing I can say will move you, if the evidence has not already convinced you that the prisoner committed this act in a moment when to all practical intents and purposes he was not responsible for his actions; a moment of such mental and moral vacuity, arising from the violent emotional agitation under which he had been suffering, as to amount to temporary madness. My friend has alluded to the 'romantic glamour' with which I have sought to invest this case. Gentlemen, I have done nothing of the kind. I have merely shown you the background of 'life'—that palpitating life which, believe me—whatever my friend may say—always lies behind the commission of a crime. Now, gentlemen, we live in a highly civilized age, and the sight of brutal violence disturbs us in a very strange way, even when we have no personal interest in the matter. But when we see it inflicted on a woman whom we love—what then? Just think of what your own feelings would have been, each of you, at the prisoner's age; and then look at him. Well! he is hardly the comfortable, shall we say bucolic, person likely to contemplate with equanimity marks of gross violence on a woman to whom he was devotedly attached. Yes, gentlemen, look at him! He has not a strong face; but neither has he a vicious face. He is just the sort of man who would easily become the prey of his emotions. You have heard the description of his eyes. My friend may laugh at the word 'funny'—*I* think it better describes the peculiar uncanny look of those who are strained to breaking-point than any other word which could have been used. I don't pretend, mind you, that his mental irresponsibility was more than a flash of darkness, in which all sense of proportion became lost; but I do contend that, just as a man who destroys himself at such a moment may be, and often is, absolved from the stigma attaching to the crime of self-murder, so he may, and frequently does, commit other crimes while in this irresponsible condition, and that he may as justly be acquitted of criminal intent and treated as a patient. I admit that this is a plea which might well be abused. It is a matter for discretion. But here you have a case in which there is every reason to give the benefit of the doubt. You heard me ask the prisoner what he thought of during those four fatal minutes. What was his answer? 'I thought of Mr.

Cokeson's face?' Gentlemen, no man could invent an answer like that; it is absolutely stamped with truth. You have seen the great affection (legitimate or not) existing between him and this woman, who came here to give evidence for him at the risk of her life. It is impossible for you to doubt his distress on the morning when he committed this act. We well know what terrible havoc such distress can make in weak and highly nervous people. It was all the work of a moment. The rest has followed, as death follows a stab to the heart, or water drops if you hold up a jug to empty it. Believe me, gentlemen, there is nothing more tragic in life than the utter impossibility of changing what you have done. Once this cheque was altered and presented, the work of four minutes—four mad minutes—the rest has been silence. But in those four minutes the boy before you has slipped through a door, hardly opened, into that great cage which never again quite lets a man go—the cage of the Law. His further acts, his failure to confess, the alteration of the counterfoil, his preparations for flight, are all evidence—not of deliberate and guilty intention when he committed the prime act from which these subsequent acts arose; no—they are merely evidence of the weak character which is clearly enough his misfortune. But is a man to be lost because he is bred and born with a weak character? Gentlemen, men like the prisoner are destroyed daily under our law for want of that human insight which sees them as they are, patients, and not criminals. If the prisoner be found guilty, and treated as though he were a criminal type, he will, as all experience shows, in all probability become one. I beg you not to return a verdict that may thrust him back into prison and brand him for ever. Gentlemen, Justice is a machine that, when someone has once given it the starting push, rolls on of itself. Is this young man to be ground to pieces under this machine for an act which at the worst was one of weakness? Is he to become a member of the luckless crews that man those dark, ill-starred ships called prisons? Is that to be his voyage—from which so few return? Or is he to have another chance, to be still looked on as one who has gone a little astray, but who will come back? I urge you, gentlemen, do not ruin this young man! For, as a result of those four minutes, ruin, utter and irretrievable, stares him in the face. He can be saved now. Imprison him as a criminal, and I affirm to you that he will be lost. He has neither the face nor the manner of one who can survive that terrible ordeal. Weigh in the scales his criminality and the suffering he has undergone. The latter is ten times heavier already. He has lain in prison under this charge for more than two months. Is he likely ever to forget that? Imagine the anguish of his mind during that time. He has had his punishment, gentlemen, you may depend. The rolling of the chariot-wheels of Justice over this boy began when it was decided to prosecute him. We are now already at the second stage. If you permit it to go on to the third I would not give—that for him.

[*He holds up finger and thumb in the form of a circle, drops his hand, and sits down.*

[*The jury stir, and consult each other's faces; then they turn towards the counsel for the Crown, who rises, and, fixing his eyes on a spot that seems to give him satisfaction, slides them every now and then towards the jury.*

Cleaver. May it please your Lordship. [*Rising on his toes.*] Gentlemen of the Jury,—The facts in this case are not disputed, and the defence, if my friend will allow me to say so, is so thin that I don't propose to waste the time of the Court by taking you over the evidence. The plea is one of temporary insanity. Well, gentlemen, I daresay it is clearer to me than it is to you why this rather—what shall we call it?—bizarre defence has been set up. The alternative would have been to plead guilty. Now, gentlemen, if the prisoner had pleaded guilty my friend would have had to rely on a simple appeal to his lordship. Instead of that, he has gone into the byways and hedges and found this—er—peculiar plea, which has enabled him to show you the proverbial woman, to put her in the box—to give, in fact, a romantic glow to this affair. I compliment my friend; I think it highly ingenious of him. By these means, he has—to a certain extent—got round the Law. He has brought the whole story of motive and stress out in court, at first hand, in a way that he would not otherwise have been able to do. But when you have once grasped that fact, gentlemen, you have grasped everything. [*With good-humoured contempt.*] For look at this plea of insanity; we can't put it lower than that. You have heard the woman. She has every reason to favour the prisoner, but what did she say? She said that the prisoner was *not* insane when she left him in the morning. If he were going out of his mind through distress, that was obviously the moment when insanity would have shown itself. You have heard the managing clerk, another witness for the defence. With some difficulty I elicited from him the admission that the prisoner, though jumpy (a word that he seemed to think you would understand, gentlemen, and I'm sure I hope you do), was *not* mad when the cheque was handed to Davis. I agree with my friend that it's unfortunate that we have not got Davis here, but the prisoner has told you the words with which Davis in turn handed him the cheque; he obviously, therefore, was *not* mad when he received it, or he would not have remembered those words. The cashier has told you that he was certainly in his senses when he cashed it. We have therefore the plea that a man who is sane at ten minutes past one, and sane at fifteen minutes past, may, for the purposes of avoiding the consequences of a crime, call himself insane between those points of time. Really, gentlemen, this is so peculiar a proposition that I am not disposed to weary you with further argument. You will form your own opinion of its value. My friend has adopted this way of saying a great deal to you—and very eloquently—on the score of youth, temptation, and the like. I might point out, however, that the offence with which the prisoner is charged is one of the most serious known to our law; and there are certain features in this case, such as the suspicion which he allowed to rest on his innocent fellow-clerk, and his relations with this married woman, which will render it difficult for you to attach too much importance to such pleading. I ask you, in short, gentlemen, for that verdict of guilty which, in the circumstances, I regard you as, unfortunately, bound to record.

[*Letting his eyes travel from the* JUDGE *and the jury to* FROME, *he sits down.*

Judge [*bending a little towards the jury, and speaking in a business-like voice*]. Members of the Jury, you have heard the evidence, and the comments on it. My only business is to make clear to you the issues you have to try. The facts are admitted, so far as the alteration of this cheque and counterfoil by the prisoner. The defence set up is that he was not in a responsible condition when he committed the crime. Well, you have heard the prisoner's story, and the evidence of the other witnesses—so far as it bears on the point of insanity. If you think that what you have heard establishes the fact that the prisoner was insane at the time of the forgery, you will find him guilty but insane.

If, on the other hand, you conclude from what you have seen and heard that the prisoner was sane—and nothing short of insanity will count—you will find him guilty. In reviewing the testimony as to his mental condition you must bear in mind very carefully the evidence as to his demeanour and conduct both before and after the act of forgery—the evidence of the prisoner himself, of the woman, of the witness—er—Cokeson, and—er—of the cashier. And in regard to that I especially direct your attention to the prisoner's admission that the idea of adding the *ty* and the nought did come into his mind at the moment when the cheque was handed to him; and also to the alteration of the counterfoil, and to his subsequent conduct generally. The bearing of all this on the question of premeditation (and premeditation will imply sanity) is very obvious. You must not allow any considerations of age or temptation to weigh with you in the finding of your verdict. Before you can come to a verdict guilty but insane, you must be well and thoroughly convinced that the condition of his mind was such as would have qualified him at the moment for a lunatic asylum. [*He pauses; then seeing that the jury are doubtful whether to retire or no, adds:*] You may retire, gentlemen, if you wish to do so.

[*The jury retire by a door behind the* JUDGE. *The* JUDGE *bends over his notes.* FALDER, *leaning from the dock, speaks excitedly to his solicitor, pointing down at* RUTH. *The solicitor in turns speaks to* FROME.

Frome [*rising*]. My lord. The prisoner is very anxious that I should ask you if your lordship would kindly request the reporters not to disclose the name of the woman witness in the Press reports of these proceedings. Your lordship will understand that the consequences might be extremely serious to her.

Judge [*pointedly—with the suspicion of a smile*]. Well, Mr. Frome, you deliberately took this course which involved bringing her here.

Frome [*with an ironic bow*]. If your lordship thinks I could have brought out the full facts in any other way?

Judge. H'm! Well.

Frome. There is very real danger to her, your lordship.

Judge. You see, I have to take your word for all that.

Frome. If your lordship would be so kind. I can assure your lordship that I am not exaggerating.

Judge. It goes very much against the grain with me that the name of a witness should ever be suppressed. [*With a glance at* FALDER, *who is gripping and clasping his hands before him, and then at* RUTH, *who is sitting perfectly rigid with her eyes fixed on* FALDER.] I'll consider your application. It must depend. I have to remember that she may have come here to commit perjury on the prisoner's behalf.

Frome. Your lordship, I really——

Judge. Yes, yes—I don't suggest anything of the sort, Mr. Frome. Leave it at that for the moment.

[*As he finishes speaking, the jury return, and file back into the box.*

Clerk of Assize. Members of the Jury, are you agreed on your verdict?

Foreman. We are.

Clerk of Assize. Is it Guilty, or Guilty but insane?

Foreman. Guilty.

[*The* JUDGE *nods; then, gathering up his notes, he looks at* FALDER, *who sits motionless.*

Frome [*rising*]. If your lordship would allow me to address you in mitigation of sentence. I don't know if your lordship thinks I can add anything to what I have said to the jury on the score of the prisoner's youth, and the great stress under which he acted.

Judge. I don't think you can, Mr. Frome.

Frome. If your lordship says so—I do most earnestly beg your lordship to give the utmost weight to my plea.

[*He sits down.*

Judge [*to the* CLERK]. Call upon him.

Clerk. Prisoner at the bar, you stand convicted of felony. Have you anything to say for yourself why the Court should not give you judgment according to Law?

[FALDER *shakes his head.*

Judge. William Falder, you have been given fair trail and found guilty, in my opinion rightly found guilty, of forgery. [*He pauses; then, consulting his notes, goes on.*] The defence was set up that you were not responsible for your actions at the moment of committing the crime. There is no doubt, I think, that this was a device to bring out at first hand the nature of the temptation to which you succumbed. For throughout the trial your counsel was in reality making an appeal for mercy. The setting up of this defence of course enabled him to put in some evidence that might weigh in that direction. Whether he was well advised to do so is another matter. He claimed that you should be treated rather as a patient than as a criminal. And this plea of his, which in the end amounted to a passionate appeal, he based in effect on an indictment of the march of Justice, which he practically accused of confirming and completing the process of criminality. Now, in considering how far I should allow weight to his appeal, I have a number of factors to take into account. I have to consider on the one hand the grave nature of your offence, the deliberate way in which you subsequently altered the counterfoil, the danger you caused to an innocent man—and that, to my mind, is a very grave point—and finally I have to consider the necessity of deterring others from following your example. On the other hand, I bear in mind that you are young, that you have hitherto borne a good character, that you were, if I am to believe your evidence and that of your witnesses, in a state of some emotional excitement when you committed this crime. I have every wish, consistently with my duty—not only to you, but to the community, to treat you with leniency. And this brings me to what are the determining factors in my mind in my consideration of your case. You are a clerk in a lawyer's office—that is a very serious aggravation in this case; no possible excuse can be made for you on the ground that you were not fully conversant with the nature of the crime you were committing and the penalties that attach to it. It is said, however, that you were carried away by your emotions. The story has been told here to-day of your relations with this—er—Mrs. Honeywill; on that story both the defence and the plea for mercy were in effect based. Now what is that story? It is that you, a young man, and she a young woman unhappily married, had formed an attachment, which you both say—with what truth I am unable to gauge—had not yet resulted in immoral relations, but which you both admit was about to result in such relationship. Your counsel has made an attempt to palliate this, on the ground that the woman is in what he describes, I think, as 'a hopeless position'. As to that I can express no opinion. She is a married woman, and the fact is patent that you committed this crime with the view of furthering an immoral design. Now, however I might wish, I am not able to justify to my conscience a plea for mercy which has a basis inimical to morality. It is vitiated *ab initio*. Your counsel has made an attempt also to show that to punish you with further imprisonment would be unjust. I do not follow him in these flights. *The Law is what it is*—a majestic edifice, sheltering all of us, each stone of which rests on another. I am concerned only with its administration. The crime you have committed is a very serious one. I cannot feel it in accordance with my duty to society to exercise the powers I have in your favour. You will go to penal servitude for three years.

[FALDER, *who throughout the* JUDGE'*s speech has looked at him steadily, lets his head fall forward on his breast.* RUTH *starts up from her seat as he is taken out by the warders. There is a bustle in court.*

Judge [*speaking to the reporters*]. Gentlemen of the Press, I think that the name of the female witness should not be reported. [*The reporters bow their acquiescence.*

Judge [*to* RUTH, *who is staring in the direction in which* FALDER *has disappeared*]. Do you understand, your name will not be mentioned?

Cokeson [*pulling her sleeve*]. The judge is speaking to you.

[RUTH *turns, stares at the* JUDGE, *and turns away.*

Judge. I shall sit rather late to-day. Call the next case.

Clerk of Assize [*to a warder*]. Put up John Booley.

[*To cries of* 'Witnesses in the case of Booley'

THE CURTAIN FALLS.

ACT III

SCENE I. *A prison. A plainly furnished room, with two large barred windows, overlooking the prisoners' exercise yard, where men, in yellow clothes marked with arrows, and yellow brimless caps, are seen in single file at a distance of four yards from each other, walking rapidly on serpentine white lines marked on the concrete floor of the yard. Two warders in blue uniforms, with peaked caps and swords, are stationed amongst them. The room has distempered walls, a bookcase with numerous official-looking books, a cupboard between the windows, a plan of the prison on the wall, a writing-table covered with documents. It is Christmas Eve.*

The GOVERNOR, *a neat, grave-looking man, with a trim, fair moustache, the eyes of a theorist, and grizzled hair, receding from the temples, is standing close to this writing-table looking at a sort of rough saw made out of a piece of metal. The hand in which he holds it is gloved, for two fingers are missing. The chief warder,* WOODER, *a tall, thin, military-looking man of sixty, with grey moustache and melancholy, monkey-like eyes, stands very upright two paces from him.*

Governor [*with a faint, abstracted smile*]. Queer-looking affair, Mr. Wooder! Where did you find it?

Wooder. In his mattress, sir. Haven't come across such a thing for two years now.

Governor [*with curiosity*]. Had he any set plan?

Wooder. He'd sawed his window-bar about that much.

[*He holds up his thumb and finger a quarter of an inch apart.*]

Governor. I'll see him this afternoon. What's his name? Moaney! An old hand, I think?

Wooder. Yes, sir—fourth spell of penal. You'd think an old lag like him would have had more sense by now. [*With pitying contempt.*] Occupied his mind, he said. Breaking in and breaking out—that's all they think about.

Governor. Who's next him?

Wooder. O'Cleary, sir.

Governor. The Irishman.

Wooder. Next to him again there's that young fellow, Falder —star class—and next him old Clipton.

Governor. Ah, yes! 'The philosopher'. I want to see him about his eyes.

Wooder. Curious thing, sir; they seem to know when there's one of these tries at escape going on. It makes them restive —there's a regular wave going through them just now.

Governor [*meditatively*]. Odd things—those waves. [*Turning to look at the prisoners exercising.*] Seem quiet enough out here!

Wooder. That Irishman, O'Cleary, began banging on his door this morning. Little thing like that's quite enough to upset the whole lot. They're just like dumb animals at times.

Governor. I've seen it with horses before thunder—it'll run right through cavalry lines.

[*The prison* CHAPLAIN *has entered. He is a dark-haired, ascetic man, in clerical undress, with a peculiarly steady, tight-lipped face, and slow, cultured speech.*

Governor [*holding up the saw*]. Seen this, Miller?

Chaplain. Useful-looking specimen.

Governor. Do for the Museum, eh! [*He goes to the cupboard and opens it, displaying to view a number of quaint ropes, hooks, and metal tools with labels tied on them.*] That'll do, thanks, Mr. Wooder.

Wooder [*saluting*]. Thank you, sir. [*He goes out.*

Governor. Account for the state of the men last day or two, Miller? Seems going through the whole place.

Chaplain. No, I don't know of anything.

Governor. By the way, will you dine with us to-morrow?

Chaplain. Christmas Day? Thanks very much.

Governor. Worries me to feel the men discontented. [*Gazing at the saw.*] Have to punish this poor devil. Can't help liking a man who tries to escape.

[*He places the saw in his pocket and locks the cupboard again.*

Chaplain. Extraordinary perverted will-power—some of them. Nothing to be done till it's broken.

Governor. And not much afterwards, I'm afraid. Ground too hard for golf? [WOODER *comes in again.*

Wooder. Visitor to speak to you, sir, I told him it wasn't usual.

Governor. What about?

Wooder. Shall I put him off, sir?

Governor [*resignedly*]. No, no. Let's see him. Don't go, Miller.

[WOODER *motions to someone without, and as the visitor comes in withdraws.*

[*The visitor is* COKESON, *who is attired in a thick overcoat to the knees, woollen gloves, and carries a top hat.*

Cokeson. I'm sorry to trouble you. But it's about a young man you've got here.

Governor. We have a good many.

Cokeson. Name of Falder, forgery. [*Producing a card, and handing it to the* GOVERNOR.] Firm of James and Walter How. Well known in the law.

Governor [*receiving the card—with a faint smile*]. What do you want to see me about, sir?

Cokeson [*suddenly seeing the prisoners at exercise*]. Why! what a sight!

Governor. Yes, we have that privilege from here; my office is being done up. [*Sitting down at his table.*] Now, please!

Cokeson [*dragging his eyes with difficulty from the window*]. I *wanted* to say a word to you; I shan't keep you long. [*Confidentially.*] Fact is, I oughtn't to be here by rights. His sister came to me—he's got no father and mother—and she was in some distress. 'My husband won't let me go and see him,' she said; 'says he's disgraced the family. And his other sister', she said, 'is an invalid.' And she asked me to come. Well, I take an interest in him. He was our junior —I go to the same chapel—and I didn't like to refuse.

Governor. I'm afraid he's not allowed a visitor yet—he's only here for his one month's separate confinement.

Cokeson. You see, I saw him while he was shut up waiting for his trial and he was lonely.

Governor [*with faint amusement*]. Ring the bell—would you, Miller. [*To* COKESON.] You'd like to hear what the doctor says about him, perhaps.

Chaplain [*ringing the bell*]. You are not accustomed to prisons, it would seem, sir.

Cokeson. No. But it's a pitiful sight. He's quite a young fellow. I said to him: 'Be patient,' I said. 'Patient!' he said. 'A day', he said, 'shut up in your cell thinking and brooding as I do, it's longer than a year outside, I can't help it,' he said; 'I try—but I'm built that way, Mr. Cokeson.' And he held his hand up to his face. I could see the tears trickling through his fingers. It wasn't nice.

Chaplain. He's a young man with rather peculiar eyes, isn't he? Not Church of England, I think?

Cokeson. No.

Chaplain. I know.

Governor [*to* WOODER, *who has come in*]. Ask the doctor to be good enough to come here for a minute. [WOODER *salutes, and goes out*.] Let's see, he's not married?

Cokeson. No. [*Confidentially*.] But there's a party he's very much attached to, not altogether *com-il-fo*. It's a sad story.

Chaplain. If it wasn't for drink and women, sir, this prison might be closed.

Cokeson [*looking at the* CHAPLAIN *over his spectacles*]. Ye-es, but I wanted to tell you about that, special. It preys on his mind.

Governor. Well!

Cokeson. Like this. The woman had a nahsty, spiteful feller for a husband, and she'd left him. Fact is, she was going away with our young friend. It's not nice—but I've looked over it. Well, after the trial she said she'd earn her living apart, and wait for him to come out. That was a great consolation to him. But after a month she came to me—I *don't* know her personally—and she said: 'I can't earn the children's living, let alone my own—I've got no friends. I'm obliged to keep out of everybody's way; else my husband'd get to know where I was. I'm very much reduced,' she said.

And she has lost flesh. 'I'll have to go in the workhouse!' It's a painful story. I said to her: 'No,' I said, 'not that! I've got a wife an' family, but sooner than you should do that I'll spare you a little myself.' 'Really,' she said—she's a nice creature—'I don't like to take it from you. I think I'd better go back to my husband.' Well, I know he's a nahsty, spiteful feller—drinks—but I didn't like to persuade her not to.

Chaplain. Surely, no.

Cokeson. Ye-es, but I'm sorry now. He's got his three years to serve. I *want* things to be pleasant for him.

Chaplain [*with a touch of impatience*]. The Law hardly shares your view, I'm afraid.

Cokeson. He's all alone there by himself. I'm afraid it'll turn him silly. And nobody wants that, I s'pose. He cried when I saw him. I don't like to see a man cry.

Chaplain. It's a very rare thing for them to give way like that.

Cokeson [*looking at him—in a tone of sudden dogged hostility*]. I keep dogs.

Chaplain. Indeed?

Cokeson. Ye-es. And I say this: I wouldn't shut one of them up all by himself, week after week, not if he'd bit me all over.

Chaplain. Unfortunately, the criminal is not a dog; he has a sense of right and wrong.

Cokeson. But that's not the way to make him feel it.

Chaplain. Ah! there I'm afraid we must differ.

Cokeson. It's the same with dogs. If you treat 'em with kindness they'll do anything for you; but to shut 'em up alone, it only makes 'em savage.

Chaplain. Surely you should allow those who have had a little more experience than yourself to know what is best for prisoners.

Cokeson [*doggedly*]. I know this young feller, I've watched him for years. He's eurotic—got no stamina. His father died of consumption. I'm thinking of his future. If he's to be kept there shut up by himself, without a cat to keep him company, it'll do him harm. I said to him: 'Where do you feel it?' 'I can't tell you, Mr. Cokeson,' he said, 'but sometimes I could beat my head against the wall.' It's not nice.

[*During this speech the* DOCTOR *has entered. He is a medium-sized, rather good-looking man, with a quick eye. He stands leaning against the window.*

Governor. This gentleman thinks the separate is telling on Q 3007—Falder, young thin fellow, star class. What do you say, Doctor Clements?

Doctor. He doesn't like it, but it's not doing him any harm, it's only a month.

Cokeson. But he was weeks before he came in here.

Doctor. We can always tell. He's lost no weight since he's been here.

Cokeson. It's his state of mind I'm speaking of.

Doctor. His mind's all right so far. He's nervous, rather melancholy. I don't see signs of anything more. I'm watching him carefully.

Cokeson [*nonplussed*]. I'm glad to hear you say that.

Chaplain [*more suavely*]. It's just at this period that we are able to make some impression on them, sir. I am speaking from my special standpoint.

Cokeson [*turning bewildered to the* GOVERNOR]. I *don't* want to be unpleasant, but I do feel it's awkward.

Governor. I'll make a point of seeing him to-day.

Cokeson. I'm much obliged to you. I thought perhaps seeing him every day you wouldn't notice it.

Governor [*rather sharply*]. If any sign of injury to his health shows itself his case will be reported at once. That's fully provided for. [*He rises.*

Cokeson [*following his own thoughts*]. Of course, what you don't see doesn't trouble you; but I don't want to have him on my mind.

Governor. I think you may safely leave it to us, sir.

Cokeson [*mollified and apologetic*]. I thought you'd understand me. I'm a plain man—never set myself up against authority. [*Expanding to the* CHAPLAIN.] Nothing personal meant. *Good* morning.

[*As he goes out the three officials do not look at each other, but their faces wear peculiar expressions.*

Chaplain. Our friend seems to think that prison is a hospital.

Cokeson [*returning suddenly with an apologetic air*]. There's just one little thing. This woman—I suppose I mustn't ask you to let him see her. It'd be a rare treat for them both. He'll be thinking about her all the time. Of course she's not his wife. But he's quite safe in here. They're a pitiful couple. You couldn't make an exception?

Governor [*wearily*]. As you say, my dear sir, I couldn't make an exception; he won't be allowed a visit till he goes to a convict prison.

Cokeson. I see. [*Rather coldly.*] Sorry to have troubled you.

[*He again goes out.*

Chaplain [*shrugging his shoulders*]. The plain man indeed, poor fellow. Come and have some lunch, Clements?

[*He and the* DOCTOR *go out talking.*

[*The* GOVERNOR, *with a sigh, sits down at his table and takes up a pen.*

THE CURTAIN FALLS.

SCENE II. *Part of the ground corridor of the prison. The walls are coloured with greenish distemper up to a stripe of deeper green about the height of a man's shoulder, and above this line are whitewashed. The floor is of blackened stones. Daylight is filtering through a heavily barred window at the end. The doors of four cells are visible. Each cell door has a little round peep-hole at the level of a man's eye, covered by a little round disc, which, raised upwards, affords a view of the cell. On the wall, close to each cell door, hangs a little square board with the prisoner's name, number, and record.*

Overhead can be seen the iron structures of the first-floor and second-floor corridors.

The WARDER INSTRUCTOR, *a bearded man in blue uniform, with an apron, and some dangling keys, is just emerging from one of the cells.*

Instructor [*speaking from the door into the cell*]. I'll have another bit for you when that's finished.

O'Cleary [*unseen—in an Irish voice*]. Little doubt o' that, sirr.

Instructor [*gossiping*]. Well, you'd rather have it than nothing, I s'pose.

O'Cleary. An' that's the blessed truth.

[*Sounds are heard of a cell door being closed and locked, and of approaching footsteps.*

Instructor [*in a sharp, changed voice*]. Look alive over it!

[*He shuts the cell door, and stands at attention.*

[*The* GOVERNOR *comes walking down the corridor, followed by* WOODER.

Governor. Anything to report?

Instructor [*saluting*]. Q 3007 [*He points to a cell.*] is behind with his work, sir. He'll lose marks to-day.

[*The* GOVERNOR *nods and passes on to the end cell. The* INSTRUCTOR *goes away.*

Governor. This is our maker of saws, isn't it?

[*He takes the saw from his pocket as* WOODER *throws open the door of the cell. The convict* MOANEY *is seen lying on his bed, athwart the cell, with his cap on. He is a raw-boned fellow, about fifty-six years old, with outstanding bat's ears and fierce, staring, steel-coloured eyes.*

Wooder. Cap off! [MOANEY *removes his cap*.] Out here!

[MOANEY *comes to the door.*

Governor [*beckoning him out into the corridor, and holding up the saw—with the manner of an officer speaking to a private*]. Anything to say about this, my man? [MOANEY *is silent*.] Come!

Moaney. It passed the time.

Governor [*pointing into the cell*]. Not enough to do, eh?

Moaney. It don't occupy your mind.

Governor [*tapping the saw*]. You might find a better way than this.

Moaney [*sullenly*]. Well! What way? I must keep my hand in against the time I get out. What's the good of anything else to me at my time of life? [*With a gradual change to civility, as his tongue warms*.] Ye know that, sir. I'll be in again within a year or two, after I've done this lot. I don't want to disgrace meself when I'm out. *You've* got your pride keeping the prison smart; well, I've got mine. [*Seeing that the* GOVERNOR *is listening with interest, he goes on, pointing to the saw*.] *I must* be doin' a little o' this. It's no harm to any one. I was five weeks makin' that saw—a bit of all right it is, too; now I'll get cells, I suppose, or seven days' bread and water. You can't help it, sir, I know that—I quite put meself in your place.

Governor. Now, look here, Moaney, if I pass it over will you give me your word not to try it on again? Think!

[*He goes into the cell, walks to the end of it, mounts the stool, and tries the window-bars.*

Governor [*returning*]. Well?

Moaney [*who has been reflecting*]. I've got another six weeks to do in here, alone. I can't do it and think o' nothing. I must have something to interest me. You've made me a sporting offer, sir, but I can't pass my word about it. I shouldn't like to deceive a gentleman. [*Pointing into the cell*.] Another four hours' steady work would have done it.

Governor. Yes, and what then? Caught, brought back, punishment. Five weeks' hard work to make this, and cells at the end of it, while they put a new bar to your window. Is it worth it, Moaney?

Moaney [*with a sort of fierceness*]. Yes, it is.

Governor [*putting his hand to his brow*]. Oh, well! Two days' cells—bread and water.

Moaney. Thank 'e, sir.

[*He turns quickly like an animal and slips into his cell.*

[*The* GOVERNOR *looks after him and shakes his head as* WOODER *closes and locks the cell door.*

Governor. Open Clipton's cell.

WOODER *opens the door of* CLIPTON'*s cell.* CLIPTON *is sitting on a stool just inside the door, at work on a pair of trousers. He is a small, thick, oldish man, with an almost shaven head, and smouldering little dark eyes behind smoked spectacles. He gets up and stands motionless in the doorway, peering at his visitors.*

Governor [*beckoning*]. Come out here a minute, Clipton.

[CLIPTON, *with a sort of dreadful quietness, comes into the corridor, the needle and thread in his hand. The* GOVERNOR *signs to* WOODER, *who goes into the cell and inspects it carefully.*

Governor. How are your eyes?

Clipton. I don't complain of them. I don't see the sun here. [*He makes a stealthy movement, protuding his neck a little.*] There's just one thing, Mr. Governor, as you're speaking to me. I wish you'd ask the cove next door here to keep a bit quieter.

Governor. What's the matter? I don't want any tales, Clipton.

Clipton. He keeps me awake. I don't know who he is. [*With contempt.*] One of this *star* class, I expect. Oughtn't to be here with *us*.

Governor [*quietly*]. Quite right, Clipton. He'll be moved when there's a cell vacant.

Clipton. He knocks about like a wild beast in the early morning. I'm not used to it—stops me getting my sleep out. In the evening too. It's not fair, Mr. Governor, as you're speaking to me. Sleep's the comfort I've got here; I'm entitled to take it out full.

[WOODER *comes out of the cell, and instantly, as though extinguished,* CLIPTON *moves with stealthy suddenness back into his cell.*

Wooder. All right, sir.

[*The* GOVERNOR *nods. The door is closed and locked.*

Governor. Which is the man who banged on his door this morning?

Wooder [*going towards* O'CLEARY'*s cell*]. This one, sir; O'Cleary.

[*He lifts the disc and glances through the peep-hole.*

Governor. Open.

[WOODER *throws open the door*. O'CLEARY, *who is seated at a little table by the door as if listening, springs up and stands at attention just inside the doorway. He is a broad-faced, middle-aged man, with a wide, thin, flexible mouth, and little holes under his high cheek-bones.*

Governor. Where's the joke, O'Cleary?

O'Cleary. The joke, your honour? I've not seen one for a long time.

Governor. Banging on your door?

O'Cleary. Oh! that!

Governor. It's womanish.

O'Cleary. An' it's that I'm becoming this two months past.

Governor. Anything to complain of?

O'Cleary. No, sirr.

Governor. You're an old hand; you ought to know better.

O'Cleary. Yes, I've been through it all.

Governor. You've got a youngster next door; you'll upset him.

O'Cleary. It cam' over me, your honour. I can't always be the same steady man.

Governor. Work all right?

O'Cleary [*taking up a rush mat he is making*]. Oh! I can do it on my head. It's the miserablest stuff—don't take the brains of a mouse. [*Working his mouth.*] It's here I feel it—the want of a little noise—a terrible little wud aise me.

Governor. You know as well as I do that if you were out in the shops you wouldn't be allowed to talk.

O'Cleary [*with a look of profound meaning*]. Not with my mouth.

Governor. Well, then?

O'Cleary. But it's the great conversation I'd be havin'.

Governor [*with a smile*]. Well, no more conversation on your door.

O'Cleary. No, sirr, I wud not have the little wit to repate meself.

Governor [*turning*]. Good night.

O'Cleary. Good night, your honour.

[*He turns into his cell. The* GOVERNOR *shuts the door.*

Governor [*looking at the record card*]. Can't help liking the poor blackguard.

Wooder. He's an amiable man, sir.

Governor [*pointing down the corridor*]. Ask the doctor to come here, Mr. Wooder.

[WOODER *salutes and goes away down the corridor.*

[*The* GOVERNOR *goes to the door of* FALDER*'s cell. He raises his uninjured hand to uncover the peep-hole; but, without uncovering it, shakes his head and drops hishand; then, after scrutinizing the record board, he opens the cell door.* FALDER, *who is standing against it, lurches forward, with a gasp.*

Governor [*beckoning him out*]. Now tell me; can't you settle down, Falder?

Falder [*in a breathless voice*]. Yes, sir.

Governor. You know what I mean? It's no good running your head against a stone wall, is it?

Falder. No, sir.

Governor. Well, come.

Falder. I try, sir.

Governor. Can't you sleep?

Falder. Very little. Between two o'clock and getting up's the worst time.

Governor. How's that?

Falder [*his lips twitch with a sort of smile*]. I don't know, sir. I was always nervous. [*Suddenly voluble.*] Everything seems to get such a size then. I feel I'll never get out as long as I live.

Governor. That's morbid, my lad. Pull yourself together.

Falder [*with an equally sudden dogged resentment*]. Yes—I've got to——

Governor. Think of all these other fellows.

Falder. They're used to it.

Governor. They all had to go through it once for the first time, just as you're doing now.

Falder. Yes, sir, I shall get to be like them in time, I suppose.

Governor [*rather taken aback*]. H'm! Well! That rests with you. Now, come. Set your mind to it, like a good fellow. You're still quite young. A man can make himself what he likes.

Falder [*wistfully*]. Yes, sir.

Governor. Take a good hold of yourself. Do you read?

Falder. I don't take the words in. [*Hanging his head.*] I know it's no good; but I can't help thinking of what's going on outside.

Governor. Private trouble?

Falder. Yes.

Governor. You mustn't think about it.

Falder [*looking back at his cell*]. How can I help it, sir?

[*He suddenly becomes motionless as* WOODER *and the* DOCTOR *approach. The* GOVERNOR *motions to him to go back into his cell.*

Falder [*quick and low*]. I'm quite right in my head, sir.

[*He goes back into his cell.*

Governor [*to the* DOCTOR]. Just go in and see him, Clements.

[*The* DOCTOR *goes into the cell. The* GOVERNOR *pushes the door to, nearly closing it, and walks towards the window.*

Wooder [*following*]. Sorry you should be troubled like this, sir. Very contented lot of men, on the whole.

Governor [*shortly*]. You think so?

Wooder. Yes, sir. It's Christmas doing it, in my opinion.

Governor [*to himself*]. Queer, that!

Wooder. Beg pardon, sir?

Governor. Christmas!

[*He turns towards the window, leaving* WOODER *looking at him with a sort of pained anxiety.*

Wooder [*suddenly*]. Do you think we make show enough, sir? If you'd like us to have more holly?

Governor. Not at all, Mr. Wooder.

Wooder. Very good, sir.

[*The* DOCTOR *has come out of* FALDER'*s cell, and the* GOVERNOR *beckons to him.*

Governor. Well?

Doctor. I can't make anything much of him. He's nervous, of course.

Governor. Is there any sort of case to report? Quite frankly, Doctor.

Doctor. Well, I don't think the separate's doing him any good; but then I could say the same of a lot of them—they'd get on better in the shops, there's no doubt.

Governor. You mean you'd have to recommend others?

Doctor. A dozen at least. It's on his nerves. There's nothing tangible. This fellow here [*pointing to* O'CLEARY'*s cell*] for instance—feels it just as much, in his way. If I once get away from physical facts—I shan't know where I am.

Conscientiously, sir, I don't know how to differentiate him. He hasn't lost weight. Nothing wrong with his eyes. His pulse is good. Talks all right. It's only another week before he goes.

Governor. It doesn't amount to melancholia?

Doctor [*shaking his head*]. I can report on him if you like; but if I do I ought to report on others.

Governor. I see. [*Looking towards* FALDER'*s cell*.] The poor devil must just stick it then.

[*As he says this he looks absently at* WOODER.

Wooder. Beg pardon, sir?

[*For answer the* GOVERNOR *stares at him, turns on his heel, and walks away*.

[*There is a sound as of beating on metal*.

Governor [*stopping*]. Mr. Wooder?

Wooder. Banging on his door, sir. I thought we should have more of that.

[*He hurries forward, passing the* GOVERNOR, *who follows slowly*.

THE CURTAIN FALLS.

SCENE III. FALDER'*s cell, a whitewashed space thirteen feet broad by seven deep, and nine feet high, with a rounded ceiling. The floor is of shiny blackened bricks. The barred window, with a ventilator, is high up in the middle of the end wall. In the middle of the opposite end wall is the narrow door. In a corner are the mattress and bedding rolled up (two blankets, two sheets, and a coverlet). Above them is a quarter-circular wooden-shelf, on which is a Bible and several little devotional books, piled in a symmetrical pyramid; there are also a black hair brush, and a bit of soap. In another corner is the wooden frame of a bed, standing on end. There is a dark ventilator under the window, and another over the door.* FALDER'*s work (a shirt to which he is putting button-holes) is hung to a nail on the wall over a small wooden table, on which the novel* Lorna Doone *lies open. Low down in the corner by the door is a thick glass screen, about a foot square, covering the gas-jet let into the wall. There is also a wooden stool, and a pair of shoes beneath it. Three bright round tins are set under the window.*

In fast-fading daylight, FALDER, *in his stockings, is seen standing motionless, with his head inclined towards the door, listening. He moves a little closer to the door, his stockinged feet making no noise. He stops at the door. He is trying harder and harder to hear something, any little thing that is going on outside. He springs suddenly upright—as if at a sound—and remains perfectly motionless. Then, with a heavy sigh, he moves to his work, and stands looking at it, with his head down; he does a stitch or two, having the air of a man so lost in sadness that each stitch is, as it were, a coming to life. Then, turning abruptly, he begins pacing the cell, moving his head, like an animal pacing its cage. He stops again at the door, listens, and, placing the palms of his hands against it with his fingers spread out, leans his forehead against the iron. Turning from it presently, he moves slowly back towards the window tracing his way with his finger along the top line of the distemper that runs round the walls. He stops under the window, and, picking up the lid of one of the tins, peers into it, as if trying to make a companion of his own face. It has grown very nearly dark. Suddenly the lid falls out of his hand with a clatter—the only sound that has broken the silence—and he stands staring intently at the wall where the stuff of the shirt is hanging rather white in the darkness—he seems to be seeing somebody or something there. There is a sharp tap and click; the cell light behind the glass screen has been turned up. The cell is brightly lighted.* FALDER *is seen gasping for breath.*

A sound from far away, as of distant, dull beating on thick metal, is suddenly audible. FALDER *shrinks back, not able to bear this sudden clamour. But the sound grows, as though some great tumbril were rolling towards the cell. And gradually it seems to hypnotize him. He begins creeping inch by inch nearer to the door. The banging sound, travelling from cell to cell, draws closer and closer;* FALDER*'s hands are seen moving as if his spirit had already joined in this beating, and the sound swells till it seems to have entered the very cell. He suddenly raises his clenched fists. Panting violently, he flings himself at his door, and beats on it.*

THE CURTAIN FALLS.

ACT IV

The scene is again COKESON*'s room, at a few minutes to ten of a March morning, two years later. The doors are all open.* SWEEDLE, *now blessed with a sprouting moustache, is getting the offices ready. He arranges papers on* COKESON*'s table; then goes to a covered washstand, raises the lid, and looks at himself in the mirror. While he is gazing his fill* RUTH HONEYWILL *comes in through the outer office and stands in the doorway.*

There seems a kind of exultation and excitement behind her habitual impassivity.

Sweedle [*suddenly seeing her, and dropping the lid of the washstand with a bang*]. Hello! It's you!

Ruth. Yes.

Sweedle. There's only me here! They don't waste their time hurrying down in the morning. Why, it must be two years since we had the pleasure of seeing you. [*Nervously.*] What have you been doing with yourself?

Ruth [*sardonically*]. Living.

Sweedle [*impressed*]. If you want to see *him* [*he points to* COKESON'*s chair*] he'll be here directly—never misses—not much. [*Delicately.*] I hope our friend's back from the country. His time's been up these three months, if I remember. [RUTH *nods.*] I was awful sorry about that. The governor made a mistake—if you ask me.

Ruth. He did.

Sweedle. He ought to have given him a chanst. And, *I* say, the judge ought to ha' let him go after that. They've forgot what human nature's like. Whereas we know.

[RUTH *gives him a honeyed smile.*

Sweedle. They come down on you like a cartload of bricks, flatten you out, and when you don't swell up again they complain of it. I know 'em—seen a lot of that sort of thing in my time. [*He shakes his head in the plenitude of wisdom.*] Why, only the other day the governor——

[*But* COKESON *has come in through the outer office; brisk with east wind, and decidedly greyer.*

Cokeson [*drawing off his coat and gloves*]. Why! it's you! [*Then motioning* SWEEDLE *out, and closing the door.*] Quite a stranger! Must be two years. D'you want to see me? I can give you a minute. Sit down! Family well?

Ruth. Yes, I'm not living where I was.

Cokeson [*eyeing her askance*]. I hope things are more comfortable at home.

Ruth. I couldn't stay with Honeywill, after all.

Cokeson. You haven't done anything rash, I hope. I should be sorry if you'd done anything rash.

Ruth. I've kept the children with me.

Cokeson [*beginning to feel that things are not so jolly as he had hoped*]. Well, I'm glad to have seen you. You've not heard from the young man, I suppose, since he came out?

Ruth. Yes, I ran across him yesterday.

Cokeson. I hope he's well.

Ruth [*with sudden fierceness*]. He can't get anything to do. It's dreadful to see him. He's just skin and bone.

Cokeson [*with genuine concern*]. Dear me! I'm sorry to hear that. [*On his guard again.*] Didn't they find him a place when his time was up?

Ruth. He was only there three weeks. It got out.

Cokeson. I'm sure I don't know what I can do for you. I don't like to be snubby.

Ruth. I can't bear his being like that.

Cokeson [*scanning her not unprosperous figure*]. I know his relations aren't very forthy about him. Perhaps *you* can do something for him, till he finds his feet.

Ruth. Not now. I could have—but not *now*.

Cokeson. I don't understand.

Ruth [*proudly*]. I've seen *him* again—that's all over.

Cokeson [*staring at her—disturbed*]. I'm a family man—I don't want to hear anything unpleasant. Excuse me—I'm very busy.

Ruth. I'd have gone home to my people in the country long ago, but they've never got over me marrying Honeywill. I never was waywise, Mr. Cokeson, but I'm proud. I was only a girl, you see, when I married him. I thought the world of him, of course . . . he used to come travelling to our farm.

Cokeson [*regretfully*]. I did hope you'd have got on better, after you saw me.

Ruth. He used me worse than ever. He couldn't break my nerve, but I lost my health; and then he began knocking the children about . . . I couldn't stand that. I wouldn't go back now, if he were dying.

Cokeson [*who had risen and is shifting about as though dodging a stream of lava*]. We mustn't be violent, must we?

Ruth [*smouldering*]. A man that can't behave better than that—— [*There is silence.*

Cokeson [*fascinated in spite of himself*]. Then there you were! And what did you do then?

Ruth [*with a shrug*]. Tried the same as when I left him before . . . making shirts . . . cheap things. It was the best I could get, but I never made more than ten shillings a week, buying my own cotton and working all day; I hardly ever got to bed till past twelve. I kept at it for nine months. [*Fiercely.*] Well, I'm not fit for that; I wasn't made for it. I'd rather die.

Cokeson. My dear woman! We mustn't talk like that.

Ruth. It was starvation for the children too—after what they'd always had. I soon got not to care. I used to be too tired. [*She is silent*.

Cokeson [*with fearful curiosity*]. And—what happened then?

Ruth [*with a laugh*]. My employer happened then—he's happened ever since.

Cokeson. Dear! Oh dear! I never came across a thing like this.

Ruth [*dully*]. He's treated me all right. But I've done with that. [*Suddenly her lips begin to quiver, and she hides them with the back of her hand*.] I never thought I'd see *him* again, you see. It was just a chance I met him by Hyde Park. We went in there and sat down, and he told me all about himself. Oh! Mr. Cokeson, give him another chance.

Cokeson [*greatly disturbed*]. Then you've both lost your livings! What a horrible position!

Ruth. If he could only get here—where there's nothing to find out about him!

Cokeson. We can't have anything derogative to the firm.

Ruth. I've no one else to go to.

Cokeson. I'll speak to the partners, but I don't think they'll take him, under the circumstances. I don't really.

Ruth. He came with me; he's down in the street.

[*She points to the window*.

Cokeson [*on his dignity*]. He shouldn't have done that until he's sent for. [*Then softening at the look on her face*.] We've got a vacancy, as it happens, but I can't promise anything.

Ruth. It would be the saving of him.

Cokeson. Well, I'll do what I can, but I'm not sanguine. Now tell him that I don't want him here till I see how things are. Leave your address? [*Repeating her*.] 83, Mullingar Street? [*He notes it on blotting-paper*.] Good morning.

Ruth. Thank you.

[*She moves towards the door, turns as if to speak but does not, and goes away*.

Cokeson [*wiping his head and forehead with a large white cotton handkerchief*]. What a business!

[*Then, looking amongst his papers, he sounds his bell*. SWEEDLE *answers it*.

Cokeson. Was that young Richards coming here to-day after the clerk's place?

Sweedle. Yes.

Cokeson. Well, keep him in the air; I don't want to see him yet.

Sweedle. What shall I tell him, sir?

Cokeson [*with asperity*]. Invent something. Use your brains. Don't stump him off altogether.

Sweedle. Shall I tell him that we've got illness, sir?

Cokeson. No! Nothing untrue, Say I'm not here to-day.

Sweedle. Yes, sir. Keep him hankering?

Cokeson. Exactly. And look here. You remember Falder? I may be having him round to see me. Now, treat him like you'd have him treat you in a similar position.

Sweedle. I naturally should do.

Cokeson. That's right. When a man's down never hit 'im. 'Tisn't necessary. Give him a hand up. That's a metaphor I recommend to you in life. It's sound policy.

Sweedle. Do you think the governors will take him on again, sir?

Cokeson. Can't say anything about that. [*At the sound of someone having entered the outer office.*] Who's there?

Sweedle [*going to the door and looking*]. It's Falder, sir.

Cokeson [*vexed*]. Dear me! That's very naughty of her. Tell him to call again. I don't want——

[*He breaks off as* FALDER *comes in.* FALDER *is thin, pale, older, his eyes have grown more restless. His clothes are very worn and loose.*

[SWEEDLE, *nodding cheerfully, withdraws.*

Cokeson. Glad to see you. You're rather previous. [*Trying to keep things pleasant.*] Shake hands! She's striking while the iron's hot. [*He wipes his forehead.*] I don't blame her. She's anxious.

[FALDER *timidly takes* COKESON'*s hand and glances towards the partners' door.*

Cokeson. No—not yet! Sit down! [FALDER *sits in the chair at the side of* COKESON'*s table, on which he places his cap.*] Now you are here I'd like you to give me a little account of yourself. [*Looking at him over his spectacles.*] How's your health?

Falder. I'm alive, Mr. Cokeson.

Cokeson [*preoccupied*]. I'm glad to hear that. About this matter. I don't like doing anything out of the ordinary; it's not my habit. I'm a plain man, and I want everything smooth and straight. But I promised your friend to speak to the partners, and I always keep my word.

Falder. I just want a chance, Mr. Cokeson. I've paid for that job a thousand times and more. I have, sir. No one knows. They say I weighed more when I came out than when I went in. They couldn't weigh me here [*he touches his head*] or here. [*He touches his heart, and gives a sort of laugh.*] Till last night I'd have thought there was nothing in here at all.

Cokeson [*concerned*]. You've not got heart disease?

Falder. Oh! they passed me sound enough.

Cokeson. But they got you a place, didn't they?

Falder. Yes; very good people, knew all about it—very kind to me. I thought I was going to get on first-rate. But one day, all of a sudden, the other clerks got wind of it. . . . I couldn't stick it, Mr. Cokeson, I couldn't, sir.

Cokeson. Easy, my dear fellow, easy.

Falder. I had one small job after that, but it didn't last.

Cokeson. How was that?

Falder. It's no good deceiving you, Mr. Cokeson. The fact is, I seem to be struggling against a thing that's all round me. I can't explain it: it's as if I was in a net; as fast as I cut it here, it grows up there. I didn't act as I ought to have, about references; but what are you to do? You must have them. And that made me afraid, and I left. In fact I'm—I'm afraid all the time now.

[*He bows his head and leans dejectedly silent over the table.*

Cokeson. I feel for you—I do really. Aren't your sisters going to do anything for you?

Falder. One's in consumption. And the other——

Cokeson. Ye . . . es. She told me her husband wasn't quite pleased with you.

Falder. When I went there—they were at supper—my sister wanted to give me a kiss—I know. But he just looked at her, and said: 'What have you come for?' Well, I pocketed my pride and I said: 'Aren't you going to give me your hand, Jim? Cis is, I know,' I said. 'Look here!' he said, 'that's all very well, but we'd better come to an understanding. I've been expecting you, and I've made up my mind. I'll give you twenty-five pounds to go to Canada with.' 'I see,' I said—'good riddance! No, thanks; keep your twenty-five pounds.' Friendship's a queer thing when you've been where I have.

Cokeson. I understand. Will you take the twenty-five pounds from me? [*Flustered, as* FALDER *regards him with a queer smile.*] Quite without prejudice; I meant it kindly.

Falder. They wouldn't let me in.

Cokeson. Oh! Ah! No! You aren't looking the thing.

Falder. I've slept in the Park three nights this week. The dawns aren't all poetry there. But meeting her—I feel a different man this morning. I've often thought the being fond of her's the best thing about me; it's sacred, somehow—and yet it did for me. That's queer, isn't it?

Cokeson. I'm sure we're all very sorry for you.

Falder. That's what I've found, Mr. Cokeson. Awfully sorry for me. [*With quiet bitterness.*] But it doesn't do to associate with criminals!

Cokeson. Come, come, it's no use calling yourself names. That never did a man any good. Put a face on it.

Falder. It's easy enough to put a face on it, sir, when you're independent. Try it when you're down like me. They talk about giving you your deserts. Well, I think I've had just a bit over.

Cokeson [*eyeing him askance over his spectacles*]. I hope they haven't made a Socialist of you.

[FALDER *is suddenly still, as if brooding over his past self; he utters a peculiar laugh.*

Cokeson. You must give them credit for the best intentions. Really you must. Nobody wishes you harm, I'm sure.

Falder. I believe that, Mr. Cokeson. Nobody wishes you harm, but they down you all the same. This feeling—— [*He stares round him, as though at something closing in.*] It's crushing me. [*With sudden impersonality.*] I know it is.

Cokeson [*horribly disturbed*]. There's nothing there! We must try and take it quiet. I'm sure I've often had you in my prayers. Now leave it to me. I'll use my gumption and take 'em when they're jolly.

[*As he speaks the two partners come in.*

Cokeson [*rather disconcerted, but trying to put them all at ease*]. I didn't expect you quite so soon. I've just been having a talk with this young man. I think you'll remember him.

James [*with a grave, keen look*]. Quite well. How are you, Falder?

Walter [*holding out his hand almost timidly*]. Very glad to see you again, Falder.

Falder [*who has recovered his self-control, takes the hand*]. Thank you, sir.

Cokeson. Just a word, Mr. James. [*To* FALDER, *pointing to the clerks' office.*] You might go in there a minute. You know your way. Our junior won't be coming this morning. His wife's just had a little family.

[FALDER *goes uncertainly out into the clerks' office.*

Cokeson [*confidentially*]. I'm bound to tell you all about it. He's quite penitent. But there's a prejudice against him. And you're not seeing him to advantage this morning; he's undernourished. It's very trying to go without your dinner.

James. Is that so, Cokeson?

Cokeson. I wanted to ask you. He's had his lesson. Now *we* know all about him, and we want a clerk. There is a young fellow applying, but I'm keeping him in the air.

James. A gaol-bird in the office, Cokeson? I don't see it.

Walter. 'The rolling of the chariot-wheels of Justice!' I've never got that out of my head.

James. I've nothing to reproach myself with in this affair. What's he been doing since he came out?

Cokeson. He's had one or two places, but he hasn't kept them. He's sensitive—quite natural. Seems to fancy everybody's down on him.

James. Bad sign. Don't like the fellow—never did from the first. 'Weak character' 's written all over him.

Walter. I think we owe him a leg up.

James. He brought it all on himself.

Walter. The doctrine of full responsibility doesn't quite hold in these days.

James [*rather grimly*]. You'll find it safer to hold it for all that, my boy.

Walter. For oneself, yes—not for other people, thanks.

James. Well! I don't want to be hard.

Cokeson. I'm glad to hear you say that. He seems to see something [*spreading his arms*] round him. 'Tisn't healthy.

James. What about the woman he was mixed up with? I saw someone uncommonly like her outside as we came in.

Cokeson. *That*! Well, I can't keep anything from you. He has met her.

James. Is she with her husband?

Cokeson. No.

James. Falder living with her, I suppose?

Cokeson [*desperately trying to retain the new-found jollity*]. I don't know that of my own knowledge. 'Tisn't my business.

James. It's *our* business, if we're going to engage him, Cokeson.

Cokeson [*reluctantly*]. I ought to tell you, perhaps. I've had the party here this morning.

James. I thought so. [*To* WALTER.] No, my dear boy, it won't do. Too shady altogether!

Cokeson. The two things together make it very awkward for you—I see that.

Walter [*tentatively*]. I don't quite know what we have to do with his private life.

James. No, no! He must make a clean sheet of it, or he can't come here.

Walter. Poor devil!

Cokeson. Will you have him in? [*And as* JAMES *nods*.] I think I can get him to see reason.

James [*grimly*]. You can leave that to me, Cokeson.

Walter [*to* JAMES, *in a low voice, while* COKESON *is summoning* FALDER]. His whole future may depend on what we do, dad.

[FALDER *comes in. He has pulled himself together, and presents a steady front*.

James. Now look here, Falder. My son and I want to give you another chance; but there are two things I must say to you. In the first place: It's no good coming here as a victim. If you've any notion that you've been unjustly treated—get rid of it. You can't play fast and loose with morality and hope to go scot-free. If society didn't take care of itself, nobody would—the sooner you realize that the better.

Falder. Yes, sir; but—may I say something?

James. Well?

Falder. I had a lot of time to think it over in prison.

[*He stops*.

Cokeson [*encouraging him*]. I'm sure you did.

Falder. There were all sorts there. And what I mean, sir, is, that if we'd been treated differently the first time, and put under somebody that could look after us a bit, and not put in prison, not a quarter of us would ever have got there.

James [*shaking his head*]. I'm afraid I've very grave doubts of that, Falder.

Falder [*with a gleam of malice*]. Yes, sir, so I found.

James. My good fellow, don't forget that you began it.

Falder. I never wanted to do wrong.

James. Perhaps not. But you did.

Falder [*with all the bitterness of his past suffering*]. It's knocked me out of time. [*Pulling himself up.*] That is, I mean, I'm not what I was.

James. This isn't encouraging for us, Falder.

Cokeson. He's putting it awkwardly, Mr. James.

Falder [*throwing over his caution from the intensity of his feeling*]. I mean it, Mr. Cokeson.

James. Now, lay aside all those thoughts, Falder, and look to the future.

Falder [*almost eagerly*]. Yes, sir, but you don't understand what prison is. It's here it gets you. [*He grips his chest.*

Cokeson [*in a whisper to* JAMES]. I told you he wanted nourishment.

Walter. Yes, but, my dear fellow, that'll pass away. Time's merciful.

Falder [*with his face twitching*]. I hope so, sir.

James [*much more gently*]. Now, my boy, what you've got to do is to put all the past behind you and build yourself up a steady reputation. And that brings me to the second thing. This woman you were mixed up with—you must give us your word, you know, to have done with that. There's no chance of your keeping straight if you're going to begin your future with such a relationship.

Falder [*looking from one to the other with a hunted expression*]. But, sir . . . but, sir . . . it's the one thing I looked forward to all that time. And she too . . . I couldn't find her before last night.

[*During this and what follows* COKESON *becomes more and more uneasy*.

James. This is painful, Falder. But you must see for yourself that it's impossible for a firm like this to close its eyes to everything. Give us this proof of your resolve to keep straight, and you can come back—not otherwise.

Falder [*after staring at* JAMES, *suddenly stiffens himself*]. I couldn't give her up. I couldn't! Oh, sir! I'm all she's got to look to. And I'm sure she's all I've got.

James. I'm very sorry, Falder, but I must be firm. It's for the benefit of you both in the long run. No good can come of this connection. It was the cause of all your disaster.

Falder. But, sir, it means—having gone through all that—getting broken up—my nerves are in an awful state—for nothing. I did it for her.

James. Come! If she's anything of a woman she'll see it for herself. She won't want to drag you down further. If there were a prospect of your being able to marry her—it might be another thing.

Falder. It's not my fault, sir, that she couldn't get rid of him—she would have if she could. That's been the whole trouble from the beginning. [*Looking suddenly at* WALTER.] . . . If anybody would help her! It's only money wanted now, I'm sure.

Cokeson [*breaking in, as* WALTER *hesitates, and is about to speak*]. I don't think we need consider that—it's rather far-fetched.

Falder [*to* WALTER, *appealing*]. He must have given her full cause since; she could prove that he drove her to leave him.

Walter. I'm inclined to do what you say, Falder, if it can be managed.

Falder. Oh, sir!

[*He goes to the window and looks down into the street.*

Cokeson [*hurriedly*]. You don't take me, Mr. Walter. I have my reasons.

Falder [*from the window*]. She's down there, sir. Will you see her? I can beckon to her from here.

[WALTER *hesitates, and looks from* COKESON *to* JAMES.

James [*with a sharp nod*]. Yes, let her come.

[FALDER *beckons from the window.*

Cokeson [*in a low fluster to* JAMES *and* WALTER]. No, Mr. James. She's not been quite what she ought to ha' been, while this young man's been away. She's lost her chance. We can't consult how to swindle the Law.

[FALDER *has come from the window. The three men look at him in a sort of awed silence.*

Falder [*with instinctive apprehension of some change—looking from one to the other*]. There's been nothing between us, sir, to prevent it. . . . What I said at the trial was true. And last night we only just sat in the Park.

[SWEEDLE *comes in from the outer office.*

Cokeson. What is it?

Sweedle. Mrs. Honeywill. [*There is silence.*

James. Show her in.

[RUTH *comes slowly in, and stands stoically with* FALDER *on one side and the three men on the other. No one speaks.* COKESON *turns to his table, bending over his papers as though the burden of the situation were forcing him back into his accustomed groove.*

James [*sharply*]. Shut the door there. [SWEEDLE *shuts the door.*] We've asked you to come up because there are certain facts to be faced in this matter. I understand you have only just met Falder again.

Ruth. Yes—only yesterday.

James. He's told us about himself, and we're very sorry for him. I've promised to take him back here if he'll make a fresh start. [*Looking steadily at* RUTH.] This is a matter that requires courage, ma'am.

[RUTH, *who is looking at* FALDER, *begins to twist her hands in front of her as though prescient of disaster*.

Falder. Mr. Walter How is good enough to say that he'll help us to get a divorce.

[RUTH *flashes a startled glance at* JAMES *and* WALTER.

James. I don't think that's practicable, Falder.

Falder. But, sir——!

James [*steadily*]. Now, Mrs. Honeywill. You're fond of him.

Ruth. Yes, sir; I love him. [*She looks miserably at* FALDER.

James. Then you don't want to stand in his way, do you?

Ruth [*in a faint voice*]. I could take care of him.

James. The best way you can take care of him will be to give him up.

Falder. Nothing shall make me give you up. You can get a divorce. There's been nothing between us, has there?

Ruth [*mournfully shaking her head—without looking at him*]. No.

Falder. We'll keep apart till it's over, sir; if you'll only help us—we promise.

James [*to* RUTH]. You see the thing plainly, don't you? You see what I mean?

Ruth [*just above a whisper*]. Yes.

Cokeson [*to himself*]. There's a dear woman.

James. The situation is impossible.

Ruth. Must I, sir?

James [*forcing himself to look at her*]. I put it to you, ma'am. His future is in your hands.

Ruth [*miserably*]. I want to do the best for him.

James [*a little huskily*]. That's right, that's right!

Falder. I don't understand. You're not going to give me up—after all this? There's something——[*Starting forward to* JAMES.] Sir, I swear solemnly there's been nothing between us.

James. I believe you, Falder. Come, my lad, be as plucky as she is.

Falder. Just now you were going to help us. [*He stares at* RUTH, *who is standing absolutely still; his face and hands twitch and quiver as the truth dawns on him.*] What is it? You've not been——

Walter. Father!

James [*hurriedly*]. There, there! That'll do, that'll do! I'll give you your chance, Falder. Don't let me know what you do with yourselves, that's all.

Falder [*as if he has not heard*]. Ruth?

[RUTH *looks at him; and* FALDER *covers his face with his hands. There is silence.*

Cokeson [*suddenly*]. There's someone out there. [*To* RUTH.] Go in here. You'll feel better by yourself for a minute.

[*He points to the clerks' room and moves towards the outer office.* FALDER *does not move.* RUTH *puts out her hand timidly. He shrinks back from the touch. She turns and goes miserably into the clerks' room. With a brusque movement he follows, seizing her by the shoulder just inside the doorway.* COKESON *shuts the door.*

James [*pointing to the outer office*]. Get rid of that, who ever it is.

Sweedle [*opening the office door, in a scared voice*]. Detective-Sergeant Wister.

[*The* DETECTIVE *enters, and closes the door behind him.*

Wister. Sorry to disturb you, sir. A clerk you had here, two years and a half ago. I arrested him in this room.

James. What about him?

Wister. I thought perhaps I might get his whereabouts from you. [*There is an awkward silence.*

Cokeson [*pleasantly, coming to the rescue*]. We're not responsible for his movements; you know that.

James. What do you want with him?

Wister. He's failed to report himself lately.

Walter. Has he to keep in touch with the police then?

Wister. We're bound to know his whereabouts. I dare say we shouldn't interfere, sir, but we've just heard there's a serious matter of obtaining employment with a forged reference. What with the two things together—we must have him.

[*Again there is silence.* WALTER *and* COKESON *steal glances at* JAMES, *who stands staring steadily at the detective.*

Cokeson [*expansively*]. We're very busy at the moment. If you could make it convenient to call again we might be able to tell you then.

James [*decisively*]. I'm a servant of the Law, but I dislike peaching. In fact, I can't do such a thing. If you want him you must find him without us.

[*As he speaks his eye falls on* FALDER'*s cap, still lying on the table, and his face contracts.*

Wister [*noting the gesture—quietly*]. Very good, sir. I ought to warn you that sheltering——

James. I shelter no one. But you mustn't come here and ask questions which it's not my business to answer.

Wister [*dryly*]. I won't trouble you further then, gentlemen.

Cokeson. I'm sorry we couldn't give you the information. You quite understand, don't you? Good morning!

[WISTER *turns to go, but instead of going to the door of the outer office he goes to the door of the clerks' room.*

Cokeson. The other door . . . the other door!

[WISTER *opens the clerks' door.* RUTH'*s voice is heard:* 'Oh, do!' *and* FALDER'*s*: 'I can't!' *There is a little pause; then, with sharp fright,* RUTH *says:* 'Who's that?' WISTER *has gone in.*

[*The three men look aghast at the door.*

Wister [*from within*]. Keep back, please!

[*He comes swiftly out with his arm twisted in* FALDER'*s. The latter gives a white, staring look at the three men.*

Walter. Let him go this time, for God's sake!

Wister. I couldn't take the responsibility, sir.

Falder [*with a queer, desperate laugh*]. Good!

[*Flinging a look back at* RUTH, *he throws up his head, and goes out through the outer office, half dragging* WISTER *after him.*

Walter [*with despair*]. That finishes him. It'll go on forever now.

[SWEEDLE *can be seen staring through the outer door. There are sounds of footsteps descending the stone stairs; suddenly a dull thud, a faint* 'My God!' *in* WISTER'*s voice.*

James. What's that?

[SWEEDLE *dashes forward. The door swings to behind him. There is dead silence.*

Walter [*starting forward to the inner room*]. The woman—she's fainting.

[*He and* COKESON *support the fainting* RUTH *from the doorway of the clerks' room.*

Cokeson [*distracted*]. Here, my dear! There, there!

Walter. Have you any brandy?

Cokeson. I've got sherry.

Walter. Get it, then. Quick!

[*He places* RUTH *in a chair—which* JAMES *has dragged forward.*

Cokeson [*with sherry*]. Here! It's good strong sherry.

[*They try to force the sherry between her lips. There is the sound of feet, and they stop to listen. The outer door is reopened—*WISTER *and* SWEEDLE *are seen carrying some burden.*

James [*hurrying forward*]. What is it?

[*They lay the burden down in the outer office, out of sight, and all but* RUTH *cluster round it, speaking in hushed voices.*

Wister. He jumped—neck's broken.

Walter. Good God!

Wister. He must have been mad to think he could give me the slip like that. And what was it—just a few months!

Walter [*bitterly*]. Was that all?

James. What a desperate thing! [*Then, in a voice unlike his own.*] Run for a doctor—you! [SWEEDLE *rushes from the outer office.*] An ambulance!

[WISTER *goes out. On* RUTH'*s face an expression of fear and horror has been seen growing, as if she dared not turn towards the voices. She now rises and steals towards them.*

Walter [*turning suddenly*]. Look!

[*The three men shrink back out of her way.* RUTH *drops on her knees by the body.*

Ruth [*in a whisper*]. What is it? He's not breathing. [*She crouches over him.*] My dear! My pretty!

[*In the outer office doorway the figures of men are seen standing.*

Ruth [*leaping to her feet*]. No, no! No, no! He's dead!

[*The figures of the men shrink back.*

Cokeson [*stealing forward. In a hoarse voice*]. There, there, poor dear woman!

[*At the sound behind her* RUTH *faces round at him.*

Cokeson. No one'll touch him now! Never again! He's safe with gentle Jesus!

[RUTH *stands as though turned to stone in the doorway, staring at* COKESON, *who, bending humbly before her, holds out his hand as one would to a lost dog.*

THE CURTAIN FALLS.

HINDLE WAKES

WILLIAM STANLEY HOUGHTON

(1881–1913)

Born Ashton-upon-Mersey, Cheshire. Educated Manchester Grammar School and elsewhere. Worked in textile industry until 1912. Contributed dramatic and literary criticism to the *Manchester Guardian*. Lived in Paris, 1912–13, but was taken ill and returned to Manchester, where he died.

His plays included *The Dear Departed* (1908); *Independent Means* (1909); *The Younger Generation* (1910); *Hindle Wakes* (1912); *The Perfect Cure* (1913); *Trust the People* (1913).

HINDLE WAKES

A PLAY IN THREE ACTS

by

Stanley Houghton

HINDLE WAKES

First produced by Miss Horniman's Repertory Company *from the Gaiety Theatre, Manchester, before the London Stage Society, at the Aldwych Theatre,* 16 *June* 1912, *with the following cast:*

Mrs. Hawthorn	Miss Ada King
Christopher Hawthorn	Mr. Charles Bibby
Fanny Hawthorn	Miss Edyth Goodall
Mrs. Jeffcote	Miss Daisy England
Nathaniel Jeffcote	Mr. Herbert Lomas
Alan Jeffcote	Mr. J. V. Bryant
Sir Timothy Farrar	Mr. Edward Landor
Beatrice Farrar	Miss Sybil Thorndike
Ada	Miss Hilda Davies

The Play produced by Mr. Lewis Casson

NOTE ON
THE LANCASHIRE DIALECT

This play is about Lancashire people. In the smaller Lancashire towns it is quite usual for well-to-do persons, and for persons who have received good educations at grammar schools and technical schools, to drop more or less into dialect when familiar, or when excited, or to point a joke. It is even usual for them to mix their speech with perfect naturalness. 'You' and 'thou' may jostle one another in the same sentence, as, for instance: 'You can't catch it, I tell thee.' As a general rule they will miss out a good many 'h's', and will pronounce vowels with an open or flat sound. The final consonants will usually be clipped. At the same time it is unnecessary laboriously to adopt any elaborate or fearsome method of pronunciation. The Lancashire dialect of to-day—except amongst the roughest class in the most out-of-the-way districts—has had many of its corners rubbed off. It varies in its accents, too, in each separate town, that it may be attempted with impunity by all save the most incompetent. The poorest attempt will probably be good enough to pass muster as 'Manchester', which has hardly a special accent of its own, but boasts a tongue composed of all the other Lancashire dialects mixed up, polished and made politer, and deprived of their raciness.

(*from the* 1*st Edition of* HINDLE WAKES)

HINDLE WAKES

ACT I

SCENE I. *The scene is triangular, representing a corner of the living-room kitchen of No.* 137, *Burnley Road, Hindle, a house rented at about 7s. 6d. a week. In the left-hand wall, low down, there is a door leading to the scullery. In the same wall, but further away from the spectator, is a window looking on to the back yard. A dresser stands in front of the window. About half-way up the right-hand wall is the door leading to the hall or passage. Nearer, against the same wall, a high cupboard for china and crockery. The fireplace is not visible, being in one of the walls not represented. However, down in the L. corner of the stage is an arm-chair, which stands by the hearth. In the middle of the room is a square table, with chairs on each side. The room is cheerful and comfortable. It is nine o'clock on a warm August evening. Through the window can be seen the darkening sky, as the blind is not drawn. Against the sky an outline of roof-tops and mill chimneys. The only light is the dim twilight from the open window. Thunder is in the air. When the curtain rises* CHRISTOPHER HAWTHORN, *a decent, white bearded man of nearly sixty, is sitting in the arm-chair smoking a pipe.* MRS. HAWTHORN, *a keen, sharp-faced woman of fifty-five, is standing gazing out of the window. There is a flash of lightning and a rumble of thunder far away.*

Mrs. Hawthorn. It's passing over. There'll be no rain.

Christopher. Ay! We could do with some rain. [*There is a flash of lightning.*] Pull down the blind and light the gas.

Mrs. Hawthorn. What for?

Christopher. It's more cosy-like with the gas.

Mrs. Hawthorn. You're not afraid of the lightning?

Christopher. I want to look at that railway guide.

Mrs. Hawthorn. What's the good? We've looked at it twice already. There's no train from Blackpool till five-past ten, and it's only just on nine now.

Christopher. Happen we've made a mistake.

Mrs. Hawthorn. Happen we've not. Besides, what's the good of a railway guide? You know trains run as they like on Bank Holiday.

Christopher. Ay! Perhaps you're right. You don't think she'll come round by Manchester?

Mrs. Hawthorn. What would she be doing coming round by Manchester?

Christopher. You can get that road from Blackpool.

Mrs. Hawthorn. Yes. If she's coming from Blackpool.

Christopher. Have you thought she may not come at all?

Mrs. Hawthorn [*grimly*]. What do you take me for?

Christopher. You never hinted.

Mrs. Hawthorn. No use putting them sort of ideas into your head. [*Another flash and a peal of thunder.*

Christopher. Well, well, those are lucky who haven't to travel at all on Bank Holiday.

Mrs. Hawthorn. Unless they've got a motor-car, like Nat Jeffcote's lad.

Christopher. Nay. *He's* not got one.

Mrs. Hawthorn. What? Why, I saw him with my own eyes setting out in it last Saturday week after the mill shut.

Christopher. Ay! He's gone off these Wakes with his pal George Ramsbottom. A couple of thick beggars, those two!

Mrs. Hawthorn. Then what do you mean telling me he's not got a motor-car?

Christopher. I said he hadn't got one of his own. It's his father's. You don't catch Nat Jeffcote parting with owt before his time. That's how he holds his lad in check, as you might say.

Mrs. Hawthorn. Alan Jeffcote's seldom short of cash. He spends plenty.

Christopher. Ay! Nat gives him what he asks for, and doesn't want to know how he spends it either. But he's *got* to ask for it first. Nat can stop supplies any time if he's a mind.

Mrs. Hawthorn. That's likely, isn't it?

Christopher. Queerer things have happened. You don't know Nat like I do. He's a bad one to get across with.

[*Another flash and gentle peal.* MRS. HAWTHORN *gets up.*

Mrs. Hawthorn. I'll light the gas.

[*She pulls down the blind and lights the gas.*

Christopher. When I met Nat this morning he told me that Alan had telegraphed from Llandudno on Saturday asking for twenty pounds.

Mrs. Hawthorn. From Llandudno?

Christopher. Ay! Reckon he's been stopping there. Run short of brass.

Mrs. Hawthorn. And did he send it?

Christopher. Of course he sent it. Nat doesn't stint the lad. [*He laughs quietly*.] Eh, but he *can* get through it, though!

Mrs. Hawthorn. Look here. What are you going to say to Fanny when she comes?

Christopher. Ask her where she's been.

Mrs. Hawthorn. Ask her where she's been! Of course we'll do that. But suppose she won't tell us?

Christopher. She's always been a good girl.

Mrs. Hawthorn. She's always gone her own road. Suppose she tells us to mind our own business?

Christopher .I reckon it *is* my business to know what she's been up to.

Mrs. Hawthorn. Don't you forget it. And don't let her forget it either. If you do, I promise you I won't!

Christopher. All right. Where's that postcard?

Mrs. Hawthorn. Little good taking heed of that.

[CHRISTOPHER *rises and gets a picture postcard from the dresser*.

Christopher [*reading*]. 'Shall be home before late on Monday. Lovely weather.' [*Looking at the picture*.] North Pier, Blackpool. Very like, too.

Mrs. Hawthorn [*suddenly*]. Let's have a look. When was it posted?

Christopher. It's dated Sunday.

Mrs. Hawthorn. That's nowt to go by. Anyone can put the wrong date. What's the post-mark? [*She scrutinises it*.] 'August 5th, summat P.M.' I can't make out the time.

Christopher. August 5th. That was yesterday, all right. There'd only be one post on Sunday.

Mrs. Hawthorn. Then she was in Blackpool up to yesterday, that's certain,

Christopher. Ay!

Mrs. Hawthorn. Well, it's a mystery.

Christopher [*shaking his head*]. Or summat worse.

Mrs. Hawthorn. Eh? You don't think *that*, eh?

Christopher. I don't know what to think.

Mrs. Hawthorn. Nor me neither.

[*They sit silent for a time. There is a rumble of thunder, far away. After it has died away a knock is heard at the front door. They turn and look at each other.* MRS. HAWTHORN *rises and goes out in silence. In a few moments* FANNY HAWTHORN *comes in, followed by* MRS. HAWTHORN. FANNY *is a sturdy, determined, dark little girl, with thick lips, a broad, short nose and big black eyes. She is dressed rather smartly, but not very tastefully. She stands by the table unpinning her hat and talking cheerfully.* MRS. HAWTHORN *stands by the door and* CHRISTOPHER *remains in his chair Both look at* FANNY *queerly.*

Fanny. Well, you didn't expect me as soon as this, I'll bet. I came round by Manchester. They said the trains would run better that way to-night. Bank Holiday, you know. I always think they let the Manchester trains through before any of the others, don't you?

Mrs. Hawthorn. We didn't see how you were to get here till past ten if you came direct. We've been looking up in the Guide.

Fanny. No. I wasn't for coming direct at any price. Mary wanted to.

Christopher. Mary!

[CHRISTOPHER *is about to rise in astonishment, but* MRS. HAWTHORN *makes signs to him behind* FANNY'*s back.*

Mrs. Hawthorn. Oh! So Mary Hollins wanted to come back the other way, did she?

Fanny. Yes. But I wasn't having any. They said the Manchester trains would be—oh! I've told you all that already.

Mrs. Hawthorn. So you've had a good time, Fanny.

Fanny. Rather! A fair treat. What do *you* think?

Mrs. Hawthorn. Was Mary Hollins with you all the time?

Fanny. Of course she was.

[*She steals a puzzled glance at* MRS. HAWTHORN.

Mrs. Hawthorn. And she came back with you to-night?

Fanny. Yes.

Mrs. Hawthorn. And where's she gone now?

Fanny. She's gone home of course. Where else should she go? [*There is a short pause.*

Christopher [*quietly*]. You're telling lies, my girl.

Fanny. What, father?

Christopher. That's not the truth you've just been saying.

Fanny. What's not the truth?

Christopher. You didn't spend the week-end in Blackpool with Mary Hollins.

Fanny. Who says I didn't?

Christopher. I say so.

Fanny. Why do you think I didn't father?

Christopher. Well, did you?

Fanny. Yes, I did. [CHRISTOPHER *turns helplessly to his wife.*

Mrs. Hawthorn. All right, Chris, wait a minute. Look here, Fanny, it's no use trying to make us believe you've been away with Mary.

Fanny. What? I can bring you any number of folk out of Hindle who saw us in Blackpool last week.

Mrs. Hawthorn. Last week, happen. Not this week-end?

Fanny. Yes.

Mrs. Hawthorn. Bring them, then.

Fanny. How can I bring them to-night? They've most of them not come back yet.

Mrs. Hawthorn. Tell us who to ask, then.

Fanny [*thinking*]. Ask Polly Birtwistle. Or Ethel Slater.

Mrs. Hawthorn. Yes. After you've got at them and given them a hint what to say.

Fanny. Of course if you'll believe that it's no use asking Mary. You'd only say she was telling lies as well.

[*There is a pause.*

Fanny. Will you go round and see Mary?

Christopher. No.

Mrs. Hawthorn. Fanny, it's no use seeing Mary. You may as well own up and tell us where you've been.

Fanny. I've been to Blackpool with Mary Hollins.

Mrs. Hawthorn. You've not. You weren't there this week-end.

Fanny. Why, I sent you a picture postcard on Sunday.

Mrs. Hawthorn. Yes, we got that. Who posted it?

Fanny. I posted it myself at the pillar-box on the Central Pier.

[*There is a pause. They do not believe her.*

Fanny [*flaring up*]. I tell you I've been all week-end at Blackpool with Mary Hollins.

Christopher [*quietly*]. No, you've not.

Fanny [*pertly*]. Well, that's settled then. There's no need to talk about it any more. [*A pause.* FANNY *nervously twists her handkerchief.*] Look here. Who's been saying I didn't?

Christopher. We know you didn't.

Fanny. But you can't know.

Mrs. Hawthorn. As certain as there's a God in Heaven we know it.

Fanny. Well, that's not so certain after all.

Christopher. Fanny! Take heed what you're saying.

Fanny. Why can't you speak out? What do you know? Tell me that.

Mrs. Hawthorn. It's not for us to tell you anything. It's for you to tell us where you've been.

Fanny [*mutinously*]. I've told you.

[*They do not speak.* FANNY *rises quickly.*

Mrs. Hawthorn. Where are you going?

Fanny. Are you trying to hinder me from going out when I please, now? I'm going to see Mary Hollins.

Mrs. Hawthorn. What for?

Fanny. To fetch her here. You shall see her whether you like it or not.

Christopher. Fanny, I've already seen Mary Hollins.

[FANNY *turns and stares at him in surprise.*

Fanny. When?

Christopher. This morning.

Fanny. She was at Blackpool this morning.

Christopher. So was I.

Fanny [*amazed*]. What were you doing there?

Christopher. I went there with Jim Hollins. We went on purpose to see Mary.

Fanny. So it's Mary as has given me away, is it?

Christopher [*nodding, slowly*]. Yes. You might say so.

Fanny [*angrily*]. I'll talk to her.

Christopher. It wasn't her fault. She couldn't help it.

Mrs. Hawthorn. Now will you tell us where you've been?

Fanny. No, I won't. I'll see Mary first. What did she say to you?

Christopher. When I told thee I went with Jim Hollins to Blackpool, I didn't tell thee quite everything, lass. [*Gently.*] Mary Hollins was drowned yesterday afternoon.

Fanny. What! [*She stares at* CHRISTOPHER *in horror.*

Christopher. It was one of them sailing boats. Run down by an excursion steamer. There was over twenty people on board. Seven of them was drowned.

Fanny. Oh! My poor Mary!

[FANNY *sinks down into her chair and stares dully at* CHRISTOPHER.

Mrs. Hawthorn. You didn't know that?

Fanny [*shaking her head*]. No, no.

[*She buries her head in her arms on the table and begins to sob.*

Mrs. Hawthorn. Now then, Fanny.

[*She is about to resume her inquisition.*

Christopher. Hold on, mother. Wait a bit. Give her a chance.

Mrs. Hawthorn [*waving him aside*]. Now then, Fanny. You see you've been telling lies all the time. [FANNY *sobs.*

Mrs. Hawthorn. Listen to me. You weren't at Blackpool this week-end.

Fanny [*to herself*]. Poor, poor Mary!

Mrs. Hawthorn [*patiently*]. You weren't at Blackpool this week-end. [FANNY *sobs.*

Mrs. Hawthorn. Were you?

Fanny [*sobbing*]. N—no.

[*She shakes her head without raising it.*

Mrs. Hawthorn. Where were you?

Fanny. Shan't tell you.

Mrs. Hawthorn. You went away for the week-end? [*No answer.*] Did you go alone? [*No answer.*] You didn't go alone, of course. [*No answer.*] Who did you go with?

Fanny. Leave me alone, mother.

Mrs. Hawthorn. Who did you go with? Did you go with a fellow? [FANNY *stops sobbing. She raises her head the tiniest bit so that she can see her mother without seeming to do so. Her eyes are just visible above her arm.* MRS. HAWTHORN *marks the movement, nevertheless, nodding.*] Yes. You went with a chap?

Fanny [*quickly dropping her head again*]. No, I didn't.

Mrs. Hawthorn [*roughly*]. You little liar, you did! You know you did! Who was he?

[MRS. HAWTHORN *seizes* FANNY *by the shoulder and shakes her in exasperation.* FANNY *sobs.*

Mrs. Hawthorn. Will you tell us who he was?

Fanny [*sharply*]. No, I won't. [*There is a slight pause.*

Christopher. This is what happens to many a lass, but I never thought to have it happen to a lass of mine!

Mrs. Hawthorn. Why didn't you get wed if you were so curious. There's plenty would have had you.

Fanny. Chance is a fine thing. Happen I wouldn't have had them!

Mrs. Hawthorn. Happen you'll be sorry for it before long. There's not so many will have you now, if this gets about.

Christopher. He ought to wed her.

Mrs. Hawthorn. Of course he ought to wed her, and shall too, or I'll know the reason why! Come now, who's the chap?

Fanny. Shan't tell you.

[*She places her hand on* FANNY*'s arm.* FANNY *turns round fiercely and flings it off.*

Fanny. Leave me alone, can't you? You ought to be thankful he did take me away. It saved my life, anyhow.

Mrs. Hawthorn. How do you make that out?

Fanny. I'd have been drowned with Mary if I hadn't gone to Llandudno.

Mrs. Hawthorn. Llandudno? Did you say——?

[*She stops short.*

Christopher. Why mother, that's——

Mrs. Hawthorn [*cutting him short*]. Be quiet, can't you?

[*She reflects for a moment, and then sits down at the other side of the table, opposite* FANNY.

Mrs. Hawthorn [*with meaning*]. When you were in Llandudno did you happen to run across Alan Jeffcote?

[FANNY *looks up and they stare hard at each other.*

Fanny [*at length*]. How did you know?

Mrs. Hawthorn [*smiling grimly*]. I didn't. You've just told me.

Fanny [*gives a low moan*]. Oh! [*She buries her head and sobs.*

Mrs. Hawthorn [*to* CHRISTOPHER]. Well. What do you think of her now?

Christopher [*dazed*]. Nat Jeffcote's lad!

Mrs. Hawthorn. Ay! Nat Jeffcote's lad. But what does that matter? If it hadn't been him it would have been some other lad.

Christopher. Nat and me were lads together. We were pals.

Mrs. Hawthorn. Well, now thy girl and Nat's lad are pals. Pull thyself together, man. What art going to do about it?

Christopher. I don't know, rightly.

Mrs. Hawthorn. Aren't you going to give her a talking-to?

Christopher. What's the good?

Mrs. Hawthorn. What's the good? Well, I like that! My father would have got a stick to me. [*She turns to* FANNY.] Did he promise to wed you?

Fanny [*in low voice*]. No.

Mrs. Hawthorn. Why not?

Fanny. Never asked him.

Mrs. Hawthorn. You little fool! Have you no common sense at all? What did you do it for if you didn't make him promise to wed you? [FANNY *does not reply.*] Do you hear me? What made you do it? [FANNY *sobs.*

Christopher. Let her be, mother.

Mrs. Hawthorn. She's turned stupid. [*To* FANNY.] When did you go? [*No answer.*] Did you go in his motor-car? [*No answer.*] Where did you stay? [*There is no answer, so she shakes* FANNY.] Will you take heed of what I'm saying? Haven't you got a tongue in your head? Tell us exactly what took place.

Fanny. I won't tell you anything more.

Mrs. Hawthorn. We'll see about that.

Christopher [*rising*]. That's enough, mother. We'll leave her alone to-night. [*He touches* FANNY *on the shoulder*.] Now then, lass, no one's going to harm thee. Stop thy crying. Thou'd better get upstairs to bed. Happen thou's fagged out.

Mrs. Hawthorn. You *are* soft. You're never going to let her off so easy?

Christopher. There's plenty of time to tackle her in the morning. Come, lass. [FANNY *rises and stands by the table, wiping her eyes*.] Get to bed and have some sleep, if thou can.

[*Without a word* FANNY *slowly goes to the door and out of the room. She does not look at either of them.*

Mrs. Hawthorn. Now then. What's to be done?

Christopher. Ay! That's it.

Mrs. Hawthorn. You'll have to waken up a bit if we're to make the most of this. I can tell you what's the first job. You'll have to go and see Nathaniel Jeffcote.

Christopher. I'll see him at the mill to-morrow.

Mrs. Hawthorn. To-morrow! You'll go and see him to-night. Go up to the house at Bank Top. If Alan's come home with Fanny he'll be there as well, and you can kill two birds with one stone.

Christopher. It's a nasty job.

Mrs. Hawthorn. It's got to be done, and the sooner the better. How would it be if I come with you?

Christopher [*hastily*]. Nay. I'll go alone.

Mrs. Hawthorn. I'm afraid you'll be too soft. It's a fine chance, and don't you forget it.

Christopher. A fine chance?

Mrs. Hawthorn. To get her wed, thou great stupid. We're not going to be content with less. We'll show them up if they turn nasty.

Christopher. He *ought* to wed her. I don't know what Nat'll say.

Mrs. Hawthorn. Look here, if you're not going to stand out for your rights, I'll come myself. I'm not afraid of Nat Jeffcote, not if he owned twenty mills like Daisy Bank.

Christopher. I'm not afraid of him, neither, though he's a bad man to tackle. [*He rises.*] Where's my hat?

[MRS. HAWTHORN *gives him his hat and stick, and he goes to the door.*

Mrs. Hawthorn. I say. I wonder if she's done this on purpose, after all. Plenty of girls have made good matches that way.

Christopher. She said they never mentioned marriage. You heard her.

Mrs. Hawthorn. Well, he mightn't have gone with her if she had. Happen she's cleverer than we think!

Christopher. She always was a deep one.

Mrs. Hawthorn. That's how Bamber's lass got hold of young Greenwood.

Christopher. But there was a——He couldn't help it, so well.

Mrs. Hawthorn. Yes. [*She reflects.*] Ah, well. You never know what may happen.

[CHRISTOPHER *goes out followed by* MRS. HAWTHORN.

THE CURTAIN FALLS.

SCENE II. *The breakfast-room at* NATHANIEL JEFFCOTE'*s house, Bank Top, Hindle Vale, is almost vast, for the house is one of those great old-fashioned places standing in ample grounds that are to be found on the outskirts of the smaller Lancashire manufacturing towns. They are inhabited by wealthy manufacturers who have resisted the temptation to live at St. Anne's-on-the-Sea, or Blackpool. In the wall facing the spectator is the door from the hall, which when the door is open can be seen distinctly, a big square place. The fire-place is in the right-hand wall, and a bow window in the left-hand one. The furniture is solid and costly, but the room is comfortable and looks as if it is intended to be lived in. A table stands in the middle, a sideboard near the door, arm-chairs near the hearth, whilst other chairs and furniture (including a bookcase filled with standard works) complete the rather ponderous interior. The* JEFFCOTES *use the breakfast-room for all meals except ceremonious ones, when the dining-room is requisitioned and an elaborate dinner is substituted for the high tea which* NATHANIEL *persists in regarding as an essential of comfort and homeliness. It is about* 10.30 *on the same Bank Holiday evening. The room is well lighted by gas, not electricity, but of course there is no fire.*

NATHANIEL JEFFCOTE *and his wife are sitting alone in the room. He is a tall, thin, gaunt, withered, domineering man of sixty. When excited or angry he drops into dialect, but otherwise his speech, though flat, is fairly accurate.* MRS. JEFFCOTE *has even more adapted herself to the responsibilities and duties imposed by the possession of wealth. She is a plump, mild, and good-natured woman. She sits under the chandelier embroidering, whilst her husband sits in an arm-chair by the empty hearth working calculations in a small shiny black notebook, which he carries about with him everywhere, in a side pocket.*

Mrs. Jeffcote. I asked Mrs. Plews to let me have a look through Hindle Lodge to-day.

Jeffcote [*looking up*]. Eh? What's that?

Mrs. Jeffcote. Mrs. Plews is leaving Hindle Lodge at Christmas.

Jeffcote. What of it?

Mrs. Jeffcote. I was thinking it would do very well for Alan when he gets married.

Jeffcote. Is Alan talking about getting married?

Mrs. Jeffcote. Beatrice was mentioning it last week.

Jeffcote. How long have they been engaged? A year?

Mrs. Jeffcote. Eleven months. I remember it was on September the 5th that it happened.

Jeffcote. How on earth can you remember that?

Mrs. Jeffcote. Because September the 5th is your birthday.

Jeffcote. Is it? [*He grunts.*] Well, eleven months isn't so long after all. Let 'em wait a bit longer.

Mrs. Jeffcote. I thought we might be speaking for the Lodge.

Jeffcote. What do they want with a house like the Lodge? Isn't there plenty of room here? We've got four living-rooms and fourteen bedrooms in this house, and there's never more than three of them going at the same time.

Mrs. Jeffcote. Really, Nat! They'll want a house of their own, no matter how many bedrooms we've got empty, and it's only natural.

Jeffcote. There's no hurry as far as I can see. Alan won't be twenty-five till next March, will he?

Mrs. Jeffcote. You were only twenty-two when you married me.

Jeffcote. I didn't marry a girl who'd been brought up like Beatrice Farrar. I married a girl who could help me to make money. Beatrice won't do that. She'll help to spend it, likely.

Mrs. Jeffcote. Well, he'll have it to spend. What's money for?

Jeffcote. Money's power. That's why I like money. Not for what it can buy.

Mrs. Jeffcote. All the same, you've always done yourself pretty well, Nat.

Jeffcote. Because it pays in the long run. And it's an outward sign. Why did I buy a motor-car? Not because I wanted to go motoring. I hate it. I bought it so that people could see Alan driving about in it, and say, 'There's Jeffcote's lad in his new car. It cost five hundred quid.' Tim Farrar was so keen on getting his knighthood for the same reason. Every one knows that him and me started life in a weaving shed. That's why we like to have something to show 'em how well we've done. That's why we put some of our brass into houses and motors and knighthoods and fancy articles of the kind. I've put a deal of brass into our Alan, and Tim Farrar's put a deal into his Beatrice, with just the same object in view.

[*There is a short pause.* JEFFCOTE *goes on with his reckoning and* MRS. JEFFCOTE *with her sewing. Then she speaks quietly.*

Mrs. Jeffcote. I was wondering what you intend to do for Alan when he gets married.

Jeffcote. Do for him? What do you mean?

Mrs. Jeffcote. He doesn't get a regular salary, does he?

Jeffcote [*suspiciously*]. Has Alan been putting you up to talk to me about this?

Mrs. Jeffcote. Well, Nat, if he has——?

Jeffcote. Why can't he talk to me himself?

Mrs. Jeffcote [*placidly continuing*]. You're not such a good one to tackle. I daresay he thought I should do it better than he would.

Jeffcote. I don't keep him short, do I?

Mrs. Jeffcote. No. But Sir Timothy will expect him to show something more definite before the wedding.

Jeffcote. Tim Farrar don't need to be afraid. I hope he'll leave his lass as much as I shall leave Alan. That lad'll be the richest man in Hindle some day.

Mrs. Jeffcote. I daresay. Some day! That's not much good to set up house on. Why don't you take him into partnership?

Jeffcote. Partnership?

Mrs. Jeffcote. You always say he works hard enough.

Jeffcote [*grudgingly*]. Well enough.

Mrs. Jeffcote. I suppose it comes to this. You don't want to take him into partnership because it would mean parting with some of that power you're so fond of.

Jeffcote. He mightn't work so well if he was his own master.

Mrs. Jeffcote. But if you gave him a junior partnership he wouldn't be his own master. You'd see to that.

Jeffcote [*jocularly dropping into dialect*]. Eh, lass! thou'd better come and manage mill thyself.

Mrs. Jeffcote. I shouldn't make such a bad job of it, neither! Remember that if you take him in you'll have less work to do yourself. He'll share the responsibility.

Jeffcote. Hold on a bit. The owd cock's not done with yet.

Mrs. Jeffcote. If Beatrice starts talking about the date——

Jeffcote. Oh, if you'll stop your worritting I daresay I'll take the lad into partnership on his wedding-day.

Mrs. Jeffcote. Can I tell Sir Timothy that?

Jeffcote. If you like. I told him myself six months ago.

Mrs. Jeffcote. You *are* a caution, Nat, indeed you are! Why couldn't you tell me so at once, instead of making a fool of me like this?

Jeffcote. I like to hear thee talking, lass.

[*Having brought off this characteristic stroke of humour*, JEFFCOTE *resumes his work. The door opens and* ADA *comes in.*

Ada. If you please, sir, there's someone to see you.

Jeffcote [*absorbed*]. Eh?

Mrs. Jeffcote. Who is it, Ada?

Ada. His name's Hawthorn, ma'am.

Mrs. Jeffcote. It'll be Christopher Hawthorn, Nat.

Jeffcote. What does he want coming so late as this? Fetch him in here. [ADA *goes out.*] Can't be owt wrong at the mill, seeing it's Bank Holiday.

[ADA *shows in* CHRISTOPHER, *who stands near the door.*

Mrs. Jeffcote. Good evening, Mr. Hawthorn.

Christopher. Good evening, Mrs. Jeffcote.

Jeffcote [*rising*]. Well, Chris!

Christopher. Well, Nat!

[*These two old comrades address each other by their first names, although master and man.*

Jeffcote. Sit down. The rain's held off.

Christopher. Ay! [*He is obviously ill at ease.*

Mrs. Jeffcote. Where have you been these Wakes?

Christopher. Nowhere.

Mrs. Jeffcote. What? Stopped at home?

Christopher. Ay! Somehow we don't seem quite as keen on Blackpool as we used to be. And the missus was badly last week with her leg, and what with one thing and another we let it drift this time round. You've not been away, either?

Mrs. Jeffcote. No, we went to Norway in June, you know.

Christopher. Ay! so you did. That must be a fine place—from the pictures.

Mrs. Jeffcote. Alan is away, though. He is motoring in North Wales. We expect him back to-night.

Jeffcote. Business is too bad to go away, Chris. I was down in Manchester Tuesday and Friday. It isn't Wakes in Manchester, thou knows!

Christopher. Anything doing?

Jeffcote. I landed ten sets of those brown jaconets on Friday. Five for October and five for November.

Christopher. For the forty-four inch looms?

Jeffcote. Ay! And hark you, Chris! they're complaining about the tint. Not bright enough, they say in India. They've sent a pattern over this mail. You'd better have a look at it to-morrow. We've got to give them what they want, I reckon.

Christopher. I don't think they do know what they want in India, Nat.

Jeffcote. You're about right there, Chris.

[*A pause.* CHRISTOPHER *looks uncomfortably at* MRS. JEFFCOTE.

Jeffcote [*at length*]. When are you going to bed, mother?

Mrs. Jeffcote [*taking the hint*]. Any time now.

Jeffcote. That's right. Just reach me the whisky before you go.

[MRS. JEFFCOTE *gets a bottle of whisky, a syphon, and glasses from the sideboard cupboard.*

Mrs. Jeffcote. Are you going to sit up for Alan?

Jeffcote. Why? Hasn't he got his latchkey?

Mrs. Jeffcote. I expect so.

Jeffcote. Then I reckon he'll be able to find the keyhole, and if he can't he won't thank me for sitting up to welcome him.

Mrs. Jeffcote [*smiling*]. You do talk some nonsense, Nat. Good night, Mr. Hawthorn.

Christopher [*rising*]. Good night, Mrs. Jeffcote.

Jeffcote. Have a drink, Chris?

Christopher. No thanks, Nat.

Jeffcote [*incredulously*]. Get away!

Christopher. Well—just a small one, then.

[JEFFCOTE *pours out two drinks.*

Jeffcote. Light your pipe, Chris.

Christopher. Ay! Thanks! [*He does so.*

Jeffcote. It's a long while since we had a quiet chat together. We don't see so much of each other as we did thirty years ago?

Christopher. No. You've other fish to fry, I reckon.

Jeffcote. I'm always right glad to see you. How long have you been taping for me, Chris?

Christopher. I came to you in '95. I remember because Joe Walmesley's shed was burnt down the same year.

Jeffcote. Ay! That was during the General Election, when Tories knocked out Mark Smethurst in Hindle. Joe was speaking at one of Mark's meetings when they come and told him his mill was afire. That was the only time I ever saw Joe Walmesley cry.

Christopher. He was fond of them looms, was Joe!

Jeffcote. You missed your way, Chris, you did indeed, when you wouldn't come in with me and put your savings into Trafalgar Mill.

Christopher. That's what the missus is never tired of telling me.

Jeffcote. You might have been my partner these fifteen years instead of only my slasher.

Christopher. You'd never have got on with a partner, Nat. You're too fond of your own way.

Jeffcote. You're right there. I've been used to it for a good while now.

Christopher. You don't remember Daisy Bank being built, Nat?

Jeffcote. No. I was living over Blackburn way then.

Christopher. I was only a lad at the time. I used to come along the river banks on Sundays with the other lads. There were no weaving sheds in Hindle Vale in those days; nothing but fields all the way to Harwood Bridge. Daisy Bank was the first shed put up outside Hindle proper. They called it Daisy Bank because of the daisies in the meadows. All the side of the brow falling away towards the river was thick with them. Thick dotted it was, like the stars in the sky of a clear night.

Jeffcote. Look here, old lad, thou didn't come up here at this time of night just to talk about daisies.

Christopher. Eh?

Jeffcote. You've come up here with a purpose, haven't you?

Christopher. That's so, Nat.

Jeffcote. I could see that. That's why I sent the missus to bed. I know you of old. What is it that's troubling you? Get it off your chest!

Christopher. It's about my lass.

Jeffcote. Hullo!

Christopher. I'm worried about her.

Jeffcote. What's she been doing?

Christopher. Getting into trouble.

Jeffcote. What sort of trouble?

Christopher [*troubled*]. Well, thou knows—there's only one sort of trouble——

Jeffcote. Ay—ay! With a lad?

Christopher. Ay! [*There is a slight pause.*] It's only by chance we found it out. The missus is in a fine way about it, I can tell you!

Jeffcote. Then it's proper serious, like?

Christopher. They've been away together, these Wakes.

Jeffcote [*whistling*]. Humph! She's a cool customer. What art going to do in the matter?

Christopher. That's what I've come up to see thee about. I wasn't for coming to-night, but missus, she was set on it.

Jeffcote. Quite right, too. I'll help thee any road I can. But you musn't take it too much to heart. It's not the first time a job like this has happened in Hindle, and it won't be the last!

Christopher. That's true. But it's poor comfort when it's your own lass that's got into trouble.

Jeffcote. There's many a couple living happy to-day as first come together in that fashion.

Christopher. Wedded, you mean?

Jeffcote. Ay! Wedded, of course. What else do you think I mean? Does the lad live in Hindle?

Christopher. Ay!

[*He does not know how to break it to* JEFFCOTE.

Jeffcote. Whose shed does he work at?

Christopher. Well, since you put it that way, he works at yours.

Jeffcote. At Daisy Bank? Do I know him?

Christopher. Ay! You know him well.

Jeffcote. Then by Gad! I'll have it out with him to-morrow. If he doesn't promise to wed thy Fanny I'll give him the sack!

Christopher [*dazed*]. Give him the sack!

Jeffcote. And I'll go further. If he'll be a decent lad and make it right with her at once, I'll see that he's well looked after at the mill. We're old pals, Chris, and I can't do no fairer than that, can I?

Christopher. No.

Jeffcote. Now, then, who's the chap?

Christopher. Thou'll be a bit surprised-like, I reckon.

Jeffcote. Spit it out!

Christopher. It's thy lad, Alan.

Jeffcote [*sharply*]. What? [*A slight pause.*] Say that again.

Christopher. Thy lad, Alan.

Jeffcote. My lad?

Christopher. Ay!

[*After a short pause,* JEFFCOTE *springs up in a blazing rage.*

Jeffcote. Damn you, Chris Hawthorn! Why the devil couldn't you tell me so before?

Christopher. I were trying to tell thee, Nat——

Jeffcote. Trying to tell me! Hasn't thou got a tongue in thy head that thou mun sit there like a bundle of grey-cloth while I'm making a fool of myself this road? [*He paces up and down in his agitation.*] Here! How do you know it's Alan? Who says it's Alan?

Christopher. Fanny.

Jeffcote. Fanny, eh? How do you know she's not lying?

Christopher [*stoutly*]. You can settle it soon enough by asking Alan. I thought to have found him here to-night.

Jeffcote. He's not come home yet?

Christopher. No.

Jeffcote. And a good job for him, too!

Christopher. Wouldn't he fetch Fanny back, think you?

Jeffcote. Would he, the dickens! He's not altogether without sense. Do you think he'd run her in the car through Hindle market-place and up Burnley Road and set her down at your house for all the folk to see?

Christopher. No.

Jeffcote [*suddenly flaring up again*]. The bally young fool! I'd like to break his silly neck for him! And that lass of thine is just as much to blame as he is! I've marked her—the hot-blooded little wench!

Christopher. I can't defend her. She's always been a bit of a mystery to her mother and me. There's that in her veins as keeps her restless and uneasy. If she sees you want her to do one thing she'll go right away and do t'other out of pure cussedness. She won't be driven, not any road. I had a dog just like her once.

Jeffcote. Eh, old lad, it's a good job you never had any boys if you don't know how to manage a girl!

Christopher. Happen I could have managed lads better. I never could clout a girl properly.

Jeffcote. I can manage my lad without clouting. Always could.

Christopher. Folk are different, you see. Happen you couldn't have managed our Fanny.

Jeffcote. I'd have had a damn good try! Where is she now?

Christopher. At the house. She was overdone, and I sent her to bed to get her out of range of the missus's tongue. She was talking rather bitter, like.

Jeffcote. She had a sharp way with her when she was Sarah Riley, had your missus, and I reckon it won't have improved with the passing of years! I shouldn't wonder if it was your missus who got the truth out of Fanny.

Christopher. So it was.

Jeffcote. And what *did* she get out of her? Let's be knowing just what took place.

Christopher. I can tell you nowt save that they stayed in Llandudno. You'll have to go to your lad for the rest of the story.

Jeffcote. All right. I'll see you to-morrow at he mill. There's nowt more to be done to-night.

Christopher. Maybe it's a queer fancy, but I'd like to have seen him to-night. There's no chance of him coming in shortly, think you?

Jeffcote. He may come in the next five minutes, or he may not come home at all. There's no telling what may happen on Bank Holiday.

Christopher. Then it's no use me waiting a while.

Jeffcote. Nay, you can't wait here. I'm going to bed. I'm not going to let this business spoil a night's rest. I'd advise you to look on it in the same light.

Christopher. Ah, Nat, but it's not so hard on you as it is on me!

Jeffcote. Is it not? How do you know what plans of mine will come to naught through this job? [*More kindly.*] Come, old lad, thou mun clear out. Thou can do nowt here.

Christopher. Well, I've not said all that my missus told me to say, and I doubt she'll be on my track, but I reckon it's a bit too previous afore we've seen the lad.

Jeffcote. If your wife wants to say anything to me, she's welcome. You'd better fetch her up here to-morrow night, and bring Fanny along as well. I'll be ready for you by then.

Christopher. To-morrow night?

Jeffcote. About nine o'clock. Do you understand?

Christopher. Ay! [*He goes to the door, and* JEFFCOTE *rises.*] My wife said——

Jeffcote [*curtly*]. I can guess all that thy wife said. You can tell her this from me. I'll see you're treated right. Do you hear? [JEFFCOTE *opens the door.*

Christopher. I can't ask for more than that.

Jeffcote. I'll see you're treated right.

[*They go into the hall out of sight.* ADA *comes into the room with a tray, which she places on the table. The tray holds bread, cheese, butter, a bottle of beer, and a tumbler.*

Jeffcote [*out of sight in the hall*]. *I*'m not afraid of thy wife, if *you* are. [*The front door bangs.* JEFFCOTE *returns into the room and sees the tray, which he examines irritably.*] What's this for?

Ada. Mr. Alan's tray, sir. We always leave it when he's out late.

Jeffcote [*flaring up*]. Take it away!

Ada. Take it away sir?

Jeffcote. Yes. Do you hear? Take the damned thing away!

Ada. What about Mr. Alan's supper, sir?

Jeffcote. Let him do without.

Ada. Yes, sir.

[ADA *takes the tray out.* JEFFCOTE *watches her, and then goes to the window to see if it is fastened.* MRS. JEFFCOTE, *mostly undressed and attired in a dressing wrap, appears in the hall.*

Mrs. Jeffcote. Nat?

Jeffcote. What do *you* want?

Mrs. Jeffcote. Is anything the matter?

Jeffcote. Why?

Mrs. Jeffcote. I thought I heard you swearing, that's all.

Jeffcote. Happen I was.

Mrs. Jeffcote. You've not quarrelled with Christopher Hawthorn?

Jeffcote. No, we're the best of friends. He only wanted my opinion about summat.

Mrs. Jeffcote. What had you got to swear about, then?

Jeffcote. I was giving him my opinion.

Mrs. Jeffcote. Well, but——

Jeffcote. That's enough. Get along to bed with you. Maybe I'll tell you all about it to-morrow. Maybe I won't!

Mrs. Jeffcote. Well, I'm glad it's no worse. I thought you were coming to blows.

[MRS. JEFFCOTE *goes out and upstairs.* JEFFCOTE *sees two glasses of whisky and soda which neither of the men has remembered to touch. He takes his own and drinks it.* ADA *appears.*

Ada. Please, sir, do you want anything else?

Jeffcote. No. Get to bed. [*She is going.*] Have the other girls gone upstairs yet?

Ada. Yes, sir.

Jeffcote. Good night.

Ada. Good night, sir.

[ADA *goes upstairs.* JEFFCOTE *slowly drinks the second glass of whisky and soda. He puts both the empty glasses on the sideboard and looks round the room. He turns out all the gases except one, which he leaves very low. He goes out into the hall, leaving the breakfast-room door open, and is seen to go out of sight to the front door, as if to assure himself that it is on the latch. Then he turns the hall gas very low indeed, and goes upstairs.*

THE CURTAIN FALLS

SCENE III. *The curtain rises again immediately. The scene is the same room about two hours later, that is to say at about one o'clock in the morning. Everything looks just the same. At first there is silence. Then is heard the scratching noise of a latchkey being inserted into the front door. The process takes some time. At last the door is heard to open, and someone stumbles in, making rather too much noise. The door is closed very quietly. A match is struck in the hall, out of sight. It goes out at once. Then a figure is dimly seen to appear in the doorway of the breakfast-room, lean against the jamb and look round. It is* ALAN JEFFCOTE, *who if he could be seen distinctly would be found a well-made, plump, easy-going young fellow, with a weak but healthy and attractive face and fair hair. He is of the type that runs to stoutness after thirty, unless diet and exercise are carefully attended to. At present he is too fond of luxury and good living to leave any doubt that this pleasant fellow of twenty-five will be a gross, fleshly man at forty. He is dressed by a good Manchester tailor, and everything he has is of the best. He does not stint his father's money. He has been to the Manchester Grammar School and Manchester University, but he has not lost the characteristic Hindle burr in his accent, though he speaks correctly as a rule. He does not ever speak affectedly, so that his speech harmonises with that of the other characters. This is important, for though he has had a far better education than any of the other characters except* BEATRICE, *he is essentially one of them, a Hindle man. He has no feeling that he is provincial, or that the provinces are not the principal assets of England. London he looks upon as a place where rich Lancashire men go for a spree, if they have not time to go to Monte Carlo or Paris. Manchester he looks upon as the centre or headquarters for Lancashire manufacturers, and therefore more important than London. But after all he thinks that Manchester is merely the office for Hindle and the other Lancashire towns, which are the actual source of wealth. Therefore Hindle, Blackburn, Bolton, Oldham, and the rest are far more important in his eyes than London or Manchester, and perhaps he is right. Anyhow, the feeling gives him sufficient assurance to stroll into the most fashionable hotels and restaurants, conscious that he can afford to pay for whatever he fancies, that he can behave himself, that he can treat the waiters with the confidence of an aristocrat born—and yet be patently a Lancashire man. He would never dream of trying to conceal the fact, nor indeed could he understand why anybody should wish to try and conceal such a thing. He is now slightly intoxicated, not seriously drunk, only what he would himself describe as 'a bit tight'. He strikes another match and lurches towards the gas, only to find that it is already lighted. He blows out the match and tries to turn up the gas. As he reaches up he knocks a small bronze vase off the end of the mantel-piece. It falls into the fire-irons with an appalling crash.*

Alan. Curse it! [*He turns up the gas and clumsily picks up and replaces the vase. He sees on the mantel-piece a couple of letters addressed to him. He tears them open, stares at them, and crams them unread into his pocket. Then he gazes at the table as if in search of something.*] Where's that tray? Where the devil's that tray? [*He shakes his head and proceeds to look in the sideboard cupboard for food. He can find none, so he turns to the whisky and soda, and fills one of the empty glasses. This he puts on the mantel-piece, and then he sits in the arm-chair by the hearth, sinks back and holds his head in his hands. He seems to be going to sleep. In the hall is observed a flickering light, coming nearer by degrees. Old* NATHANIEL JEFFCOTE *appears, a lean picturesque figure in pyjamas and dressing-gown, carrying in one hand a lighted bedroom candle and in the other a poker. He comes to the door of the room, stands at the threshold and contemplates his son. At length* ALAN *seems to feel that he is not alone, for he slowly steals a glance round to the door, and encounters his father's stern gaze.*] Hello! [*He smiles amiably.*] Thought you were in bed.

Jeffcote. So it's you, is it? What are you making all this din about?

Alan. 'S not my fault. You don't s'pose I did it on purpose, do you?

Jeffcote. I'll not have you coming in and raising Cain at this time of night. It's enough to waken the dead!

Alan. I can't help it. They go and stick that beastly thing up there! [*He points to the vase.*] Can't blame me for knocking it over. 'S not my fault. [*He hiccoughs.*] I can't help it.

Jeffcote. Are you drunk?

Alan [*rising and standing with his back to the hearth in a dignified way*]. You've never seen me drunk yet!

[*He hiccoughs.* JEFFCOTE *approaches him and scrutinises him by the light of the candle.*

Jeffcote. I've never seen thee nearer drunk, anyhow. Thou didn't drive the car home in this state, surely?

Alan. No fear!

Jeffcote. Where have you left it?

Alan. At George and Dragon, in Hindle.

Jeffcote. I see. You've been at George and Dragon? Didn't they chuck you out at eleven?

Alan. Ay! Then we went round to the Liberal Club.

Jeffcote. Who's 'we'?

Alan. Me and George Ramsbottom.

Jeffcote. Has George Ramsbottom been with you this week-end?

Alan. No. I met him at the Midland at Manchester. We had a bit of dinner together.

Jeffcote. Ah! Where's George Ramsbottom been during the week-end?

Alan. After his own devices.

Jeffcote. Humph! Like thyself, no doubt?

Alan. Happen!

Jeffcote. What's thou been up to these Wakes?

Alan. Nothing. Why?

Jeffcote [*holding the candle up to* ALAN'*s face*]. Hast been with a girl?

Alan [*flinching slightly*]. No.

Jeffcote. Thou hardened young liar!

Alan [*staggered*]. Why?

Jeffcote [*looking hard at him*]. Chris Hawthorn's been here to-night.

Alan [*vaguely*]. Chris Hawthorn?

Jeffcote. Ay! [ALAN *cannot bear his father's gaze. He is not able to keep up the pretence of coolness any longer. He turns towards the arm-chair and stumbles into it, his attitude of collapse denoting surrender.*] Thou cursed young fool! I could find it in my heart to take a strap to thee, so I could. Why hadn't thou the sense to pay for thy pleasures, instead of getting mixed up with a straight girl! I've never kept thee short of brass. And if thou must have a straight girl, thou might have kept off one from the mill. Let alone her father's one of my oldest friends.

Alan. What does he say?

Jeffcote. Say? What dost thou think he said? Does thou think as he come up here to return thanks?

Alan. But—but, how did he know?

Jeffcote. The lass has told them, so it appears.

Alan. She promised not to.

Jeffcote. Happen she did. And what then?

Alan. What's going to be done?

Jeffcote. I said I'd see him treated right.

Alan [*brightening*]. What'll they take?

Jeffcote [*dangerously*]. I said I'd see them treated right. If thou expects I'm going to square it with a cheque, and that thou's going to slip away scot free, thou's sadly mistaken.

Alan. What do you want me to do?

Jeffcote. I know what thou's going to do. Thou's going to wed the lass.

Alan. What do you say?

Jeffcote. Thou's heard me all right.

Alan. Wed her? Fanny Hawthorn!

Jeffcote. Ay! Fanny Hawthorn.

Alan. But I cannot.

Jeffcote. Why not?

Alan. You know—Beatrice—I can't!

Jeffcote. Thou mun tell Beatrice it's off.

Alan. How can I do that?

Jeffcote. That's thy look-out.

Alan [*rising and holding on to the mantel-piece*]. Look here. I can't do it. It isn't fair to Beatrice.

Jeffcote. It's a pity thou didn't think of that before thou went to Llandudno!

Alan. But what can I tell her?

Jeffcote. Thou mun tell her the truth if thou can't find owt better to say.

Alan. The truth!

[ALAN *again collapses in the chair. A pause.*

Jeffcote. What's done is done. We've got to stand by it.

Alan. Father! I don't want to wed Fanny. I want to wed Beatrice.

Jeffcote. Dost thou love Beatrice?

Alan. Yes.

Jeffcote. I'm glad of it. It's right that thou should suffer as well as her.

[ALAN *is overcome, and drops into dialect as he pleads.*

Alan. Father, thou'll not make me do it! Thou'll not make me do it! I cannot. I'd have all the folk in Hindle laughing at me.

[ALAN *breaks down, excitement and drink combined being too much for him.*

Jeffcote [*brusquely*]. Come now, pull thyself together.

Alan. Ay! It's easy talking that road.

Jeffcote. Thou art a man, now. Not a kid!

Alan. It's me that's got to go through it. It doesn't hurt thee if I wed Fanny Hawthorn.

Jeffcote. Does it not?

Alan. No.

Jeffcote. So thou thinks it easy for me to see thee wed Fanny Hawthorn? Hearken! Dost know how I began life? Dost know that I started as tenter in Walmesley's shed when I were eight years of age, and that when the time comes I shall leave the biggest fortune ever made in the cotton trade in Hindle? Dost know what my thought has been when labouring these thirty years to get all that brass together? Not what pleasure I could get out of spending, but what power and influence I were piling up the while. I was set on founding a great firm that would be famous not only all over Lancashire but all over the world, like Horrockses or Calverts or Hornbys of Blackburn. Dost think as I weren't right glad when thou goes and gets engaged to Tim Farrar's lass? Tim Farrar as were Mayor of Hindle and got knighted when the King come to open the new Town Hall. Tim Farrar that owns Lane End Shed, next biggest place to Daisy Bank in Hindle. Why, it were the dearest wish of my heart to see thee wed Tim Farrar's lass; and, happen, to see thee running both mills afore I died. And now what falls out? Lad as I'd looked to to keep on the tradition and build the business bigger still, goes and weds one of my own weavers! Dost think that's no disappointment to me? Hearken! I'd put down ten thousand quid if thou could honestly wed Beatrice Farrar. But thou can't honestly wed her, not if I put down a million. There's only one lass thou can honestly wed now, and that's Fanny Hawthorn, and by God I'm going to see that thou does it!

[JEFFCOTE *stalks out of the room with his candle and his poker, which he has never put down, and* ALAN *remains huddled up and motionless in a corner of the arm-char.*

THE CURTAIN FALLS

ACT II

The scene is again the breakfast room at the JEFFCOTES' *house. It is shortly after* 8 *p.m. on the day following that on which the First Act took place. The evening meal, tea, is just over. Only* MR. *and* MRS. JEFFCOTE *have partaken of it.* ADA *has almost finished clearing away, there is a loaded tray on the sideboard and the coloured cloth is not yet spread, although the white cloth has been removed.* MRS. JEFFCOTE *is sitting by the hearth, and* JEFFCOTE *is standing with his back to the empty fireplace filling his pipe. It is not yet dark, but the light is fading.*

Jeffcote [*to* ADA]. Come now, lass, be sharp with your siding away.

[ADA *is about to spread the coloured cloth.* MRS. JEFFCOTE *rises and assists her.*

Mrs. Jeffcote. Give me that end, Ada.

[*They spread the cloth whilst* JEFFCOTE *lights his pipe, and then* ADA *hurries out with the tray.*

Jeffcote. That girl wants wakening up.

Mrs. Jeffcote. What are you in such a hurry about, Nat?

Jeffcote. I've got summat to say to you.

Mrs. Jeffcote. Something to say to me. Why couldn't you say it whilst we were having tea?

Jeffcote. It's not quite the sort of think to say before the servant.

Mrs. Jeffcote [*surprised*]. Why, Nat, what is it?

Jeffcote. Last night you were talking of taking Hindle Lodge for Alan?

Mrs. Jeffcote. Yes. I was going to call on Mrs. Plews this afternoon, only it came on wet.

Jeffcote [*briefly*]. Don't go.

Mrs. Jeffcote. Why not?

Jeffcote. There's no need.

Mrs. Jeffcote. Surely, Nat, you've not changed your mind again?

Jeffcote. Alan won't want to live in a place like Hindle Lodge.

Mrs. Jeffcote. His wife will.

Jeffcote. How do you know that?

Mrs. Jeffcote. I've asked her.

Jeffcote. Nay, you've not.

Mrs. Jeffcote. Why, Nat, I mentioned it to Beatrice only a week ago.

Jeffcote. Happen you did. Alan's not going to marry Beatrice.

Mrs. Jeffcote [*dumbfoundered*]. Not going to marry——
[*She stops.*

Jeffcote. That's what I said.

Mrs. Jeffcote. Why? Have they quarrelled?

Jeffcote. No.

Mrs. Jeffcote. Then, what's the matter? What has happened? When did you get to know about it?

Jeffcote. I first got to know about it last night.

Mrs. Jeffcote. That was what you were talking to Alan about when you went downstairs last night?

Jeffcote. Ay!

Mrs. Jeffcote. And you said you were lecturing him on coming home so late. Why didn't you tell me the truth?

Jeffcote. I knew you'd learn it soon enough, and I didn't want to spoil your night's rest.

Mrs. Jeffcote. Why didn't you tell me to-day, then?

Jeffcote. I've been at the Mill all day.

Mrs. Jeffcote. You could have told me as soon as you came home.

Jeffcote. I didn't want to spoil your tea for you.

Mrs. Jeffcote [*wiping her eyes*]. As if that mattered!

Jeffcote. Well, then, I didn't want to spoil *my* tea.

Mrs. Jeffcote. Oh! Nat, what is it that's happened?

Jeffcote. To put it in a nutshell, Alan's not going to marry Beatrice because another girl has a better right to him.

Mrs. Jeffcote. But how can that be? He's been engaged to Beatrice for nearly a year.

Jeffcote [*grimly*]. Ay! He's only been engaged to Beatrice. With the other girl he's gone a step further.

Mrs. Jeffcote. He's not gone and got wed already.

Jeffcote. No. He's not got wed. He dispensed with the ceremony.

Mrs. Jeffcote. Dispensed with it?

Jeffcote. Did without.

Mrs. Jeffcote [*shocked*]. Oh, Nat!

Jeffcote. Ay. He spent last week-end with a girl at Llandudno.

Mrs. Jeffcote. The creature!

Jeffcote. Eh?

Mrs. Jeffcote [*indignantly*]. Why are such women allowed to exist?

Jeffcote [*scratching his head*]. Thou mun ask me another. I never looked on it in that light before.

Mrs. Jeffcote. And at Llandudno, too, of all places! Why, I've been there many a time.

Jeffcote. What's that got to do with it?

Mrs. Jeffcote. I shall never be able to fancy it again! And I'm so fond of the place.

Jeffcote. That's a pity. Happen you'll get over the feeling when they're married.

Mrs. Jeffcote. But Nat, it's impossible! Alan can't marry a woman of that sort!

Jeffcote. She's not a woman of that sort. She's a straight girl.

Mrs. Jeffcote. How can you call her that?

Jeffcote. Well, you know what I mean. It's not a matter of business with her.

Mrs. Jeffcote. I don't see that that makes things any better. There might have been some excuse for her if it had been a matter of business. Really, Nat, you must see that the woman is not fit to marry Alan!

Jeffcote. Not quite so fast. You don't even know who she is yet.

Mrs. Jeffcote. Whoever she is, if she's not above going away for the week-end with a man she can't be fit to marry our son.

Jeffcote. Not even when our son's the man she's been away with?

Mrs. Jeffcote. That has nothing to do with the case. It is evident that she is a girl with absolutely no principles.

Jeffcote. Dash it all! At that rate some folk might say that Alan's not fit to marry her because of what he's done.

Mrs. Jeffcote. Well, if you can't see the difference—— [*He does not choose to. She shrugs her shoulders and continues.*] I'm surprised at you, Nat, I really am. You seem to take a delight in being perverse and making difficulties.

Jeffcote. Upon my soul, mother, I'd no idea thou were such an unscrupulous one before. Don't you want to do what's right.

Mrs. Jeffcote. Can't you offer the girl some money?

Jeffcote. Would you think that right treatment?

Mrs. Jeffcote. She wouldn't object. She'd jump at it.

Jeffcote. Shall I tell you who she is?

Mrs. Jeffcote. Of course you'll tell me who she is. Though that won't make me much wiser, for I don't suppose I've ever heard her name before.

Jeffcote. What makes you think that?

Mrs. Jeffcote. I'm sure nobody I know would do a think like that.

Jeffcote. She's not exactly a friend of yours, but her father is a very old friend of mine. His name's Christopher Hawthorn.

Mrs. Jeffcote [*open-mouthed*]. What!

Jeffcote. And the lass is his daughter Fanny.

Mrs. Jeffcote. Fanny Hawthorn! Do you mean to tell me that the lad's going to marry one of our own weavers? Why, Nat, you must be out of your senses!

Jeffcote [*stubbornly*]. Think so?

Mrs. Jeffcote. Why, all the folk in Hindle will be laughing at us.

Jeffcote. Anything else?

Mrs. Jeffcote. I should just think I have got something else. What about Timothy Farrar, for instance? Have you thought what he'll say?

Jeffcote. What does it matter what Tim Farrar says?

Mrs. Jeffcote. There's Beatrice.

Ada. No, ma'am.

Mrs. Jeffcote. Are they in the drawing-room?

Ada. Yes, ma'am.

Mrs. Jeffcote. Very well. [ADA *withdraws*.

Mrs. Jeffcote. Dear me, Nat, this is very awkward. Why doesn't Alan come home? It's too bad of him, it is indeed.

Jeffcote. He's ashamed to face his mother, happen?

Mrs. Jeffcote. He should know his mother better than that.

Jeffcote. Then he's trying to drive it too late to go up to Farrar's to-night.

Mrs. Jeffcote. That's more likely.

Jeffcote. Very well. He's reckoned without his dad. If he's too much of a coward to face the music himself, I'll do it for him.

Mrs. Jeffcote. What are you going to do?

Jeffcote. Just go and send Tim Farrar in here, while you keep Beatrice company in the other room.

Mrs. Jeffcote. Are you going to tell him?

Jeffcote. Ay!

Mrs. Jeffcote. But what shall I say to Beatrice?

Jeffcote. Say nowt.

Mrs. Jeffcote. But I can't talk to her just as if nothing has happened. It would be like deceiving her. I'm not cut out for a hypocrite.

Jeffcote. All right. Tell her everything. She'll have to know some time.

Mrs. Jeffcote [*pleading*]. Need she ever know?

Jeffcote. Whatever falls out, it's not going to be hushed up.

Mrs. Jeffcote. Strike a light, Nat. [*He lights the gas*.] Do I look as if I'd been crying?

Jeffcote. Why? Have you been crying?

Mrs. Jeffcote. No.

Jeffcote. It doesn't show. Nothing to speak of.

[MRS. JEFFCOTE *goes out, and* JEFFCOTE *lights the other gas-jets, until the room is brightly illuminated. He gets out the whisky and soda*. SIR TIMOTHY FARRAR, *a portly, red-faced, rough Lancashire man of fifty-nine or so, with a scrubby growth of hair under his chin, appears in the doorway. He is much the coarsest and commonest person in the play*.

Jeffcote [*curtly*]. How do, Tim.

Sir Timothy. How do, Nat.

Jeffcote [*nodding to a chair*]. Sit you down.

Sir Timothy [*choosing the best chair*]. Ay—ay!

Jeffcote [*holding out a cigar-box*]. The old brand.

Sir Timothy [*choosing the best cigar with deliberation*]. I'll have a drop of whisky, too, Nat.

Jeffcote. Help yourself. [JEFFCOTE *places the whisky handy, and then closes the door*.] So they've made you Chairman of Hindle Education Committee, Tim?

Sir Timothy. Ay! Why not? Thou knows I were reet mon for the job.

Jeffcote. Thou's not done much studying since thou were eight year of age.

Sir Timothy. Happen I haven't. But I'm going to take damn good care that Hindle new Technical School is the finest in Lancashire. Or Yorkshire either, if it comes to that!

Jeffcote. Why not finest in England whilst you are about it?

Sir Timothy. If it's finest in Lancashire and Yorkshire it goes without saying it's finest in England. They don't know how to spend money on them in the South. Besides, what should they want with Technical Schools in them parts? They don't *make* anything to speak of.

Jeffcote. They're a poor lot, it's true.

Sir Timothy. I were in London all last week.

Jeffcote. Corporation business?

Sir Timothy. Ay!

Jeffcote. Expenses paid?

Sir Timothy. Ay!

Jeffcote. That's the style.

Sir Timothy. Where's the lad?

Jeffcote. Not got home yet.

Sir Timothy. Beatrice were expecting him to telephone all day, but he didn't. So as soon as we'd done eating she were on pins and needles to look him up.

Jeffcote. He was coming round to your place to-night.

Sir Timothy. I told the lass he'd be sure to. She hasn't seen him for ten days, thou knows, and that seems a long time when it's before the wedding. It doesn't seem so long afterwards. That reminds me! Have you seen *The Winning Post* this week?

Jeffcote. Nay. I rarely look at it.

Sir Timothy. There's a tale in this week—it'll suit thee down to the ground.

Jeffcote. Hold on a bit. There's something I've a mind to tell you.

Sir Timothy. Let me get mine off my chest first. It's about a fellow who took a girl away for the week-end——

Jeffcote. So's mine.

Sir Timothy. Oh! It's the same one. [*He is disappointed*.

Jeffcote. Nay, it isn't.

Sir Timothy. How do you know?

Jeffcote. Mine's true.

Sir Timothy. True, is it? [*He considers*.] Well, let's hear it. Who's the fellow?

Jeffcote. Chap out of Hindle.

Sir Timothy [*looking him in the face*]. Here! Who's been giving me away?

Jeffcote. Eh?

Sir Timothy. I say who's been giving me away?

Jeffcote. Thee? [*He stares at* SIR TIMOTHY *and then breaks in to a roar of laughter*.] Thou's given thyself away, Tim Farrar. I wasn't talking about thee at all.

Sir Timothy [*wiping his brow*]. Eh! I thought as someone had seen us at Brighton. I don't mind thee knowing, but if the wrong person gets hold of that sort of thing all Hindle is apt to hear about it. Well, who's the chap?

Jeffcote. Our Alan.

Sir Timothy. What! The young devil! I'd like to give him a reet good hiding.

Jeffcote. Come. Thou'rt a nice man to talk, after what I've just learned.

Sir Timothy. Hang it all, it's different with me! I'm not engaged to be wed. Why, I haven't even got a wife living. [*Fuming*.] The young beggar!

Jeffcote. I though I'd better tell thee first.

Sir Timothy. Ay—ay! I'll talk pretty straight to him.

Jeffcote. Perhaps you'll choose to tell Beatrice yourself.

Sir Timothy. Tell who?

Jeffcote. Beatrice.

Sir Timothy. Why? What's it got to do with her?

Jeffcote. Someone will have to tell her. She'll have to know sooner or later.

Sir Timothy. God bless my soul, Nat Jeffcote! Hast thou told thy missus everything thou did before thou got wed?

Jeffcote. I'd nowt to tell her.

Sir Timothy. I always thought there was summat queer about thee, Nat. [*He shakes his head*.] Well, I'm not going to have Bee told of this affair, and that's flat. It's all over and done with.

Jeffcote. It's not all over. You don't understand. This girl is a decent girl, thou knows. Daughter of Chris Hawthorn.

Sir Timothy. What! Him as slashes for thee?

Jeffcote. Ay!

Sir Timothy. I've seen her. A sulky-looking wench. Well, I cannot see what difference it makes who the girl was. I reckon Alan's not going to marry her.

Jeffcote. That's just what he is going to do.

Sir Timothy. What!

Jeffcote. You heard what I said.

Sir Timothy. But he's going to marry my Beatrice.

Jeffcote. If he does he'll be had up for bigamy.

Sir Timothy. Do you mean to say he's going to throw her over?

Jeffcote. There's no need to put it that way.

Sir Timothy. There's no other way to put it if he weds Fanny Hawthorn.

Jeffcote. What else can he do?

Sir Timothy. There's ways and means.

Jeffcote. For instance——

Sir Timothy. It's only a question of money.

Jeffcote. Have you forgotten who she is?

Sir Timothy. She's one of thy weavers. That'll cost thee a trifle more.

Jeffcote. She's daughter of one of my oldest friends.

Sir Timothy. I'm one of thy oldest friends, likewise. What about my lass? Have you thought what a fool she'll look?

Jeffcote. I'm sorry. But t'other girl must come first. I think well enough of Beatrice to know she'll see it in that light when it's put to her.

Sir Timothy. And who's going to put it to her, I should like to know?

Jeffcote. You can put it to her yourself, if you've a mind.

Sir Timothy. Dang it! It's a nice awkward thing to talk to a lass about. Here! before I go any further with this job I want to see Alan, and know for certain what he's going to do.

Jeffcote. He'll do what I tell him.

Sir Timothy. I doubt it! I know he's a fool, but I don't think he's such a fool as all that. [*The door opens and* ALAN *looks in*.] Why—talk of the devil——

Alan. Hello, Sir Timothy! Has Bee come with you?

Jeffcote. She's with your mother in the drawing-room.

Alan. Right.

[ALAN *is withdrawing when* JEFFCOTE *calls him back*.

Jeffcote. Here! I say! Just wait awhile. We've summat to say to you. [ALAN *comes in reluctantly*.] Anything fresh in Manchester?

Alan. No.

Jeffcote. Nowt for us in that cable?

Alan. No.

Jeffcote. You're very late.

Alan. I got something to eat in Manchester.

[*He is for withdrawing again.*

Jeffcote. Hold on a bit. You'd better shut the door and sit down.

Sir Timothy. Now then, what's all this I hear tell about thee?

Alan [*to* JEFFCOTE]. Have you been telling him?

Jeffcote. Ay!

Alan. You'd no right to!

Jeffcote. Hello!

Alan. It was my business.

Jeffcote. It was your business right enough, but if I'd left it to you it wouldn't have been done. I can see that you weren't going up to Farrar's to-night.

Alan. No, I wasn't.

Jeffcote [*grimly*]. I knew it.

Alan. And that's just why you hadn't any right to tell Sir Timothy.

Jeffcote. You young fool! What was the good of hanging back? Sir Timothy had got to be told some time, I reckon.

Alan. Why?

Jeffcote. Why? You don't suppose he's going to see you throw his Beatrice over without knowing why?

Alan. Who says I'm going to throw his Beatrice over?

Jeffcote [*looking hard at him*]. I say so.

Alan. Happen it would be better if you'd stick to what con-concerns you in future.

Jeffcote [*rising*]. What the deuce dost thou mean by talking to me that road?

Sir Timothy [*rising*]. Here! Hold on a bit. Don't go shouting the lad down, Nat Jeffcote. I want to hear what he's got to say.

Alan. If father hadn't opened his mouth there'd have been no call to say anything. It wasn't me who started to make difficulties.

Sir Timothy. I'll bet it wasn't. You'd have let the thing slide?

Alan. I'd have tried to settle it.

Sir Timothy. Then I take it thou's no desire to wed Fanny Hawthorn?

Alan. I don't think it's necessary.

Sir Timothy. No more do I.

Jeffcote [*to* ALAN]. I thought we had this out last night. Were you so drunk that you couldn't take in what I said?

Alan. No.

Jeffcote. Why did you not speak out then?

Alan. You never gave me a chance. You did all the talking yourself.

Sir Timothy. I'd be ashamed to say that. I'd like to see the man as could shut *my* mouth when I'd had too much to drink. *Thou* couldn't do it, Nat, fond of shouting as thou art!

Alan. He's not your father.

Sir Timothy. Art afraid of him?

Alan. No.

Sir Timothy. Then stand up to him. I'll back thee up.

Alan. I've told him I'm not going to wed Fanny. What more does he want?

Jeffcote. You've made up your mind?

Alan. Yes.

Jeffcote. Very well. I've rarely been beat up to now, and I'm not going to be beat by my own lad!

Sir Timothy. Hang it all, Nat, thou cannot take him by the scruff of the neck and force him to wed where he doesn't want to!

Jeffcote. No, that's true. And no one can force me to leave my brass where I don't want to.

Sir Timothy. Thou's not serious?

Jeffcote. I am that.

Sir Timothy. Thou wouldn't care to leave Daisy Bank outside the family.

Jeffcote. It wouldn't go outside the family if I left it to his cousin Travis.

Sir Timothy [*grimacing*]. Thou art a queer chap, Nat!

Alan. So it comes to this. If I don't marry Fanny you'll leave your brass to Travis?

Jeffcote. That's it.

Alan. I see. [*He thinks for a moment*.] And would Travis be expected to take Fanny over along with the mill? [JEFFCOTE *winces, and makes as if to reply angrily, but he thinks better of it and remains grimly silent. A pause*.] Very well. Leave it to Travis. I'm going to stick to Beatrice.

Jeffcote. Right. You haven't thought what you and Beatrice are going to live on, have you?

Alan. I'm not such a fool that I can't earn my own living.

Jeffcote. What you'll earn won't go very far if you have to keep a girl like Beatrice.

Alan. Beatrice and I can manage like you and mother did.

Jeffcote. No, you can't. You haven't been brought up to it.

Alan. Then Sir Timothy will help us.

Jeffcote. Sir Timothy? Oh, ay! [*He laughs sardonically.*] I'd like to hear what Tim Farrar thinks of the situation now.

Sir Timothy [*scratching his head*]. It's not straight of thee, Nat. Thou's not acting right.

Jeffcote. I've put thee in a bit of a hole, like?

Sir Timothy. Thou's made it very awkward for me.

Alan. I like that! It was you who told me to stand up to father. You said you'd back me up.

Sir Timothy. Oh, ay! I'll back thee up all right. But there's no good in losing our tempers over this job, thou knows. I don't want to see a split 'twixt thee and thy father.

Alan. If I don't mind, I don't see why you should.

Sir Timothy. Lord bless thee! If thou art bent on a row, have it thy own way. But thy father's one of my oldest friends, think on, and I'm not going to part from him for thy sake. *Thou* can quarrel with him if thou's a mind to, but don't expect me to do the same.

Alan. You're trying to draw out, now.

Sir Timothy. I'll stand in at anything in reason, but I'll be no party to a bust-up. Besides, now I come to think of it, I'm not sure thou's treated my Beatrice right.

Alan. Hello!

Sir Timothy. No, I'm not. When a chap's engaged he ought to behave himself. From the way thou's been carrying on thou might be married already.

Alan. Look here! You knew all this five minutes ago, and when you told me to stand up to my father. What's happened to change you?

Sir Timothy. Thou's very much mistaken if thou thinks I've changed my mind because thy father's leaving the Mill to thy cousin Travis. I'm not the man to do that sort of thing. Besides, what do I care about thy father's brass? I'm worth as much as he is.

Jeffcote [*pleasantly*]. That's a lie, Tim Farrar.

Sir Thomas. Lie or not, I'm worth enough to be able to snap my fingers at thy brass. I'll not see my lass insulted by thy lad, not if thou were ten times as rich as thou makes out!

Alan [*exasperated*]. But don't you see——

Sir Timothy. No, I don't.

Jeffcote. Yes, you do. You're only trying to draw a red herring across the track.

Sir Timothy. Be damned to that for a tale!

Jeffcote. It's right.

Sir Timothy. Dost take me for a mean beggar?

Jeffcote. No. I take thee for a business man. I never think of thee as owt else.

Sir Timothy [*with heat*]. Dost tell me thou can believe I don't wish Alan to marry Bee just because of what thou's said about leaving thy brass?

Jeffcote. I do.

[*A pause*. SIR TIMOTHY *looks hard at* JEFFCOTE.

Sir Timothy. Well! And why not?

Jeffcote. Don't ask me. I don't object.

Alan. Aren't you ashamed to say that?

Sir Timothy. No. And if thou'd been in weaving as long as I have, thou wouldn't either. Thou's got to keep an eye on the main chance.

Alan. But you've got plenty of money yourself. Quite enough for the two of us.

Sir Timothy [*whimsically*]. Well, blow me if thou aren't the best business man of the lot! Thou comes along and asks me for my daughter and my money. And what does thou offer in exchange? Nowt but thyself! It isn't good enough, my lad.

Alan. Good enough or not, it's the best I can do.

Sir Timothy. It won't do for me.

Alan. I shan't bother about you.

Sir Timothy. Eh? What's that?

Alan. I don't want to marry you. I shall leave it to Beatrice.

Sir Timothy. Bee'll do what I tell her. Thou can take that from me.

Alan. No thanks. I'll ask her myself. I don't care a hang for the pair of you. I'm going to stick to Beatrice if she'll have me. You can cut us off with a shilling if you've a mind to, both of you.

Sir Timothy [*worried*]. Hang it! Thou knows I cannot do that with my Bee. I call it taking a mean advantage of me, that I do!

Jeffcote. Why cannot you cut off your lass?

Sir Timothy. Thou knows well enough that I cannot.

Jeffcote. I could.

Sir Timothy. I don't doubt it. But, thank God, I'm not like thee, Nat Jeffcote. I sometimes think thou'st got a stone where thy heart should be by rights.

Jeffcote. Happen, I've got a pair of scales.

Sir Timothy. That's nowt to boast of. I'd as soon have the stone. [*The door opens and* MRS. JEFFCOTE *looks in.*

Mrs. Jeffcote [*seeing* ALAN]. Beatrice wants to speak to you, Alan.

[MRS. JEFFCOTE *enters, followed by* BEATRICE FARRAR *a determined straightforward girl of about twenty-three.*

Sir Timothy [*to* BEATRICE]. Now my lass——

Beatrice. Father, I want to speak to Alan.

Sir Timothy. I'd like to have a word with thee first, Bee.

Beatrice. Afterwards, father.

Sir Timothy. Ay! But it'll be too late afterwards, happen!

Jeffcote. Come, Tim, thou can't meddle with this job.

Sir Timothy [*worried*]. I call it a bit thick!

Beatrice. Please, father.

Mrs. Jeffcote. Come into the drawing-room, Sir Timothy. You can smoke there, you know.

Sir Timothy [*grumbling*]. A bit thick!

[*He is led out by* MRS. JEFFCOTE. JEFFCOTE *is following, when he turns in the doorway.*

Jeffcote. I'll overlook all you've said to-night if you'll be guided by me. But it's your last chance, mind.

Alan. All right.

Jeffcote [*half to himself*]. I never fancied thy cousin Travis. [SIR TIMOTHY *returns to the doorway.*

Sir Timothy [*indignantly*]. Here! What's all this? Thou wouldn't let me stop behind! What's thou been saying to Alan?

Jeffcote. Telling him not to make a fool of himself.

Sir Timothy. I don't call it fair——

Jeffcote. Come along. Don't *thee* make a fool of thyself, either.

[JEFFCOTE *draws* SIR TIMOTHY *out of the room. After they have gone* ALAN *closes the door, and then turns slowly to* BEATRICE. *They do not speak at first. At last* BEATRICE *almost whispers.*

Beatrice. Alan!

Alan. So they've told you?

Beatrice. Yes.

Alan. Perhaps it's as well. I should have hated telling you.

Beatrice. Alan, why did you——?

Alan. I don't know. It was her lips.

Beatrice. Her lips?

Alan. I suppose so.

Beatrice. I—I see.

Alan. I'm not a proper cad, Bee. I haven't been telling her one tale and you another. It was all an accident, like.

Beatrice. You mean it wasn't arranged?

Alan. No, indeed, it wasn't. I shouldn't like you to think that, Bee. I ran across her at Blackpool.

Beatrice. You didn't go to Blackpool to meet her?

Alan. On my oath I didn't! I went there in the car with George Ramsbottom.

Beatrice. What became of him?

Alan. Him? Oh! George is a pal. He made himself scarce.

Beatrice. Just as you would have done, I suppose, if he had been in your place?

Alan. Of course! What else can a fellow do? Two's company, you know. But old George would be all right. I daresay he picked up something himself.

Beatrice. You knew her before you met her at Blackpool?

Alan. Of course. There's not so many pretty girls in Hindle that you can miss one like Fanny Hawthorn. I knew her well enough, but on the straight, mind you. I thought she looked gay, that was all. I'd hardly spoken to her before I ran into her at the Tower at Blackpool.

Beatrice. So you met her at the Tower?

Alan. Yes. We'd just had dinner at the Metropole Grill-room, George and I, and I daresay we had drunk about as much champagne as was good for us. We looked in at the Tower for a lark, and we ran into Fanny in the Ball-room. She had a girl with her—Mary—Mary—something or other. I forget. Anyhow, George took Mary on, and I went with Fanny.

Beatrice. Yes?

Alan. Next day I got her to come with me in the car. We went to Llandudno.

Beatrice. Yes?

Alan. There's not much more to say.

Beatrice. And I've got to be satisfied with that?

Alan. What else do you want me to tell you?

Beatrice. Didn't you ever think of me?

Alan. Yes, Bee, I suppose I did. But you weren't there, you see, and she was. That was what did it. Being near her and looking at her lips. Then I forgot everything else. Oh! I know. I'm a beast. I couldn't help it. I suppose you can never understand. It's too much to expect you to see th difference.

Beatrice. Between me and Fanny?

Alan. Yes. Fanny was just an amusement—a lark. I thought of her as a girl to have a bit of fun with. Going off with her was like going off and getting tight for once in a way. You wouldn't care for me to do that, but if I did you wouldn't think very seriously about it. You wouldn't want to break off our engagement for that. I wonder if you can look on this affair of Fanny's as something like getting tight—only worse. I'm ashamed of myself, just as I should be if you caught me drunk. I can't defend myself. I feel just an utter swine. What I felt for Fanny was simply—base—horrible—

Beatrice. And how had you always thought of me?

Alan. Oh, Bee, what I felt for you was something—higher—finer——

Beatrice. Was it? Or are you only trying to make yourself believe that?

Alan. No. I respected you.

Beatrice [*thinking*]. I wonder which feeling a woman would rather arouse. And I wonder which is most like love?

Alan. All the time, Bee, I have never loved anyone else but you.

Beatrice. You say so now. But, forgive me, dear, how am I to know? You have given Fanny the greater proof.

Alan. I'm trying to show you that Fanny was one thing, you were another. Can't you understand that a fellow may love one girl and amuse himself with another? [*Despondently.*] No, I don't suppose you ever can?

Beatrice. I think I can. We were different kinds of women. On separate planes. It didn't matter to the one how you treated the other.

Alan. That's it. Going away with Fanny was just a fancy—a sort of freak.

Beatrice. But you have never given me any proof half so great as that.

Alan. Haven't I? I'll give it you now. You know that father says I am to marry Fanny?

Beatrice. Your mother told me he wished it.

Alan. Wished it? He's set his mind on it. He won't leave me a farthing unless I marry her.

Beatrice. What did you tell him?

Alan. If you can't guess that you haven't much confidence in me.

Beatrice. That's hardly my fault, is it?

Alan. No. Well, I told him I'd see him damned first—or words to that effect.

Beatrice [*with a movement of pleasure*]. You did?

Alan. Yes. Is that good enough for you, Bee? You wanted proof that it is you I love. I've chucked away everything I had to expect in the world rather than give you up. Isn't that good enough for you.

Beatrice. Alan!

Alan [*quickly clasping her*]. Bee, in a way I've been faithful to you all the time. I tried hard enough to forget all about you, but I couldn't. Often and often I thought about you. Sometimes I thought about you when I was kissing Fanny. I tried to pretend she was you. She never guessed, of course. She thought it was her I was kissing. But it wasn't. It was you. Oh, the awfulness of having another girl in my arms and wanting you! [BEATRICE *does not answer. She closes her eyes, overcome.*] Bee, you'll stick to me, although I shan't have a penny? I'll get to work, though. I'll work for you. You won't have any cause to reproach me. If only you'll stick to me. If only you'll tell me you forgive me!

Beatrice [*at length*]. Could you have forgiven me if I had done the same as you?

Alan [*surprised*]. But—you—you couldn't do it!

Beatrice. Fanny Hawthorn did.

Alan. She's not your class.

Beatrice. She's a woman.

Alan. That's just it. It's different with a woman.

Beatrice. Yet you expect me to forgive you. It doesn't seem fair!

Alan. It isn't fair. But it's usual.

Beatrice. It's what everybody agrees to.

Alan. You always say that you aren't one of these advanced women. You ought to agree to it as well.

Beatrice. I do. I can see that there is a difference between men and women in cases of this sort.

Alan. You can?

Beatrice. Men haven't so much self-control.

Alan. Don't be cruel, Bee. There's no need to rub it in!

Beatrice. I'm not being personal, Alan. I'm old-fashioned enough to really believe there is that difference. You see, men have never had to exercise self-control like women have. And so I'm old-fashioned enough to be able to forgive you.

Alan. To forgive me, and marry me, in spite of what has happened, and in spite of your father and mine?

Beatrice. I care nothing for my father or yours. I care a good deal for what has happened, but it shows, I think, that you need me even more than I need you. For I do need you, Alan. So much that nothing on earth could make me break off our engagement, if I felt that it was at all possible to let it go on. But it isn't. It's impossible.

Alan. Impossible? Why do you say that? Of course it's not impossible.

Beatrice. Yes, it is. Because to all intents and purposes you are already married.

Alan. No, Bee!

Beatrice. You say I'm old-fashioned. Old-fashioned people used to think that when a man treated a girl as you have treated Fanny it was his duty to marry her.

Alan. You aren't going to talk to me like father, Bee?

Beatrice. Yes. But with your father it is only a fad. You know it isn't that with me. I love you, and I believe that you love me. And yet I am asking you to give me up for Fanny. You may be sure that only the very strongest reasons could make me do that.

Alan. Reasons! Reasons! Don't talk about reasons, when you are doing a thing like this!

Beatrice. You may not be able to understand my reasons. You have always laughed at me because I go to church and believe things that you don't believe.

Alan. I may have laughed, but I've never tried to interfere with you.

Beatrice. Nor I with you. We mustn't begin it now, either of us.

Alan. Is this what your religion leads you to? Do you call it a Christian thing to leave me in the lurch with Fanny Hawthorn? When I need you so much more than I've ever done before?

Beatrice. I don't know. It's not what I can argue about. I was born to look at things just in the way I do, and I can't help believing what I do.

Alan. And what you believe comes before me?

Beatrice. It comes before everything. [*A pause*.] Alan, promise that you'll do what I wish.

Alan. You love me?

Beatrice. If I love anything on earth I love you.

Alan. And you want me to marry Fanny?

Beatrice. Yes. Oh, Alan! Can't you see what a splendid sacrifice you have it in your power to make? Not only to do the right thing, but to give up so much in order to do it. [*A pause*.] Alan, promise me.

Alan [*nodding sullenly*]. Very well.

Beatrice [*gladly*]. You have sufficient courage and strength?

Alan. I'll do what you ask, but only because I can see that your talk is all humbug. You don't love me. You are shocked by what I did, and you're glad to find a good excuse for getting rid of me. All right. I understand.

Beatrice [*in agony*]. You don't—you don't understand.

Alan. Faugh! You might have spared me all that goody-goody business.

Beatrice [*faintly*]. Please——

Alan. You don't care for me a bit.

Beatrice [*passionately*]. Alan! You don't know what it's costing me.

[ALAN *looks at her keenly, and then seizes her violently and kisses her several times. She yields to him and returns his embrace.*

Alan [*speaking quickly and excitedly*]. Bee, you're talking nonsense. You can't give me up—you can't give me up, however much you try.

[BEATRICE *tears herself away from him.*

Beatrice. You don't know me. I can. I will. I shall never be your wife.

Alan. I won't take that for an answer—Bee——

Beatrice. No, no, no! Never, never! Whilst Fanny Hawthorn has a better right to you than I have.

[*There is a long pause. At length comes a knock at the door.*

Alan. Hello! [JEFFCOTE *puts his head inside.*

Jeffcote. Nine o'clock.

Alan. What of it?

Jeffcote. Hawthorns are due up here at nine.

Alan [*shortly*]. Oh!

Beatrice. Is my father there?

Jeffcote. Ay! [*Calling.*] Tim!

[SIR TIMOTHY *appears in the doorway.*

Sir Timothy. Well? Fixed it up, eh?

Beatrice. Alan and I are not going to be married, father.

[*There is a pause.*

Jeffcote. Ah!

Sir Timothy. I'm sure it's all for the best, lass.

Beatrice. Are you quite ready, father? I want you to take me home.

Sir Timothy. Ay—ay! Shall I get thee a cab, Bee?

Beatrice. I'd rather walk, please. [BEATRICE *goes to the door.*] I'll write to you, Alan.

[*She goes out, followed by* SIR TIMOTHY.

Jeffcote. So you've thought better of it?

Alan. Seems so.

Jeffcote. And you'll wed Fanny Hawthorn, I take it?

Alan [*laconically*]. Ay!

Jeffcote. Thou'rt a good lad, Alan. I'm right pleased with thee. [ALAN *bursts into a loud peal of mirthless laughter.* JEFFCOTE *stares at* ALAN *in surprise.*] What's the matter?

Alan. Nothing, father.

[*He flings himself listlessly into an arm-chair.* JEFFCOTE *after another look at him, scratches his head and goes out.*

THE CURTAIN FALLS

ACT III

The scene is the same as in the previous Act, the time a few minutes later. The room is empty. ADA *opens the door and shows in* MRS. HAWTHORN, CHRISTOPHER, *and* FANNY, *who file in silently and awkwardly. Instead of a hat,* FANNY *is wearing the shawl that Lancashire weavers commonly wear when going to the Mill.*

Ada [*glancing back at them from the door*]. Will you take a seat, please.

[ADA *goes out.* CHRISTOPHER *and* MRS. HAWTHORN *sit on chairs placed against the back wall.* FANNY *remains standing.*

Mrs. Hawthorn. Fanny, sit you down.

[FANNY *silently seats herself. They are all three in a row along the back wall, very stiff and awkward. Presently* JEFFCOTE *enters. The* HAWTHORNS *all rise. He greets the three drily.*

Jeffcote [*nodding*]. Evening, Chris. [*To* MRS. HAWTHORN.] Good evening. [*He stops in front of* FANNY.] Good evening, lass.

[*He eyes her from tip to toe with a searching stare. She returns it quite simply and boldly.*

Jeffcote [*satisfied*]. Ay!

[*He turns away to the hearth where he takes his stand just as* MRS. JEFFCOTE *comes in. She is stiff and ill at ease.*

Mrs. Jeffcote [*to them all without looking at them*]. Good evening.

[MRS. HAWTHORN *and* CHRISTOPHER *murmur a greeting, and* MRS. JEFFCOTE *passes on to the fire, having cut them as nearly as she dared.* ALAN *lounges in sheepishly. He does not say anything, but nods to the three in a subdued way, and sits down sullenly on the L., far away from his father and mother.*

Jeffcote [*to the* HAWTHORNS]. Sit down. [*They are about to sit against the wall as before, but he stops them.*] Not there. Draw up to the table. [*They seat themselves round the table. The disposition of the characters is as follows. On the extreme L. is* ALAN, *in a big arm-chair. Sitting on the left of the table is* FANNY. *Behind the table,* MRS. HAWTHORN. *On the right of the table,* CHRISTOPHER. *Further to the right, in an arm-chair near the hearth, is* MRS. JEFFCOTE. *As for* JEFFCOTE, *he stands up with his back to the empty fireplace. Thus he can dominate the scene and walk about if he feels inclined.*] Well, here we are, all of us. We know what's brought us together. It's not a nice job, but it's got to be gone through, so we may as well get to business right away.

Christopher. Ay!

Jeffcote. We don't need to say owt about what's happened, do we?

Mrs. Hawthorn. No, I don't see as we need.

Mrs. Jeffcote. Excuse me, I think we do. I know hardly anything of what has happened.

Mrs. Hawthorn. It's admitted by them both.

Mrs. Jeffcote. But what is admitted by them both? It's rather important to know that.

Mrs. Hawthorn. You're hoping that we won't be able to prove owt against Alan. You think that happen he'll be able to wriggle out of it.

Jeffcote. There'll be no wriggling out. Alan has got to pay what he owes, and I don't think there's any doubt what that is. It's true I've only heard his version. What's Fanny told you?

Christopher. Nowt.

Jeffcote. Nowt?

Christopher. Nowt.

Jeffcote. How's that?

Mrs. Hawthorn. She's turned stupid, that's why.

Jeffcote. I'll have to have a go at her, then. [*To* FANNY.] It seems my lad met you one night in Blackpool and asked you to go to Llandudno with him?

Fanny. Yes. What then?

Jeffcote. He was drunk?

Fanny. No. He wasn't what you'd call drunk.

Jeffcote. As near as makes no matter, I'll bet.

Fanny. Anyhow, he was sober enough next morning when we went away.

Jeffcote. And where did you stay at Llandudno? Did he take you to an hotel? [FANNY *does not reply*.

Mrs. Hawthorn [*sharply*]. Now then, Fanny.

Jeffcote. Come lass, open thy mouth.

Alan. All right, father. I'll answer for Fanny. We stopped at St. Elvies Hotel, Saturday till Monday.

Jeffcote. What did you stop as?

Alan. Man and wife.

Mrs. Hawthorn [*gratified*]. Ah!

Alan. You'll find it in the register if you go there and look it up.

Jeffcote [*to* MRS. JEFFCOTE]. There. Are you satisfied?

Mrs. Jeffcote. Quite, thank you, Nat. That was all I wanted to know. I didn't want there to be any mistake.

Christopher. There's one thing bothering me. That postcard. It was posted in Blackpool on Sunday. I don't see how you managed it if you left on Saturday.

Fanny. I wrote it beforehand and left it for Mary to post on Sunday morning.

Mrs. Hawthorn. So Mary was in at all this!

Fanny. If Mary hadn't been drowned you'd never have found out about it. I'd never have opened my mouth, and Alan knows that.

Mrs. Hawthorn. Well, Mary's got her reward, poor lass!

Christopher. There's more in this than chance, it seems to me.

Mrs. Hawthorn. The ways of the Lord are mysterious and

wonderful. We can't pretend to understand them. He used Mary as an instrument for His purpose.

Jeffcote. Happen. But if He did it seems cruel hard on Mary, like. However, it's all over and done with, and can't be mended now, worse luck! These two young ones have made fools of themselves. That don't matter so much. The worst feature of it is they've made a fool of me. We've got to decide what's to be done. [*To* MRS. HAWTHORN.] I gave Chris a message for you last night.

Mrs. Hawthorn. Yes, you said as how you'd see us treated right.

Jeffcote. That's it. That's what I'm going to do. Now what do you reckon is the right way to settle this job?

Mrs. Hawthorn. He ought to marry her. I'll never be satisfied with owt less.

Jeffcote. That's your idea, too, Chris?

Christopher. Ay!

Jeffcote. It's mine as well. [MRS. HAWTHORN *nods eagerly.*] Before I knew who the chap was I said he should wed her, and I'm not going back on that now I find he's my own son. The missus there doesn't see it in the same light, but she'll have to make the best of it. She's in a minority of one, as they say.

Mrs. Hawthorn. Then we may take it that Alan's agreeable?

Jeffcote. Whether he's agreeable or not I cannot say. He's willing, and that'll have to be enough for you.

Mrs. Hawthorn. You'll excuse me mentioning it, but what about the other girl?

Jeffcote. What other girl? Has he been carrying on with another one as well?

Mrs. Jeffcote. She means Beatrice. Alan was engaged to Miss Farrar.

Mrs. Hawthorn. Yes, that's it. What about her?

Jeffcote. That's off now. No need to talk of that.

Christopher. The lad's no longer engaged to her?

Mrs. Jeffcote. No.

Mrs. Hawthorn. And he's quite free to wed our Fanny?

Jeffcote. He is so far as we know.

Mrs. Hawthorn. Then the sooner it's done the better.

Jeffcote. We've only to get the licence.

Christopher [*brokenly*]. I'm sure—I'm sure—we're very grateful.

Mrs. Hawthorn [*wiping her eyes*]. Yes, we are indeed. Though, of course, it's only what we'd a right to expect.

Christopher. I'm sure, Mrs. Jeffcote, that you'll try and look on Fanny more kindly in time.

Mrs. Jeffcote. I hope I shall, Mr. Hawthorn. Perhaps it's all for the best. More unlikely matches have turned out all right in the end.

Mrs. Hawthorn. I'm sure there's nothing can be said against Fanny save that she's got a will of her own. And after all, there's a many of us have that.

Christopher. She's always been a good girl up to now. You can put trust in her, Alan.

Jeffcote. It's evidently high time Alan got wed, that's all I can say, and it may as well be to Fanny as to anyone else. She's had to work at the loom for her living, and that does no woman any harm. My missus has worked at the loom in her time, though you'd never think it to look at her now, and if Fanny turns out half as good as her, Alan won't have done so badly. Now we've got to settle when the wedding's to be.

Mrs. Jeffcote. What *sort* of wedding is it to be?

Jeffcote. You women had better fix that up.

Mrs. Jeffcote. It ought to be quiet.

Jeffcote. It'll be quiet, you may lay your shirt on that! We shan't hold a reception at the Town Hall this journey.

Mrs. Jeffcote. I should prefer it to take place at the Registrar's.

Mrs. Hawthorn. No. I'll never agree to that. Not on any account.

Mrs. Jeffcote. Why not?

Mrs. Hawthorn. No. In church if you please, with the banns and everything. There's been enough irregular work about this job already. We'll have it done properly this time.

Alan. I should like to hear what Fanny says.

Mrs. Hawthorn. Fanny'll do what's thought best for her.

Alan. Anyhow, we'll hear what she thinks about it, if you please.

Fanny. I was just wondering where I come in.

Mrs. Hawthorn. Where you come in? You're a nice one to talk! You'd have been in a fine mess, happen, if you hadn't had us to look after you. You ought to be very thankful to us all, instead of sitting there hard like.

Jeffcote. You'd better leave it to us, lass. We'll settle this job for you.

Fanny. It's very good of you. You'll hire the parson and get the licence and make all the arrangements on your own without consulting me, and I shall have nothing to do save turn up meek as a lamb at the church or registry office or whatever it is.

Jeffcote. That's about all you'll be required to do.

Fanny. You'll look rather foolish if that's just what I won't do.

Mrs. Hawthorn. Don't talk silly, Fanny.

Jeffcote. What does she mean by that?

Mrs. Hawthorn. Nothing. She's only showing off, like. Don't heed her.

Mrs. Jeffcote. I beg your pardon. We will heed her, if you please. We'll see what it is she means by that.

Jeffcote. Hark you, lass. I'm having no hanky-panky work now. You'll have to do what you're bid, or maybe you'll find yourself in the cart.

Christopher. Fanny, you'll not turn stupid now?

Fanny. It doesn't suit me to let you settle my affairs without so much as consulting me.

Mrs. Hawthorn. Consulting you! What is there to consult you about, I'd like to know? You want to marry Alan, I suppose, and all we're talking about is the best way to bring it about.

Fanny. That's just where you make the mistake. I don't want to marry Alan.

Jeffcote. Eh?

Fanny. And what's more, I haven't the least intention of marrying him.

Mrs. Hawthorn. She's taken leave of her senses!

[*They are all surprised*. ALAN *is puzzled*. MRS. JEFFCOTE *visibly brightens*.

Jeffcote. Now then, what the devil do you mean by that?

Fanny. I mean what I say, and I'll trouble you to talk to me without swearing at me. I'm not one of the family yet.

Jeffcote. Well, I'm hanged!

[*He is much more polite to* FANNY *after this, for she has impressed him. But now he rubs his head and looks round queerly at the others*.

Christopher. Why won't you wed him? Have you got summat against him?

Fanny. That's my affair.

Mrs. Hawthorn. But you must give us a reason.

[FANNY *remains obstinately silent*.

Christopher. It's no good talking to her when she's in this mood. I know her better than you do. She won't open her mouth, no, not if she was going to be hung.

Jeffcote. Dost thou mean to tell me that all us folk are to stand here and let this girl beat us?

Christopher. Fanny'll get her own way.

Jeffcote. We'll see.

Mrs. Jeffcote. Why shouldn't she have her own way? I don't think we have any right to press her; I don't really.

Mrs. Hawthorn. All you're after is to get Alan out of the hole he's in. You don't care about Fanny.

Mrs. Jeffcote. I'm sorry for Fanny, but of course I care more about my own child.

Mrs. Hawthorn. Well, and so do we.

Mrs. Jeffcote. After all she knows better than we do whether she wants to marry Alan.

Jeffcote. Now then, Alan, what's the meaning of this?

Alan. I don't know, father.

Jeffcote. You've not been getting at her to-day and wheedling her into this?

Alan. Good Lord, no! What would have been the good of that? Besides I never thought of it.

Jeffcote. Well, I can't account for it!

Alan. Look here, father, just let me have a talk to her alone. It's not likely she'll care to speak with all you folk sitting round.

Jeffcote. Do you reckon she'll open her mouth to you?

Alan. I can try, though it's true she never takes much notice of what I say.

Jeffcote. We'll give you fifteen minutes. [*He looks at his watch.*] If thou cannot talk a lass round in that time thou ought to be jolly well ashamed of thyself. I know I could have done it when I was thy age. Mother, you'd better show Chris and his missus into t'other room for a bit.

[MRS. JEFFCOTE *goes to the door.*

Mrs. Jeffcote. Will you come this way, please.

[MRS. JEFFCOTE *goes out, followed by* CHRISTOPHER.

Mrs. Hawthorn. Now, Fanny, think on what you're doing. For God's sake, have a bit of common sense!

[FANNY *is silent.* MRS. HAWTHORN *goes out.*

Jeffcote. Fifteen minutes. And if you're not done then we shall come in whether or not. [JEFFCOTE *goes out.*

Alan. Look here, Fanny, what's all this nonsense about?

Fanny. What nonsense?

Alan. Why won't you marry me? My father's serious enough. He means it when he says he wants you to. He's as stupid as a mule when he once gets an idea into his head.

Fanny. As if I didn't know that. He's like you, for that matter!

Alan. Well, then, what are you afraid of?

Fanny. Afraid? Who says I am afraid?

Alan. I don't see what else it can be.

Fanny. You can't understand a girl not jumping at you when she gets the chance, can you?

Alan. I can't understand you not taking me when you get the chance.

Fanny. How is it you aren't going to marry Beatrice Farrar?

Alan. I can't marry both of you.

Fanny. Weren't you fond of her?

Alan. Very.

Fanny. But you were fonder of me—Eh?

Alan. Well——

Fanny. Come now, you must have been or you wouldn't have given her up for me.

Alan. I gave her up because my father made me.

Fanny. Made you? Good Lord, a chap of your age!

Alan. My father's a man who will have his own way.

Fanny. You can tell him to go and hang himself. He hasn't got any hold over you.

Alan. That's just what he has. He can keep me short of brass.

Fanny. Earn some brass.

Alan. Ay! I can earn some brass, but it'll mean hard work and it'll take time. And, after all, I shan't earn anything like what I get now.

Fanny. Then all you want to wed me for is what you'll get with me? I'm to be given away with a pound of tea, as it were?

Alan. No. You know I like you, Fanny—I'm fond of you.

Fanny. You didn't give up Beatrice Farrar because of me, but because of the money.

Alan. If it comes to that, I didn't really give her up at all. I may as well be straight with you. It was she that gave me up.

Fanny. What did she do that for? Her father's plenty of money, and she can get round *him*, I'll bet, if you can't get round *yours*.

Alan. She gave me up because she thought it was her duty to.

Fanny. You mean because she didn't fancy my leavings.

Alan. No. Because she thought you had the right to marry me.

Fanny. Glory! She must be queer!

Alan. It was jolly fine of her. You ought to be the first to see that.

Fanny. Fine to give you up? [*She shrugs her shoulders, and then admits grudgingly*.] Well, I reckon it was a sacrifice of a sort. That is, if she loves you. If I loved a chap I wouldn't do that.

Alan. You would. You're doing it now.

Fanny. Eh?

Alan. Women are more unselfish than men and no mistake!

Fanny. What are you getting at?

Alan. I know why you won't marry me.

Fanny. Do you? [*She smiles*.] Well, spit it out, lad!

Alan. You're doing it for my sake.

Fanny. How do you make that out?

Alan. You don't want to spoil my life.

Fanny. Thanks! Much obliged for the compliment.

Alan. I'm not intending to say anything unkind, but of course it's as clear as daylight that you'd damage my prospects, and all that sort of thing. You can see that, can't you?

Fanny. Ay! I can see it now you point it out. I hadn't thought of it before.

Alan. Then, that isn't why you refuse me?

Fanny. Sorry to disappoint you, but it's not.

Alan. I didn't see what else it could be.

Fanny. Don't you kid yourself, my lad! It isn't because I'm afraid of spoiling *your* life that I'm refusing you, but because I'm afraid of spoiling *mine*! That didn't occur to you?

Alan. It didn't.

Fanny. You never thought that anybody else could be as selfish as yourself.

Alan. I may be very conceited, but I don't see how you can hurt yourself by wedding me. You'd come in for plenty of brass, anyhow.

Fanny. I don't know as money's much to go by when it comes to a job of this sort. It's more important to get the right chap.

Alan. You like me well enough?

Fanny. Suppose it didn't last? Weddings brought about this road have a knack of turning out badly. Would you ever forget it was your father bade you marry me? No fear! You'd bear me a grudge all my life for that.

Alan. Hang it! I'm not such a cad as you make out.

Fanny. You wouldn't be able to help it. It mostly happens that road. Look at old Mrs. Eastwood—hers was a case like ours. Old Joe Eastwood's father made them wed. And she's been separated from him these thirty years, living all alone in that big house at Valley Edge. Got any amount of brass, she has, but she's so lonesome-like she does her own housework for the sake of something to occupy her time. The tradesfolk catch her washing the front steps. You don't find me making a mess of my life like that.

Alan. Look here, Fanny, I promise you I'll treat you fair all the time. You don't need to fear that folk'll look down on you. We shall have too much money for that.

Fanny. I can manage all right on twenty-five bob a week.

Alan. Happen you can. It's not the brass altogether. You do like me, as well, don't you?

Fanny. Have you only just thought of that part of the bargain?

Alan. Don't be silly. I thought of it long ago. You *do* like me? You wouldn't have gone to Llandudno with me if you hadn't liked me?

Fanny. Oh! Yes, I liked you.

Alan. And don't you like me now?

Fanny. You're a nice, clean, well-made lad. Oh, ay! I like you right enough.

Alan. Then, Fanny, for God's sake marry me, and let's get this job settled.

Fanny. Not me!

Alan. But you must. Don't you see it's your duty to.

Fanny. Oh! come now, *you* aren't going to start preaching to me?

Alan. No. I don't mean duty in the way Beatrice did. I mean your duty to me. You've got me into a hole, and it's only fair you should get me out.

Fanny. I like your cheek!

Alan. But just look here. I'm going to fall between two stools. It's all up with Beatrice, of course. And if you won't have me I shall have parted from her to no purpose; besides getting kicked out of the house by my father, more than likely!

Fanny. Nay, nay! He'll not punish you for this. He doesn't know it's your fault I'm not willing to wed you.

Alan. He may. It's not fair, but it would be father all over to do that.

Fanny. He'll be only too pleased to get shut of me without eating his own words. He'll forgive you on the spot, and you can make it up with Beatrice to-morrow.

Alan. I can never make it up with Bee!

Fanny. Get away!

Alan. You won't understand a girl like Bee. I couldn't think of even trying for months, and then it may be too late. I'm not the only pebble on the beach. And I'm a damaged one, at that!

Fanny. She's fond of you, you said?

Alan. Yes. I think she's very fond of me.

Fanny. Then she'll make it up in a fortnight.

Alan [*moodily*]. You said *you* were fond of me once, but it hasn't taken you long to alter.

Fanny. All women aren't built alike. Beatrice is religious. She'll be sorry for you. I was fond of you in a way.

Alan. But you didn't ever really love me?

Fanny. Love you? Good heavens, of course not! Why on earth should I love you? You were just someone to have a bit of fun with. You were an amusement—a lark.

Alan [*shocked*]. Fanny! Is that all you cared for me?

Fanny. How much more did you care for me?

Alan. But it's not the same. I'm a man.

Fanny. You're a man, and I was your little fancy. Well, I'm a woman, and *you* were *my* little fancy. You wouldn't prevent a woman enjoying herself as well as a man, if she takes it into her head?

Alan. But do you mean to say that you didn't care any more for me than a fellow cares for any girl he happens to pick up?

Fanny. Yes. Are you shocked?

Alan. It's a bit thick; it is really!

Fanny. You're a beauty to talk!

Alan. It sounds so jolly immoral. I never thought of a girl looking on a chap just like that! I made sure you wanted to marry me if you got the chance.

Fanny. No fear! You're not good enough for me. The chap Fanny Hawthorn weds has got to be made of different stuff from you, my lad. My husband, if ever I have one, will be a man, not a fellow who'll throw over his girl at his father's bidding! Strikes me the sons of these rich manufacturers are all much alike. They seem a bit weak in the upper storey. It's their fathers' brass that's too much for them, happen! They don't know how to spend it properly. They're like chaps who can't carry their drink because they aren't used to it. The brass gets into their heads, like!

Alan. Hang it, Fanny, I'm not quite a fool.

Fanny. No. You're not a fool altogether. But there's summat lacking. You're not man enough for me. You're a nice lad, and I'm fond of you. But I couldn't ever marry you. We've had a right good time together, I'll never forget that. It *has* been a right good time, and no mistake! We've enjoyed ourselves proper! But all good times have to come to an end, and ours is over now. Come along now, and bid me farewell.

Alan. I can't make you out rightly, Fanny, but you're a damn good sort, and I wish there were more like you!

Fanny [*holding out her hand*]. Good-bye, old lad.

Alan [*grasping her hand*]. Good-bye, Fanny! And good luck! [*A slight pause.*

Fanny. And now call them in again.

Alan [*looking at his watch*]. Time's not up yet.

Fanny. Never heed! Let's get it over.

[ALAN *goes out, and* FANNY *returns to her chair and sits down. Presently* ALAN *comes in and stands by the door, whilst* MRS. JEFFCOTE, MRS. HAWTHORN, *and* CHRISTOPHER *file in and resume their original positions. Last of all comes* JEFFCOTE, *and* ALAN *leaves the door and goes back to his chair.* JEFFCOTE *comes straight behind the table.*

Jeffcote. Well? What's it to be? [ALAN *and* FANNY *look at each other.*] Come. What's it to be? You, Fanny, have you come to your senses?

Fanny. I've never left them, so far as I know.

Jeffcote. Are you going to wed our Alan or are you not?

Fanny. I'm not.

Jeffcote. Ah!

Mrs. Hawthorn. Well!

Alan. It's no good, father. I can't help it. I've done all I can. She won't have me.

Jeffcote. I'm beat this time! I wash my hands of it! There's no fathoming a woman. And these are the creatures that want us to give them votes!

[*After this* JEFFCOTE *does not attempt to influence the discussion.*

Mrs. Hawthorn [*in a shrill voice*]. Do you tell us you're throwing away a chance like this?

Fanny. You've heard.

Mrs. Hawthorn. I call it wicked, I do, indeed! I can see you are downright bad, through and through! There's one thing I tell you straight. Our house is no place for thee after this.

Fanny. You're not really angry with me because of what I've done. It's because I'm not going to have any of Mr. Jeffcote's money that you want to turn me out of the house.

Mrs. Hawthorn. It's not! It's because you choose to be a girl who's lost her reputation, instead of letting Alan make you into an honest woman.

Fanny. How can he do that?

Mrs. Hawthorn. By wedding you, of course.

Fanny. You called him a blackguard this morning.

Mrs. Hawthorn. So he is a blackguard.

Fanny. I don't see how marrying a blackguard is going to turn me into an honest woman!

Mrs. Hawthorn. If he marries you he won't be a blackguard any longer.

Fanny. Then it looks as if I'm asked to wed him to turn him into an honest man?

Alan. It's no use bandying words about what's over and done with. I want to know what's all this talk of turning Fanny out of doors?

Christopher. Take no heed of it! My missus don't rightly know what she's saying just now.

Mrs. Hawthorn. Don't she? You're making a big mistake if you think that. Fanny can go home and fetch her things, and after that she may pack off!

Christopher. That she'll not!

Mrs. Hawthorn. Then I'll make it so hot for her in the house, and for thee, too, that thou'll be glad to see the back of her!

Fanny. This hasn't got anything to do with Mr. and Mrs. Jeffcote, has it? [FANNY *rises.*

Alan. It's got something to do with me, though! I'm not going to see you without a home.

Fanny [*smiling*]. It's right good of you, Alan, but I shan't starve. I'm not without a trade at my finger tips, thou knows. I'm a Lancashire lass, and so long as there's weaving sheds in Lancashire I shall earn enough brass to keep me going. I wouldn't live at home again after this, not anyhow! I'm going to be on my own in future. [*To* CHRISTOPHER.] You've no call to be afraid. I'm not going to disgrace you. But so long as I've to live my own life I don't see why I shouldn't choose what it's to be.

Christopher [*rising*]. We're in the road here! Come, Sarah!

Jeffcote. I'm sorry, Chris. I've done my best for thee.

Christopher. Ay! I know. I'm grateful to thee, Nat. [*To* MRS. JEFFCOTE.] Good night, ma'am.

Mrs. Jeffcote. Good night. [MRS. HAWTHORN *and* CHRISTOPHER *go out, the former seething with suppressed resentment. Neither says anything to* ALAN. JEFFCOTE *opens the door for them and follows them into the hall. As* FANNY *is going out* MRS. JEFFCOTE *speaks.*] Good-bye, Fanny Hawthorn. If ever you want help, come to me.

Fanny. Ah! You didn't want us to wed?

Mrs. Jeffcote. No.

Fanny. You were straight enough.

Mrs. Jeffcote. I'm sure this is the best way out. I couldn't see any hope the other way.

Fanny. Good-bye.

[MRS. JEFFCOTE *holds out her hand, and they shake hands. Then* FANNY *goes out with* ALAN. *There is a slight pause.* MRS. JEFFCOTE *goes to the door and looks into the hall, and then returns to her chair.*

Mrs. Jeffcote. Have they gone?

Jeffcote. Ay!

[JEFFCOTE *sits down in an arm-chair and fills his pipe.*

Mrs. Jeffcote. Where's Alan?

Jeffcote. Don't know.

Mrs. Jeffcote. What are you going to do about him?

Jeffcote. Don't know.

[ALAN *opens the door and looks in. He is wearing a light burberry mackintosh and a soft felt hat.*

Mrs. Jeffcote. Where are you going to, Alan?

Alan. I'm just running round to Farrar's.

Jeffcote [*surprised*]. To Farrar's?

Alan. To see Beatrice.

Mrs. Jeffcote [*not surprised*]. You're going to ask her to marry you?

Alan [*laconically*]. Happen I am!

Jeffcote. Well, I'm damned! Dost thou reckon she'll have thee?

Alan. That remains to be seen.

Jeffcote. Aren't you reckoning without me?

Alan. Can't help that. [JEFFCOTE *grunts.*] Hang it! Be fair. I've done my best. It's not my fault that Fanny won't have me.

Jeffcote. Well, if Beatrice Farrar can fancy thee, it's not for me to be too particular.

Alan. Thank you, father.

Jeffcote. Get along! I'm disgusted with thee!

[ALAN *slips out of the door.*

Mrs. Jeffcote. Beatrice will have him.

Jeffcote. How do you know that?

Mrs. Jeffcote. She loves him; she told me.

Jeffcote. There's no accounting for tastes! [*He ruminates.*] So Beatrice loves him, does she? Eh! But women are queer folk! Who'd have thought that Fanny would refuse to wed him?

Mrs. Jeffcote. It *is* strange. It makes you feel there *is* something in Providence after all.

THE CURTAIN FALLS